THE LOEB CLASSICAL LIBRARY

FOUNDED BY JAMES LOEB 1911

EDITED BY

JEFFREY HENDERSON

EURIPIDES

VIII

LCL 506

EURIPIDES

FRAGMENTS

Oedipus–Chrysippus
Other Fragments

EDITED AND TRANSLATED BY

CHRISTOPHER COLLARD
AND
MARTIN CROPP

HARVARD UNIVERSITY PRESS
CAMBRIDGE, MASSACHUSETTS
LONDON, ENGLAND
2008

S/o Blkwl. 2/9 24.10

First published 2008

LOEB CLASSICAL LIBRARY® is a registered trademark
of the President and Fellows of Harvard College

Library of Congress Control Number 2007043817
CIP data available from the Library of Congress

ISBN 978-0-674-99631-1

*Composed in ZephGreek and ZephText by
Technologies 'N Typography, Merrimac, Massachusetts.
Printed on acid-free paper and bound by
Edwards Brothers, Ann Arbor, Michigan*

CONTENTS

CONTENTS

CONTENTS

PREFACE

We were invited to contribute these volumes to the Loeb Classical Library at the generous suggestion of Sir Hugh Lloyd-Jones, whose editions of the Aeschylean and Sophoclean fragments provided a template. We had earlier cut our teeth for such work in two volumes which offer selected fragmentary plays on a much larger scale (*SFP* in our Abbreviations list). We have been immeasurably aided in this new task by two recent and complete major editions of Euripides' fragments by François Jouan and the late Hermann Van Looy (ed. Budé) and Richard Kannicht (*TrGF* 5). We briefly describe and admire the extraordinary achievement of these editions in our Introduction under "Collection and Study of the Fragments"; here we express our warmest gratitude to the editors themselves for their encouragement and help.

Amongst other recent editors of the fragmentary texts we salute especially Colin Austin (Austin, *NFE* in the Abbreviations list), James Diggle (Diggle, *TrGFS*), and Wolfgang Luppe, a prolific editor of papyri whom we cite very frequently. Our bibliographies name the many editors of individual plays on whose work we have drawn, and other scholars who have contributed to the surge in fragment studies on which we remark in the Introduction (note 23 there mentions some bibliographical surveys of this work).

Martin Cropp's work for these volumes has been facilitated by research grants from the University of Calgary. Jason McClure assisted him in checking refererences and preparing the Index, and Elizabeth Cropp read most of our introductions and translations with improving effect. Thanks for various kinds of personal support and practical help go also to Bill Allan, James Diggle, John Gibert, Doreen Innes, Jim Neville and Peter Toohey. We happily record appreciation of a quite different kind, not least for much wondering patience, to our wives, Jean Collard and Elizabeth Cropp.

Lastly, Christopher Collard would like it known how much is owed to Martin Cropp's expertise in preparing the copy for publication.

Christopher Collard, Oxford
Martin Cropp, Calgary

This Edition

We reproduce Kannicht's numbering of the testimonia and fragments (itself based on Nauck's) and likewise the established ordering of the plays alphabetically by their Greek rather than Latin/English titles; thus the numerical sequence of the fragments is maintained, but those titles beginning with C, Ch, H, Ph and Th in Latin and English appear 'out of order' since these letters represent K, X, aspirated I, Φ and Θ in Greek (and there are other minor discrepancies). The fragments of *Pirithous, Rhadamanthys,*

PREFACE

Tennes and *Sisyphus* which are assigned to Critias in *TrGF* 1 are here added at the end of the edition. We preface each play with a select bibliography, usually divided between editions and other studies and discussions, and a brief introduction surveying so far as possible (and with varying emphases according to the nature of the evidence) the play's mythical background, its plot and reconstruction, and its general character, chronology, and impact on subsequent literary and artistic traditions. These introductions also list 'Brief fragments' (single contextless words or phrases, or incomprehensible papyri, which we have omitted from the main series) and 'Other ascriptions' (i.e. other fragments which scholars have assigned inconclusively to the play). The introductions are followed by a selection of Kannicht's testimonia (including only those which contribute substantially to our knowledge of the play's content) and all of the play's fragments other than the 'Brief fragments' just mentioned. The apparatus accompanying the Greek texts lists the principal sources (excluding those which are derivative or otherwise of little importance) and notes only those textual uncertainities, with a very limited number of conjectural suggestions, which have a substantial bearing on the sense; most such points are explained briefly in the notes to the translations. For complete information on the sources, history and constitution of the texts the reader should in all cases consult Kannicht's edition and those specialized editions of individual plays which are mentioned in our introductions to the plays.

PREFACE

The following markers are used in Greek texts:

[ ]	gaps in papyri due to physical damage (text within square brackets, if any, is editorial reconstruction)
... ...	dots beneath spaces represent letters missing or illegible in papyri (incomplete letters printed with reasonable confidence are not so marked in this edition)
⟨ ⟩	text or speaker identifications omitted in the source(s) and supplied or left incomplete by editors
{ }	text judged inauthentic
† †	text judged incurably corrupt
—	unidentified speaker
*	fragment (F) or testimony (test.) identified as Euripidean but attributed conjecturally to this play
**	fragment (F) or testimony (test.) attributed conjecturally to Euripides

The English translation uses the last five markers similarly, but parenthesis marks enclose all editorial supplements and completions of sense as well as actual parentheses, and all gaps and omissions are represented by three dots on the line. Translations of papyrus texts occasionally reflect supplements not included in the facing Greek text but recorded in the apparatus below it.

CHRONOLOGY

Exact or near-exact dates of production derived from Athenian public records are available for the nine extant and fourteen fragmentary plays listed in section (*a*) below. Those listed in section (*b*) can be dated more or less closely from several kinds of evidence, of which two are of special importance. First, quotation or parody by Aristophanes and other contemporary comic playwrights provides latest dates for a dozen tragedies in this group, although these are not necessarily close approximations—there are for example parodies of *Telephus* (438) in Aristophanes' *Acharnians* (425) and again in his *Women at the Thesmophoria* (411). Secondly, close or distant approximations for the dates of nearly twenty more tragedies can be estimated from metrical features of the fragments, especially the increasing frequency over time of 'resolutions' (substitutions of two short for one long or *anceps* syllable) in Euripides' iambic trimeters, the increasing variety of word-shapes accommodated by these resolutions, and his use of trochaic tetrameters in dialogue scenes, of which the earliest dated instance is in *Trojan Women* (415).[1]

---

[1] Further chronological details are given in the introductions to the plays. For general guidance on the estimates from metrical data see Cropp–Fick 1–30, 60–1, 66, 69. Several factors make the

» preceding a date = 'before', following = 'or later'

m dates inferred mainly or wholly from metrical evidence

q dates inferred mainly or wholly from quotations or parodies in Comedy (usually Aristophanes)

Capital letters (*ALCESTIS* etc.) denote extant plays.

(a) Dates Derived from Athenian Public Records

455	*Peliades*
438	*Cretan Women, Alcmeon in Psophis, Telephus, ALCESTIS*
431	*MEDEA, Dictys, Philoctetes, Theristae*
428	*HIPPOLYTUS*
415	*Alexander, Palamedes, TROJAN WOMEN, Sisyphus*
412	*Andromeda, HELEN*
411–407	*Hypsipyle, PHOENICIAN WOMEN, Antiope* (?)[2]
408	*ORESTES*
posthumous	*Alcmeon in Corinth, BACCHAE, IPHIGENIA AT AULIS*

statistical estimates necessarily tentative and inexact (see especially Cropp–Fick 2, 23); they are however accurate for most of those plays whose dates can be confirmed from other evidence (*ibid.* 18–19, 23).

[2] Metrical evidence suggests an earlier date for *Antiope* (427–419).

(b) Approximate Dates

c. 450?	*Rhesus* (lost)
» 431	*Aegeus, Cretans* (m), *Hippolytus Veiled*
c. 430	CHILDREN OF HERACLES
» 425	*Bellerophon* (q), *Danae* (m), *Thyestes* (q), *Ino* (q), *Oeneus* (q), *Phoenix* (q), *Protesilaus* (m)
426–412	*Melanippe Captive* (m, q)
c. 425	*Cresphontes,* ANDROMACHE
» 423	*Aeolus* (q), HECUBA (q)[3]
c. 423	SUPPLIANT WOMEN
423 »	*Temenidae* (m)[4]
» 422	*Stheneboea* (q), *Theseus* (q)
422?	*Erechtheus*[5]
c. 420	*Phaethon* (m), ELECTRA (m)
420 »	*Antigone* (m), *Ixion* (?)
419 »	*Meleager* (m), *Oedipus* (m)
c. 417	HERACLES (m)
» 414	*Pleisthenes* (q)

[3] *Aeolus* and *Hecuba* are quoted in Aristophanes' *Clouds* which was produced in 423, but the extant text of *Clouds* shows signs of revision. *Aeolus* might therefore be as late as 421 (the date of *Peace* which also quotes it), and *Hecuba* as late as 417 (the latest possible date for the revision of *Clouds*).

[4] If *Temenus, Temenidae* and *Archelaus* formed a trilogy, all should be dated after the accession of Archelaus in 413. See Introduction to *Archelaus*.

[5] The date 422 for *Erechtheus* is inferred uncertainly from Plutarch. Metrical evidence suggests 421–410.

414 »	*Auge* (m), *Polyidus* (m)
c. 413	*IPHIGENIA IN TAURIS* (m), *ION* (m)
412 »	*Archelaus* (and *Temenus*, *Temen-idae*?)[4]
» 411 (421–411?)	*Melanippe Wise* (q)
» 410 (421–410?)	*Alcmene* (m)

(c) Unknown Dates

TRAGEDIES. *Alope*, *Licymnius* (» 448?), *Oenomaus*, *Peleus*, *Scyrians* (» 431?), *Temenus*,[4] *Phrixus A* and *B*, *Chrysippus*, and the doubtfully ascribed *Pirithous*, *Rhadamanthys*, *Tennes*.

SATYR PLAYS. *Autolycus A and B*, *Busiris*, *Epeus*, *Eurystheus*, *CYCLOPS* (c. 408?), *Lamia*, *Sciron*, *Syleus* (437–424?)

ABBREVIATIONS

AC	*L'Antiquité Classique*
Aélion (1983)	R. Aélion, *Euripide héritier d'Eschyle*, 2 vols. (Paris, 1983)
Aélion (1986)	R. Aélion, *Quelques grands mythes héroiques dans l'oeuvre d'Euripide* (Paris, 1986)
AJA	*American Journal of Archaeology*
AJP	*American Journal of Philology*
APF	*Archiv für Papyrusforschung*
Austin, *NFE*	C. Austin, *Nova Fragmenta Euripidea in Papyris Reperta* (Berlin, 1968)
Bastianini–Casanova, *Euripide e i papiri*	G. Bastianini, A. Casanova (eds.), *Euripide e i papiri: atti del Convegno Internazionale di Studi, Firenze, 10–11 giugno 2004* (Florence, 2005)
BICS	*Bulletin of the Institute of Classical Studies* (London)
CAG	*Commentaria in Aristotelem Graeca*, 23 vols. (Berlin, 1882–1909)
CCC	*Civiltà Classica e Cristiana*

CPG	*Corpus Pareomiographorum Graecorum*, ed. E. von Leutsch, F. Schneidewin, 2 vols. (Göttingen, 1839, 1851)
CQ	*Classical Quarterly*
CRAI	*Comptes rendus de l'Académie des Inscriptions et Belles-Lettres* (Paris)
Cropp–Fick	M. Cropp, G. Fick. *Resolutions and Chronology in Euripides: the Fragmentary Tragedies* (London, 1985: *BICS* Suppl. 43)
Diggle, *TrGFS*	J. Diggle, *Tragicorum Graecorum Fragmenta Selecta* (Oxford, 1998)
DK	H. Diels, W. Kranz, *Die Fragmente der Vorsokratiker* (Berlin, 1951–2⁶)
ed. Budé	F. Jouan, H. van Looy, *Euripide, Tome VIII: Fragments*, 4 vols. (Paris, 1998–2003)
Egli	F. Egli, *Euripides im Kontext zeitgenössischer intellektueller Strömungen* (Munich-Leipzig, 2003)
FGrH	*Die Fragmente der griechischen Historiker*, ed. F. Jacoby, 3 vols. in 15 (Berlin, 1923–58)
Fragmenta Dramatica	H. Hofmann, A. Harder (eds.), *Fragmenta Dramatica: Beiträge zur Interpretation der griechischen Tragikerfragmente etc.* (Göttingen, 1991)

Gantz	T. Gantz, *Early Greek Myth: a Guide to Literary and Artistic Sources* (Baltimore, 1993)
Gramm. Gr.	*Grammatici Graeci*, ed. G. Uhlig and others, 4 vols. in 6 (Leipzig, 1867–1910)
GRBS	*Greek, Roman and Byzantine Studies*
HSCP	*Harvard Studies in Classical Philology*
Huys, *The Tale*	M. Huys, *The Tale of the Hero who was Exposed at Birth in Euripidean Tragedy: a Study of Motifs* (Leuven, 1995)
ICS	*Illinois Classical Studies*
IEG	*Iambi et Elegi Graeci*, ed. M. L. West (Oxford, 1989–91²)
IG	*Inscriptiones Graecae*
JHS	*Journal of Hellenic Studies*
Jouan (1966)	F. Jouan, *Euripides et les légendes des chants cypriens* (Paris, 1966)
Krumeich	R. Krumeich, N. Pechstein, B. Seidensticker (eds.), *Das griechische Satyrspiel* (Darmstadt, 1999)
LIMC	*Lexicon Iconographicum Mythologiae Classicae*, 8 vols., each in two parts (Zürich, 1981–98)
LSJ	H. G. Liddell, R. Scott, *A Greek–English Lexicon*, revised by H. Stuart-Jones, with Supplement (Oxford, 1968⁹)

Matthiessen	K. Matthiessen, *Die Tragödien des Euripides* (Munich, 2002)
McHardy, *Lost Dramas*	F. McHardy, J. Robson, D. Harvey (eds.), *Lost Dramas of Classical Athens: Greek Tragic Fragments* (Exeter, 2005)
MDAI(A)	*Mitteilungen des Deutschen Archäologischen Instituts, Athenische Abteilung*
Musa Tragica	B. Gauly and others, *Musa Tragica: Die griechische Tragödie von Thespis bis Ezechiel: Ausgewählte Zeugnisse und Fragmente* (Göttingen, 1991)
Nauck *or* N	A. Nauck, *Tragicorum Graecorum Fragmenta* (Leipzig, 1889²: reprinted with *Supplementum continens nova fragmenta Euripidea etc.*, ed. B. Snell, Hildesheim, 1964)
Nauck–Snell *or* N–Sn	Supplement to Nauck (see above)
OGCMA	*The Oxford Guide to Classical Mythology in the Arts, 1300–1990s*, ed. J. D. Reid, 2 vols. *(Oxford, 1993)*
Page, *GLP*	D. L. Page, *Select Papyri, III: Literary Papyri, Poetry* (London and Cambridge, MA, 1941: Loeb Classical Library no. 360)

ABBREVIATIONS

PCG	*Poetae Comici Graeci*, ed. R. Kassel, C. Austin, 8 vols. in 10 (Berlin, 1983–)
Pechstein	N. Pechstein, *Euripides Satyrographos: Ein Kommentar zu den Euripideischen Satyrspielfragmenten* (Stuttgart–Leipzig, 1998)
P.	Papyrus (followed usually by the name of the place or the collection with which the papyrus is associated, and by the number assigned to the papyrus)
P. Oxy.	Oxyrhynchus Papyrus
PG	*Patrologiae cursus completus . . . series Graeca*, ed. J.-P. Migne, 161 vols. (Paris, 1857–66)
PMG	*Poetae Melici Graeci*, ed. D. L. Page (Oxford, 1962)
PMGF	*Poetarum Melicorum Graecorum Fragmenta*, ed. M. Davies (Oxford, 1991–)
PSI	Pubblicazioni della Società italiana per la ricerca dei papiri greci e latini in Egitto
RAAN	*Rendiconti dell'Accademia di Archeologia, Lettere e Belle Arti di Napoli*
Rau, *Paratragodia*	P. Rau, *Paratragodia: Untersuchung einer komischen Form des Aristophanes* (Munich, 1967: *Zetemata* 45)

RFIC	*Rivista di Filologia e di Istruzione Classica*
Rhet. Gr.	*Rhetores Graeci* ed. C. Walz, 9 vols. (Stuttgart, 1832–6); ed. L. Spengel, 3 vols. (Leipzig, 1853–6)
RhM	*Rheinisches Museum*
SBAW	*Sitzungsberichte der Bayerischen Akademie der Wissenschaften*
Séchan	L. Séchan, *Études sur la tragédie grecque dans ses rapports avec la céramique* (Paris, 1926)
SFP	*Euripides: Selected Fragmentary Plays*, Vol. 1 ed. C. Collard, M. J. Cropp, K. H. Lee (Warminster, 1995: corrected reprint with Addenda, Oxford, 2008); Vol. 2 ed. C. Collard, M. J. Cropp, J. Gibert (Oxford, 2004)
SIFC	*Studi Italiani di Filologia Classica*
Sourvinou-Inwood	C. Sourvinou-Inwood, *Tragedy and Athenian Religion* (Lanham, 2003)
TAPA	*Transactions of the American Philological Association*
Taplin	O. Taplin, *Pots and Plays: Interactions between Tragedy and Greek Vase-painting of the Fourth Century B.C.* (Los Angeles, 2007)
Todisco	L. Todisco and others, *La Ceramica figurata a soggetto tragico in Magna Grecia e in Sicilia* (Rome, 2003)

Trendall–Webster   A. D. Trendall, T. B. L. Webster, *Illustrations of Greek Drama* (London, 1971)

TrGF   *Tragicorum Graecorum Fragmenta*, ed. B. Snell, R. Kannicht, S. Radt, 5 vols. in 6 (Göttingen, 1971–2004)

Van Looy (1964)   H. Van Looy, *Zes verloren Tragedies van Euripides* (Brussels, 1964)

Van Rossum-Steenbeek   M. van Rossum-Steenbeek, *Greek Readers' Digests: Studies on a Selection of Subliterary Papyri* (Leiden, 1998: *Mnemosyne* Suppl. 175)

Voelke   P. Voelke, *Un théâtre en marge: aspects figuratifs et configurationels de drame satyrique dans l'Athènes classique* (Bari, 2001)

Webster   T. B. L. Webster, *The Tragedies of Euripides* (London, 1967)

Wilamowitz, *Analecta*   U. von Wilamowitz-Moellendorff, *Analecta Euripidea* (Berlin, 1875)

Wilamowitz, *Kleine Schriften*   U. von Wilamowitz-Moellendorff, *Kleine Schriften*, 6 vols. in 7 (Berlin, 1935–72)

ZPE   *Zeitschrift für Papyrologie und Epigraphik*

EURIPIDES

OEDIPUS

Austin, *NFE* 59–65; H. Van Looy in ed. Budé VIII.2.429–58; C. Collard in *SFP* II.105–32.

C. Robert, *Oidipus* (Berlin, 1915), I.305–31, II.107–18; E. L. de Kock, *Acta Classica* 5 (1962), 15–37; J. Vaio, *GRBS* 5 (1964), 43–55; Webster 241–6; J. Dingel, *Museum Helveticum* 27 (1970), 90–6; L. di Gregorio, *CCC* 1 (1980), 49–94; Aélion (1986), 42–61; M. Hose, *ZPE* 81 (1990), 9–15; Gantz 488–506, esp. 492–502; *LIMC* VII.i.1–15 'Oidipous'; H. Lloyd-Jones, *CQ* 52 (2002), 1–14 (= *Further Academic Papers* (Oxford, 2005), 18–35); C. Collard in McHardy, *Lost Dramas* 57–62 (orig. 1996, publ. 2004).

To us Oedipus' tragedy is so familiar that we risk assuming it was the same in antiquity. While the remains of early poetry and art afford much evidence for his curse upon his sons Eteocles and Polynices and their mutual fratricide in the war of the Seven against Thebes (Gantz 502–19), his own life story is barely represented in them, perhaps through accident. Homer, Odyssey 11.271–80 tells concisely the terrible fates of himself and his mother Jocasta; Hesiod, Theogony 326 mentions the Sphinx but not Oedipus' victory over her; and only a trace of the 6th-century epic Oedipodea *has reached us (see the Loeb Greek Epic Fragments, ed. M. L. West, 38–43): on this*

2

dearth of early material see Gantz 497–8. There is little even in the 5th century before tragedy; the mythographer Pherecydes (FGrH 3 F 95) tells that Oedipus was given the throne of Thebes and Laius' widow after Laius' death, and lists Oedipus' further marriages and children after the death of Jocasta. When Pindar, Olympians 2.38–40 has Oedipus fulfil an ancient oracle in killing his father Laius, he may already be following Aeschylus' dramatization (below). In short, we do not know how frequently Oedipus' story had been told, and whether it had broadly the shape and detail fixed for us now as canonical by Sophocles.

Euripides' Oedipus, produced probably after 415 B.C (see below), dramatized the same span of events as had Sophocles' Oedipus Tyrannus nearly twenty years earlier, and probably as Aeschylus' Oedipus more than fifty years earlier (Aeschylus' outline may be inferred from vv. 772–91 of the Seven Against Thebes, its sequel in the trilogy of 467 B.C.). Euripides and Sophocles gave Oedipus the same past: he was exposed as a baby after the god Apollo warned Laius that any child he got would kill him (cf. our F 539a); he was saved and brought up by Polybus, king of Corinth. Later he killed Laius unwittingly, destroyed the Sphinx, and became king. He was subsequently revealed as the child exposed long ago, and thus as a parricide and incestuous husband, and in consequence suffered blinding. In Aeschylus he may have lived on at Thebes, as he does in Euripides' Phoenician Women (cf. Pherecydes above); in Sophocles, as probably in Euripides (F 554b), he goes into exile after power at Thebes passes to Jocasta's brother Creon.

Euripides differed markedly from Sophocles, however: (1) he included a long narrative of the Sphinx's riddle

(F 540, 540a) and, it seems, of how Oedipus solved it; (2) Oedipus is blinded not by his own hand but by servants of the dead Laius while he is still known at Thebes only as the son of Polybus of Corinth (F 541); (3) when the truth of Oedipus' life is revealed, Jocasta does not kill herself as in Sophocles (and Homer) from shame, but lives on, resolved to share his guilt and suffering (F *545a.9–12, cf. F 551.2; in Phoenician Women *she tends Oedipus in seclusion at Thebes, and kills herself only after their twin sons Eteocles and Polynices have died at each other's hands). These three distinctive features seem consistent with one very late secondary source, John Malalas (6th c. A.D.), who says that the play was about 'Oedipus and Jocasta and the Sphinx' (test. ii below).*

Other secondary sources and a few fragments have prompted much speculation about the play's course and character.[1] The narratives in Hyginus' Fables as so often tempt association with Euripides. In Fab. 66.2 he tells how the baby Oedipus was found by Periboea the wife of Polybus and brought up at Corinth; scholars, most influentially Robert (1915, I.326–7), have long adduced a 2nd c. B.C. 'Homeric' cup (LIMC 'Oidipous' no. 4), which depicts her discovery (the figures are named). Furthermore, in Fab. 67.7 Hyginus tells that when Oedipus, as king of Thebes, learned of the death of Polybus, Periboea arrived to alleviate his grief by disclosing that she and Polybus

---

[1] For surveys of evidence and reconstructions see Hose, Collard in *Lost Dramas*, Van Looy 430–4. The remarkable 'Pisander' Scholion on *Phoenician Women* 1760 has been shown by de Kock and Lloyd-Jones to be an unreliable, if suggestive, guide to Euripides' play.

were not his parents. Hose infers from Hyginus 67.7, with a detail from Phoenician Women *44–5 and the Scholia there (also the 'Pisander' Scholion on* Phoen. *1760), that Oedipus on becoming king of Thebes had sent to Polybus as a gift the chariot in which Laius had been riding when Oedipus killed him. Hose suggests it was in this chariot that Periboea came to Thebes, that it was recognised and prompted the inference that Oedipus had been Laius' killer, so that he was blinded as a regicide (F 541 with note), and that Periboea's disclosures led to his further punishment with exile (a regular penalty for those polluted by their own actions, e.g. Bellerophon in* Stheneboea *test. iia.7–9).*

*All this provides a plausible outline of the plot, with mechanisms of discovery and reversal for Oedipus through goodwill and accident like the arrival of Polybus' servant in Sophocles (*Oedipus *924ff.); but it leaves the account of the Sphinx both unlocated and unexplained. Some reconstructors have made it an early and 'live' episode, with a triumphant Oedipus soon overturned in a severe compression of 'dramatic time' (see especially Dingel, Aélion); these scholars and e.g. M. Huys (APF 43 [1997], 17–18) can support their case from Homer,* Odyssey *11.274, where the gods make Oedipus' parricide known 'immediately' after his marriage to his mother. Others suppose a retrospective narrative of the Sphinx, either by one of Laius' servants who in F 541 help to blind Oedipus (Vaio, 1964), or by Creon (Webster, Van Looy), or by Oedipus himself telling Periboea (Hose; compare Oedipus' 'flashback' to Laius' death in Sophocles'* Oedipus *798–813).*

*Only Creon had authority to order the blinding of Oedipus; an Etruscan vase of the 2nd century B.C. (*LIMC

'Oidipous' no. 85) may illustrate such a scene, but it shows it done in the presence of Jocasta and Oedipus' children, which is theatrically impossible. In F 551 Jocasta speaks of 'envy' as having destroyed Oedipus and herself; this, and the musings on self-interest (F 552–3), have been compared with Sophocles' Oedipus 380–6, 618–24, where Oedipus suspects that Creon wishes to depose him; so in Euripides Creon may have seized the throne when Oedipus was blinded (compare Sophocles, 1416–8). A three-cornered agon scene might develop in the play's last full episode between Oedipus, Jocasta and a Creon intent on punishing Oedipus additionally with exile (F 554a, perhaps F **555 if authentic); here too Jocasta's determination to stand by him would justify John Malalas' statement of her importance (above). Such a scene would plausibly accommodate most of the remaining fragments, gnomological and otherwise contextless, on the values of true marriage: F 543, 545, 545a, 546–8 and perhaps 542 and 544 (for such accumulations by gnomologists of fragments from one episode see our General Introduction, pp. xix–xx). A most intriguing fragment is F 554b which, if the text is sound (see note there), may allude to Oedipus' expectation of refuge in Athens (in Sophocles' Oedipus at Colonus 84–110 he appears to be confident of this from an oracle). For the unlocated F 556 see the note on the translation.

We should like to know what part, if any, Euripides gave the gods in Oedipus' passage from birth to catastrophe. In Aeschylus and Sophocles their role, communicated through oracles, was great. Euripides' F 539a may repeat from them that Oedipus was doomed because his father Laius defied Apollo's oracle; but F 549, 550 and 554, on life's uncertainties, may indicate that Euripides attributed the causation largely to chance.

Brief fragment: F 557 'limp' (perhaps of limbs—the defeated Sphinx, or the blinded Oedipus?). Other ascriptions: F 912 (see note there); F 1029.4–5 (see on F 542.3 here); adesp. F 8 (a tragic Oedipus: 'My father, sharer in my marriage, compelled me to die pitiably'). Adesp. fr. 284 N is now Diogenes of Sinope, TrGF 88 F 4.

A date later than 415 is suggested by the trochaic tetrameters in F 545 and *545a, a verse form found in other Euripidean dialogues only from Trojan Women *(415) onward; the metrical style of the iambic trimeters suggests the range 419–406 (Cropp–Fick 70, 85).*

Oedipus' life in the ancient theatre was busy: we have many titles for 5th and 4th c. tragedies (see TrGF 2.336). Any distinctive influence of Euripides' play is difficult to trace. It was alluded to, if not travestied, in Eubulus' comedy Oedipus *(mid-4th c.). Oedipus' encounter with the Sphinx was burlesqued in 4th–3rd c. South Italian farces (Trendall–Webster IV.32). We cannot define Seneca's debt to Euripides in his* Oedipus *(see the edition by K. Töchterle, Heidelberg, 1994, 10–14). For the Oedipus myth from antiquity to the present see SFP II.113 and above all L. Edmunds,* Oedipus *(London, 2006) with comprehensive bibliography; also OGCMA II.754–62.*

ΟΙΔΙΠΟΥΣ

test. ii

ὁ γὰρ σοφώτατος Εὐριπίδης ποιητικῶς ἐξέθετο δρᾶμα περὶ τοῦ Οἰδίποδος καὶ τῆς Ἰοκάστης καὶ τῆς Σφιγγός.

John Malalas, *Chronicles* 2.17 Thurn = 2.42 Jeffreys–Scott

test. iii (Hypothesis)

fr. 4   Ο]ἰδίπους, [οὗ ἀρχή·

Φοί]βου ποτ' οὐκ [ἐῶντος ἔσπειρεν

    ] τέκν[ο]ν· ἡ [δ' ὑπόθεσις·

about 33 lines lost

fr. 18.i   4 line-ends with a few letters each, then (5):

               ἐ]πὶ γήρως

               ]——

P. Oxy. 2455 fr. 4.40–2 and fr. 18 col. i.1–6

OEDIPUS

test. ii

The very learned Euripides produced a poetic drama about Oedipus and Jocasta and the Sphinx.

test. iii (Hypothesis)

Oedipus, (which begins) 'Although Phoebus (forbade it, Laius) once (fathered) a child'. The (plot is as follows) . . . *(about 37 lines almost entirely lost)* . . . into old age . . .[1] *(end of hypothesis)*

[1] Perhaps referring to the life which Jocasta intends to endure supporting the blind Oedipus at the end of the play (F *545a).

539a (= fr. adesp. 378 N)

Φοίβου ποτ᾽ οὐκ ἐῶντος ἔσπειρεν τέκνον . . .

Partially preserved in P. Oxy. 2455 (test. iii above); complete in
Plutarch, *Moralia* 205c and *Life of Cicero* 27.4

540

fr. 1   πυρσ]ώδη τε βοστρύχ[ων] φόβην·
οὐρὰν δ᾽ ὑπί]λασ᾽ ὑπὸ λεοντόπουν βάσιν
καθέζετ᾽, εἶτα] δ᾽ ἀποφέρουσ᾽ ὠκύπτερον
        ]ν ἐπιπα…ιριζ[.]ν χρόνῳ
5   ]ν διήλεσε..φυλλων φόβην
ὅταν μεθῇ τε] προσβάλῃ τ᾽ αὐγαῖς πτερόν·
εἰ μὲν πρὸς ἵπ]πους Ἡλίου, χρυσωπὸν ἦ[ν
νώτισμα θηρ]ός· εἰ δὲ [πρ]ὸς [νέ]φος [βάλοι,
κυανωπὸν ὤ]ς τις ἾΙρ[ις ἀντηύ]γει [σέλας.
remains from centres of six more lines

540, 540a, 540b: P. Oxy. 2459 frs. 1–3, ed. E. Turner (1962), cf.
H. Lloyd-Jones, *Gnomon* 35 (1963), 446–7; re-ed. Austin, *NFE*
60–1. We omit the tiny frs. 4 and 5.

540 (= fr. 1): vv. 2–3 (οὐρὰν—καθίζετο) Aelian, *Nature of Ani-
mals* 12.7; v. 2: Erotian υ 23 and (οὐρὰν ὑπήλας) Athenaeus
15.701b; vv. 7–9: Stobaeus 4.20.68 (= Plutarch fr. 136 Sandbach)

1 πυρσ]ώδη Diggle   5 διήλασε conj. Turner: -σ᾽
ἐριφύλλων Lloyd-Jones   7 ἵπ]πους P. Oxy.: αὐγὰς Stob.

10

OEDIPUS

539a (= fr. adesp. 378 N)
(Beginning of the play)

Although Phoebus forbade it, (Laius) once fathered a child.[1]

[1] I.e. Oedipus. Plutarch records that Cicero altered 'a child' to 'children' in quoting the line on sight of a certain Voconius accompanied by his three ugly daughters (for the ugliness of the blinded Oedipus see F *545a.4).

540

. . . and (fiery) mane of hair; she curled her tail beneath her lion's legs and sat; and (then) putting away her swift-flying . . . *(wording defective and unintelligible)* . . . in time . . . she ground down(?) the foliage(?) (of leafy . . . ?) (whenever   5
she unfurled) and moved her wing to the rays. If the creature held her back towards the horses of the Sun, its hue was golden, but if towards cloud, it shone back a dark-blue gleam like a rainbow.[1]

[1] The narrator's identity is disputed: see Introduction. The Sphinx has the body and legs of a lion, and wings, but the face of a girl (F 540a.5). Much of the text and translation is uncertain, and in v. 5 the verb 'ground down', if correct, is extraordinary; Turner's conjecture might perhaps mean 'thrust through' or 'spread', but none of these words seems to suit 'foliage'. A further problem is that the word meaning 'foliage' has to be translated 'mane' in v. 1.

540a

fr. 2   *remains of one line*

2   ]μον ἐλίπομεν [

        ]πων ἵσταντ᾽ ἀ[

       σ]υρίξασ᾽ ἱ....[

5   ] αἴνιγμ᾽ ἡ μιαι[φόνος κόρη

      ἐ]πειποῦσ᾽ ἐξάμετ[ρ᾽ ἀφῆκ᾽ ἔπη

   ἔστι τι φωνῇ]εν· ξύνεσιν δ᾽ ἔχο[ν

   τέτραπον ἠδὲ δί]πουν τι τρίπο[υν

        ]νῇ τρισὶ δ᾽ [

10   ]ίν δ᾽ ἄρσεν κα[ὶ

      ].ευεις ἢ πάλιν β[

      ]ὸν ὕμνον οπ[

     ] ὑμεῖς λέξ[ατε

   remains of one more line

P. Oxy. 2459 fr. 2 (see under F 540 above)

6 end Barrett   7–10 supplements draw on a version of
the Sphinx's riddle found in Athenaeus 10.456b and elsewhere
7 beg. Lloyd-Jones (φωνῇ]εν Snell)

540b

fr. 3 *Remains of six lines including 3* ἀν]ταγωνιστῇ[

P. Oxy. 2459 fr. 3 (see under F 540 above)

540a

... we left ... they were placing themselves[1] ... (the
Sphinx) hissing ... the murderous (maiden) pronouncing   5
her riddle (uttered) hexameter (verses): '(There is a thing
with a voice); it has intelligence ... a thing (four-footed and
two)-footed (and?) three-footed ... (on?) three ... male ...
and ... '[2] ... again ... song ... You (are to) say ...   10

[1] Bystanders, perhaps the 'You' addressed in 13?   [2] The
Sphinx's riddle in Athenaeus 10.456b (see opposite) reads: 'it is
two-footed and four-footed and three-footed on the ground; it has
a single voice; of all creatures that move, making their way on the
ground and up into the sky and down into the sea, it alone changes
its form. Whenever it goes supported on most feet, however, the
speed in its limbs is feeblest.' Answer: man, walking normally, or
crawling as a baby, or walking with a stick.

540b

... to (her?) antagonist ...[1]

[1] Probably Oedipus, attempting or solving the riddle.

EURIPIDES

541

ἡμεῖς δὲ Πολύβου παῖδ᾽ ἐρείσαντες πέδῳ
ἐξομματοῦμεν καὶ διόλλυμεν κόρας.

Schol. on *Phoenician Women* 61

542

οὗτοι νόμισμα λευκὸς ἄργυρος μόνον
καὶ χρυσός ἐστιν, ἀλλὰ κἀρετὴ βροτοῖς
νόμισμα κεῖται πᾶσιν, ᾗ χρῆσθαι χρεών.

Stobaeus 3.1.3; Orion, Euripidean Appendix 21 Haffner (garbled); vv. 1–2 (omitting καὶ—ἐστιν) Philodemus, *On Rhetoric*, P. Herc. 1669 col. XXVII.5–10 (I.262.5–10 Sudhaus; cf. T. di Mateo, *SIFC* 18 [2000], 200–8); vv. 1–2 (partly unmetrical, and attributed to Sophocles): Clement of Alexandria, *Miscellanies* 4.5.24.6

3 authenticity doubted by Nauck; Gomperz substituted F 1029.4–5 (see note on the translation)

543

μεγάλη τυραννὶς ἀνδρὶ τέκνα καὶ γυνή
⟨   ⟩
ἴσην γὰρ ἀνδρὶ συμφορὰν εἶναι λέγω
τέκνων θ᾽ ἁμαρτεῖν καὶ πάτρας καὶ χρημάτων

Stobaeus 4.22.1; v. 1 = [Menander], *Monostichs* 506 Jaekel

1–2 lacuna Weil

OEDIPUS

541

SERVANT OF LAIUS

We pressed the son of Polybus to the ground, destroying his eyes and blinding him.[1]

[1] On this fragment and its possible reflection in art, see the Introduction.

542

Truly, pale silver and gold are not the only currency, but virtue too is an established currency for all men, which they should use.[1]

[1] The authenticity of v. 3 was doubted because two of the sources, Philodemus and Clement, do not cite it. Gomperz substituted F 1029.4–5 to give 'but virtue too is an established currency for men, but (while currency wears away with use,) the more you are willing to practise virtue, the more it will increase and be perfected.'

543

⟨OEDIPUS⟩

Children and a wife are a great kingdom for a man[1] ... for to lose children and fatherland and wealth is a disaster for a man equal, I say, to losing a good wife, in that his wealth

[1] The sense is either that they are a highly valuable asset, or that they have a strong hold over him. The tenor of vv. 2–3, and of F 545, 545a and 546, suggests that 'kingdom' is preferable to the negative alternative 'tyranny' (cf. F 544).

EURIPIDES

ἀλόχου τε κεδνῆς, ὡς μόνων τῶν χρημάτων
⟨   ⟩
5   ἢ κρεῖσσόν ἐστιν ἀνδρί, σῶφρον· ἢν λάβῃ . . .

4–5 lacuna Welcker and others   5 ἢ Stob. ed. Trincavelli: ἢ
or ἡ Stob. mss.

544

ἄλλως δὲ πάντων δυσμαχώτατον γυνή.

Stobaeus 4.22.140

545

⟨ΙΟΚΑΣΤΗ⟩

πᾶσα γὰρ δούλη πέφυκεν ἀνδρὸς ἡ σώφρων γυνή,
ἡ δὲ μὴ σώφρων ἀνοίᾳ τὸν ξυνόνθ᾽ ὑπερφρονεῖ.

Stobaeus 4.22.85; Clement of Alexandria, *Miscellanies*
4.8.63.3 (corrupt and possibly altered for contrast with F 546,
which Clement cites next); v. 1: Stobaeus 4.22.2 (directly after F
543). Inserted between vv. 10 and 11 of F *545a by Robert.

2 ἡ δὲ Stob. ms. S, Clem.: εἰ δὲ Stob. mss. MA (and Blaydes,
with εἰ σώφρων in v. 1)

*545a (= 909 N)

⟨ΙΟΚΑΣΤΗ⟩

οὐδεμίαν ὤνησε κάλλος εἰς πόσιν ξυνάορον,
ἀρετὴ δ᾽ ὤνησε πολλάς· πᾶσα γὰρ κεδνὴ γυνή,
ἥτις ἀνδρὶ συντέτηκε, σωφρονεῖν ἐπίσταται.
πρῶτα μὲν γὰρ τοῦθ᾽ ὑπάρχει· κἂν ἄμορφος ᾖ
    πόσις,

alone . . . Truly, it is better for a man, if he gets a virtuous (wife) . . .[2]

[2] Many editors have tried to preserve the unity of all 5 verses through emendation.

544

And besides, a woman is the hardest of all things to fight.

545

⟨JOCASTA⟩

Every sensible wife is her husband's slave; the wife without sense despises her partner out of folly.[1]

[1] Blaydes preferred 'Every wife is her husband's slave if she is sensible; but if she is not sensible she despises . . . '. Robert proposed to insert this couplet between vv. 10 and 11 of F *545a: see note there.

*545a (= 909 N)

⟨JOCASTA⟩

Beauty benefits no wife with her husband, but virtue benefits many. Every good wife who has melted in union with her husband knows how to be sensible. For this is the first fundamental: even if a husband is unhandsome, to a wife

5 χρὴ δοκεῖν εὔμορφον εἶναι τῇ γε νοῦν κεκτημένῃ,
οὐ γὰρ ὀφθαλμὸς τὸ ⟨ταῦτα⟩ κρῖνόν ἐστιν, ἀλλὰ
νοῦς.
εὖ λέγειν δ᾽, ὅταν τι λέξῃ, χρὴ δοκεῖν, κἂν μὴ λέγῃ,
κἀκπονεῖν ἂν τῷ ξυνόντι πρὸς χάριν μέλλῃ πονεῖν.
ἡδὺ δ᾽, ἢν κακὸν πάθῃ τι, συσκυθρωπάζειν πόσει
10 ἄλοχον ἐν κοινῷ τε λύπης ἡδονῆς τ᾽ ἔχειν μέρος.
σοὶ δ᾽ ἔγωγε καὶ νοσοῦντι συννοσοῦσ᾽ ἀνέξομαι
καὶ κακῶν τῶν σῶν ξυνοίσω, κοὐδὲν ἔσται μοι
πικρόν.

Clement of Alexandria, *Miscellanies* 4.20.125.1–126.4, citing
7–8, 9–10, 11–12, 1–3, 4–6 separately and in that order; reordered
and made continuous by Musgrave; assigned to *Oedipus* by K. F.
Hermann.

2 κεδνὴ Nauck: ἀγαθὴ (unmetrical) Clem.   4 γὰρ
Grotius: γε Clem.   6 ⟨ταῦτα⟩ Musgrave   κρῖνόν Sylburg: κρίνειν Clem.: οὐ γὰρ ὀφθαλμοῦ τὸ κρίνειν ἐστὶν ἀλλὰ
νοῦς ⟨ὁρᾷ⟩ (Wilamowitz) Nauck (. . . ἀλλὰ νοῦ Cropp)
8 πονεῖν Collard: λέγειν Clem.: τελεῖν Wecklein: τάχα Kannicht
9 πάθῃ Blaydes, Nauck: πράξῃ Clem.   10 Robert inserted
F 545 after this verse

546

⟨ΧΟΡΟΣ?⟩
πᾶσα γὰρ ἀνδρὸς κακίων ἄλοχος,
κἂν ὁ κάκιστος
γήμῃ τὴν εὐδοκιμοῦσαν.

OEDIPUS

with sense at all he ought to seem handsome; for it is not   5
the eye that judges (these things), but the mind.[1] She must
think, whenever he says anything, that he speaks well, even
if he does not; and work to achieve whatever she means to
work at[2] to please her partner. It is pleasing too, if he expe-
riences some trouble, for a wife to put on a gloomy face
with her husband, and to join in sharing his pain and plea-
sure.[3] (*to Oedipus*) You and I: I will endure sharing your   10
guilt as my own, and help to bear your troubles; and noth-
ing will be (too) harsh for me.

[1] The defective line is variously mended, sometimes with
Clement's wording retained, e.g. 'it is not the eye's to judge, but
the mind <that sees>' (Nauck, Wilamowitz: ' . . . but the mind's',
Cropp).   [2] 'to work at', Collard: Clement's 'to say' is clearly
wrong; 'to accomplish', Wecklein; 'quickly', Kannicht.   [3] Cf.
Phrixus A/B F 822.35–8 and F 823. The thought and wording of
Menander, *Men at Arbitration* 817–21 (a wife) and 914–22 (her
husband) may echo our passage (cf. F 554b). Robert's insertion
here of F 545, prompted in part by the separation of vv. 9–10 and
11–12 in Clement, is possible but no more.

546

<CHORUS?>

Every wife is worse than her husband, even if the worst of
men marries one of good repute.

Clement of Alexandria, *Miscellanies* 4.8.63.2; vv. 1–3 (κα-
κίων—εὐδοκιμοῦσαν) Stobaeus 4.22.187

1 κακίων Clem., Stob. (metrically unlikely): χείρων (same
sense) anon., Heimsoeth   2 κάκιστος Stob. κράτιστος
Clem.

19

547

ἑνὸς ⟨δ'⟩ ἔρωτος ὄντος οὐ μί' ἡδονή·
οἱ μὲν κακῶν ἐρῶσιν, οἱ δὲ τῶν καλῶν.

Stobaeus 1.9.2

548

⟨ΙΟΚΑΣΤΗ?⟩

νοῦν χρὴ θεᾶσθαι, νοῦν· τί τῆς εὐμορφίας
ὄφελος, ὅταν τις μὴ φρένας καλὰς ἔχῃ;

Stobaeus 4.21.19

1 θεᾶσθαι, νοῦν· τί Elmsley: θεάσασθαι οὐδέν τι Stob. mss.
SMA (θεᾶσθαι ms. Paris. 1985)

549

⟨ΟΙΔΙΠΟΥΣ?⟩

ἀλλ' ἦμαρ ⟨ἕν⟩ τοι μεταβολὰς πολλὰς ἔχει.

Stobaeus 4.41.45

550

⟨ΟΙΔΙΠΟΥΣ?⟩

ἐκ τῶν ἀέλπτων ἡ χάρις μείζων βροτοῖς
{φανεῖσα μᾶλλον ἢ τὸ προσδοκώμενον}.

Stobaeus 4.47.4; v. 2 deleted by Herwerden

547

Although love is a single thing, it has no single pleasure:
some love what is bad, others what is good.[1]

[1] Jocasta's love for Oedipus defended? By herself? By him?

548

⟨JOCASTA?⟩

It is the mind one must watch, the mind! What use is hand-
someness, when a man does not have good sense?[1]

[1] Jocasta continues her defence? *Antiope* F 212 is very similar
except that it refers to a woman's beauty.

549

⟨OEDIPUS?⟩

But (one) day holds many changes, I tell you![1]

[1] This fragment and the next may come from the same context
as F 554 and perhaps 554b.

550

⟨OEDIPUS?⟩

Men's joy is greater from what is unexpected {when (this),
rather than the expected, appears}.

EURIPIDES

551

⟨ΙΟΚΑΣΤΗ?⟩

φθόνος δ᾿ ὁ πολλῶν φρένα διαφθείρων βροτῶν
ἀπώλεσ᾿ αὐτὸν κἀμὲ συνδιώλεσεν.

Stobaeus 3.38.9

552

πότερα γενέσθαι δῆτα χρησιμώτερον
συνετὸν ἄτολμον ἢ θρασύν τε κἀμαθῆ;
τὸ μὲν γὰρ αὐτῶν σκαιὸν ἀλλ᾿ ἀμύνεται,
τὸ δ᾿ ἡσυχαῖον ἀργόν· ἐν δ᾿ ἀμφοῖν νόσος.

Stobaeus 3.7.9

553

⟨ΟΙΔΙΠΟΥΣ?⟩

ἐκμαρτυρεῖν γὰρ ἄνδρα τὰς αὑτοῦ τύχας
εἰς πάντας ἀμαθές, τὸ δ᾿ ἐπικρύπτεσθαι σοφόν.

Stobaeus 4.45.6

554

πολλάς γ᾿ ὁ δαίμων τοῦ βίου μεταστάσεις
ἔδωκεν ἡμῖν μεταβολάς τε τῆς τύχης.

Stobaeus 4.41.44

22

OEDIPUS

551

<JOCASTA?>

Envy which corrupts the mind of many men has destroyed
him, and destroyed me with him.[1]

[1] Probably Creon's envy of Oedipus: see Introduction. This
fragment may have preceded F 549 and 550.

552

Is it indeed more useful to be intelligent and without dar-
ing, or rash and stupid? The one of these is foolish, but de-
fends itself, while the other, which is peaceable, is lazy.
There is weakness in both, however.[1]

[1] The value terms in this fragment were common in Athenian
political language: cf. e.g. *Antiope* F 193–4 (and the brief F 226).

553

<OEDIPUS?>

It is stupid for a man to testify to his misfortunes in front of
everybody; concealment is wise.[1]

[1] For the sentiment cf. *Cretan Women* F 460 with note.

554

The god gives us many changes in our life, and many alter-
ations in our fortune.

EURIPIDES

554a (= 1049 N)

⟨ΚΡΕΩΝ?⟩

ἐγὼ γὰρ ὅστις μὴ δίκαιος ὢν ἀνὴρ
βωμὸν προσίζει, τὸν νόμον χαίρειν ἐῶν
πρὸς τὴν δίκην ἄγοιμ' ἂν οὐ τρέσας θεούς·
κακὸν γὰρ ἄνδρα χρὴ κακῶς πάσχειν ἀεί.

Stobaeus 4.5.11; v. 4: *CPG* II.757.3 and 'Tübinger Theosophist' §86 Erbse

554b

⟨ΟΙΔΙΠΟΥΣ?⟩

ὦ πόλισμα Κεκροπίας χθονός,
ὦ ταναὸς αἰθήρ, ὦ . . .

Menander, *Woman from Samos* 325–6, where a marginal note in P. Bodmer 25 attributes the words to the play and possibly to Oedipus himself.

1 Κεκροπίας Men.: Καδμείας Cropp, Van Looy

**555

ἀλλ' ἡ Δίκη γὰρ καὶ κατὰ σκότον βλέπει.

Stobaeus 1.3.6, attached to a part-line of Callimachus (*Aetia* F 239.5 *Suppl. Hell.*) which is attributed to Euripides' *Oedipus*.

σκότον Kannicht: -ους Stob.

OEDIPUS

554a (= 1049 N)

⟨CREON?⟩

I'd myself take away to face justice any man who sits in sanctuary at an altar without just cause, and would leave the law aside; and I'd not fear the gods: for a bad man should always suffer badly.[1]

[1] Perhaps Creon insisting on summary justice and exile for the already blinded Oedipus (now actually in sanctuary?), after his revelation as a parricide: see Introduction. For the general idea cf. *Ion* 1314–9.

554b

⟨OEDIPUS?⟩

O city of Cecrops' land, O sky outspread, O . . .[1]

[1] Almost certainly Oedipus, calling either on Athens ('Cecrops' land') as his place of exile (see Introduction), or on Thebes ('Cadmus' land', as Cropp and Van Looy suggest) as witness of his terrible fate.

**555

The truth is, Justice sees even in darkness.[1]

[1] A commonplace, so (if from this play at all) perhaps not dark humour at the expense of the blinded Oedipus.

556

τόν θ' ὑμνοποιὸν δόνα[χ' ὃν ἐκτρέφει Μέ]λας
ποταμός, ἀηδόν' εὐπνόων αὐλῶν σοφήν.

Theon, Commentary on Pindar, *Pythians* 12.25–6 (P. Oxy.
2536 col. i.28–30); v. 2: ἀηδόνα 'metaphorical' attributed to Eur.
Oedipus in Hesychius α 1500 Latte, to 'tragic poets' in Photius α
441 Theodoridis

1 δόνα[χ' ὃν Turner, ἐκτρέφει Gentili, Μέ]λας Lobel

556

. . . and the reed, maker of song, (which the Black) River (produces), the skilful nightingale of pipes sweetly blown.[1]

[1] The Black River in Boeotia was famous for the quality of its pipe reeds. For 'nightingale' see on *Palamedes* F 588.3.

OENEUS

H. Van Looy in ed. Budé VIII.2.459–75.

Webster 113, 299–300; *LIMC* I.i.306–8 'Agrios',
VII.i.915–9 'Oineus'; Gantz 334–5.

*Two principal sources for the myth broadly coincide and
suggest the outline of Euripides' play (Scholia on Aris-
tophanes,* Acharnians *418–9 = test. iia below, and Hyginus,*
Fab. *175 = test. *iiib below; cf. Gantz 334–5). Oeneus king
of Calydon in Aetolia was by his second wife Periboea
the father of Tydeus, the fearsome warrior (the tragedy of
his first wife, Althaea, and their son Meleager resulting
from Oeneus' offence against Artemis was the subject of*
Meleager*). Tydeus had to flee Calydon when he shed kin-
dred blood (F 558.2–3); he became one of the Seven against
Thebes and was killed there (F 558.4–5, 559; cf. Alcmeon
in Psophis F *69, Meleager F 537). After Tydeus' death,
Oeneus' brother Agrius deposed him (test. iia) and Agrius'
sons maltreated him (F 562, cf. 564), or Agrius drove him
from Calydon into poverty (Hyginus). Tydeus' son Dio-
medes learned of this, and returned to Calydon, either
from the vengeance taken upon Thebes by the sons of the
Seven (cf. F 559), or from the Trojan War (Hyginus). Dio-
medes was accompanied by Sthenelus, son of another of the
Seven, Capaneus (Hyginus); together they killed one of*

28

Agrius' sons and drove Agrius out (*Hyginus*), or killed Agrius himself (*Schol.* Acharnians). Diomedes then restored Oeneus to the throne.

Variant details of the myth in the Scholia on Homer, Iliad *14.115* and in Apollodorus *1.8.6* seem not to fit well with this outline. The Homeric scholia have Tydeus himself, not Diomedes, killing cousins (i.e. sons of Agrius) who were plotting against Oeneus. Apollodorus has Diomedes aided not by Sthenelus but by Alcmeon (yet another of the sons of the Seven); because of Oeneus' old age Diomedes does not restore the throne to him, but gives it to Oeneus' son Andraemon; then Diomedes takes Oeneus to the Peloponnese, where Oeneus is ambushed and killed by the surviving sons of Agrius. Also, unconfident attempts have been made to trace back to Euripides some elements of two Roman tragedies whose titles alone suggest very different plots: that of Accius' Diomedes is unknown, but did feature a tyrant (Agrius? See frs. 1, 4 Dangel); Pacuvius' Periboea features an elderly, wretched and perhaps ill-treated man (frs. 1, 3–4, 5–6, 10 d'Anna), but also Melanippus a son of Agrius whom a woman (Periboea? see above) tries to enlist to help end the terrible dispute (fr. 12, cf. fr. 27 d'Anna).

How far Euripides' plot took Oeneus' story, and whether up to his death (Apollodorus, above), neither the principal testimonia nor the fragments themselves allow us to judge. Diomedes delivered the prologue, most likely at his return to Calydon (F 558, ?559). Probably one of Oeneus' faithful servants informed him and Sthenelus of Oeneus' maltreatment (F 562, cf. 561; 564 is addressed to 'strangers': see the note there), before Diomedes spoke with Oeneus himself (F 565, perhaps also 563 and 566). These

29

fragments would have led the action into at least a second episode; the vengeance upon Agrius and his sons (perhaps through the sort of intrigue common in such Euripidean plots), its likely report by a messenger, and the restoration of Oeneus would follow easily enough; indeed these elements may be reflected in a composite scene on a Paestan hydria of c. 340 B.C. (LIMC 'Agrios' no. 1 = 'Oineus' no. 55, Trendall–Webster III.3.41, Todisco P 13, Taplin no. 70), in which Agrius (named) in tragic costume sits bound on an altar and is threatened both by a Fury figure and by a young man dressed as a traveller (the returned Diomedes?), who is about to offer a sword to an elderly king in tragic costume (Oeneus?); a similar scene, but with no named figure, on a Capuan amphora of the same date is assigned uncertainly either to our play or to Sophocles' Thyestes (LIMC 'Oineus' no. 56, Todisco C 38). As so often, we are frustrated for the tone of the play's end, either happy or still threatening. It is not possible to locate in this outline F 560, 567, 568 and the brief F 569 and 570.

Brief fragments: F 569 'unspread' (apparently a metaphor from leather stretched for tanning, perhaps referring to the lack of proper bedding for the maltreated Oeneus), F 570 'on tip toe'. Other ascription: adesp. F 625 (papyrus fragments perhaps from an Oeneus or Meleager = Page, GLP no. 28, rejected most recently by T. Stephanopoulos, ZPE 73 (1988), 237–41).

Date: before 425, the year of Aristophanes' Acharnians (see test. iia).

Sophocles appears to have written a satyr drama Oeneus: *see TrGF 4, F **1130; Diggle, TrGFS 77–8; Krumeich 368–74; there would probably have been word-play*

upon Oeneus' name ('Wine-man') in connection with
Dionysus-Bacchus. Plays named Oeneus are known from
Philocles (5th c.) and Chaeremon (4th c.). For the Roman
Pacuvius' Periboea and Accius' Diomedes see above.

ΟΙΝΕΥΣ

test. iia

'τὰ ποῖα τρύχη; μῶν ἐν οἷς Οἰνεὺς ὁδὶ | ὁ δύσποτμος
γεραιὸς ἠγωνίζετο;' γέγραπται τῷ Εὐριπίδῃ δρᾶμα Οἰ-
νεύς. μετὰ δὲ τὸν θάνατον Τυδέως καὶ ἐπιστράτευσιν
Διομήδους κατὰ Θηβαίων ἀφῃρέθη τὴν βασιλείαν Οἰ-
νεὺς διὰ τὸ γῆρας ὑπὸ τῶν Ἀγρίου παίδων καὶ περιῄει
ταπεινός, ἄχρις οὗ ἐπανελθὼν ὁ Διομήδης Ἄγριον μὲν
ἀνεῖλε, τὴν βασιλείαν δὲ Οἰνεῖ παραδέδωκε.

Aristophanes, *Acharnians* 418–9 and Schol. on 418a; see note
on the translation opposite.

test. *iiib

AGRIVS. Agrius Porthaonis filius ut uidit Oeneum fratrem
orbum liberis factum, egentem regno expulit atque ipse reg-
num possedit. (2) Interim Diomedes Tydei filius et Deipyles
Ilio deuicto ut audiuit auum suum regno pulsum, peruenit in
Aetoliam cum Sthenelo Capanei filio et armis contendit cum
†Opopa† Agrii filio, quo interfecto Agrium e regno expulit
atque Oeneo auo suo regnum restituit. (3) Postque Agrius
regno expulsus ipse se interfecit.

Hyginus, *Fab.* 175

32

OENEUS

test. iia

'What tatters?—not the ones in which Oeneus, that ill-starred old man, performed in competition here?' (*Acharnians* 418–9). A play *Oeneus* was written by Euripides. After the death of Tydeus and Diomedes' campaign against the Thebans, Oeneus was deprived of his kingdom by the sons of Agrius because of his old age; he went about abjectly, until Diomedes on his return killed Agrius and handed the kingship to Oeneus.[1]

[1] Oeneus' tattered beggary in Euripides' play is recorded in another now fragmentary commentary on *Acharnians* 419 (P. Oxy. 856, also in *TrGF* test. iia), and in *Frogs* 1063 and Scholia.

test. *iiib

AGRIUS. When Agrius, son of Porthaon, saw his brother Oeneus had been made childless, he drove him from the kingdom in poverty and took possession of it himself. (2) Meanwhile, when Diomedes, son of Tydeus and Deipyle, after Troy's defeat heard that his grandfather had been driven from the kingdom, he came to Aetolia with Sthenelus, son of Capaneus, and fought a battle with †Opopas† the son of Agrius; after killing him he drove Agrius from the kingdom and restored it to his grandfather Oeneus. (3) Later, expelled from the kingdom, Agrius killed himself.

EURIPIDES

558

ΔΙΟΜΗΔΗΣ

Ὦ γῆς πατρῴας χαῖρε φίλτατον πέδον
Καλυδῶνος, ἔνθεν αἷμα συγγενὲς φυγὼν
Τυδεύς, τόκος μὲν Οἰνέως, πατὴρ δ' ἐμός,
ᾤκησεν Ἄργος, παῖδα δ' Ἀδράστου λαβὼν
5 συνῆψε γένναν . . .

Aristotle, *Rhetoric* 1417a15–16 names the prologue of *Oeneus*
for its concision; a commentator in *CAG* XXI.2.245–8 Rabe cites
the verses themselves.

559

⟨ΔΙΟΜΗΔΗΣ⟩

ἐγὼ δὲ πατρὸς αἷμ' ἐτιμωρησάμην
σὺν τοῖς ἐφηβήσασι τῶν ὀλωλότων.

Erotian τ 17

560

ἀλλ' ἄλλος ἄλλοις μᾶλλον ἥδεται τρόποις.

Clement of Alexandria, *Miscellanies* 6.2.7.5

561

οἰκεῖα γεωργεῖς ταῦτα, ἢ δεσπότης μὲν αὐτῶν ἕτερος, σὺ
δὲ τρέφοντα τοῦτον τρέφεις, ὥσπερ τὸν τοῦ Εὐριπίδου
Οἰνέα;

Philostratus, *On Heroes* 4.1; Kannicht and others have ex-
tracted τρέφω (or τρέφεις) τρέφοντα as original Euripidean
wording.

OENEUS

558

(Beginning of the play)

DIOMEDES

Greetings, dearest soil of my fatherland Calydon, from where Tydeus, son of Oeneus and my own father, fled after shedding the blood of kin;[1] he went to live in Argos, took Adrastus' daughter in marriage, and linked their families . . . [2]

[1] Mythographers give various names for the victims, either accidental or deliberate (see Gantz 334). [2] Cf. *Suppliant Women* 133–48, *Phoenician Women* 417–25, *Hypsipyle* F 753c.8–21.

559

⟨DIOMEDES⟩

I avenged my father's blood in company with the sons of those who had perished, once they had reached manhood.[1]

[1] For the sons of the Seven against Thebes ('Epigoni') see Introduction to *Alcmeon in Psophis*.

560

Yet one person enjoys some kinds of behaviour more, and another, others.

561

Do you farm this as your own, or is another its master, and do you maintain this one who maintains you, like Euripides' Oeneus?[1]

[1] The comparison suggests that some such words were said to a faithful servant of Oeneus who worked to keep his master, perhaps by Diomedes when restoring Oeneus to his throne. Euripides' own words may have included 'I maintain (*or* you maintain) . . . who maintains (you)'.

562

πυκνοῖς δ' ἔβαλλον Βακχίου τοξεύμασιν
κάρα γέροντος· τὸν βαλόντα δὲ στέφειν
ἐγὼ 'τετάγμην, ἆθλα κοσσάβων διδούς.

Athenaeus 15.666c

563

σχολὴ μὲν οὐχί, τῷ δὲ δυστυχοῦντί πως
τερπνὸν τὸ λέξαι κἀποκλαύσασθαι πάλιν.

Stobaeus 4.48.16; Chrysippus, *On Passions* fr. 467 von Arnim

2 λέξαι κἀποκλαύσασθαι πάλιν Stob.: κλαῦσαι κἀπο-
δύρασθαι τύχας Chrys. (preferred by some editors but perhaps
due to confusion with the similarly worded *Prometheus Bound*
637)

564

ὅταν κακοὶ πράξωσιν, ὦ ξένοι, καλῶς,
ἄγαν κρατοῦντες κοὐ νομίζοντες δίκην
δώσειν, ἔδρασαν πάντ' ἐφέντες ἡδονῇ.

Stobaeus 4.42.4

565

⟨ΔΙΟΜΗΔΗΣ⟩

σὺ δ' ὧδ' ἔρημος ξυμμάχων ἀπόλλυσαι;

36

OENEUS

562

They threw frequent shots of wine at the old man's head. I had been appointed to crown the one who hit it, giving the prize for cottabus.[1]

[1] Oeneus' servant tells how Oeneus was humiliated: his (bald?) head became the target instead of the saucer or metal disk at which cottabus players aimed the last drops of wine from their cups (cf. *Pleisthenes* F 631, *Stheneboea* F 664). Penelope's suitor Eurymachus similarly abuses Odysseus, disguised as a beggar, in Aeschylus' *Bone-Gatherers*, F 179 (also cited by Athenaeus).

563

No, I have no leisure, but retelling and weeping again is somehow pleasurable for any unfortunate person.[1]

[1] Possibly Oeneus is speaking. Renewed lament may be pleasing (cf. *Andromeda* F 119 with note) or displeasing (e.g. Sophocles, *Oedipus at Colonus* 363–4). Chrysippus' version means 'weeping and lamenting their misfortunes'.

564

When bad men prosper, strangers, they are over-mighty and do not think they will pay a penalty: they give way to pleasure and commit all kinds of crimes.[1]

[1] If Oeneus is speaking (cf. on F 563), he has not recognized his grandson Diomedes among the 'strangers' (or were they disguised?); but the speaker may be Oeneus' servant, as in F 562. The text and syntax of this fragment are suspect.

565

⟨DIOMEDES⟩

Are you being destroyed like this because you are without allies?

EURIPIDES

⟨ΟΙΝΕΥΣ⟩

οἱ μὲν γὰρ οὐκέτ᾽ εἰσίν, οἱ δ᾽ ὄντες κακοί.

Schol. on Aristophanes, *Frogs* 71–2; v. 2 (= *Frogs* 72) became a saying, e.g. Gregory of Cyprus 3.22a *CPG*, varied at Cicero, *Letters to Atticus* 1.20.3

566

ὡς οὐδὲν ἀνδρὶ πιστὸν ἄλλο πλὴν τέκνων·
κέρδους δ᾽ ἕκατι καὶ τὸ συγγενὲς νοσεῖ.

Stobaeus 4.24.3; v. 1 assigned to Diomedes, v. 2 to Oeneus by Herwerden (cf. F 565)

567

τὰς βροτῶν
γνώμας †σκοπῶν† ὥστε Μαγνῆτις λίθος
τὴν δόξαν ἕλκει καὶ μεθίησιν πάλιν.

Photius η 224 Theodoridis = Suda η 459; v. 2 Μαγνῆτις λίθος 'named by Euripides', Plato, *Ion* 533d

2 ἐπισπῶν Hartung

568

. . . καὶ γάρ εἰμ᾽ ἄγαν
ὀχληρός, οὐ δοκῶν με κοιράνους στυγεῖν.

Aristophanes, *Acharnians* 471–2 and Schol. ('an obscure parody from *Oeneus*')

‹OENEUS›

Yes: some are no longer alive, and those that live are worthless.[1]

---

[1] The line was used by Aristophanes to highlight the lack of 'good' poets in Athens to encourage its citizens in the final crisis of the Peloponesian War.

566

A man has nothing to rely upon except children; and even kinship weakens when profit is the issue.[1]

---

[1] Vv. 1 and 2 may have been divided between Diomedes and Oeneus (Herwerden), as F 565.

567

†Looking at† men's opinions, (he?) attracts and then releases their belief like Magnesian stone.[1]

---

[1] Text and interpretation are wholly insecure. Photius records an ancient distinction between magnetic iron-stone ('stone of Heracles') and silver ('stone of Magnesia'), and cites our fragment as illustrating the power of silver over those who view it and waver; but elsewhere in antiquity 'stone of Magnesia' also meant iron-stone. In the transmitted Greek, 'Looking at' is both inappropriate and unmetrical: Hartung suggested 'drawing', a word Photius himself uses in his illustration; then probably the sentence describes a powerful speaker.

568

. . . for I am too troublesome, not thinking that (our) rulers hate me.[1]

---

[1] Ancient commentators could not understand the point of Aristophanes' parody (see opposite), so a context for this fragment can hardly be guessed. An ascription of the same verse to *Telephus*, mentioned in the scholia, is probably without foundation.

OENOMAUS

H. Van Looy in ed. Budé VIII.3.477–86.

Séchan 447–66; Webster 115; *LIMC* V.i.434–40 'Hippodameia I', VII.i.19–23 'Oinomaos'; Gantz 540–3.

The seven gnomic fragments reveal almost nothing, but presumably the play was about Pelops' race against Oenomaus for the hand of his daughter Hippodamia, a story well established in archaic Greek poetry (cf. [Hesiod] F 259(a)) and art, and best known to us from Pindar's First Olympian *and several mythographic summaries (see Gantz's thorough survey). Oenomaus obstructed his daughter's marriage, either fearing his son-in-law would kill him or being in love with her himself; he had invincible chariot horses (a gift from his father, the god Ares), and therefore challenged Hippodamia's suitors to a chariot race from Pisa to the Isthmus of Corinth in which the loser was to be killed. Oenomaus invariably won until Pelops defeated and killed him, either by obtaining an even more invincible chariot team from Poseidon (Pindar) or more commonly (at least from the early 5th century) by having Oenomaus' charioteer Myrtilus sabotage the wheels of the king's chariot. Pelops later killed Myrtilus when he assaulted Hippodamia, or claimed the sexual reward she or Pelops had promised him; as he died, Myrtilus cursed the family of Pelops with devastating effect on his sons Atreus and Thyestes and their children.*

OENOMAUS

Sophocles produced an Oenomaus *of which eight fragments survive, the most informative being Hippodamia's striking description of how she was struck with love by Pelops' gaze (F 474). Among the Euripidean fragments, F 571 seems to come from a relatively sympathetic Oenomaus, concerned for his daughter's welfare (though this does not preclude abusive behaviour on his part: cf. Cercyon in* Alope*), and F 572–3 and 575 could have contributed to such a portrayal. Some scholars are therefore inclined to think that Sophocles' play focused on* erôs *(Hippodamia's desire for Pelops, Oenomaus' and Myrtilus' desire for her: cf. Apollodorus, Epit. 2.3–9), while Euripides contrasted a protective Oenomaus with a ruthless and treacherous Pelops, perhaps reflecting anti-Peloponnesian sentiment at Athens (cf. Webster, Van Looy). But all this remains speculative, as is any attempt to link the many 4th-century vase-paintings on this subject with one or other of the lost plays (cf. Taplin 199–200).*

Oenomaus, Chrysippus *and* Phoenician Women *are mentioned together in a fragmentary hypothesis to* Phoenician Women, *probably as having related content rather than as making a trilogy (see Introduction to* Chrysippus). *The metrical style of the* Oenomaus *fragments, with no resolutions in 24 trimeters, makes a date as late as* Phoenician Women *(c. 409) seem unlikely, though the inference from seven gnomic fragments is not secure. Sophocles'* Oenomaus *seems to have preceded Aristophanes'* Birds *of 414 (Soph. F 476 =* Birds *1337–9). Antiphanes and Eubulus each produced a comic* Oenomaus *or* Pelops *in the 4th century (one fragment of each survives), and Accius a Latin tragedy in the 2nd (eleven fragments); the relationship of these with the earlier tragedies is unknown.*

ΟΙΝΟΜΑΟΣ

571

<ΟΙΝΟΜΑΟΣ?>

ἀμηχανῶ δ' ἔγωγε κοὐκ ἔχω μαθεῖν,
εἴτ' οὖν ἄμεινόν ἐστι γίγνεσθαι τέκνα
θνητοῖσιν εἴτ' ἄπαιδα καρποῦσθαι βίον.
ὁρῶ γὰρ οἷς μὲν οὐκ ἔφυσαν, ἀθλίους,
5 ὅσοισι δ' εἰσίν, οὐδὲν εὐτυχεστέρους·
καὶ γὰρ κακοὶ γεγῶτες ἐχθίστη νόσος,
κἂν αὖ γένωνται σώφρονες—κακὸν μέγα—
λυποῦσι τὸν φύσαντα μὴ πάθωσί τι.

Stobaeus 4.24.17

572

ἕν ἐστι πάντων πρῶτον εἰδέναι τόδε,
φέρειν τὰ συμπίπτοντα μὴ παλιγκότως·
χοὗτός γ' ἀνὴρ ἄριστος, αἵ τε συμφοραὶ
ἧσσον δάκνουσιν. ἀλλὰ ταῦτα γὰρ λέγειν
5 ἐπιστάμεσθα, δρᾶν δ' ἀμηχάνως ἔχει.

Stobaeus 4.35.8

1 τόδε Stobaean excerpts in ms. Brussels 11360, and various
scholars: τουτί Stob.: βροτῷ Nauck

OENOMAUS

571

I myself am uncertain and cannot learn for sure whether it
is indeed better for men to get children, or to enjoy a child-
less life. For I see that those who have no children are mis-
erable, while all those who have them are in no way more
fortunate: if their children turn out bad, they are a most   5
hateful affliction, and if on the other hand they are well
behaved—a great distress, this—they make their father
anxious that something may happen to them.[1]

[1] Similar reasoning: F 908.3–6, 908a, *Medea* 1090–1115.

572

This one thing is the most important of all to know: to bear
the things that befall us without resentment.[1] Such a man
excels in virtue, and his misfortunes torment him less. But
of course, though we know how to say this, we cannot
do it.[2]

[1] Cf. *Antiope* F 175.12–15, *Hippolytus* 203–7.   [2] Cf.
Alexandros F 45, *Alcestis* 1077–80.

573

ἀλλ' ἔστι γὰρ δὴ κἀν κακοῖσιν ἡδονὴ
θνητοῖς, ὀδυρμοὶ δακρύων τ' ἐπιρροαί·
ἀλγηδόνας δὲ ταῦτα κουφίζει φρενῶν,
καὶ καρδίας ἔλυσε τοὺς ἄγαν πόνους.

Stobaeus 4.54.8

574

τεκμαιρόμεσθα τοῖς παροῦσι τἀφανῆ.

Clement of Alexandria, *Miscellanies* 6.2.18.1

575

ὅστις δὲ θνητῶν βούλεται δυσώνυμον
εἰς γῆρας ἐλθεῖν, οὐ λογίζεται καλῶς·
μακρὸς γὰρ αἰὼν μυρίους τίκτει πόνους.

Stobaeus 4.50.39

576

ὁ πλεῖστα πράσσων πλεῖσθ' ἁμαρτάνει βροτῶν.

Stobaeus 4.16.13

577

ἐγὼ μὲν εὖτ' ἂν τοὺς κακοὺς ὁρῶ βροτῶν
πίπτοντας, εἶναί φημι δαιμόνων γένος.

Orion 5.5 Haffner

573

Yet there is a pleasure that men can take in their woes, the pleasure of lamentation and floods of tears.[1] These things lighten the pains within their minds and ease the excessive suffering of their hearts.

[1] A traditional commonplace: see on *Andromeda* F 119.

574

We judge what is obscure by the evidence that is before us.[1]

[1] Cf. *Phoenix* F 811. The wording in both fragments recalls Alcmaeon of Croton's (mid-5th c.?) assertion of the value of scientific reasoning based on observation: cf. Alcmaeon 24 B 1 DK; Egli 77–8.

575

Anyone who wants to reach ill-famed old age is not thinking straight; for a long life begets innumerable troubles.

576

The man who tries to do most[1] makes the most mistakes.

[1] The Greek wording here suggests *polypragmosynê*, usually excessive activity or ambition (cf. *Philoctetes* F 787.2 with note), but implicitly defended as a quality of the Athenian democracy by Pericles in Thuc. 2.40.2 (cf. 1.70.8).

577

Whenever I see a bad man fall, I affirm that the race of gods indeed exists.[1]

[1] Again a traditional commonplace, e.g. Homer, *Odyssey* 24.351–2, Eur. *Suppliant Women* 731–3, *Bacchae* 1325–6; but contrast *Bellerophon* F 286.

PALAMEDES

F. Jouan in ed. Budé VIII.2.487–513; R. Falcetto, *Euripide. Palamede* (Alessandria, 2002); C. Collard in *SFP* II.92–103.

Jouan (1966), 339–63; F. Stoessl, *Wiener Studien* 79 (1966), 93–101; Webster 174–6; G. Koniaris, *HSCP* 77 (1973), 87–92; M. Szarmach, *Eos* 63 (1975), 249–71; R. Scodel, *The Trojan Trilogy of Euripides* (Göttingen, 1980), 43–54; Aélion (1983), I.47–59; Gantz 603–8; S. Woodford, *JHS* 114 (1994), 164–9 and *LIMC* VII.i.145–9 'Palamedes'; D. Sutton, *Two Lost Plays of Euripides* (New York, 1984), 111–55; W. Luppe, *APF* 50 (2004), 217–8; R. Kannicht in A. Bierl (ed.), *Antike Literatur in neuer Deutung. Festschrift für J. Latacz* (Munich–Leipzig, 2004), 196–7; J. L. L. Cruces, *Philologus* 149 (2005), 158–61.

Palamedes the son of Nauplius the Argonaut was a human counterpart of the intellectual and inventive god Prometheus who gave men many skills; he became a byword for cleverness (Aristophanes, Frogs *1451 = test. iv; F 588). He was one of the Greeks at Troy, having unmasked the madness which Odysseus pretended in order to avoid going there (Cypria F 19 West); with his invention of writing and numbering, and of board games, he helped the Greeks organize their food supplies (Sophocles,* Nauplius *F *432,* Plato, Republic *522d = test. *vi below; cf. F 578) and prevent boredom when they were held back at Aulis (Soph-*

46

ocles, Palamedes *F 479 and* Nauplius *F 429; Gorgias,* Palamedes *30). His resulting popularity added jealousy to Odysseus' resentment (Xenophon,* Memorabilia *4.2.33 = test. *vb), and his ridicule of Agamemnon's leadership (test. *vi, cf. F 581) won enmity from him as well. Together with Diomedes these two destroyed Palamedes—by drowning according to early myth (Cypria F 27 West), but through a 'stratagem' of Odysseus in the version developed by 5th c. tragedy (Polyaenus = test. *va below, cf. test. *vi; Kannicht [bibl. above], 197). They accused him of negotiating treacherously with Priam of Troy, for a reward of gold; they planted both gold and a forged letter to incriminate him, and 'found' both of these themselves; and Palamedes was summarily arraigned and stoned to death. This story is fullest in the Scholia on Euripides, Orestes 432; there are different details in Hyginus, Fab. 105, cf. Apollodorus, Epitome 3.8. Odysseus' destruction of Palamedes is grimly recalled in Euripides, Philoctetes F 789d.(8)–(9); cf. also Virgil, Aeneid 2.81–5.*

Palamedes' story continued, however. He had been accompanied to Troy by his brother Oeax, who after his death sent a message to their father Nauplius back in Greece. Nauplius came to Troy and threatened Agamemnon with vengeance. This continuation was in Aeschylus' Palamedes (F 191) and Sophocles' Nauplius (P. Oxy. 3653 fr. 1.4–5 in TrGF 4².756, cf. F 431, 433); it stands also in the Scholia on Orestes (above), and Nauplius' presence at Troy in Euripides' play now appears to be confirmed by an unpublished Michigan papyrus hypothesis (Luppe in bibl. above); cf. also F 588a for Oeax, who the papyrus says was thrown into the sea by the Greeks but rescued by the Nereids. Such an ending for the play had long ago been suggested by Stoessl (1966).

47

   *Almost all the fragments fit into this outline, but the
first, F 578, is already well into the story: Palamedes is de-
fending himself against the false accusation, no doubt in a
trial scene with Agamemnon and Odysseus; F 579–85 al-
most certainly come from it too. F 588 (Chorus of Greeks)
voices bitter grief for Palamedes' death. F 588a reveals how
Oeax informed Nauplius: he scratched a message on oar
blades and launched them into the sea. It seems likely that a
god's intervention (perhaps revealed later: by Poseidon, fa-
ther of Nauplius?), rather than mere good fortune, carried
the oars swiftly to Nauplius (during a choral ode gener-
ous with 'dramatic time'?), so that the play ended with
Nauplius' threats to Agamemnon, perhaps with a god (Po-
seidon?) appearing to confirm them in a prophecy to (at
least) Nauplius and Oeax. This would suit well the start of*
Trojan Women, *which followed* Palamedes *in the produc-
tion of 415, where Poseidon proposes his own vengeance
upon the Greeks through destructive storms; the* Orestes
*scholia relate that Nauplius lured the Greek ships on to
rocks in a storm (cf. Sophocles,* Nauplius *F 435). The re-
maining F 586 (from a choral ode evoking Dionysus' wor-
ship near Troy) and F 589 (night patrols with bells) cannot
be firmly located (but see the note on F 589).*

   *Brief fragments: F 587 'a sword-hilt inlaid with gold',
F 590 'door-bars'. Other ascriptions: F 878 (an imminent
victim of impalement or stoning), F 910 (see* Antiope, *at
end), and the now jettisoned F [886, 887] = 582 N = Aris-
tophanes,* Frogs *1446–8; also adesp. F 470 (now Aeschylus,
Palamedes **F 181) and 591c (Palamedes 'hooded'); and
two fragments reconstructed by Cruces (2005) from Suda
π 44 ('Palamedes'): 'the kinds of . . . thing I have seen in a
long time' and 'envy attacks the greatest . . . men'.*

No help towards reconstruction comes from ancient art, which does not portray or reflect Palamedes' manner of death in tragedy (see Woodford).

Palamedes *was produced with* Alexander, Trojan Women *and* Sisyphus *in 415 B.C.; for the trilogy and the nature of* Alexander *and* Palamedes *see our Introduction to* Alexander *and especially Koniaris and Scodel. Euripides' failure to win the prize for tragedy occasioned a jibe by Aristophanes against the* Palamedes *(Women at the Thesmophoria 847–8 = test. iiib), and later astonished Aelian, Historical Miscellanies 2.8 (= test. iia). The Introduction to Isocrates' Busiris states that 'the entire theatre wept' because Euripides was alluding to Socrates through the fate of the intellectual Palamedes (= test. iic below); this might relate to a revival after Socrates' death in 399 B.C., but some have applied the statement to the (undated) prosecution of the sophist Protagoras who had been in Athens in 421: see Sutton (1984), 133–55, M. Hose,* Drama und Gesellschaft *(Stuttgart, 1995), 45–7.*

In addition to Aeschylus, Sophocles and Euripides, Astydamas II dramatized Palamedes' story in the 4th century, and there may have been a comedy by Philemon. The 5th c. sophist and orator Gorgias wrote a 'display' defence speech for Palamedes (above), and Alcidamas slightly later a prosecution speech for Odysseus. OGCMA II.801–2 includes Canova's sculpture of Palamedes unmasking Odysseus' pretended madness (above). T. E. Jenkins, Classical and Modern Literature *25.2 (2005), 29–53 compares the myth of 'writing's invention, narrative and erasure' for Lévi-Strauss, Derrida, and Palamedes as depicted in antiquity, with much on Euripides.*

ΠΑΛΑΜΗΔΗΣ

test. iic

λέγεται . . . ὅτι Εὐριπίδου βουλομένου εἰπεῖν περὶ αὐτοῦ (τοῦ Σωκράτους) καὶ δεδιότος ἀναπλάσασθαι Παλαμήδην, ἵνα διὰ τούτου σχοίη καιρὸν τοῦ αἰνίξασθαι εἰς τὸν Σωκράτη καὶ εἰς τοὺς Ἀθηναίους· 'ἐκάνετε, ἐκάνετε τῶν Ἑλλήνων τὸν ἄριστον', ὅ ἐστιν ἐφονεύσατε. καὶ νοῆσαν τὸ θέατρον ἅπαν ἐδάκρυσε, διότι περὶ Σωκράτους ἠνίττετο.

Introduction to Isocrates, *Busiris* 24–30

test. *va

οἶον δὲ κἀκεῖνο στρατήγημα Ὀδυσσέως οἱ τραγῳδοὶ ᾄδουσι· Παλαμήδην ἐνίκησεν Ὀδυσσεὺς ἐν δικαστηρίῳ τῶν Ἀχαιῶν ὑποβαλὼν αὐτοῦ τῇ σκηνῇ βαρβαρικὸν χρυσίον, καὶ ὁ σοφώτατος τῶν Ἑλλήνων ἐκεῖνος ἥλω προδοσίας . . .

Polyaenus, *On Stratagems*, Preface 12

PALAMEDES

test. iic

It is said . . . that when Euripides wanted to speak about him (Socrates) and was afraid to do so, he portrayed Palamedes, so as to have the opportunity through him of alluding darkly to Socrates and the Athenians: 'You have killed, you have killed the best of the Greeks'—that is, you have murdered him. The entire theatre understood this and wept, because of the allusion to Socrates.[1]

[1] See Introduction above, and F 588.

test.*va

. . . just as the tragic poets sing too of that stratagem of Odysseus: he overcame Palamedes in a trial before the Achaeans after hiding barbarian gold under the man's tent; and that wisest of the Greeks was convicted of treachery . . . [1]

[1] More briefly, and earlier, Xenophon, *Memorabilia* 4.2.33 (= test.*vb).

test. *vi

παγγέλοιον . . . στρατηγὸν Ἀγαμέμνονα ἐν ταῖς τραγῳ-
δίαις Παλαμήδης ἑκάστοτε ἀποφαίνει. ἢ οὐκ ἐννενόηκας
ὅτι φησὶν ἀριθμὸν εὑρὼν τάς τε τάξεις τῷ στρατοπέδῳ
καταστῆσαι ἐν Ἰλίῳ καὶ ἐξαριθμῆσαι ναῦς τε καὶ τἄλλα
πάντα, ὡς πρὸ τοῦ ἀναριθμήτων ὄντων καὶ τοῦ Ἀγα-
μέμνονος, ὡς ἔοικεν, οὐδ᾽ ὅσους πόδας εἶχεν εἰδότος,
εἴπερ ἀριθμεῖν μὴ ἠπίστατο;

Plato, *Republic* 522d

578

ΠΑΛΑΜΗΔΗΣ

τὰ τῆς γε λήθης φάρμακ᾽ ὀρθώσας μόνος,
ἄφωνα καὶ φωνοῦντα, συλλαβὰς τιθείς,
ἐξηῦρον ἀνθρώποισι γράμματ᾽ εἰδέναι,
ὥστ᾽ οὐ παρόντα ποντίας ὑπὲρ πλακὸς
5   τἀκεῖ κατ᾽ οἴκους πάντ᾽ ἐπίστασθαι καλῶς,
παισίν τε τὸν θνῄσκοντα χρημάτων μέτρον
γράψαντα λείπειν, τὸν λαβόντα δ᾽ εἰδέναι.
ἃ δ᾽ εἰς ἔριν πίπτουσιν ἀνθρώποις κακά,
δέλτος διαιρεῖ, κοὐκ ἐᾷ ψευδῆ λέγειν.

Stobaeus 2.4.8

1 ὀρθώσας Stob.: ἀρθρώσας Naber   2 τιθείς Stob.: τε
θείς Heath   6 τε τὸν θνῄσκοντα Wecklein: τ᾽
ἀποθνῄσκοντα Stob.   7 γράψαντα λείπειν Scaliger:
γράψαντας εἰπεῖν Stob.   See also C. Neri, *Eikasmos* 18 (2007),
167–71.

PALAMEDES

test.*vi

Palamedes in tragedy shows up Agamemnon on every occasion as a laughable commander. Or haven't you reflected that Palamedes says that through the invention of number he organized the army's divisions at Troy, and counted the ships and everything else, since previously they were uncounted, and that Agamemnon, it seems, did not even know how many feet he had, since he didn't know how to count.[1]

[1] It is uncertain whether the last part of this represents something in the play, or is largely Plato's humour.

F 578–585 are almost certainly from the trial scene:

578

PALAMEDES

On my own I established[1] remedies for forgetfulness, which are without speech and (yet) speak, by creating syllables;[2] I invented writing for men's knowledge, so a man absent over the ocean's plain might have good knowledge of all matters back there in his house, and the dying man[3] might write down the size of his wealth[4] when bequeathing it to his sons, and the receiver know it. And the troubles that afflict men when they fall to quarrelling—a written tablet does away with these and prevents the telling of lies.

5

[1] An unusual sense for the Greek verb; Naber conjectured 'articulated', which perhaps accommodates the sense of v. 2 more easily.   [2] Or perhaps 'consonants and vowels, by creating syllables', or (with Heath's alteration) 'by creating consonants and vowels and syllables'.   [3] I.e. any dying man. Stobaeus has 'and when he dies', referring to the absent seafarer of vv. 4–5, but his form of the verb 'die' is unparalleled in tragedy.   [4] Or perhaps the 'measurement', i.e. division, of his wealth.

EURIPIDES

579

πάλαι πάλαι δή σ' ἐξερωτῆσαι θέλων,
σχολή μ' ἀπεῖργε.

Schol. on Homer, *Iliad* 2.353; Anon., *On Figures*, *Rhet. Gr.*
III.152.4 Spengel; Eustathius on *Iliad* 2.353

1 πάλαι πάλαι Nauck: Λάϊε πάλαι Schol. Hom. b: πάλαι
(once) Schol. Hom. Ge, Anon., Eustath.

580

Ἀγάμεμνον, ἀνθρώποισι πᾶσαν αἱ τύχαι
μορφὴν ἔχουσι, συντρέχει δ' εἰς ἓν τόδε·
†τούτου† δὲ πάντες, οἵ τε μουσικῆς φίλοι
ὅσοι τε χωρὶς ζῶσι, χρημάτων ὕπερ
5 μοχθοῦσιν, ὃς δ' ἂν πλεῖστ' ἔχῃ σοφώτατος.

Stobaeus 4.31.14 mss. MA (placed after 31.29 in ms. S, and re-
peated after 31.30 in mss. MA)

1–2 so Dobree: πᾶσιν αἱ τύχαι . . . εἰς χρήματα Stob. 29/30:
πᾶσι χρήματα . . . εἰς ἓν τόδε Stob. 14: τάδε (for τόδε) Hense
3 τούτου Stob. 29/30: τούτων Stob. 14: βροτοὶ Herwerden

581

στρατηλάται τἂν μυρίοι γενοίμεθα,
σοφὸς δ' ἂν εἷς τις ἢ δύ' ἐν μακρῷ χρόνῳ.

Stobaeus 4.13.6

54

579

Long, long indeed have I wanted to question you thoroughly, but my time prevented me.[1]

[1] Probably Agamemnon, delayed from questioning Palamedes about Odysseus' accusation; 'my time' (lit. 'leisure') then means his *lack* of free time. Less probably Palamedes, prevented by his intellectual activities from questioning Agamemnon and Odysseus, as Kannicht suggests.

580

Agamemnon, men's fortunes take every form, but there is concurrence upon one thing: †of this† all, both those friendly to the arts, and those who live without them, labour for wealth; and whoever has most, is wisest.[1]

[1] Probably Odysseus accuses Palamedes of openness to Priam's bribery, despite being a 'friend of the arts' (cf. F 588). The ends of vv. 1–2 are muddled in Stobaeus, and the text insecure; Hense's 'but these circumstances concur on one point' is attractive. In v. 3 '†of this†' lacks syntax but has been defended as anticipating 'for wealth'; Herwerden's emendation (the best among many) gives 'All mortals . . .'

581

Countless men among us might become commanders, but just one or two in a long time would become wise ones.[1]

[1] Perhaps Palamedes impugning Agamemnon's leadership (cf. test.*vi above).

EURIPIDES

(582 N = Aristophanes, *Frogs* 1446–8 = F [886–7] *TrGF*)

583

ὅστις λέγει μὲν εὖ, τὰ δ᾽ ἔργ᾽ ἐφ᾽ οἷς λέγει
αἴσχρ᾽ ἐστί, τούτου τὸ σοφὸν οὐκ αἰνῶ ποτέ.

Orion 1.6 Haffner; Stobaeus 2.15.15

584

εἷς τοι δίκαιος μυρίων οὐκ ἐνδίκων
κρατεῖ, τὸ θεῖον τὴν δίκην τε συλλαβών.

Stobaeus 3.9.12

*585

τοῦ γὰρ δικαίου κἂν βροτοῖσι κἂν θεοῖς
ἀθάνατος αἰεὶ δόξα διατελεῖ μόνου.

Stobaeus 3.9.20, attributed to 'Philemon from *Palamedes*' (cf. Philemon F 60 *PCG*); assigned to Euripides by Meineke

586

ΧΟΡΟΣ

†οὐ σὰν† Διονύσου
†κομᾶν† ὃς ἄν᾽ Ἴδαν
τέρπεται σὺν ματρὶ φίλᾳ
τυμπάνων ἰάκχοις.

Strabo 10.3.14, attributed to the Chorus
2 †κομᾶν† ὃς editors: κομᾶνος Stob.

(582 N = Aristophanes, *Frogs* 1446–8 = F [886–7] *TrGF*)

583

One who makes a fine speech when the actions upon which he speaks are shameful—I never praise this man's wisdom.[1]

[1] Either Odysseus or Palamedes might say this against the other. The sentiment is common: cf. *Alexander* F 56 with note, *Meleager* F 528.2.

584

One just man masters countless thousands who are not just, if he has the gods and justice with him.

*585

A just man's reputation, and his alone, continues for ever undying among both men and gods.

586

CHORUS

† . . . (hair?)† of Dionysus, who upon Ida delights with the dear mother in the revel-cries of tambourines.[1]

[1] The Chorus evokes the loud, ecstatic rites honouring Dionysus and the 'Great Mother' Cybele on Mt. Ida above Troy (cf. especially *Helen* 1301–68); these lyric lines may be from the Chorus' self-identification on their first entry (cf. F 589). Vv. 1–2 are hopelessly corrupt, but there may be a reference to the wild tossing of hair in Dionysiac rites (e.g. *Bacchae* 241).

588

⟨ΧΟΡΟΣ⟩

. . . ἐκάνετ᾽ ἐκάνετε τὰν
πάνσοφον, ὦ Δαναοί,
τὰν οὐδέν᾽ ἀλγύνουσαν ἀηδόνα Μουσᾶν.

Philostratus, *On Heroes* 34.6; Diogenes Laertius 2.44; cf. test.
iic above

588a

. . . Εὐριπίδης ἐν τῷ Παλαμήδει ἐποίησε τὸν Οἴακα τὸν
ἀδελφὸν Παλαμήδους ἐπιγράψαι εἰς πλάτας τὸν θάνατον
αὐτοῦ, ἵνα φερόμεναι ἑαυταῖς ἔλθωσιν εἰς τὸν Ναύπλιον
τὸν πατέρα αὐτοῦ καὶ ἀπαγγείλωσι τὸν θάνατον αὐτοῦ.

Schol. on Aristophanes, *Women at the Thesmophoria* 770: see
note on the translation.

589

‘διεκωδώνισε’ . . . ἡ δὲ μεταφορὰ . . . ἀπὸ τῶν περι-
πολούντων σὺν κώδωσι νυκτὸς τὰς φυλακάς, ⟨ὡς⟩ Εὐριπί-
δης Παλαμήδει . . .

Harpocration p. 96.13 Dindorf; cf. Aristophanes, *Birds* 841–2
with Schol., Suda κ 2221

PALAMEDES

588

⟨CHORUS⟩

. . . you have killed, you have killed, O you Danaans, that all-wise nightingale of the Muses, that harmed no man.[1]

[1] Palamedes as 'nightingale of the Muses', the voice of the arts: cf. F 580.3–4. For this fragment see Introduction above.

588a

. . . Euripides in *Palamedes* had Palamedes' brother Oeax inscribe his death on oar-blades, so that they would be carried of their own accord to his father Nauplius and report Palamedes' death.[1]

[1] Aristophanes, *Women at the Thesmophoria* 768–84 burlesques an incident from our play (where it was presumably narrated rather than staged): Euripides' imprisoned kinsman records his plight on wooden tablets and throws them outdoors in the hope of rescue. Vv. 776–84 appear to parody impassioned anapaestic verses of Euripides: 'Hands of mine, you must put your hand to an effective job. Tablets of planed board, accept the knife's scratchings, harbingers of my troubles! Damn, this R is troublesome. There we go, there we go! What a scratch! Be off then, travel every road, this way, that way, and better hurry!' (tr. J. Henderson)

589

'He carried bells around' . . . the metaphor (is) from those who go round the watch-points at night with bells (as in) Euripides, *Palamedes* . . .[1]

[1] To test and wake sleeping guards, and to prompt a response (as the Aristophanic scholia explain). The detail may come from the Chorus's entry song (cf. F 586).

PELIADES,
'DAUGHTERS OF PELIAS'

H. Van Looy in ed. Budé VIII.2.515–30.

Séchan 467–81; Webster 32–6, 300; H. Meyer, *Medeia und die Peliaden* (Rome, 1980); M. Schmidt, *Gnomon* 50 (1984), 59–67 (review of Meyer); Aélion (1986), 143–5; *LIMC* VII.i.270–3 'Peliades' and 273–7 'Pelias'; Gantz 365–8; D. Pralon, *Pallas* 45 (1996), 69–83.

Pelias and Neleus were twins borne to Poseidon by the Thessalian princess Tyro, who then married her uncle Cretheus and had other sons including Aeson and Pheres (cf. Homer, Odyssey 11.235–59). Neleus became the ruler of Pylos in Messenia, while Pelias usurped the kingdom of Iolcus in Thessaly from his half-brother Aeson (Pindar, Pythians 4.106–15). Fearing that Aeson's son Jason would reclaim the kingdom, Pelias sent Jason on his famous quest for the Golden Fleece. Jason completed the quest with the aid of the Argonauts and of the sorceress Medea, daughter of the king of Colchis; he then returned with Medea to Iolcus where she contrived the death of Pelias. Medea assured the daughters of Pelias that she could rejuvenate their elderly father if he was dismembered and boiled in a magic cauldron, and she demonstrated her power to do this by rejuvenating an aged ram in the same way. The daugh-

60

ters gladly proceeded to kill their father, whereupon Medea refrained from reviving him.

This episode, known in coherent form from Hellenistic and Roman sources, is alluded to by Pindar at *Pythians* 4.250 (cf. Pherecydes FGrH 3 F 105). The fragmentary hypothesis (test. *iiia¹ below) and a late rhetorical summary by Moses of Chorene (test. iiib below) confirm that it was the subject of Euripides' play but do not reveal much about how he dramatized it; neither do the brief allusions to the episode in Euripides' *Medea, produced 24 years later (cf. Med. 9–10, 486–7, 504–5, 734), nor the fragments themselves which are largely gnomic. Some features found in Hyginus,* Fab. 24 *and (much elaborated) in Diodorus 4.50–3 have however been attributed to a dramatic, perhaps Euripidean, origin. These place the action at the palace of Pelias (cf. F 601?), with Jason's return as yet undeclared and the Argo hidden in a nearby anchorage; in Diodorus, Jason has learned of Pelias' mistreatment of his family from a local man. Medea disguises herself as a priestess of Artemis in order to establish her authority and work her deception (cf. Hera's disguise as a priestess in Aeschylus'* Xantriae *or* Semele, *F **168). Alcestis alone of the daughters resists Medea's project, and Medea later contrives a signal from the rooftop to summon Jason (cf. Aeschylus' use of the rooftop for the sighting of the beacon signal in* Agamemnon *three years earlier). If these features, or some of them, are Euripidean, we might ascribe F 603 to a dialogue between Pelias and Alcestis; this fragment at any rate confirms that one of the daughters had an individual role, and of these only Alcestis has much substance as a mythical figure. See also the note on F 601.*

Despite the play's title the daughters of Pelias need not have formed the play's chorus (cf. Children of Heracles*); their small number and Alcestis' separate role make it unlikely that they did so. Moses of Chorene makes the rejuvenation of the ram illusory (the girls are deceived as the boiling water shakes the cauldron), but this is probably a later rationalization. Presumably Jason and Medea left Iolcus for Corinth at the end of the play, but how this came about, and how the killing of Pelias was received in Iolcus, can only be guessed; the mythographic accounts vary on these points and on the fate of the daughters of Pelias themselves (sometimes exiled to Arcadia, sometimes exculpated and suitably married, as Alcestis herself certainly was). The kingdom of Iolcus is usually said to have passed to Pelias' son Acastus; in Moses' summary Medea argues that Pelias has no son to succeed him, but this could be because Acastus was himself an Argonaut and at this moment was presumed dead.*

Brief fragments: F 611 'to revile in return', F 612 'to butcher', F 613 'accurately', F 614 'a concern' or 'an obligation'(?), F 615 'loosening' or 'resolvable', F 616 'young (of animals)'. Other ascriptions: F 858; adesp. F *188c 'Aeson's son, from the bloodline of Cretheus'.

The ancient Life of Euripides *records that* Peliades *was part of Euripides' first production at the City Dionysia in 455 B.C.; its companion plays are not known. The story appears with some frequency in Attic vase-paintings of the late 6th and the 5th centuries, and occasionally in Etruscan and Roman art (see* LIMC *'Peliades' nos. 4–13, Pelias nos. 10–23, with Meyer and M. Schmidt). Nearly all the depictions feature the cauldron with the ram and/or Pelias, and none has overtly 'dramatic' features, although a few of the later 5th c. Attic ones which seem to emphasize the reluctance of one or more daughters or of Pelias himself have been thought to show tragic influence. Sophocles'* Rhizotomoi ('Root-Cutters') *may have dramatized the same episode, but this idea is insecurely based on a single fragment featuring Medea and her magic (Soph. F 534). A didascalic inscription records that Isocrates' adopted son Aphareus came third at the City Dionysia of 341 B.C. with his own* Peliades, Orestes *and* Auge *(TrGF 1 73 F 1). One fragment of a 4th c. comic 'Pelias' by Diphilus is known (F 64 PCG), and one from a Latin tragedy by Gracchus (p. 266 Ribbeck). For a few representations in Renaissance and later art see OGCMA II.643–50 under 'Medea'.*

ΠΕΛΙΑΔΕΣ

test. *iiia[1] (Hypothesis)

one line with a few letters

τος αὐτοῦ κρ[

.ως τὴν ἐλπ[

ἐκκομίζουσαν[

5   ....]στατην ε[..]α[

.]ωσαμένη καὶ τὸ [*c. 12 letters* παρά-

δοξον ὡς ἔστιν δυ[

μασιν δείξασα· κρ[ιὸν

ἤδη λα[βο]ῦσα κατὰ μ[έλη

10 κα[τέθ]ηκεν εἰς λ[έ]βη[τα

one more line with a few letters

P. Oxy. 2455 fr. 18 col. ii, ed. E. Turner (1962); re-ed. W. Luppe, *Anagennesis* 3 (1983), 125–41 and *ZPE* 60 (1985), 16–20. Test. *iiia[2] (P. IFAO inv. PSP 248.1–2) has a few words from what was probably the end of a similar hypothesis.

PELIADES,
'DAUGHTERS OF PELIAS'

test. *iiia[1] (Hypothesis)

. . . (a few letters) . . . his . . . the (hope?) . . . bringing out . . .
(one line with no clear sense) . . . . . . and showing by (her de-   5
vices) that the (seemingly un)believable was (possible). She
took a (ram that was) already (old) and (dismembered it and)
placed it in a cauldron . . . [1]

[1] As supplemented by Luppe in vv. 6–10 (see below).

6–10 καὶ τὸ [δοκοῦν εἶναι παρά]δοξον ὡς ἔστιν δυ[νατὸν
μηχανή]μασιν δείξασα· κρ[ιὸν γὰρ παλαιὸν] ἤδη λα[βο]ῦσα
κατὰ μ[έλη διεῖλεν καὶ] κα[τέθ]ηκεν εἰς λ[έ]βη[τα Luppe (e.g.)

test. iiib

Euripides . . . de Medea . . . ait . . . illam Iasonem quendam in-
secutam nauem conscendisse et e Scythia prouincia in Thes-
saliam uenisse. Ibi artes magicas exercuit: decreuerat enim
regem qui terrae imperabat dolosis consiliis perdere. (2)
Idcirco persuasit filias eius ad senectutem patris respiciens et
quia mascula proles, quae in paternum regnum succederet, ei
deesset, 'si ipsae uultis, equidem illum in iuuenilem aetatem
restituere possum.' (3) His dictis statim pergit eis demon-
strare, qua ratione res patrari possit: arietem laniauit et in le-
betem coniecit ignemque subdidit. Atque feruente cum moti-
bus lebete, arietem uiuum declarauit. (4) Hoc modo filiabus
deceptis Medea Peliam laniandum curauit: eratque, inquit
(sc. Euripides), in lebete et nil amplius.

Moses of Chorene, *Progymnasmata* 3.4 (in Armenian: cf. un-
der *Auge* test. ii b)

601

Μήδεια πρὸς μὲν δώμασιν τυραννικοῖς . . .

Schol. on *Medea* 693, citing this as the play's first line

602

τί χρῆμα δράσας; φράζε μοι σαφέστερον.

Schol. on *Medea* 693

test. iiib

Euripides . . . relates . . . about Medea that she followed a certain Jason and boarded a ship, and thus came from the province of Scythia to Thessaly. There she exercised her magical arts; for she had determined to destroy the king who ruled the country by her deceptive schemes. (2) For that purpose, considering their father's advanced age and the fact that he had no male offspring to succeed him as king, she spoke peruasively to his daughters saying 'if you yourselves are willing, I for my part can restore him to a youthful age'. (3) This said, she immediately proceeded to show them how this could be achieved. She dismembered a ram and threw it into a cauldron and set a fire under it; and as the cauldron boiled and shook, she declared the ram to be alive. (4) Having thus deceived the daughters, Medea undertook the dismembering of Pelias; and, says he (i.e. Euripides), once he was in the cauldron, that was that.

601

(Beginning of the play)

Medea . . . near the royal palace . . .[1]

[1] The palace may be Pelias's, the play being set before it, and many scholars have followed F. Vater in supposing the words are addressed to Medea by an accomplice, possibly Jason himself (see Introduction above). If so, Euripides here uniquely, so far as we know, opens a play with a dialogue scene; but a narrative speech about Medea seems at least equally likely, and the palace could even be her father's in Colchis where her story began.

602

By doing what? Explain this to me more clearly.[1]

[1] The verse is identical with *Medea* 693, as the scholiast on *Medea* points out in quoting both this fragment and F 601. Such repetitions are not rare in Euripides.

EURIPIDES

603

αἰνῶ· διδάξαι δ' ὦ τέκνον σε βούλομαι·
ὅταν μὲν ᾖς παῖς, μὴ πλέον παιδὸς φρονεῖν,
ἐν παρθένοις δὲ παρθένου τρόπους ἔχειν,
ὅταν δ' ὑπ' ἀνδρὸς χλαῖναν εὐγενοῦς πέσῃς,
(one line lost)
5   τὰ δ' ἄλλ' ἀφεῖναι μηχανήματ' ἀνδράσιν.

Stobaeus 4.23.25

4–5 ⟨τἄνδον φυλάσσειν ἐν δόμοις καθημένην⟩ Headlam
(e.g.)

604

πρὸς κέντρα μὴ λάκτιζε τοῖς κρατοῦσί σου.

Stobaeus 3.3.22; Schol. on Pindar, *Pythians* 2.94–5

605

τὸ δ' ἔσχατον δὴ τοῦτο θαυμαστὸν βροτοῖς,
τυραννίς—οὐχ εὕροις ἂν ἀθλιώτερον·
φίλους τε πορθεῖν καὶ κατακτανεῖν χρεών,
πλεῖστος φόβος πρόσεστι μὴ δράσωσί τι.

Stobaeus 4.8.9

606

οὐ γὰρ τὰ τῶν θεῶν ἄδικα, τἀνθρώπεια δὲ
κακοῖς νοσοῦντα σύγχυσιν πολλὴν ἔχει.

Stobaeus 2.8.2; Orion, Euripidean Appendix 5 Haffner

PELIADES

603

I approve—but I want to give you some advice, my girl.
When you are a child, don't have ideas beyond a child's;
amongst the maidens, stick to a maiden's behaviour; and
when you have slipped beneath a well-born husband's
blanket . . . *(a line missing)* . . . and leave all other projects
to the men.[1]

[1] Probably Pelias addresses his eldest daughter, Alcestis. The
lost line must have contained something like Headlam's 'sit at
home and take care of domestic matters'.

604

Don't kick against the pricks when others control you.[1]

[1] A proverbial warning as in Pindar, *Pythians* 2.94–6, Aeschy-
lus, *Agamemnon* 1624, Eur. *Bacchae* 794–5 etc.

605

As for this highest state that men so admire, tyranny—you
could find no sadder one. The tyrant must ruin his friends
and put them to death; he lives in very great fear that they
will do him harm.[1]

[1] A common criticism of tyranny, e.g. *Suppliant Women* 444–
6, Herodotus 3.80.4–5, Plato, *Republic* 567a–b.

606

It is not the actions of the gods that are unjust, but men's
which are corrupted by evil and thoroughly confounded.

---

1 οὐ γὰρ τὰ τῶν θεῶν West: οὐκ ἔστι τὰ τῶν θεῶν Stob. (τὰ
θεῶν Orion)   τἀνθρώπεια Pflugk: ἐν ἀνθρώποισι Stob.,
Orion

607

ὁρῶσι δ᾽ οἱ διδόντες εἰς τὰ χρήματα.

Stobaeus 4.31.38

608

ἐν τοῖσι μὲν δεινοῖσιν ὡς φίλοι φίλων·
ὅταν δὲ πράξωσ᾽ εὖ, διωθοῦνται χάριν
αὐτοὶ δι᾽ αὑτοὺς εὐτυχεῖν ἡγούμενοι.

Stobaeus 2.46.10

609

ὁ γὰρ ξυνὼν κακὸς μὲν ἦν τύχῃ γεγώς,
τοιούσδε τοὺς ξυνόντας ἐκπαιδεύεται,
χρηστοὺς δὲ χρηστός· ἀλλὰ τὰς ὁμιλίας
ἐσθλὰς διώκειν, ὦ νέοι, σπουδάζετε.

Stobaeus 2.31.4 and 2.33.3

610

φθείρου· τὸ γὰρ δρᾶν οὐκ ἔχων λόγους ἔχεις.

Stobaeus 2.15.20

607

But those who give look (only) to wealth.[1]

[1] I.e. to the wealth of the recipient and the expected benefit to themselves: cf. *Danae* F 326.6–7. 'Give' might mean 'give their daughters in marriage'.

608

When they are in trouble they are your greatest friends;[1] but when they are doing well, they repudiate their obligation, considering their good fortune to be of their own making.

[1] Literally 'as friends amongst friends', i.e. more than ordinary friends. Cf. Menander F 701 *PCG* (= *Monostichs* 42): 'The rescued man is always naturally ungrateful'; also *Temenidae* F 735.

609

A companion who happens to be badly bred trains his companions to be like himself, while a good one makes them good; come then, young men, make sure you seek the company of honourable men.[1]

[1] Cf. *Erechtheus* F 362.21–3 with note.

610

Get lost! You can do nothing—you can only talk.

71

PELEUS

H. Van Looy in ed. Budé VIII.2.531–40.

Webster 85–6; E. M. Papamichael, *Dodone* 12 (1983), 142–6; Gantz 220–32, esp. 231–2, 688–9; *LIMC* VII.i.251–69 'Peleus'.

Peleus son of Aeacus twice shed kindred blood; after the second, involuntary killing he took refuge with Acastus the king of Iolcus in Thessaly, and was purified by him. Acastus' wife tried to seduce him, was repulsed, and accused him falsely of seduction to Acastus (the seduction stood in Hesiod F 208). To punish Peleus, Acastus did not execute the man he had purified, but took him hunting on Mt. Pelion and contrived to leave him there unarmed at night and in danger from wild beasts; but he was rescued by the centaurs under Chiron (so Apollodorus 3.13.3). Peleus' virtuous rejection of Acastus' wife eventually won him, with Chiron's help, marriage to the seagoddess Thetis (cf. Aristophanes, Clouds 1061–7), and they became the parents of Achilles.

The very few fragments permit no reconstruction whatever, but it seems likely that Peleus' recourse to Acastus, the failed seduction, and then Peleus' survival of what Acastus had devised against him provided Euripides with a characteristic plot (compare especially the story of Bellerophon in

72

Stheneboea); this has been argued by Papamichael (1983) and Van Looy 533–4. Peleus' future marriage to Thetis may have been foretold at the play's end.

Another version of the story had Peleus rescued from Acastus by his grandson Neoptolemus, and this may have been followed by Sophocles in his Peleus *(Gantz 688–9), where Peleus is an old man, but rejuvenated (Soph. F 487); but whether Sophocles dramatized or retold the seduction is unknown. Euripides F 619 has nevertheless been linked with Sophocles' play and its possible plot, as the speaker there is apparently an old man (but this could be Chiron rather than Peleus?).*

Brief fragment: F 624 'it assists'. Other ascription: fr. 620 N = fr. 1018 (a).1–3 PMG (the earth's final destruction in fire), attributed to Euripides' Peleus *at Stobaeus 1.5.10, with which the preceding citations 8 and 9 on the power of Fate have been associated (these are now adesp. F 503 and 504). The attribution of P. Berlin 17154 is firmly rejected by Kannicht, TrGF 2.321 and Van Looy 536.*

There is no external evidence for the play's date, and too little survives to apply metrical criteria. Euripides' and Sophocles' plays are the only tragedies known with this title.

ΠΗΛΕΥΣ

617

οὐκ ἔστιν ἀνθρώποισι τοιοῦτος σκότος,
οὐ δῶμα γαίας κληστόν, ἔνθα τὴν φύσιν
ὁ δυσγενὴς κρύψας ἂν †εἴη σοφός†.

Stobaeus 4.30.8

2 δῶμα Stob.: χῶμα Meineke   3 see note opposite

617a (= 1025 N)

⟨ΠΗΛΕΥΣ⟩

θεοῦ γὰρ οὐδεὶς χωρὶς εὐτυχεῖ βροτῶν,
οὐδ᾽ εἰς τὸ μεῖον ἦλθε· τὰς θνητῶν δ᾽ ἐγὼ
χαίρειν κελεύω θεῶν ἄτερ προθυμίας.

Stobaeus 1.1.17, without attribution; v. 1: John Lydus, *On Months* 4.7 and *Palatine Anthology* 10.107.1 (both with *Scyrians* F 684.1–3 attached); [Menander], *Monostichs* 344 Jaekel

618

τὸν ὄλβον οὐδὲν οὐδαμοῦ κρίνω βροτοῖς,
ὅν γ᾽ ἐξαλείφει ῥᾷον ἢ γραφὴν θεός.

Stobaeus 4.31.62

PELEUS

617

Men have no such darkness, no house in the earth[1] shut
fast, where the base man[2] might(?) hide his nature †(and)
be wise†.[3]

[1] Or perhaps 'mound of earth' (Meineke).   [2] I.e. Acastus
(see Introduction).   [3] Faulty syntax and metre, and poor
sense; it has been amended unconvincingly, or the words deleted.

617a (= 1025 N)

⟨PELEUS⟩

Without god, no man has good fortune, and none is dimin-
ished. I myself dismiss those eager ventures of men that
lack the gods' aid.

618

I judge prosperity as nothing whatever to men's advantage;
a god wipes it away more easily than a painting![1]

[1] A familiar metaphor for human misfortune, e.g. F 1041 and
especially Aeschylus, *Agamemnon* 1328–9.

619

τὸ γῆρας, ὦ παῖ, τῶν νεωτέρων φρενῶν
σοφώτερον πέφυκε κἀσφαλέστερον,
ἐμπειρία τε τῆς ἀπειρίας κρατεῖ.

Stobaeus 4.50.17; v. 3: [Menander], *Monostichs* 242 Jaekel

(620 N = fr. adesp. 100.1–3 *PMG*)

621

⟨ΑΓΓΕΛΟΣ⟩

. . . τὰ δ᾽ ἔνθενδ᾽ οὐκέτ᾽ ἂν φράσαι λόγῳ
δακρύων δυναίμην χωρίς.

John Lydus, *On Months* 3.25

622

πάρεσμεν, ἀλλ᾽ οὐκ ἠσθάνου παρόντα με.

Etymologicum Genuinum AB under 'ἦσθα' (i.e. ἦσθα =
ᾔδεισθα: the lexicon's source appears to have had not ἠσθάνου
but ἦσθ᾽ ἂν οὐ)

(623 N = Sophocles, *Peleus* F 491)

619

Old age, my son, is wiser, and safer, than younger heads,
and experience overcomes inexperience.[1]

[1] For the thought see on *Melanippe* F 508.

(620 N = fr. adesp. 100.1–3 *PMG*)

621

‹MESSENGER›

. . . but what followed, I could no longer recount without
weeping.[1]

[1] No doubt the Messenger, describing Peleus' maltreatment
by Acastus.

622

I am present; but you did not perceive my presence.

(623 N = Sophocles, *Peleus* F 491)

PLEISTHENES

H. Van Looy in ed. Budé VIII.2.541–8.

Wilamowitz, *Kleine Schriften* 4.185–7 = *Hermes* 40 (1905), 131–4; Webster 236–7; Gantz 552–6; M. Papathomopoulos, *REG* 105 (1992), 45–58 (myth).

Not much can be said about the subject of this play. Pleisthenes is an obscure figure, unknown or ignored in the Homeric poems but apparently identified in the Hesiodic Catalogue of Women *(F 194) as a son of Atreus; in this tradition Pleisthenes and (probably) Aerope, rather than Atreus and Aerope, were the parents of Agamemnon and Menelaus.*[1] *In* Cretan Women *Euripides seems to have had Pleisthenes take Aerope as his wife after her expulsion from Crete (see our Introduction to that play). In 5th-century poetry Agamemnon and Menelaus could be referred to both as Atreus' sons and as Pleisthenes' offspring (see e.g. Aeschylus,* Agamemnon *1569, 1602). According to the*

---

[1] Alternatively Pleisthenes is a son, or bastard son, of Pelops, and thus Atreus' brother or half-brother (Schol. on Pindar, *Olympians* 1.89). A Pleisthenes son of Thyestes (Hyginus, *Fab.* 88.1, Seneca, *Thyestes* 726) and a Pleisthenes son of Menelaus and Helen (*Cypria* fr. 10 Davies) are best regarded as separate inventions.

Byzantine scholar John Tzetzes, 'Hesiod' explained that the two had become Atreus' heirs after Pleisthenes died prematurely, and that Pleisthenes had been lame and sexually ambiguous;[2] but it is not clear whether these details really stem from early mythical traditions (as Papathomopoulos argues) or from later rationalizations of conflicting legends about their parentage.

One might guess that Euripides' play was about Pleisthenes' relationship with Aerope and his early death, but no evidence confirms this. Instead, a possible plot has been found in a brief summary in Hyginus, Fab. 86: 'Thyestes . . . because he had lain with Atreus' wife Aerope was expelled by Atreus from his kingdom; but he sent Atreus' son Pleisthenes, whom he had raised as his own son, to kill Atreus. Atreus, believing him to be his brother's son, unknowingly killed his own son.' In the absence of any alternative, many scholars have been inclined to follow Musgrave's guess that this reflects Euripides' plot, but the story may well have been, as Wilamowitz put it, 'one of the wild contrivances of late tragedy'.

The fragments and testimonia of the play itself give no clear guidance. It would appear to have included an apologia for the killing of someone's father (F 625, difficult to relate to Hyginus' summary), a ruler giving political advice (F 626, father to son?), comments (negative?) on oracle-mongers and sacrifices (F 627, 628), defiance of a persecutor or punisher (F 629), and a man connected with Sardis renouncing his connection with Argos (see F 630

---

[2] See the *addendum* to F 194 in the Oxford Classical Text of Hesiod, ed. 2 (1983), 232 (= F 137(c) in the Loeb *Hesiod* (2007)).

with note). The lyric fragment about a symposium (F 631) need not refer to an event within the play.

Brief fragment: F 633 'censure'. Other ascriptions: none.

If Aristophanes, Birds *1232 is an echo of F 628 (see note there),* Pleisthenes *will have been produced before 414 (perhaps not long before, but the occurrence of three resolutions in the 14 extant trimeters, with two in the single verse F 625, does not prove this: cf. Cropp–Fick 89).*

No literary or artistic descendants of the play have been identified.

ΠΛΕΙΣΘΕΝΗΣ

625

οὐ τὸν σὸν ἔκταν πατέρα, πολέμιόν γε μήν.

Schol. on Homer, *Iliad* 4.319 (= Herodian, *On Prosody in the Iliad* p. 46.11 Lentz)

626

δήμῳ δὲ μήτε πᾶν ἀναρτήσῃς κράτος,
μήτ' αὖ κακώσῃς, πλοῦτον ἔντιμον τιθείς.
μηδ' ἄνδρα δήμῳ πιστὸν ἐκβάλῃς ποτὲ
μηδ' αὖξε καιροῦ μεῖζον', οὐ γὰρ ἀσφαλές,
5   μή σοι τύραννος λαμπρὸς ἐξ αὐτοῦ φανῇ.
κώλυε δ' ἄνδρα παρὰ δίκην τιμώμενον·
πόλει γὰρ εὐτυχοῦντες οἱ κακοὶ νόσος.

Stobaeus 4.7.1

PLEISTHENES

625

I did not kill your father, but rather an enemy.[1]

[1] Without a context the sense is unclear; perhaps an equivocation, 'not *your* father, but *my* enemy.'

626

Do not attach power wholly to the people, nor on the other hand degrade them by privileging wealth. Never expel a man who is trusted by the people, and do not let him grow greater than he should be, for that is unsafe, in case he should turn into a manifest tyrant. Check a man who gains   5
esteem unjustly, for base men prospering are an affliction to a city.[1]

[1] Lit. 'a disease', i.e. they corrupt public life because their success encourages others to seek success by similar means: cf. *Polyidus* F 644 with note.

EURIPIDES

627

εἰσὶν γὰρ εἰσὶ διφθέραι μελεγγραφεῖς
πολλῶν γέμουσαι Λοξίου γηρυμάτων.

Tzetzes, Schol. on his own *Chiliades* 12.338 (p. 596 Leone)

μελεγγραφεῖς Tzetz.: μελαγγραφεῖς Bergk

628

μηλοσφαγεῖτε δαιμόνων ἐπ᾽ ἐσχάραις.

Ammonius, *On similar and different words* 113; cf.
Aristophanes, *Birds* 1232 μηλοσφαγεῖν τε βουθύτοις ἐπ᾽ ἐσχά-
ραις

629

. . . καὶ κάταιθε χὦτι λῇς ποίει.

Etymologicum Genuinum AB λ 93 Alpers

630

ἐγὼ δὲ Σαρδιανός, οὐκέτ᾽ Ἀργόλας.

Stephanus of Byzantium "Ἄργος᾽ (p. 113.9 Meineke)

οὐκέτ᾽ Barnes: ⟨οὐ⟩ γὰρ οὐκέτι Steph.: οὐ γὰρ Hartung

627

There are, truly there are, parchments inscribed with song,[1] laden with many utterances of Loxias.[2]

[1] I.e. in dactylic verse. Written oracle collections were common in the 5th century: see e.g. Herodotus 7.6.3–5, Thucydides 2.8.2; J. Fontenrose, *The Delphic Oracle* (Berkeley, 1978), 152–65. Bergk's conjecture turns 'inscribed with song' (a doubtful word-formation) into 'inscribed in black (ink)'.   [2] A title of the oracular Apollo; etymology unknown, but commonly associated with the word *loxos*, 'oblique'.

628

Slaughter (*or* 'You slaughter') sheep on the altars of the gods.[1]

[1] This verse seems to be echoed in Aristophanes, *Birds* 1232 'and to slaughter sheep on sacrificial altars'; *Birds* was produced in 414 B.C.

629

. . . and burn (me?), and do (to me?) what you will.[1]

[1] Probably a defiant challenge to an oppressor, like *Cretans* F 472e.35–9, *Syleus* F 687.1–2.

630

I am a Sardian, no longer an Argive.[1]

[1] Either 'no longer' (Barnes) or 'assuredly not' (Hartung); the manuscripts of Stephanus combine the two phrases unmetrically. A man renouncing Argos in favour of Sardis may well belong to the family of Pelops, who migrated from Lydia to Greece.

631

πολὺς δὲ κοσσάβων ἀραγ-
μὸς Κύπριδος προσῳδὸν ἀ-
χεῖ μέλος ἐν δόμοισιν.

Athenaeus 15.668b

632

πολλῶν δὲ χρήματ᾽ αἴτι᾽ ἀνθρώποις κακῶν.

Stobaeus 4.31.73

631

Much ringing of wine-drops made a song appealing to
Cypris resound through the house.[1]

[1] The ringing is caused by symposiasts propelling drops of
wine at metal disks in the game of cottabus (see on *Oeneus* F 562).
A hit could be taken as a portent of sexual success (hence 'appeal-
ing to Cypris').

632

Money is the cause of many evils for men.

POLYIDUS

H. Van Looy in ed. Budé VIII.2.549–65.

Webster 161–2; Aélion (1983), I.297–9; *LIMC* IV.i.273–4 'Glaukos II' and VIII.i.1010–11 'Polyidos'; Gantz 270–1.

The earliest mention of the seer Polyidus ('Much-knowing') has him vainly deterring his son Euchenor from fighting while at Troy, and foreboding his death (Homer, Iliad 13.663–72). In the Hesiodic Catalogue of Women F 136.5–7, however, Euchenor's father is (apparently) named Coeranus, who for Pindar, Olympians 13.75, for Sophocles, Seers (or Polyidus) F 395, and for Euripides in this play (test. iva (3) below) is father to Polyidus himself. The same very damaged Hesiodic fragment names Polyidus among the descendants of the famous seer Melampus, together with the latter's daughters Manto ('Prophetess') and Pronoe ('Forethought'). The incident for which Polyidus was best known to poets and mythographers, and which gave Euripides his plot, indeed had his divinatory skills at its heart.

The story is told most fully, without attribution to Euripides, in Hyginus, Fab. 136 (test. iva below): in brief, Polyidus' skills enabled him to find Glaucus the son of king Minos of Crete when the boy went missing and then, al-

*though he was judged dead, to restore him to life. There is
a similar narrative in Apollodorus 3.3.17–20, but with a
slightly different ending (test. ivb below). An incident early
in the story is explicitly recorded for Euripides by Aelian,
Nature of Animals 5.2 (test. iii below). It seems likely that
all three tragedians followed essentially the same outline,
first Aeschylus in his Cretan Women (F 116–20) and then
Sophocles in his Seers (F **389a–*400); the story's cur-
rency in their time is attested by an Attic cup of c. 470–460
B.C. depicting and naming its two prominent figures Minos
and Polyidus (LIMC 'Glaukos II' no. 1).*

*Unfortunately the dozen Euripidean fragments can be
placed only loosely within the outline. Polyidus' proof of
his skills, necessary before Minos can invite (or challenge)
him to find Glaucus, is not represented, although F 634
and 635 allude to it: he 'explained' the portent of a three-
coloured cow by likening it to a ripening mulberry (test.
iva.1–3; cf. Aeschylus F 116, Sophocles F 395). We do how-
ever glimpse him using divination from birds to find the
dead Glaucus (F 636, test. iii, test. iva.(4); cf. Sophocles F
396). The boy's death is reflected in F 638 and 638a, his
seemingly elaborate funeral and tomb in F 639–40, and
Minos' grief in F 641, 644–5, 645b.[1] Also unrepresented
are Polyidus' incarceration in Glaucus' tomb and the epi-
sode of the snakes which led to the boy's restoration to life
and their joint release (test. iva.5–7; cf. the Attic cup noted*

---

[1] Plutarch, *Moralia* 132e, however, has Minos in his grief
omitting music and wreaths from the funeral sacrifices. Kannicht
(*TrGF* 5.625) records a suggestion by Wilamowitz that this detail
came from Euripides' play, but see adesp. F 166 and 419 under
'Other ascriptions'.

*above). There is nothing too of Minos' rewarding Polyidus
and sending him home (test. iva.7), or of Apollodorus' vari-
ant (test. ivb) that Minos first made Polyidus teach Glaucus
his divinatory skills, only for Polyidus before he left to con-
trive that Glaucus should forget them (so keeping them se-
cret to Melampus' dynasty). F 643 and 644 speak critically
of a 'bad man', cf. 645.2 'perjury' and 646 'mislead': these
tones look to come from the altercation when Polyidus re-
bukes Minos' behaviour over the funeral and is incarcer-
ated (see esp. Webster 161–2). It is frustrating that such an
evidently colourful drama remains so misty.*

*Brief fragment: F 646 'mislead' (see above: possibly
confused with* Hippolytus Veiled *F 435). Other ascrip-
tions: adesp. F 166 (Minos addresses the dead Glaucus on
the huge size he intends for his tomb; almost certainly of
Hellenistic date) and adesp. F 419 (Minos buries Cretan
pipes with Glaucus); for adesp. F 279h, an inscription from
Roman Ostia on the brevity of life, see Van Looy 564 n. 23.*

*Metrical criteria point to a late date (Webster 161),
probably after 412 (Cropp–Fick 89). Apart from the plays
by Aeschylus and Sophocles, no other tragedies with this
name or subject are known (unless adesp. F 166 and 419
derive from one). Aristophanes' comedy* Polyidus *may
have burlesqued Euripides' play, especially if Euripides
had attempted to stage the incarceration in the tomb (see
Gantz 271 on this scene on the Attic cup).*

ΠΟΛΥΙΔΟΣ

Hypothesis

Scrappy remnants including the title-line Πολύειδος, οὗ ἀρχή and the phrases καὶ Κοιρα[ν . . .]ἔπλευσε

P. Michigan, unpublished: see W. Luppe, *APF* 50 (2004), 218

test. iii

ἐν τῇ Κρήτῃ γλαῦκα μὴ γίνεσθαί φασι τὸ παράπαν, ἀλλὰ καὶ ἐσκομισθεῖσαν ἔξωθεν ἀποθνῄσκειν. ἔοικε δὲ ὁ Εὐριπίδης ἀβασανίστως πεποιηκέναι τὸν Πολύειδον ὁρῶντα τήνδε τὴν ὄρνιν καὶ ἐξ αὐτῆς τεκμηράμενον ὅτι εὑρήσει τὸν Γλαῦκον τὸν τεθνεῶτα τοῦ Μίνω υἱόν.

Aelian, *Nature of Animals* 5.2

test. iva

⟨POLYIDUS⟩. Glaucus Minois et Pasiphaae filius, dum ludit pila, cecidit in dolium melle plenum. Quem cum parentes quaererent, Apollinem sciscitati sunt de puero; quibus Apollo respondit, 'monstrum uobis natum est; quod si quis soluerit, puerum uobis restituet.' (2) Minos sorte audita coepit monstrum a suis quaerere; cui dixerunt natum esse uitulum, qui

POLYIDUS

Hypothesis

Polyidus, which begins . . . and Coera(nus?) . . . sailed . . .[1]

[1] Coeranus: the father of Polyidus (see Introduction); 'sailed' may have related to Polyidus' voyage to Crete (from his home in Corinth?).

test. iii

They say that the owl is totally non-existent in Crete, and that if it is brought in from outside, it dies. Euripides seems not to have examined the facts when he made Polyidus see this bird and infer from it that he would find Glaucus, the dead son of Minos.[1]

[1] 'Owl' is Greek *glauk-*, i.e. Glauc(us); cf. test. iva (4) below.

test. iva

Glaucus, son of Minos and Pasiphae, fell into a storage jar full of honey while playing ball. When his parents sought after him, they inquired about the boy from Apollo, and Apollo answered them: 'You have a portentous creature born for you; if anyone explains it, he will restore the boy to you.' (2) When he heard the oracle, Minos began to seek the portent from his people, who told him that a calf had been born which changed

ter in die colorem mutaret per quaternas horas: primum al-
bum, secundo rubeum, deinde nigrum. (3) Minos autem ad
monstrum soluendum augures conuocauit, qui cum non
inuenirentur, Polyidus Coerani filius †Bizanti† monstrum de-
monstrauit: eum arbori moro similem esse; nam primum al-
bum est, deinde rubrum, cum permaturauit nigrum. (4) Tunc
Minos ait ei, 'ex Apollinis responso filium mihi oportet resti-
tuas.' Quod Polyidus dum auguratur uidit noctuam super cel-
lam uinariam sedentem atque apes fugantem. augurio accep-
to puerum exanimem de dolio eduxit. (5) Cui Minos ait,
'corpore inuento nunc spiritum restitue'. quod Polyidus cum
negaret posse fieri, Minos iubet eum cum puero in monumen-
to includi et gladium poni. (6) Qui cum inclusi essent, draco
repente ad corpus pueri processit; quod Polyidus aestimans
eum uelle consumere, gladio repente percussit et occidit.
Altera serpens parem quaerens uidit eam interfectam et pro-
gressa herbam attulit, atque eius tactu serpenti spiritum resti-
tuit. (7) Idemque Polyidus fecit. Qui cum intus uociferaren-
tur, quidam praeteriens Minoi nuntiauit, qui monumentum
iussit aperiri et filium incolumem recuperauit, Polyidum cum
multis muneribus in patriam remisit.

Hyginus, *Fab*. 136

test. ivb

ἀπολαβὼν δὲ Μίνως τὸν παῖδα οὐδ᾽ οὕτως εἰς Ἄργος
ἀπιέναι τὸν Πολύιδον εἴα, πρὶν ἢ τὴν μαντείαν διδάξαι
τὸν Γλαῦκον· ἀναγκασθεὶς δὲ Πολύιδος διδάσκει. καὶ
ἐπειδὴ ἀπέπλει, κελεύει τὸν Γλαῦκον εἰς τὸ στόμα
ἐμπτύσαι· καὶ τοῦτο ποιήσας Γλαῦκος τῆς μαντείας
ἐπελάθετο.

its colour three times a day, every four hours, first white, then ruddy, and after that black. (3) Then Minos called augurs together to explain the portent; when they could not be found, Polyidus the son of Coeranus †of Byzantium† made the portent clear: it was like a mulberry tree; for it was first white, then red, and when it matured, black. (4) Then Minos said to him, 'In accord with Apollo's oracle, you must restore my son to me.' While Polyidus was seeking signs, he saw an owl perched above a wine cellar, and driving bees away. He accepted the sign, and brought the boy lifeless from the storage jar. (5) Minos said to him, 'You have found his body: now restore his life's breath.' When Polyidus said that this was impossible, Minos ordered him to be shut up together with the boy inside a tomb, and a sword to be put there. (6) When they had been shut inside, a serpent suddenly approached the boy's body; thinking that it wished to devour it, Polyidus struck it instantly with the sword and slew it. Another serpent, seeking its mate, saw that that it had been killed; it went and brought a herb to it, and with its touch restored the breath of life to the serpent. (7) Polyidus accordingly did the same *(i.e. to the boy)*. When they cried out from inside the tomb, a passer-by reported it to Minos; he ordered the tomb to be opened and recovered his son safe and well, and sent Polyidus back to his homeland with many rewards.

test. ivb

Although he had recovered his son, Minos even so would not allow Polyidus to go off to Argos before he had taught Glaucus divination; so Polyidus taught him under compulsion. When he was about to sail away, he ordered Glaucus to spit into his mouth; and when Glaucus did this he forgot divination.

Apollodorus 3.3.20

634

ὅστις νέμει κάλλιστα τὴν αὑτοῦ φύσιν,
οὗτος σοφὸς πέφυκε πρὸς τὸ συμφέρον.

Stobaeus 3.3.20; Arsenius 40.15 *CPG*

τὴν αὑτοῦ φύσιν Stob. mss. MA: τοῖς αὑτοῦ φίλοις Stob. ed.
Trincavelli, Arsen.

635

⟨ΠΟΛΤΙΔΟΣ?⟩

οἱ τὰς τέχνας δ' ἔχοντες ἀθλιώτεροι
τῆς φαυλότητος· ⟨τό⟩ τε γὰρ ἐν κοινῷ ψέγειν
ἅπασι κεῖσθαι δυστυχὲς ⟨κ⟩οὐκ εὐτυχές . . .

Stobaeus 4.18.15

2 ⟨τό⟩ τε γὰρ Wagner, Badham: καὶ γὰρ Musgrave: see note
opposite

636

ΠΟΛΤΙΔΟΣ

ἔα ἔα·
ὁρῶ τιν' ἀκταῖς νομάδα κυματόφθορον
ἁλιαίετον· τὸν παῖδα χερσεύει μόρος.
εἰ μὲν γὰρ ἐκ γῆς εἰς θάλασσαν ἔπτατο

Hermogenes, *On Figures* 2.5 (*Rhet. Gr.* VI.344.5 Rabe) cit-
ing vv. 4–6, with unpublished Schol. citing vv. 1–8 in full; other
sources repeat phrases from vv. 4–5

2 τιν' Blaydes, West: τὸν Schol. Herm.   κυματόφθορον
Blaydes, West: κυματοφθόρον Schol. Herm.

634

The man who manages his own nature best is wise to his own advantage.[1]

[1] The variant 'who pays best attention to his friends' may be a simple miscopying.

635

‹POLYIDUS?›

Those who possess skills are more wretched than those who are weak in them; for it is their misfortune, and not good fortune, to be open to everyone's common blame . . .[1]

[1] Probably Polyidus excusing himself when told by Minos to divine the whereabouts of the missing Glaucus (test. iva (4)). The Greek translates insecurely, even with Wagner's restoration of better syntax (Musgrave restored only metre), and may be defective.

636

POLYIDUS

Look, look there! I see on the shore a sea-eagle, that is driven over the waves and pastures on them: death has the boy on dry land. For if the bird, whose home is the waves,

EURIPIDES

5 ὁ κύματ᾿ οἰκῶν ὄρνις, ἡρμήνευσεν ἂν
   τὸν παῖδ᾿ ἐν ὑγροῖς κύμασιν τεθνηκέναι·
   νῦν δ᾿ ἐκλιπὼν ἤθη τε καὶ νομὸν βίου
   δεῦρ᾿ ἔπτατ᾿· οὔκουν ἔσθ᾿ ὁ παῖς ἐν οἴδμασιν.

(637 N = 645b below)

638

τίς δ᾿ οἶδεν εἰ τὸ ζῆν μέν ἐστι κατθανεῖν,
τὸ κατθανεῖν δὲ ζῆν κάτω νομίζεται;

Schol. on *Hippolytus* 191 (omitting the last two words), with
the only attribution to *Polyidus*; attributed elsewhere to *Hippolytus* (a plain error) or *Phrixus* (cf. F 833), or just to Euripides
(earliest Plato, *Gorgias* 492e, but implicit in Aristophanes' travesty at *Frogs* 1476–8); the whole fr. is cited very frequently, with
minor variations.

638a (= 645a N–Sn)

⟨ΧΟΡΟΣ?⟩

δύστανοι καὶ πολύμοχθοι
ματέρες ῞Αιδᾳ τίκτουσαι
τέκνα . . .

Photius α 553 Theodoridis

had flown from land out to sea, this would have indicated 5
that the boy is dead among the watery waves; but now it
has abandoned its life's habits and haunts, and has flown
here: therefore the boy is not in the swell of the sea.[1]

[1] The first bird-sign seen by Polyidus, not the one from the
owl named by Hyginus in test. iva (4). In v. 2 the Schol. on
Hermogenes has 'that sea-eagle which pastures and plunders the
waves'.

(637 N = 645b below)

638

Who knows if life is death, and if in the underworld death
is considered life?[1]

[1] Possibly Polyidus, challenged by Minos: see test. iva (4–5)
and Introduction. This conceit was famous throughout antiq-
uity: see note opposite, and cf. especially *Hippolytus* 191–7,
Phrixus A/B F 833, *Phoenix* F 816.6–11. Egli 110–2 notes its 'Or-
phic' character.

638a (= 645a N–Sn)

‹CHORUS?›

Wretched and much-enduring mothers, giving birth to
children for Hades . . .[1]

[1] The words may be self-referential, if the Chorus is composed
of women, or may evoke the misery of bereaved mothers in an
apostrophe (in this case, particularly Pasiphae the mother of
Glaucus).

639

μάτην γὰρ οἴκῳ σῷ τόδ' ἐκβαίη τέλος.

Schol. on Homer, *Iliad* 10.56, and Eustathius there; other citations

γὰρ sources: γ' ἂν Matthiae   οἴκῳ σῷ Valckenaer: οἴκῳ σὸν Schol.: many other conjectures

640

. . . ἀνθρώπων δὲ μαίνονται φρένες,
δαπάνας ὅταν θανοῦσι πέμπωσιν κενάς.

Stobaeus 4.55.1

641

πλουτεῖς, τὰ δ' ἄλλα μὴ δόκει ξυνιέναι·
ἐν τῷ γὰρ ὄλβῳ φαυλότης ἔνεστί τις,
πενία δὲ σοφίαν ἔλαχε διὰ τὸ συγγενές.

Stobaeus 4.32.7; v. 3: Clement of Alexandria, *Miscellanies* 4.5.24.4; other citations, some with adaptations.

3 συγγενές Clem.: δυστυχές Stob.

642

οὐ γάρ ⟨τι⟩ παρὰ κρατῆρα καὶ θοίνην μόνον
τὰ χρήματ' ἀνθρώποισιν ἡδονὰς ἔχει,
ἀλλ' ἐν κακοῖσι δύναμιν οὐ μικρὰν φέρει.

Stobaeus 4.31.12; Arsenius 41.59 *CPG*, seemingly attributing the fragment to the tragedian Polyidus (= *TrGF* no. 78 F 2?)

639

May this expenditure turn out profitless for your house![1]

[1] This and F 640 were probably spoken angrily by Polyidus when Minos ordered him to be shut in Glaucus' tomb (test. iva (5)). Matthiae's alteration creates not a wish but confidence: 'This expenditure would indeed turn out profitless . . .'

640

. . . men's wits go mad when they spend on empty offerings to the dead.[1]

[1] Cf. *Andromeda* F 154 with note.

641

You have riches, but you should not think that you under-stand the rest of things: there is a certain weakness in wealth, while poverty has inherent wisdom because the two are akin.[1]

[1] Polyidus speaks? The words recall his F 635. The general idea also at *Archelaus* F 235; cf. *Telephus* F 715.2.

642

It's not (at all) just at the wine-bowl and banquet that money affords men pleasures; it provides no little strength amid troubles.

643

βαρύ τι φόρημ' οἴησις ἀνθρώπου κακοῦ.

Stobaeus 3.22.1, attributed to Euripides' *Glaucus* (cf. F 644, 645b) amid confused lemmata; the three fragments were reassigned by Musgrave.

βαρύ τι Wagner, φόρημ' Salmasius: βαρὺ τὸ φρόνημ' Stob.

644

ὅταν κακός τις ἐν πόλει πράσσῃ καλῶς,
νοσεῖν τίθησι τὰς ἀμεινόνων φρένας,
παράδειγμ' ἐχόντας τῶν κακῶν ἐξουσίαν.

Stobaeus 4.4.3, assigned to Eur. *Glaucus* (see on F 643)

645

συγγνώμονάς τοι τοὺς θεοὺς εἶναι δοκεῖς,
ὅταν τις ὅρκῳ θάνατον ἐκφυγεῖν θέλῃ
ἢ δεσμὸν ἢ βίαια πολεμίων κακά,
ἢ τοῖσιν αὐθένταισι κοινωνῇ δόμων;
5 ἢ τἄρα θνητῶν εἰσιν ἀσυνετώτεροι,
εἰ τἀπιεικῆ πρόσθεν ἡγοῦνται δίκης.

Stobaeus 1.3.40 without lemma, but assigned in a marginal note to Eur. *Polyidus*; vv. 1–3: Stobaeus 3.28.3 attributed just to Euripides

1 δοκεῖς (δοκεῖς; Valckenaer) or δόκει or δοκεῖ Stob. mss.
4 τοῖσιν Valckenaer: παισὶν Stob.   5 ἢ τἄρα Valckenaer
(ἤτἄρα Nauck): ἢ τἄρα Stob.   6 εἰ Valckenaer: ἢ Stob.: οἱ
Usener

POLYIDUS

643

An opinionated bad man is quite a heavy burden.

644

When a bad man does well in a city, he corrupts the minds of his betters, who have as their example the power given to bad men.[1]

[1] Against the advancement of 'bad men' see also *Erechtheus* F 362.28–31, *Pleisthenes* F 626.6–7.

645

Do you think the gods show pardon when someone chooses through perjury to escape death, or bonds, or violent harm from enemies, or when he shares his house with murderers? In that case, truly they are less intelligent than mortal men, if they consider that fairness comes before 5 justice.[1]

[1] Text and interpretation must be insecure when context and speaker are unknown. In v. 1 Stobaeus offers 'You think', 'Think!' or 'He thinks': the first seems likelier than the second, but the third is possible. In vv. 5–6 Stobaeus appears to offer 'Either in that case truly they are less intelligent . . . or they consider . . .', i.e. two alternative criticisms of the gods for pardoning perjury: but are they genuine or sardonic? Kannicht in *TrGF* follows Nauck in v. 5 and Usener in v. 6: 'for otherwise truly they are less intelligent . . . in that they (the gods) consider . . .' We print Valckenaer's text throughout.

EURIPIDES

(645a N–Sn = 638a above)

645b (= 637 N)

φεῦ φεῦ, τὸ γῆρας ὡς ἔχει πολλὰς νόσους.

Stobaeus 4.50.33, assigned to Euripides' *Glaucus* (see on F 643); *Florilegium Monacense* 129 Meineke, unattributed

POLYIDUS

(645a N–Sn = 638a above)

645b (= 637 N)
Alas, alas: old age has many afflictions![1]

[1] Minos, most likely.

PROTESILAUS

F. Jouan in ed. Budé VIII.2.567–89.

M. Mayer, *Hermes* 20 (1885), 101–35; Jouan (1966), 317–36; Webster 97–8; W. Burkert, *Homo Necans* (Berkeley, 1983), 243–7 (myth and cult); A. Ruiz de Elvira, *Cuadernos de Filologia Clásica (Estudios latínos)* 1 (1991), 139–58; *LIMC* VII.i.554–60 'Protesilaos'.

The Thessalian hero Protesilaus, first of the Greeks to fall at Troy, is recalled in the Iliad *(2.695–710); the lost* Cypria, *according to Proclus' summary (p. 77 West), gave an account of his death. The* Iliad *relates that he left a grieving wife and a half-built house in his home town of Phylace. By the early 5th century there were cults of Protesilaus at Phylace (Pindar,* Isthmians *1.58–9), at his supposed burial site at Elaeus on the shore opposite Troy (Herodotus 9.116–20), and at Scione in Chalcidice whose coins claimed him as its founder (LIMC nos. 4–6). Protesilaus' continuing presence at Elaeus is the subject of Philostratus' dialogue* On Heroes *(2nd c. A.D.).*

According to the Cypria *(F 18 Davies) Protesilaus' wife was Meleager's daughter Polydora, but in Euripides and all later literature she is Laodamia, daughter of Acastus of Iolcus (heir of Jason's adversary Pelias). His posthumous reunion with her is not attested before Euripides but may*

have been a fundamental part of his myth, in which the
'Dionysiac' elements of a dying-reviving god and a sacred
marriage have been detected. This reunion was certainly
the basis of Euripides' play, in which the underworld gods
permitted Protesilaus to return to life for a single day in or-
der to visit his wife. The scholia to Aristides and Lucian
on which we rely for this information (see test. ii below
with note) give no further detail, but elements of Euripides'
plot are probably reflected more or less closely in mytho-
graphic summaries of the story (especially Apollodorus,
Epit. 3.29–30 and Eustathius on Iliad 2.700–2 and the
slightly confused Hyginus, Fab. 103–4: see TrGF test.
*iiia–b), in numerous references to it in later Greek and
Latin literature, and in two sculptured sarcophagi of the
2nd century A.D. (LIMC nos. 26–7 = TrGF test. *iiic):
for analysis of all these see primarily Mayer. Recurring
features are that Laodamia indulged her longing for her
husband by making an image of him (a motif apparently al-
luded to in Alcestis 348–52) and that she killed herself after
his enforced return to Hades. Further dramatic substance
has been detected (less certainly) in Hyginus, Fab. 104
where Laodamia disguises her devotion to the image as
religious ritual (depicted as Bacchic on the Naples sar-
cophagus, LIMC no. 26; cf. Statius, Silvae 2.7.124–7) but a
servant 'early in the morning' observes her embracing it in
her chamber and reports this to her father, who orders it to
be burned so as to limit her grief.

Mayer argued persuasively that this crisis must have
preceded Laodamia's reunion with her husband. The
play's action, then, would have begun with the servant's re-
port to Acastus, a confrontation between Acastus and
Laodamia in which she defended her devotion to the image

EURIPIDES

*(F 655), and Acastus' order for the image to be burned
(for such an opening sequence compare the discovery,
'trial' and condemnation of Melanippe's newborn sons in
Melanippe Wise). Protesilaus presumably then arrived
with Hermes (F 646a) in a 'second prologue' and found
Laodamia in her chamber as the Naples sarcophagus sug-
gests (although the Vatican sarcophagus shows a meeting
at the house entrance); it seems necessary for the play's ac-
tion that he should have returned in his original youthful
form (cf. Lucian 77.28.2) rather than as a mere ghost as in
some accounts, and it could also be that Laodamia mistak-
enly supposed, at least at first, that he had survived the
war at Troy after all (Apollodorus). A confrontation be-
tween Protesilaus and Acastus (F 647) presumably took
place later as Protesilaus prepared to leave, and may well
have been the context for F 653 (Acastus denigrating mar-
riage) and F 654 (a choral comment on their dispute). After
Protesilaus' departure Laodamia determined to kill her-
self (F 656), and her suicide will have been reported to
Acastus by a servant (F 657 may well be the conclusion of
this report, as Wilamowitz suggested, rather than part of
the debate between Protesilaus and Acastus). Hyginus has
Laodamia throwing herself on the pyre built to burn the
image, but this is probably a romantic variation on an orig-
inal heroic suicide by the sword (Eustathius; the Naples
sarcophagus).*

*The remaining short fragments (F 648–52) can be ac-
commodated within such a framework in various ways, but
their placing is largely a matter of speculation (presumably
F 649 and 651 consoled Laodamia for her husband's death,
and F 652 was said about her by Acastus). Jouan (1966 and
2000) attempts a full plot-reconstruction which accommo-*

dates all of them and includes some other features from later accounts which may or may not be Euripidean: a role for Aphrodite speaking the prologue (Eustathius attributes Protesilaus' yearning for his wife—or in an alternative version hers for him—to Aphrodite's 'wrath', perhaps due to their unfulfilled marriage); a role for Laodamia's nurse (pictured on the Naples sarcophagus); a chorus of local women (cf. Ovid, Heroides 13. 35–6?); Laodamia pressed by her father to marry again (Eustathius' alternative version); Protesilaus persuading her to join him in Hades (Lucian, Philostratus, Eustathius).

Brief fragments: none. Other ascriptions: none of any extent.

The absence of resolutions in the fragments (all of them iambic trimeters) suggests a date before 425, perhaps close to Alcestis *with its image motif (see above), but our limited acquaintance with both plot and fragments makes it impossible to tell whether Euripides gave the story any of the humorous or paradoxical tones that we find in that 'prosatyric' play. No other tragedies are recorded, but Anaxandrides (mid-4th c.) produced a comic* Protesilaus *(F 41–2 PCG). Hellenistic poetry on the subject is almost totally lost, but it was a familar topic in Latin poetry, notably Catullus 68.73–86, Ovid, Heroides 13, and Statius, Silvae 2.7.120–31. Treatments in modern drama, opera and poetry are few and mostly obscure (OGCMA II.937), but note Wordsworth's narrative* Laodamia *(see* Shorter Poems, 1807–1820, *ed. C. Ketcham [Ithaca, 1991], 142–52, 360–9).*

ΠΡΩΤΕΣΙΛΑΟΣ

test. ii

Πρωτεσίλαος δρᾶμα γέγραπται Εὐριπίδῃ. λέγει δὲ ὅτι γαμήσας καὶ μίαν ἡμέραν μόνην συγγενόμενος τῇ γυναικὶ αὐτοῦ ἠναγκάσθη μετὰ τῶν Ἑλλήνων κατὰ τῆς Τροίας ἐλθεῖν, καὶ πρῶτος ἐπιβὰς τῆς Τροίας ἐτελεύτησεν. καί φησιν ὅτι τοὺς κάτω δαίμονας ᾐτήσατο καὶ ἀφείθη μίαν ἡμέραν, καὶ συνεγένετο τῇ γυναικὶ αὐτοῦ.

Schol. on Aelius Aristides 3.365; similarly Schol. on Lucian 26.1

1 λέγει δὲ or λέγει or λέγεται δὲ Schol. Aristid. mss. (λέγεται δὲ Schol. Lucian)   5 φησιν or φασιν Schol. Aristid. mss. (φασιν Schol. Lucian)

646a

‹ΕΡΜΗΣ›

ἕπου δὲ μοῦνον ἀμπρεύοντί μοι.

Photius, *Lexicon* a 1251 Theodoridis (= Phrynichus, *Sophistic Preparation* fr. 171 de Borries)

PROTESILAUS

test. ii

Protesilaus is a drama written by Euripides. And he says that after marrying and consorting with his wife for just one day he was compelled to go with the Greeks against Troy, and died after being the first of them to land at Troy. He also says that he entreated the powers below and was released for one day, and consorted with his wife.[1]

[1] The variants 'He says' and 'And it is said' in the second sentence, and 'They say' in the third, make it a little uncertain that all of this refers to Euripides: see F. Lenz, *Mnemosyne* 21 (1968), 163–70.

646a

⟨ HERMES ⟩
(to Protesilaus)
Just follow me as I guide you.

EURIPIDES

647

ἀξίως δ' ἐμὸς
γαμβρὸς κέκλησαι, παῖδά μοι ξυνοικίσας.

Photius, *Lexicon*, 'πενθερά' (II.74 Naber) = Suda π 963
(= Aelius Dionysius, *Attic Vocabulary* π 34 Erbse), also citing
Alcmeon in Psophis F 72

648

οὐ γὰρ θέμις βέβηλον ἅπτεσθαι δόμων.

Schol. on Sophocles, *Oedipus at Colonus* 10 ≈ Suda β 218

649

πέπονθεν οἷα καὶ σὲ καὶ πάντας μένει.

Stobaeus 4.56.8

650

πόλλ' ἐλπίδες ψεύδουσιν ἄλογοι βροτούς.

Stobaeus 4.47.5

651

οὐ θαῦμ' ἔλεξας θνητὸν ὄντα δυστυχεῖν.

Stobaeus 4.34.51

652

⟨ΑΚΑΣΤΟΣ?⟩
ὦ παῖδες, οἷον φίλτρον ἀνθρώποις φρενός.

Stobaeus 4.24.10

647

PROTESILAUS
(to Acastus)

You are rightly called my father-in-law, since you settled
your daughter on me.

648

For it is unlawful for one who is polluted to be in contact
with the house.[1]

[1] Perhaps Protesilaus hesitating to enter his house, being
polluted by death; but Kannicht notes that δόμων might mean
'rooms', i.e. Laodamia's chamber or shrine from which unpurified
people (such as the servant who observed her from outside) were
prohibited.

649

He has suffered such things as await you and every one.[1]

[1] I.e. death: cf. e.g. *Hypsipyle* F 757.921–7.

650

Mortals are much deceived by groundless hopes.

651

What you have said is nothing strange, that a mortal should
suffer misfortune.

652

⟨ACASTUS?⟩

O children, how you can beguile men's hearts![1]

[1] Cf. *Alcmene* F 103 with note.

113

653

δοκεῖ μὲν] οὖν μοι σκα[ι]ὸς ⸴⸴[
ὅστις γυν]αικὸς οὕνεκ' ἂν λά[β-
            ]του [π]ανδοκεῖ το ⸴[
κοινὸν γὰρ] εἶναι χρῆν γυναι[κεῖον λέχος
5   ο]ὕτως εὐγένεια τ[

P. Oxy. 3214.9–14 (citing *Protesilaus*), ed. M. Haslam (1977),
cf. M. West, *ZPE* 26 (1977), 40, W. Luppe, *ZPE* 29 (1978), 33–5,
H. Oranje, *ZPE* 37 (1980), 169–72; v. 4: Clement of Alexandria,
Miscellanies 6.2.24.6

1 εὐ[ήθης τ' ἀνήρ West   2 λά[βοι πόνους West (λά[βῃ
Luppe)   3 τόκ[ους μόνον Luppe: τόκ[ου σποράν Kannicht
5 βροτοῖσι· χο]ὕτως West (ἄπασι Luppe)   τ[' ἂν κρατοῖ
West

654

δυοῖν λεγόντοιν, θατέρου θυμουμένου,
ὁ μὴ ἀντιτείνων τοῖς λόγοις σοφώτερος.

Stobaeus 3.19.3 and 3.3.40; [Plutarch], *Moralia* 10a

655

ΛΑΟΔΑΜΕΙΑ

οὐκ ἂν προδοίην καίπερ ἄψυχον φίλον.

[Dio Chrysostom] 37.46 (now ascribed to Favorinus)

653

(A man who) takes on (troubles) for the sake of having
a wife (seems) to me stupid (and simple-minded; for a
woman merely) acts as a host (to his offspring, *or* to his
seed). A woman's bed should be commonly available (to
men, *or* to all), and in this way nobility (would prevail) . . . [1]

[1] For the supplements see the apparatus opposite. The papy-
rus (a Euripidean gnomology) probably contained at least one fur-
ther line belonging to this excerpt. The thought seems to be that
women contribute nothing to the quality of their children, and
that without marriage nobility would not be mistakenly associated
with heredity. For the woman's passive part in breeding, cf. Aes-
chylus, *Eumenides* 658–61, Eur. *Orestes* 552–4, and for the oppo-
site view e.g. *Bellerophon* F 298, *Meleager* F 520. For the debate
between true and inherited nobility, *Electra* 384–5, *Alexander* F
61b, *Melanippe Captive* F 495.40ff., etc.

654

When two men speak and one of them is incensed, the
other is wiser not to combat his words.

655

LAODAMIA

I shall not forsake a loved one, even though he is lifeless.

656

⟨ ΛΑΟΔΑΜΕΙΑ ⟩

†δητ . σα† λαιμὸν ἢ πεσοῦσ' ἀπ' ἰσθμίου
⟨   ⟩ κευθμῶνα πηγαῖόν ⟨θ'⟩ ὕδωρ

Proverbs in ms. Paris suppl. gr. 676 (ed. L. Cohn, 1887 = *CPG*
Suppl. I, 1961), no. 95

1 †δητ . σα†: παίσασα Gomperz, Nauck
2 ⟨ἄβυσσον (or κελαινὸν) ἐς⟩ Gomperz: ⟨φρέατος ἐς⟩
Nauck   ⟨θ'⟩ Gomperz, Nauck

657

ὅστις δὲ πάσας συντιθεὶς ψέγει λόγῳ
γυναῖκας ἑξῆς, σκαιός ἐστι κοὐ σοφός·
πολλῶν γὰρ οὐσῶν τὴν μὲν εὑρήσεις κακήν,
τὴν δ' ὥσπερ ἥδε λῆμ' ἔχουσαν εὐγενές.

Stobaeus 4.22.76, and without attribution in two 2nd c. A.D.
papyrus anthologies

656

⟨LAODAMIA⟩

. . . -ing my throat or throwing myself from a well-head . . .
recess (and) spring-water.[1]

[1] Very uncertain text and sense; perhaps Laodamia contemplates ways of killing herself. In v. 1 something like Gomperz's 'striking' is needed. For v. 2 he suggested 'into a fathomless (*or* dark) recess and spring-water' (hendiadys), and Nauck 'into a well's watery recess' (for this method of suicide cf. e.g. *Phoenix* test. iva[1]).

657

Anyone who puts all women together and blames them indiscriminately is foolish and not wise. There are many of them, and you will find one bad while another is of noble character, as this one is (*or* was).[1]

[1] Cf. *Melanippe Captive* F 494.26–9.

RHESUS

A Rhesus *has been transmitted in the Euripidean corpus at least since the mid-3rd century* B.C. *An ancient hypothesis accompanying its text (hypoth. (b) Diggle =* Rhesus *test. ia in TrGF 5) shows that 'some' Hellenistic scholars thought it might be inauthentic, but this opinion clearly did not prevail. The hypothesis notes that the records of the Athenian dramatic festivals did include the production of a* Rhesus *by Euripides, and a scholion on* Rhesus *528 (= test. ib in TrGF 5) suggests that his play was known from these records to be an early work. It is now widely accepted, in view of its style and dramatic design, that the extant* Rhesus *is not by Euripides and is probably a 4th-century play that somehow came to be mistaken for his; there are no obvious candidates for its authorship.*

No certain fragments of Euripides' play survive, but the same hypothesis quotes the beginnings of two iambic prologues that were associated with the extant Rhesus *in the Hellenistic period. The first is attributed to 'Dicaearchus [Nauck's restoration of a corruptly transmitted name] setting out the hypothesis of* Rhesus*', i.e. to the collection of plot summaries of the plays of Sophocles and Euripides made by Aristotle's pupil Dicaearchus or derived from his work; this is fr. dub. 1108 N, a first line quoted in the usual manner of the Dicaearchan collection:*

νῦν εὐσέληνον φέγγος ἡ διφρήλατος . . .
'Now the chariot-driving (goddess) . . . fair moonlight'

(this might refer to the Moon dispensing moonlight, or to the Dawn dispersing or about to disperse it).

The second quotation is attributed in the transmitted hypothesis (hardly by the Dicaearchan source, as some scholars think) to 'some copies (of the extant play)'; this is TrGF *adesp. F 8l = Eur. fr. dub.* 1109 N, eleven lines in which Hera urges Athena to consider assisting the Achaeans against the threat of Hector's advance. The hypothesis describes this speech as 'prosaic and wholly inappropriate for Euripides', and suggests plausibly that it was due to actors revising the text, which has no iambic prologue of its own. The status of the prologue represented by fr. 1108 N (above) is less clear. It is tempting to think that it comes from Euripides' own play, but this would mean that his text survived until the late 4th century (so that Dicaearchus knew and publicized it), but then vanished completely and was displaced by the extant play within two generations. It seems more likely that the text was lost much earlier (probably before Euripides' death), that Dicaearchus was referring to the extant play in the (already common) belief that it was Euripides', and that the prologue known to him was another substitute prologue.

For further details and select bibliography see Kannicht in TrGF 5.642–3 and D. Kovacs in the Loeb Euripides VI (2002), 352–4 and 452–5 (with English translation of hypothesis (b)); also V. Liapis, GRBS 42 (2001), 313–28 on the hypothesis, and in D. Jacob and E. Papazoglou (eds.), ΘΥΜΕΛΗ· Μελέτες χαρισμένες . . . Ν. Χουρμουζιάδη (Iraklion, 2004), 159–88 on the prove-

nance of the extant play. For 4th c. vases featuring the story (but presumably not Euripides' play) see Taplin nos. 53–4 citing previous bibliography.

STHENEBOEA

C. Collard in *SFP* I.79–97, 284 (~ II.365); Diggle, *TrGFS* 128–31 (test. iia, F 661, 670); F. Jouan in ed. Budé VIII.3.1–27.

Wilamowitz, *Kleine Schriften* I.274–81; B. Zühlke, *Philologus* 105 (1961), 1–15, 198–215; K. Vysoký, *Zprávy Jednoty Klasických Filologu* 5 (1963), 73–80 (German résumé, *Bibliotheca Classica Orientalis* 9 [1964], 175); D. Korzeniewski, *Philologus* 108 (1964), 45–65; Trendall–Webster III.3.43–5; J. Moret, *Antike Kunst* 15 (1972), 95–106; A.-M. Braet, *AC* 42 (1973), 82–112; E. M. Papamichael, *Dodone* 12 (1983), 45–74, 139–52; Aélion (1986), 187–91; F. Jouan, *Sacris Erudiri* 31 (1989–90), 187–208; Gantz 311–6; *LIMC* VII.i.214–30, esp. 224–30 'Pegasos', 525–6 'Proitos', 810–1 'Stheneboea'; Taplin 201–4.

Evidence for Stheneboea's wretched story earlier than Euripides' play is sparse. In Homer, Iliad *6.155–66 it is given only in part, and merely as the incident which precipitated the heroic triumphs and later the tragedy of Bellerophon (see* Bellerophon *with our Introduction). Homer has her as daughter of a king of Lycia, but named Anticleia, and as married to Proetus king of Argos. In [Hesiod],* Catalogue of Women *F 129 she has a different 'Greek' father but the same husband, and the name used by Euripides and later*

121

writers; her tale itself is not told (or is lost from the fragment).

Homer's narrative goes this far: Stheneboea became passionately enamoured of the virtuous Bellerophon; he rejected her advances; she falsely accused him to Proetus of seduction; because Proetus scrupled to kill him out of hand, he sent him off to his brother-in-law in Lycia with secret written instructions to contrive his death. We possess however an entire narrative hypothesis to Euripides' play (test. iia below), thanks to the Byzantine scholar Ioannes Logothetes of about A.D. 1100, who provides also the long fragment from Bellerophon's prologue speech (F 661).[1] Euripides used the Homeric part-story, but his Proetus is king of Tiryns, not Argos, and Bellerophon is there after being purified by Proetus for a kin-killing in Corinth (this is the one detail added to Homer by the Scholia on Iliad 6.155). Euripides also named the king of Lycia as Iobates (test. iia.16), as had [Hesiod] F 43a.88; he was the name-character of a play by Sophocles which is unfortunately almost a blank.

Bellerophon in his prologue narrates Stheneboea's attempt to seduce him, and her nurse's part in it (F 661.5–14; Stheneboea's passion is evoked in F 663–5); he has already resolved to flee from Proetus' troubled house (F 661.5–6, 26–31). The fragment ends there, and nothing survives of Stheneboea's accusation and Proetus' instructions to Iobates in Lycia. Bellerophon was set by Iobates to challenge the Chimaera and other monstrous foes; his victories

---

[1] Ioannes similarly preserves the hypothesis and F 481 of *Melanippe Wise*, and the hypothesis to *Pirithous* (see Appendix to this edition).

were narrated by Homer (above) and commemorated by Hesiod, Theogony 325 *and* Catalogue F 453a.87, *and in the 5th century by Pindar*, Olympians 13.63–92. *Homer does not record that Bellerophon was aided by the winged horse Pegasus, which according to Pindar (above) the gods had given him, but in the later poets and Euripides he has the horse, as in* Bellerophon (F 306–309a).

When the fragments resume, Bellerophon has already returned to Tiryns and is telling of his victory over the Chimaera (F 665a). Though few, they illustrate what the hypothesis reveals of his intended retaliation: reproach for Proetus (F 667?), but a grim deception of Stheneboea. On learning from her of Proetus' further plans against him, he both accuses her (F *666) and tricks her into flying off with him over the sea because of her infatuation (F 669), only to throw her off; and she is drowned. Her body is found by fishermen (F 670 is from their report; it gives a charming picture of their simple life quite untypical of the usual tragic messenger's style); it is brought to Proetus (F 671). Bellerophon again returns to Tiryns to justify his punishment of both husband and wife (test. iia.31–6, unrepresented in the fragments).

For Aristophanes (Frogs 1043–55), Stheneboea and the Phaedra of Euripides' Hippolytus plays were 'whores' (1043): no poet should dramatize them because they disgrace upright men, and corrupt adolescents. Such 'bad' women are vindictive when rejected; they are Greek analogues of 'Potiphar's Wife' (see especially Papamichael (1983) and Jouan (1989–90), who give much bibliography); and both Stheneboea and Phaedra have their nurses as go-betweens. While Hippolytus' integrity brings on his own destruction, Bellerophon retaliates with murder. It

123

is worth noting that in F 671, as the play ends, Proetus is made to repeat Bellerophon's condemnation of 'bad women' in his prologue, F 661.5.

The play spans two and possibly three designs on others' lives, and two returns by Bellerophon from 'over the sea', the latter made credible by Pegasus and his speed. So remarkable is Euripides' expansion of dramatic time in the play that before the hypothesis and the almost complete prologue speech were recovered, and Wilamowitz pronounced on them (in 1908: see bibliography above), reconstructors placed Bellerophon's victory over the Chimaera and his first return to Tiryns before the play began. This idea recurred when Zühlke (1961) and Korzeniewski (1964) suggested that Bellerophon narrated both these incidents in a part of his prologue now lost; but all other scholars named in the bibliography accept the structure described above.[2]

Bellerophon (especially with Pegasus and the Chimaera), Proetus and his letter and Stheneboea were extremely popular with artists from the late 5th century into the Roman period, but only one depiction almost certainly reflects the play, an Apulian stamnos of c. 400 B.C. which shows Proetus giving the letter to Bellerophon while Stheneboea gently touches Proetus' arm, and in the presence of Pegasus, in front of a doorway which suggest a theatrical inspiration: see Taplin no. 72 (Trendall–Webster III.3.45, LIMC 'Proitos' no. 3, Todisco Ap 3b). Less closely related is a Paestan vessel of c. 340 B.C. (Taplin no. 73,

---

[2] J. Pòrtulas, in F. de Martino (ed.), *El caliu de l'oikos* (Bari, 2004), 503–22 gives the most recent survey of attempted reconstructions (see *L'Année Philologique* 75 [2004], 216).

Trendall–Webster III.3.44, LIMC 'Proitos' no. 5, Todisco
P 5); remotely if at all related, Taplin no. 74. Much disputed
is a fragment of a mid-4th c. Gnathia crater, perhaps re-
flecting Bellerophon's first return with Stheneboea and her
Nurse listening in doorways (LIMC 'Pegasos' no. 240 =
'Proitos' no. 13, Todisco Ap 94; cf. Trendall–Webster [posi-
tive], Aélion 188–9 and Taplin no. 88 [very doubtful]).

   Brief fragments: none. Other ascriptions: Bellerophon
F 305; F 889 (see note on F 661.13); adesp. F 60 'What if
(s)he falls into the watery depths?' (= Aristophanes, Peace
140, where the scholia suggest it may refer to Stheneboea's
fall from Pegasus); adesp. F 292 'Hail, master of this land of
Tiryns!' (attributed to the fisherman of F 670 by some, e.g.
Jouan in ed. Budé fr. 10). Part of a dactylic tetrameter, 'I
see Melos . . . to the right of Crete', in the margin of PSI
1192 (Sophocles, Oedipus 179–200) is ascribed improba-
bly to Cretans by C. Austin in Bastianini and Casanova,
Euripide e i papiri 167–8.

   *F 663 and 665 were exploited in Aristophanes' Wasps
of 422, and F 664 by Cratinus (whose last production
was in 424); the metrical criteria permit a date in the
420s or earlier (Cropp–Fick 90–1). Stheneboea is named as
Proetus' wife in a fragmentary commentary on Eupolis'
Prospaltians of 429 B.C. (F 259.125–7 PCG: see I. Storey,
Eupolis [Oxford, 2003], 231–3); this may point to produc-
tion a little earlier than the mid-420s, and among others of
Euripides' earlier plays which featured 'bad women': see
Jouan (1989–90) and in ed. Budé, Webster 64–86.

   The content of Sophocles' Iobates (above) and Astyda-
mas II's Bellerophon (4th c.) is unknown; neither may have
touched Stheneboea's story, nor did any Roman play. For
the modern period see OGCMA I.274–6.

ΣΘΕΝΕΒΟΙΑ

test. iia (Hypothesis)

Σθ[ε]ν[έ]βοια, ἧς ἀρχή·

οὐκ ἔστιν ὅσ]τις πάντ᾿ ἀνὴρ εὐδαιμονεῖ·

[ἡ δ᾿] ὑπόθεσις·

Προῖτος Ἄβαντος μὲν ἦν υἱός, Ἀκρισίου

5   δὲ ἀδελφός, βασιλεὺς δὲ Τείρυνθος.

Σθενεβοίαν δὲ γήμας ἐξ αὐτῆς ἐγέν-

νησε παῖδας. Βελλεροφόντην δὲ φεύ-

γοντα ἐκ Κορίνθου διὰ φόνον αὐτὸς

μὲν ἥγνισε τοῦ μύσους, ἡ γυνὴ δὲ αὐ-

10   τοῦ τὸν ξένον ἠγάπησε. τυχεῖν δὲ οὐ

δυναμένη τῶν ἐπιθυμημάτων δι-

P. Oxy. 2455, ed. E. Turner (1962), frs. 5.7–21, 24 + 95, and
6.1–9 (very damaged: P. Strasbourg 2676 ed. J. Schwartz, *ZPE* 4
[1969], 43–4 has beginnings of lines 1–4 from the same papyrus);
lines 4–36 in full with minor varations: Ioannes Logothetes, Com-
mentary on [Hermogenes], *Means of Rhetorical Effectiveness* 30

126

STHENEBOEA

test. iia (Hypothesis)

Stheneboea, which begins, '(There is no) man (who) is com-
pletely fortunate'; (the) plot is as follows: Proetus was the son
of Abas, brother of Acrisius, and king of Tiryns. He married   5
Stheneboea and had children by her. When Bellerophon fled
Corinth because of a killing, Proetus purified him of the
pollution[1] but his wife fell in love with their guest. When she   10
was unable to achieve her desires, she traduced the Corin-

---

[1] Cf. F 661.17–18. Exile for kin-killing or involuntary kill-
ing was usual, e.g. *Melanippe Wise* test. i.8–9, *Hippolytus* 34–7;
such purification too was regular, e.g. *Alcmeon in Psophis* test.
**iic.

(ed. H. Rabe, *RhM* 63 [1908], 147), and (mutilated) Gregory of
Corinth, Commentary on the same treatise, *Rhet. Gr.* VII.1321
Walz. See also van Rossum-Steenbeek 209–11, Diggle, *TrGFS*
128–9.

2 = F 661.1 below   7 A numeral (Cropp) or names
(Diggle) may be missing after παῖδας; three names are given in
Hesiod F 129.24.   8 αὐτὸς Wilamowitz: αὐτὸν Ioann.,
Greg. [P. Oxy.]   11 ἐπιθυμημάτων Ioann.: ἐπιθυμηθέν-
των Greg. (ἐπιθυ[P. Oxy.)

ἔβαλεν ὡς ἐπιθέμενον ἑαυτῇ τὸν
Κορίνθιον [ξένο]ν. πιστεύσας δὲ
ὁ Προῖτος αὐτὸν εἰς Καρίαν ἐξ-
15 έπεμψεν, ἵνα ἀπόληται. δέλτον
γὰρ αὐτῷ δοὺς ἐκέλευσε πρὸς Ἰοβάτην
διακομίζειν. ὁ δὲ τοῖς γεγραμμένοις
ἀκόλουθα πράττων προσέταξεν αὐτῷ
διακινδυνεῦσαι πρὸς τὴν Χίμαιραν.
20 ὁ δὲ ἀγωνισάμενος τὸ θηρίον ἀνεῖλε.
πάλιν δὲ ἐπιστρέψας εἰς τὴν Τείρυνθα
τὸν ⟨μὲν⟩ Προῖτον κατεμέμψατο, ἀνέσει-
σε δὲ τὴν Σθενέβοιαν ὡς ⟨εἰς⟩ τὴν Καρίαν ἀπά-
ξων. μαθὼν δὲ παρ᾽ αὐτῆς ἐκ Προίτου δευτέ-
25 ραν ἐπιβουλὴν φθάσας ἀνεχώρησεν. ἀνα-
θέμενος δὲ ἐπὶ τὸν Πήγασον τὴν Σθενέ-
βοιαν μετέωρος ἐπὶ τὴν θάλασσαν ἤρθη.
κατὰ Μῆλον δὲ τὴν νῆσον γενόμενος ἐκεί-
νην ἀπέρριψεν. αὐτὴν μὲν οὖν ἀπο-
30 θανοῦσαν ἁλιεῖς εὑρόντες εἰς Τείρυν-
θα διεκόμισαν. πάλιν δὲ ἐπιστρέψας
ὁ Βελλεροφόντης πρὸς τὸν Προῖτον αὐ-
τὸς ὡμολόγησε πεπραχέναι ταῦτα·
δὶς γὰρ ἐπιβουλευθεὶς παρ᾽ ἀμφοτέρων

thian (guest) as having assaulted her. Trusting (her), Proetus
sent him to Caria to be killed: he had given him a tablet-letter   15
and told him to take it to Iobates, who followed what was writ-
ten and ordered Bellerophon to risk himself against the Chi-
maera. Belleropohon fought and killed the creature, however;   20
returning to Tiryns he denounced Proetus, but excited
Stheneboea with the idea of taking her back to Caria. When he
learned from her of a second plot by Proetus, he forestalled it
by going away. He mounted Stheneboea on Pegasus and rose   25
high over the sea; when he was close to the island of Melos[2] he
threw her off. After her death fishermen found and carried
her to Tiryns. Returning again to Proetus, Bellerophon him-   30
self admitted his actions; having twice been the subject of

[2] The sizable island of Melos is about 100 miles from Tiryns,
and probably appeared as 'in the direction of Melos' in Euripides'
play. Only fishermen from the coast near Tiryns would know to
take the body there.

---

13 [Κορίνθιον ξένο]ν in P. Oxy. Kannicht: [Βελλεροφόντη]ν
Luppe: simply Κορίνθιον Ioann., Greg.   13–14 πιστ[εύ-
σας in P. Oxy. Luppe: πεισθεὶς Ioann., Greg.   24 παρ' αὐτῆς
Wilamowitz: παρ' αὐτοῦ Ioann. [P. Oxy., Greg.]   34 παρ'
Luppe: ὑπ' Ioann., Greg. [P. Oxy.]

35 δίκην εἰληφέναι τὴν πρέπουσαν, τῆς
μὲν εἰς τὸ ζῆν, τοῦ δὲ εἰς τὸ λυπεῖσθαι.

—

test. iib²

ἡ δὲ Σθενέβοια μετὰ τὰ τρόπαια τὰ κατὰ Λυκίαν νικητοῦ
Βελλεροφόντου ὑποστρέψαντος καὶ Προῖτον αἰτιωμένου,
ὡς κατ᾽ αὐτοῦ μελετήσαντος ἄδικον θάνατον, ἀναιρεῖται
τρόπῳ τοιούτῳ. προσποιεῖται Βελλεροφόντης ταύτης
ἐρᾶν· ἡ δὲ νικωμένη τῷ ἔρωτι, ἀφεῖσα τὸν οἶκον τοῦ
Προίτου, ἔξεισι λάθρᾳ, καὶ κατὰ νώτου Πηγάσου συν-
εποχεῖται Βελλεροφόντῃ, ὃς διαέριος μέσῳ πελάγους
φερόμενος τῶν νώτων τοῦ ἵππου ἀποσφαιρίσας αὐτὴν
τοῖς ὕδασιν ἀπέπνιξεν.

Tzetzes on Aristophanes, *Frogs* 1051

661

ΒΕΛΛΕΡΟΦΟΝΤΗΣ

οὐκ ἔστιν ὅστις πάντ᾽ ἀνὴρ εὐδαιμονεῖ.
ἢ γὰρ πεφυκὼς ἐσθλὸς οὐκ ἔχει βίον,
ἢ δυσγενὴς ὢν πλουσίαν ἀροῖ πλάκα.
πολλοὺς δὲ πλούτῳ καὶ γένει γαυρουμένους
5 γυνὴ κατῄσχυν᾽ ἐν δόμοισι νηπία.
τοιάδε Προῖτος ⟨γῆς⟩ ἄναξ νόσῳ νοσεῖ·

Ioannes Logothetes (see under test. iia above; Gregory
omits), after ending his quotation of the hypothesis with
'Bellerophon is brought on stage soliloquizing'; vv. 1–3 (= F 661
N): Aristophanes, *Frogs* 1217–9 with Schol.; v. 1 = Menander,

plots, he had exacted the appropriate justice from both—from   35
her with her life, and from him with his painful grief. *(end of hypothesis)*

test. iib[2]

When Bellerophon returned victorious after his triumphs in Lycia and accused Proetus of planning an unjust death for him, Stheneboea was killed in the following way. Bellerophon pretended to fall in love with her; she was overcome by love, abandoned Proetus' house and left it secretly, and rode off with Bellerophon mounted on Pegasus' back. When Bellerophon was borne high in the air well out to sea, he sent her tumbling from the horse's back, and drowned her in the waters.

661
(Beginning of the play)

BELLEROPHON

There is no man who is fortunate in all respects: either he has noble birth but no livelihood, or he is of low birth but ploughs rich acres; and many who pride themselves on wealth and birth are disgraced by a foolish wife in their house. Such is the affliction[1] besetting Proetus, (this   5

---

[1] Lit. 'disease', used repeatedly of improper love and its consequences, e.g. *Hippolytus Veiled* F 428.2, *Melanippe* F 497.1.

Shield 407, much cited or repeated throughout antiquity; vv. 4–5 (= F 662 N): Stobaeus 4.22.46 and 125; vv. 24–5 (= F 672 N): Aeschines 1.151 and later citations

ξένον γὰρ ἱκέτην τῆσδ᾽ ἔμ᾽ ἐλθόντα στέγης
(one or more lines missing)
λόγοισι πείθει καὶ δόλῳ θηρεύεται
κρυφαῖον εὐνῆς εἰς ὁμιλίαν πεσεῖν.
10 ἀεὶ γὰρ ἥπερ τῷδ᾽ ἐφέστηκεν λόγῳ
τροφὸς γεραιὰ καὶ ξυνίστησιν λέχος,
ὑμνεῖ τὸν αὐτὸν μῦθον· 'ὦ κακῶς φρονῶν,
πιθοῦ· τί μαίνῃ; τλῆθι δεσποίνης ἐμῆς
(one or more lines missing)
κτήσῃ δ᾽ ἄνακτος δώμαθ᾽ ἓν πεισθεὶς βραχύ.'
15 ἐγὼ δὲ θεσμοὺς Ζῆνά θ᾽ ἱκέσιον σέβων
Προῖτόν τε τιμῶν, ὅς μ᾽ ἐδέξατ᾽ εἰς δόμους
λιπόντα γαῖαν Σισύφου φόνον τ᾽ ἐμῆς
ἔνιψε χειρὸς αἷμ᾽ ἐπισφάξας νέον,
οὐπώποτ᾽ ἠθέλησα δέξασθαι λόγους,
20 οὐδ᾽ εἰς νοσοῦντας ὑβρίσαι δόμους ξένος,
μισῶν ἔρωτα δεινόν, ὃς φθείρει βροτούς.
†διπλοῖ γὰρ ἔρωτες ἐντρέφονται χθονί†
ὁ μὲν γεγὼς ἔχθιστος εἰς Ἅιδην φέρει,
ὁ δ᾽ εἰς τὸ σῶφρον ἐπ᾽ ἀρετήν τ᾽ ἄγων ἔρως
25 ζηλωτὸς ἀνθρώποισιν, ὧν εἴην ἐγώ.
†οὐκοῦν νομίζω καὶ θανεῖν γε σωφρονῶν.†

7 lacuna Korzeniewski   13 lacuna Rabe: F 889 inserted
by Gronewald   14 κτήσῃ Rabe: κτῆσαι Ioann.   δώμαθ᾽
ἓν πεισθεὶς Wilamowitz: δῶμα πεισθείς τι Ioann.   22–
3 deleted by Wilamowitz (24–5 by Holford-Strevens, 22–5 by
Diggle)   22 διπλοῖ γὰρ εἴσ᾽ ἔρωτες ἔντροφοι χθονί
Mekler   26 corruption is certain, loss of text probable

land's) king: for when I came as a stranger in supplication
of his roof . . . (*one or more lines missing*) . . . (Stheneboea)
tried words to persuade me and guile to snare me into slip-
ping covertly into the intimacy of her bed: for her old
nurse, who is in charge of this talk and tries to bring us to- 10
gether, always sings the same tune: 'Your thinking is bad!
Be persuaded! Why this madness? Have the courage . . .
(*one or more lines missing*)[2] . . . of my mistress, and you will
gain the king's palace, once you are persuaded in this one
small thing.' But I respect the ordinances of Zeus the god
of suppliants and honour Proetus, who received me in his 15
house when I left Sisyphus' land,[3] and washed the blood-
shed from my hand by sacrificing new blood over it;[4] I have
never yet been willing to accept her words or to violate an
afflicted house when I am its guest, hating as I do the 20
dreadful love which destroys men. †For there are two
loves bred on earth†: one, which is most inimical, leads to
Hades, but the love which leads towards morality and vir-
tue is something men may envy[5]—among whose number I
wish I may myself be! †Therefore I do not consider . . . † 25

[2] Gronewald filled the lacuna with F 889: 'have the courage <to
slip into the couch and marriage-bed> of my mistress', but the
repetition from vv. 9 and 11 is unwelcome. Rabe's change in v. 14
from 'gain' (imperative) to 'you will gain' assumes the loss of some
such sense, however.   [3] Corinth (cf. test. iia.8), the kingdom
of his grandfather Sisyphus.   [4] Polluting blood was cleansed
by new blood from a pure animal: Aeschylus, *Eumenides* 280–3
etc.   [5] For 'two kinds of love' cf. *Theseus* F 388 with note.
The corruption in v. 22 and the supposedly 'Christian' ethos of vv.
22–3 have led to deletions (see textual apparatus). For the style of
analysis compare e.g. *Bellerophon* F 285.3–5.

EURIPIDES

ἀλλ᾽ εἰς ἀγροὺς γὰρ ἐξιὼν βουλεύσομαι·
οὐ γάρ με λύει τοῖσδ᾽ ἐφημένον δόμοις
κακορροθεῖσθαι μὴ θέλοντ᾽ εἶναι κακόν,
30 οὐδ᾽ αὖ κατειπεῖν καὶ γυναικὶ προσβαλεῖν
κηλῖδα Προίτου καὶ διασπάσαι δόμον.

27 ἀγροὺς Diggle: -ὸν Ioann.   ἐξιὼν βουλεύσομαι
Wilamowitz: ἐξιέναι βουλήσομαι Ioann.

(662 N = 661.4–5 above)

663
ποιητὴν ἄρα
Ἔρως διδάσκει, κἂν ἄμουσος ᾖ τὸ πρίν.

Plutarch, *Moralia* 762b, cf. 405e, 622c; v. 2 (κἂν—πρίν):
Aristophanes, *Wasps* 1074 with Schol.; many other partial cita-
tions and allusions

664
πεσὸν δέ νιν λέληθεν οὐδὲν ἐκ χερός,
ἀλλ᾽ εὐθὺς αὐδᾷ ‘τῷ Κορινθίῳ ξένῳ’.

Athenaeus 10.427e; v. 2 (τῷ—ξένῳ): Aristophanes, *Women at
the Thesmophoria* 404 with Schol., and travestied by Cratinus F
299 *PCG*, cf. Hesychius κ 3629 Latte

665
τοιαῦτ᾽ ἀλύει· νουθετούμενος δ᾽ ἔρως
μᾶλλον πιέζει.

Aristophanes, *Wasps* 111–2 with Schol.; (νουθετούμενος—
πιέζει) Chrysippus, *On Passions* fr. 475 von Arnim; Plutarch,
Moralia 71a

134

So now I will go out into the country and deliberate. There is no profit for me in sitting in this house and being abused because I am unwilling to be evil, nor in denouncing and setting a stain on Proetus' wife, and tearing his house apart.

30

(662 N = 661.4–5 above)

663

After all, Love teaches a poet, even if he's previously lacking in skill.[1]

[1] Possibly Stheneboea's nurse pursues her inducement of Bellerophon. Love teaches courage in the amorous Phaedra, *Hippolytus Veiled* F 430; 'love teaches a poet', Plato, *Symposium* 196d8ff., where the end of our v. 2 is cited.

664

Nothing fallen from her hand escapes her, but at once she says 'To my guest from Corinth!'[1]

[1] Probably the nurse again, describing Stheneboea's thwarted passion. According to Athenaeus, Stheneboea follows the custom of 'toasting' dead friends with fallen table-scraps, believing that Bellerophon has gone to his death in Lycia. Aristophanes and Cratinus both turned the passage to comic advantage; Cratinus apparently makes a woman play the wholly masculine game of cottabus (see on *Oeneus* F 562, *Pleisthenes* F 631) and throw wine-drops with an obscene variation on Stheneboea's toast, 'to my prick from Corinth'; cf. *Syleus* F 693, note on the Greek.

665

Such is her raging madness; but when desire is reproved, it becomes more pressing.

135

665a

⟨ΒΕΛΛΕΡΟΦΟΝΤΗΣ⟩

παίω Χιμαίρας εἰς σφαγάς, πυρὸς δ᾽ ἀθὴρ
βάλλει με καὶ τοῦδ᾽ αἰθαλοῖ πυκνὸν πτερόν.

Photius α 475 Theodoridis

*666

⟨ΒΕΛΛΕΡΟΦΟΝΤΗΣ⟩

ὦ παγκακίστη καὶ γυνή, τί γὰρ λέγων
μεῖζόν σε τοῦδ᾽ ὄνειδος ἐξείποι τις ἄν;

Stobaeus 4.22.168, attributed to 'Bellerophon', i.e. the character (Meineke) rather than the play (others)

667

τίς ἄνδρα τιμᾷ ξεναπάτην;

Photius, *Lexicon*, 'ξεναπάτας' (II.455 Naber)

668

ἄνευ τύχης γάρ, ὥσπερ ἡ παροιμία,
πόνος μονωθεὶς οὐκέτ᾽ ἀλγύνει βροτούς.

Stobaeus 3.29.36

2 ἀλγύνει Stob.: ὠφελεῖ Blaydes

665a

⟨BELLEROPHON⟩

I strike into the Chimaera's throat, and a beard of flame
strikes and scorches the sturdy wing of Pegasus here.

*666

⟨BELLEROPHON⟩

You—utterly evil, and a woman! What could one say to
pronounce on you a greater reproach than this?[1]

[1] Bellerophon reproaches Stheneboea's nurse? Cf. Hippol-
ytus' denouncing women to Phaedra's nurse, *Hipp.* 616–68. The
similarly worded Carcinus II F 3 may be a reflection of our frag-
ment.

667

Who honours a man who deceives a guest?[1]

[1] Probably Bellerophon abusing Proetus (cf. test. iia.12–15).
Alternatively ' . . . deceives a host?', again more likely Bellerophon
defending his own conduct than Proetus maintaining Stheneo-
boea's false accusation.

668

Without luck, as the proverb goes, misery on its own no
longer causes men pain.[1]

[1] I.e. continuous misery ceases to be painful: cf. *Bellerophon* F
285.15–17, *Heracles* 1292–3. The translation is not certain, how-
ever: some scholars have preferred 'toil' to 'misery' and 'helps'
(Blaydes) instead of 'causes pain', thus restoring a much com-
moner association of luck and work, e.g. *Archelaus* F 233, *Cretan
Women* F 461, Philemon F 56 *PCG*.

EURIPIDES

669

‹—›

πέλας δὲ ταύτης δεινὸς ἵδρυται Κράγος
ἔνθηρος, ᾗ λῃστῆρσι φρουρεῖται ‹πόρος›
κλύδωνι δεινῷ καὶ βροτοστόνῳ βρέμων.

‹ΒΕΛΛΕΡΟΦΟΝΤΗΣ›

πτηνὸς πορεύσει πῶλος· οὐ ναυσθλώσομαι.

Schol. on Aristophanes, *Peace* 126 (= v. 4), recording alternative attribution to *Bellerophon*

1 Κράγος Meineke: κράτος Schol.   2 ᾗ λῃστῆρσι Meineke (λῃσταῖσι Blaydes): ἢ λῃστὴς Schol.
2–3 ‹πόρος› . . . βρέμων Meineke: βρέμει Schol.
3 βροτοστόνῳ Schol.: βροτοκτόνῳ Meineke: βαρυστόνῳ Dindorf

670

βίος δὲ πορφυρέως θαλάσσιος
οὐκ εὐτράπεζος, ἀλλ᾽ ἐπάκτιοι φάτναι.
ὑγρὰ δὲ μήτηρ, οὐ πεδοστιβὴς τροφὸς
θάλασσα· τήνδ᾽ ἀροῦμεν, ἐκ ταύτης βίος
5 βρόχοισι καὶ πέδαισιν οἴκαδ᾽ ἔρχεται.

Athenaeus 10.421f

1 πορφυρέως Lobeck: -οῦς Ath.

669

⟨—⟩

Near this is situated fearsome Cragus with its wild beasts,
where (the passage) is watched by robbers, and roars with
a fearsome surge to cause men grief.[1]

⟨BELLEROPHON⟩

My winged steed shall make the crossing; I will not go by
ship.

---

[1] The first speaker may be Stheneboea, a native of Lycia, fear-
ful of the journey back there with Bellerophon (cf. test. iia.22–5).
Cragus is a mountain on the west coast of Lycia; its 'wild beasts' in-
cluded the Chimaera. The text is corrupt in vv. 1–3; we follow
Meineke, except for his 'fearsome man-killing surge'; note also
Dindorf's 'deep-groaning surge'.

670

A purple-fisher's livelihood from the sea yields no luxuri-
ous fare; his table is on the shore. The watery sea is his
mother, a nurse not trodden by feet: it is this we plough,
from this a living comes to our homes by means of lines and
traps.[1]

---

[1] A fisherman reports the recovery of Stheneboea's body from
the sea (test. iia.29–31). Purple-fish (shellfish) provided both food
and, when sun-dried, dye. In vv. 3–4 the metaphors are 'oracular'
in their riddling style but not rare, e.g. the land is a nurse in *Phoe-
nician Women* 686; cf. Theocritus fr. 3.2, 'for the man with a living
from the sea, his nets are his ploughs'.

671

κομίζετ᾽ εἴσω τήνδε· πιστεύειν δὲ χρὴ
γυναικὶ μηδὲν ὅστις εὖ φρονεῖ βροτῶν.

Stobaeus 4.28.6

(672 N = 661.24–5 above)

671

‹PROETUS›

Carry her inside.[1] A sensible man should never put any
trust in a woman.

[1] *Bellerophon* F 311 has a similar 'stage direction'.

(672 N = 661.24–5 above)

SISYPHUS

Pechstein 185–217; Krumeich 442–8; H. Van Looy in ed.
Budé VIII.3.29–38.

Gantz 173–6; *LIMC* VII.1. 781–7b 'Sisyphos I'

*A satyr play of this name concluded Euripides' 'Trojan'
trilogy of 415 B.C. (see Introductions to* Alexander *and*
Palamedes). *The evidence to suggest its content is both
minimal and disputed, but its chief figure must have been
the notorious trickster Sisyphus (Gantz 173–6), who also
appeared in one of the* Autolycus *plays (see test. *va there);
cf. brief fragment F 674 below.*

*Scholars are divided on how to assign frs. 5 and 7 of
P. Oxy. 2455 (the large but badly damaged collection of
Euripidean narrative hypotheses in alphabetical order)
among play-titles beginning with 'S'. Many scholars now
give fr. 5 to* Sciron *(see test. iia there) and fr. 7 to* Sisyphus
*(test. *iii below), but Pechstein 199–204 does the opposite,
and others reach no decision (the debate may be followed
in Van Looy 35–8). If fr. 7 does belong to* Sisyphus, *its last
word 'escape' may be linked with F 673 (below), addressed
to Heracles, to suggest that the play ended with his arrival
to release the satyrs from the servitude which is regular in
satyr plays (e.g.* Sciron *and* Syleus). *Heracles' name has ac-
cordingly been supplied in fr. 7.2—and it appears too in fr.*

142

5.2, *probably also as a rescuer. Because no certainly known mythical incident links Heracles and Sisyphus, however, everything is in doubt;*[1] *and even F 673 is sometimes transferred to Syleus. Further, a 'Homeric cup' of c. 100 B.C. (LIMC no. 2.a) depicting Sisyphus with Autolycus, Hermes and Anticleia (all named), is referred either to our play or to* Autolycus *(test. *vb there). The play's content must therefore remain entirely speculation.*

Brief fragment: F 674 'twisting' (a devious speaker, presumably Sisyphus: cf. Autolycus test. *va.3).

There is a further very long-lived and unresolved dispute about the play's content and nature: does the single large book fragment of a Sisyphus play assigned in whole or part in antiquity itself to both Euripides and Critias in fact stem from our play? TrGF 1.180–2 lodges it with Critias as 43 F 19. The issue is bound up with the similarly uncertain Pirithous: *see the Appendix at the end of this volume.*

One or two plays called Sisyphus *were credited to Aeschylus (probably satyric), and one to Sophocles; their content is uncertain. Comedies with his name survive in small fragments from both Greek and Roman playwrights. For Sisyphus' modern afterlife see OGCMA II.1008–9.*

[1] Probus on Virgil, *Georgics* 3.267–8, however, records a story that Sisyphus stole the flesh-eating horses of Diomedes when Heracles was bringing them to Eurystheus (cf. *Alcestis* 481–98, 1020–2, *Heracles* 380–8).

ΣΙΣΥΦΟΣ

test. *iii (Hypothesis)

οἱ μὲ]ν οὖν σάτυροι κα[

　]εους· Ἑρμῆς δεσθη[

　]ων ἐπέζευξεν [

　]φυγὼν δ' ἐντεῦθε[ν

5　]μαχόμ[ε]νος σὺν .[.].ῳ

ἐπι]φανεὶς δὲ τοῖς σατύροις παρ[

ξέπ]ληξεν αὐτούς· ὧν μὲν οἱ .[

　]σ[..].ηθησαν εἶναι [

　]τας ἐμπρήσειν [

10　]ς δήσειν τωκε[

　].τους φυγεῖν [

P. Oxy. 2455 fr. 7, ed. E. Turner (1962); cf. Austin, *NFE* 93, no. 17

2 Ἡρακλ]έους Barrett　　　7 ἐ]ξέπ]ληξεν Turner
11 το]ύτους Turner

144

SISYPHUS

test. *iii (Hypothesis)

. . . now the satyrs . . . (Heracles);[1] but Hermes . . . yoked . . .
Escaping from here . . . fighting with . . . appearing to the sa-   5
tyrs . . . he (terrified) them. Some of them . . . to be . . . to (be
about to?) burn . . . to (be about to?) bind . . . . . . (them?)[2] to   10
escape . . . *(end of hypothesis)*

[1] Barrett supplied the name of Heracles (see Introduction); if
correctly, 'Escaping etc.' may well describe him too, perhaps 'es-
caping' from one of his famous Labours (F 673?) and happening
to pass by.   [2] The satyrs (see Introduction).

673

χαίρω γέ σ', ὦ βέλτιστον Ἀλκμήνης τέκος,
<   > τόν τε μιαρὸν ἐξολωλότα.

Etymologicum Genuinum B (= *Etym. Magnum* p. 808.5
Gaisford) = Suda χ 174; attributed to *Syleus* by Hartung and
Wilamowitz (see Introduction)

2 ⟨ἐλθόντα⟩ Valckenaer: ⟨νικῶντα⟩ West

673

I do rejoice, O most excellent son of Alcmene,[1] that you (have come?)[2] and (that?) the foul creature has been destroyed . . .

[1] Heracles (see Introduction).   [2] Valckenaer's supplement reflects a statement in the fragment's source that it embodies 'a Boeotian greeting'. West prefers 'are victorious'.

SCIRON

Pechstein 218–42; Krumeich 449–56; H. Van Looy in ed. Budé VIII.3.39–46.

D. F. Sutton, *The Greek Satyr-Play* (Meisenheim-am-Glan, 1980), 62–5; W. Luppe, *Studi Classici e Orientali* 32 (1982), 231–3, *Anagennesis* 4 (1986), 223–43, *APF* 40 (1994), 13–19; *Eos* 84 (1996), 231–6; Gantz 252; *LIMC* VII.i.925–9 under 'Theseus'; G. Conrad, *Der Silen* (Trier, 1997), 189–95.

Sciron was a pest whom the hero Theseus killed. The play was satyric, and had the outline common to many such plays, rescue of the satyrs from slavery to a monstrous or cruel master (e.g. Cyclops, Busiris, Syleus, cf. Voelke 72–83; for Theseus in such satyric rescues and punishments see Voelke 340–2). The plot can be inferred with some confidence from test. iia (below) and from Plutarch, Theseus *10: the satyrs, led as usual by their 'father' Silenus, were in servitude to Sciron; they tended, not their master's animals for his enjoyment, but passers-by whom they lured with prostitutes at various prices (test. iia.12, F 675–6)— this for their own profit, in their regular acquisitiveness (Conrad 191–3). Sciron then killed these unfortunate men until Theseus came by, destroyed Sciron, and freed the satyrs. Whether Heracles, Theseus' close friend, appeared at*

148

the play's end depends on the ascription of test. iia fr. 5 to this play rather than to Sisyphus *(see Introduction there); but it is hard to see what role Heracles might have had if the hero Theseus had already triumphed over Sciron (see especially Luppe, Conrad 193–5).*

Brief fragments: F 677 'nor (or 'not even') the thigh-bones of fawns' (possibly the satyrs' diet?), F 680 'to accompany', F 681 'door-bars'. Other ascriptions: F 879 (also ascribed to Busiris*), F 1084 (also to* Alcmeon in Psophis*).*

There is no means of dating the play. A comedy of this title was written by Epicharmus in the 5th century, and one by Alexis in the 4th. The episode of Theseus and Sciron, particularly Theseus' throwing him into the sea, was popular in art from c. 500 B.C. (LIMC nos. 97–122), but no depiction including satyrs has been found. The modern period has largely ignored the story (OGCMA II.1022).

ΣΚΙΡΩΝ

test. iia (Hypothesis)

fr. 6   Σκείρων [σατυρικός, οὗ ἀρχή·

Ἑρμῆ, σὺ γὰρ δὴ [

ἔχεις· ἡ δ᾽ ὑ[πόθεσις·

Σκείρων τῶν κατειστ[

5   θη· πετρῶνα καταλαβ[ὼν

ἀπὸ λῃστείας βίον εἶχ[εν ἀσεβῆ, παῖς

Ποσειδῶνος ὤν· καὶ τὴ[ν τῶν στενῶν αὐ-

τὸς ἔμβασιν οὐ θεωρῶν, [ἔχων δὲ πρόσκο-

πον καὶ διάκονον τῆς ὕβ[ρεως Σιληνόν,

10   κείνῳ μὲν ἐπέτρεψ[εν τὴν ὁδὸν φρου-

ρεῖν, αὐτὸς δὲ ἐχωρίσθ[η. ἔπειτα δ᾽ εἰς τὴν

ἐρημίαν σάτυ[ρ]οι εἰσκ[ωμάσαντες μετὰ

ἑταιρῶν θη[

beginnings of vv. 14–17, including 16 μετὰ χεῖρα[ς

150

SCIRON

test. iia (Hypothesis)

fr. 6: *Sciron*, (satyric, which begins) 'Hermes, for you indeed
hold . . .' The (plot is as follows): Sciron . . . of those . . . He oc-
cupied a ravine . . . and got an (impious)[1] livelihood from rob-   5
bery; he was (a son) of Poseidon.[2] He did not (himself) watch
the entrance (to the narrow defile), but (had as his spy) and
servant in wanton violence (Silenus); he entrusted him with
(guarding the path), while he himself went away. (Then) the   10
satyrs (brought their wild revels into the) solitude (with) pros-
titutes . . . (*nothing distinct in vv. 14–15*) . . . into (*or* between)
(his?) arms . . .

[1] An attractive supplement, given 'wanton violence' in 9; but
Diggle in Bastianini–Casanova, *Euripide e i papiri* 52–3 declines
it on grounds of prose rhythm and suggests 'a livelihood (here)'.
[2] Poseidon's offspring were often the anti-heroes of satyr plays
(e.g. *Cyclops, Busiris*).

P. Oxy. 2455 fr. 6 and fr. 5.1–6, ed. E. Turner (1962), re-ed.
Austin, *NFE* 94 (no. 18), van Rossum-Steenbeek 209, 211. Fr. 6.2
= F 674a below. Ascription of the text in fr. 5 to *Sciron* is disputed:
see on *Sisyphus*, Introduction.

fr. 6.6 εἶχ[εν ἀσεβῆ, παῖς Snell: εἶχ[εν ἐνταῦθα Diggle

fr. 6.7–12 suppl. Barrett, Austin (e.g.)

151

EURIPIDES

end of possibly the same hypothesis:

fr. 5   *a few letters*

   ἐ]πιφαν[εὶ]ς δ᾽ Ἡρα[κλῆς

   ]ενος ὑπὸ τοῦ συ[

   ] λαβών· καὶ το [

5] ... ν αὐτοῦ κα[ὶ] τη[

   ]θη————

test. iib

(*a*) τέταρτον ἔκτεινε Σκείρωνα τὸν Κορίνθιον τοῦ Πέλο-
πος, ὡς δὲ ἔνιοι Ποσειδῶνος. οὗτος ἐν τῇ Μεγαρικῇ
κατέχων τὰς ἀφ᾽ ἑαυτοῦ κληθείσας πέτρας Σκειρωνίδας,
ἠνάγκαζε τοὺς παριόντας νίζειν αὐτοῦ τοὺς πόδας, καὶ
νίζοντας εἰς τὸν βυθὸν αὐτοὺς ἔρριπτε βορὰν ὑπερμεγέ-
θει χελώνῃ. Θησεὺς δὲ ἁρπάσας αὐτὸν τῶν ποδῶν ἔρρι-
ψεν ⟨εἰς τὴν θάλασσαν⟩.

(*b*) οὗτος γὰρ εἰώθει τοὺς παριόντας ἀναγκάζειν ἀπο-
νίπτειν ἑαυτὸν ἐπί τινος ἀποκρήμνου τόπου, λακτίσματι
δ᾽ ἄφνω τύπτων περιεκύλιε κατὰ τῶν κρημνῶν εἰς θάλατ-
ταν κατὰ τὴν ὀνομαζομένην Χελώνην.

(*a*) Apollodorus, *Epitome* 1.2   (*b*) Diodorus 4.59.4

152

SCIRON

fr. 5: *centres of six lines possibly from the same hypothesis, including 2 . . . Heracles appeared . . . 4 . . . seizing . . . (end of hypothesis)*

test. iib

(a) Fourth, (Theseus) killed Sciron the Corinthian, son of Pelops, but as some say, of Poseidon. He occupied the crags called the Scironides after him, in the Megarian land; he compelled passers-by to wash his feet, and as they washed them he threw them into a chasm as meat for an enormous turtle. Theseus seized him by the feet and threw him (into the sea).[1]

(b) . . . Sciron had a habit of compelling passers-by to wash (the dust) from (his feet) on top of a sheer cliff; then he gave them a sudden kick and tumbled them down from the cliff into the sea at the (place) named Chelone.[2]

[1] The road from Athens to Corinth passed through Megara along the shore.   [2] Greek 'Turtle'.

674a

⟨ΣΙΛΗΝΟΣ⟩

Ἑρμῆ, σὺ γὰρ δὴ [   ] ἔχεις

See test. iia.2 above; speaker identified by Kassel

675

καὶ τὰς μὲν ἄξῃ, πῶλον ἢν διδῷς ἕνα,
τὰς δὲ, ξυνωρίδ᾽· αἱ δέ κἀπὶ τεσσάρων
φοιτῶσιν ἵππων ἀργυρῶν. φιλοῦσι δὲ
τὰς ἐξ Ἀθηνῶν παρθένους, ὅταν φέρῃ
5 πολλάς ⟨τις⟩ . . .

Pollux 9.75

676

σχεδὸν χαμεύνη σύμμετρος Κορινθίας
παιδός, κνεφάλλου δ᾽ οὐχ ὑπερτείνεις πόδα.

Pollux 10.35

SCIRON

674a
(Beginning of the play)

〈SILENUS〉

Hermes, for you indeed . . . hold . . .[1]

[1] *Antiope* F 179 has a similar opening prayer to a god. Silenus perhaps appeals to Hermes for some luck or trick (cf. *Autolycus* test. iv), either to lure the passers-by or for his own escape; he is the prologue speaker also in *Cyclops*.

675

You can take these (women) with you if you pay one 'colt', and those, if you pay a 'pair in harness'; and these others actually go for four 'silver horses'. Men like the 'girls from Athens', when (someone) has plenty with him . . .[1]

[1] The speaker refers to coins of rising value, identified by the images stamped on them. Their names pun on the sexual activities of the prostitutes (so Pollux implies; cf. test. iia.13); see also the next fragment. For such sexual play in satyric drama see Voelke 225–7.

676

. . . (you are) almost the same size as a Corinthian girl's mattress, and your foot won't stretch beyond the cushion.[1]

[1] Possibly Silenus offering a prostitute to Theseus, whom he at first takes for an ordinary passer-by. The prostitutes of Corinth were famous for their skills; v. 2 alludes both to this and to another of Theseus' exploits, his killing of Procrustes who 'tailored' passers-by to the size of the bed he offered them.

678

ἔστι τοι καλὸν

κακοὺς κολάζειν.

Stobaeus 4.5.6

679

. . . ἢ προσπηγνύναι

κράδαις ἐριναῖς . . .

Athenaeus 3.76c

SCIRON

678

It is certainly good to punish vile men.[1]

[1] A reference to Theseus' good deeds; cf. the wording of F
**953a.17.

679

. . . or fix (them) to the branches of wild fig trees . . .[1]

[1] A reference to Theseus' killing of the robber Sinis (cf. *Hippolytus* 977); he tore travellers apart by tying them to bent-over trees, which he then released.

SCYRIANS

F. Jouan in ed. Budé VIII.3.51–74.

A. Körte, *Hermes* 69 (1934), 1–12; Jouan (1966), 204–18; Webster 95–7; G. Aricò in I. Gallo (ed.), *Studi Salernitani in memoria di R. Cantarella* (Salerno, 1981), 215–30; *LIMC* I.i.55–69 'Achilleus (Aufenthalt auf Skyros)'; Gantz 580–2.

Early Greek epics told of Achilles' son Neoptolemus being born and raised on the island of Scyros (Homer, Iliad *19.326, Odyssey 11.506–9), where Achilles had landed while returning from the Greeks' first abortive expedition against Mysia and married king Lycomedes' daughter Deidameia (the* Cypria *in Proclus' summary, cf.* Little Iliad *F 4 West). According to a different story, first clearly attested in a mid-5th century painting of Polygnotus described by Pausanias 1.22.6 (but attributed by the scholia on* Iliad *19.326 to 'the Cyclic poets', and hence by A. Severyns and F. Jouan to the* Cypria*), the adolescent Achilles seduced Deidameia while concealed in Lycomedes' household disguised as a girl; his mother Thetis had sent him to Scyros so that he would avoid dying in the war at Troy, but Odysseus and other Greek leaders intent on recruiting him came to Scyros and got him to betray his identity by adding weapons to the gifts they offered to Lycomedes' 'daughters'*

159

and/or by sounding a call to arms on the trumpet. Summaries of this story are found in Apollodorus 3.13.8 (= test. iib), Hyginus Fab. 96, and the scholia on Iliad 19.326.

The incomplete papyrus hypothesis of Scyrians *published in 1933 (= test. iia below), with which Apollodorus shares some common features, shows that Euripides' play told this latter story in some form. Its preserved text includes only the antecedents to the play's action, but (as Körte observed) lines 17–20 suggest some likely key points in the dramatic design. Deidameia is notably Lycomedes' only daughter (cf. also F 682), and Lycomedes is unaware of Achilles' identity (in most accounts she is one of a group of daughters amongst whom Achilles is easily hidden, and often Lycomedes assists in this concealment). Further, Deidameia is motherless, so it is probably her nurse who in an early scene reveals her condition to Lycomedes and agrees with him to keep it quiet (F 682–3; the nurse may have spoken the prologue speech, and if so she must have been aware of Achilles' identity as well as the seduction). The hypothesis also makes no mention of Deidameia giving birth before the beginning of the play, and F 682 probably refers to her being in labour, so the birth of the child and the revelation of Achilles' paternity will have coincided with the arrival of the Greek representatives and the revelation of his identity. Beyond this the direct evidence adds only a role for Diomedes as Odyssseus' companion (test. iia.18) and a scene in which Odysseus challenged Achilles to accept his role as a hero (F **683a, and probably the unattributed F 880, printed after F 684 below), but it is very likely that after the two revelations the play dramatized a conflict of duties and inclinations for Achilles and his final, fatal decision to leave Deidameia and their* son and sail for Troy. Possibly this decision was divinely imposed, like Neoptolemus' decision in Sophocles' Philoctetes. The name of the play implies a male chorus, probably advisers of Lycomedes who would have provided a forum for the debate over Achilles' future.

Brief fragments: F 685 'oar-thongs', F 686 'couriers'. Other ascriptions: F 880 (see above), F 885, F 906.

There are no firm grounds for dating Scyrians, but scholars have been inclined to place it in the first half of Euripides' career (see e.g. Webster 86, Jouan in ed. Budé 60–2). The legends treated in Euripides' play and in Sophocles' Scyrians (about the similar story of the fetching of Neoptolemus from Scyros) may have been of special interest at Athens after the island was settled by Athenians, and Theseus' bones 'discovered' there by Cimon, in the years following the Persian Wars. Two mid-5th century Athenian art-works are known to have treated the story (LIMC nos. 95 and 176, neither connected with Euripides' play). The rich later artistic tradition concerning Achilles' sojourn on Scyros may have included Euripidean elements eclectically, as may Ovid's brief narratives (Ars Amatoria 1.681–704, Metamorphoses 13.162–70) and the lengthy epic reworking of the story in Statius, Achilleid 1.198–396, 560–920 (cf. Körte 7–12). No other Greek or Latin plays are known, but the story provided a very popular subject for paintings and operas in the 17th and 18th centuries (see OGCMA I.5–9).

ΣΚΥΡΙΟΙ

test. iia (Hypothesis)

Σκύριοι, ὧν ἀρχή·

10 ὦ Τυνδαρεία παῖ Λάκαινα [

ἡ δ᾽ ὑπόθεσις·

Θέτιδος τοῦ παιδὸς Ἀχιλλέω[ς τὴν εἱμαρ-

μένην ἐπεγνωκυίας, τῆ[ς πρὸς Ἴλι-

ον στρατείας αὐτὸν ἀ[πείργειν θέ-

15 λουσα κόρης ἐσθῆτ[ι κρύψασα παρέθε-

το Λυκομήδει τῷ Σκυρί[ων δυνά-

στῃ. τρέφων δ᾽ ἐκεῖνος [θυγατέρα

μητρὸς ὀρφανὴν ὄνομα [Δηϊδάμει-

αν, ταύτῃ συνεπαρθένευε[ν αὐτὸν ἀ-

20 γνο[ούμ]ενον ὅς ἐστιν. ὁ δ[ὲ

ος [. . . .]κλέψας τὴν Δηϊδά[μειαν ἔγ-

PSI XII.1286 col. ii.9–27 (following the hypothesis to *Rhadamanthys*), ed. C. Gallavotti (1951: previously *RFIC* 11

162

SCYRIANS

test. iia (Hypothesis)

Scyrians, which begins, 'O daughter of Tyndareus from Sparta   10
. . .'; the plot is as follows: Thetis, having learned of (the des-
tiny) of her son Achilles, wanted (to keep) him out of the ex-
pedition (against Troy), and so (she concealed) him in a girl's
clothing (and deposited him) with Lycomedes the (ruler)   15
of the Scyrians. Lycomedes was raising (a daughter) named
(Deidameia) whose mother had died, and he brought (Achil-
les) up as a girl together with her, his real identity being unrec-
ognized; and Achilles . . . [1] seduced Deidameia and made her   20

---

[1] Latte's 'secret(ly)' is rejected by Diggle in Bastianini–Casa-
nova, *Euripide e i papiri* 53, who suggests 'with force'.

(1933), 177–88); cf. Austin, *NFE* 95–6, W. Luppe, *Anagennesis* 2
(1982), 265–71, van Rossum-Steenbeek 202–3. Line 10 = F681a
below.

20–1 ὁ δ[ὲ λαθραῖ]ος [ὑπο]κλέψας Latte: ὁ δ[ὲ μετ᾽ ἰσχύ]ος
[χάριν] κλέψας Diggle

κυ[ον ἐπ]οίησεν. οἱ δὲ περὶ τ[ὸν Ἀγαμέ-
μνον[α] χρησμῶν αὐτοὺς κ[ελευόν-
των χ[ωρ]ὶς Ἀχιλλέως μὴ π[οιεῖσθαι
25   τὴν στ[ρα]τεί[α]ν.( )[...]..[
Διομήδ[..] καιν[
καταν[ο]ήσαν[τες

25–6 τ[ὸν Ὀδυ]σσ[έα σὺν] Διομήδ[ει] καὶ Ν[έστορι
ἀπέστειλαν (e.g.) Luppe

681a
ὦ Τυνδάρεια παῖ, Λάκαινα [

See test. iia.2 above

682

<ΤΡΟΦΟΣ>
ἡ παῖς νοσεῖ σου κἀπικινδύνως ἔχει.

<ΛΥΚΟΜΗΔΗΣ>
πρὸς τοῦ; τίς αὐτὴν πημονὴ δαμάζεται;
μῶν κρυμὸς αὐτῆς πλευρὰ γυμνάζει χολῆς;

Sextus Empiricus, *Against the Experts* 1.308; divided by
Heath and Valckenaer between an unidentified speaker (the
Nurse: Welcker) and Lycomedes

683
σοφοὶ δὲ συγκρύπτουσιν οἰκείας βλάβας.

Orion 1.10 Haffner; Stobaeus 4.45.8; cf. [Menander], *Mono-
stichs* 719 Jaekel

pregnant. Agamemnon and his comrades (were told) by an
oracle not (to make their expedition) without Achilles . . .   25
Diomedes . . . [2] (they,) learning . . .

[2] In vv. 25–6 Luppe suggests '(they despatched Odysseus
with) Diomedes and (Nestor)', although a dramatic role for
Nestor seems unlikely.

681a
(Beginning of the play)
O daughter of Tyndareus from Sparta . . . [1]

[1] I.e. Helen, invoked resentfully as the cause of the Trojan
War. The prologue speaker may have been Deidameia's nurse.

682

⟨NURSE⟩
Your daughter is sick and in a dangerous condition.

⟨LYCOMEDES⟩
What is the cause? What ailment is overcoming her? Is
some chill in her bile troubling her chest?[1]

[1] The source (Sextus) explains that Lycomedes guesses his
daughter may be suffering from pleurisy. Greek medical writers
do not associate pleurisy specifically with chilled bile, but Lyco-
medes need not be speaking as an expert.

683
Wise people join in concealing damage within their own
family.[1]

[1] Cf. *Cretan Women* F 460 with note.

EURIPIDES

**683a (= fr. adesp. 9 N)

ΟΔΥΣΣΕΥΣ

σὺ δ', ὦ τὸ λαμπρὸν φῶς ἀποσβεννὺς γένους,
ξαίνεις, ἀρίστου πατρὸς Ἑλλήνων γεγώς;

Plutarch, *Moralia* 34d and (with attribution to *Scyrians*) 72e; assigned to Sophocles' *Scyrians* by Bergk, to Euripides' by Wilamowitz

684

⟨ΛΥΚΟΜΗΔΗΣ?⟩

φεῦ, τῶν βροτείων—ὡς ἀνώμαλοι—τυχῶν·
οἱ μὲν γὰρ εὖ πράσσουσι, τοῖς δὲ συμφοραὶ
σκληραὶ πάρεισιν εὐσεβοῦσιν εἰς θεούς
καὶ πάντ' ἀκριβῶς κἀπὶ φροντίδων βίον
5   οὕτω δικαίως ζῶσιν αἰσχύνης ἄτερ.

Stobaeus 4.41.16; vv. 1–3: John Lydus, *On Months* 4.7 and 4.100; *Palatine Anthology* 10.107.2–4

1 τυχῶν and preceding punctuation Collard, cf. *Hipp.* 936 cited by Kannicht: τύχαι sources   3 εὐσεβοῦσιν εἰς Stob. (-σι πρὸς others): εὐσεβοῦσί γ' εἰς Jouan

PROBABLY FROM SCYRIANS

880

οὐκ ἐν γυναιξὶ τοὺς νεανίας χρεὼν
ἀλλ' ἐν σιδήρῳ κἀν ὅπλοις τιμὰς ἔχειν.

Chrysippus, *On Negatives* fr. 180.8 von Arnim; assigned to *Scyrians* by Bergk

SCYRIANS

**683a (= fr. adesp. 9 N)

ODYSSEUS
(to Achilles)

And you, extinguisher of your family's brilliant light, are you combing wool—you, born of the most valiant father in Greece?[1]

[1] Girls typically assisted their mothers and female slaves in preparing, spinning and weaving wool for clothing etc. This reproach, probably from Euripides' play, seems to be echoed by Ovid in his own voice at *Ars Amatoria* 1.690–6. The uncertain F 880 (see after F 684) probably comes from the same scene.

684

‹LYCOMEDES?›

Ah, the fortunes of men—how uneven they are! Some of them fare well, while others meet harsh misfortunes although they show respect to the gods and live their whole life with care and prudence, quite justly and without disgrace.

PROBABLY FROM *SCYRIANS*

880

Young men should get honours not amongst women but amidst arms and weaponry.[1]

[1] Probably Odysseus exhorting Achilles: see Introduction and F **683a above.

SYLEUS

Pechstein 243–83; Krumeich 457–73; H. Van Looy in ed. Budé VIII.3.75–90.

U. von Wilamowitz-Moellendorff, *Euripides: Herakles* (1895², repr. Darmstadt, 1959), I.38 n. 72 and II.73–5 n. 134; B. A. van Groningen, *Mnemosyne* 58 (1930), 293–9; N. C. Chourmouziades, *Satyrika* (Athens, 1974), 120–57 (in Greek); *LIMC* VII.i.825–7 'Syleus'; Gantz 434–7, 440–1; Voelke 216–7, 330–8.

Heracles killed his friend Iphitus the son of Eurytus while Iphitus was his guest (test. ii.4–5 below; for other versions of the killing see Gantz 434–7). Seized by the madness with which Hera regularly tormented him, he sought oracular guidance and was told that he must pay Eurytus a penalty through common servitude somewhere for three years (test. iiic below). In many accounts, generally later than Euripides, he serves Omphale queen of Lydia (as in Euripides' contemporary Ion of Chios' satyr play Omphale);[1] but in Euripides he serves Syleus, a son of Poseidon who lived in northern Greece (Herodotus 7.115.2 etc.: see on

[1] See P. E. Easterling, 'Looking for Omphale', in V. Jennings and A. Katsaros (eds.), *The World of Ion of Chios* (Leiden, 2007), 282–92 at 285.

date below). Syleus was a pest (his name means 'Despoiler, Robber'), typical of many such destroyed by Heracles (cf. Busiris; Voelke 329–39) or Theseus (cf. Sciron): Syleus compelled passers-by to toil in his vineyard before killing them.

Euripides seems to have begun his play with Heracles being sold by Hermes as a slave to Syleus (test. ii.6, iiia, iiic below); Philo in his moral essay *Every Good Man Is Free* 98–104 (test. iiib below) not only preserves F 687–691 from this opening scene, in dramatic sequence, but links their content in order to contrast a virtuous man's automatic instinct for freedom and goodness with the repressive nature of an ignoble man (see Philo 98, 104). Accordingly Heracles in the play would not endure his evil master Syleus (cf. F 692), and turned his great strength against him. He destroyed his vines and burned them to roast his best bull; he challenged him to a drinking contest with his own best wine (test. iiib (103), F 691, cf. test. iiia). Then he used his great club (F 688.4) to kill Syleus, it appears (F 693; cf. test. iiic); instead of killing also Syleus' daughter Xenodoce (as test. iiic has it), he saved her (test. ii.16–17), but only to enjoy her (F 694).

Reconstructors have readily imposed an episodic structure on this outline (see Chourmouziades 156–7, Pechstein 275–83, and esp. Krumeich 472–3 and Van Looy 81–3). Incidents with the great hero humiliated by being sold, with his argument with his persecutors and then his violent rebellion, and with eating and drinking followed by sex, served the satyric ethos excellently. The few fragments contain however no mention of the satyrs themselves. They would as usual have formed the chorus, and would have been like Heracles in servitude to a cruel master (another *satyric commonplace, cf. e.g.* Sisyphus *test. *iii.6–11 and* Sciron, *Introduction)—and similarly in the vineyard, where they would have thirsted for wine (another commonplace: Voelke 183–202); indeed it has been suggested that* Theristae *('Harvesters') was an alternative title for* Syleus.

*No fewer than seven Attic vase paintings of the early 5th century (*LIMC *nos. 1–7) show Heracles amid the vines, and some of them an angry Syleus (cf. F 691) and a young woman, probably Xenodoce—but none has satyrs. Their number demonstrates the popularity of the story before Euripides, but no other drama, even a comedy, is known. Nevertheless, Euripides' play lasted well, for it boasts the most numerous certain fragments and the fullest secondary evidence of all his lost satyr plays.*

Brief fragment: F 686a (three letters from the play's first line = test. ii.2). Other ascriptions: F 907b (= fr. *10 Van Looy: noisy feasting by Heracles matching details in test. iiia and F 691); Auge F 272a; Sisyphus F 673; adesp. F 90 (hospitality offered), 165 (invitation to sex, using the colloquial verb of F 694), 327 (virtuous self-possession), 416 (Heracles asleep, clasping his club).

A date in the 430s has been inferred from the play's location, if the corrupt place-name in test. iiic is correctly restored as Phyllis in northern Greece; there was much Athenian invasion and colonization there in the period (see Wilamowitz in the bibliography above).

The story of Syleus left hardly a mark on later literary tradition.

ΣΥΛΕΥΣ

test. ii (Hypothesis)

Συλεὺς Σατυ]ρικό[ς, οὗ ἀρχή·

]ν ὑψ[

ἡ δ' ὑπό]θεσις·

Ἡρακλεῖ φονε]ύσαντι τὸν ἑαυτ[οῦ ξένον

5   Ἴφιτον τὸν Ε]ὐρύτου Ζεὺς ἐπ[έταξεν

ἀπ]εμποληθέντι [

]· εἰ δὲ τὸν πόν[ον

]ν ἐνιαυτὸν δ[

remains of four further lines, then this fragment breaks off

end of the same hypothesis:

....] καὶ τὸν Συλέα[·] ἀνασ[

θυγα]τέρα τοῦ προειρημ[ένου

15   ]νος διωκομένην [

]· τούτου[ς] μὲν οὖν [, Ξενο-

δό]κην δὲ ἔσωσεν———

SYLEUS

test. ii (Hypothesis)

(*Syleus*, saty)ric, (which begins ... *(first line not preserved)* ...
(the) plot is as follows: (when Heracles had kill)ed his own
(guest Iphitus the son) of Eurytus, Zeus (enjoined on him that   5
he should) be sold (off, *i.e. into slavery*) ... and if ... the labour
... for a year ... *(letters from four further lines)* ...

(end of the same hypothesis) ... and Syleus. (Heracles) ...
(the daugh)ter of the aforenamed ... being pursued ... So   15
(Heracles) ... these ... and saved (Xenodoce).[1] *(end of hy-
pothesis)*

[1] Xenodoce ('Guest-Hostess') and Xenodice ('Guest-Justice')
have both been restored here, and both occur at the end of test.
iiic. The mildly colloquial meaning of the first seems ironically
appropriate to the girl's rape.

---

vv. 1–12: P. Strasbourg Gr. 2676 fr. A (a), ed. J. Schwartz, *ZPE*
4 (1969), 43–4 and H.-J. Mette, *ibid*. 173 (who identified it with
Euripides' play); subsequently shown to be from the same papy-
rus roll as vv. 13–17, P. Oxy. 2455 fr. 8 (= Austin, *NFE* 96, no. 20);
both re-ed. by W. Luppe, *SIFC* III.2 (1984), 35–9, cf. van
Rossum-Steenbeek 213–5.

4–5 so Mette and Luppe: cf. Sophocles, *Women of Trachis*
248–79   16–17 so Luppe (with Ξενοδί]κην or Ξενοδό]κην:
see note above), following Harder, Chourmouziades

EURIPIDES

test. iiia (= T 221b, *TrGF* 5.137)

ἡ σατυρικὴ δὲ ποίησις . . . ἀμιγῆ καὶ χαρίεντα καὶ
θυμελικὸν ἔχει τὸν γέλωτα, οἷον· Ἡρακλῆς πραθεὶς τῷ
Συλεῖ ὡς γεωργὸς δοῦλος ἐστάλη εἰς τὸν ἀγρὸν τὸν
ἀμπελῶνα ἐργάσασθαι, ἀνεσπακὼς δὲ δικέλλῃ προρρί-
ζους τὰς ἀμπέλους ἁπάσας νωτοφορήσας τε αὐτὰς εἰς τὸ
οἴκημα τοῦ ἀγροῦ θωμοὺς μεγάλους ἐποίησε, τὸν κρείττω
τε τῶν βοῶν θύσας κατεθοινᾶτο, καὶ τὸν πιθεῶνα δὲ
διαρρήξας καὶ τὸν κάλλιστον πίθον ἀποπωμάσας τὰς
θύρας τε ὡς τράπεζαν θεὶς ἦσθε καὶ ἔπινεν ᾄδων, καὶ τῷ
προεστῶτι δὲ τοῦ ἀγροῦ δριμὺ ἐνορῶν φέρειν ἐκέλευεν
ὡραῖά τε καὶ πλακοῦντας· καὶ τέλος ὅλον ποταμὸν πρὸς
τὴν ἔπαυλιν τρέψας τὰ πάντα κατέκλυσεν ὁ δοῦλος ἐκεῖ-
νος ὁ τεχνικώτατος γεωργός. τοιαῦτα τὰ σατυρικὰ δρά-
ματα . . .

Tzetzes, *Prolegomena on Comedy* II.59–70 (pp. 35–6 Koster)

test. iiib

(98) τῆς δὲ σπουδαίων ἐλευθερίας μάρτυρές εἰσι ποιηταὶ
. . . (99) ἴδε γοῦν οἷα παρ' Εὐριπίδῃ φησὶν ὁ Ἡρακλῆς·
'πίμπρα . . . λόγον' (F 687). τῷ γὰρ ὄντι θωπεία μὲν καὶ
κολακεία καὶ ὑπόκρισις . . . δουλοπρεπέστατα, τὸ δὲ
ἀνόθως καὶ γνησίως . . . ἐλευθεροστομεῖν εὐγενέσιν ἁρ-
μόττον. (100) πάλιν τὸν αὐτὸν σπουδαῖον οὐχ ὁρᾷς ὅτι
οὐδὲ πωλούμενος θεράπων εἶναι δοκεῖ, καταπλήττων τοὺς
ὁρῶντας ὡς οὐ μόνον ἐλεύθερος ὢν ἀλλὰ καὶ δεσπότης
ἐσόμενος τοῦ πριαμένου; (101) ὁ γοῦν Ἑρμῆς πυνθανο-

test. iiia (= T 221b, *TrGF* 5.137)

The humour in satyric drama is pure, pleasing and theatrical; for example: Heracles was sold to Syleus and sent as a slave labourer into the farmland to work in the vineyard. He rooted up all the vines completely with a mattock and carried them on his back to the farmhouse and made them into a great heap; he sacrificed the better of the oxen and made a feast of it;[1] he broke into the cellar and took the top off the the best jar, set up the doors as a table, and began eating and drinking, and singing; with a fierce look at the farm's master he ordered him to bring seasonal fruits and cakes. In the end he diverted a complete river towards the farm buildings and flooded everything—that most ingenious farm slave![2] That is what satyr plays are like . . .

[1] Roasting the ox on the heaped-up wood.   [2] A later hand in the ms. has here substituted 'There is a play of Euripides like this' for the words 'that most ingenious farm slave!'

test. iiib

(98) The freedom of virtuous men (is) attested by poets . . . (99) So look for instance at the sort of things Heracles says in Euripides . . . (*F 687 quoted*) . . . For in reality wheedling and flattery and hypocrisy . . . are the clearest marks of a slave, while speaking freely . . . with genuine sincerity befits nobility of birth. (100) Again, do you see that the same virtuous man seems not to be servile even when being sold, astounding those who watch as being not only free but about to become the master of the one who buys him? (101) For instance, to

Philo, *Every Good Man Is Free* 98–104; see also apparatus to F 687–691 below

EURIPIDES

μένῳ Συλεῖ εἰ φαῦλός ἐστιν ἀποκρίνεται· 'ἥκιστα . . .
δραστήριος' (F 688)· 'οὐδεὶς δὲ . . . πρὸς ἐμβολήν' (F 689)·
εἶτ᾽ ἐπιλέγει· 'τὸ εἶδος . . . θέλοις' (F 690). (102) ἐπεὶ δὲ καὶ
πριαμένου Συλέως εἰς ἀγρὸν ἐπέμφθη, διέδειξεν ἔργοις
τὸ τῆς φύσεως ἀδούλωτον· τὸν μὲν γὰρ ἄριστον τῶν ἐκεῖ
ταύρων καταθύσας Διὶ πρόφασιν εὐωχεῖτο, πολὺν δ᾽
οἶνον ἐκφορήσας ἀθρόον εὖ μάλα κατακλιθεὶς ἠκρατί-
ζετο. (103) Συλεῖ δὲ ἀφικομένῳ καὶ δυσανασχετοῦντι ἐπί
τε τῇ βλάβῃ καὶ τῇ τοῦ θεράποντος ῥαθυμίᾳ καὶ τῇ
περιττῇ καταφρονήσει μηδὲν μήτε τῆς χρόας μήτε ὧν
ἔπραττε μεταβαλὼν εὐτολμότατά φησιν· 'κλίθητι . . . ἔσῃ'
(F 691). (104) τοῦτον οὖν δοῦλον ἢ κύριον ἀποφαντέον τοῦ
δεσπότου, μὴ μόνον ἀπελευθεριάζειν ἀλλὰ καὶ ἐπι-
τάγματα ἐπιτάσσειν τῷ κτησαμένῳ καὶ εἰ ἀφηνιάζοι
τύπτειν καὶ προπηλακίζειν, εἰ δὲ καὶ βοηθοὺς ἐπάγοιτο,
πάντας ἄρδην ἀπολλύναι τολμῶντα;

(101) Συλεῖ εἰ Kannicht: μὲν εἰ Philo ms. M (πυνθανομένοις
ἡμῖν ὡς most mss.)

test. iiic

κατασχεθεὶς δὲ δεινῇ νόσῳ διὰ τὸν Ἰφίτου φόνον . . .
λαμβάνει χρησμὸν Ἡρακλῆς, ὃς ἔλεγεν ἀπαλλαγὴν
αὐτῷ τῆς νόσου ἔσεσθαι πραθέντι καὶ τρία ἔτη λατρεύ-
σαντι καὶ δόντι ποινὴν τοῦ φόνου τὴν τιμὴν Εὐρύτῳ. (3)
τοῦ δὲ χρησμοῦ δοθέντος Ἑρμῆς Ἡρακλέα πιπράσκει.
καὶ αὐτὸν ὠνεῖται Ὀμφάλη Ἰαρδάνου, βασιλεύουσα Λυ-

Apollodorus 2.6.2–3 (test. iiic in *TrGF* adds briefer versions,
Tzetzes, *Chiliades* 2.415–38 and Diodorus 4.31)

176

(Syleus')[1] question whether (Heracles) is a weakling, Hermes replies . . . (*F 688, 689*) . . . , then continues . . . (*F 690*) . . . (102) Besides, when Heracles was sent on to the farmland after Syleus had bought him, he demonstrated by his actions that slavishness was not in his nature. He sacrificed the finest of the bulls there, nominally to Zeus, and feasted himself well; and he brought out a good deal of wine, laid himself down very comfortably, and drank it all off neat. (103) When Syleus arrived and grew angry at the loss, and at his servant's idleness and extreme contempt, Heracles did not at all change colour, nor what he was doing, but said very boldly . . . (*F 691*) . . . (104) So should we describe the man as slave to his master, or lord over him, who dares not only to take such liberties but also to issue instructions to his owner, and to hit and treat him roughly if he resists, and if he should bring in helpers, to destroy them all utterly?

[1] Kannicht suggests adding Syleus' name here; the ms. has simply 'the one asking' (some have thought him to be Heracles).

test. iiic

Heracles was gripped by a dreadful affliction because he had murdered Iphitus . . . he received an oracle which told him he would be released from the affliction if he were sold, worked in servitude for three years, and paid Eurytus the sale-price as a penalty for the murder. (3) After the oracle had been given, Hermes sold Heracles, who was bought by Omphale the daughter of Iardanus and queen of the Lydians[1] . . . and he

[1] Heracles' servitude to Omphale rather than Syleus became the dominant version of the myth: see Introduction.

δῶν . . . Συλέα δὲ ἐν †Αὐλίδι† τοὺς παριόντας ξένους
σκάπτειν ἀναγκάζοντα, σὺν ταῖς ῥίζαις τὰς ἀμπέλους
καύσας μετὰ τῆς Ξενοδόκης ἀπέκτεινε.

(3) †Αὐλίδι†: see note 2 opposite.

687

ΗΡΑΚΛΗΣ

πίμπρη, κάταιθε σάρκας, ἐμπλήσθητί μου
πίνων κελαινὸν αἷμα· πρόσθε γὰρ κάτω
γῆς εἶσιν ἄστρα, γῆ δ᾽ ἄνεισ᾽ ἐς αἰθέρα,
πρὶν ἐξ ἐμοῦ σοι θῶπ᾽ ἀπαντῆσαι λόγον.

Philo (test. iiib above) 99 with attribution to *Syleus* implied,
and without attribution in three other works, with minor varia-
tions; Eusebius, *Preparation for the Gospel* 6.6.2; Theophanes
Syriacus 1.64; vv. 1–2: Psellus, *Poems* 21.275–6 Westerink; v. 1:
Artemidorus, *Dream-Interpretation* 4.59.

688

ΕΡΜΗΣ

ἥκιστα φαῦλος, ἀλλὰ πᾶν τοὐναντίον·
τὸ σχῆμα σεμνὸς κοὐ ταπεινὸς οὐδ᾽ ἄγαν
εὔογκος ὡς ἂν δοῦλος, ἀλλὰ καὶ στολὴν
ἰδόντι λαμπρὸς καὶ ξύλῳ δραστήριος.

Philo (test. iiib above) 101

killed Syleus, who †at Aulis† [2] compelled passing strangers to dig (his land), and Xenodoce with him, after burning Syleus' vines together with their roots.

[2] 'Aulis' is incorrect, as Syleus did not live there. It is variously changed, but unconvincingly, to e.g. 'Lydia' (ruled by Omphale), 'Phyllis' (a place in Macedonia: see Introduction on the play's date), or just 'a valley'.

687

HERACLES

Set fire to me, burn my flesh up, sate yourself with drinking my dark blood![1] The stars will go down below the earth, and the earth rise up into the heaven, before you meet with any fawning talk from me!

[1] For such defiance see on *Pleisthenes* F 629.

688

HERMES

Not in the least a weakling, but completely the opposite: proud in his bearing, and not meek nor too bulky as a slave would be, but both splendid in his garb and effective with a club.[1]

[1] Heracles is clad as usual with a lion-skin, and carries his great club.

689

⟨ΕΡΜΗΣ⟩

οὐδεὶς δ' ἐς οἴκους δεσπότης ἀμείνονας
αὐτοῦ πρίασθαι βούλεται· σὲ δ' εἰσορῶν
πᾶς τις δέδοικεν. ὄμμα γὰρ πυρὸς γέμεις,
ταῦρος λέοντος ὡς βλέπων πρὸς ἐμβολήν.

Philo (test. iiib above) 101; separated from F 688 by Grotius;
Philo perhaps implies an interval between F 689 and 690, but
they may be joined (Musgrave).

1 δεσπότης Musgrave: -ας Philo

690

⟨ΕΡΜΗΣ⟩

. . . τό ⟨γ'⟩ εἶδος αὐτὸ σοῦ κατηγορεῖ
σιγῶντος ὡς εἴης ἂν οὐχ ὑπήκοος,
τάσσειν δὲ μᾶλλον ἢ 'πιτάσσεσθαι θέλοις.

Philo (test. iiib above) 101: see on F 689 (Musgrave)

1 ⟨γ'⟩ Elmsley: ⟨ἐπεὶ⟩ τό ⟨γ'⟩ εἶδος, with F 690 joined to 689,
van Groningen: ⟨καίτοι⟩ etc., with or without join, Collard

691

ΗΡΑΚΛΗΣ

κλίθητι καὶ πίωμεν· ἐν τούτῳ δέ μου
τὴν πεῖραν εὐθὺς λάμβαν'· εἰ κρείσσων ἔσῃ.

Philo (test. iiib above) 103

SYLEUS

689

⟨HERMES⟩

No master wants to buy men better than himself for his house;[1] and every man is afraid when he sees *you*: your eyes are full of fire, like a bull facing attack by a lion.[2]

[1] Cf. *Alexander* F 51, *Archelaus* F 251. Philo has 'No one wants to buy masters better than himself for his house'; but Syleus is buying only a slave.　　[2] A similar comparison at *Heracles* 869.

690

⟨HERMES⟩

. . .[1] your very appearance, though you are silent, declares that you would not be obedient, but would prefer giving instructions to being instructed.

[1] Perhaps supply 'For' (van Groningen) or 'And yet' (Collard).

691

HERACLES

Lie down and let's drink! Test me at once to see if you'll be better at it than I am!

692

τοῖς μὲν δικαίοις ἔνδικος, τοῖς δ' αὖ κακοῖς
πάντων μέγιστος πολέμιος κατὰ χθόνα.

Stobaeus 4.5.1

693

ΗΡΑΚΛΗΣ
εἶα δή, φίλον ξύλον,
ἔγειρέ μοι σεαυτὸ καὶ γίγνου θρασύ.

George Choeroboscus (on the use of εἶα) in *Etymologicum
Genuinum* B (= *Etym. Magnum* p. 294.45 Gaisford); cited by
other grammarians, sometimes beginning at ἔγειρε and with
slight variations. A terse entry in Hesychius τ 1626 (τύλον =
'penis') prompted Meineke to suggest that Euripides wrote τύλον
rather than ξύλον here, but Hesychius may reflect a coarse comic
adaptation of the verse: cf. on *Stheneboea* F 664.2.

694

⟨ΗΡΑΚΛΗΣ⟩
βαυβῶμεν εἰσελθόντες· ἀπόμορξαι σέθεν
τὰ δάκρυα.

Anecdota Graeca I.85.10 Bekker = Aristophanes of Byzan-
tium fr. 15 Slater

SYLEUS

692

(Heracles) . . . just towards those who are just, but to those who are bad, the greatest of all their enemies on earth.

693

HERACLES

Come on then, my dear club, stir yourself, please, and be bold![1]

[1] Heracles prepares his club for violent action against Syleus' vines or more probably the man himself and any helpers (test. iiib (104)). For his 'dear' club cf. Bellerophon addressing his horse Pegasus, *Bellerophon* F 306. Alternatively (see note to the Greek text), Heracles is preparing himself to bed Xenodoce (F 694).

694

⟨HERACLES⟩

Let's go in and cuddle up![1] Wipe away your tears!

[1] The Greek verb is vulgar and euphemistic. Heracles is addressing Syleus' daughter Xenodoce, whom he spared from death only to enjoy her (test. ii.16–17).

TELEPHUS

E. W. Handley and J. Rea, *The Telephus of Euripides* (London, 1957); H. J. Mette, *Der verlorene Aischylos* (Berlin, 1963), 81–94; Austin, *NFE* 66–82; M. Cropp in *SFP* I.17–52, 282 (~ II.363–4); F. Jouan in ed. Budé VIII.2.91–132; C. Preiser, *Euripides: Telephos* (Hildesheim, 2000).

Jouan (1966), 222–55; Webster 43–8, 302; Rau, *Paratragodia* 19–50; Trendall–Webster III.3.47–9; C. Bauchhenss-Thüriedl, *Der Mythos von Telephos in der antiken Bildkunst* (Würzburg, 1971); G. Mengano Cavalli, *Atti dell' Accademia Pontaniana* 31 (1982), 315–37; Aélion (1983), I.31–42; *LIMC* I.i.260–2 'Agamemnon, Téléphos et Oreste', VII.i.856–70 'Telephos' (esp. nos. 51–88); M. Ditifeci, *Prometheus* 10 (1984), 210–20; M. Heath, *CQ* 37 (1987), 272–80; E. Keuls in J.-P. Descoeudres (ed.), *Eumousia: Studies . . . A. Cambitoglou* (Sydney, 1990), 87–94; Gantz 428–31, 576–80; Matthiessen 272–3.

Telephus was the son of Heracles and of Auge, daughter of king Aleus of Tegea in Arcadia; Euripides dramatized his birth story in Auge, *a much later play than* Telephus. *Auge became the wife of king Teuthras of Mysia and Telephus eventually his heir (cf. F 697.9–15, and our Introduction to* Auge *on the varying mythical traditions). When the Greeks under Agamemnon attacked Mysia during their*

185

abortive first expedition against Troy, Telephus led a successful resistance but stumbled while pursuing the invaders and was wounded in the leg by Achilles. The wound festered, and Telephus was advised by an oracle of Apollo that only 'the one that had wounded him' could heal him; so he went to Argos, where the Greeks were by now assembling for a second expedition, and was healed by Achilles in return for undertaking to guide the Greeks to Troy. This story was told in the epic Cypria *according to Proclus' summary, and was dramatized in Aeschylus'* Telephus *(Aesch. F 238–40) where Telephus may have taken Agamemnon's young son Orestes to the family hearth or altar to assist his supplication, like Themistocles seeking refuge with the Molossian king Admetus (Thucydides 1.136). Little is known about Aeschylus' play, and still less about Sophocles'* Telephus *(Soph. F 727, a single word; date unknown),[1] but Euripides'* Telephus *is relatively well documented, not least because of Aristophanes' parodies of scenes from it in* Acharnians *204–625 (cf. TrGF test. iva, va) and* Women at the Thesmophoria *466–764 (cf. test. vb); these plays and the ancient commentaries on them provide nearly half of the book fragments of* Telephus. *In* Acharnians *(425 B.C.) Dicaeopolis borrows Telephus' beggar costume from Euripides in order to get the chorus's sympathy as he speaks against the war with Sparta. In*

---

[1] An early 4th c. inscription commemorating the production of a *Telepheia* by Sophocles may be the only evidence of his composing a trilogy (*Sons of Aleus, Mysians, Telephus*?), but the interpretation of the title is disputed and this Sophocles might perhaps be the grandson of the famous tragedian. See *TrGF* 1 DID B 5 and 4. 434.

Women at the Thesmophoria *(411 B.C.) Euripides' kins-man dresses himself as a woman in order to persuade the female chorus that Euripides' criticisms of women are more than justified, but is exposed and takes refuge at an altar with threats to kill a 'baby'—actually a wineskin—that he has seized from one of them (Dicaeopolis similarly threatens a charcoal basket to get the attention of the cho-rus in* Acharnians). *Telephus' beggar role (reminiscent of Odysseus in the* Odyssey*), his 'disguised speech' (cf.* Melanippe Wise *test. iia) and his threat to kill Orestes seem to have been the most distinctive elements in Euripides' plot, although the first two go unmentioned in Hyginus,* Fab. 101 *(= test. *iiic below) which is the nearest approxi-mation we have to a summary.*[2]

A rough plot outline can be established incorporating the elements just mentioned and many of the fragments.[3] *The action was probably set in front of Agamemnon's pal-ace, the Chorus comprising Argive elders. F 696 is the be-ginning of Telephus' prologue speech, which must have included F 697–8 explaining his disguise and probably also F 705a explaining his wound (whereas F 705 is a false explanation given later to the Greeks). Telephus' plan for using his disguise is not entirely clear, but he may have en-countered Clytemnestra and gained her assistance in using Orestes as an aid to his supplication in a scene following the prologue speech (for her possible role in the play see*

[2] P. Oxy. 2455 fr. 12 (= test. *iiib) probably provides a few dam-aged and uninformative lines from a hypothesis.   [3] This out-line diverges at some points from the order of the fragments in *TrGF* which Nauck established. The papyrus F 727a includes fragments from several different points in the play.

further below on iconography; F 699 perhaps has Telephus addressing her as his advisor, but she can hardly have advised violence against Orestes as Hyginus suggests). The next certain scene contained Telephus' speech in disguise which Aristophanes parodied (F 702a, 703), but there are also signs of a dispute between Agamemnon and Menelaus about the need for a second expedition (F 722–3; see also F 713, 719 with notes) which may have prompted Telephus to intervene and deliver the speech. It included a defence of the Mysians' attack on the invading Greeks (F 708–11) and may also have called for peace between Greece and Troy as Dicaeopolis calls for peace between Athens and Sparta. F 712 and 712a are reactions to the speech, and F 706 belongs either before it or at the start of a further speech. The shape of the whole scene (or scenes?) remains unclear, but eventually Telephus' identity was somehow revealed (perhaps following, or causing, a search for a suspected enemy presence, F 727a fr. 1), and Telephus then somehow managed to seize the baby Orestes and take refuge with him at the altar. A negotiation probably followed, leading ultimately to an agreement that Telephus would guide the Greeks to Troy if Achilles would heal him; Webster plausibly suggested that the oracle only mentioned Telephus cryptically (not by name as in Hyginus), and that Odysseus recognized its meaning and used Telephus' Greek ancestry (cf. F 727c.31–2) to justify his helping the Greeks against his Trojan allies; if so, the oracle may have been brought from Delphi just after Telephus' seizure of Orestes, either by Odysseus himself or by a herald. The conclusion of the negotiation may be represented in F **727b, if it belongs in this play, and F 727c certainly gives the end of a choral song celebrating the agreement and the beginning of a

*scene in which Achilles arriving from Scyros was asked by
Odysseus, and later presumably by Telephus himself, to
perform the healing; but probably two impediments arose,
first Achilles' resistance to the idea of aiding an enemy
(cf. F 716, 718?), then his ignorance of medicine which
Odysseus resolved by recognizing the spear as the destined
healer (cf. Hyginus). F 727a fr. 13 may bring us very close
to the end of the play with Achilles and Telephus reconciled
and perhaps exiting together like Theseus and Heracles at
the end of* Heracles; *but the exact form of the ending is un-
clear (F 724 might be from a description or report of the
healing, or from Odysseus' interpretation of the oracle).*

*The remaining fragments (F 700–2, 707, 714–5, 717,
720–1, 727) cannot be placed with confidence, though
plausible guesses have been made for most of them (see
notes to the translations). Brief fragments: F 704 'Mysian
Telephus', F 725 'lying (i.e. flattened) wheat' or 'wheat con-
cealing an ambush'?, F 626 'a wine-cooler'; also P. Oxy.
2460 (= F 727a) frs. 2–8, 11–12, 14–16, 21–51. Other as-
criptions: Oeneus F 568 (see note there); F 883, 885, 888,
**898a (~ Acharnians 203), 915, 918 (~ Ach. 659–64), 975,
1043a, 1066; adesp. F *57 (see on F 699 below); also Ach.
384 = 436 'to equip myself to be as pitiful as possible', 449
(= fr. adesp. 44 N) 'Leave this stone-built dwelling', 456
'Know that you are troublesome; get away from this house',
and* Women at the Thesmophoria *76–7 'On this day it will
be decided whether Euripides (i.e. Telephus?) lives on or is
no more', 693–5 'But here, upon the (sacrificial) thigh-
bones, struck by this dagger in his blood-filled veins he
(i.e. Orestes?) shall stain the altar'. Further identifications
have been speculatively detected in both comedies.*

More than a dozen Attic and South Italian vase paint-

EURIPIDES

*ings and a few other art works from the 4th century proba-
bly reflect (with variations) Euripides' altar scene, with
Telephus threatening Orestes and Agamemnon threaten-
ing Telephus.[4] Clytemnestra appears frequently in these,
often restraining Agamemnon's attack; this encourages the
view that she had a role in the play, although such evidence
needs to be treated with caution.*

The hypothesis to Alcestis *ascribed to Aristophanes of
Byzantium (= Telephus test. ii) records that Euripides was
awarded second place behind Sophocles at the Dionysia of
438 B.C. with* Cretan Women, Alcmeon in Psophis, *Tele-
phus and* Alcestis. *The bold disguising of the hero as a beg-
gar, his criticisms of Greek hostility towards the barbarian
Mysians and Trojans, and the melodramatic altar scene
made the play memorable and perhaps controversial as
Aristophanes' parodies suggest (it is recalled also in* Clouds
and Frogs: *test. i, iiia, ivb). But there was also tragic dig-
nity in the healing of the hero's grievous wound (see F 724
with note) and his reconciliation with Achilles and the
Greeks. Telephus remained popular as a dramatic sub-
ject, though little or nothing is known of the tragedies of*

[4] See *TrGF* test. *vc; LIMC* 'Agamemnon' nos. 12–19, 'Tele-
phos' nos. 53–69; Taplin nos. 75–7; Todisco, Index, 'Euripide:
Telefo'. Clytemnestra is named on one such vase painted by
Assteas and published in 1983 (Todisco P 2, Taplin no. 77). The al-
tar scene is repeated with further variations on many Etruscan
cremation urns of the 3rd and 2nd centuries (*LIMC* 'Agamemnon'
nos. 20–6, 'Telephos' nos. 72–6). The parody scene in *Women at
the Thesmophoria* appears with some strikingly similar features
on a 4th c. Apulian vase (*TrGF* test. vb2; *LIMC* 'Telephos' no. 81).

190

this name produced by Euripides' younger contemporaries and successors (Iophon, Agathon, Cleophon, Moschion), nor of the Doric comedies by Dinolochus (5th c.) and Rhinthon (3rd c.). The Latin tragedies of Ennius and Accius (seven and fifteen brief fragments respectively) may have followed Euripides, but there is no more recent tradition.

ΤΗΛΕΦΟΣ

test. *iiic

Telephus Herculis et Auges filius ab Achille in pugna Chironis hasta percussus dicitur. Ex quo uulnere cum in dies taetro cruciatu angeretur, petit sortem ab Apolline, quod esset remedium; responsum est ei neminem mederi posse nisi eandem hastam qua uulneratus est. (2) Hoc Telephus ut audiuit, ad regem Agamemnonem uenit et monitu Clytaemnestrae Orestem infantem de cunabulis rapuit, minitans se eum occisurum esse nisi sibi Achiui mederentur. (3) Achiuis autem quod responsum erat sine Telephi ductu Troiam capi non posse, facile cum eo in gratiam redierunt et ab Achille petierunt ut eum sanaret; quibus Achilles respondit se artem medicam non nosse. (4) Tunc Ulixes ait, 'non te dicit Apollo sed auctorem uulneris hastam nominat'; quam cum rasissent, remediatus est. (5) A quo cum peterent ut secum ad Troiam expugnandam iret, non impetrarunt, quod is Laodicen Priami filiam uxorem haberet; sed ob beneficium quod eum sanarunt, eos deduxit, locos autem et itinera demonstrauit; inde in Moesiam est profectus.

Hyginus, *Fab*. 101

TELEPHUS

test. *iiic

Telephus, son of Hercules and Auge, is said to have been struck by Achilles in battle with Chiron's spear. Since he was afflicted daily by hideous torment from this wound, he sought an oracle from Apollo as to what the remedy might be. The response was that no one could heal him but the same spear with which he had been wounded. (2) When Telephus heard this, he came to king Agamemnon and on Clytemnestra's advice seized the infant Orestes from his cradle, threatening to kill him unless the Achaeans healed him. (3) The Achaeans for their part had received an oracle that Troy could not be taken without Telephus' guidance, and so they readily made friends with him and asked Achilles to cure him; but Achilles replied that he did not know the art of medicine. (4) Then Ulysses said, 'Apollo does not mean you, but names the spear as the author of the wound'; and when they had scraped the spear, he was healed. (5) When they asked Telephus to go with them to sack Troy they did not persuade him, for he was married to Priam's daughter Laodice; but in return for their help in curing him he guided them and pointed out places and routes; then he departed to Moesia (i.e. Mysia).

EURIPIDES

696

ΤΗΛΕΦΟΣ

ὦ γαῖα πατρὶς ἣν Πέλοψ ὁρίζεται,
χαῖρ’, ὅς τε πέτραν Ἀρκάδων δυσχείμερον
Πὰν ἐμβατεύεις, ἔνθεν εὔχομαι γένος·
Αὔγη γὰρ Ἀλέου παῖς με τῷ Τιρυνθίῳ
5 τίκτει λαθραίως Ἡρακλεῖ· ξύνοιδ’ ὄρος
Παρθένιον, ἔνθα μητέρ’ ὠδίνων ἐμὴν
ἔλυσεν Εἰλείθυια, γίγνομαι δ’ ἐγώ.
καὶ πόλλ’ ἐμόχθησ’, ἀλλὰ συντεμῶ λόγον.
ἦλθον δὲ Μυσῶν πεδίον, ἔνθ’ εὑρὼν ἐμὴν
10 μητέρα κατοικῶ, καὶ δίδωσί μοι κράτη
Τεύθρας ὁ Μυσός, Τήλεφον δ’ ἐπώνυμον
καλοῦσί μ’ ἀστοὶ Μυσίαν κατὰ χθόνα·
τηλοῦ γὰρ οἰκῶν βίοτον ἐξιδρυσάμην.
Ἕλλην δὲ βαρβάροισιν ἦρχε †τεκτονων†
15 πολλοῖς σὺν ὅπλοις πρὶν ⟨γ’⟩ Ἀχαϊκὸς μολὼν
στρατὸς τὰ Μυσῶν πεδί’ ἐπ[ι]στρωφῶν πατεῖ.

P. Milan 1, ed. S. Daris (1966) after A. Calderini, *Aegyptus* 15
(1935), 239–45; cf. Page, *GLP* 130–2 (no. 17), Austin, *NFE* 67–8,
Diggle, *TrGFS* 132–3; vv. 1–7 (ὦ γαῖα—Εἰλείθυια): Dionysius of
Halicarnassus, *On Arrangement of Words* 26; v. 13: Schol. on
Aristophanes, *Clouds* 138 (= F 884 N)

14 ηρχετεκτονων P: ἦρχον εὐκλεῶς Calderini: ἦρχετ’
ἐκπονῶν Grégoire   16 so Maehler, reading στρατος δε‘α΄
Μυσων πεδιον επε[ι]στροφον πατει in the papyrus

696
(Beginning of the play)

TELEPHUS

O fatherland, which Pelops marked out as his own, greetings—and you, Pan, who haunt Arcadia's stormy massif from where I claim descent; for Aleus' daughter Auge bore me secretly to Heracles of Tiryns—my witness is Mount   5
Parthenion, where Eileithyia released my mother from her labour and I was born.[1] Many hardships I endured, but I will cut short my story: I came to the Mysian plain, where I found my mother and made my home. Teuthras the Mysian gave me authority, and people throughout Mysia   10
call me by the fitting name of Telephus, for I settled far from home when I made my life here.[2] A Greek led barbarians † . . . †[3] abundantly armed—till the Achaean host came   15
roaming and trampling over the Mysian plain.

---

[1] See Introduction to *Auge* for the various accounts of Telephus' birth.   [2] Telephus' name is here connected with the Greek *tēle-* 'far away'; for such etymologies in Euripidean prologues cf. *Alexander* F 42d, *Antiope* F 181–2, *Melanippe Captive* F 489 etc. Elsewhere it is derived from the 'teat' (*thēlē*) of the 'deer' (*elaphos*) which was said to have suckled him.   [3] The Greek word is meaningless: Calderini suggested 'I, a Greek, led barbarians (gloriously)', Grégoire 'A Greek took the lead in striving for barbarians'.

697

⟨ΤΗΛΕΦΟΣ⟩

πτώχ᾽ ἀμφίβληστρα σώματος λαβὼν ῥάκη
ἀλκτήρια †τύχης†

[Diogenes the Cynic], *Letters* 34.2 (*Epistol. Gr.* p. 248 Hercher)

1 ἀμφίβληστρα Burges: ἀμφίβλητα [Diog.]
2 ἀλκτήρι(α) ⟨   ⟩ τύχης Kannicht: ⟨   καὶ⟩ τύχης
ἀλκτήρια Diggle

698

⟨ΤΗΛΕΦΟΣ⟩

δεῖ γάρ με δόξαι πτωχὸν ⟨   ⟩
εἶναι μὲν ὅσπερ εἰμί, φαίνεσθαι δὲ μή.

Aristophanes, *Acharnians* 440–1 with Schol.

1 πτωχὸν εἶναι τήμερον Aristoph.: πτωχὸν ἐν τῇδ᾽ ἡμέρᾳ
Blaydes

699

ἄνασσα πράγους τοῦδε καὶ βουλεύματος

Aristophanes, *Lysistrata* 706 with Schol.; some think the Schol. also attributes *Lys.* 707 (= adesp. F *57: see note opposite) to *Telephus*.

697

⟨TELEPHUS⟩

. . . with beggar's rags clothing my body as protections
†from fortune† . . . [1]

[1] The Greek in v. 2 is unmetrical, and 'fortune' alone can
hardly mean 'misfortune' here. Possibly a phrase has been dis-
rupted in quotation as Kannicht and Diggle suppose, and an ad-
jective qualifying 'fortune' lost.

698

⟨TELEPHUS⟩

For I must seem . . . a beggar,[1] to be who I am but not
appear to be so.

[1] Aristophanes wrote 'must seem to be a beggar today', but the
last two words would be unmetrical in tragedy and the syntax is
awkward even with an adjustment such as Blaydes' 'I must seem a
beggar on this day, must be who I am etc.'. Possibly Euripides' two
verses were not adjacent.

699

Mistress of this affair and plan . . .[1]

[1] Often attributed to Telephus addressing Clytemnestra. If
so, the plan is to supplicate Agamemnon, not to use Orestes as a
hostage (see Introduction); but an address to a goddess such as
Athena (Buchwald) is equally possible. Aristophanes' next line
('why, tell me, have you come out of the house scowling?') is prob-
ably not included in the scholiast's attribution to *Telephus*.

EURIPIDES

700

<ΤΗΛΕΦΟΣ>

ὦ Φοῖβ' Ἄπολλον Λύκιε, τί ποτέ μ' ἐργάσῃ;

Aristophanes, *Knights* 1240 with Schol.

701

μοχθεῖν ἀνάγκη τοὺς θέλοντας εὐτυχεῖν.

Stobaeus 3.29.10 and (subjoined to Sophocles F 397) 3.29.25a; also in several gnomic anthologies without attribution

702

τόλμα σύ, κἄν τι τραχὺ νείμωσιν θεοί.

Stobaeus 4.10.10

1 τόλμα σύ Nauck: τόλμ' ἀεὶ or τόλμης ἀεὶ Stob.   τραχὺ νείμωσιν Bothe: τρηχὺ νέμωσι(ν) Stob.

702a

(*a*) καὶ στολισθεὶς τοῖς Τηλέφου ῥακώμασι παρῳδεῖ τὸν ἐκείνου λόγον.

(*b*) ΔΙΚΑΙΟΠΟΛΙΣ

δεῖ γάρ με λέξαι τῷ χορῷ λέξιν μακράν.

(*a*) Hypothesis to Aristophanes' *Acharnians* I.9–10
(*b*) Aristophanes, *Acharnians* 416

700

⟨TELEPHUS⟩

O Lycian Phoebus Apollo, whatever will you do to me?[1]

[1] Probably Telephus fears (after his exposure?) that the Lycian Apollo has endangered his life by sending him to Argos. The 'wolf-slaying' Apollo Lycius worshipped at Argos (cf. Sophocles, *Electra* 6–7) may also be relevant if it was at his altar that Telephus took refuge.

701

Those who want success must strive for it.

702

Bear up, even if the gods give you some harsh treatment.

702a

(*a*) And dressed in Telephus' rags he (i.e. Dicaeopolis) parodies his speech.

(*b*) For I (Dicaeopolis) must deliver a lengthy speech to the chorus.

F 703 and 708–11 belong to the speech mentioned in F 702a, and F 705–7 probably to the same scene. F 705a may belong here, but see note on it below.

703

⟨ΤΗΛΕΦΟΣ⟩

μή μοι φθονήσητ', ἄνδρες Ἑλλήνων ἄκροι,
εἰ πτωχὸς ὢν τέτληκ' ἐν ἐσθλοῖσιν λέγειν.

Schol. on Aristophanes, *Acharnians* 497; v. 1 = Alexis fr. 63.7
PCG

705

⟨ΤΗΛΕΦΟΣ⟩

κώπης ἀνάσσων κἀποβὰς εἰς Μυσίαν
ἐτραυματίσθη⟨ν⟩ πολεμίῳ βραχίονι.

Aristotle, *Rhetoric* 1405a29 (citing v. 1), with Anonymous
Commentary in *CAG* XXI.2.169 (citing κώπης ἀνάσσειν and
ἀποβὰς—βραχίονι) and Stephanus' commentary in *CAG*
XXI.2.313, 315 (citing κώπης ἀνάσσων and ἀποβὰς εἰς
Μυσίαν)

705a

⟨ΤΗΛΕΦΟΣ?⟩

ληστὰς ἐλαύνων καὶ κατασπέρχων δορί

Aristophanes, *Acharnians* 1188 with Schol.

706

⟨ΤΗΛΕΦΟΣ⟩

Ἀγάμεμνον, οὐδ' εἰ πέλεκυν ἐν χεροῖν ἔχων
μέλλοι τις εἰς τράχηλον ἐμβαλεῖν ἐμόν,
σιγήσομαι δίκαιά γ' ἀντειπεῖν ἔχων.

Stobaeus 3.13.3

703

⟨TELEPHUS⟩

Do not feel resentment towards me, leaders of the Greeks,
if I have dared to speak among nobles when I am a beggar.

705

⟨TELEPHUS⟩

Ruling an oar[1] I landed in Mysia, and there was wounded
by a hostile arm.

[1] Aristotle cites this phrase as too elevated to describe a rower.
Aeschylus calls rowers 'oar-rulers' (*Persians* 377). M. L. West ex-
plains such usages as reflecting a Semitic idiom in which the
equivalent word (*b*el*) denotes ownership or responsibility (*The
East Face of Helicon* [Oxford, 1997], 545–6).

705a

⟨TELEPHUS?⟩

. . . pursuing the raiders and harrying them with my spear.[1]

[1] Possibly part of Telephus' false explanation of his wound
along with F 705, but more likely part of his prologue speech, the
'raiders' being the Greek invaders of Mysia.

706

⟨TELEPHUS⟩

Agamemnon, not even if someone with an axe in his hands
were about to strike it on my neck, shall I keep silent; for I
have a just reply to make.[1]

[1] Aristophanes parodies this by having his chorus take up
Dicaeopolis' offer to speak with his head on a butcher's block
(*Acharnians* 317–8, 352–67). The Locrians were said to require
those proposing new laws to speak with their heads in a noose
(Demosthenes 24.139).

EURIPIDES

707

⟨ΤΗΛΕΦΟΣ?⟩

εὖ σοι γένοιτο, Τηλέφῳ δ᾽ ἀγὼ φρονῶ.

Schol. on Aristophanes, *Acharnians* 446 (a paraphrase of this verse); Athenaeus 5.186c

εὖ σοι γένοιτο Ath. (εὐδαιμονοίης Aristoph.): καλῶς ἔχοιμι Schol. (ἔχοι μοι Dobree, ἔχει μοι? Nauck)

708

⟨ΤΗΛΕΦΟΣ⟩

ἐρεῖ τις, οὐ χρῆν.

Aristophanes, *Acharnians* 540 with Schol.

**708a

⟨ΤΗΛΕΦΟΣ⟩

φέρ᾽ εἰ ⟨   ⟩ ἐκπλεύσας σκάφει

Aristophanes, *Acharnians* 541, attributed to *Telephus* by Wilamowitz following Hartung and Bakhuyzen

709

⟨ΤΗΛΕΦΟΣ⟩

καθῆσθ᾽ ἂν ἐν δόμοισιν; ἦ πολλοῦ γε δεῖ.

Aristophanes, *Acharnians* 543 with Schol.

TELEPHUS

707

⟨TELEPHUS?⟩

May it go well for you, and as I intend for Telephus.[1]

[1] Dicaeopolis thanks Euripides for his help in a similar verse, *Acharnians* 446 (this favours Athenaeus' phrasing of the Euripidean fragment). The vague 'as I intend . . .' suggests someone concealing his true meaning, i.e. Telephus himself speaking in disguise.

708

⟨TELEPHUS⟩

Someone will say, 'he should not have'.[1]

[1] F 708–10 are all imitated in Dicaeopolis' defence of Spartan conduct, *Acharnians* 540–56. F 711 very probably belongs with them in Telephus' argument.

**708a

⟨TELEPHUS⟩

Come now, suppose . . . having sailed out in a boat . . . .

709

⟨TELEPHUS⟩

Would you have sat at home? No, far from it!

EURIPIDES

710

⟨ΤΗΛΕΦΟΣ⟩
τὸν δὲ Τήλεφον
οὐκ οἰόμεσθα;

Aristophanes, *Acharnians* 555–6 with Schol.; paraphrased by Aelius Aristides, *Oration* 2.59

711

⟨ΤΗΛΕΦΟΣ⟩
εἶτα δὴ θυμούμεθα
παθόντες οὐδὲν μᾶλλον ἢ δεδρακότες;

Schol. on Aristophanes, *Women at the Thesmophoria* 518–9

712

ἅπασαν ἡμῶν τὴν πόλιν κακορροθεῖ.

Aristophanes, *Acharnians* 577 with Schol.

**712a

οὗτος σὺ τολμᾷς πτωχὸς ὢν λέγειν τάδε;

Aristophanes, *Acharnians* 577b, attributed to *Telephus* by Bakhuyzen and van Leeuwen

713

ὦ πόλις Ἄργους, κλύεθ' οἷα λέγει;

Aristophanes, *Knights* 813 and *Wealth* 601, both with Schol.

TELEPHUS

710

⟨TELEPHUS⟩

. . . and do we not think Telephus (would say the same)?[1]

[1] The completion of the sentence is inferred from the Scholia to Aelius Aristides.

711

⟨TELEPHUS⟩

And then we are angry, when we have no more suffered (harm) than done it?

712

He is vilifying our whole city.[1]

[1] In *Acharnians* the Chorus-leader reacts to Dicaeopolis' speech with these words, and Lamachus follows with the words of F **712a. In *Telephus* perhaps the Chorus-leader (the 'city' being Argos) followed by Agamemnon?

**712a

You—do you, a beggar, dare to say these things?

713

O city of Argos, do you hear what he is saying?[1]

[1] Metre anapaestic, context and speaker debated: either a reaction to Telephus' speech (by the Chorus?), or Agamemnon attacking Menelaus as in F 722–3 (also anapaestic).

EURIPIDES

714

<ΤΗΛΕΦΟΣ>

τί γάρ με πλοῦτος ὠφελεῖ †νόσον;
σμίκρ᾽ ἂν θέλοιμι καὶ καθ᾽ ἡμέραν ἔχων
ἄλυπος οἰκεῖν μᾶλλον ἢ πλουτῶν νοσεῖν.

Crantor fr. 7a Mette in Sextus Empiricus, *Against the Experts*
11.56; vv. 2–3: Stobaeus 4.31.64 and 4.33.11

1 νοσοῦντά γε Fabricius: ⟨ x – ∪ x ⟩ τί γάρ με πλοῦτος
ὠφελεῖ; Austin (νόσον deleted by Wilamowitz)

715

οὐκ ἄρ᾽ Ὀδυσσεύς ἐστιν αἱμύλος μόνος·
χρεία διδάσκει, κἂν βραδύς τις ᾖ, σοφόν.

Stobaeus 3.29.55; v. 1: Plutarch, *Lysander* 20.5; v. 2 conflated
with *Stheneboea* F 663 is cited as proverbial in Suda χ 465, per-
haps with attribution to Menander's *Man from Carthage* (fr. 229
Koerte)

716

<ΤΗΛΕΦΟΣ>

σὺ δ᾽ εἶκ᾽ ἀνάγκῃ καὶ θεοῖσι μὴ μάχου·
τόλμα δὲ προσβλέπειν με καὶ φρονήματος
χάλα. τά τοι μέγιστα πολλάκις θεὸς
ταπείν᾽ ἔθηκε καὶ συνέστειλεν πάλιν.
traces of two more lines in the papyrus

vv. 1–4: Stobaeus 3.22.32; vv. 2–6 (2–3 letters of each) P. Oxy.
2460 (= F 727a) fr. 32

TELEPHUS

714

<TELEPHUS>

What help does wealth give me †(for?) my ailment†?[1] I would rather have the little I need for my daily life and live without pain, than be wealthy and afflicted by illness.

[1] The sense is clear despite minor textual difficulty (an incomplete verse, slightly incoherent syntax). With v. 2 compare *Hecuba* 317–8.

715

Not only Odysseus, then, is a crafty speaker. Need makes a man clever, even if he is slow to learn.[1]

[1] A comment on Telephus' eloquence, probably while still disguised.

716

<TELEPHUS>

(to Achilles)

But you, yield to necessity and do not fight the gods; bring yourself to face me, and temper your pride! Often god lowers the mightiest and puts them back in their place.

717

τί δ', ὦ τάλας, σοὶ τῷδε πείθεσθαι μέλει;

Schol. on Aristophanes, *Acharnians* 454

σοὶ . . . μέλει Schol. Lh: σὺ . . . μέλλεις Schol. ΕΓ (μέλεις Wilamowitz)

718

ὥρα σε θυμοῦ κρείσσονα γνώμην ἔχειν.

Stobaeus 3.20.36

719

Ἕλληνες ὄντες βαρβάροις δουλεύσομεν;

Clement of Alexandria, *Miscellanies* 6.2.16.5; adapted by Thrasymachus 85 B 2 DK and [Callisthenes], *History of Alexander the Great* rec. β 1.25

720

κακῶς ὄλοιτ' ἄν· ἄξιον γὰρ Ἑλλάδι.

Schol. on Aristophanes, *Acharnians* 8

721

κακός τίς ἐστι προξένῳ σοι χρώμενος.

Ammonius, *On similar and different words* 411

722

⟨ΑΓΑΜΕΜΝΩΝ⟩
ἴθ' ὅποι χρῄζεις· οὐκ ἀπολοῦμαι
τῆς σῆς Ἑλένης οὕνεκα.

Schol. and Tzetzes on Aristophanes, *Clouds* 891

717

Why, poor fool, do you trouble to obey him?[1]

[1] Often speculatively attributed to Achilles objecting to Telephus' leadership.

718

It is time for you to let your mind rule your temper.[1]

[1] Perhaps Odysseus persuading Achilles to help Telephus.

719

Shall we who are Greeks be slaves to barbarians?[1]

[1] More likely Menelaus insisting on pursuing the war against Troy (cf. *Iphigenia at Aulis* 1400–1) than Agamemnon or Achilles questioning Telephus' leadership.

720

He (*or* she) may perish miserably; Greece deserves this.[1]

[1] Context unknown; the reference might be to Telephus, or Paris, or Helen.

721

A bad man is using you as a sponsor.[1]

[1] Probably a warning to Agamemnon (or Clytemnestra?) about Telephus.

722

⟨AGAMEMNON⟩
(*to Menelaus*)
Go where you want—I'll not die for your Helen's sakè!

723

⟨ΑΓΑΜΕΜΝΩΝ⟩

Σπάρτην ἔλαχες, κείνην κόσμει·
τὰς δὲ Μυκήνας ἡμεῖς ἰδίᾳ.

Stobaeus 3.39.9; v. 1 was often used or paraphrased as a proverb, e.g. Cicero, *Letters to Atticus* 4.6.2 (cf. 1.20.3), Plutarch, *Moralia* 472e, 602b

724

πριστοῖσι λόγχης θέλγεται ῥινήμασιν.

Plutarch, *Moralia* 46f

727

⟨ΤΗΛΕΦΟΣ?⟩

ἀπέπτυσ᾽ ἐχθροῦ φωτὸς ἔχθιστον τέκος.

Schol. on Aristophanes, *Peace* 528

727a

fr. 1   *Centres of iambic trimeters (1–6), then ends of anapaestic dimeters (7–11):*

   ] .παντλεῖν εἰτι[
   ]τοί[ν]υν πάντες [
   ]εν κατ᾽ ἄστυ· μη[
   ].... μηδεν..[
5   ἰ]δόντες δ᾽ αὐτὸν ενφ[
   ]μας οἷς μέλει τ[

P. Oxy. 2460, ed. J. Rea (1962) after Handley–Rea (1957); cf. Mette (1963), Austin, *NFE* 75–80, Preiser 143–61

723

⟨AGAMEMNON⟩
(to Menelaus)

You inherited Sparta—govern her! I possess Mycenae in my own right.

724

It is soothed by filings shaved from the spearhead.[1]

[1] A 'magical' cure for Telephus' wound insofar as only the filings from Achilles' spearhead could effect it; but the healing properties of metal filings are noted in later medical texts. For discussion of the cure and traditions about it see Preiser, commentary and *RhM* 144 (2001), 277–86, arguing that Euripides invented this method for the healing by Achilles. A few later art works depict the healing by the touch of the spearpoint (*LIMC* 'Telephos' nos. 86–8) or by filings from it (no. 85); perhaps also a lost 5th c. painting by Parrhasios (no. 84).

727

⟨TELEPHUS?⟩

I spurn the most hated child of a hated father.[1]

[1] Probably Telephus backing his threat to kill Orestes.

727a

fr. 1: *end of a speech calling for a search, then self-exhortation by the Chorus to pursue it?*

. . . to relieve(?) . . . now then, all . . . through the town . . . nothing/no one . . . and on seeing him . . . . . . us/you to   5
whom . . . is/are of concern . . .

---

1 ἀπαντλεῖν or ἐπαντλεῖν Rea   6 ἡ]μᾶς or ὑ]μᾶς Rea

⟨ΧΟΡΟΣ?⟩

]..[ ]τερον πάντες ται[

]. πόλιν μαστεύωμ[εν

].ις; τί δοκεῖ; πῶ[ς ἂν

10 τε]λέσαιμεν ἄρισ[τα;

]μασ[τ]εύειν χρή [

fr. 9 *remains of three lines, then beginning of a speech:*

45 εἶ]έν· τί δή σοι χρησ[

]ωλον βολαίας τη[

π]ότερά σ' ἔτρωσαν .[

ἤ] τις φανεῖ τοῦδ' απα[

]..[....]τε τὸν βα[λόντα

50]ν φησὶν ἰᾶ[σθαι

46 κ]ῶλον or χ]ωλὸν Rea

fr. 10 *remains of one line*

⟨ΑΓΑΜΕΜΝΩΝ?⟩

τί οὖν σ' ἀπείργε[ι

⟨ΤΗΛΕΦΟΣ?⟩

τὸ μὴ προδοῦναι [

⟨ΑΓΑΜΕΜΝΩΝ?⟩

ο]ὔ [π]ού τις ἐχ[θ]ρῶν [

⟨ΤΗΛΕΦΟΣ?⟩

55 ο]ὐκ οἶδα· δει[μ]αίν[ω δὲ

⟨ΑΓΑΜΕΜΝΩΝ?⟩

κλαίω[ν] πλανήσεις [

212

‹CHORUS?›

. . . let all of us . . . seek (him throughout?) the city . . . What
seems best? How might we best accomplish . . . . . . (we) 10
must seek . . .

fr. 9: *Agamemnon(?) questions Telephus about his need for
healing:*

Well, then; what . . . to you . . . . . . leg (*or* lamed) . . . (from/ 45
of?) . . . netted (*or* struck?) . . . Did they wound you . . . or
will someone reveal . . . of this . . . the one who struck
(you?) . . . says . . . to heal . . . 50

fr. 10: *perhaps from the subsequent dialogue:*

remains of one line

‹AGAMEMNON?›

So what prevents you . . . ?

‹TELEPHUS?›

Not to betray . . .

‹AGAMEMNON?›

Surely no enemy . . . ?

‹TELEPHUS?›

I do not know; but I fear . . . 55

‹AGAMEMNON?›

You will suffer for it if you deceive (us) . . .

EURIPIDES

⟨ΤΗΛΕΦΟΣ?⟩

κ]α[ὶ] σεμνὸς ̣.[

remains of two lines

⟨ΑΓΑΜΕΜΝΩΝ?⟩

60 ἧσσόν γ᾽ ἂν οὖν [

⟨ΤΗΛΕΦΟΣ?⟩

Ἀγαμεμνον[

⟨ΑΓΑΜΕΜΝΩΝ?⟩

βλ[ά]πτειν τὸ κο[ιν]ὸν ̣[

⟨ΤΗΛΕΦΟΣ?⟩

ο]ὐκ οἶσθ᾽ Ὀδυσσ[

⟨ΑΓΑΜΕΜΝΩΝ?⟩

ἀλ]λ᾽ ἐν χρόνω[ι ̣] ̣ ̣αισ[

⟨ΤΗΛΕΦΟΣ?⟩

65 *remains of one line*

⟨ΑΓΑΜΕΜΝΩΝ?⟩

]μω[̣] ἀκοῦσαι καιρὸς [

⟨ΤΗΛΕΦΟΣ?⟩

̣ ̣]δ᾽ ἀ[γ]ρίου του φωτὸς[

remains of four more lines

Speaker changes are visible for vv. 52–6, 59–61, 63, possible but not preserved elsewhere

fr. 13 *beginning of one line*

214

<TELEPHUS?>

(And) . . . arrogant . . .

remains of two lines

<AGAMEMNON?>
. . . would . . . less, no doubt, in that case . . .   60

<TELEPHUS?>

Agamemnon . . .

<AGAMEMNON?>

To harm the common . . .

<TELEPHUS?>
Do you not know . . . Odysseus . . . ?

<AGAMEMNON?>

(But) in time. . . .

<TELEPHUS?>
remains of one line   65

<AGAMEMNON?>
. . . (it is) time to listen . . .

<TELEPHUS?>
. . . (from/of?>) a savage man . . .

remains of four more lines

fr. 13: *probably dialogue from near the end of the play:*

beginning of one line

⟨ΑΧΙΛΛΕΥΣ?⟩

95 τ]έχνῃ γεμ[

⟨ΤΗΛΕΦΟΣ?⟩

ὅ]μως δ' ὀνη.[

⟨ΑΧΙΛΛΕΥΣ?⟩

οὐ]κ ἀξιώσω [

⟨ΤΗΛΕΦΟΣ?⟩

ὦ] φίλτατ', ὦ .[

⟨ΑΧΙΛΛΕΥΣ?⟩

στ]είχοντί νυ[ν

⟨ΤΗΛΕΦΟΣ?⟩

100 ἰδ]ού· πορευο[

⟨ΑΧΙΛΛΕΥΣ?⟩

φρ]ουρεῖτέ νυ[ν
trace of one more line

Speaker changes are visible for 95, 98, possible but not pre-
served elsewhere

100 πορευό[μεσθα, πορεύο[μαι?   101 or φρ]ούρει τε

**727b

Dialogue trimeters (1–15), then anapaests:

⟨ΟΔΥΣΣΕΥΣ?⟩

remains of two lines
            ]ς Τήλε[φ].ς ταπε[
    ] να[ύτα]ις καὶ κ[υ]βερνή[ταις
5   *remains of one line*

216

⟨ACHILLES?⟩

By skill . . .   95

⟨TELEPHUS?⟩

But nevertheless . . .

⟨ACHILLES?⟩

I shall not think fit . . .

⟨TELEPHUS?⟩

⟨O⟩ dearest friend, O . . .

⟨ACHILLES?⟩

. . . (for him?) as he goes, now . . .

⟨TELEPHUS?⟩

Look, we are (*or* I am) going . . .   100

⟨ACHILLES?⟩

Keep watch (over him?), now . . .

**727b[1]

⟨ODYSSEUS?⟩

. . . (*remains of two lines*) . . . Telephus . . . (to/for?) the sail-
ors and steersmen . . . (*remains of one line*) . . . . . . let him go   5

---

[1] Ascription of this fragment to *Telephus* is doubtful, division
of vv. 1–15 between two speakers—and their identification—also
conjectural (vv. 16–19 are anapaestic and so assignable to a cho-
rus). The content suggests this may be the end of a scene in which
Telephus agreed to guide the Greek fleet in return for his healing.

EURIPIDES

]μεν [σύ]μβουλο[ς] ἐλθέτω.[
] γὰρ ἡμῶν ὡς ὁ [μῦ]θος εσται[
π]ρῶτα καὶ νόμ[ο]ις Ἑλληνικ[οῖς
]υσι χρῆσθαι τ[ῆ]ς τύχης αμ[
10   ]οισιν ἐμπε[σ]εῖν· ἀστὸς γὰ[ρ] ὡς
] κηρύκειον .[.] δάκνει πλέον·
]κοις ἂν τῆσδ᾽ ἀφ᾽ ἑσπέρας γνάθο[ς
]ηνεθωμεθ᾽ [ἀ]μνηστεῖν σε χρή.

⟨ΤΗΛΕΦΟΣ?⟩

]τα· σοὶ δ᾽ ὑπεξελεῖν πάρα,
15   εἴ τι] μὴ πρόσχο[ρδ]ον, ὡς ἀνὴρ μόλῃ.

⟨ΧΟΡΟΣ?⟩

]υν τούτοις τ[ῷ]ι μὲν ξείνῳ
]ιν πομποὺ[ς] παρατασσέσθω·
καὶ να]ύαρχός τις [ἀν]ὴρ ἔσται·
].κτουτ.[...].ος ἐγὼ πᾶν

P. Rylands 482, ed. C. H. Roberts with D. L. Page (1938); cf.
T. B. L. Webster, *Bulletin of the Rylands Library* 22 (1938), 543–
9; B. Snell, *Gnomon* 15 (1939), 538–40; Page, *GLP* 140–5 (no.
21); Handley–Rea 20–2; Mette (1963); Austin, *NFE* 80–1.

6 σὺ] μὲν . . . ἐλθὲ Roberts–Page: ἐλθέτω Snell
11 κηρύκειον Roberts–Page: κηρυκεῖον P. Ryl.   then e.g. ο[ὐ,
ο[ῦ, ε[ἰ   12 οὐ . . . δά]κοι σ᾽ ἂν . . . γνάθο[ς (e.g.) Snell
(γνάθο[ις Collard)   13 τάδ᾽] ἦν ε⟨ὖ⟩θωμεθ᾽ Roberts–Page
14 speaker change suggested by Snell (at 13 Webster, at 12 Mette)

(*or imperative* you go) (as?) a counsellor . . . For our . . . as the report (*or* saying) goes . . . first, and to use Greek laws . . . fortune, to fall upon . . . ; for as a citizen . . . the herald's staff . . . (it?) afflicts (you?) more . . . (its?) jaw[2] would not (afflict you further?) from this evening . . . [3] you should (not?) forget . . .

‹TELEPHUS?›

. . . and it is up to you to remove . . . (if anything is) not in harmony, so that the man may come.

‹CHORUS?›

. . . (for *or* with?) these (for?) the foreigner . . . let him appoint escorts; and he will be a kind of admiral . . . I . . all . . .

[2] Probably a metaphor for Telephus' festering wound; cf. *Medea* 1201. Collard's 'with its jaws' is also possible. [3] The first eight letters of the Greek text make no sense. The first editors' correction gives 'if we arrange (these things) well'.

EURIPIDES

727c

col. i   *a few line-ends*

col. ii   ἢ Νότ[ου ἢ] Ζεφύροιο δεινὰ

26   πέμψ[ει Τ]ρῳάδας ἀκτάς,

σύ τε π[ηδ]αλίῳ παρεδρεύω[ν

φράσει[ς τῷ] κατὰ πρῷραν

εὐθὺς Ἰλ[ίο]υ πόρον

30   Ἀτρείδα[ις] ἰδέσθαι.

σὲ γὰρ Τε[γ]εᾶτις ἡμῖν,

Ἑλλάς, οὐχὶ Μυσία, τίκτει

ναύταν σύν τινι δὴ θεῶν

καὶ πεμπτῆρ' ἁλίων ἐρετμῶν.

ΑΧΙΛΛΕΥΣ

35   μῶν καὶ σὺ καινὸς ποντίας ἀπὸ χθονὸς

ἥκεις, Ὀδυσσεῦ; ποῦ 'στι σύλλογος φίλων;

τί μέλλετ'; οὐ χρῆν ἥσυχον κεῖσθαι π[ό]δα.

ΟΔΥΣΣΕΥΣ

δοκεῖ στρατεύειν καὶ μέλει τοῖς ἐν τέλει

τάδ'· ἐν δέοντι δ' ἦλθες, ὦ παῖ Πηλέως.

ΑΧΙΛΛΕΥΣ

40   οὐ μὴν ἐπ' ἀκταῖς γ' ἐστὶ κωπήρης στρατός,

οὔτ' οὖν ὁπλίτης ἐξετάζεται παρών.

ΟΔΥΣΣΕΥΣ

ἀλλ' αὐτίκα· σπεύδειν γὰρ ἐν καιρῷ χρεών.

TELEPHUS

727c

⟨CHORUS⟩

col. i: *a few line-ends*

col. ii: . . . the formidable (breath?) of Notus or Zephyrus[1]   25
will bring (our fleet) to Trojan shores; and you (i.e.
Telephus), stationed at the steering-oar, will indicate for
the prow-man's observation a course that will take the sons
of Atreus direct to Troy. For a Tegean mother, Greek not   30
Mysian, bore you to be—surely with some god's aid—a
sailor and a guide for our oared ships.

ACHILLES

Are you too newly arrived here from your island home,   35
Odysseus?[2] Where are our comrades gathered? Why do
you all delay? You ought not to be lying idle here.

ODYSSEUS

We have agreed to start the campaign, and those in charge
are seeing to it. You have come just at the right moment,
son of Peleus.

ACHILLES

And yet our rowing force is not on the shore, nor indeed is   40
our infantry present and being inspected.

ODYSSEUS

It will be soon enough; one should press on when the time
is right.

[1] I.e. south and west winds, 'formidable' because of their
strength and divine origin. Some editors prefer Murray's 'squall of
Notus and Zephyrus'.   [2] Achilles arriving from Scyros as-
sumes that Odysseus has just arrived from Ithaca.

EURIPIDES

ΑΧΙΛΛΕΥΣ

αἰεί ποτ᾽ ἐστὲ νωχελεῖς καὶ μέλλετε,
ῥήσεις θ᾽ ἕκαστος μυρίας καθήμενος
45 λέγει, τὸ δ᾽ ἔργον [ο]ὐδαμοῦ περαίνεται.
κἀ[γ]ὼ μέν, ὡς ὁρᾶ[τ]ε, δρᾶν ἕτοιμος ὢν
ἥκω, στρατός τε Μ[υρ]μιδῶν, καὶ πλεύσ[ομαι
τὰ [τ]ῶν Ἀτρειδ[ῶν οὐ μένων] μελλήμ[ατα.

col. iii *speaker-notations indicate further dialogue between
Odysseus and Achilles*

P. Berlin 9908, ed. U. von Wilamowitz-Moellendorff and W.
Schubart (1907); cf. A. C. Pearson, *The Fragments of Sophocles*
(Cambridge, 1917), I.97–100; Page, *GLP* 12–15 (no. 3); Handley–
Rea (1957), 11–12; Mette (1963); Austin, *NFE* 81–2; Diggle,
TrGFS 133–4; Preiser 162–4. Attributed by Wilamowitz to Soph-
ocles' *Gathering of the Achaeans*, but identified with P. Oxy. 2460
(= F 727a) frs. 17–20 and hence with *Telephus* by Handley–Rea

25 δεινὰ P. Berl.: δίνα Murray

ACHILLES

You people are always sluggish, always delaying; each of you sits and makes a thousand speeches, while nothing gets done to finish the job. For my part, as you can see,[3] I have   45 come prepared for action, and my Myrmidon force with me; and I shall sail (without waiting on) Atreus' sons' delays.

col. iii: *speaker notations remain from continuing dialogue between Odysseus and Achilles*

[3] This suggests that Achilles was costumed in armour.

TEMENIDAE ('SONS OF TEMENUS') *and* TEMENUS

H. Van Looy in ed. Budé VIII.3.133–54. See also under test. i–iv below.

Webster 252–5; L. di Gregorio, *CCC* 8 (1987), 279–318; A. Harder in *Fragmenta Dramatica* 117–35.

Temenus, a descendant of Heracles' son Hyllus, was tradi-tionally the leader of the Return of the Heraclidae (cf. In-troductions to Archelaus *and* Cresphontes*). The myths of the Return, the division of the Peloponnese, and the subsequent history of these dynasties were continually re-invented to suit the interests of competing Greek states, and are known to us largely through summaries in late sources such as Diodorus 4.57–8, Apollodorus 2.8.2–5 and Pausanias 2.18.6–8, 4.3.3–5. Several episodes concerning Temenus and his sons might have provided dramatic mate-rial for Euripides, including the Return itself, the division of the Peloponnese, a further war between Temenus and Orestes' heir Tisamenus (based in Achaea after his expul-sion from Mycenae by the Heraclidae: Pausanias 2.38.1), conflicts between Temenus and his sons (Diodorus 7.13, Nicolaus FGrH 90 F 30, Pausanias 2.19.1), their abduction and accidental killing of their sister Hyrnetho (Pausanias 2.28), events leading to the exile of Archelaus (see Intro-*

225

duction to Archelaus*), and the establishment of Temenid kingdoms at Sicyon and Epidaurus.*

The largely gnomic fragments give little indication of our plays' subjects, except that some prominence is given to the division of the Peloponnese (F 727e, 730?, 742?), military matters (F 728, 731, 732?, 734, 743, 744), and easily related topics such as patriotism, fortune, nobility, toil and death. The papyrus hypothesis fragments (connected with the plays in question by reasonably secure inferences) pose more problems than they solve. Test. i and ii both describe the division and must refer to different plays, but test. i at least seems to contain background information rather than dramatic events (F 727e is probably prologue material of a similar nature). Test. iii probably describes Tisamenus preparing for a campaign, and test. iv gives more about possibly the same campaign, but it is not clear whether this is the original invasion of the Heraclidae or some later war. Test. iv appears to describe an embarkation of Peloponnesian forces against the Heraclidae which is otherwise entirely unknown—a difficulty addressed by Luppe's adjustments transferring the embarkation to the Heraclidae themselves (see notes to test. iv below: it seems likely enough that the battle in question is the one that decided the Return itself, and that Temenus' declaration about his kingship is made in anticipation of this success; the prominence thus given to Archelaus is consistent with test. vi). The mention of Archelaus in both test. i and test. iv is notable but hard to interpret. Also notable, as Harder points out, is the absence of any trace of the story of Hyrnetho, which Webster took to be the subject of Temenidae.

Harder inferred tentatively that Temenus is represented in test. ii (and F 727e) and told the story of the division of the Peloponnese and the collusion of Temenus

with Cresphontes which gave the latter Messenia, while
Temenidae, *represented in test. i and iii–iv (together mak-*
ing an unusually long hypothesis), concerned a later con-
flict between Temenus and Tisamenus. She argues against
taking test. iii as the beginning of a hypothesis (as its word-
ing suggested to Turner and others). Luppe, on the other
hand, accepts test. iii as a beginning and infers that three
different plays are represented by (respectively) test. i, test.
ii, and test. iii–iv (the last concerning the Return itself), the
additional play perhaps being a second Temenidae. *Scul-*
lion, arguing for the possibility that the two plays formed a
trilogy with the late Archelaus *(see our Introduction to*
Archelaus), *supposes that* Temenus *was concerned with*
the conquest of the Peloponnese and the award of Argos to
Archelaus, *and* Temenidae *with Archelaus' conflict with*
his brothers which led to his exile. All of this remains un-
certain and is unlikely to be resolved without new evi-
dence.

Brief fragments: Temenus *test. ii with F 741a (= P. Oxy.*
2455 fr. 8, a hypothesis heading naming the play and giv-
ing the word 'slain in war' or simply 'military' from its first
line); also Temenus *F 747 'auspiciously', F 748 'distribu-*
tion', F 749 'unfortified', F 750 (as Peliades F 614) 'a con-
cern' or 'an obligation'?, F 751 'a spasm of pain', F 752
'Chalyboi' (= 'Chalybes', the Pontic people). Other ascrip-
tions: F 989, F 995.

There is no external evidence for the date of either play.
Metrical evidence favours a date after 423 for Temeni-
dae but offers no guidance for Temenus. *If the two plays*
formed a trilogy with the Archelaus *(see above), they will*
of course have shared its late date.

No other poetic or artistic treatment of this group of sto-
ries is known.

ΤΗΜΕΝΙΔΑΙ or ΤΗΜΕΝΟΣ

test. i (Hypothesis)

remains of two lines

κεδ.ν[...] ἡμιόνου μονοφθάλ[μου

ὑπέμνησεν χρησμοῦ τὸν Τήμ[ε]ν[ον, ὃς

5 ἐκέλευσεν τῆς εἰς Ἄργος κ[αθό]δου λαβεῖ[ν

α]ὐτοὺς [ὁδηγ]ὸν τὸν τρ[ιό]φθαλμον. δι[α-

μερίσα]ντος δὲ τοῦ Ὀξύλου [τ]ὴν Πελο-

πόννησον εἰς] μέρη τρία, τ[ὴν μ]ὲν Ἀργεί-

αν Τήμενος ἀπ]ῄτησ[ε]ν [ὁ] πρεσ[βύ]τατος,

10 τὴν δὲ] Μεσσηνίαν ἔ[λα]βεν Κρ[εσφόν-

της   ] τὴν δ[ὲ] Λακ[ω-

νίαν οἱ Ἀριστο]δήμ[ου] παῖδες· ἀδικη-

remains of three more lines including 14 π]αίδων,

15 Ἀρχέλαον

P. Oxy. 2455 fr. 9, ed. E. Turner (1962); cf. Austin, *NFE* 12; A.
Harder, *ZPE* 35 (1979), 11–12 and *Euripides' Kresphontes and
Archelaos* (Leiden, 1985), 288–9, cf. H. Hofmann, A. Harder

228

TEMENIDAE ('SONS OF TEMENUS') *or* TEMENUS

test. i (Hypothesis)

. . . *(remains of two lines)* . . . on a one-eyed ass reminded Temenus of the oracle which had told them to take as their (guide) for the return to Argos 'the Three-eyed One'.[1] And 5 when Oxylus divided the Peloponnese into three parts, Temenus the eldest (i.e. of the Heraclidae) requested the Argolid, and Cresphontes took Messenia, and the sons of Aris- 10 todemus Laconia . . . treated unjustly *(form and syntax uncertain)* . . . *(remains of one line)* . . . of the sons . . . Archelaus . . .

---

[1] The Heraclidae recognized their 'three-eyed' guide when they met Oxylus riding an ass or horse that was blind in one eye (alternatively, he himself was blind in one eye). He was said to have been re-established in his ancestral kingdom of Elis in return for his assistance to the Heraclidae (Strabo 8.3.33).

(eds.), *Fragmenta Dramatica* (Göttingen, 1991), 120–1; W. Luppe, *Prometheus* 13 (1987), 193–8, 202–3; van Rossum-Steenbeek 216

test. ii (Hypothesis)

Σ]πάρτην ...[.]νδ[

]μενος δὲ παρ[ὰ] τῶν [

]το.(.) Τήμενος μερι.[

εἰλή]φει· παρ᾽ ἑκόντων τ[

5   ]νος ἐκλήρωσεν· ἔλαχεν [δὲ

Κρεσφόντ]ης τὴν Μεσσηνίαν· τοῖς [δὲ

Ἀριστοδήμου] παισὶν Ἀγασθένει καὶ Ὀρ[

    ]τη[   ]εν τῷ κλήρῳ

remains of two more lines

P. Oxy. 2455 fr. 10, ed. Turner; cf. Austin, *NFE* 98; Harder (1979), 12–13 and (1985), 279, cf. (1991), 121 (all under test. i above); W. Luppe, *Prometheus* 13 (1987), 198–203; van Rossum-Steenbeek 216

3–4 Τήμενος μερίσ[ας τὴν χώραν ἣν εἰλή]φει Luppe (μερίζ[ων Kannicht)   4–5 τ[ὸ Ἄργος ἑλόμε]νος Luppe

test. iii (Hypothesis)

remains of three lines

    ]νης υἱὸς ὢν Ὀρέσ[του

5   Ἀγαμέ]μνονος· βασιλεὺς [

remains of one line

    ]ων ἔγνω τὴν πε[

    ]θουμένην· συμβούλου[

        ] τοῖς Τ[η]μένου παισ[ὶ]ν [

TEMENIDAE *or* TEMENUS

test. ii (Hypothesis)

. . . Sparta . . . from the . . . Temenus (dividing up the country which he had captured, having taken Argos for himself)[1] from . . . with their consent, cast lots; (and Cresphontes) drew 5 Messenia, while to (Aristodemus') sons Agasthenes and Or- . . .[2] by the lot . . . *(remains of two more lines)* . . .

[1] See apparatus opposite.   [2] Usually the sons of Aristodemus are Eurysthenes and Procles.

test. iii (Hypothesis)

. . . *(remains of three lines)* . . . being the son (of) Orestes . . . of (Agame)mnon[1] . . . king . . . . . . *(remains of one line)* . . . learned 5 that the . . . was being . . . [2] . . . adviser(s) . . . for the sons of

[1] Perhaps 'Tisamenus, being the son of Orestes and grandson of Agamemnon' (Luppe).   [2] Perhaps 'that the Peloponnese was now being devastated' (Turner), or 'that the area around Argos was being restored' (Luppe).

P. Oxy. 2455 fr. 11, ed. Turner; cf. Austin, *NFE* 97–8; Harder (1979), 13–14, cf. (1991), 121–2 (both under test. i above); W. Luppe, *Acta Antiqua Academiae Scientiarum Hungaricae* 32 (1989), 243–8 and *APF* 41 (1995), 25–33; van Rossum-Steenbeek 217

4–5 Τ(ε)ισαμε]νὸς υἱὸς ὢν Ὀρέσ[του, ὑϊδοῦς δὲ Ἀγα-μέ]μνονος Luppe   7–8 τὴν Πε[λόποννησον πορ]θουμέ-νην Turner (ἤδη πορ]θουμένην Kannicht): τὴν πε[ρὶ (τὸ) Ἄργος χώραν ὀρ]θουμένην Luppe

10   ]εν κατάσκοπον εἰς Σπάρτ[ην

Μ]εσσήνην πῶς ἔχει τὰ τη[

]ν πολυπραγμονησα[

ε]ὐτυχούντων συ[

]ωκα· φαύλως δὲ [

15   ]. συμμαχ[

remains of two more lines

10 ἀπέστειλ]εν (e.g.) Diggle

test. iv (Hypothesis)

οὗτοι μὲν οὖν βιασάμενοι τὸν πατέρα

τοῖς Ἡρακλέους παισὶν συγκατελοχίσ-

θησαν. ‹ἀν›αβιβασάμενοι δὲ τὸ τῶν

Πελοποννησίων στράτευμα ἐπ' αὐτοὺς

5 διεβίβασαν, ὧν Ὀρέστου παῖς ‹Τισαμενὸς . . . › Τήμε-

νος ὁ τῶν Ἡρακλειδῶν πρεσβύτατος

ἐκτάττων τὸ στράτευμα τὴν βασιλείαν ἔφη-

σεν παραδώσειν τ[ῷ] εἰς τὴν μάχην

P. Mich. inv. 1319, ed. E. Turner, *Papyrologica Lugduno-Batava* 17 (1968), 133–6; the text was copied twice, by different hands, on either side of the papyrus; parts of vv. 7–11 were identified with P. Oxy. 2455 fr. 107 by Harder (1979), 7–14, cf. (1985), 289–90 and (1991), 122–3 (all under test. i above); W. Luppe, *Philologus* 122 (1978), 243–8, *ZPE* 45 (1982), 15–19 and 149 (2004), 10–14; J. Rusten, *ZPE* 40 (1980), 39–42; van Rossum-Steenbeek 203

Temenus, (he dispatched) an observer to Sparta ... Messene 10
(to see) in what condition the ... were ... acting ambitiously
... prospering ... but ... poorly ... ally/allies/alliance 15
(*remains of two more lines*) ...

test. iv (Hypothesis)

Thus these, after doing violence to the father, now joined
forces with the sons of Heracles.[1] And they (i.e. the Pelo-
ponnesian leaders?) embarked the army of the Pelopon-
nesians and transported it against them, their (leader be-
ing Tisamenus) son of Orestes.[2] As Temenus, the eldest of 5
the Heraclidae was drawing up his army he declared that he
would bestow the kingship on whichever of his sons fought

---

[1] Without a context it is difficult to guess the identity of 'these'.
Luppe (2004) thinks of the sons of Aegimius assisting the Return
of the Heraclidae (cf. Kannicht, *TrGF* 5.723), although a conflict
between them and their father is otherwise unknown. The phras-
ing suggests that 'the father' may be Heracles himself, and that
'these' may be a people (rather than individuals) who, having once
been in conflict with Heracles, are now in alliance with his descen-
dants ('sons').   [2] The text is defective owing to confusion
of the names Tisamenus and Temenus. Luppe (2004) suggests
that the confusion is more widespread and that the sentence origi-
nally read: 'And they (i.e. the Heraclidae) embarked their army
and transported it against the Peloponnesians, whose (leader was
Tisamenus) son of Orestes. And as Temenus ...'

3–5 ⟨Τισαμενὸς.⟩ Τήμενος ⟨δὲ⟩ Handley in Turner: ⟨ἀν⟩α-
βιβασάμενοι δὲ τὸ στράτευμα ἐπὶ τοὺς Πελοποννησίους
διεβίβασαν, ὧν Ὀρέστου παῖς ⟨Τεισαμενὸς ἡγεμόνευεν. ὁ δὲ⟩
Τήμενος ... Luppe (2004)

EURIPIDES

ἀριστεύσαντι τῶν υἱῶν. τὸ

10 μὲν οὖν κρῖμα τῆς μάχης ἐγέ-
νετο κατὰ τοὺς Ἡρακλείδας,
ἄριστος δὲ ἐκρίνετο Ἀρχέλαος
ὁ πρεσβύτατος τῶν [[   ]]
Τημενιδ[ῶν]· π[ ]δ

13 erasure uncertainly inferred: τῶν δ[ὲ ἄλλω]ν Luppe

test. vi

ἐπεὶ διὰ τίνα αἰτίαν . . . οὐδ' Εὐριπίδου κατηγορῶ τῷ μὲν
Ἀρχελάῳ περιτεθεικότος τὰς Τημένου πράξεις . . . ; ὅτι
πᾶς ποιητὴς ψυχαγωγίας μᾶλλον ἢ ἀληθείας ἐστὶ στο-
χαστής.

Agatharchides, *On the Red Sea* (extracts in Photius' *Library*)
1.8

727e (= 1083 N)

περὶ δὲ τῆς φύσεως τῶν τόπων καὶ τούτων καὶ τῶν
Μεσσηνιακῶν ταῦτα μὲν ἀποδεκτέον λέγοντος Εὐριπί-
δου· τὴν γὰρ Λακωνικήν φησιν ἔχειν

πολὺν μὲν ἄροτον, ἐκπονεῖν δ' οὐ ῥᾴδιον·
κοίλη γὰρ ὄρεσι περίδρομος τραχεῖά τε
δυσείσβολός τε πολεμίοις,

τὴν δὲ Μεσσηνίαν

234

best in the battle. Now the decisive moment in the battle oc-   10
curred where the Heraclidae were fighting, and Archelaus,
the eldest of Temenus' sons, was judged the best warrior . . .

test. vi

And for what reason . . . do I also not denounce Euripides for
having reassigned the exploits of Temenus to Archelaus . . . ?[1]
Because every poet aims for imaginative appeal rather than
truth.

[1] The reference may be to Archelaus' role in the battle re-
ferred to in test. iv.

727e (= 1083 N)

Concerning the nature of both this (i.e. the Laconian) and the
Messenian region one may accept the following from Euripi-
des' description. He says that Laconia has

arable land in abundance, but hard to work; for it is
set deep within encircling mountains, rough, and
hard for enemies to invade,

while Messenia is

Strabo 8.5.6; for assignment to *Temenidae* or *Temenus* see
Harder (1985), 278–9 and (1991), 134–5 (both under test. i
above)

καλλίκαρπον . . .

5   κατάρρυτόν τε μυρίοισι νάμασιν
    καὶ βουσὶ καὶ ποίμναισιν εὐβοτωτάτην,
    οὔτ' ἐν πνοαῖσι χείματος δυσχείμερον
    οὔτ' αὖ τεθρίπποις Ἡλίου θερμὴν ἄγαν·

καὶ ὑποβὰς τῶν πάλων φησίν, ὧν οἱ Ἡρακλεῖδαι περὶ
τῆς χώρας ἐποιήσαντο, τὸν μὲν πρότερον γενέσθαι

    γαίας Λακαίνης κύριον, φαύλου χθονός,

τὸν δὲ δεύτερον τῆς Μεσσήνης

10   ἀρετὴν ἐχούσης μεῖζον' ἢ λόγῳ φράσαι,

οἵαν καὶ ὁ Τυρταῖος φράζει. τὴν δὲ Λακωνικὴν καὶ τὴν
Μεσσηνίαν ὁρίζειν αὐτοῦ φήσαντος

    Παμισὸν εἰς θάλασσαν ἐξορμώμενον

οὐ συγχωρητέον, ὃς διὰ μέσης ῥεῖ τῆς Μεσσηνίας,
οὐδαμοῦ τῆς νῦν Λακωνικῆς ἁπτόμενος. οὐκ εὖ δὲ οὐδ'
ὅτι—τῆς Μεσσηνίας ὁμοίως ἐπιθαλαττιδίας οὔσης τῇ
Λακωνικῇ—φησιν αὐτὴν

    πρόσω . . . ναυτίλοισιν

εἶναι. ἀλλ' οὐδὲ τὴν Ἦλιν εὖ διορίζει·

    πρόσω δὲ βάντι ποταμὸν Ἦλις ἡ Διὸς
    γείτων κάθηται.

fruitful . . . and watered by innumerable streams,   5
rich in pasturage for cattle and flocks, neither
harshly beset by winter's winds, nor overheated by
the Sun's chariot;

and a little later he says that the first of the lots which the
Heraclidae cast for the region was

valid for the Laconian land, a poor country,

and the second for Messene

blessed with excellence beyond what words can tell,   10

as Tyrtaeus also describes it.[1] But when he says that Laconia
and Messenia are divided by

Pamisos, hurrying forth to the sea

one cannot agree, as the Pamisos flows through the middle of
Messenia, not touching what is now Laconia at any point. And
neither—given that Messenia is just as coastal as Laconia—
does he do well to say that it is

distant . . . for sailors.

And neither does he define Elis well with:

passing beyond the river one reaches Elis, which lies
close to Zeus.[2]

[1] Tyrtaeus fr. 5.3 *IEG*.   [2] I.e. to the great sanctuary of
Zeus at Olympia.

ΤΗΜΕΝΙΔΑΙ

728

φιλεῖ τοι πόλεμος οὐ πάντ᾽ εὐτυχεῖν,
ἐσθλῶν δὲ χαίρει πτώμασιν νεανιῶν,
κακοὺς δὲ μισεῖ. τῇ πόλει μὲν οὖν νόσος
τόδ᾽ ἐστί, τοῖς δὲ κατθανοῦσιν εὐκλεές.

Stobaeus 4.9.1

729

εἰκὸς δὲ παντὶ καὶ λόγῳ καὶ μηχανῇ
πατρίδος ἐρῶντας ἐκπονεῖν σωτηρίαν.

Stobaeus 3.39.1

730

ἅπασα Πελοπόννησος εὐτυχεῖ πόλις.

Pollux 9.27

731

οὐκ ἔστι κρεῖσσον ἄλλο πλὴν κρατεῖν δορί.

Stobaeus 4.10.2

TEMENIDAE
('SONS OF TEMENUS')

728

War does not usually achieve all its aims, but rejoices in the deaths of brave young men and spurns cowardly ones.[1] This is an affliction for the city, but glorious for those that have died.

[1] For the sentiment cf. Aeschylus F 100, Sophocles F 724.

729

It is to be expected that men should love their country and strive for its preservation with every kind of argument and device.

730

All the land of the Peloponnese is prosperous.[1]

[1] Cited by Pollux as an example of *polis* meaning 'land'.

731

Nothing is better than to conquer by the spear.

732

ῥώμη δέ γ᾽ ἀμαθὴς πολλάκις τίκτει βλάβην.

Stobaeus 4.13.18

733

τοῖς πᾶσιν ἀνθρώποισι κατθανεῖν μένει,
κοινὸν δ᾽ ἔχοντες αὐτὸ κοινὰ πάσχομεν
πάντες· τὸ γὰρ χρεὼν μεῖζον ἢ τὸ μὴ χρεών.

Stobaeus 4.56.29

734

ἀρετὴ δὲ κἂν θάνῃ τις οὐκ ἀπόλλυται,
ζῇ δ᾽ οὐκέτ᾽ ὄντος σώματος· κακοῖσι δὲ
ἅπαντα φροῦδα συνθανόνθ᾽ ὑπὸ χθονός.

Stobaeus 3.1.4; v. 1: Sextus Empiricus, *Against the Experts*
1.271

735

ἀσύνετος ὅστις ἐν φόβῳ μὲν ἀσθενής,
λαβὼν δὲ μικρὸν τῆς τύχης φρονεῖ μέγα.

Stobaeus 3.4.10

736

ὡς σκαιὸς ἀνὴρ καὶ ξένοισιν ἄξενος
καὶ μνημονεύων οὐδὲν ὧν ἐχρῆν φίλον.
σπάνιον δ᾽ ἄρ᾽ ἦν θανοῦσιν ἀσφαλεῖς φίλοι,
κἂν ὁμόθεν ὦσι· τὸ γὰρ ἔχειν πλέον κρατεῖ

732

Yet strength without intelligence often breeds damage.

733

Death waits for every man; that is our common lot, and all of us suffer it in common. What is fated is greater than what is not fated.

734

Virtue does not perish even if a man dies, but lives on when his body is no more. With cowards everything dies and is lost beneath the earth.[1]

[1] For the sentiment cf. *Meleager* F 518 with note.

735

It's a foolish man who is feeble when he's afraid, but arrogant when he gets a little good fortune.[1]

[1] Cf. *Peliades* F 608.

736

How uncouth the man is, and inhospitable to his guests, remembering none of the things a friend should remember! But friends who stay loyal to the dead are a rarity, it seems, even if they are from the same family; for greed is

5 τῆς εὐσεβείας· ἡ δ᾽ ἐν ὀφθαλμοῖς χάρις
   ἀπόλωλ᾽, ὅταν τις ἐκ δόμων ἀνὴρ θάνῃ.

Stobaeus 4.58.6–7, giving vv. 1–4 as from *Temenidae*, then vv.
5–6 separately as from Euripides; editors either print vv. 1–2 and
3–6 separately (Grotius) or vv. 1–6 all together (Nauck).

737

καλόν γ᾽ ἀληθὴς κἀτενὴς παρρησία.

Stobaeus 3.13.2

738

πολλοὶ γεγῶτες ἄνδρες οὐκ ἔχουσ᾽ ὅπως
δείξουσιν αὐτοὺς τῶν κακῶν ἐξουσίᾳ.

Stobaeus 4.42.11

739

φεῦ φεῦ, τὸ φῦναι πατρὸς εὐγενοῦς ἄπο
ὅσην ἔχει φρόνησιν ἀξίωμά τε.
κἂν γὰρ πένης ὢν τυγχάνῃ, χρηστὸς γεγὼς
τιμὴν ἔχει τιν᾽, ἀναμετρούμενος δέ πως
5 τὸ τοῦ πατρὸς γενναῖον †ὠφελεῖ τρόπῳ†.

Stobaeus 4.29.41

stronger than duty, and the respect a man has face to face is   5
gone once he has died and departed from his home.[1]

> [1] Possibly two fragments (see apparatus opposite); but vv. 1–2
> alone are hardly relevant to the topic of Stobaeus' chapter, 'That
> most people are quickly forgotten after their death'.

737

Honest and direct plain speaking is a fine thing indeed.

738

Many fine men have no way of proving themselves, be-
cause of the power wielded by worthless ones.

739

Ah, what pride and worth does birth from a well-born fa-
ther bring! Even if a man is poor, he has some honour if he
is of reputable stock, and by recollecting, as it were, his fa-
ther's nobility †he is of use to his behaviour†.[1]

> [1] The end is incoherent, but the sense of the whole is illus-
> trated by Aristotle, *Rhetoric* 1390b14–21, where it is observed
> that a well-born man will naturally want to gain more honour
> (*timē*) than he has inherited from his forebears, and will look down
> on those of his contemporaries who only match his own forebears
> in honour (cf. 'pride' in v. 1 here). For similar wording cf. *Auge* F
> 274, and for the thought in vv. 1–4 *Archelaus* F 232, and F 1066.

EURIPIDES

740

⟨ΧΟΡΟΣ?⟩

ἦλθεν δ᾽
ἐπὶ χρυσόκερων ἔλαφον, μεγάλων
ἄθλων ἕνα δεινὸν ὑποστάς,
κατ᾽ ἔναυλ᾽ ὀρέων ἀβάτους ἐπιὼν
5   λειμῶνας ⟨ἀ⟩ποίμνιά τ᾽ ἄλση.

Aelian, *Nature of Animals* 7.39 (= Aristophanes of Byzantium
fr. 378 Slater)

4–5 So Nauck (⟨ἀ⟩ποίμνιά Meineke): κατ᾽ ἐναύλων (or
κατέναυλα) ὀρέων ἀβάτους ἐπί τε λειμῶνας ποιμ(έ)νιά τ᾽ ἄλση
Aelian

244

740

⟨CHORUS?⟩

And he (Heracles) went against the golden-antlered hind, one daunting challenge amongst his great labours, in mountain regions traversing untrodden meadows and ungrazed thickets.[1]

[1] The capture of the Cerynean hind, Heracles' third labour in the canonical order, also described by a Euripidean chorus in *Heracles* 375–9.

ΤΗΜΕΝΟΣ

742

ἄλλη πρὸς ἄλλο γαῖα χρησιμωτέρα.

Stobaeus 4.15.14

743

τὸ δὲ στρατηγεῖν τοῦτ' ἐγὼ κρίνω· καλῶς
γνῶναι τὸν ἐχθρὸν ᾗ μάλισθ' ἁλώσιμος.

Stobaeus 4.13.16

744

ἄρξεις ἄρ' οὕτω· χρὴ δὲ τὸν στρατηλάτην
ὁμῶς δίκαιον ὄντα ποιμαίνειν στρατόν.

Stobaeus 4.13.17

745

τολμᾶν δὲ χρεών· ὁ γὰρ ἐν καιρῷ
μόχθος πολλὴν εὐδαιμονίαν
τίκτει θνητοῖσι τελευτῶν.

Stobaeus 4.10.3

TEMENUS

742
Different lands are good for different uses.

743
Generalship in my judgment amounts to this: to know where your enemy is most vulnerable.

744
This, then, is how you will command; and an army's leader, if he is just, should care for his men in the same way.

745
You must show fortitude; exertion at the right moment breeds abundant good fortune for men in the end.

746

αἰδὼς γὰρ ὀργῆς πλείον' ὠφελεῖ βροτούς.

Stobaeus 3.31.1

*746a

τῷ γὰρ πονοῦντι καὶ θεὸς συλλαμβάνει.

Clement of Alexandria, *Miscellanies* 6.2.10.6 with ascription to Euripides' *Ktimenus* (*Temenus*, Gataker); the same verse is ascribed elsewhere to *Hippolytus Veiled* (see F 432.2)

746

Shame does people more good than anger.

*746a

God gives a helping hand to the man who strives.

HYPSIPYLE

B. Grenfell and A. Hunt in *Oxyrhynchus Papyri* VI (1908), 19–106 (P. Oxy. 852); W. Morel, *De Euripidis Hypsipyla* (Leipzig, 1921); G. Italie, *Euripidis Hypsipyla* (Berlin, 1923); U. Scatena, *Studio sull' Ipsipile Euripidea* (Rome, 1934); G. W. Bond, *Euripides: Hypsipyle* (Oxford, 1963); W. E. H. Cockle, *Euripides: Hypsipyle* (Rome, 1987); Diggle, *TrGFS* 135–49; H. Van Looy in ed. Budé VIII.3.155–223; M. Cropp in *SFP* II.169–258.

C. Robert, *Hermes* 44 (1909), 376–402; T. B. L. Webster in *The Classical Tradition . . . Studies . . . H. Caplan* (Ithaca, 1966), 83–97; Webster 211–5; Trendall–Webster III.3.25–6; G. Giangrande, *Museum Philologum Londiniense* 2 (1977), 165–75; E. Simon, *Archäologischer Anzeiger* (1979), 31–45; C. Brillante in *Omaggio a Piero Treves* (Padua, 1983), 43–55; Aélion (1983), I.187–95 and (1986), 119–35; *LIMC* II.i.472–5 'Archemoros', III.i.59–62 'Euneos et Thoas', VIII.i.645–50 'Hypsipyle'; Gantz 345–6, 511–2; F. Zeitlin in T. Carpenter and C. Faraone (eds.), *Masks of Dionysus* (Ithaca, 1993), 147–82; W. Burkert in A. Bierl (ed.), *Orchestra: Drama, Mythos, Logos* (Stuttgart, 1994), 44–9; M. Cropp in E. Csapo and M. Miller (eds.), *Poetry, Theory, Praxis: Essays . . . William J. Slater* (Oxford, 2003), 129–45; C. O. Pache, *Baby and Child Heroes in Ancient Greece* (Urbana, 2004), 95–134 (myth and sources).

Hypsipyle *was one of Euripides' latest and most elaborate tragedies. Its heroine was the daughter of Thoas, a son of the god Dionysus and king of the island of Lemnos. As a young woman she had borne twin sons to Jason during the Argonauts' visit to Lemnos, but Jason took these sons with him to Colchis and Hypsipyle later had to flee the island after refusing to kill her father when the other women of Lemnos massacred their menfolk. Seized by marauders, she was sold as a slave to Lycurgus, priest at the rural sanctuary of Zeus at Nemea, and later became nurse to Opheltes, son of Lycurgus and his wife Eurydice. Meanwhile Jason died, probably at Colchis, and left his sons to be raised by his comrade Orpheus in Thrace. They were eventually reunited there with their grandfather, returned with him to Lemnos, and set out to find their mother. In the play, they reach Nemea just as the army of the Seven is passing by on its march to Thebes, and Hypsipyle admits them to the house without recognizing them. She also agrees to guide the Argive seer Amphiaraus to a spring where he can find fresh water for a sacrifice, but at the spring she negligently allows the infant Opheltes to be killed by a serpent. His mother wishes to punish Hypsipyle with death, but Amphiaraus persuades Eurydice to accept the boy's fate, interpreting it as a portent for the Seven and advising that a funeral should be celebrated with games; these will be perpetuated as the Nemean Games and the boy remembered in cult as Archemorus, 'First to die' (see F 757.908–18 with note 4). Hypsipyle's sons compete in the games, a recognition is effected, and thus redeemed she returns with them to Lemnos at the end of the play.*

Hypsipyle's involvement in the events at Nemea seems to have been invented by Euripides, for earlier sources connect her only with events on Lemnos (especially Homer,

Iliad 7.468–9; Pindar Olympians 4.19–23, cf. Pythians 4.252–8), while early accounts of the origin of the Nemean Games feature only the death of Opheltes/Archemorus and Amphiaraus' settlement (Bacchylides 9.10–17, Simonides F 553 PMG, Pindar, Nemeans 8.51, 10.28); in these accounts the woman responsible for the boy's death is either his own mother or an anonymous nurse. Euripides' adaptation of the story may have been intended in part to associate Athens indirectly with the institution of the Nemean Games, for Lemnos was an Athenian dependency and Hypsipyle's son Euneos was regarded as the founder of the Athenian priestly family of the Euneidae: cf. Robert (1909), Burkert (1994), Cropp (2003).

P. Oxy. 852 (see Note on the text below) provides substantial parts of the first half of the play, which begins with Hypsipyle telling her personal history in a prologue speech (F 752, 752a–b). As she re-enters the house Euneos and Thoas arrive seeking a night's shelter (F 752c); she responds to their knock, bringing the baby with her, and persuades them to accept the house's hospitality even though the priest is away from home (F 752d–e). They presumably enter the house, and Hypsipyle remains singing to the baby as the Chorus of friendly local women arrives with news that the Seven and their army have reached Nemea (F 752f); the parodos sequence is a lyric exchange, the women trying to interest Hypsipyle in these current events, she dwelling on her unhappiness (F 752g, 752h.1–9; cf. Electra 167–212). Episode 1 sees the arrival of Amphiaraus requesting help in finding a spring (F 752h); he explains the expedition and his own connection with it (F 752k: cf. our introduction to Alcmeon in Psophis), and Hypsipyle agrees to help him (F 753), taking the baby with her and *probably spurning warnings about this from the Chorus (F 753a). The Chorus sings a stasimon about the origin of the expedition (F 753c), then Hysipyle returns in distress saying that the baby has been seized by the serpent when she incautiously left him playing on the ground (F 753d, 754, F 754a). Her thoughts of escape (F 754b) are forestalled by the entrance of Eurydice from the house (F 754c), and so she must explain what has happened and seek forgiveness (F 755a, 757.800–830). Eurydice is bent on putting Hypsipyle to death until Amphiaraus intervenes with his explanations and advice (F 757.831–949).*

The remainder of the play is more obscure. F 758a–b represent a second or possibly third stasimon celebrating the power and blessings of Dionysus. Nearly 300 lines later F 758c–d seem to be from a speech of Hypsipyle concerned with her servitude and yearning for her sons, and a further hundred-line interval brings us to the reunion scene (F 759a col. ii). Nothing survives after this except an indication that Dionysus himself appeared, no doubt validating Hypsipyle's release and directing the family's future. How the recognition between mother and sons came about is unclear; some later accounts mention a continuing threat to Hypsipyle from Eurydice or from Lycurgus on his return, or even from her own unrecognized sons, but this is difficult to accommodate in the play after Amphiaraus' seemingly decisive intervention, nor is there any hint of it in Amphiaraus' parting words (F 759a.1584–6). Probably the focus was on the games, the recognition process, and the redemption of Hypsipyle from slavery. The games will have been reported by a messenger, and the twins' identity may have been revealed when they were proclaimed by name as sons of Jason and Hypsipyle after winning the foot-race (see test. va below with note). A gold ornament in the shape of a vine or grape-bunch probably served as a proof of their identity (see test. iv below with note).

Brief fragments: F 753b, 756a, 759b are scraps of P. Oxy. 852 (for F 753e and F 755a see under F 753d and F 754c respectively); F 766 'burgeonings', F 767 'bears' (girls serving Artemis at Brauron), F 769 'her who played the castanets' (cf. F 752f.8). Other ascriptions: F 856 (= Aristophanes, Frogs 1309–12), TrGF adesp. F 37a ('Aeetes' golden fleece': not to be identified with F 752f.22–3), adesp. F 634 (someone threatened for causing a child's death).

The play is one of Euripides' late 'romantic' and senti-mental dramas in which heroines survive perils and escape servitude or other misery through reunion with lost sons or brothers: cf. Iphigenia in Tauris, Ion, Melanippe Captive, Antiope. Also notable are its mythic expansiveness (cf. es-pecially Phoenician Women, Iphigenia at Aulis), its con-cern with Attic cult and genealogy (Erechtheus, Iphigenia in Tauris, Ion), and Dionysiac elements (Antiope, Bacchae). A scholion on Aristophanes, Frogs 53 (= test. ii) dates it later than 412 along with Phoenissae and Antiope (but not necessarily as a trilogy, although Webster and Zeitlin have noted some interesting thematic similarities); this dating is supported by the play's metrical features as well as its dramatic style and content.

The impact of Hypsipyle can be seen in several parodies and allusions in Aristophanes' Frogs (cf. F 752, 763, 765, 765a–b; also F 752f.8ff. with Frogs 1304ff.), in the influ-ence of Euripides' plot on the mythographic tradition, and in iconography, especially the Darius Painter's fine mid-4th c. vase focused on Amphiaraus' intervention (= test. vi, cf. Trendall-Webster III.3.26, Todisco Ap 179, Taplin no. 79) and the lost Hellenistic relief featuring the recognition which is described in Palatine Anthology 3.10 (= test. iv below). But the only major literary descendant is Statius' reworking of the story in Books 4–6 of his Thebaid; Hypsipyle's affair with Jason remained a much more popular subject, as for example in Apollonius Rhodius' Argonautica, Ovid's Heroides and Valerius Flaccus' Argonautica, as well as much later European poetry and music (cf. OGCMA I.617–8); it was probably the subject also of Aeschylus' Hypsipyle (his Nemea may have been about the death of Archemorus but is unlikely to have involved the Lemnian princess).

Note on the text: This is the best preserved of all the fragmentary tragedies, thanks to the discovery of P. Oxy. 852 (with P. Oxy. 985, the document on whose reverse side the play text was written) in 1905. Its content and physical features have allowed the fairly precise reconstruction of the papyrus roll presented by Cockle in his 1987 edition. The ancient line numbering (shown by the survival of some of the ancient notations marking every hundredth line of the play) is given here, where possible, either exactly (e.g. 375) or approximately (e.g. ~135). References such as P. Oxy. 852 col. 3 are to the columns of the whole papyrus roll (thirty in all).

ΥΨΙΠΥΛΗ

test. iiia (Hypothesis)

Ὑ[ψι]πύλη ἧς ἀρχή·
Δ]ι[όνυσ]ος ὃς θ[ύρσοισ]ι{ν} καὶ νε[βρ]ῶν
   δοραῖς [   ] ἡ δ᾽ ὑπ[όθεσις·

about fourteen lines largely lost (perhaps including P. Oxy.
fr. 15 with successive line-beginnings Ἀμ]φιαρα[and
π]αραγε[ν-), then:

κρήνην ἔδ‹ε›ιξ[ε   δρά-
20 κ[ο]ντος διεσπ[......]αδε [
   τ[ό]πους οἱ γεγονότες [.....].. παῖδες παρ[ῆσ]αν
   ἐπὶ τὴν τῆς μητρὸς ζήτησιν καὶ κατα-
   λύσαντες παρὰ τῇ τοῦ Λυκούργου γυναικὶ
   τὸν ἐπιτάφιον τοῦ παιδὸς ἠθέλησαν ἀ-
25 γωνίσασθαι· ἡ δ[ὲ] τ[ο]ὺς π[ρ]οειρημέν[ο]υ[ς
   ξενοδοχήσασα τούτους μὲν ἐπήνεσ[ε]ν,
   τὴν μητέρα δ᾽ αὐτῶν ἀποκτείνειν [ἤμελ-
   λεν [ὥ]ς ἑκουσίω[ς ἀπ]ολωλεκυ[ί]ας α[ὐ-
   τῆ[ς τὸ] τέκνον· Ἀ[μφια]ράου δὲ ....[
30 σαμ[....] τουτω[...] χ[ά]ριν ἔδω[κε

remaining text largely lost; P. Oxy. 3652 col. ii yields scattered

256

HYPSIPYLE

test. iiia (Hypothesis)

Hypsipyle, which begins: '(Dionysus), who with (thyrsuses)
and fawnskins . . . '; the plot (is as follows) . . . *(about fourteen
lines largely lost, perhaps including* . . . Amphiaraus . . . arriv-
ing . . .) . . . (Hypsipyle) showed (them) the spring . . . (torn
asunder by?) a serpent . . . the sons born . . . arrived (in the) vi-   20
cinity in search of their mother, and having lodged with
Lycurgus' wife wanted to compete in the boy's funeral games;
and she having received the aforesaid youths as guests ap-   25
proved them, but (planned) to kill their mother (as) having
killed (her) son on purpose. But when Amphiaraus . . . (she?)
thanked him . . . *(several lines lost)* . . . the(ir?) mother . . . they   30
found . . . *(several lines lost)* . . . Archemorus . . . *(several lines
lost)* . . . prophesied . . . *(end of hypothesis)*

P. Oxy. 2455 frs. 14–15, ed. E. Turner (1962), with P. Oxy. 3652
cols. i and ii.1–15, ed. H. M. Cockle (1984); cf. W. Luppe, *ZPE* 52
(1983), 43–4 and 72 (1988) 27–33; van Rossum-Steenbeek 204–5,
219–21; Diggle *TrGFS* 135

2–3 = F 752.1 below

words 6 τὴν μητέρα, 7 εὗρον, 13 Ἀρ]χεμορ[, *and the final
line in P. Oxy. 2455 (also the last line of this hypothesis) has*
ἐθ]έσπισ[εν

test. iv

ἐν δὲ τῷ κατὰ δύσιν πλευρῷ ἐστὶν ἐν ἀρχῇ τοῦ ι΄ πίνακος
Εὔνοος γεγλυμμένος καὶ Θόας, οὓς ἐγέννησεν Ὑψιπύλη,
ἀναγνωριζόμενοι τῇ μητρὶ καὶ τὴν χρυσῆν δεικνύντες
ἄμπελον, ὅπερ ἦν αὐτοῖς τοῦ γένους σύμβολον, καὶ
ῥυόμενοι αὐτὴν τῆς διὰ τὸν Ἀρχεμόρου θάνατον παρ᾽
Εὐρυδίκῃ τιμωρίας·

    Φαῖνε, Θόαν, Βάκχοιο φυτὸν τόδε· ματέρα γάρ σου
       ῥύσῃ τοῦ θανάτου, οἰκέτιν Ὑψιπύλαν·
    ἃ τὸν ἀπ᾽ Εὐρυδίκας ἔτλη χόλον, ἦμος ἀφαυρὸν
       ὕδρος ὁ γᾶς γενέτας ὤλεσεν Ἀρχέμορον.
5   στεῖχε δὲ καὶ σὺ λιπὼν Ἀσωπίδος ἀφνεὸν οὖθαρ,
       γειναμένην ἄξων Λῆμνον ἐς ἠγαθέην.

Palatine Anthology 3.10

    3 ἀφαυρὸν Beckby: ἀφοῦθαρ *Anth.*   5 ἀφνεὸν οὖθαρ
Lumb: νέαν κούραν *Anth.*

test. va

Quibus ludis duo filii quos ex Iasone habuit intererant, quos
fugiens reliquit in Lemno: qui et ipsi matrem quaerentes cur-
rendo uicerunt. Quorum nomina praeco cum pronuntiasset
Iasonis et Hypsipyles filios esse, mater eos agnouit: quam
agnitam exorato rege mox Lemnum reduxerunt.

    Vatican Mythographer 2.141 (p. 123 Bode); similarly
Lactantius Placidus on Statius, *Thebaid* 4.740

test. iv

On the west side (*i.e. of the monument at Cyzicus to Apollonis, mother of Attalus and Eumenes of Pergamum*), at the beginning of the tenth plaque are carved Eunoos and Thoas, the sons of Hypsipyle, making themselves known to their mother and displaying the golden vine which was their family's emblem, and rescuing her from the vengeance of Eurydice prompted by the death of Archemorus.

(*Inscription:*) 'Reveal, Thoas, this plant of Dionysus; thus you will rescue your mother from death, the slave Hypsipyle, who endured Eurydice's wrath when the serpent, offspring of the earth, killed helpless Archemorus. And you too go on your way, leaving Asopia's rich land to bring your mother to holy 5 Lemnos.'[1]

---

[1] Much of the detail here may well be Euripidean, although in the play Eurydice probably forgave Hypsipyle before she and her sons recognized each other (see Introduction above).

test. va

Amongst the competitors at these games were Hypsipyle's two sons, whom she had borne to Jason and left in Lemnos when she fled. They too had gone in search of their mother, and now were victorious in the foot-race. The herald proclaimed their names, and that they were the sons of Jason and Hypsipyle, and so their mother recognized them. Once they had recognized her, they obtained the king's agreement and soon took her back to Lemnos.[1]

---

[1] The recognition process described here may be Euripidean, although the involvement of the king is doubtful.

EURIPIDES

752

⟨ΤΨΙΠΤΛΗ⟩

Διόνυσος, ὃς θύρσοισι καὶ νεβρῶν δοραῖς
καθαπτὸς ἐν πεύκαισι Παρνασσὸν κάτα
πηδᾷ χορεύων παρθένοις σὺν Δελφίσιν . . .

Aristophanes, *Frogs* 1211–13 with Schol.; Schol. on Aristophanes, *Clouds* 603; vv. 1–3 (Διόνυσος—χορεύων): Macrobius, *Saturnalia* 1.18.4; v. 1: see test. iii a.2–3 above; v. 2: several lexical sources

752a

⟨ΤΨΙΠΤΛΗ⟩

Σταφ[υλ-
Πεπαρ . . . . [
τούτων . . . . . [
ὥραις γε . . ονγ[
5 Ἥρας . εδοιδ . [
Διονυσο . . νολ[
τρίτος Διονυ[σ
Χίου παρα[
οι . ντατ[
10 Λῆμνον . [
ἐγὼ δε . [
beginnings of four more lines

P. Hamburg 118b col. ii, ed. E. Siegmann (1954); cf. H. Lloyd-Jones in Bond, *Hypsipyle* 157–60

752

(Beginning of the play)

HYPSIPYLE

Dionysus, who girded with thyrsuses and fawnskins leaps
in the torch-lit dance across Parnassus with the girls of
Delphi . . .

752a

A few lines later in the prologue speech:

⟨HYPSIPYLE⟩

. . . Staphylos . . . Peparethos . . . of these . . . seasons . . .
Hera('s?) . . . Dionysus . . . a third . . . Dionysus . . . Chios . . .   5
(one line) . . . Lemnos . . . and I . . .[1]   10

---

[1] Hypsipyle probably listed four sons of Dionysus (F 752) and
Ariadne (cf. Apollodorus, *Epit.* 1.9): Staphylos (personification of
the grape-bunch), Peparethos (identified with the wine-produc-
ing island of that name, now Skopelos), Oenopion ('Son of Wine-
face', often associated with Chios), and Thoas (Hypsipyle's father,
ruler of Lemnos). Alternatively, Peparethos was named as
Staphylos' island (cf. Diodorus 5.79).

EURIPIDES

752b

*Ends of twelve lines from later in Hypsipyle's pro-
logue speech, including* 1 ἀπ]όπτολιν   2]ι τύχαις
5 Συμ]πληγάδων   6].φάος   7]αζω ζυγῷ

P. Oxy. 852 (see play-bibliography and *Note on the text* above)
col. 2, frs. 96 + 70

752c (= 764 N)

⟨ΘΟΑΣ⟩

ἰδού, πρὸς αἰθέρ᾽ ἐξαμίλλησαι κόρας,
γραπτούς ⟨τ᾽ ἐν αἰετ⟩οῖσι πρόσβλεψον τύπους.

Galen, *Commentary on Hippocrates, On Joints* 3.23 (XVIII.
1.519.10–11 Kühn)

1 κόρας Hermann: -αι Galen mss.: -αις Musgrave
2 ⟨τ᾽ ἐν αἰετ⟩οῖσι Nauck (⟨ἐν αἰετ⟩οῖσι Valckenaer): οῖσι Galen
mss.

752d

⟨ΥΨΙΠΥΛΗ⟩

remains of one line
ἥξε[ι .....]σπ.[..... ἀ]θύρμα[τ]α
ἃ σὰς [ὀ]δυρμῶν ἐκγαλη[νιεῖ φ]ρένας.
(~ 134)   ὑμεῖς ἐκρούσατ᾽, ὦ νεανία[ι, πύλα]ς;
5   ὦ μακαρία σφῷν ἡ τεκο[ῦσ᾽, ἥ]τις ποτ᾽ ἦν·
τί τῶ[ν]δε μελάθρων δε[όμε]νοι προσήλθετον;

P. Oxy. 852 col. 3, fr. 1.i

HYPSIPYLE

752b

Later in the prologue speech:

⟨HYPSIPYLE⟩

. . . abroad/exiled . . . (mis?)fortunes . . . *(two lines)* . . .
Clashing Rocks . . . light/salvation . . . yoke . . .   5

752c (= 764N)

⟨THOAS⟩

(to Euneos as they enter) Look—run your eyes up towards
the sky, and take a look at the painted reliefs on the pedi-
ment.[1]

[1] The brothers admire the decoration of the temple of Zeus as
they arrive in Nemea (cf. *Iphigenia in Tauris* 67ff., *Ion* 184ff.,
Helen 68ff.).

752d

⟨HYPSIPYLE⟩

*(to the baby Opheltes as she opens the door to the strang-
ers)* . . . will come . . . toys which (will) calm your mind from
crying. *(to Euneos and Thoas)* Was it you, young men, who
knocked at the door? *(noticing their looks)* O happy the
mother that bore you, whoever she was![1] Why have you   5
come to this house, and what do you want from it?

[1] Dramatic irony, as Hypsipyle unknowingly refers to herself.

ΘΟΑΣ

στέγ[η]ς κεχρήμεθ' [ἐ]ν[τὸς ἀ]χθῆναι, γύναι,
εἰ δυ[να]τὸν ἡ[μῖ]ν νύκτ' ἐ[ναυλίσ]αι μίαν.

(~ 139) ἔχο[με]ν δ' ὅ[σ]ων δεῖ κ[α]ὶ οὐχὶ λυ[π]ηροὶ δό[μοις
10 ἐσό[μ]εθα τοῖσδε, τὸ δὲ σὸν ὡς ἔχει μ[εν]εῖ.

⟨ΥΨΙΠΥΛΗ⟩

ἀδέσ]ποτος μ[ὲν ο]ἶκ[ο]ς ἀρσένων κυ[ρε]ῖ
    about 20 letters   ] δώμ[α]τα

10 ἔχει ed. pr.: ἔχεις P. Oxy.

752e

⟨ΥΨΙΠΥΛΗ⟩

traces of one line
Λυκοῦρ[γ-
γυνὴ δ[

ΘΟΑΣ

οὐκ ἐν ξε[νῶσι
5 πρὸς δ' α[

⟨ΥΨΙΠΥΛΗ⟩

ἤκιστ[α
ξένο[
ἀεὶ δε[
ἀλλ' εἰς ν[
10 *remains of one more line*

P. Oxy. 852 col. 3, fr. 2

5 πρὸς δ' ἄ[λλο δή τι δῶμ' Turner (e.g.)

264

THOAS

We need to be given shelter in the house, woman, if we
may, (to stay) one night. We have what we need and will be
(no) trouble to this (household); you for your part will stay
just as you are.[2]   10

⟨HYPSIPYLE⟩

(Our family) is (without) its master . . . the house . . .

[2] A less obvious dramatic irony: the twins will in fact rescue
Hypsipyle from her servitude.

752e

Later in the same dialogue:

⟨HYPSIPYLE⟩

. . . Lycurgus . . . his wife . . .

THOAS

. . . not . . . in the guest-quarters . . . but to (some other
house) . . .   5

⟨HYPSIPYLE⟩

By no means . . . guest(s?) . . . always . . . But . . . into . . .

752f

⟨ΤΨΙΠΤΛΗ⟩

remains of one line-end
c. 9 letters]ος ἰδέσθαι
.......]...χον ὡς ἐνόπτρου
(∼ 190)   ......]οφαῆ τιν' αὐγὰν
5   ......] αὔξημα τὸ σὸν
..(.)].νησωμαι, τέκνον, εὐ-
ωποῖς ἢ θεραπείαις.
ἰδού, κτύπος ὅδε κορτάλων
(∼ 195)   (one(?) line omitted in the papyrus)
οὐ τάδε πήνας, οὐ τάδε κερκίδος
10   ἱστοτόνου παραμύθια Λήμνια
Μοῦσα θέλει με κρέκειν, ὅτι δ' εἰς ὕπνον
ἢ χάριν ἢ θεραπεύματα πρόσφορα
(∼ 200)   π]αιδὶ πρέπει νεαρῷ
τάδε μελῳδὸς αὐδῶ.

⟨ΧΟΡΟΣ⟩

στρ.   τί σὺ παρὰ προθύροις, φίλα;
16   πότερα δώματος εἰσόδους
σαίρει[ς], ἢ δρόσον ἐπὶ πέδῳ
(∼ 205)   βάλλεις οἷά τε δούλα;
ἢ τὰν Ἀργὼ τὰν διὰ σοῦ
20   στόματος αἰεὶ κληζομέναν
πεντηκόντερον ᾄδεις,
ἢ τὸ χρυσεόμαλλον
(∼ 210)   ἱερὸν δέρος ὃ περὶ δρυὸς

266

HYPSIPYLE

752f

<HYPSIPYLE>
(singing to the baby Opheltes) . . . to look at . . . like a mir-
ror's (bright?)-lit gleam . . . your growth I may . . . , child, 5
or with my cheerful tending. Look, here is the sound of
castanets[1] . . . *(a line omitted)* . . . These are not Lemnian
songs, relieving the labour of weft-thread and web-
stretching shuttle,[2] that the Muse desires me to sing, but 10
what serves for a tender young boy, to lull him or charm
him or tend to his needs—this is the song I tunefully sing.

<CHORUS>
(entering, singing)
Why are you here at the doorway, dear friend? Are you 15
sweeping the house's entrance, or sprinkling water on the
ground, as a slave-woman will? Are you singing now of
Argo, that fifty-oared vessel that your voice is always cele-
brating, or the sacred golden fleece which the eye of the 20
serpent, coiled round the boughs of the tree, keeps under

---

[1] A mundane touch, mocked by Aristophanes in *Frogs* 1305–7.
[2] I.e., the kind of weaving-songs that Hypsipyle used to sing as a
girl in her mother's household.

P. Oxy. 852 col. 4, fr. 1.ii

4 λευκ]οφαῆ (e.g.) Turner   8 a marginal note ἄν(ω)
'above' indicates an omitted line added in the now lost upper mar-
gin

ὄζοις ὄμμα δράκοντος
25 φρουρεῖ, μναμοσύνα δέ σοι
τᾶς ἀγχιάλοιο Λήμνου,
τὰν Αἰγαῖος ἐλί[σ]σων
(~ 215) κυμοκτύπος ἀχεῖ;
δεῦρο †ταν† λειμῶνα Νέμει[ον·
30 ἀσ[τ]ράπτει χαλκέο[ι]σιν ὅπλο[ις
Ἀργείων π[ε]δίον πᾶ[ν·
ἐπὶ τὸ τᾶ[ς] κιθάρας ἔρυμα
(~ 220) τᾶς Ἀμφιονίας ἔργον [
ὠ[κυ]πόδας Ἄ[δρ]ασ[το]ς [
35 ὁ [δ'] ἐκάλεσε μένο[ς
ποικίλα σάματα [
τόξα τε χρύσεα [
(~ 225) κα[ὶ] μονοβάμονε[ς
ἀειρόμενοι χθ[ον
remains of one more line

29 δ' ἂν (suggested by Turner) Dodds (δ' ἀνὰ Collard)
31 Ἀργείων von Arnim: Ἀργεῖον P. Oxy.

752g

⟨ΥΨΙΠΤΛΗ⟩

(~ 250)   *traces of one line*
      c. 8 letters Θ]ρηκίαν
      .....]σ[.]μενης ὀρούσας
      ἐπ' οἶδμα γαλανείας
5   πρυμνήσι' ἀνάψαι,
(~ 255) τὸν ἁ τοῦ ποταμοῦ παρ-

guard? And does your memory dwell on Lemnos lying by   25
the sea, which the Aegean encircles and beats with echoing
waves? Come here †to the† Nemean meadow. All of the
plain is flashing with the Argives' arms of bronze.[3] Against   30
the bastion, the work of Amphion's lyre[4] . . . swift-footed
Adrastus . . . (and) he has summoned the might . . . intricate   35
devices . . . and golden bows . . . and single-stepping[5] . . .
raising (from?) the ground . . . *(remainder of the choral
strophe lost)*

[3] 'All of the Argive plain is flashing with bronze arms', P. Oxy.:
but the army is at Nemea, and it is natural for the chorus to iden-
tify the army's origin before explaining its destination.
[4] Amphion used his lyre-music to assemble the stones for the
fortifications of Thebes: cf. *Antiope* F 223.90–5.   [5] Probably
a reference to horses with individual riders, or to one-horse chari-
ots; then the next phrase would have them raising dust from the
ground.

752g

⟨HYPSIPYLE⟩

(first half of Hypsipyle's sung response lost) . . . Thracian
(sea?)[1] . . . leaping forth over the calmly lapping water to
fasten the stern-cables, Peleus whom the river's maiden   5

[1] The sea between Thessaly and Lemnos.

P. Oxy. 852 col. 5, fr. 1.iii

EURIPIDES

θένος Αἴγιν᾽ ἐτέκνωσεν
Πηλέα, μέσῳ δὲ παρ᾽ ἱστῷ
Ἀσιάδ᾽ ἔλεγον ἰήιον
10 Θρῆσσ᾽ ἐβόα κίθαρις {Ὀρφέως}
μακροπόλων πιτύλων
(~ 260) ἐρέταισι κελεύσματα μελπομένα,
τότε μὲν ταχύπλουν,
τότε δ᾽ εἰλατίνας ἀνάπαυμα πλάτα[ς.
15 τ[ά]δε μοι τάδε θυμὸς ἰδεῖν ἵεται,
(~ 265) Δαναῶν δὲ πόνους
ἕτερος ἀναβοάτω.

ΧΟΡΟΣ

ἀντ. παρὰ σοφῶν ἔκλυον λόγο[υ]ς
πρότερον ὡς ἐπὶ κυμάτων
20 πόλιν καὶ πατρίους δόμου[ς
(~ 270) Φοίνικος Τυρία παῖς
Εὐρώπα λιποῦσ᾽ ἐπέβα
Διοτρόφον Κρῆταν ἱερὰν
Κουρήτων τροφὸν ἀνδρῶν,
25 ἃ τέκνων ἀρότοισ[ι]ν
(~ 275) τρισσοῖς ἔλιπεν κρά[τος
χώρας τ᾽ ὄλβιον ἀρχάν.
Ἀργείαν θ᾽ ἑτέραν κλύω
λέκ]τρῳ βασίλειαν Ἰώ

9 Ἀσιάδ᾽ ἔλεγον Beazley: Ἀσιὰς ἔλεγεν P. Oxy. (ἔλεγον
Wilamowitz)   21 Φοίνικος West: Φοινίκας P. Oxy.

270

daughter Aegina bore;[2] and by the mast amidships the
Thracian lyre cried out a mournful Asian plaint,[3] singing   10
commands to the rowers for their long-sweeping strokes,
now fast ahead, now at rest from the pinewood oar. These
things, yes these, does my spirit yearn to see; but as for the   15
Danaans' labours, let someone else acclaim them.

CHORUS

From learned storytellers I have heard how once Phoenix's
daughter from Tyre, Europa, left city and father's home[4]   20
and went on the waves to sacred Crete, nurse of Zeus and
the Curetes;[5] to her threefold harvest of children she left   25
power and prosperous government of the land. And an-
other princess, I hear, the Argive Io, at her mating ex-

---

[2] Hypsipyle recalls the Argo and its heroes arriving on
Lemnos, including Achilles' father Peleus and (8–14) the lyre-
player Orpheus (for whom see also F 759a.1616–23).   [3] Or
with Wilamowitz's reading, 'the Asian lyre from Thrace (i.e. Or-
pheus' Asian lyre, cf. F 757.1622) cried out a mournful plaint' (or
'a hymn of thanks for their landfall' Kannicht, taking the adjective
iêion to refer to the cry *ié paiân*).   [4] With P. Oxy.'s reading,
'how once the Tyrian girl Europa left city and father's home in
Phoenicia . . . ' Zeus took the form of a bull to carry Europa across
the sea from Tyre to Crete; their sons were Minos, Rhadamanthys
and Sarpedon. Cf. *Cretans* F 472.1–3, *Phrixus* F 820.
[5] Young male devotees of Zeus: cf. *Cretans* F 472.13–15 with
note.

30   ...]φας ἀμφὶς ἀμεῖψαι
(~ 280) κερ]ασφόρον ἄταν.
       ταῦ]τ᾿ ἦν θεὸς εἰς φροντίδα θῇ σοι
       ...].[.]ς δή, φίλα, τὸ μέσον
       c. 9 letters] ἀπολείψει
35   c. 8 letters π]ατέρος πατέρα
(~ 285) c. 9 letters]τεχει σέθεν
       c. 9 letters] ὠκύπορο[ς] μετανίσεται
       remains of nine more lines

       30]φας read by Cockle: πάτ]ρας Turner: perhaps μορ]φᾶς
Diggle   33 στέρξει]ς Radermacher

752h

       ⟨ΤΨΙΠΤΛΗ⟩

       trace of one line
(~ 310) νεμον ἄγαγέ ποτε .[
       κυναγόν τε Π⟨ρ⟩όκριν τὰν πόσις ἔκτα
       κατεθρήνησεν ἀοιδαῖς [
5   θάνατος ἔλαχε· τὰ δ᾿ ἐμὰ πάθε[α
(~ 315) τίς ἂν ἢ γόος ἢ μέλος ἢ κιθάρας
       ἐπὶ δάκρυσι μοῦσ᾿ ἀνοδυρομένα
       μετὰ Καλλιόπας
       ἐπὶ πόνους ἂν ἔλθοι;

       ⟨ΧΟΡΟΣ⟩

10   ὦ Ζεῦ Νεμέας τῆσδ᾿ ἄλσος ἔχων

       P. Oxy. 852 col. 6, frs. 1.iv etc.

changed the horn-bearing affliction (of her form?).[6] If god 30
puts (these things) into your thoughts, (you will) surely
(cherish?) moderation, dear friend . . . will (not?) desert
you . . . your father's father . . . of/for you . . . will come in 35
pursuit . . . *(remainder of the choral antistrophe lost)* . . .

[6] Io was turned into a cow when Zeus desired her, and wan-
dered the earth until in Egypt he restored her human form and
impregnated her with a son Epaphus. In v. 30 we translate
Diggle's conjecture.

752h

⟨HYPSIPYLE⟩

(most of this lyric response lost) . . . once brought . . . and
the huntress Procris, whom her husband killed . . . la-
mented with songs . . . death claimed (her);[1] but my suffer- 5
ings—what cry or song or lyre's music, lamenting them be-
side my tears with Calliope's aid, will come to mourn my
troubles?

(Amphiaraus approaches by a side-entrance)

⟨CHORUS⟩

O Zeus, possessor of this Nemean grove, what busi- 10

[1] Erechtheus' daughter Procris was accidentally killed while
hunting with her husband Cephalus (in some accounts by
Cephalus himself).

273

(~ 320)   τίνος ἐμπορίᾳ τούσδ᾽ ἐγγὺς ὁρῶ
πελάτας ξείνους Δωρίδι πέπλων
ἐσθῆτι σαφεῖς πρὸς τούσδε δόμους
στείχοντας ἐρῆμον ἀν᾽ ἄλσος;

ΑΜΦΙΑΡΑΟΣ

15 ὡς ἐχθρὸν ἀνθρώποισιν αἵ τ᾽ ἐκδημίαι
(~ 325) ὅταν τε χρείαν εἰσπεσὼν ὁδοιπόρος
ἀγροὺς ἐρήμους καὶ μονοικήτους ἴδῃ
ἄπολις ἀνερμήνευτος ἀπορίαν ἔχων
ὅπῃ τράπηται· κἀμὲ γὰρ τὸ δ[υ]σχερὲς
20 τοῦτ᾽ εἰσβέβηκεν· ἄσμενος δ᾽ εἶδον δόμ[ους
(~ 330) τούσδ᾽ ἐν Διὸς λειμῶνι Νεμεάδος χθον[ός.
καί σ᾽, εἴτε δούλη τοῖσδ᾽ ἐφέστηκας δόμ[οις
εἴτ᾽ οὐχὶ δοῦλον σῶμ᾽ ἔχουσ᾽, ἐρήσομαι·
τίνος τάδ᾽ ἀνδρῶν μηλοβοσκὰ δώματ[α
25 Φλειουντίας γῆς, ὦ ξένη, νομίζεται;

ΥΨΙΠΤΛΗ

(~ 335) ὄ]λβια Λυκούργου μέλαθρα κλῄζεται τά[δε,
ὅ]ς ἐξ ἁπάσης αἱρεθεὶς Ἀσωπίας
κλῃδοῦχός ἐστι τοὐπιχωρίου Διός.

ΑΜΦΙΑΡΑΟΣ

ῥ]υτὸν λαβεῖν [χ]ρῄ[ζοι]μ᾽ ἂν ἐν κρωσσοῖς ὕδωρ
30 χ]έρνιβα θεοῖσιν ὅ[σιον] ὡς χεαίμεθα.
(~ 340) στατῶν γὰρ ὑδάτων [ν]άματ᾽ οὐ διειπετῆ,
στρατοῦ δὲ πλήθει πάντα συνταράσσεται.

ΥΨΙΠΤΛΗ

τίν]ες μολόντες καὶ χ[θ]ονὸς ποίας ἄπο;

274

ness brings these newcomers I see close by, distinctively dressed in Dorian clothing,[2] and coming towards this house through the lonely grove?

AMPHIARAUS

How hateful it is for men to journey abroad, and those 15
times when a traveller, falling into need, sees barren countryside with solitary dwellings, while he is displaced, unguided, unknowing where to turn. This is my predicament,
in fact, and I was glad when I saw this house in Zeus's 20
meadow here in Nemean territory. And now I shall ask
you, whether you are a slave standing here by the house, or
whether you are no slave: who is considered the owner of
this pastoral dwelling in Phlius' country?[3] 25

HYPSIPYLE

These are known as the wealthy halls of Lycurgus, who was
chosen from all of Asopia[4] to be the temple-keeper of our
local Zeus.

AMPHIARAUS

(I would like to ask) to take some running water in pitchers, so we may pour a (proper) libation to the gods. The 30
trickles of stagnant water are not clear, and are being all
churned up by our numerous host.

HYPSIPYLE

(Who) are you all, and what country do you come from?

---

[2] A simple knee-length tunic, appropriate to Amphiaraus' disciplined character.   [3] The Nemean sanctuary lay between the
small towns of Phlius and Cleonae.   [4] The valley of the river
Asopus, in which Phlius lay.

⟨ΑΜΦΙΑΡΑΟΣ⟩

ἐκ τῶν Μυκηνῶν [ἐσ]μεν, Ἀργεῖοι γέν[ος,

35 ὅ]ρια δ᾽ ὑπερβαίνοντες εἰς ἄλλην χθόνα

(~ 345) στρ]ατοῦ πρ[ο]θῦσαι βουλόμεσθα Δαν[α]ϊδῶ[ν.

⟨ΤΥΙΠΤΛΗ⟩

ὑ]μεῖς [πορ]εύεσθ᾽[ἆ]ρα πρὸς Κάδμου πύλας;

⟨ΑΜΦΙΑΡΑΟΣ⟩

c. 8 letters].ρομ[..... ε]ὐτυχῶς, γύναι.

⟨ΤΥΙΠΤΛΗ⟩

c. 11 letters]λε[.....] σου θέμι[ς μ]αθεῖν;

⟨ΑΜΦΙΑΡΑΟΣ⟩

40 .....] κατάγομ[εν φυγ]άδα Π[ολυνεί]κη πάτρας.

⟨ΤΥΙΠΤΛΗ⟩

(~ 350) ...]ω[c. 15 letters]ὰς θηρᾶ.[

ΑΜΦΙΑΡΑΟΣ

παῖ[ς] Οἰκ[λέους c. 8 letters] Ἀμφιάρ[εως

⟨ΤΥΙΠΤΛΗ⟩

ὦ μεγάλ[α c. 11 letters]ια και[

⟨ΑΜΦΙΑΡΑΟΣ⟩

πῶς δ᾽ οιλ[c. 12 letters]σα.[

38 a marginal note ειδη[may indicate line-beginning εἰ δή or
similar   39 λέ[γ᾽, εἴ τί] σου Diggle   40 ἡμεῖς] Cockle:
Θήβας] Diggle

‹AMPHIARAUS›

We are from Mycenae, Argives by race; and as we cross the
border into another country we wish to make sacrifice for   35
our Danaid army.

‹HYPSIPYLE›

So you are making for the gates of Cadmus?

‹AMPHIARAUS›

(Yes, if) . . . successfully, lady.

‹HYPSIPYLE›

(Tell me . . . if) I may learn it from you.

‹AMPHIARAUS›

We are restoring Polynices (to Thebes?), a fugitive from
his homeland   40

‹HYPSIPYLE›

. . . pursue . . .

AMPHIARAUS

The son of Oicles . . . Amphiaraus . . .

‹HYPSIPYLE›

O great . . .

‹AMPHIARAUS›

And how . . .

752i

Five more line-beginnings from the same dialogue, including:

2 <ΑΜΦ.> ὄνομα   3 <ΤΨΙΠ.> ἡ Λημν[

P. Oxy. 852 col. 7, fr. 4

752k

beginnings of three dialogue lines, then:

ΤΨΙΠΤΛΗ

(375) πόθεν μ[

ΑΜΦΙΑΡΑΟΣ

5   ἔγημ' ὁ κλε[ινὸς

ΤΨΙΠΤΛΗ

εἶς ἦν τις ω[

ΑΜΦΙΑΡΑΟΣ

ταύτῃ δίδωσ[ι

ΤΨΙΠΤΛΗ

θεοὶ θεῶν γὰ[ρ

ΑΜΦΙΑΡΑΟΣ

(380) Πολύδωρος οὗ[ν

ΤΨΙΠΤΛΗ

10   εἴ που θεᾶς φὺ[ς

P. Oxy. 852 col. 7, frs. 1.v etc.; vv. 20–1 (= fr. adesp. 350 N): Plutarch, *Moralia* 20d

752i

Five more line-beginnings from the same dialogue, including:

2 (AMPH.) . . . name . . .   3 (HYPS.) Lemnos/The Lemnian . . .

752k

From the same dialogue, three line-beginnings, then:

HYPSIPYLE

Whence/Why . . .[1]

AMPHIARAUS

The (famous) . . . married . . .   5

HYPSIPYLE

He/There was one . . .

AMPHIARAUS

. . . gave to her . . .

HYPSIPYLE

The gods . . . the gods' . . .

AMPHIARAUS

So Polydorus[2] . . .

HYPSIPYLE

If born from a goddess . . .   10

---

[1] Hypsipyle asks why Amphiaraus joined the expedition. In vv. 5–17 he explains that he is doing so, despite knowing he will die at Thebes, because of the persuasion of his wife Eriphyle who was bribed by Polynices with the necklace of Harmonia (see Introduction to *Alcmeon in Psophis*).   [2] Son of Cadmus and Harmonia, and father of Labdacus (Gantz 483–4).

ΑΜΦΙΑΡΑΟΣ

τούτου δὲ παι[

ΤΨΙΠΤΛΗ

.]ει.[. ἡ]δύ τοί[

ΑΜΦΙΑΡΑΟΣ

ὃν καὶ σ[υ]νείπο[

ΤΨΙΠΤΛΗ

(385)   εἰς χρησμὸν οὖν σοι θα[

ΑΜΦΙΑΡΑΟΣ

15   χρὴ γὰρ στρατεύειν μ᾽ ει[

ΤΨΙΠΤΛΗ

ἐ]δέξατ᾽ οὖν ἑκοῦσα δυ[

⟨ΑΜΦΙΑΡΑΟΣ⟩

ἐδέ]ξαθ᾽, ἥκω δ᾽ [οὔ]ποτ᾽ ἐκ[

⟨ΤΨΙΠΤΛΗ⟩

...]αι σαφῶς [..]θανατ[

⟨ΑΜΦΙΑΡΑΟΣ⟩

(390)   ... ἔ]στιν αι[...].[ ].[

⟨ΤΨΙΠΤΛΗ⟩

20   τί δῆτα θύειν δεῖ σε κατθανούμενον;

⟨ΑΜΦΙΑΡΑΟΣ⟩

ἄμεινον· οὐδεὶς κάματος εὐσεβεῖν θεούς.

fourteen more lines (= vv. 393–406) largely lost

AMPHIARAUS

And his (son(s)) . . .

HYPSIPYLE

. . . pleasing . . .

AMPHIARAUS

One whom also (I/we/they agreed?) . . .

HYPSIPYLE

So . . . to the/an oracle . . . for you . . .

AMPHIARAUS

Yes, for I must join the campaign . . .   15

HYPSIPYLE

She accepted willingly, then . . .

⟨**AMPHIARAUS**⟩

She accepted it—and I am never coming . . .

⟨**HYPSIPYLE**⟩

. . . plainly . . . death . . .

⟨**AMPHIARAUS**⟩

. . . is . . .

⟨**HYPSIPYLE**⟩

Then why should you sacrifice, if you are going to die?   20

⟨**AMPHIARAUS**⟩

It is better to do so; respecting the gods is no burden.

remainder of this dialogue largely lost

---

13 σ[υ]νείπο[corrected from σ[υ]νηγο[: perhaps συνεῖπο[ν
or συνειπό[μεσθα Kannicht

753

⟨ΤΥΙΠΤΛΗ⟩

δείξω μὲν Ἀργείοισιν Ἀχελῴου ῥόον.

Macrobius, *Saturnalia* 5.18.2 (= Didymus, *Tragic Words* fr. 2, p. 85 Schmidt)

753a

Beginnings of twelve lines of dialogue, including:
1 — τί φ[ή]ς; ἐκε[2 — ἐκεῖ λο.α.[3 — ὦ
παντά- λα[ινα

P. Oxy 852 col. 8, frs. 23 + 37, fr. 24

2 perhaps λοχαγ[οί Cockle

753c

ΧΟΡΟΣ

remains of 10 (or 11?) lyric lines including
2 πολυκά[ρπων?   3 σταχύω[ν   4 δρ]οσιζομεν[
5 δώτορες ει.[8 Πλευρ[ων   9 ἀλατευ[, *then:*

11   φυγὰς [....].. Ἄργος [
    νν[*c. 12 letters*].[.] ἐν κοίταισι παρ' αὐλα[
    ἐριδ[.... ἀ]μειβόμενοι
(~ 559) σιδ[*c. 8 letters*]εσια
15   σφαγα[....].ον
    κλισίας π[ερ]ὶ νυκτέρου
    γενναίων π[α]τέρων

P. Oxy. 852 col. 10, frs. 7, 8 + 9 etc.

HYPSIPYLE

753

⟨HYPSIPYLE⟩
I'll show the Argives Achelous' stream.[1]

[1] The great river Achelous could be regarded as the source or parent of minor rivers and springs throughout Greece.

753a

Beginnings of twelve lines in which (probably) the Chorus questions Hypsipyle's decision to go to the spring, including:
1 — What are you saying? . . . there(?) . . .   2 — There (the commanders?) . . .   3 — You foolhardy (*or much afflicted?*) woman . . .

753c

CHORUS
From the first Stasimon, remains of ten or eleven lines including:
2 (fruit?)ful   3 (of?) corn-ears/harvest   4 moistening   5 givers   8 Pleuron(ian?)   9 wander(ing?), *then:*
. . . a fugitive . . . Argos . . . amongst the beddings by the courtyard, exchanging quarrel(s?) . . . iron *or* sword . . . slaughter . . . over a couch for the night, the fugitives . . .   15 their noble fathers' temper in conflict.[1] And King Adrastus

[1] The Chorus recalls the fight between the exiled Polynices and Tydeus when they arrived at Adrastus' palace in Argos. Adrastus identified them as the lion and the boar that Apollo's oracle had said should marry his daughters. Cf. *Suppliant Women* 131–50, *Phoenician Women* 408–23.

φ[υ]γάδες δορὶ θυμόν.

(~ 564)   Φοίβου δ' ἐν[ο]πὰ[ς] βα[σ]ιλεὺς ἐνύχευ-
20   ε[ν] Ἄδραστος ἔχων
          τέκνα θηρσὶν [ζ]εῦ[ξ]αι
          remains of one line
                    ] ἀμπετάσας

753d

Part of a lyric exchange between Hypsipyle and the Cho-
rus, vv. 1–9 very damaged but including 4 ὤ μοι (a cry
from Hypsipyle), then:

⟨ΤΨΙΠΤΛΗ?⟩
10   ] ποῦ μάλα;

ΧΟΡΟΣ
          ἤδη [τόδ'] ἐγγύς, οὐχὶ μα[κράν
(~ 590)   λε]ύσσειν ἀλλασο[

⟨ΤΨΙΠΤΛΗ⟩
          γυνα]ῖκες οἵας ειθεν‥[
          οἴ] ἐγώ·

⟨ΧΟΡΟΣ⟩
15   ] τί θροεῖς;

⟨ΤΨΙΠΤΛΗ⟩
          ] ὠλόμαν·

remains of one more line, and a few lines later in F 753e,
screams from Hypsipyle:
(~ 610)   ἐὲ ἐ[έ … ἐὲ ἐ[έ

P. Oxy. col. 10, frs. 12, 14, 13, 10

lay pondering in the night the injunction he had from
Phoebus, (to yoke) his daughters with wild beasts . . . *(one*   20
line) . . . throwing open . . .

753d

*Part of a lyric exchange between Hypsipyle (returning
from the spring without the baby) and the Chorus, vv. 1–9
very damaged but including 4 O me! from Hypsipyle, then:*

⟨HYPSIPYLE?⟩

Just where?   10

CHORUS

Already (this) is close by, not far off, to see . . .

⟨HYPSIPYLE⟩

. . . women, what . . . Woe is me!

⟨CHORUS⟩

What does this cry mean?   15

⟨HYPSIPYLE⟩

I am lost!

*remains of one more line, and a few lines later in F 753e,
screams from Hypsipyle*

754

⟨ΥΨΙΠΤΛΗ⟩

ἕτερον ἐφ᾽ ἑτέρῳ †αἱρόμενος†
ἄγρευμ᾽ ἀνθέων ἡδομένᾳ ψυχᾷ,
τὸ νήπιον ἄπληστον ἔχων.

Plutarch, *Moralia* 93d and 661e–f

1 αἱρόμενος Plut. 93d most mss.: αἱρούμενος others: ἱέμενος
Plut. 661f: δρεπόμενος Wecklein

754a

⟨ΥΨΙΠΤΛΗ?⟩

κρήνη [σ]κιαζ[
δράκων πάροικ[ος
γοργωπὰ λεύσσω[ν
πήληκα σείων, οὗ φοβ[
5 ποιμένες επεισιγ᾽ εν[.].[
   παν[..]μα δρᾶσαι καὶ ῥυ.[

⟨ΧΟΡΟΣ?⟩

φ[εῦ·
γυ]ναικὶ πάντα γίγνε[ται
.....]ς ἥκει· φύλακα δ᾽ οὐ π[
remains of four more lines

P. Oxy. 852 col. 12, frs. 18, 19

5 ἐπεὶ σῖγ᾽ or ἔπεισί γ᾽ Wilamowitz

754

Probably from the same sung dialogue:

⟨HYPSIPYLE⟩

... †picking† one quarry[1] of flowers after another with joy-
ful spirit, his child's mind unsatisfied.

[1] Or perhaps 'starting one hunt for . . .' The various participles
transmitted in the mss. of Plutarch are all metrically difficult (with
preceding hiatus); they may have displaced a different word such
as Wecklein's 'plucking'.

754a

Spoken dialogue later in the same scene:

⟨HYPSIPYLE?⟩

... a spring (is shaded?) ... a serpent living by it ... staring
fiercely ... shaking its helm, (in fear?) of which ... shep-
herds ... *(text uncertain)*[1] ...... to do ... and ...   5

⟨CHORUS?⟩

Alas, for a woman everything is ... comes ... but ... not ...
guardian ... *(remains of four more lines)* ...

[1] Wilamowitz noted that the text might yield either 'when
silently' or '(it) approaches)', either presumably referring to the
serpent.

754b

⟨ΤΨΙΠΤΛΗ⟩

traces of one line

ἕστηκα μ.π.[

(~ 670) ἀνά[ξι’] ἕξειν· οἱ φόβοι δ[..]τικτο..[

ΧΟΡΟΣ

4 ἐνελπ[..́.]υτι[...]’ ἔχεις ἐν[..]..[

ΤΨΙΠΤΛΗ

7 δέδο[ι]κα θ[α]νάτῳ παιδὸς οἷα πείσομ[αι.

ΧΟΡΟΣ

8 οὔκουν ἄπειρός γ’, ὦ τάλαινα, σ[υμφορῶν.

ΤΨΙΠΤΛΗ

9 ἔγνωκα κἀγὼ τοῦτο καὶ φυλάξ[ομαι.

ΧΟΡΟΣ

6 τί δῆτά γ’ ἐξεύρηκας εἰς ἀλκ[ὴν κακῶν;

ΤΨΙΠΤΛΗ

5 φεύγειν στ.[.]ων των[..]δρ[

ΧΟΡΟΣ

10 ποῖ δῆτα τρέψῃ; τίς σε δ[έ]ξεται πό[λ]ις;

ΤΨΙΠΤΛΗ

πόδες κριν[ο]ῦσι τοῦτο κα[ὶ π]ροθυμία.

P Oxy. 852 col. 12, frs. 20 + 21 + 44

7ff. so ordered by Wecklein   5 στε[γ]ῶν τῶν[δ’
ἔ]δρ[αν(α) Bury in ed. pr.

HYPSIPYLE

754b
(a few lines later)

〈HYPSIPYLE〉

(traces of one line) . . . I stand . . . to get undeserved (sufferings). My fears . . .

CHORUS

. . . optimistic . . . you have . . .   4

HYPSIPYLE

I fear what I shall suffer because of the child's death.   7

CHORUS

Well, you are not inexperienced in misfortunes, poor woman.   8

〈HYPSIPYLE〉

I too know that, and shall protect myself.   9

CHORUS

Then what have you found to defend yourself (from harm)?   6

HYPSIPYLE

To flee (the shelter of this house?) . . .   5

〈CHORUS〉

Where will you turn, then? What community will receive you?   10

HYPSIPYLE

My feet and urgent flight will determine this.

EURIPIDES

ΧΟΡΟΣ

φυλάσ[σ]εται[ι] γῆ φρου[ρίο]ισιν ἐν κύκλῳ.

ΤΨΙΠΤΛΗ

(~ 680) [ν]ικᾷ[ς]· ἐῶ δὴ τοῦτ[ό] ⟨γ᾽⟩· ἀλλ᾽ [ἀ]πέρχομαι.

ΧΟΡΟΣ

σκόπει, φίλας [γ]ὰρ τά[σδε] συμβούλους ἔχεις.

ΤΨΙΠΤΛΗ

15 τί δε........[.]ιμ[..τ]ις ἐξάξε[ι] με γῆς;

⟨ΧΟΡΟΣ⟩

c. 12 letters]...[......] δούλους ἄγειν.

remains of one more line

754c

remains of two lines including 2 δέσ]ποινα[, *then:*

⟨ΕΥΡΥΔΙΚΗ?⟩

.......].ι κλῇθρ[᾽] ὤσ[......].ουσε[

(~ 695) .....]ωμαι δωμάτων [......].τιδα

5 .....]τ᾽ ἔξω δμωῒς ἡ τροφ[ὸς τέ]κνου

.....] δίδωσιν οὐδ᾽ ἔσω βαίν[ει δό]μων.

*remains of four lines, with speaker changes at 9 (= 700)
and perhaps 10, then:*

⟨ΕΥΡΥΔΙΚΗ?⟩

11 π]έλας θυρῶν ἆ[ρ᾽] ὕπνον ἐκτελεῖ γλυκ[ύν,

ἢ π]α[ι]δὸς εἴργε[ι] δάκρυ᾽ ἔχουσ᾽ ἐν ἀγκάλ[αις;

290

HYPSIPYLE

CHORUS
The land is watched by guard-posts all around it.

HYPSIPYLE
You win—I'll give up that plan; but still I'll leave.

CHORUS
But look; you have your friends here to advise you.

HYPSIPYLE
But what . . . (who) will take me out of the country?   15

CHORUS
. . . to take slaves.

remains of one more line

754c

A few lines later, remains of two lines including 2 mistress, *then:*

⟨EURYDICE?⟩
(Release?) the door-bolts (for me?), so that (going out from?) the palace I may . . . The slave-woman who nurses my child . . . outside . . . is giving . . . and is not going about   5 within (the house).

remains of four lines with one or two speaker-changes, then:

⟨EURYDICE?⟩
Is he finishing a pleasant sleep by the doorway, or is she   11 holding the boy in her arms to stop him crying?

P. Oxy. 852 col. 12, frs. 34 etc.

3 χαλᾶτέ μ]οι Bury in ed. pr.   ὡς [ἂν ἐξελ]θοῦσ' ἐ[γώ Dale adapting Bury

⟨ΤΨΙΠΤΛΗ?⟩

(~ 704) ..]π[.]τ᾽ ἀπ᾽ οἴ[κ]ων· οἴχε[τα]ι φίλας τέκν[ον
remains of five more lines, including 14 δ]ηλήματο[ς or
κ]ηλήματο[ς   15 λόγων   16 ἐ]π᾽ ἀγκάλαισί[μου
17 ἀπωλόμ[ην   18 ἐ]κ χερῶν
Several further scraps from the next column of P. Oxy. (= F
755a) represent the continuation of this scene before a
more coherent text resumes in F 757.

(755 N = 765b, Brief fragment)

(756 N = 765a below)

757

End of a long speech of Hypsipyle defending herself, in-
cluding line-beginnings: 801 καὶ χ[έρ]νιβ[802 ἐῶ
803 ἀπεννε[επ-   804 ἀρετὴν ξενο[805 δοκῶ δὲ
ταῦ[τα?   806 ἢν μὴ σὺ πεισθ[ῆς and line-ends
810 κακόν   812 ἄφρων, then:

820 κεῖται .[..].[
καλαῖσι τονο[
Φ[οί]βου τὰ λε[
καὶ μὴ δι᾽ ὀρ[γῆς
(25) χρόνῳ δὲ βούλ[-
825 τὸ τῶν γυναι[κῶν
καὶ πα[ῖ]δα τ[
κἂν διαριθμ[
ἢν δ᾽ ἐξαμα[ρτ

⟨HYPSIPYLE?⟩

. . . from the house; the child is gone . . . dear . . . mischief
(*or* magic) . . . words . . . upon (my) arms . . . I am ruined . . .   15
out of (my?) hands . . .

(755 N = 765b, Brief fragment)

(756 N = 765a below)

757

*Later in the same scene, end of a long speech of Hypsipyle
defending herself, including:*
801 and the libation . . .   802 I leave aside . . .
803 . . . forbid . . .   804 virtue (to?) strange(rs?) . . .
805 and I consider (these things?) . . .   806 if you are
not persuaded . . .   810 . . . evil   812 . . . foolish,
then 820ff.: he lies . . . with/in fine . . . Phoebus' . . . and do
not through anger . . . but take time to think . . . women's . . .   825
and the child . . . and if (you) reckon carefully . . . but if
(you) make an error . . .

---

vv. 800–31, 835–949: P. Oxy. 852 cols. 14–16, frs. 27 etc. and
60 + 87; see also below on vv. 830–50, 920–7 and 946–9

827–8 διαριθμ[ήσηι . . . ἐξαμά[ρτηις Cropp

EURIPIDES

ΧΟΡΟΣ

(30) γενν[αῖ᾽ ἔ]λε[ξας
830 ἐν σώφροσιν [γ]ὰρ κἄμ᾽ ἀριθμεῖσθα[ι θέλω.

ΕΥΡΥΔΙΚΗ

τί ταῦτ[α] κομψῶς ἀντιλάζυσαι λό[γων
c. 10 letters] εχουσα μηκύνεις μ[ακράν,
κτανοῦσ᾽ Ὀφέ]λτην, τῶν ἐμῶν ὄσσω[ν χαράν;
(35) c. 10 letters] . . μηδ᾽ ἀναμν[ησ-
835 . ν.π[. . .] . . . [(.)]μοι παιδί θ᾽ ὃν διώ[λεσας.

⟨ΥΨΙΠΥΛΗ⟩

οὕτω δοκεῖ μ᾽, ὦ [π]ότνι᾽, ἀποκτείνε[ιν ἄρα
ὀργῇ πρὶν ὀρθῶς πρᾶγμ[α] διαμαθε[ῖν τόδε;
σιγᾷς, ἀμείβῃ δ᾽ οὐδέν; ὦ τάλαιν᾽ ἐγ[ώ·
(40) ὡς τοῦ θανεῖν μὲν οὕνεκ᾽ οὐ μέγα στ[έν]ω,
840 εἰ δὲ κτανεῖν τὸ τέκνον οὐκ ὀρθῶς δοκῶ,
τοὐμὸν τιθήνημ᾽, ὃν ἐπ᾽ ἐμαῖσιν ἀγκάλαις
πλὴν οὐ τεκοῦσα τἆλλα γ᾽ ὡς ἐμὸν τέκνον
στέργουσ᾽ ἔφερβον, ὠφέλημ᾽ ἐμοὶ μέγα.
(45) ὦ πρῷρα †καὶ λευκαῖνον ἐξ ἅλμης ὕδωρ†
845 Ἀργοῦς, ἰὼ παῖδ᾽, ὡς ἀπόλλυμαι κακῶς.
ὦ μάντι πατρὸς Οἰκλέους, θανούμεθα.
ἄρηξον, ἐλθέ, μή μ᾽ ἴδῃς ὑπ᾽ αἰτίας
αἰσχρᾶς θανοῦσαν, διὰ σὲ γὰρ διόλλυμαι.
(50) ἔλθ᾽, οἶσθα γὰρ δὴ τἀμά, καὶ σὲ μάρτυρα
850 σαφέστατον δέξαιτ᾽ ἂν ἥδ᾽ ἐμῶν κακῶν.

294

HYPSIPYLE

CHORUS

You have spoken nobly . . . For I too want to be counted
amongst those with good sense.   830

⟨EURYDICE⟩

Why do you seize on words so cleverly (and) . . . spin them
out at length (when you have killed) Opheltes, (the joy) of
my eyes? . . . and do not remind me (of my troubles?)[1] . . .
for me and my son whom (you have killed).   835

⟨HYPSIPYLE⟩

Do you (then) mean to kill me thus in anger, mistress, be-
fore you have properly learned the truth of this matter?
You are silent, and give me no reply? O, how I suffer! I do
not greatly complain that I must die, but if I wrongly seem
to have killed the child, my nursling, whom I fed and cher-   840
ished in my arms in every way except that I did not bear
him—and he was a great blessing to me. O prow †and
water whitening from the brine† of Argo![2] O my two sons, I
face a terrible death! O seer, son of Oicles, I am about to   845
die: defend me, come, don't see me die so shamefully ac-
cused, for I die because of you! Come—you know what I
have done, and she would accept you as the truest wit-
ness of my misfortune. *(to Eurydice's servants, despairing)* 850

---

[1] Diggle's adaptation of Petersen's '(of my child)'.   [2] The
Greek is slightly incoherent. Collard's tentative alteration gives 'O
prow of Argo, and water whitening from its onset.'

830–50 (centres): P. Petrie II.49c, ed. J. Mahaffy (1893), re-
ed. H. J. Milne (1927 = P. Lit. Lond. 74)   834 μηδ’
ἀναμν[ήσῃς τέκνον Petersen (κακῶν Diggle)   836 end
ἄρα Diggle   844 ἐξ ὁρμῆς Collard

ἄγετε, φίλων γὰρ οὐδέν᾽ εἰσορῶ πέλας
ὅστις με σώσει· κενὰ δ᾽ [ἐ]πηδέσθην ἄρα.

ΑΜΦΙΑΡΑΟΣ

ἐπίσχες, ὦ πέμπουσα τ[ή]νδ᾽ ἐπὶ σφαγά[ς,
(55) δόμων ἄνασσα· τῷ γὰρ εὐπρεπεῖ σ᾽ ἰδὼν
855 τοὐλεύθερόν σοι προστίθημι τῇ φύσει.

ΥΨΙΠΥΛΗ

ὦ πρός σε γονάτων—ἱκέτις, Ἀμφιάρεω, πίτνω—
κ]αὶ πρὸς [γ]ενείο[υ τ]ῆς τ᾽ Ἀπόλλωνος τέχνης,
κ]αιρὸν γὰρ ἥκεις τοῖς ἐμοῖσιν ἐν κακοῖς,
(60) ῥ]ῦσαί με· διὰ γὰρ σὴν ἀπόλλυμαι χάριν.
860 μέλλω τε θνήσκειν, δεσμίαν τέ μ᾽ εἰσορᾷς
πρὸς σοῖσι γόνασιν, ἢ τόθ᾽ εἱπόμην ξένοις·
ὅσια δὲ πράξεις ὅσιος ὤν· πρ[ο]δοὺς δέ με
ὄνειδος Ἀργείοισιν Ἕλλησίν τ᾽ ἔσῃ.
(65) ἀλλ᾽ ὦ δι᾽ ἁ[γνῶ]ν ἐμπύρων λεύσσων τύχας
865 Δαναοῖσιν, [εἰπ]ὲ τῇδε συμφορὰν τέκνου·
παρὼν γὰ[ρ οἶσ]θα· φησὶ δ᾽ ἥδ᾽ ἑκουσίως
κτανεῖν μ[ε π]αῖδα κἀπιβουλεῦσαι δόμοις.

ΑΜΦΙΑΡΑΟΣ

εἰδὼς ἀφῖγμαι τὴν τύχην θ᾽ ὑπειδόμην
(70) τὴν σὴν ἃ πείσῃ τ᾽ ἐκπεπνευκότος τέκνου.
870 ἥκ[ω] δ᾽ ἀρήξων συμφοραῖσι ταῖσι σαῖς,
τὸ μ[ὲ]ν βίαιον οὐκ ἔχων, τὸ δ᾽ εὐσεβές.
αἰ[σ]χρὸν γὰρ εὖ μὲν ἐξεπίστασθαι παθεῖν,

Take me, then; I see no friend nearby to save me. My
deference, it seems, was wasted.
(Amphiaraus re-enters from the direction of the spring)

AMPHIARAUS

Wait, you who are sending this woman to be slaughtered,
mistress of this house—for your dignified bearing shows
me you are of free birth.   855

HYPSIPYLE
(kneeling before him)

O, by your knees—I fall as your suppliant, Amphiaraus—
and by your chin and the skill you have from Apollo;[3] for
you have come just in time for me in my troubles. Save me,
for I am to die because of my service to you. I am facing
death, you see me bound at your knees, who went with you 860
strangers then and assisted you. You will act righteously
since you are righteous; but if you forsake me, you will
bring reproach on the people of Argos and of Greece.
Come, you who perceive events for the Danaans through
(pure) burnt offerings, (tell) her what happened to her son. 865
You (know) since you were there, yet she claims I plotted
against her family and killed her boy on purpose.

AMPHIARAUS

I have come well acquainted with and had guessed your
situation and what you would suffer because of the child's
death. I am here now to defend you in your misfortune, re- 870
lying not on force but on piety. It would be shameful to

---

[3] A suppliant conventionally grasps the knees and chin of the
person supplicated, and appeals to their authority. Hypsipyle is
bound (v. 860), so she presumably uses the terminology without
enacting it.

δρᾶσαι δὲ μηδὲν εὖ παθόντα πρὸς σέθεν.
(75) πρῶτον μὲν οὖν σὸν δεῖξον, ὦ ξένη, κάρα·
875 σῶφρον γὰρ ὄμμα τοὐμόν—Ἑλλήνων λόγος
πολὺς διήκει—καὶ πέφυχ᾿ οὕτω, γύναι,
κοσμεῖν τ᾿ ἐμαυτὸν καὶ τὰ διαφέρονθ᾿ ὁρᾶν.
ἔπειτ᾿ ἄκουσον, τοῦ τάχους δὲ τοῦδ᾿ ἄνες·
(80) εἰς μὲν γὰρ ἄλλο πᾶν ἁμαρτάνειν χρεών,
880 ψυχὴν δ᾿ ἐς ἀνδρὸς ἢ γυναικὸς οὐ καλόν.

ΕΥΡΥΔΙΚΗ

ὦ ξένε πρὸς Ἄργει πλησία[ν] ναίων χθόνα,
πάντων ἀκούουσ᾿ οἶδά σ᾿ ὄ[ν]τα σώφρονα·
οὐ γάρ ποτ᾿ εἰς τόδ᾿ ὄμμ᾿ ἂν ἔβλ[ε]ψας παρών.
(85) νῦν δ᾿, εἴ τι βούλῃ, καὶ κλύε[ι]ν σέθεν θέλω
885 καὶ σ᾿ ἐκδιδάσκειν· οὐκ ἀνάξιος γὰρ εἶ.

ΑΜΦΙΑΡΑΟΣ

γύναι, τὸ τῆσδε τῆς ταλαιπώρου κ[α]κὸν
ἀγρίως φέρουσάν σ᾿ ἤπιον θ[έσθαι θέλ]ω,
οὐ τήνδε μᾶλ[λ]ον ἢ τὸ τῆς δ[ί]κης ὁ[ρ]ῶν.
(90) αἰσχύνομα[ι] δὲ Φοῖβον, οὗ δι᾿ ἐμπύρ[ω]ν
890 τέχνην ἐπασκῶ, ψεῦδος ε[ἴ τ]ι λέξομεν.
ταύτην ἐγὼ ᾿ξέπεισα κρηναῖον [γά]νος
δεῖξαι δι᾿ ἁγνῶν ῥευμάτων [...].υχ.[
στρατιᾶς πρόθυμ᾿, Ἀργεῖον ὡς δ[.].νην πυρ[
six lines wholly or largely lost, then:
900 ἡμ]εῖς δε[.]. ᾿[
...]αι θέλ[οντες
δρ]άκων ασ[

298

know all about accepting services, but not to do any service in return for yours. *(to Eurydice)* So first, lady, let me see your face;[4] my eye is disciplined—that is much mentioned in Hellas—and I have been bred to govern myself and to observe what matters. Then next, listen to me and give up this haste; one may be permitted to err in anything else, but with a man's or a woman's life this cannot be approved. 880

EURYDICE
(unveiling herself)
O stranger from the neighbouring land towards Argos, from all reports I know you are a disciplined man, or you would never have stood before me and looked upon my face. And now, if you wish it, I am ready to listen and explain things to you. You are not unworthy of that. 885

AMPHIARAUS
Lady, you are reacting cruelly to this poor woman's misfortune, but I would like to make you lenient, not considering her so much as the interests of justice. I shall be ashamed before Phoebus, whose art I practise with burnt offerings, if I say anything false. I myself persuaded this woman to 890 show me the bright spring-water . . . through its pure streams . . . a sacrifice for the army, so that(?) . . . Argive . . . . . . *(six lines wholly or largely lost)* . . . And we . . . wanting 900

[4] Eurydice has modestly drawn her veil over her face when confronted by an unfamiliar man. Amphiaraus assures her that he will respect her modesty.

901 σῶσ]αι von Arnim

ἠκόντισ' ἁ[

(105) καί νιν δρομ[

905 εἵλιξεν ἀμφ[

ἡμεῖς δ' ἰδό[ντες

ἐγὼ δ' ἐτόξευσ['

ἀρχὴ γὰρ ἡμῖν [

(110) Ἀρχέμορος ε.[

910 σύ τ' οὐχὶ σαυτὴ[ν

ὄρνιθα δ' Ἀργείο[ισι

καὶ μὴ ....[

ἀλλουχ[

(115) πολλοὶ δ[

915 Κάδμου[

νόστου κυρησ[

Ἄδραστος ἵξετ' αρ[

ἑπτὰ στρατηγ[

(120) τὰ μὲν γενόμεν[α

920 ἃ δ' αὖ παραινῶ, [ταῦτά μοι δέξαι, γύναι.

ἔφυ μὲν οὐδεὶς ὅ[στις οὐ πονεῖ βροτῶν·

θάπτει τε τέκ[να χἄτερα κτᾶται νέα,

αὐτός τε θνῄσκε[ι· καὶ τάδ' ἄχθονται βροτοὶ

(125) εἰς γῆν φέροντες [γῆν. ἀναγκαίως δ' ἔχει

925 βίον θερίζειν ὥ[στε κάρπιμον στάχυν,

καὶ τὸν μὲν εἶ[ναι, τὸν δὲ μή· τί ταῦτα δεῖ

στένειν ἅπε[ρ δεῖ κατὰ φύσιν διεκπερᾶν;

ἃ δ' εἰκὸς Ἀργο[

(130) θάψαι δὸς ἡμ[ῖν

930 οὐ γὰρ καθ' ἡμ[

(to rescue him?) . . . the serpent . . . shot forth . . . and . . .
him (rapidly?) . . . coiled around . . . And we, seeing . . . and   905
I shot (an arrow) . . . For . . . the beginning for us . . . [5]
Archemorus . . . and you . . . not . . . yourself . . . but an omen   910
for the Argives . . . and don't . . . but not(?) . . . many . . .
Cadmus' . . . (will?) achieve a homecoming . . . Adrastus   915
will come (to Argos?) . . . the seven commanders . . .

What happened (you now can understand clearly); but
now, lady, please accept this counsel that I offer you. No   920
mortal was ever born who does not suffer; he buries chil-
dren and gets other new ones, and dies himself, and mor-
tals grieve at these things, bringing earth to earth. But it is
our inevitable lot to harvest life like a fruitful crop, for one   925
of us to live, one not: why should we lament these things,
which by our very nature we must endure? But what it is
proper . . . Argos . . . Allow us to bury . . . [6] For not in . . . but   930

---

[5] In vv. 908–18 Amphiaraus interprets Opheltes' death as 'be-
ginning' (Greek arche-) the events that led to the fated deaths
(moroi) at Thebes of all the Argive leaders except Adrastus.
Opheltes is thus to be renamed *Archemorus*, 'First to die'.

[6] In vv. 929–40 Amphiaraus gives instructions for the funeral
of Opheltes/Archemorus and the games that will perpetuate his
memory at Nemea.

---

917 ἰξεταρ[P. Oxy.: ἥξει τ᾽ Ἀρ[γος Page   919 τὰ μὲν
γενόμεν[α δὴ σαφῶς ἐπίστασαι ed. pr. (e.g.)   920–7 (= fr.
757.1–8 N): Clement of Alexandria, *Miscellanies* 4.7.53.3 (vv.
920–3 and 926–7 ταῦτα—διεκπερᾶν); [Plutarch], *Moralia* 110f–
111a and Stob. 4.44.12 (vv. 921–7); vv. 925–6 are cited elsewhere,
and vv. 921–7 translated by Cicero, *Tusculan Disputations* 3.59;
Clement and [Plutarch] add a further verse, deleted by most edi-
tors (see F 1043a)

ἀλλ᾽ εἰς τὸν αἰε[ὶ
τοῖ[ς σο]ῖς βρότ. [
κλεινὸς γὰρ ἔσ[ται
(135) ἀγῶνά τ᾽ αὐτῷ[
935 στεφάνους διδ[
ζηλωτὸς ἔστ[αι
ἐν τῷδε με.[
μνησθήσετα[ι
(140) ἐπωνομάσθη[
940 Νεμέας κατ᾽ ἄλσ[ος
ἀναιτία γάρ· τοισ[
σὺν γὰρ καλῷ σο[
θήσει σε καὶ παιδ᾽ [

ΕΥΡΥΔΙΚΗ

(145) ὦ παῖ, τὸ μέν σοι τ[
945 ..] ἧσσον ἢ μην[
πρὸς τὰς φύσεις [χρὴ καὶ τὰ πράγματα σκοπεῖν
καὶ τὰς διαίτας τῶ[ν κακῶν τε κἀγαθῶν,
π[ει]θὼ δὲ τοῖς μὲ[ν σώφροσιν πολλὴν ἔχειν,
(150) το[ῖς μὴ δικ]αίοις [δ᾽ οὐδὲ συμβάλλειν χρεών.

946–9 (= fr. 759 N): Orion 7.5 Haffner

(758 N = 760a below)

758a

*Near-beginnings of five iambic trimeters including 1084
ἔοικε, 1085 Διόνυσος, then opening of a choral stasimon
with line-beginnings as follows:*

for eternal (time) . . . (your) . . . mortal . . . For he will be fa-
mous . . . and . . . a contest for him . . . giv(ing?) crowns . . .   935
he will be envied . . . in this . . . will be remembered . . . was
given the name . . . in the grove of Nemea . . . For she is   940
blameless . . . For with good . . . (for you?) . . . will make you
and your son . . .

EURYDICE

My son, the . . . for you . . . less than . . . We should look at   945
the natures of the good and the bad, and at their actions
and their ways of life, putting much trust in those who are
temperate, and not consorting at all with the unrighteous.

(758 N = 760a below)

758a

Five dialogue lines including 1084 . . . it seems . . . 1085 . . .
Dionysus . . . , *then line-beginnings from the opening of a
choral song celebrating Dionysus:*[1]

---

[1] The topics seem to be a yearning to commune with the
god and enjoy his gifts, then (1103ff., antistrophe?) an 'Orphic'
theogony/cosmogony giving prominence to the birth and ultimate
supremacy of Dionysus, as in the poem discussed in the Derveni
Papyrus (cf. R. Janko, *Classical Philology* 96 (2001), 1–32 and *ZPE*
141 (2002), 1–62; Aristophanes, *Birds* 690–702 is a parody of such
narratives). F 758b evokes the actual experience of Dionysiac
worship.

τίς ποτ᾽ [1100   τάχ᾽ ἂν ε[

1090 θαλαμο[χάριν α[

βάλλει ὑπ[(19)   ἀντάπο[

ἀνά τ᾽ αἰθ[έρ-   (ἀντ.?) ὦ πότνια θεῶ[ν

(10) τί τὸ σῆμα [   ]άος ἄσκοπον [

βότρυς α [1105   ]έρι πρωτόγονο[

1095 ἀναδίδω[σι   ]θελ᾽ Ἔρως ὅτε νυ[

ῥεῖ δὲ γά[   ]ν τ᾽ ἐτράφη τότε [

στάζει[(25)   ] α θεῶν γένο[ς

(15) νέκταρ[traces of one more line

λιβάνου[

P. Oxy. 852 col. 19, frs. 57 + 81

1096 γά[λακτι ed. pr.   1104 φ]άος ed. pr.: χ]άος re-
sisted by Morel   1105 ἀ]έρι ed. pr.: αἰ]θ]έρι Morel
1106 νὺ[ξ ed. pr. (or νυ[κτ-)

758b

From the same stasimon, some 20 lines later:

] υραι θέλομεν[

] σμύρνας καπν[

θα]λάμοις Βρόμιο[ ]ει[

] ἀπ᾽ οἴνας

5   ] τε φίλαι

νάρ]θηκα φέρουσα τριπέ[τηλον

]ας παρὰ χειρὸς ἐδε[ξ-

]ς ἐς οἴκους

]ερον· ὡς δ᾽ ἐπ᾽ ἐπώμ[ιον

10   κυ]παρισσόροφον χερὶ ν[

304

CHORUS

Who/what ever . . . chamber(s?) . . .casts (*or* strikes) . . . up   1090
to (*or* through) the heaven . . . What (is?) the sign . . . grape-
bunch . . . gives forth . . . . . . and flows (with milk?) . . . drips   1095
. . . nectar . . . of frankincense . . . perhaps . . . . . . joy/grace   1100
. . . reward . . . ?

O mistress . . . of the gods . . . inscrutable (light)[2] . . .
first-born[3] (in) mist (*or* heaven) . . . Erôs willed, when   1105
(Night) . . . and was nurtured then . . . family of gods . . .

[2] Either the primeval darkness (an oxymoron), or the dazzling brightness of the aether. The first editors' 'light' makes a more striking phrase than the alternative 'chaos' (primeval void).
[3] Perhaps Protogonos, a name of the primeval deity according to 'Orphic' doctrine. Both 'mist' (*aēr*) and 'heaven' (*aithēr*) were variously identified as primeval entities.

758b

From the same stasimon, some 20 lines later:

⟨CHORUS⟩

. . . (on the breeze *or* with the lyre) we want . . . myrrh-
smoke . . . (in the?) chamber . . . Bromius[1] . . . from the vine
. . . dear . . . , bearing the trefoil wand[2] . . . received from the   5
hand . . . into the/my home . . . and as . . . onto my shoulder-[3]

[1] 'Roarer', a title of Dionysus.   [2] The bacchant's thyrsus or ritual staff, wrapped in three-lobed ivy-leaves.   [3] Probably a reference to the fawnskin, draped over the bacchant's shoulder.

P. Oxy. 852 col. 20, frs. 58 etc.

1] αὖραι (or αὗραι) or] λύραι

ἔ]σωθεν
]τι...[.]..[....]μόν[
]ας ἁμᾶς [
]ο κτῆμα ..[..´]τασ[
15   ]ς οὐχὶ θιγ[
]ν οἴκοις
] ἐξάγετα[ι ......].α
]ον γενο.[
]εῖπε τ᾽ ἄ[....]εμις
20   ]μεν σα.[....]χρη πέρας
]η χάριν [....]ασθαι
]ιδ᾽ ἀπομ[

758c

*From a scene more than 300 lines later, middles and ends
of iambic trimeters:*

⟨ΤΥΨΙΠΤΛΗ?⟩
traces of one line
] ἄνδρα κατέφυγεν[
]θειν ἐστὶν εἰς τα[.]δε.[
]ους ἀνέθεσαν· τὰς συν[
5   ] οὐκ ἔχουσι συμμάχους
]ς Ἀμφιάρεως· σωσαι[
]θις ὥσπερεὶ νεὼς [
λ]α[μ]βάνω[

P. Oxy 852 col. 25, fr. 63

. . . cypress-roofed[4] . . . in my hand . . . . . . within . . . *(one il-* 10
legible line) . . . our/my . . . (the?) possession . . . not touch 15
. . . home(s) . . . brings (*or* is brought) forth . . . *(remains*
of one line) . . . and said . . . limit . . . joy/grace . . . *(remains* 20
of one more line) . . .

[4] Probably a ritual chamber: cf. *Cretans* F 472.4–8, *Antiope* F
203.

758c
Spoken lines from a scene more than 300 lines later:[1]

⟨HYPSIPYLE?⟩
. . . *(traces of one line)* . . . took refuge . . . man . . . is . . . into
. . . (they) dedicated/attributed . . . (they) do not have (*or*
not having) allies . . . Amphiaraus; . . . save . . . like a ship's 5
. . . I(?) take/find . . .

[1] Probably just before the recognition. This and the next frag-
ment seem to refer to Hypsipyle's servitude, her separation from
her sons, and Amphiaraus' assistance to her. Hypsipyle appears to
speak some, possibly all, of the lines.

EURIPIDES

758d

Several lines later, trimeter-ends:

remains of four line-ends

5   ]λ' ο[ὔ]ρι' ἀζήλῳ κα[κῷ

ἦ]λθε καρδίας ἔσ[ω

]σδ' [ἔ]χοις νεανι[

]λθ' ὁμοῦ παρόνθ' ὁ.[

ζῶ]σιν ἢ τεθνᾶσι δ[ή

10   ]λλα δυστυχοῦν[

] δουλείαν πικρ[άν

]ς ἀνηνύτους λό[γους

]αύσομαι σεδω[

]καταστήσειας ἄ[ν

15   πρό]σθ' ἐλευθέραν .[

]ρος εἶ σύ μοι, τερ[

]οφῳ δοίης χά[ριν

remains of two more lines

P. Oxy. 852 col. 26, frs. 61 + 82

7 τού]σδ' [ἔ]χοις νεανί[ας von Arnim   10 πο]λλὰ von Arnim (or ἀ]λλὰ, Kannicht)   13 π]αύσομαι E. Petersen: κλ]αύσομαι von Arnim   16 τερ[read in ed. pr. (τέρ[ας, τερ[ασκόπος?]: τέκ[νον von Arnim, E. Petersen   17 σ]οφῷ ed. pr.: τρ]οφῷ von Arnim

(759 N = 757.946–9 above)

759a

Some 45 lines later, scattered line-ends from vv. ~ 1530–78 (col. 27 = fr. 64 col. i) yielding only the words Ἠδωνίσι

758d

Several lines later:
... favourable ... (to/through?) unenviable trouble ... oc-   5
curred within my heart ... you might have (these) young
men ... being present together ... they are (*or* are they)
alive or dead ... suffering (many?) misfortunes ...... bit-   10
ter servitude ... unavailing (words) ... I shall cease (*or* I
shall weep) ... you ... you would establish/render ... (for-
merly) free ...... you are ... to me[1] ... you might give   15
thanks ...[2]

[1] Perhaps 'to me, my son ... ' (von Arnim, Petersen).
[2] Perhaps 'give thanks to (*or* with) a wise ...' (first editors), or 'give
thanks to your nurse' (von Arnim).

(759 N = 757.946–9 above)

759a

*Some 45 lines later, scattered line-ends from vv. ~1530–78
yielding only the words* Edonian women *and* (Mount)

and Πάγγαιον *from marginal notes at vv. 50–1 (~ 1571–2), then in col. 28 (= fr. 64 col. ii):*

⟨ΥΨΙΠΤΛΗ⟩

τέκνα τ᾽ ἀνὰ μίαν ὁδὸν
1580 ἀνάπ[α]λιν ἐτρόχασεν
(60) ἐπὶ φόβον ἐπὶ {τε} χάριν
ἑλίξας, χρόνῳ δ᾽
ἐξέλαμψεν εὐάμερος.

ΑΜΦΙΑΡΑΟΣ

τὴν μὲν παρ᾽ ἡ[μ]ῶν, ὦ γύναι, φέρῃ χάριν·
1585 ἐπεὶ δ᾽ ἐμοὶ πρόθυμος ἦσθ᾽ ὅτ᾽ ᾐτόμην,
(65) ἀπέδωκα κἀγὼ σοὶ πρόθυμ᾽ ἐς παῖδε σώ.
σῴζου δὲ δὴ σύ, σφὼ δὲ τήνδε μητέρα,
καὶ χαίρεθ᾽· ἡμε[ῖ]ς δ᾽, ὥσπερ ὡρμήμεσθα δή,
στράτευμ᾽ ἄγοντες ἥξομεν Θήβας ἔπι.

ΥΨΙΠΤΛΗ

1590 εὐδαιμονοίης, ἄξιος γάρ, ὦ ξένε.

ΕΥΝΗΟΣ

(70) εὐδαιμονοίης δῆτα. τῶν δὲ σῶν κακῶν,
τάλαινα μῆτερ, θεῶν τις ὡς ἄπληστος ἦ⟨ν⟩.

ΥΨΙΠΤΛΗ

αἰαῖ, φυγὰς ἐμέθεν ἃς ἔφυγον,
ὦ τέκνον, εἰ μάθοις, Λήμνου ποντίας,
1595 πολιὸν ὅτι πατέρος οὐκ ἔτεμον κάρα.

P. Oxy 852 cols. 27–29, frs. 64 etc.

Pangaeus *(both associated with the worship of Dionysus in Thrace) from marginal notes at vv. ~1571–2; then from the reunion celebration of Hypsipyle, Euneos, Thoas (mute) and Amphiaraus:*

⟨HYPSIPYLE⟩
(singing joyfully) . . . (our fortune?) has driven (me) and
my sons along a single path, this way and that, swerving us   1580
now towards fear, now towards gladness, but in time has
shone out bright and fair.

AMPHIARAUS
(speaking) Lady, you now have the favour that I owed you.
As you were generous to me when I made my request, so   1585
I have repaid you generously concerning your two sons.
Keep yourself safe, now—and you two protect your
mother; and prosper, while we, as we set out to do, will lead
our army on and come to Thebes.
(Amphiaraus departs)

HYPSIPYLE
(speaking)
Good fortune to you, for you are worthy of it, stranger.   1590

EUNEOS
(speaking)
Good fortune indeed—but as for you, poor mother, how
greedily some god has fed on your misfortunes!

HYPSIPYLE
(singing her replies)
Alas, the flight that I fled, my son—if you only knew it—
from sea-girt Lemnos, because I did not cut off my father's
grey head![1]   1595

---

[1] See Introduction above on the Lemnian massacre and
Hypsipyle's role in it.

EURIPIDES

ΕΥΝΗΟΣ

(75) ἦ γάρ σ' ἔταξαν πατέρα σὸν κατακτανεῖν;

ΤΨΙΠΤΛΗ

φόβος ἔχει με τῶν τότε κακῶν· ἰὼ
τέκνον, οἷά τε Γοργάδες ἐν λέκτροις
ἔκανον εὐνέτας.

ΕΥΝΗΟΣ

1600 σὺ δ' ἐξέκλεψας πῶς πόδ' ὥστε μὴ θανεῖν;

ΤΨΙΠΤΛΗ

(80) ἀκτὰς βαρυβρόμους ἱκόμαν
ἐπί τ' οἶδμα θαλάσσιον, ὀρνίθων
ἔρημον κοίταν.

ΕΥΝΗΟΣ

κἀκεῖθεν ἦλθες δεῦρο πῶς, τίνι στόλῳ;

ΤΨΙΠΤΛΗ

1605 ναῦται κώπαις
(85) Ναύπλιον εἰς λιμένα ξενικὸν πόρον
ἄγαγόν με
δουλοσύ[ν]ας τ' ἐπέβασαν, <ἰ>ὼ τέ[κ]νον,
ἐνθάδε νάϊον, μέλεον ἐμπολάν.

ΕΥΝΗΟΣ

οἴμοι κακῶν σῶν.

ΤΨΙΠΤΛΗ

1610 μὴ στέν' ἐπ' εὐτυχίαισιν.
(90) ἀλλὰ σὺ πῶς ἐτράφης ὅδε τ', ἐν τίνι
χειρί, τέκνον; ὦ τέκνον,
ἔνεπ' ἔνεπε ματρὶ σᾷ.

EUNEOS

Did they really order you to kill your father?

HYPSIPYLE

I am gripped by fear of those evil events—O my son, like
Gorgons they slew their husbands in their beds!

EUNEOS

And you—how did you steal away and so escape death? 1600

HYPSIPYLE

I came to the deep-resounding shore and the swelling sea,
the lonely refuge of birds.

EUNEOS

And how did you come here from there, what transport did
you use?

HYPSIPYLE

Seafarers, rowing, took me on a foreign voyage to Nau- 1605
plion harbour and sold me into slavery—O my son—in this
land, ship-borne, a pitiful piece of merchandise.

EUNEOS

Alas for your hardships—

HYPSIPYLE

　　　　　　Don't grieve at what turned out well! 1610
But how were you and your brother raised, my son, and in
whose care? Tell, tell this to your mother, O my son!

EURIPIDES

ΕΤΝΗΟΣ

Ἀργώ με καὶ τόνδ' ἤγαγ' εἰς Κόλχων πόλιν.

ΤΨΙΠΤΛΗ

1615   ἀπομαστίδιόν γ' ἐμῶν στέρνων.

ΕΤΝΗΟΣ

(95)   ἐπεὶ δ' Ἰάσων ἔθαν' ἐμός, μῆτερ, πατήρ—

ΤΨΙΠΤΛΗ

οἴμοι κακὰ λέγεις δάκρυά τ' ὄμμασιν,
τέκνον, ἐμοῖς δίδως.

ΕΤΝΗΟΣ

Ὀρφεύς με καὶ τόνδ' ἤγαγ' εἰς Θρῄκης τόπον.

ΤΨΙΠΤΛΗ

1620   τίνα πατέρι ποτὲ χάριν ἀθλίῳ
(100)   τιθέμενος; ἔνεπέ μοι, τέκνον.

ΕΤΝΗΟΣ

μοῦσάν με κιθάρας Ἀσιάδος διδάσκεται,
τοῦτ[ο]ν δ' ἐς Ἄρεως ὅπλ' ἐκόσμησεν μάχης.

ΤΨΙΠΤΛΗ

δι' Αἰγαίου δὲ τίνα πόρον ἐμ[ό]λετ'
1625   ἀκτὰν Λημνίαν;

ΕΤΝΗΟΣ

(105)   Θόας [κ]ομίζει σὸς πατὴρ †δυοῖν τέκνω†.

1626 δυοῖν τέκνω P. Oxy.: δισσὼ (or παιδὸς) τέκνω Wecklein:
τὼ σὼ τέκνω Collard

314

EUNEOS

Argo took us to the Colchians' city.

HYPSIPYLE

Yes, just lately weaned as you were from my breast!   1615

EUNEOS

And when my father Jason died, mother . . .[2]

HYPSIPYLE

Alas, you tell me of evils and bring tears to my eyes, my son.

EUNEOS

. . . Orpheus took us to the region of Thrace.

HYPSIPYLE

What service was he doing for your hapless father? Tell   1620
me, my son!

EUNEOS

He taught me the music of the Asian lyre, and trained my
brother in Ares' martial arms.[3]

HYPSIPYLE

And how did you travel across the Aegean to Lemnos'
shore?   1625

EUNEOS

Thoas your father conveyed †the children of two†.[4]

---

[2] In this account Jason appears to have died at Colchis: see Introduction above.   [3] The politically fundamental functions of music and warfare are divided between the twins, as between Amphion and Zethus in *Antiope* (especially F 223.86–95). For Euneos' connection with music at Athens see Introduction above.
[4] Restoration uncertain: 'the twin sons' or 'his son's sons', Wecklein; 'your two sons', Collard.

ΤΨΙΠΤΛΗ

ἦ γὰ[ρ] σέσ[ω]τ[α]ι;

ΕΤΝΗΟΣ
> Βα[κ]χ[ίου] γε μηχαναῖς.

ΤΨΙΠΤΛΗ
>]βό[..]ι πόνων
>].ι προσδοκία βιοτᾶς
> ἐ]πόρευσε ματρί παῖδα σῇ
>]ιε μοι

1630
(110)

ΕΤΝΗΟΣ
κει[   ] Θόαντος οἰνωπὸν βότρυν.

col. 29 (= fr. 64 col. iii): scattered traces of line-beginnings, with speaker-notation διοννς at v. 41 (~ 1673). The final column of P. Oxy. (vv. ~ 1687–end) is entirely lost.

UNPLACED FRAGMENTS

760

ἔξω γὰρ ὀργῆς πᾶς ἀνὴρ σοφώτερος.

Stobaeus 3.20.31 (also Stob. 3.20.12, combined with Archelaus F 259 and adesp. F 523)

760a (= 758 N)

κακοῖς τὸ κέρδος τῆς δίκης ὑπέρτερον.

Stobaeus 3.10.26

HYPSIPYLE

Is he really safe, then?

EUNEOS

Yes, through Bacchus' contriving.

HYPSIPYLE

. . . (of/from?) hardships . . . expectation of life . . . brought
(his?) son for your mother . . . (to/for?) me.   1630

EUNEOS

. . . Thoas'(?) wine-dark grape-bunch.[5]

[5] Possibly a gold ornament used as a recognition token (see Introduction above).

*The remaining text is almost entirely lost, except for the
speaker-notation* DIONYSUS *at v. ~1673.*

UNPLACED FRAGMENTS

760

Every man is wiser when he avoids anger.

760a (= 758N)

To bad people profit is more important than fairness.

EURIPIDES

761

ἄελπτον οὐδέν, πάντα δ᾽ ἐλπίζειν χρεών.

Stobaeus 4.46.16

762

εὔφημα καὶ σᾶ καὶ κατεσφραγισμένα

Eustathius on Homer, *Iliad* 13.773 citing Aelius Dionysius σ 1 Erbse

εὔφημα Eustath.: εὔσημα Valckenaer

763

ἆρ᾽ ἐκδιδάσκω τὸ σαφές;

Aristophanes, *Frogs* 64 with Schol.

(764 N = 752c above)

765

⟨ΧΟΡΟΣ⟩
οἰνάνθα τρέφει τὸν ἱερὸν βότρυν

Schol. and Tzetzes on Aristophanes, *Frogs* 1320

765a (= 756 N)

⟨ΤΥΙΠΤΛΗ⟩
περίβαλλ᾽, ὦ τέκνον, ὠλένας.

Aristophanes, *Frogs* 1322 with Schol.

761

Nothing is beyond expectation; one should expect every-thing.

762

. . . auspicious, safely kept and stamped with a seal . . .[1]

[1] Possibly referring to the recognition token(s). Valckenaer therefore suggested altering 'auspicious' to 'well marked'.

763

Am I giving you clear information?

(764 N = 752c above)

765

<CHORUS>

. . . the vine-shoot nurtures its sacred cluster . . .[1]

[1] A lyric phrase, possibly from the same hymn as F 758a–b.

765a (= 756 N)

<HYPSIPYLE>
(singing)

Throw your arms around me, my child![1]

[1] Almost certainly from the recognition scene.

765b

ἀνὰ τὸ δωδεκαμήχανον ἄστρον   .

Aristophanes, *Frogs* 1327 with Schol.; Suda δ 1442 Adler

765c (= 942 N)

οὐδὲν γὰρ ἀσφαλές ἐστι τῆς τύχης, ὡς Εὐριπίδης ἐν Ὑψιπύλη.

John Lydus, *On Months* 4.7 and 4.100

(768 N = 752h.15 above)

(770 N = 752f.13 above)

765b

. . . like(?) the star with twelve devices . . .[1]

[1] Sense and reference unclear: possibly the sun passing through the zodiac. In Aristophanes' parody Aeschylus accuses Euripides of composing his lyrics 'in the manner of Cyrene's twelve devices' (i.e. her versatile sexual technique).

765c (= 942 N)

Nothing in the realm of fortune is secure, as Euripides (says) in *Hypsipyle*.

(768 N = 752h.15 above)

(770 N = 752f.13 above)

PHAETHON

F. Blass, *Dissertatio de Phaethontis Euripideae fragmentis Claromontanis* (Kiel, 1885); J. Diggle, *Euripides: Phaethon* (Cambridge, 1970), supplemented in *AC* 65 (1996), 189–99; reviews of Diggle by H. Lloyd-Jones, *CR* 21 (1971), 341–5 (= *Academic Papers: Greek Epic, Lyric and Tragedy* [Oxford, 1990], 452–7) and R. Kannicht, *Gnomon* 44 (1972), 1–12; C. Collard in *SFP* I.195–238; Diggle, *TrGFS* 150–60 (vv. 1–7, 45–126, 158–76, 214–88); H. Van Looy in ed. Budé VIII.3.225–67.

Wilamowitz, *Kleine Schriften* I.110–47 (= *Hermes* 18 [1883], 396–434), and *Sappho und Simonides* (Berlin, 1913), 38–9; H. Weil, *REG* 2 (1889), 323–8; A. Lesky, *Wiener Studien* 50 (1932), 1–25 (= *Gesammelte Schriften* 111–30); Webster 220–32; K. Reckford, *TAPA* 103 (1972), 405–32; L. Burelli in L. Braccesi (ed.), *I Tragici Greci e l'Occidente* (Bologna, 1979), 131–9; Aélion (1983), I.303–11; A. Barigazzi, *Prometheus* 15 (1990), 97–110; Gantz 31–4; *LIMC* VI.i.69–70 'Klymene II', and VII.i.350–4 'Phaethon I'; A. Debiasi, *Anemos* 2 (2001), 285–319; Matthiessen 268–70.

Phaethon was destroyed when he lost control of his father Helios the sun god's fiery chariot; Zeus blasted him from the sky with lightning to save the world from incineration.

*His tragedy was widely retold in later antiquity, most fully
in Ovid,* Metamorphoses *1.750–2.400 and Nonnus,* Dio-
nysiaca *38.90–434 (both concentrate on the chariot ride),
and summarily in the Scholia on Homer,* Odyssey *17.208,
Diodorus 5.23, and Hyginus,* Fab. *152A, 154, and else-
where. Evidence for the myth from the archaic and classi-
cal periods is scanty, and the fragmentary* Phaethon *is in
fact the only extensive text to survive; there is nothing at all
in art until Hellenistic and Roman times (see below). Aes-
chylus'* Daughters of Helios, *which seems to have treated
largely the same incidents as Euripides, has disappeared
except for a few scattered lines (F 68–73a).*

The Phaethon *of Euripides and many later accounts is
the son of Helios and the nymph Clymene, daughter of
Oceanus; but in the earliest, almost isolated occurrence of
his name his parents are Eos (Dawn) and Cephalus, and as
a beautiful youth he is abducted by Aphrodite and made
her temple keeper ([Hesiod],* Theogony *986–91, cf. Pau-
sanias 1.3.1). Most scholars (but not Lloyd-Jones 341–3)
now accept Diggle's argument that these discrepant stories
are irreconcilable, and that this other Phaethon is a 'differ-
ent figure' (Gantz 31). On all these matters see Diggle
(1970), 3–32, 180–220 and (1996), 189–90, 199; Gantz 31–
4, 238; LIMC VII.i.350–2; Aélion (1983) I.303–5, 308–9;
Van Looy 225–32.*

*The principal play fragments are preserved on palimp-
sest parchment, but are intermittently damaged or defec-
tive (see Note on the text below); they include two complete
choral lyrics, one an evocative dawn song (63–94, over-
lapped by a papyrus text), the other a wedding hymn (227–
44). The few book fragments can almost all be fitted into*

*or around these fuller remains with the aid of the later
sources.*

*The play's setting is coloured and affected throughout
by the divine: it is Oceanus' land (111), close to Helios' sta-
bles for his sun chariot (5), and so at the remotest eastern
boundary of the mythical world. Strabo 1.2.27, the source
of vv. 1–7, says that this closeness is 'woven into the whole
play'. The scene is before the palace of king Merops (a mor-
tal), to whom Clymene is now married (test. ii.1–4 below,
and v. 1); she has told neither him nor Phaethon the boy's
true father. The action begins before dawn on the day on
which Merops will begin the marriage of Phaethon (95–
118) to a goddess (241, cf. 236–7; also 24?). Clymene real-
izes that on this day she must tell Phaethon about Helios
(although she will keep it hidden from Merops); Phaethon
distrusts her, but accepts her advice to secure confirmation
from Helios by asking for a gift that only a true father
would give (1–62, the prologue scene, incomplete and dam-
aged). Merops inaugurates the marriage (63–118, choral
entry song and prayers, Merops' ceremonious entry and
announcement; largely undamaged), and a strained dis-
cussion between him and Phaethon reveals his determina-
tion upon the marriage and Phaethon's misgivings (119–67
and F 777, parts of the first episode; very badly damaged
and defective). Clymene is absent from this episode, and
at its end Phaethon leaves to visit Helios. Then a messen-
ger, probably Phaethon's tutor (see (B) below), reports to
Clymene Phaethon's death in the chariot drive which was
Helios' reluctant gift to him (168–77 and F 786, two book
fragments from the second episode). Phaethon's still smoul-
dering corpse is brought to Clymene (off-stage?: see (C)*

*below); her attempt to conceal it from Merops fails when he
enters with a second chorus singing a wedding hymn; his
grief and anger threaten her life; he interrogates the Tu-
tor, why the death occurred (178–327, third episode, ur-
gently paced and extraordinarily various in content and
manner; incomplete, with start and end badly damaged
or defective). After this, scholars infer from F 782–5 a
fourth episode running into the exodos (see D, E below):
Merops learns the whole truth about Phaethon and con-
fronts Clymene; a god saves her from death, and will have
prophesied Phaethon's burial and future cult.*

*Brief fragments: F 783 (= fr. 5 Diggle) 'golden mass' (of
the Sun), uncertainly located in the play; similarly F 783b
(780 N = fr. 2 Diggle), a reference to the 'three Hyades', a
constellation; both seem likely to belong to the ending.
Other ascriptions: F 896, 971 (see notes to these), 982.*

*Some aspects of the play: (A) The main characters and
factors are clear enough after the first episode (after 167):
Clymene is anxious, Phaethon misgives everything, Mer-
ops is joyful and obsessively determined. Clymene's secret
is revealed to Phaethon, but he does not pass it to Merops,
probably because of their apparent disagreement; indeed
they may have been given a formal agon scene, but we
cannot tell how long it was. (B) The messenger was al-
most certainly Phaethon's tutor, who would plausibly ac-
company him (Lesky 2/112); the Tutor is interrogated by
Merops later in the play (317). (C) The display of a disfig-
ured corpse was common enough, but not one described
as smouldering (214–5); it may have been kept just off-
stage (216, 219–21 permit this manoeuvre), with concealed
smoke effects like those presumed at* Suppliant Women
1009–71 and Trojan Women *1271–99. (D) When Merops*

*goes to investigate the smoke from Phaethon's body, the Chorus sing of their anxiety for Clymene when it is found (270–88): these tones, and the few remaining words and book fragments, suggest the onset of a final crisis and resolution typical of Euripides' invention (not reflected in the later narrative sources, however). (E) The crisis appears when Merops returns from the body, singing a monody (now sadly damaged) of grief for his 'son' and the lost marriage (289–310). Clymene was saved from his anger, almost certainly not through his own mercy but probably by her father Oceanus (see most recently Van Looy 243, Matthiessen 269; cf. vv. 281–4); a god is needed to forecast Phaethon's cult, and the transformation of his half-sisters the Daughters of Helios into poplars, their tears turning to amber (see Aeschylus, Daughters of Helios F 71–73a, Pliny, Natural History 37.2.31–2, Hyginus, and cf. F 782). (F) Phaethon's burial place in most ancient sources is near the river Eridanus or Padus (modern Po) in the West (first at Aeschylus F 71 cited by Pliny, Natural History 37.2.31–2; cf. e.g. Schol. on Homer, Odyssey 17.208, Hyginus; Burelli adduces Hippolytus 737–41); but Pliny 37.2.33 cites an authority for its location in 'Ethiopia' (test. *iv below), i.e. in the East where the play is set (see Diggle [1970], 27–32 and 44–6 for this likelihood); it would suit the economy of the play's location (Strabo above), if Phaethon were given funeral near where he fell. (G) The myth-version in which Aphrodite abducted Phaethon ([Hesiod], above) and her invocation in the wedding hymn (230–9) long induced agreement that Phaethon's bride was the 'goddess' referred to in v. 241 (cf. 236–7 with notes), especially after Wilamowitz (1883), 413, 432–3 and (1913), 38; so e.g. Lesky, Webster 227–9, Debiasi (2001), 317–9. But*

Aphrodite was a great goddess, beyond any mortal's aspiration, even that of the child of the Sun god and a nymph; and many now follow Diggle (1970, 155–60) in accepting Weil's suggestion that the intended bride was one of Helios' daughters who were Phaethon's half-sisters (e.g. Aélion 307, Van Looy 238, Matthiessen 268). (H) Was the play less a tragedy than a very human turmoil quietened only by a god? (Reckford marks the similarities especially with Ion, *and with* Hippolytus *where a similarly 'athletic' youth [cf. our F **785] is destroyed in a chariot.) The fears and desires of Clymene, Phaethon and Merops are entirely natural and work ironically to their mutual dangers (Webster 232). Phaethon's self-destruction is more than a youth's foolish presumption in demanding to drive the chariot: he was no doubt unsettled by Clymene's revelation and by Merops' blind determination. Despite the setting, there is little evidence in the fragments of divine control (rather the reverse!), and it is argued that Phaethon's death is due in part to irrational chance (Barigazzi, on the basis of Plutarch's interpretation of the story,* Moralia *498a).*

Date: the only reliable indication comes from the metrical criteria, which point either side of 420: see Diggle (1970), 47–9; Cropp–Fick 87, and cf. Webster 220.

Only one subsequent tragedy is known, and by title only, by the mid-4th c. Theodorides (see TrGF 1².249, 342). An Apulian crater of c. A.D. 350 (LIMC 'Klymene II' no. 1, Trendall–Webster III.5.5, Todisco Ap 84) may reflect a dramatic scene, but almost certainly not from Euripides (see adesp. F 5f; Diggle (1996), 189). Among late works of art depicting incidents from the myth generally see especially two 2nd/3rd c. Roman sarcophagi, LIMC 'Phaethon I' nos. 7 and 9 (= Diggle [1970], 214–7, nos. 3 and 4 with

Pl. 6). Goethe was inspired by the first major recovery of the play text in 1820 to translate, study and imitate the play; see Wilamowitz (1883), 397 and Kannicht (1972), 4 n. 4; in general OGCMA II.888–92.

Note on the text: The main source for the text of Phaethon *is the parchment Paris Bibl. Nat. ms. Gr. 107B, which has vv. 8–157 and 178–327, variously complete or badly damaged, in palimpsest form. It has deteriorated since its first transcription in 1819 and the first competent edition by Blass (1885): see Diggle (1970), 33–4 with Pls. I–V and (1996), 190–1; Kannicht (1972), 2 and TrGF 5.801–2. We cite this text as* P *and its many corrections as* Pᶜ, *and use the continuous line-numbering of Diggle (1970). In the text and translation we add in brackets Kannicht's fragment numbers (F 771 etc.) and his line numbers within the longer fragments. Unplaced fragments are identified by Kannicht's numbers, with Diggle's given in brackets in text and translation, e.g.* *786 (fr. 3 Diggle).*

ΦΑΕΘΩΝ

test. ii (Hypothesis)

an uncertain number of lines missing from the start, then:

δ[. . . .]σης· τ[*fifteen letters?*   Μέ-
ροπι δὲ μετα[*sixteen letters?*   ἐγέν-
νησεν· πάντων δὲ [π]α[τ]έρα ἔφη[σε(ν)] τ[ὸν
κατὰ νόμους συ[νοικ]οῦντα εἶναι[·] γε-
5   νηθέντι δ᾽ ἐν ἡλικίᾳ τῷ Φαέθοντι
τὴν ἀλήθειαν ἐξέφηνεν· ἀπιστοῦντι
δὲ ὡς ἔστιν Ἡλ[ί]ου παῖς προσέταξεν
ἐ[λ]θεῖν πρὸς τὰς ἱπ[ποστ]άσεις τοῦ θεο[ῦ
γει]τνιώσας· καὶ δῶρ[ο]ν αἰτήσασθα[ι ὃ
10 ἂν ἐθελ]ήσῃ[ι]· [π]αραγενηθεὶς δὲ κ[.

remains of three further lines

P. Oxy. 2455 fr. 14 col. xv, ed. E. Turner (1962), re-ed. Austin,
NFE 99; W. Luppe, *Philologus* 127 (1983), 135–9, cf. *ZPE* 52
(1983), 43–4; Diggle (1970), 53 and *TrGFS* 150; van Rossum-
Steenbeek 222–3.

PHAETHON

test. ii (Hypothesis)

. . . and to Merops after (this) (*or* after [him], i.e. Phaethon)
she bore . . .;[1] she (said) that the man living legally with her was
the father of (them) all. When Phaethon was of age, however,
she revealed the truth to him, and when he disbelieved that he   5
was the son of Helios, she told him to go to the god's stables,
which were in the neighbourhood, and to request . . . (any) gift
(he wanted); when he got there . . .

[1] Clymene's marriage to Merops (Strabo 1.2.27, source of vv.
1–5) was stated in the preceding lines.

---

2 μετὰ [ταῦτα Turner μετὰ [τοῦτον Kannicht   ἐγέν]νη-
σεν Diggle   3 ἔφη[σε(ν)] Luppe   4 συ[νοικ]οῦντα
editors: συ[μβι]οῦντα Turner   9–10 ὃ | ἂν ἐθελ]ήσῃ[ι
Diggle

EURIPIDES

test. *iii

Ac ne illa quidem promissa seruanda sunt, quae non sunt iis ipsis utilia, quibus illa promiseris. Sol Phaethonti filio . . . facturum se esse dixit quidquid optasset. Optauit ut in currum patris tolleretur; sublatus est; atque ante quam constitit ictu fulminis deflagrauit. Quanto melius fuerat in hoc promissum patris non esse seruatum!

Cicero, *On Duties* 3.94

test. *iv

Chares uero Phaethontem in Aethiopia Ἄμμωνος νήσῳ obisse, ibi et delubrum eius esse atque oraculum, electrumque gigni.

Chares of Mytilene, *FGrH* 125 F 8 in Pliny, *Natural History* 37.2.33

1–5 (F 771)

From the prologue speech:

⟨ΚΛΥΜΕΝΗ⟩

 . . . Μέροπι τῆσδ᾿ ἄνακτι γῆς,
ἣν ἐκ τεθρίππων ἁρμάτων πρώτην χθόνα
Ἥλιος ἀνίσχων χρυσέᾳ βάλλει φλογί.
καλοῦσι δ᾿ αὐτὴν γείτονες μελάμβροτοι
5 Ἕω φαεννὰς Ἡλίου θ᾿ ἱπποστάσεις.

Strabo 1.2.27

332

PHAETHON

test. *iii

Also, not even those promises are to be kept which are not beneficial to those you have made them to. The Sun told his son Phaethon . . . that he would do whatever he wished. Phaethon wished he might be taken up in his father's chariot; he was borne aloft, and before he came to a stop he was burned up by a bolt of lightning. How much better it had been in this case for the father's promise not to have been kept!

test. *iv

Chares however (said that) Phaethon met his end in Ethiopia on the island of Ammon, and that there he has both a shrine and an oracle, and amber is produced.[1]

---

[1] Amber was said to have originated in the tears wept for Phaethon by his half-sisters (cf. Introduction (E) and (F), and F 782 with note).

1–5 (F 771)

⟨CLYMENE⟩

(speaking the prologue before Merops' palace)
. . . (I was given in marriage) to Merops the king of this land, which is the first soil that Helios as he rises strikes with a flame of gold from his four-horsed chariot. Its black neighbours call the land the bright stables of Dawn and Helios.[1]

---

[1] Ethiopia is here loosely the remote East (see on *Archelaus* F 228.3–4). Dawn and Helios with his chariot are paired at *Iphigenia at Aulis* 157–9. For Strabo's comment on the dramatic importance of these lines see Introduction above.

6–7 (F 772)

⟨ΚΛΥΜΕΝΗ⟩

θερμὴ δ' ἄνακτος φλὸξ ὑπερτέλλουσα γῆς
καίει τὰ πόρσω, τἀγγύθεν δ' εὔκρατ' ἔχει.

v. 6: Stobaeus 1.25.6; v. 7: Vitruvius 9.1.13; joined as one fragment by Barnes

8–44 (F 772a)

The end of the prologue speech and start of Clymene's dialogue with the newly entering Phaethon are lost; continuous text begins with the ends of 37 trimeters (with changes of speaker indicated by dicola after vv. 9, 13, 22, 41, showing that the dialogue was irregular), including:

8 θεῶν 9 ἐ]κπέμπων πατήρ 10 λέχος 13 λέχη
19 γα]μηλίους 20 πατρί 22 πατήρ 24 θεᾶς(?)
λέχη 25 ἀεὶ λέγεις 26 θεούς 27 ἐ]λπίσιν
30 φιλεῖ(ν?) 31 γάμοι 38 ἐν]νέπουσά μοι
39 πατρός 41 φίλον 42 τ]ὰ φίλτατα
four lines lost before the next fragment

8–157, 178–327: Paris Bibl. Nat. ms. Gr. 107B (see *Note on the text*, after the Introduction above)

45–120 (F 773)

End of the prologue scene, parodos of the Chorus, and start of the first episode:

⟨ΚΛΥΜΕΝΗ⟩

45 μνησθεὶς ὅ μοί ποτ' εἶφ' ὅτ' ἠυνάσθη θεός,
αἰτοῦ τί χρήζεις ἕν· πέρα γὰρ οὐ θέμις

PHAETHON

6–7 (F 772)

‹CLYMENE›

(continuing her prologue speech)

The (Sun-)lord's hot flame rises high above the earth and scorches its remote parts, but keeps those near here moderate.[1]

---

[1] Tolerable to white men, implicitly contrasted with their 'black neighbours' (v. 4).

8–44 (F 772a)

Line-ends from a dialogue between Clymene and Phaethon, who has come out of the palace to join her, including:
8 of gods   9 father[1] sending . . . out   10 marriage(-bed)
13 marriage-(beds)   19 marital   20 to (your?) father
22 (your?) father   24 marriage (to a goddess?)[2]   25 you always say   26 gods   27 (in *or* with) hopes   30 (to?) love *or* he loves   31 marriage(s)   38 telling me
39 of (your?) father   41 dear   42 (his? *or* my?) dearest (son?)
four lines lost before the next fragment

---

[1] Here and in vv. 20, 22 and 39 either Merops or Helios: Clymene is revealing his true father Helios to the disbelieving Phaethon (cf. 51–3, 61–2).   [2] See vv. 227–44 with notes, and Introduction (G).

45–120 (F 773)

Dialogue between Clymene and Phaethon continues:

‹CLYMENE›

Mention what the god once said when he lay with me, and   45
request one single thing you wish; for further than that,

λαβεῖν σε· κἂν μὲν τυγχάνῃς [ὅσων ἐρᾷς]
θεοῦ πέφυκας· εἰ δὲ μή, ψευδὴς ἐγώ.

ΦΑΕΘΩΝ

(5)   πῶς οὖν πρόσειμι δῶμα θερμὸν Ἡλίου;

ΚΛΥΜΕΝΗ

50   κείνῳ μελήσει σῶμα μὴ βλάπτειν τὸ σόν.

ΦΑΕΘΩΝ

εἴπερ πατὴρ πέφυκεν, οὐ κακῶς λέγεις.

ΚΛΥΜΕΝΗ

σάφ᾽ ἴσθι· πεύσῃ δ᾽ αὐτὸ τῷ χρόνῳ σαφῶς.

ΦΑΕΘΩΝ

ἀρκεῖ· πέποιθα γάρ σε μὴ ψευδῆ λέγειν.
(10) ἀλλ᾽ ἕρπ᾽ ἐς οἴκους· καὶ γὰρ αἵδ᾽ ἔξω δόμων
55   δμῳαὶ περῶσιν αἱ πατρὸς κατὰ σταθμὰ
σαίρουσι δῶμα καὶ δόμων κειμήλια
καθ᾽ ἡμέραν φοιβῶσι κἀπιχωρίοις
ὀσμαῖσι θυμιῶσιν εἰσόδους δόμων.
(15) ὅταν δ᾽ ὕπνον γεραιὸς ἐκλιπὼν πατὴρ
60   πύλας ἀμείψῃ καὶ λόγους γάμων πέρι
λέξῃ πρὸς ἡμᾶς, Ἡλίου μολὼν δόμους
τοὺς σοὺς ἐλέγξω, μῆτερ, εἰ σαφεῖς λόγοι.

47 [ὅσων ἐρᾷς] Diggle (1996: previously [ὅπερ θέλεις]): [εὖ
ἴσθ᾽ ὅτι] West   55 κατὰ σταθμὰ Diggle: κατασταθμ.(.)(.)
Pᶜ (-οὺς conj. Blass): -στομ.(.)(.) P

you have no right to receive. And if you get (what you de-
sire),[1] you are the god's son; but if not, then I lie.

PHAETHON
How then shall I approach Helios' palace and its heat?[2]

CLYMENE
It will be his concern not to harm you bodily.   50

PHAETHON
If he really is my father, what you say is well.

CLYMENE
Be certain of it: you will learn it in due time for a certainty.

PHAETHON
Enough; I am convinced you speak no lies.
*(The Chorus of slave women begins to
come out from the palace)*
But now go in to the house, for here are slave women mak-
ing their way outside from it, who sweep the house in my
father's mansions, and daily purify its precious things, and   55
fume its entries with native scents.[3] When my elderly fa-
ther has left sleep behind and passed through the doors,
and has had his say[4] to me about marriage, I shall go to   60
Helios' palace, mother, and test the certainty of what you
said.
(Clymene and Phaethon enter the palace)

---

[1] Or '(the thing you wish)', Diggle; 'if you get (it), (be sure that)
. . .', West.   [2] An early signal for the audience of Phaethon's
catastrophe.   [3] Frankincense etc.   [4] A hint that
Merops' words will be resisted (cf. 158–9, 164–7).

EURIPIDES

ΧΟΡΟΣ

στρ. α   ἤδη μὲν ἀρτιφανὴς

(20)   Ἀὼς ἱ[ππεύει] κατὰ γᾶν,

65   ὑπὲρ δ᾽ ἐμᾶς κεφαλᾶς

       Πλειά[δων πέφευγε χορός],

       μέλπει δ᾽ ἐν δένδρεσι λεπ-

          τὰν ἀηδὼν ἁρμονίαν

(25)   ὀρθρευομένα γόοις

70   Ἴτυν Ἴτυν πολύθρηνον.

ἀντ. α   σύριγγας δ᾽ οὐριβάται

       κινοῦσιν ποιμνᾶν ἐλάται,

       ἔγρονται δ᾽ εἰς βοτάναν

(30)   ξανθᾶν πώλων συζυγίαι·

75   ἤδη δ᾽ εἰς ἔργα κυνα-

          γοὶ στείχουσιν θηροφόνοι,

       παγαῖς τ᾽ ἐπ᾽ Ὠκεανοῦ

       μελιβόας κύκνος ἀχεῖ.

στρ. β   ἄκατοι δ᾽ ἀνάγονται ὑπ᾽ εἰρεσίας

80   ἀνέμων τ᾽ εὐαέσσιν ῥοθίοις,

63–97 P. Berlin 9771, ed. W. Schubart and U. von Wilamowitz (1907), with many lines damaged or defective; P itself is largely illegible or defective in 63–6 and 82–5.   64 ἱ[ππεύει] Wilamowitz in P. Berl.: [P]   κατα γαν Pᶜ: [P, P. Berl.] 66 so P. Berl. supplemented by Diggle: [P]   67 δ᾽ ἐν Burges: δε P. Berl., P   76 θ[ηροφόνοι στ]είχουσι P. Berl.

⟨CHORUS⟩

Already the Dawn just appearing⁵ (drives her chariot) over
the earth, and above my head (the chorus) of the Pleiades   65
(has fled);⁶ the nightingale sings her subtle harmony in the
trees, awake at dawn with her lament of many tears for
'Itys, Itys'.⁷   70

Drovers of their flocks, who walk the mountains, stir their
pipes, and teams of chestnut mares wake for grazing; al-
ready hunters with beasts to kill are going to their work; on 75
Ocean's streams the swan sounds its tuneful cry.⁸

Vessels are put to sea under oars and at the winds' favour-
able bluster, and (sailors) as they raise the sails cry loudly 80

---

⁵ For appreciations of this dawn song see M. Hose, *Studien zum
Chor bei Euripides* (Stuttgart, 1990), I.121–31, and Collard in
SFP I.226–8.   ⁶ For the Pleiades see on 171 below. The met-
aphors in 'drives her chariot', 'chorus' and 'has fled' are common-
place for heavenly transits.   ⁷ Itys was the son of Tereus and
Procne, who became a nightingale after killing Itys in revenge for
Tereus's rape of her sister Philomela; she lamented her son with
the cry '*itys*'. Cf. *Cresphontes* F 448a.82–6 with note; Aeschylus,
Agamemnon 1142–5; Sophocles, *Electra* 147–9.   ⁸ For the
swan's singing cf. e.g. *Iphigenia in Tauris* 1104–5, *Ion* 164–9.
There is no implication here like that of the English 'swan-song'.

---

79 ἄκατοι Dobree, Matthiae: ακοντοι P: [P. Berl.]   εἰρεσίας P
(-ας Pᶜ): -αις P. Berl.

(37) &ἀνὰ δ᾽ ἱστία ν[αῦται] ἀειράμενοι
&ἀχοῦσιν '["Επου,] πότνι᾽ αὔρ[α],
[ἡμῖν ὑπ᾽] ἀκύμονι πομπᾷ
(40) σιγώντων ἀνέμων
85 [ποτὶ τέκνα] τε καὶ φιλίας ἀλόχους.'
σινδὼν δὲ πρότονον ἐπὶ μέσον πελάζει.

ἀντ. β   τὰ μὲν οὖν ἑτέροισι μέριμνα πέλει,
κόσμον δ᾽ ὑμεναίων δεσποσύνων
(45) ἐμὲ καὶ τὸ δίκαιον ἄγει καὶ ἔρως
90 ὑμνεῖν· δμωσὶν γὰρ ἀνάκτων
εὐαμερίαι προσιοῦσαι
μολπᾷ θάρσος ἄγουσ᾽
ἐπιχάρματά τ᾽· εἰ δὲ τύχα τι τέκοι,
(50) βαρὺν βαρεῖα φόβον ἔπεμψεν οἴκοις.

ἐπῳδ.   ὁρίζεται δὲ τόδε φάος γάμων τέλει,
96 τὸ δή ποτ᾽ εὐχαῖς ἐγὼ
λισσομένα προσέβαν ὑμέναιον ἀεῖσαι
(55) φίλον φίλων δεσποτᾶν·
θεὸς ἔδωκε, χρόνος ἔκρανε
100 λέχος ἐμοῖσιν ἀρχέταις.
ἴτω τελεία γάμων ἀοιδά.

81 ν[αῦται] Kranz (only αν[and] ἀειράμενοι P. Berl.: only
ἀνὰ δ᾽ ἱστία[P)   82 ἀχοῦσιν Wilamowitz: ἀχέουσιν P.
Berl.: [P]: ἰαχοῦσιν (or ἰάχουσιν) Diggle   82–3 ["Επου,]
... [ἡμῖν ὑπ᾽] Austin (ὑπ᾽ Volmer)

340

'(Escort us,)⁹ breeze, our mistress, on a calm voyage with
quiet winds (towards) our dear (children) and wives'; and   85
the canvas comes close to the forestay's middle.¹⁰

Those things are others' concern; but both right and desire
lead me to sing praise honouring a marriage for my mas-
ters; for happy times approaching for their lords bring con-   90
fidence and joy to servants in their song—but if ever some
misfortune should befall, it is heavy in sending heavy fear
on the house.

This day is marked for the fulfilment of a marriage which I   95
long since entreated and prayed for, and I have come for-
ward to sing a wedding hymn out of love for my loving mas-
ters. God has given, and time has achieved, marriage for
those who rule me. Let the singing to fulfil the marriage   100
come on!

⁹ Austin's supplement seems the best of many giving this
sense.   ¹⁰ The breeze fills the canvas sail.

85 [ποτὶ τέκνα] Kranz: [P. Berl.]   87 πέλει (or μέλει?) P: τὰ
μ[ὲ]ν ἐτέρων ἐτέ[ροισι μέλει P. Berl. supplemented by Ruben-
sohn   88 κόσμον δ' ὑμεναίων Hartung: κοσμεῖν ὑμεναίων
δὲ P. Berl., P   91 εὐαμερίαι M. Schmidt: εὐάμεροι Pᶜ (ειαμ-
P):]υἡμεροι P. Berl.   92 ἄγουσ' Burges: αιουσ P: [P. Berl.]
93 τ': τε P. Berl., om. P   95 τέλει P. Berl.: τέλος P
101 ἴτω Pᶜ: ἰὼ P

ἀλλ' ὅδε γὰρ δὴ βασιλεὺς πρὸ δόμων
(60)   κῆρύξ θ' ἱερὸς καὶ παῖς Φαέθων
    βαίνουσι τριπλοῦν ζεῦγος, ἔχειν χρὴ
105   στόμ' ἐν ἡσυχίᾳ·
    περὶ γὰρ μεγάλων γνώμας δείξει
    παῖδ' ὑμεναίοις ὁσίοισι θέλων
(65)   ζεῦξαι νύμφης τε λεπάδνοις.

<ΚΗΡΥΞ>

    Ὠκεανοῦ πεδίων οἰκήτορες, εὐφαμεῖτ' ὦ
111   ἐκτόπιοί τε δόμων ἀπαείρετε· ὦ ἴτε λαοί.
(70)   κηρύσσω †δ' ὁσίαν βασιλήιον αὐτῷ δ' αὐδὰν†
115   εὐτεκνίαν τε γάμοις, ὧν ἔξοδος ἅδ' ἔνεχ' ἥκει,
    παιδὸς πατρός τε τῇδ' ἐν ἡμέρᾳ λέχη
(75)   κρᾶναι θελόντων· ἀλλὰ σῖγ' ἔστω λεώς.

<ΜΕΡΟΨ>

one line missing, then:
120   ] εἰ γὰρ εὖ λέγω
then five lines missing before the next fragment

104 τριπλοῦν P: διπλοῦν Pᶜ   107 ὁσίοισι Page; ὥς
φησι P   θέλων Pᶜ: λέγων P   114 αὐτῷ Blass (αυτω P):
αἰτῶ Hermann   115 εὐτεκνίαν P: εὐτυχίαν Wilamowitz

121–157 (F 774)

*Beginnings of 37 dialogue trimeters, three coinciding with
a book fragment:*

<ΜΕΡΟΨ>

124   ναῦν [τοι μί' ἄγκυρ' οὐχ ὁμῶς σῴζειν φιλεῖ

342

PHAETHON

A ceremonious entry from the palace begins; the Chorus chants:

Yet I must keep my tongue still, for here indeed in front of the palace come the king and his sacred herald, and Phaethon his son, three joined in company: the king will   105
reveal his mind upon great matters, in his wish to link his son in holy marriage, in ties to a bride.

⟨HERALD⟩

You inhabitants of Oceanus' lands, keep auspicious silence! Make your way outside your homes! Come, you   110
people! I proclaim †the holy royal . . . (?) . . . voice†[11] and fine children for the marriage which is the object of this procession, now that son and father on this day wish to ac-   115
complish the marriage. Let the people stand silent!

⟨MEROPS⟩

. . . for if my words are well . . .   120

five lines missing before the next fragment

[11] Hopelessly corrupt; for the best conjectures see Diggle (1970) and (1996), and Kannicht in *TrGF*. It seems that the Herald is proclaiming holy silence (cf. 110, 118) on the king's behalf; but the coupling of this with a wish for 'fine children for the marriage' makes a very difficult compression (unless Wilamowitz's 'happiness' replaces 'fine children'); a line or more of text may have been lost.

121–157 (F 774)
Merops continues, perhaps in a monologue; beginnings of 37 lines, three coinciding with a book fragment (124–6):

⟨MEROPS⟩

For sure, just as one anchor does not usually keep a ship

EURIPIDES

τῷ τρεῖς [ἀφέντι· προστάτης θ᾽ ἁπλοῦς πόλει
σφαλερ[ός, ὑπὼν δὲ κάλλος οὐ κακὸν πέλει.
and others giving these initial words:

127 ἰσχὺν   128 γήμας   129 γάμοις   131 δώσει
132 νέος   133 ἥβης   136 γέρων   137 νέαι
or νέᾳ   139 δεινὸν   142 πεσὼν   144 κλέψει
146 κῆδος   148 ἕξεις   150 καὶ ζῶν   151 γαμεῖς

vv. 124–6: Stobaeus 4.1.3, without lemma in ms. A, attached to
4.1.2 (= F 775a below) without new lemma in mss. MS; separated
by Gesner and identified in P by Blass

124 οὐχ ὁμῶς Badham: οὐδαμῶς Stob.: οὐκ ἴσως Burges
125 τῷ Burges: ὡς P, Stob.   126 πέλει Barnes: πόλει Stob.

*Three lines missing after v. 157, then a gap of uncertain
length (pages missing in P), to which editors assign the fol-
lowing four book fragments:*

158–9 (F 775)

⟨ΦΑΕΘΩΝ⟩

ἐλεύθερος δ᾽ ὢν δοῦλός ἐστι τοῦ λέχους,
πεπραμένον τὸ σῶμα τῆς φερνῆς ἔχων.

Eustathius on Homer, *Odyssey* 13.15; v. 159: Plutarch,
Moralia 498a; assigned to Phaethon by Matthiae

344

safe in the same way[1] as the man who has let down three, so
a single man at the head of a city is fallible, while another in   125
his support is no bad thing.

and others including these words:

127 strength   128 having married   129 (by *or* in)
marriage   131 will give   132 young (man?)   133 of
(his?) prime   136 old (man)   137 young (women?)
or to a young (woman)   139 dreadful   142 having
fallen   144 will steal   146 a relation(ship?)   148 you
will have   150 and . . . living   151 you will marry

---

[1] Badham's correction here is more economical than Burges'
'equally'.

---

*Four fragments from later in the first episode show Merops
and Phaethon exchanging their very different views of the
marriage:*

158–9 (F 775)

⟨PHAETHON⟩

Though he is free, he is a slave of his marriage bed, when
he has sold his body for the dowry.[1]

---

[1] Cf. *Melanippe* F 502 with note.

160–2 (F 775a = 784 N)

⟨ΜΕΡΟΨ⟩

ἐν τοῖσι μώροις τοῦτ᾽ ἐγὼ κρίνω βροτῶν,
ὅστις τὰ πατέρων παισὶ μὴ φρονοῦσιν εὖ
ἢ καὶ πολίταις παραδίδωσ᾽ ἐξουσίαν.

Stobaeus 4.1.2 (see on 124–6 above); assigned to Merops by Rau

161 τὰ πατέρων West: τῶν πατέρων Stob.: πατρῷα Diggle

164–7 (F 776)

⟨ΦΑΕΘΩΝ⟩

δεινόν γε, τοῖς πλουτοῦσι τοῦτο δ᾽ ἔμφυτον,
σκαιοῖσιν εἶναι· τί ποτε τοῦδ᾽ ἐπαίτιον;
ἆρ᾽ ὄλβος αὐτοῖς ὅτι τυφλὸς συνηρετεῖ
τυφλὰς ἔχουσι τὰς φρένας †καὶ τῆς τύχης†;

Stobaeus 4.31.54; assigned to Phaethon by Goethe

165 τοῦδ᾽ ἐπαίτιον Wecklein: τοῦτό τ᾽ αἴτιον Stob.
166 συνηρετεῖ Meineke: συνηρεφεῖ Stob.   167 text completing the sentence perhaps lost after this line (Musgrave)

163 (F 777)

⟨ΦΑΕΘΩΝ?⟩

ὡς πανταχοῦ γε πατρὶς ἡ βόσκουσα γῆ.

Stobaeus 3.40.2; Florilegium Monacense 146 Meineke

PHAETHON

160–2 (F 775a = 784 N)

⟨MEROPS⟩

I judge this among the follies of men, if one hands over a
father's property to sons who lack good sense,[1] or again au-
thority to citizens.

[1] Cf. *Phoenix* F 803b.1–2.

164–7 (F 776)

⟨PHAETHON⟩

Dreadful!—but this is native in the rich, to be foolish.
Whatever is responsible for this? Is it that wealth in its
blindness befriends them when their wits are blind †and
. . . of fortune†?[1]

[1] Wealth is often personified as 'blind' because it bestows itself
indiscriminately; cf. especially Aristophanes, *Wealth* 87–9. The
text of this brief fragment is remarkably damaged; the end of v.
167 is senseless, and the quotation probably curtailed.

163 (F 777)

⟨PHAETHON?⟩

. . . for the nourishing earth is a fatherland everywhere![1]

[1] Probably Phaethon threatened with exile by an angry
Merops, or contemplating it to escape marriage.

EURIPIDES

(778 N = 783a below)

The first stasimon is lost; two book fragments are all that remains of the second episode:

168–177 (F 779)

⟨ΤΡΟΦΕΥΣ⟩

τῷ Φαέθοντι παραδιδοὺς τὰς ἡνίας ὁ Ἥλιός φησιν·

'ἔλα δὲ μήτε Λιβυκὸν αἰθέρ' εἰσβαλὼν
(κρᾶσιν γὰρ ὑγρὰν οὐκ ἔχων ἁψῖδα σὴν
170   κάτω διήσει) ⟨μήτε . . .
a short gap
ἵει δ' ἐφ' ἑπτὰ Πλειάδων ἔχων δρόμον.'
(5) τοσαῦτ' ἀκούσας παῖς ἔμαρψεν ἡνίας·
κρούσας δὲ πλευρὰ πτεροφόρων ὀχημάτων
μεθῆκεν, αἱ δ' ἔπταντ' ἐπ' αἰθέρος πτυχάς.
175   πατὴρ δ' ὄπισθε νῶτα Σειρίου βεβὼς
ἵππευε παῖδα νουθετῶν· 'Ἐκεῖσ' ἔλα,
(10) τῇδε στρέφ' ἄρμα, τῇδε . . .'

[Longinus], *On The Sublime* 15.4; assigned to the Tutor by Lesky

348

PHAETHON

(778 N = 783a *below*)

After a now missing choral ode, a report of Phaethon's di-
sastrous chariot drive is brought to Clymene (probably
now accompanied by some of her slave women) by his
Tutor:

168–177 (F 779)

⟨TUTOR⟩

Handing the reins to Phaethon the Sun says,

'Drive neither entering the heaven above Libya—for be-
cause it has no admixture of wet it will let your wheels
fall[1]—(nor . . . *some words and possibly one or more lines*   170
missing . . .); steer and hold a course for the seven
Pleiads.'[2] When he had heard that much, the boy seized
the reins; he struck the flanks of the chariot's winged
horses and set them going, and the mares flew to heaven's
folds. Behind him his father mounted Sirius[3] and rode ad-
vising the boy, 'Drive over there! Turn the chariot this way,   175
this way!'[4]

[1] Above the 'African' desert the air is so dry (cf. *Electra* 734–6)
that it gives no support. Euripides draws here upon early Greek
physical speculation: cf. Egli 69–71.   [2] A prominent con-
stellation, named merely for colour: cf. 66 above, *Andromeda* F
124.4.   [3] One of the Sun's horses, like Aethops in F 896.
[4] The Tutor has heard the Sun's preliminary instructions, and
presumably now 'invents' his subsequent ones when the drive is
under way.

EURIPIDES

*786 (fr. 3 Diggle)

ΚΛΥΜΕΝΗ

φίλος δέ μοι

ἄλουτος ἐν φάραγξι σήπεται νέκυς.

Plutarch, *Moralia* 665c; assigned to *Phaethon* by Heath, to this place by Wilamowitz

The second stasimon is missing; from the third episode:

178–213 (F 779a)

Damaged ends of 36 dialogue trimeters, including:

178 προθυμίᾳ   181 δυστυχεῖς   184 πλοῦτον
187 ἴχνος   188 ἅπαντ᾽ ἐρῶ   189 χθονὸς σκότου
190 πόλει   191 τυ]ράννιδι   193 ἐ]λευθεροι(ς?)
194 πλούσιον   195 πόλις   196 νόμος
197 ἐπήνεσα   198 σοφή   199 π]ράγματα
201 ἀμηχανοι(ς?)   202 πλοκή   205 κακοῖς
206 σκότῳ   207 ποίῳ τάφῳ   209 δι᾽ ἀστέως
210 κ]ειμήλιον   211 νεκροί   212 τύχας
213 πειρατέος (or -ον)

five or six lines missing before the next fragment

---

¹ A formula, probably in the first line of an answer.
² Possibly the end of a sentence.   ³ If 'scheme' is correct, Clymene may be thinking already of a way to conceal Phaethon's death and body from Merops, as later at 221–4 (cf. 207 and 213); if 'lock of hair', she will cut a lock from her head and leave it with the body in token of her grief (perhaps the 'memorial' of 210).

350

PHAETHON

*786 (fr. 3 Diggle)

CLYMENE

. . . and my dear (son's) body rots away unwashed in a ravine.[1]

---

[1] Clymene so far has been told only of Phaethon's death from Zeus' thunderbolt, not that his body still smoulders (this comes in the next episode, 214–5). Plutarch uses the fragment to illustrate the custom of leaving those killed by lightning where they fell, without benefit of washing or funeral of any kind.

The rest of the second episode, all of the second choral ode, and the start of the third episode are missing; then:

178–213 (F 779a)

Ends of 36 dialogue lines including the following words (Clymene is almost certainly one of the speakers, cf. 197, 202):

178 by/in (your?) eagerness   181 unlucky (*plural, or* you (*sing.*) are unlucky)   184 wealth   187 track 188 I shall say everything   189 earth's darkness 190 for/to the city   191 in absolute rule   193 free 194 rich   195 city   196 law   197 I thank you![1] 198 wise (*or* clever, *fem.*)   199 matters   201 helpless (*or* impossible)[2]   202 scheme (*or* lock of hair)[3] 205 in troubles   206 in darkness   207 in/with what kind of funeral   209 through the city   210 memorial (*or* relic)   211 corpses   212 fortunes   213 must be attempted

five or six lines missing before the next fragment

EURIPIDES

214–327 (F 781)

Complete continuous text resumes with the end of a speech by Clymene:

⟨ΚΛΥΜΕΝΗ⟩

πυροῦσσ᾽ Ἐρινὺς ἐν †νεκροις θ.ρ.( )νναι†
215 ζώσης δ᾽ ἀνίησ᾽ ἀτμὸν ἐμφανῆ ⟨φλογός⟩.
ἀπωλόμην· οὐκ οἴσετ᾽ εἰς δόμους νέκυν;
πόσις πόσις μοι πλησίον γαμηλίους
(5) μολπὰς ἀϋτεῖ παρθένοις ἡγούμενος.
οὐ θᾶσσον; οὐ σταλαγμὸν ἐξομόρξετε,
220 εἴ πού τίς ἐστιν αἵματος χαμαὶ πεσών;
ἐπείγετ᾽ ἤδη, δμωΐδες· κρύψω δέ νιν
ξεστοῖσι θαλάμοις, ἔνθ᾽ ἐμῷ κεῖται πόσει
(10) χρυσός, μόνη δὲ κλῇθρ᾽ ἐγὼ σφραγίζομαι.
    ὦ καλλιφεγγὲς Ἥλι᾽, ὥς μ᾽ ἀπώλεσας
225 καὶ τόνδ᾽· Ἀπόλλων δ᾽ ἐν βροτοῖς ὀρθῶς καλῇ,
ὅστις τὰ σιγῶντ᾽ ὀνόματ᾽ οἶδε δαιμόνων.

214 πυροῦσσ᾽ Hermann: πυροσθ P: πυρός τ᾽ Rau   νεκρῷ
Hartung   θρασύνεται Diggle (e.g.)   215 ζώσης (Ellis)
δ᾽ Diggle: ζωσαηδ P   ⟨φλογός⟩ Rau
217–8 γαμηλίους | μολπὰς Hermann: -ίους or -ίοις | μολπαῖς P
219 θᾶσσον; οὐ σταλαγμὸν Dobree, Hermann: θασσεουσο-
μολγον P   221 ἐπείγετ᾽ ἤδη Page: επειγετεα P
224–5 Schol. on *Orestes* 1388; Macrobius, *Saturnalia* 1.17.9
224 καλλιφεγγὲς P: χρυσο- Macrob., Schol.   225 ὀρθῶς
Bekker: ορθοσ P   καὶ τόνδ᾽ Ἀπόλλων εἰκότως κλήζῃ
βροτοῖς (or similar) Schol.: ὅθεν σ᾽ Ἀπόλλων ἐμφανῶς κλήζει
βροτός Macrob.

352

PHAETHON

214–327 (F 781)

Phaethon's body has been brought to Clymene; continuous text resumes with the end of a speech by her:

<CLYMENE>

A Fury all of fire (wantons?) on the dead and sends up a visible exhalation of living (flame).[1] I am destroyed! (*to her* 215 *slave women*) Take the body into the house! My husband, my husband is close at hand, chanting marriage songs as he leads maiden girls! More quickly! Wipe up any drip of blood if it has fallen somewhere on the ground! Hurry now, 220 you slave women! And I will hide the body in the chambers of dressed stone where my husband's gold is laid up and I alone have the seal for the doors.[2]

O Helios with your beautiful light, you have destroyed me and Phaethon here![3] You are rightly called Apollo among men, where any knows the unspoken meaning of 225 gods' names![4]

---

[1] For the dramatic context see Introduction and the note on v. 202.   [2] A ring-seal, pressed into wax over the doors' join, to indicate authorized entry and closure.   [3] 'light . . . destroyed': a black paradox.   [4] Apollo's name suggests the Greek verb 'destroy' (224), an etymology used powerfully by Aeschylus in *Agamemnon* 1080–2. For such devices generally see e.g. on *Alexander* F 42d, *Auge* test. iib. Here Apollo is identified with Helios the Sun, as earlier (probably) in Aeschylus, *Suppliants* 212–4, cf. *Seven against Thebes* 859.

EURIPIDES

ΧΟΡΟΣ ⟨ΠΑΡΘΕΝΩΝ⟩

στρ.   Ὑμὴν Ὑμήν.
(15)   τὰν Διὸς οὐρανίαν ⟨ἀ⟩είδομεν,
       τὰν ἐρώτων πότνιαν, τὰν παρθένοις
230   γαμήλιον Ἀφροδίταν.
       πότνια, σοὶ τάδ᾽ ἐγὼ νυμφεῖ᾽ ἀείδω,
       Κύπρι θεῶν καλλίστα,
(20)   τῷ τε νεόζυγι σῷ
           πώλῳ τὸν ἐν αἰθέρι κρύπτεις,
235   σῶν γάμων γένναν·

ἀντ.   ἃ τὸν μέγαν
       τᾶσδε πόλεως βασιλῆ νυμφεύεαι
(25)   ἀστερωποῖσιν δόμοισι χρυσέοις
       ἀρχὸν φίλον Ἀφροδίτα·

231 νυμφεῖ᾽ (Hermann) ἀείδω Wilamowitz: only νυμφα . (. .)
now legible in P   233 νεόζυγι σῷ Hermann: νεοζυγιστω
or -σιω P   234 κρύπτεις read in P by Bekker: P no longer
legible   236–9 ὃς . . . νυμφεύεται (P) . . . Ἀφροδίτᾳ
(Hermann) Lloyd-Jones   237 νυμφεύεαι (or -σεαι) Diggle
νυμφεύεται Pᶜ   238 χρυσέοις Hermann: χρυσέων P:
δόμοις χρυσέ⟨οις θε⟩ῶν Willink

---

5 Both the marriage cry and its personification (more com-
monly named Hymenaeus), invoked together at *Trojan Women*
331. In myth Aphrodite is sometimes his mother; he disappeared
on his wedding night, and is therefore identified plausibly here in
233–5. (Some scholars identify the 'boy' of 233 as the Phaethon
whom Aphrodite abducted as her temple keeper [see Introduc-

354

PHAETHON

Merops enters with attendants, leading a second chorus singing a wedding hymn:

CHORUS OF MAIDEN GIRLS

Hymen, Hymen![5] We sing Zeus's daughter celestial, mistress of loves, goddess of marriage for maiden girls, Aphrodite! Mistress, to you I sing this marriage song, Cypris most beautiful of goddesses, and to your newly-wed boy, whom you keep hidden in the heaven, offspring of your marriage,

you who will betroth the great king of this city,[6] a ruler dear to the starry golden palace,[7] Aphrodite! O blessed man,

230

235

tion, at start], others as Eros, who neither married nor was hidden in heaven; these identifications also involve widespread and difficult alterations to the text.) [6] If both 'great king' and 'blessed man' refer to Phaethon, then he is a 'great king' because he is a prince about to share his father's kingdom, and Aphrodite will 'betroth' him so that he 'will ally (himself) in marriage with a goddess' (242): this is Diggle's text and interpretation, which we follow. If both terms refer instead to Merops, then Diggle's text translates in 236 with difficulty as '(Aphrodite) will make a marriage on behalf of *the great king*', and in 241 it is Merops who 'will ally himself to a goddess through *marriage*' (this sense is given as readily by P's unaltered text there). Collard in *SFP* I argued that in 236 Merops and in 240 Phaethon can be meant (in Diggle's text); Lloyd-Jones had suggested in 236 'who (= Hymen) will betroth (Phaethon)' and in 239 (awkwardly) 'dear to the . . . palace, to Aphrodite'. For Phaethon's bride, probably a daughter of Helios, see Introduction (G). [7] The palace of the gods in heaven (Willink's ingenious metrical conjecture explicitly adds the word 'gods' ').

355

240   ὦ μάκαρ, ὦ βασιλέως μείζων ἔτ᾽ ὄλβον,
       ὃς θεᾷ κηδεύσεις
       καὶ μόνος ἀθανάτων
(30)   γαμβρὸς δι᾽ ἀπείρονα γαῖαν
       θνατὸς ὑμνήσῃ.

ΜΕΡΟΨ

245   χώρει σὺ καὶ τάσδ᾽ εἰς δόμους ἄγων κόρας
       γυναῖκ᾽ ἄνωχθι πᾶσι τοῖς κατὰ σταθμὰ
       θεοῖς χορεῦσαι κἀγκυκλώσασθαι δόμοις
(35)   σεμνοῖσιν ὑμεναίοισιν, Ἑστίας θ᾽ ἕδος,
       ἀφ᾽ ἧς γε σώφρων πᾶς τις ἄρχεται θεοῖς
250   εὐχὰς πο[ιεῖσθαι
       four lines missing
(42)   θεᾶς προσελθεῖν τέμενος ἐξ ἐμῶν δόμων.

ΘΕΡΑΠΩΝ

       ὦ δέσποτ᾽, ἔστρεψ᾽ ἐκ δόμων ταχὺν πόδα.
       οὗ γὰρ σὺ σῴζῃ σεμνὰ θησαυρίσματα
(45)   χρυσοῦ, δι᾽ ἁρμῶν ἐξαμείβεται πύλης
255   καπνοῦ μέλαιν᾽ ἄησις ἔνδοθεν στέγης.
       προσθεὶς πρόσωπον φλόγα μὲν οὐχ ὁρῶ πυρός,

240 ὦ μάκαρ, ὦ βασιλέως Hermann: ὦ μακάρων βασιλεὺς P
241 θεᾷ Diggle: θεαν P   244 ὑμνήσῃ Hermann: ὑμνήσεται
P   246 σταθμὰ Blass: στόμα P (cf. 55)   249 γε Burges:
τι P   πᾶς τις Blaydes, θεοῖς Blass: πασανσ . . θε . ι read in P by
Blass   250 πο[ιεῖσθαι Burges   252 δεσποτα Pᶜ (sup-
plying θεραπων): πατερ P   253 σῴζῃ Hermann: ζωση P
(cf. 215)   256 a preceding verse perhaps lost (West)

greater still in happiness than a king, who will ally yourself   240
in marriage with a goddess, and will be praised in song
throughout the boundless earth as mortals' only connec-
tion with immortals in marriage.[8]

MEROPS
(to an attendant)

You—go and take these girls into the house, and order my   245
wife to begin dances for all the gods throughout the palace,
and to circle in them inside the house in fine wedding
hymns, and . . . the altar of Hestia,[9] with whom every
prudent man begins prayers to the gods . . . . . . *(four lines*   250
missing) . . . to approach the goddess's[10] precinct from
my house.

*As Merops' attendant leads the second chorus into the pal-
ace, a servant enters hurriedly:*

SERVANT

Master, I have turned my step quickly from the palace; for
where you keep your splendid treasures of gold, a black
draught of smoke is issuing through the door's joins from
inside the building.[11] Though I put my face close I saw no   255

---

[8] An enthusiastic exaggeration: see on Peleus in *Peleus*. The en-
tire text and interpretation of this wedding hymn are endlessly
disputed: see especially Diggle (1970, 1996), Kannicht (1972 and
TrGF 5.817–9), Lloyd-Jones, and E. Contiades-Tsitsoni, *ZPE* 102
(1994), 52–60, who studies it in relation to the comparable hymns
in *Women of Troy* 308–41 and *Iphigenia at Aulis* 1036–79.
[9] Goddess of the hearth, the centre of a house's well-being.
[10] Probably Aphrodite (cf. 230, 239).   [11] Cf. 221–3.
Difficulties and abruptness in P's text hereabouts have caused a
good deal of emendation, and suspicion that text may be lost.

γέμοντα δ' οἶκον μέλανος ἔνδοθεν καπνοῦ.
ἀλλ' ἔσιθ' ἐς οἶκον, μή τιν' Ἥφαιστος χόλον
(50) δόμοις ἐπεισφρεὶς μέλαθρα συμφλέξῃ πυρὶ
260 ἐν τοῖσιν ἡδίστοισι Φαέθοντος γάμοις.

ΜΕΡΟΨ

πῶς φῄς; ὅρα μὴ θυμάτων πυρουμένων
κατ' οἶκον ἀτμὸν κεῖσ' ἀποσταλέντ' ἴδῃς.

ΘΕΡΑΠΩΝ

ἅπαντα ταῦτ' ᾔθρησ'· ἀκαπνώτως ἔχει.

ΜΕΡΟΨ

(55) οἶδεν δ' ἐμὴ τάδ' ἢ οὐκ ἐπίσταται δάμαρ;

ΘΕΡΑΠΩΝ

265 θυηπολοῦσα θεοῖς ἐκεῖσ' ἔχει φρένας.

ΜΕΡΟΨ

ἀλλ' εἶμ', ἐπεί τοι καὶ φιλεῖ τὰ τοιάδε
ληφθέντα φαύλως ἐς μέγαν χειμῶν' ἄγειν.
σὺ δ' ὦ πυρὸς δέσποινα Δήμητρος κόρη
(60) Ἥφαιστέ τ', εἴητ' εὐμενεῖς δόμοις ἐμοῖς.

ΧΟΡΟΣ

270 τάλαιν' ἐγὼ τάλαινα ποῖ
πόδα πτερόεντα καταστάσω;

257 καπνοῦ Elmsley: καταινου P   ἔξωθεν Hermann:
ἔκτοθεν δ' ἐγὼ Diggle   263 so Diggle (ᾔθρησ'· ἀκαπνώτως
<δ'> Wilamowitz: ηθρησεκανπωτους P)   267 ἄγειν
Hermann: αδι P

fiery flame but the treasure house full of black smoke inside. Go into the palace, in case Hephaestus may be visiting some anger on the house and consuming the palace in fire amid Phaethon's most happy marriage!   260

MEROPS

How do you mean? Be sure you may not be seeing the drift from sacrifices burning in the palace and sent in that direction.

SERVANT

I had an eye to all that; there is no smoke there.

MEROPS

Does my wife know of this, or is she unaware?

SERVANT

She is sacrificing to the gods and has her mind on that.   265

MEROPS

Then I will go, since such things taken lightly do usually lead to a great storm—and may you, fire's mistress, daughter of Demeter,[12] and you, Hephaestus, be kind to my house!

Merops and the Servant hasten into the palace. The Chorus sings in wild distress:

CHORUS

Where am I to set my foot in winged flight, in my misery,   270

---

[12] Persephone, who was sometimes merged with another underworld deity Hecate in the latter's association with fire and light (cf. *Alexander* F *62h).

ἀν' αἰθέρ' ἢ γᾶς ὑπὸ κεῦθος ἄφαν-
  τον ἐξαμαυρωθῶ;
275 ἰώ μοί μοι. κακὰ φανήσεται·
(66) βασίλεια τάλαινα παῖς τ' ἔσω
  κρυφαῖος νέκυς,
  ὀτοτοτοῖ, κεραύνιαί τ' ἐκ Διὸς
  πυριβόλοι πλαγαὶ λέχεά θ' Ἁλίου.
280 ὦ δυστάλαινα τῶν ἀμετρήτων κακῶν,
(71) Ὠκεανοῦ κόρα,
  †πατρὸς ἴθι πρόσπεσε
  γόνυ λιταῖς σφαγὰς
  σφαγὰς οἰκτρὰς ἀρκέσαι σᾶς δειρᾶς†.

МЕРОΨ

(off-stage)

(75) ἰώ μοί μοι.

ΧΟΡΟΣ

285 ἠκούσατ' ἀρχὰς δεσπότου στεναγμάτων;

МЕРОΨ

ἰὼ τέκνον.

ΧΟΡΟΣ

καλεῖ τὸν οὐ κλύοντα δυστυχῆ γόνον.
  ]άτων ὁρᾶν σαφῆ.

---

272 ἀν' αἰθέρ' Nauck: τιναθερ P   ἄφαντον P: -ος Heiland
ἐξαμαυρωθῶ Hermann: -ώσω P   282 γόνυ λιταῖς
Hermann: γονυται P   283 οἰκτρὰς Burges: -αι P

my misery? Should I vanish up into the heaven, or down
into an invisible hiding place in the earth?[13] Alas, alas for
me! Evil things will be revealed: the wretched queen and   275
her dead son hidden within—oh, dreadful!—and the fiery
lightning-strokes hurled by Zeus, and her union with
Helios! O you poor, wretched woman in your measureless   280
troubles! Daughter of Oceanus, †go, fall at your father's†
knee with prayers †to avert a pitiable death, death for
your neck.†[14]

MEROPS
(inside the palace)

Alas, alas for me!

CHORUS

Did you hear the beginning of our master's laments?   285

MEROPS

O–oh! My child!

CHORUS

He calls upon his ill-fated son, who does not hear . . .
(words missing) . . . clear to see.

[13] Such imagined escapes from imminent disaster are fre-
quent in tragedy, e.g. *Hecuba* 1099–1102, *Ion* 1238–9. Heiland's
conjecture giving 'invisibly into a hiding-place' is deemed more
stylish by some.   [14] The naming of Clymene's father
Oceanus here is taken by many to anticipate his later appearance
to save her: see Introduction (E). 'Your neck' suggests that the
Chorus fears Clymene may hang herself or cut her throat, before
Merops himself threatens her with death. The translation gives
only the likely sense of 282–3, which are corrupt beyond confident
repair.

EURIPIDES

Three lines missing, then beginnings of 22 lines of a mon-
ody sung by Merops (289–310), including:

289 αἰα[ῖ   290 ὃς ὑμεν[αι-   291 εὐκελαδ[
296 ὑμεναι[308 καλεῖτε   309 ὃς ἐμὰν [
310 κακὰ

then beginnings of 17 trimeters from a dialogue between
Merops and the Tutor:

ΧΟΡΟΣ

311 ὅδ᾽ ἐκ δό[μων
(106) παιδὸς

ΜΕΡΟΨ

εἶέν· θυρ[
ὧς εἰσο[
315 *a few letters*
(110) θεᾶς δε[

ΤΡΟΦΕΥΣ

ὤμοι·[

ΜΕΡΟΨ

στέναζ[ε

ΤΡΟΦΕΥΣ

αἰαῖ·[

ΜΕΡΟΨ

320 διπλᾶ δ[

PHAETHON

*Three lines missing, then beginnings of 22 lines from a
monody sung by Merops (now returned from the palace),*[15]
including:
289 Cry sorrow!   290 who . . . the marriage-   291 glo-
rious   296 the marriage-   308 Summon . . . [16]
309 who . . . my . . .   310 evil troubles
*then beginnings of 17 lines of a spoken exchange between
Merops and the Tutor:*

CHORUS

Here from the house . . . (comes?) his son's (tutor?) . . .

MEROPS

Well . . . the doors[17] . . . so that (we may know?) . . . *one line
with a few letters* . . . of the goddess . . .   315

(the Tutor enters)

TUTOR

O me, alas! . . .

MEROPS

Lament . . . !

TUTOR

Cry sorrow!

MEROPS

. . . double . . .   320

[15] Merops' off-stage cries (284, 286) and on-stage monody
(289–310) following the discovery of his dead son have a close par-
allel in Polymestor's shock at *Hecuba* 1035–1108.
[16] I.e. summon the Tutor as a witness to explain Phaethon's death.
[17] Probably 'open the doors', an inbuilt stage direction for the
body's display.

EURIPIDES

ΤΡΟΦΕΥΣ

(115) τί γὰρ λε[

ΜΕΡΟΨ

τίς παιδ[

ΤΡΟΦΕΥΣ

εἰδὼς α[

ΜΕΡΟΨ

ἵν' ἀντα[

ΤΡΟΦΕΥΣ

325 σμικρο[

ΜΕΡΟΨ

(120) κρεισσ[

ΤΡΟΦΕΥΣ

ὃς σεθ[

UNPLACED FRAGMENTS

782 (fr. 6 Diggle)

ψυκτήρια

δένδρη φίλαισιν ὠλέναισι δέξεται.

Athenaeus 11.503c; text may be missing before or after ψυκτήρια, which Athen. cites as a noun

TUTOR

For what . . . (to say?)

MEROPS

Who . . . (my) son . . . ?

TUTOR

. . . knowing . . .

MEROPS

So that . . .

TUTOR

. . . small . . .   325

MEROPS

. . . better . . .

TUTOR

. . . who . . . you (*or* your) . . .

UNPLACED FRAGMENTS

782 (fr. 6 Diggle)

. . . cooling trees will receive (Phaethon) with loving arms
. . .[1]

[1] Most probably a reference to Phaethon's burial place, the
trees being the poplars into which his half-sisters the Daughters of
Helios were transformed (see Introduction (E)).

EURIPIDES

**783a (fr. 1 Diggle = 778 N)

ΜΕΡΟΨ

εὐδαιμονίζων ὄχλος ἐξέπληξέ ⟨με⟩.

Plutarch, *Moralia* 456a

⟨με⟩ Meineke

(784 N = 775a above)

**785 (fr. 4 Diggle)

ΚΛΥΜΕΝΗ

μισῶ δε ⟨   ⟩ εὐάγκαλον
τόξον κρανείας, γυμνάσια δ᾽ οἴχοιτ᾽ ἀεί.

Plutarch, *Moralia* 608e

(786: see after F 779)

PHAETHON

**783a (fr. 1 Diggle = 778 N)

MEROPS

The crowd with its felicitations unsettled (me)![1]

[1] Merops explains his blind enthusiasm for Phaethon's wedding to a goddess, and probably therefore his inattention to the anxieties of Phaethon and Clymene.

(784 N = 775a above)

**785 (fr. 4 Diggle)

CLYMENE

I hate . . . the handy cornel bow—and good riddance for ever to training schools![1]

[1] Plutarch says that Clymene feared being hurt by reminders of her dead son's youthful activities ('training schools' may pick up a now lost earlier reference to his also practising chariot-driving). The densely hard cornel wood was favoured for spear shafts and arrows.

(786: see after F 779)

PHILOCTETES

C. W. Müller, *Euripides. Philoktet* (Berlin–New York, 2000) and *Philoktet. Beiträge zur Wiedergewinnung einer Tragödie des Euripides* (Stuttgart, 1997), both reviewed by C. Collard, *Gnomon* 78 (2006), 106–13; F. Jouan in ed. Budé VIII.3.269–312; C. Collard in *SFP* II.1–34.

L. A. Milani, *Il mito di Filottete nella letteratura classica e nell' arte figurata* (Rome, 1879); N. Wecklein, *SBAW* 1888.1.127–39; W. H. Friedrich, *Philologus* 94 (1941), 157–64; Jouan (1966), 308–17; Webster 57–61; W. M. Calder in O. Mörkholm, N. M. Waggoner (eds.), *Greek Numismatics . . . in honor of Margaret Thompson* (Wetteren, 1979), 53–62; O. Mandel, *Philoctetes and the Fall of Troy* (Lincoln NA, 1981); Aélion (1983), I.61–72; M. T. Luzzato, *Prometheus* 9 (1983), 199–220; G. Avezzù, *Il ferimento e il rito. La storia di Filottete* (Bari, 1988); S. D. Olson, *Hesperia* 60 (1991), 269–85; *LIMC* VII.i.376–85 'Philoktetes'; E. Simon in H. Cancik (ed.), *Geschichte–Tradition–Reflexion. Festschrift . . . M. Hengel* (Tübingen, 1996), II.15–39; D. Fontannaz, *Antike Kunst* 43 (2000), 53–69; C. W. Müller, *RhM* 145 (2002), 61–7; F. Jouan, *REG* 115 (2002), 409–16; R. Scanzo, *Maia* 55 (2003), 481–500.

The grim story of Philoctetes' affliction when at Troy with a noisome, unhealing wound, his abandonment by the dis-

gusted Greeks on the island of Lemnos, and after ten years the necessity, revealed to the Greeks by the captured Trojan seer Helenus, to recover, heal and rehabilitate him because Troy could only be taken with the bow which Heracles had given him: this story was widely told or alluded to in early epic (Homer, Iliad 2.718–25; Cypria, Arg. 9 West; Little Iliad, Arg. 2 West) and in lyric (Pindar, Pythians 1.50–5, Bacchylides fr. 7). It was dramatized before Euripides by Aeschylus (F 249–257; of little use for reconstruction), and after him by Sophocles in the surviving Philoctetes, and by others (see below: Sophocles' fragmentary Philoctetes at Troy, F 697–703, set after his retrieval from Lemnos, is undated).

Many later accounts throw light generally on the entire myth,[1] but art gives only a little help for Euripides. The primary evidence for the play is thin—only a damaged hypothesis (test. iiia below) and just 40 or so lines in fewer than 20 book fragments—but for reconstruction, and especially appreciation, there is a secondary resource of singular value. The rhetorician Dio of Prusa ('Chrysostom', c. A.D. 100) wrote a comparison of the tragedies of Aeschylus, Sophocles and Euripides in his Oration 52, stating that they had 'all the same subject' (52.2). Dio's Oration 11 may reflect details from Aeschylus (see Jouan 2002), and he paraphrased the start of Euripides' play in Oration 59. Dio's extensive evidence has been carefully reedited and assessed by Müller (2000), and is presented with great concision by Kannicht in TrGF as test. iiib, ivb–d and v (all reproduced below) and as F 787–789 and 789b–d. Thanks to Dio, the incidents can be followed in reasonable fullness

---

[1] See Avezzù, Gantz 589–90, 635–9, Müller (2000), 25–65 and (1997), Jouan 269–72, Scanzo.

*(but not through entrances and exits and episodic struc-
ture) as far as the play's first critical turn (see (1) below);
thereafter much remains speculative (see (2) below). We
give here only a summary reconstruction, with comments.*[2]

(1) *The scene is Lemnos, in front of Philoctetes' cave
(compare Sophocles); Odysseus' prologue-soliloquy (F
787–789, 789a, 787–9, 789b) shows that he has come to
recover Philoctetes if he can, prompted by duty and ambi-
tion, but unconfident despite being disguised by the god-
dess Athena. The crippled and ragged Philoctetes appears
(again, compare Sophocles); the unrecognized Odysseus
pretends to be an outcast from the Greeks like Philoctetes
himself, and plays so far upon Philoctetes' sympathy and
resentment (for the latter, Sophocles again) that he is in-
vited to share the miserable resources of the cave (F 789d,
790, **790a, probably 792). A choral ode would follow
this first major development. Major uncertainties here: (a)
Odysseus is accompanied to Lemnos by Diomedes (test.
ivc), but we do not know whether Odysseus even men-
tioned him in his soliloquy. (b) The play's chorus is of
Lemnian men who in their entry song express guilt that
they have long neglected Philoctetes (test. ivd, F 789c, pos-
sibly also F 792a), but we do not know whether they en-
tered directly after the prologue speech, with the initial
encounter between Odysseus and Philoctetes forming the
first episode, or (much less probably) after that meeting; F
791 may come from their entry song, or from the first*

---

[2] Müller reviewed all previous studies and his two volumes af-
ford the most detailed basis for reconstruction. His results are
subsumed in Jouan (ed. Budé 279–99) and Collard (*SFP* II.3–11),
and assessed by Collard (2006), 110–3.

*stasimon. (c) An individual Lemnian, the shepherd Actor,
has occasionally helped Philoctetes in the past (test. ivb)
and makes an entry, probably in the first episode after the
encounter of Odysseus and Philoctetes, possibly in a sepa-
rate second episode (so Müller, giving the first episode to
Actor and the Chorus, with Odysseus overhearing); recon-
structors suggest that Actor brings Philoctetes the major
news, confirming Odysseus' own knowledge (test. ivc, cf. F
789b (4)), that Trojan envoys are coming to try to win
Philoctetes and his bow to their side.*

*(2) The rest of the action. The Trojans arrive,[3] and there
is a debate scene between their leader (F 794) and Philocte-
tes, into which Odysseus breaks (still unrecognized), en-
couraging the Greek Philoctetes to resist the 'barbarians'
(F 796; the denunciation of prophecy in F 795 is probably
a further part of his deception of Philoctetes). After the
Trojans leave in failure, there would be a choral ode; and
now Odysseus must himself win over Philoctetes, which he
does, states Dio, using the same phrase of Aeschylus' and
Sophocles' plays, 'by forcible persuasion'. It is likely that
Diomedes here played his part, somehow compounding
Odysseus' deception with a false promise to Philoctetes to
take him back to Greece (Wecklein's suggestion; compare
Sophocles). Philoctetes probably suffered a renewed attack
from his wound, perhaps when about to prepare for the
false departure (cf. Sophocles again); the bow was taken
from him, most likely after Odysseus and Diomedes had*

---

[3] Imagined on a 2nd. c. B.C. urn from Volterra: *LIMC* no. 57,
Müller (1997) Pl. 5, (2000) fig. 5.

led or carried him into the cave.[4] When they came out, an angry scene followed, in which Odysseus, now revealed and in possession of the bow, compelled Philoctetes by argument to come to Troy (F 798, 799, 799a, perhaps in a further debate scene: see on F 797); at the end Philoctetes was taken on shipboard (test. iiia.21). Major uncertainties here: (a) Odysseus may not have mentioned Diomedes in his prologue (above): was his appearance a theatrical surprise, and was he disguised too, like the false merchant in Sophocles? (b) If Philoctetes' attack of agony and the taking of the bow were off-stage, were they narrated by Diomedes, or even by Actor (whom some reconstructors wish to give a further role)? (c) How far was the 'forcible persuasion' physical, like Odysseus' maltreatment of Philoctetes in Sophocles? If it was literally 'forcible', did Diomedes aid the violence? (d) When Philoctetes is finally compelled, a confirming god has been suggested, like Heracles in Sophocles, but most reconstructors now find this unnecessary. (e) The taking of the bow and the final argument and departure may have filled an extended exodos, interrupted only by brief choral lyrics or spoken comment (F 800), rather than a further episode, a formal ode, and then a final scene.

Brief fragments: F 801 'he breathed life away' (perhaps referring to Palamedes' death, cf. F 789d (8)); both F 802 'you understand' and F 803 ('peak, critical point') are lexicographic and insecure in sense; for F 801a see on F 888. Other ascriptions: adesp. F 579 (= F 7 Müller: see note on F 789d (11)); Cyclops 104 'grim' (Odysseus: = F 24 Müller);

[4] The taking is vividly imagined, but outdoors, on a 1st c. B.C./A.D. silver cup now in Copenhagen: *LIMC* no. 69; Müller (1997) Pls. 12–14, (2000) fig. 7.

Cyclops 707 'through a tunnelled cave' (= F 5 Müller, cf. Soph. Phil. 19).

As to the temper of the play, Dio (test. v) admired the clarity of the language, the quality of the argumentative scenes, and the moral benefit to readers. The contrast between a callously manipulative and ambitious Odysseus and an embittered, deceived and sympathetic Philoctetes was powerful. The progress of events was realistic (Dio again), with 'political' issues of patriotism, ambition, and individual responsibility and service most prominent (see Olson [1991] and Müller [1997], 11–42). The divine is barely visible in the testimonia and fragments (apart from Athena's disguise of Odysseus) beneath a very human sequence of motives and emotions; but the plot's outcome confirms divine prophecy (as in Sophocles; cf. F 800 here).

Date: 431 B.C. (test. ii), with Medea and Dictys (see Introduction there). Müller (2002) speculates why Euripides (and Sophocles) were defeated in this year by Euphorion the son of Aeschylus.

The tragedies of Aeschylus, Euripides and Sophocles assured the story's later popularity. Theodectes followed them in the 4th century, and later notably the Roman Accius, whose fragments give some help in reconstructing Euripides. Other episodes (apparently) were dramatized by Euripides' contemporaries Achaeus and Philocles. Comedians in both the 5th and 4th centuries used the myth. The rich literary and artistic heritage is superbly documented and illustrated (into the modern period) by Müller (1997, 2000), subsuming the earlier work of Milani (1879), Mandel (1981), Avezzù (1988), LIMC (1994), Simon (1996); cf. OGCMA II.892–4.

ΦΙΛΟΚΤΗΤΗΣ

test. iiia (Hypothesis)

traces of one line
  ..ρα[...]σας Φιλοκτ[ή]τ[8–9 *letters*]οι
λευ....ς ἐν τοῖς τ[ό]ποις [ἐν οἷς ἐδ]ή-
χθη· περιαλγῆ δ᾽ α[ὐτὸν γενόμ]ενον
5 ἐπὶ τὴν παρακειμένην Λ[ῆ]μνον δια-
κομ[ίσ]αντες εἴασαν· ὁ δ[ὲ] τὸν δεκαετῆ
χρό[ν]ον διέζησεν ἀτυχῶν, ὡς ἂν βίον
ἔχ[ων] τὸν ἔλεον τῶν ἐντυγχαν[ό]ντων·
ἔ[π]ε[ι]τα καὶ Ἕλενος εἶπεν τοῖς Τρωσὶ τοῖς
10 Ἡρακλέο[υς] τόξοις ἀσφαλίσασθα[ι] τὴν πό-
λιν, καὶ λ[η]φθεὶς δ᾽ αἰχμάλωτος τὴν αὐ-
τὴν ποιεῖσθ]αι συμμαχ[ία]ν] ἐ[θέσπ]ισεν
9–10 *letters*] τὸν Φιλοκτ[ήτ-
7 *letters*] Ὀδυσσεὺς εκ[
15 ..... ἐσ]τείλατο μὲν ἐμφ[
7 *letters*] Ἀθηνᾶς βου[λ-

a few letters from lines 17–18, then about 13 lines missing, then a separate fragment with a few letters from line 19 followed by:

374

PHILOCTETES

test. iiia (Hypothesis)

. . . Philoctetes . . . in the place (where) he was bitten;[1] (when
he was) in agony they took him across to nearby Lemnos and   5
let him be. He lived in miserable need for the duration of the
ten years,[2] as he would when he had as his livelihood the pity
of those who encountered him. (Then) Helenus both told
the Trojans to make the city safe with Heracles' bow, and when   10
he was taken prisoner (pronounced that they [the Greeks]
should make)[3] the same alliance . . . Philoctetes . . . Odys-
seus (set sail) . . . . . . Athena counselling(?) him . . . (about 16   15

---

[1] At Chryse's altar: cf. F 789d (9), Soph. *Philoctetes* 1326–8.
[2] The length of the Trojan War.   [3] Supplemented by Turner,
Luppe: see F 789b (2).

P. Oxy. 2455 fr. 17, ed. E. Turner (1962); cf. Austin, *NFE* 100,
van Rossum-Steenbeek 223, W. Luppe, *Anagennesis* 3 (1983),
187–200 and *Würzburger Jahrbücher* 19 (1993), 47–53, C. W.
Müller, *ZPE* 98 (1993), 19–24 and *Eur. Philoktet* (2000), 144–7,
224–30.

12 ἐ[θέσπ]ισεν Turner, Luppe   15 ἐσ]τείλατο Müller

20

]ην ἀσφάλει-

αν ἀναγκάζει[ν εἰς τὴν ν]αῦν συνακ[ο]λουθεῖν.

———

21 ἀναγκάζει[ν εἰς Luppe: -ει[πρὸς Turner

test. iiib

ἐνέτυχον τραγῳδίαις . . . Αἰσχύλου καὶ Σοφοκλέους καὶ
Εὐριπίδου, πάντων περὶ τὴν αὐτὴν ὑπόθεσιν. ἦν γὰρ ἡ
τῶν Φιλοκτήτου τόξων εἴτε κλοπὴ εἴτε ἁρπαγὴ‹ν› δεῖ
λέγειν· πλὴν ἀφαιρούμενός γε τῶν ὅπλων ἦν Φιλοκτήτης
ὑπὸ τοῦ Ὀδυσσέως καὶ αὐτὸς εἰς τὴν Τροίαν ἀναγόμενος,
τὸ μὲν πλέον ἄκων, τὸ δέ τι καὶ πειθοῖ ἀναγκαίᾳ, ἐπειδὴ
τῶν ὅπλων ἐστέρητο, ἃ τοῦτο μὲν βίον αὐτῷ παρεῖχεν ἐν
τῇ νήσῳ, τοῦτο δὲ θάρσος ἐν τῇ τοιαύτῃ νόσῳ, ἅμα δὲ
εὔκλειαν.

Dio Chrysostom, *Orations* 52.2, ed. Müller (2000), 150

test. ivb

οὐδὲ ἐξ ἅπαντος ἦν μήτε προσελθεῖν αὐτῷ μηδένα
Λημνίων μήτε ἐπιμεληθῆναι μηδέν· δοκεῖ γάρ μοι οὐδ' ἂν
διεγένετο τὰ δέκα ἔτη μηδεμιᾶς τυγχάνων βοηθείας, ἀλλ'
εἰκὸς μὲν τυγχάνειν αὐτόν, σπανίως δὲ καὶ οὐδενὸς
μεγάλου, καὶ μηδένα αἱρεῖσθαι οἰκίᾳ ὑποδέξασθαι καὶ
νοσηλεύειν διὰ τὴν δυσχέρειαν τῆς νόσου. αὐτὸς γοῦν ὁ
Εὐριπίδης τὸν Ἄκτορα εἰσάγει, ἕνα Λημνίων, ὡς γνώ-
ριμον τῷ Φιλοκτήτῃ προσιόντα καὶ πολλάκις συμβε-
βληκότα.

Dio 52.8, ed. Müller (2000), 152–3

lines largely or wholly lost) . . . safety to compel him (i.e.   20
Philoctetes) to accompany them (onto the) ship. *(end of hypothesis)*

test. iiib

I came upon tragedies . . . of Aeschylus and Sophocles and Euripides, all upon the same subject: it was the theft or, one should say, seizure of Philoctetes' bow—except that Philoctetes had his weapons taken from him by Odysseus and was himself brought back to Troy, unwillingly for the greater part but in some sense actually by forcible persuasion, since he had been deprived of the weapons which provided him with life on the island as well as with courage in such an affliction, and at the same time with fame.

test. ivb

. . . and it was altogether impossible that none of the Lemnians had either visited him or had any concern for him: it seems to me, he would not even have survived the ten years without getting some help; but it was likely that he did get it, rarely and to no great extent, and that no one chose to receive him in his home and to treat his condition because of the affliction's unpleasantness. Euripides himself at any rate brings Actor on stage, one of the Lemnians, approaching Philoctetes as an acquaintance and having often met him.[1]

[1] See Introduction (1(c)). Hyginus, *Fab.* 102.2 names Actor as a king's shepherd who sustains Philoctetes.

EURIPIDES

test. ivc

φησί τε (ὁ Εὐριπίδης) ὑπὸ τῆς Ἀθηνᾶς ἠλλοιῶσθαι, ὥστε
ἐντυχόντα τῷ Φιλοκτήτῃ μὴ γνωσθῆναι ὑπ᾽ αὐτοῦ, μιμη-
σάμενος κατὰ τοῦτο Ὅμηρον . . . φησί τε πρεσβείαν
μέλλειν παρὰ τῶν Τρώων ἀφικνεῖσθαι πρὸς τὸν Φιλοκτή-
την, δεησομένην αὐτόν τε καὶ τὰ ὅπλα ἐκείνοις παρα-
σχεῖν ἐπὶ τῇ τῆς Τροίας βασιλείᾳ, ποικιλώτερον τὸ
δρᾶμα κατασκευάζων καὶ ἀνευρίσκων λόγων ἀφορμάς,
καθ᾽ ἃς εἰς τὰ ἐναντία ἐπιχειρῶν εὐπορώτατος καὶ παρ᾽
ὁντινοῦν ἱκανώτατος φαίνεται, (14) καὶ οὐ μόνον πεποίηκε
τὸν Ὀδυσσέα παραγιγνόμενον, ἀλλὰ μετὰ τοῦ Διομή-
δους, ὁμηρικῶς καὶ τοῦτο . . .

Dio 52.13–14, ed. Müller (2000), 156–8

test. ivd

ὅ τε Σοφοκλῆς . . . τὸν χορὸν οὐχ ὥσπερ ὁ Αἰσχύλος καὶ
Εὐριπίδης ἐκ τῶν ἐπιχωρίων πεποίηκεν, ἀλλὰ τῶν ἐν τῇ
νηὶ συμπλεόντων τῷ Ὀδυσσεῖ καὶ τῷ Νεοπτολέμῳ . . .
(17) . . . τά τε μέλη οὐκ ἔχει πολὺ τὸ γνωμικὸν οὐδὲ πρὸς
ἀρετὴν παράκλησιν, ὥσπερ τὰ τοῦ Εὐριπίδου . . .

Dio 52.15–17, ed. Müller (2000), 158–60

test. v

ἥ τε τοῦ Εὐριπίδου σύνεσις καὶ περὶ πάντα ἐπιμέλεια,
ὥστε μήτε ἀπίθανόν τι καὶ παρημελημένον ἐᾶσαι μήτε
ἁπλῶς τοῖς πράγμασι χρῆσθαι, ἀλλὰ μετὰ πάσης ἐν τῷ
εἰπεῖν δυνάμεως, ὥσπερ ἀντίστροφός ἐστι τῇ τοῦ Αἰσχύ-

test. ivc

He (Euripides) says that he (Odysseus) has been transformed
by Athena, so as not to be recognized by Philoctetes when he
encounters him, in this respect copying Homer[1] . . . and he
says that an embassy is about to come from the Trojans to
Philoctetes, to ask him to put himself and his weapons at their
disposal with the kingship of Troy as reward, making his play
more complex and inventing occasions for argument, in which
he appears most resourceful in his efforts for contrast and
most capable in comparison with anyone else; (14) and he has
not made Odysseus come there on his own, but in the com-
pany of Diomedes, this too in a Homeric manner.[2]

[1] *Odyssey* 13.397–403, 429–38. Dio 52.5 says that in Aeschy-
lus Odysseus was not transformed by Athena, but begged her to
prevent the recognition.   [2] Homer does not give this detail,
but cf. *Little Iliad* arg. (2) West with Apollodorus Epit. 5.8, and
Hyginus, *fab.* 102.3. Hyginus, *Fab.* 102.3 also pairs Diomedes
with Odysseus in the attempt.

test. ivd

(Sophocles) composed his chorus not from the inhabitants (of
Lemnos), as did Aeschylus and Euripides, but from those who
sailed on shipboard with Odysseus and Neoptolemus . . . (17)
. . . and his lyrics do not have much of the gnomic or of incen-
tive to virtue like those of Euripides . . .

test. v

Euripides' intelligence and concern for everything, so as not
to permit anything which is unconvincing and lacks care, nor
simply to employ the incidents, but with every power in the

Dio 52.11 and 14, ed. Müller (2000), 154–6 and 158

EURIPIDES

λου <ποιήσει>, πολιτικωτάτη καὶ ῥητορικωτάτη οὖσα καὶ
τοῖς ἐντυγχάνουσι πλείστην ὠφέλειαν παρασχεῖν δυνα-
μένη . . . (14) . . . καὶ τὸ ὅλον, ὡς ἔφην, δι' ὅλου τοῦ
δράματος πλείστην μὲν ἐν τοῖς πράγμασι σύνεσιν καὶ
πιθανότητα ἐπιδείκνυται, ἀμήχανον δὲ καὶ θαυμαστὴν ἐν
τοῖς λόγοις δύναμιν, καὶ τά τε ἰαμβεῖα σαφῶς καὶ κατὰ
φύσιν καὶ πολιτικῶς ἔχοντα, καὶ τὰ μέλη οὐ μόνον
ἡδονήν, ἀλλὰ καὶ πολλὴν πρὸς ἀρετὴν παράκλησιν.

(11) <ποιήσει> Müller: <ἁπλότητι> Reiske

(787–789)

Under this composite number TrGF *places Dio 52.11–12 and
59.1–2 together as evidence for Odysseus' prologue speech,
which included F 789a, 787, 788, 789, and 789b. Dio 52.12
and 59.1 reflect and partially paraphrase F 787 and 788
(52.12 quotes F 788.1); 59.2 reflects F 789. See further the
summary opposite.*

telling—in this he is just the reverse of Aeschylus' (poetic manner)[1]—these qualities are very true to ordinary life and eloquent, and able to provide very great benefit to those who come upon them . . . (14) . . . and altogether, as I said, throughout the play he displays very great intelligence and conviction in the incidents, an irresistible and wonderful power in the words, with his iambic dialogue kept clear and natural and true to ordinary life, and his lyrics affording not only pleasure but also great incentive to virtue.

[1] Müller's supplement; '(simplicity)', Reiske.

(787–789)

Extracts from Dio's paraphrase and appreciation of Odysseus' prologue speech, which included F 789a, 787, 788, 789, and 789b:

The speech is full of 'political' and personal introspection, as Odysseus doubts his reputation among the Greeks for supreme intelligence and cleverness; he wonders why some men are always ready to undertake risks when they could live quietly, and explains this as the instinct of the well-born man to gain honour and glory. This is his own nature, always to exert himself in a new challenge, fearing to lose the glory of his previous achievements.[1]

[1] Plato, *Republic* 10.620c–d seems to have had in mind the individual fragments 787–9.

EURIPIDES

789a (= 793 N)

⟨ΟΔΥΣΣΕΥΣ⟩

'μακάριος ὅστις εὐτυχῶν οἴκοι μένει·
ἐν γῇ δ' ὁ φόρτος, κοὺ πάλιν ναυτίλλεται.

Stobaeus 4.17.18; v. 1: Stobaeus 3.39.13, and imitated or adapted in Clement of Alexandria, *Miscellanies* 6.2.7.7, Menander F 82 *PCG*, Stobaeus 3.39.14 (attributed to Sophocles), and paroemiographers. Placed early in Odysseus' prologue speech, if not at its beginning, by Müller; assigned to Diomedes (disguised as a sea trader: see Introduction) and placed later in the play by Luzzato, Olson.

2 κοὺ Gesner: καὶ Stob.: καὶ πόλιν Schott

787

ΟΔΥΣΣΕΥΣ

πῶς δ' ἂν φρονοίην, ᾧ παρῆν ἀπραγμόνως
ἐν τοῖσι πολλοῖς ἠριθμημένῳ στρατοῦ
ἴσον μετασχεῖν τῷ σοφωτάτῳ τύχης;

Plutarch, *Moralia* 544c (followed by F 789); vv. 1–3 (πῶς—μετασχεῖν): Aristotle, *Nicomachean Ethics* 1142a3–5 (followed by F 788.2; so too *CAG* XX.340.4, paraphrased in *CAG* XIX.2.123.28)

PHILOCTETES

789a (= 793 N)

⟨ODYSSEUS⟩

'Blessed the man who rests happily at home.'[1] His cargo is safely on land, and he does not go to sea again.[2]

[1] Evidently a common saying (see the Greek apparatus).
[2] Odysseus begins his prologue speech by referring to the dilemma he faced, whether to sail off again on a further dangerous mission (cf. F 787, 789, 789b (2)). Stobaeus' text in v. 2 (without the negative) is interpreted by some as a contrast with v. 1, 'his cargo is safely on land, and (yet) he goes to sea again!' Schott suggested 'and he steers his *city*' (rather than a ship).

787

ODYSSEUS

How would I be in my right mind,[1] when I could be counted among the army's masses and without exertion share equally in fortune with the cleverest man?

[1] I.e., if I kept on taking risks: cf. F 787–789 above, and for the idea *Antiope* F 193, *Hippolytus* 1012–20, Sophocles, *Oedipus* 584–602.

EURIPIDES

788

ΟΔΥΣΣΕΥΣ

οὐδὲν γὰρ οὕτω γαῦρον ὡς ἀνὴρ ἔφυ·
τοὺς γὰρ περισσοὺς καί τι πράσσοντας πλέον
τιμῶμεν ἄνδρας τ᾽ ἐν πόλει νομίζομεν.

Paraphrased in Dio 59.1 (see F 787–789 above); v. 1: Dio
52.12; P. Herc. 1384 col. 32.3–5 (see A. Antoni, *Cronache
Ercolanesi* 34 [2004], 34–5); Schol. on Aristophanes, *Frogs* 282;
Plutarch, *Moralia* 779d; v. 2: see on F 787; vv. 2–3: Stobaeus
3.29.15 (continued into F 789)

789

ΟΔΥΣΣΕΥΣ

ὀκνῶν δὲ μόχθων τῶν πρὶν ἐκχέαι χάριν
καὶ τοὺς παρόντας οὐκ ἀπωθοῦμαι πόνους.

Plutarch, *Moralia* 544c (see on F 787); paraphrased in Dio
59.2 (see F 787–789 above); v. 1: Stobaeus 3.29.16, continued
without new lemma from F 788.2–3; v. 2 adulterated in P. Herc.
1384 col. 32.1–3 (see on F 788)

(789a: see before F 787 above)

(789b (1): a sentence from Dio 52.12 introducing
test. ivc above)

789b (2)

ΟΔΥΣΣΕΥΣ

νῦν οὖν κατὰ πρᾶξιν πάνυ ἐπισφαλῆ καὶ χαλεπὴν δεῦρο
ἐλήλυθα εἰς Λῆμνον, ὅπως Φιλοκτήτην καὶ τὰ Ἡρακλέ-

788

ODYSSEUS

. . . for there's nothing so vain by nature as a man: we honour those who go beyond the ordinary and seek greater success, and count them real men in a city.

789

ODYSSEUS

In my reluctance to waste the credit for my former efforts, I don't refuse these present tasks either.

(789a: see before F 787 above)

(789b (1): a sentence from Dio 52.12 introducing test. ivc above)

789b (2)

Dio's paraphrase (cf. the composite F 787–789 above) continues in Or. 59.2–4:

ODYSSEUS

Now therefore I have come here to Lemnos for an altogether dangerous and difficult task, to bring Philoctetes and the bow

EURIPIDES

ους τόξα κομίζοιμι τοῖς συμμάχοις. ὁ γὰρ δὴ μαντικώτα-
τος Φρυγῶν Ἕλενος ὁ Πριάμου κατεμήνυσεν, ὡς ἔτυχεν
αἰχμάλωτος ληφθείς, ἄνευ τούτων μήποτ' ἂν ἁλῶναι τὴν
πόλιν. (3) πρὸς μὲν δὴ τοὺς βασιλέας οὐχ ὡμολόγησα
τὴν πρᾶξιν, ἐπιστάμενος τὴν τοῦ ἀνδρὸς ἔχθραν, ᾧ γε
αὐτὸς αἴτιος ἐγενόμην καταλειφθῆναι, ὅτε δηχθεὶς ἔτυχεν
ὑπὸ χαλεπῆς καὶ ἀνιάτου ἐχίδνης. οὐκ ἂν οὖν ᾤμην οὐδὲ
πειθὼ τοιαύτην ἐξευρεῖν, ὑφ' ἧς ἄν ποτε ἐκεῖνος ἐμοὶ
πρᾴως ἔσχεν, ἀλλ' εὐθὺς ἀποθανεῖσθαί ᾤμην ὑπ' αὐτοῦ.
ὕστερον δέ, τῆς Ἀθηνᾶς μοι παρακελευσαμένης καθ'
ὕπνους, ὥσπερ εἴωθε, θαρροῦντα ἐπὶ τὸν ἄνδρα ἰέναι
(αὐτὴ γὰρ ἀλλάξειν μου τὸ εἶδος καὶ τὴν φωνήν, ὥστε
λαθεῖν αὐτῷ ξυγγενόμενον), οὕτω δὴ ἀφῖγμαι θαρρήσας.
(4) πυνθάνομαι δὲ καὶ παρὰ τῶν Φρυγῶν πρέσβεις ἀπ-
εστάλθαι κρύφα, ἐάν πως δύνωνται τὸν Φιλοκτήτην πεί-
σαντες δώροις ἅμα καὶ διὰ τὴν ἔχθραν τὴν πρὸς ἡμᾶς
ἀναλαβεῖν εἰς τὴν πόλιν αὐτὸν καὶ τὰ τόξα. τοιούτου
προκειμένου ἄθλου πῶς οὐ πάντα χρὴ ἄνδρα γίγνεσθαι
πρόθυμον; ὡς διαμαρτάνοντι τῆς πράξεως ταύτης πάντα
τὰ πρότερον εἰργασμένα μάτην πεπονῆσθαι ἔοικεν.

Dio 59.2–4, ed. Müller (2000), 172–4

789c

εὐθὺς ἀπολογοῦνται περὶ τῆς πρότερον ἀμελείας, ὅτι δὴ
τοσούτων ἐτῶν οὔτε προσέλθοιεν πρὸς τὸν Φιλοκτήτην
οὔτε βοηθήσειαν οὐδὲν αὐτῷ.

Dio 52.7, ed. Müller (2000), 152

of Heracles to the allies: this is because Helenus, son of Priam and the Phrygians' best seer, disclosed when he happened to be captured, that without them the city (of Troy) would never be taken. (3) Now I did not give the (Greek) kings my agreement to the task, knowing Philoctetes' hatred—I had myself been the cause of his abandonment, when it happened that he was bitten by a cruel and deadly viper. So I didn't think I would find the sort of persuasiveness either, under which the man would ever have been merciful to me; no, I thought I would immediately be killed by Philoctetes. Later however, once Athena had ordered me (in my sleep, as was her custom) to go confidently after the man—for she said she would change my appearance and voice, so as to be undetected when I met him—well, this is how I have come with confidence. (4) And I discover that envoys have been sent secretly from the Phrygians too, in case they may be able to persuade Philoctetes with gifts as well as on the ground of his enmity towards us, and take him and the bow back to Troy. When such a prize has been placed before him, how should every man not be eager? Also, if I fail in this task, it seems that all my former achievements will have been wasted effort.

789c

Dio describes the entry of the Chorus:

They (the Chorus) immediately apologize for their former neglect, namely that in so many years they neither approached Philoctetes nor gave him any help.

EURIPIDES

789d

(5) ΟΔΥΣΣΕΥΣ. παπαῖ· πρόσεισιν ὁ ἀνήρ. αὐτὸς ὅδε ὁ Ποίαντος παῖς, οὐκ ἄδηλος τῇ ξυμφορᾷ, μόλις καὶ χαλεπῶς προβαίνων. ὢ τοῦ χαλεποῦ καὶ δεινοῦ ὁράματος οὕτως· τό τε γὰρ εἶδος ὑπὸ τῆς νόσου φοβερὸν ἥ τε στολὴ ἀήθης· δοραὶ θηρίων καλύπτουσιν αὐτόν. ἀλλὰ σὺ ἄμυνον, ὢ δέσποινα Ἀθηνᾶ, καὶ μὴ μάτην φανῇς ἡμῖν ὑποσχομένη τὴν σωτηρίαν.

(6) ΦΙΛΟΚΤΗΤΗΣ. τί δὴ βουλόμενος, ὅστις εἶ ποτε σύ, ἢ τίνα τόλμαν λαβών, πότερον ἁρπαγῆς χάριν ἥκεις ἐπὶ τήνδε τὴν ἄπορον στέγην ἢ κατάσκοπος τῆς ἡμετέρας δυστυχίας;

ΟΔ. οὔτοι γε ὁρᾷς ἄνδρα ὑβριστήν.

ΦΙ. οὐ μὴν εἰωθώς γε πρότερον δεῦρο ἥκεις.

ΟΔ. οὐ γὰρ εἰωθώς· εἴη δὲ καὶ νῦν ἐν καιρῷ ἀφῖχθαι.

ΦΙ. πολλὴν ἔοικας φράζειν ἀλογίαν τῆς δεῦρο ὁδοῦ.

ΟΔ. εὖ τοίνυν ἴσθι οὐ χωρὶς αἰτίας με ἥκοντα καὶ σοί γε οὐκ ἀλλότριον φανησόμενον.

(7) ΦΙ. πόθεν δή; τοῦτο γὰρ πρῶτον εἰκός με εἰδέναι.

ΟΔ. ἀλλ᾽ εἰμὶ Ἀργεῖος τῶν ἐπὶ Τροίαν πλευσάντων.

ΦΙ. πόθεν; εἰπὲ πάλιν, ὡς εἰδῶ σαφέστερον.

ΟΔ. οὐκοῦν δεύτερον ἀκούεις· τῶν ἐπ᾽ Ἴλιον στρατευσάντων Ἀχαιῶν εἶναί φημι.

Dio 59.5–11, ed. Müller (2000), 184–96

(6) <φίλον καὶ> οὐκ ἀλλότριον Müller

789d

ODYSSEUS (*seeing Philoctetes slowly approaching*). Oh no! The man approaches! Here is the son of Poeas himself, his wretched condition quite evident, barely making his way forward, and in difficulty. Oh, what a hard and terrible sight he is, like this: his appearance under his affliction is frightening, and his dress extraordinary, with the hides of wild beasts covering him. Now, Athena my mistress, defend me, and do not let your promise to me of safety seem empty!

PHILOCTETES. What is it you want, whoever you are, or what (6) audacity are you set on? Is it for robbery that you come to this resourceless dwelling, or as a spy on my misfortune?

OD. You are seeing no man of violence, be sure of that!

PH. I swear you've not had the habit before of coming here.

OD. No, no habit; but I wish to have come opportunely all the same.

PH. There seems a great lack of sense in your coming, from what you say.

OD. Well, you should know that I haven't come without cause, and that I'll prove no stranger to yourself.[1]

PH. Where from, then? It's reasonable I should know this first. (7)

OD. Well, I am an Argive, from those who sailed against Troy.

PH. From where? Tell me again, so that I may know quite clearly.

OD. A second time, then, you hear it: I say that I am one of the Achaeans who campaigned against Troy.

---

[1] '(a friend and) no stranger' Müller.

EURIPIDES

ΦΙ. καλῶς δῆτα ἔφησθα ἐμὸς εἶναι φίλος, ὁπότε γε τῶν
ἐμοὶ πολεμιωτάτων Ἀργείων πέφηνας. τούτων δὴ τῆς
ἀδικίας αὐτίκα μάλα ὑφέξεις δίκην.

ΟΔ. ἀλλ᾽ ὦ πρὸς θεῶν ἐπίσχες ἀφεῖναι τὸ βέλος.

ΦΙ. οὐ δυνατόν, εἴπερ Ἕλλην ὢν τυγχάνεις, τὸ μὴ ἀπολω-
λέναι σε ἐν τῇδε τῇ ἡμέρᾳ.

(8) ΟΔ. ἀλλὰ πέπονθά γε ὑπ᾽ αὐτῶν τοιαῦτα, ἐξ ὧν δικαίως
σοὶ μὲν ἂν φίλος εἴην, ἐκείνων δὲ ἐχθρός.

ΦΙ. καὶ τί δὴ τοῦτό ἐστιν, ὃ πέπονθας οὕτως χαλεπόν;

ΟΔ. φυγάδα με ἤλασεν Ὀδυσσεὺς ἐκ τοῦ στρατοῦ.

ΦΙ. τί δὲ ἔδρασας, ἐφ᾽ ὅτῳ τῆσδε τῆς δίκης ἔτυχες;

ΟΔ. οἶμαί σε γιγνώσκειν τὸν Ναυπλίου παῖδα Παλα-
μήδην.

ΦΙ. οὐ γὰρ δὴ τῶν ἐπιτυχόντων οὐδὲ ὀλίγου ἄξιος συν-
έπλει οὔτε τῷ στρατῷ οὔτε τοῖς ἡγεμόσιν.

ΟΔ. τὸν δὴ τοιοῦτον ἄνδρα ὁ κοινὸς τῶν Ἑλλήνων λυμεὼν
διέφθειρεν.

ΦΙ. πότερον ἐκ τοῦ φανεροῦ μάχῃ κρατήσας ἢ μετὰ δόλου
τινός;

ΟΔ. προδοσίαν ἐπενεγκὼν τοῦ στρατοῦ τοῖς Πριαμίδαις.

ΦΙ. ἦν δὲ κατ᾽ ἀλήθειαν οὕτως ἔχον ἢ πέπονθε κατ-
εψευσμένος;

ΟΔ. πῶς δ᾽ ἂν δικαίως γένοιτο τῶν ὑπ᾽ ἐκείνου γιγνομένων
ὁτιοῦν;

PH. Then you did well to say you are a friend of mine, when you've revealed you're one of the Argives—my worst enemies! You'll pay the price of their injustice right away!

OD. No! In the name of heaven, hold back from shooting that arrow!

PH. Impossible, if you really are a Greek, that you do not die this day!

OD. But I've suffered such things at their hands as would justly (8) make me your friend, and their enemy.

PH. And what is it that you've suffered, and is so hard?

OD. Exile: Odysseus drove me from the army.

PH. And you did what, to meet with this punishment?

OD. You know, I think, Nauplius' son Palamedes.[2]

PH. Yes, certainly: he was no ordinary comrade on the voyage, and of no little worth to both army and commanders.

OD. Yes, it was just such a man that that blight on all the Greeks destroyed.

PH. Did he overcome him openly in a fight, or through some trick?

OD. He charged him with betraying the army to the sons of Priam.

PH. Was there truth in that, or did he suffer from a false accusation?

OD. How could anything whatever of that man's actions be just?

[2] See *Palamedes* test. *va, *vb, F 588.

(9) ΦΙ. ὦ μηδενὸς ἀποσχόμενος τῶν χαλεπωτάτων, λόγῳ τε
καὶ ἔργῳ πανουργότατε ἀνθρώπων Ὀδυσσεῦ, οἷον αὖ
τοῦτον ἄνδρα ἀνῄρηκας, ὃς οὐδὲν ἧττον ὠφέλιμος ἦν τοῖς
ξυμμάχοις ἤπερ οἶμαι σύ, τὰ κάλλιστα καὶ σοφώτατα
ἀνευρίσκων καὶ συντιθείς· ὥσπερ ἀμέλει κἀμὲ ἐξέθηκας,
ὑπὲρ τῆς κοινῆς σωτηρίας τε καὶ νίκης περιπεσόντα τῇδε
τῇ ξυμφορᾷ, δεικνύντα τὸν Χρύσης βωμόν, οὗ θύσαντες
κρατήσειν ἔμελλον τῶν πολεμίων· εἰ δὲ μή, μάτην ἐγίγνε-
το ἡ στρατεία. ἀλλὰ τί δή σοι προσῆκον τῆς Παλα-
μήδους τύχης;

(10) ΟΔ. εὖ ἴσθι ὅτι ἐπὶ πάντας τοὺς ἐκείνου φίλους ἦλθε τὸ
κακὸν καὶ πάντες ἀπολώλασιν, ὅστις μὴ φυγεῖν ἠδυνήθη.
οὕτω δὲ κἀγὼ τῆς παροιχομένης νυκτὸς διαπλεύσας
μόνος δεῦρο ἐσώθην. σχεδὸν μὲν οὖν ἐν ὅσῃ ἔγωγε χρείᾳ
καθέστηκας αὐτός. εἰ δ᾽ οὖν ἔχεις τινὰ μηχανήν, ξυμπρο-
θυμηθεὶς ἡμῖν περὶ τὸν οἴκαδε ἀπόπλουν ἡμᾶς τε εὖ
πεποιηκὼς ἔσῃ καὶ ἅμα ἄγγελον ἀποπέμψεις πρὸς τοὺς
σεαυτοῦ οἴκαδε τῶν σοὶ προσόντων κακῶν.

(11) ΦΙ. ἀλλ᾽, ὦ δύστηνε, πρὸς τοιοῦτον ἕτερον ἥκεις ξύμ-
μαχον, αὐτόν τε ἄπορον καὶ ἔρημον φίλων ἐπὶ τῆσδε τῆς
ἀκτῆς ἐρριμμένον, γλίσχρως καὶ μόλις ἀπὸ τῶνδε τῶν
τόξων πορίζοντα καὶ τροφὴν καὶ ἐσθῆτα, ὡς ὁρᾷς· ἣ γὰρ
ἦν ἡμῖν ἐσθὴς πρότερον, ὑπὸ τοῦ χρόνου ἀνάλωται. εἰ δὲ
δὴ τοῦδ᾽ ἐθελήσεις κοινωνεῖν τοῦ βίου μεθ᾽ ἡμῶν ἐνθάδε,
ἕως ἂν ἑτέρα σοι παραπέσῃ σωτηρία ποθέν, οὐκ ἂν

PH. *(cursing the real Odysseus)* You—you keep from none of (9)
the cruellest wrongs, Odysseus! You are the most villainous of
men in word and deed! What a man you've again done away
with in Palamedes—he was not less useful to the allies than
you were yourself, I think, in his invention and contrivance of
the finest and cleverest things—exactly as you once got rid of
me too, after I had met with this disaster of mine in the inter-
est of common safety and victory, when I revealed Chryse's al-
tar:[3] if the Greeks offered sacrifice there, they were destined
to overcome their enemy, but if not, their campaign would be
wasted.

But just what connection do you have with Palamedes'
fate?

OD. Know that the evil came upon all his friends, and that all (10)
have been destroyed except any who was able to escape. This
was how I too sailed across last night and came safely here on
my own. Now, I'm almost in such great need as you yourself;
so, if you do have any means, if you join keenly in helping my
voyage home, you will have done me a good turn and at the
same time will be sending a messenger to your own people at
home of the troubles you have now.

PH. But, you poor wretch, you have come to another man like (11)
yourself as an ally,[4] with no resources of his own and deprived
of friends when cast out on this shore, barely and with dif-
ficulty providing himself with food and clothing with this bow
here, as you see; for the clothing I had before has worn away
with the time. Still, if you're willing to share the life here with
me, until some other safety falls your way from somewhere,

---

[3] See note 1 on test. iiia above.   [4] Müller inserts here adesp.
F 579 (his F 7), 'you are weak and you have come to one who is
weak'.

EURIPIDES

φθονοῖμεν. δυσχερῆ γε μὴν τἄνδον ὁράματα, ὦ ξένε,
τελαμῶνές τε ⟨   ⟩ ἀνάπλεῳ καὶ ἄλλα σημεῖα τῆς νόσου·
αὐτός τε οὐχ ἡδὺς ξυγγενέσθαι, ὅταν ἡ ὀδύνη προσπέσῃ.
καίτοι λελώφηκε τῷ χρόνῳ τὸ πολὺ τῆς νόσου, κατ᾽
ἀρχὰς δὲ οὐδαμῶς ἀνεκτὸς ἦν.

(11) ⟨αἵματος⟩ ἀνάπλεῳ Bothe, Müller

790

⟨ΦΙΛΟΚΤΗΤΗΣ⟩
δύσμορφα μέντοι τἄνδον εἰσιδεῖν, ξένε.

Plutarch, *Moralia* 521a; assigned to the play by D. Canter, noting the paraphrase in F 789d (11)

**790a (= fr. adesp. 389 N)

⟨ΦΙΛΟΚΤΗΤΗΣ⟩
οὐκ ἔστ᾽ ἐν ἄντροις λευκός, ὦ ξέν᾽, ἄργυρος.

Plutarch, *Moralia* 553a; assigned to the play by Hilberg, comparing F 789d (11)

(791 N = 792a below)

792

⟨ΦΙΛΟΚΤΗΤΗΣ⟩
φαγέδαιναν ἥ μου σάρκα θοινᾶται ποδός

Aristotle, *Poetics* 1458b23–4

φαγέδαιναν Butler: φαγέδαινα* one ms. of Plut., φαγέδαινα
others: φαγέδαινά ⟨γ᾽⟩ Barnes

394

PHILOCTETES

I'd not grudge it. I have to tell you, the sights inside[5] are hard
to bear, bandages full of (blood?) and other signs of my afflic-
tion; and I'm not pleasant myself to be with, when the pain
strikes. And yet much of the affliction has eased with the time,
though at the start it was in no way tolerable.

[5] I.e. inside the cave: cf. F 790 below.

790

⟨PHILOCTETES⟩
Things inside, however, are an ugly sight, stranger.

**790a (= fr. adesp. 389 N)

⟨PHILOCTETES⟩
There is no pale silver[1] in the cave, stranger!

[1] Cf. *Oedipus* F 542.1 with note.

(791 N = 792a below)

792

⟨PHILOCTETES⟩
. . . ulcer which feasts on the flesh of my foot . . .

EURIPIDES

792a (= 791 N)

ΧΟΡΟΣ

ἅλις, ὦ βιοτά· πέραινε,
πρίν τινα συντυχίαν
ἢ κτεάτεσσιν ἐμοῖς ἢ σώματι τῷδε γενέσθαι.

Stobaeus 4.52.29, attributed to the Chorus

(793 N = 789a above)

794

⟨ΠΡΕΣΒΥΣ ΤΡΩΣ⟩

ὁρᾶτε δ᾽ ὡς κἀν θεοῖσι κερδαίνειν καλόν,
θαυμάζεται δ᾽ ὁ πλεῖστον ἐν ναοῖς ἔχων
χρυσόν· τί δῆτα καὶ σὲ κωλύει ⟨λαβεῖν⟩
κέρδος, παρόν γε, κἀξομοιοῦσθαι θεοῖς;

[Justin], *On Monarchy* 5.8; assigned to a Trojan Envoy by
Valckenaer

3 ⟨λαβεῖν⟩ Sylburg   4 comma after γε Barnes, rejected
by Heath

PHILOCTETES

792a (= 791 N)

CHORUS

Life, enough! Make an end, before some misfortune happens to my herds or myself here!

(793 N = 789a above)

794

⟨TROJAN ENVOY⟩[1]
(to Philoctetes)

You see[2] that making a profit is honourable among the gods too, and that the one with most gold in his temples is admired! What prevents you too from (taking) profit, then, when it is quite possible, and from making yourself like the gods?[3]

---

[1] Identified by some editors as Paris, comparing the recognizably Trojan youth shown leaving Philoctetes on the 2nd. c. B.C. relief urns, *LIMC* nos. 57–9 (see Introduction (2)).   [2] Or imperative 'See': either way, a generalizing plural.   [3] Or 'when it is possible to make yourself like the gods' (Heath).

EURIPIDES

(795: see after 796)

796

⟨ΟΔΥΣΣΕΥΣ⟩

ὑπέρ γε μέντοι παντὸς Ἑλλήνων στρατοῦ
αἰσχρὸν σιωπᾶν, βαρβάρους δ' ἐᾶν λέγειν.

v. 1 and separately v. 2 (αἰσχρὸν σιωπᾶν): Plutarch, *Moralia*
1108b; end of v. 2 reconstructed by Musgrave from later adapta-
tions (Ἰσοκρά[τ]ην δ' ἐᾶν λέγειν Philodemus, *Rhetoric* II, P.
Herc. 1015 + 832 col. XLVIII 22 + 36.3–5. p. 50 Sudhaus = Schol.
on Hermogenes, *On Issues*, *Rhet. Gr.* 4.298.4 Walz, cf. Latin ver-
sions by Cicero, *Orator* 3.141 [including both *Isocratem* and *bar-
baros*] and Quintilian 3.14 [*Isocratem*]; Ξενοκράτην δ' ἐᾶν
λέγειν Diogenes Laertius 5.3). Assigned to *Philoctetes* by D. Can-
ter, and to Odysseus by Valckenaer.

795

⟨ΟΔΥΣΣΕΥΣ⟩

τί δῆτα θάκοις μαντικοῖς ἐνήμενοι
σαφῶς διόμνυσθ' εἰδέναι τὰ δαιμόνων,
οἱ τῶνδε χειρώνακτες ἄνθρωποι λόγων;
ὅστις γὰρ αὐχεῖ θεῶν ἐπίστασθαι πέρι,
5 οὐδέν τι μᾶλλον οἶδεν ἢ πείθειν λέγων.

Stobaeus 2.1.2

1 μαντικοῖς Musgrave: ἀργικοῖς Stob.: ἀρχικοῖς Valckenaer
3 οἱ τῶνδε Stob.: ὦ τῶνδε Kannicht: δαιμόνων; | οὐ τῶνδε Nauck
ἄνθρωποι Stob.: ἀνθρώποις Meineke   lacuna after 3 Müller
5 πείθειν Musgrave: πείθει Stob.

PHILOCTETES

(795: see after 796)

796

<ODYSSEUS>

Shameful to keep silent, however, when the whole Greek army is at issue, but to allow barbarians to speak.[1]

---

[1] Best placed before Odysseus' first argument, F 795. The two lines were regularly adapted by later writers, substituting a real individual's name for 'barbarians'.

795

<ODYSSEUS>[1]

Why then, seated on your prophetic[2] thrones, do you swear you know the gods' will clearly, you people who are past-masters[3] of these words? The man who vaunts knowledge of the gods knows nothing more than how to be persuasive in speaking.

---

[1] Almost certainly Odysseus, undermining the Trojan's attempt to lure Philoctetes to the Trojan side with the very prophecy of Helenus which prompted Odysseus' own mission.
[2] Stobaeus' 'lazy' was a copyist's slip; Valckenaer changed only one letter with 'ruling' (i.e. with controlling influence), but Musgrave's 'prophetic' gives clearer sense.   [3] This attempts the contemptuous implication of the Greek (lit. 'handicraftsmen, artisans'); but the syntax is difficult, and remains so with Meineke's '(you) the pastmasters . . . of these words for mankind'. It is eased by Kannicht's 'O you people who . . . ' Nauck and Müller make v. 3 a new sentence: 'Men are no masters of these words' (Nauck), or 'Those who are pastmasters of these words . . . ' with the rest of the sentence lost (Müller).

797

λέξω δ' ἐγώ, κἄν μου διαφθείρας δοκῇ
λόγους ὑποφθὰς αὐτὸς ἠδικηκέναι·
ἀλλ' ἐξ ἐμοῦ γὰρ τἄμ' ἐπιστήσῃ κλυών,
ὁ δ' αὐτὸς αὐτὸν ἐμφανῆ θήσει λέγων.

Anaximenes, Rhetoric 18.15 (from [Aristotle], Rhetoric for Alexander 1433b10–14); Latin version (13th–14th c.) ed. M. Grabmann, SBAW 1931–2.4.55

1 διαφθείρας Anax. (corrumpens Lat.): διαφθεῖραι Munro 2 ὑποφθὰς Weil (preveniens Lat.): ὑποστὰς Anax.   3 ἐπιστήσῃ Collard (cf. Tro. 687, Soph. OC 53, 290): μαθήσῃ Anax. (unmetrical): addisces Lat.   4 ἐμφανῆ θήσει Jacobs (demonstrabit Lat.): †ἐμφανιεῖ σοι† Anax.

798

πατρὶς καλῶς πράσσουσα τὸν τυχόντ' ἀεὶ
μείζω τίθησι, δυστυχοῦσα δ' ἀσθενῆ.

Stobaeus 3.40.1

1 τὸν τυχόντ' Matthiae: τὸν εὐτυχοῦντ' Stob.   2 δυστυχοῦσα Stob. ms. Paris 1985: -οῦντα all other mss.

799

ὥσπερ δὲ θνητὸν καὶ τὸ σῶμ' ἡμῶν ἔφυ,
οὕτω προσήκει μηδὲ τὴν ὀργὴν ἔχειν
ἀθάνατον ὅστις σωφρονεῖν ἐπίσταται.

Stobaeus 3.20.17; Gnomica Basileensia 404b Kindstrand

797

I'll speak for myself, even if in destroying my argument
through anticipation he seems to have done me an injus-
tice; but you'll know my case further when you've heard it,
and he'll make his own clear when he speaks for himself.[1]

[1] A very perplexing fragment. Anaximenes quotes it to illus-
trate the rhetorical ploy of weakening an opponent's case by antic-
ipating it, and the opponent's counter-ploy of drawing attention to
the attempt. The context may be the debate between the Trojan,
Philoctetes and Odysseus, or the final debate probably between
Odysseus, Diomedes and Philoctetes. Any of these three may be
the speaker, and 'you' in v. 3 may be Philoctetes in the first debate
or (more likely) the Chorus in the second: see Introduction (2).
The medieval Latin translation confirms the sense of the Greek
text in vv. 1 and 3, and suggests the required sense in vv. 2 and 4.

798

His fatherland's prosperity makes the ordinary man
greater, but its misfortune makes him weak.[1]

[1] For this antithesis cf. Thucydides 2.60.2.

799

Just as our body too is born to die, so it is fitting for the man
who understands moderation not to keep his anger undy-
ing either.[1]

[1] Similarly e.g. adesp. F 79; probably a well-used maxim.

EURIPIDES

799a

ἀνδρὸς κακῶς πράσσοντος ἐκποδὼν φίλοι.

Schol. on *Phoenician Women* 402; cited thus in many authors without attribution, with φίλου κακῶς πράξαντος in Aristides, *Orations* 1.60 and Schol. on 20.18

800

φεῦ·
μηδέν ποτ᾽ εἴην ἄλλο πλὴν θεοῖς φίλος,
ὡς πᾶν τελοῦσι, κἂν βραδύνωσιν, χρόνῳ.

Orion 5.4 and Euripidean Appendix 1 Haffner; v. 1: Suda μ 875

2 πᾶν τελοῦσι Nauck: πάντ᾽ ἔχωσι Orion

799a

When a man does badly, friends keep out of his way.[1]

[1] Cynicism frequent in Euripides, e.g. *Heracles* 559, *Medea* 561.

800

Oh, alas! May I never be anything but dear to the gods, for in time they fulfil everything, even if they are slow.[1]

[1] The gods inevitable if slow, e.g. *Ion* 1615; similarly Time's revelations, *Aeolus* F **38a with note; Justice's fulfilment, *Antiope* F 222 with note, *Phrixus A/B* F 835.4, F 979.

PHOENIX

F. Jouan in ed. Budé VIII.3.313–28.

Webster 84–5; Trendall–Webster III.3.42; E. M. Papamichael, *Dodone* 11 (1982), 213–34; F. Jouan, *Sacris Erudiri* 31 (1989–90), 187–208; Gantz 618; *LIMC* VIII.i.984–5 'Phoinix II'; Taplin 214.

The episode dramatized by Euripides is unrecorded between its earliest mention in Homer, Iliad *9.447–77, and our play; Sophocles'* Phoenix *probably preceded Euripides', but its content is unknown, like that of one or two such plays by Euripides' contemporary Ion of Chios (TrGF 1.105–8). The sources for the story are set out fully by Papamichael; cf. Gantz, LIMC and Jouan in ed. Budé 314–9.*

Phoenix's father Amyntor came to prefer a concubine's bed to that of his wife, who pleaded with her son to lie with the woman and so disgust her with Amyntor. Phoenix obeyed, but his father quickly found out and cursed him with childlessness (which the gods brought about); therefore Phoenix left his home, despite his family's attempt to dissuade him, and found refuge with Peleus, who made him tutor to the young Achilles. That is Homer's account in Iliad *9.437–43, 478–84, but four further verses (9.458–61), preserved only by Plutarch,* Moralia *26f and said by him to* have been struck from the poem by one of its great Alexandrian editors Aristarchus, and deleted by all modern editors, tell that Phoenix had first meditated killing his father, only to be deterred by a god. There is nothing of this last detail in the evidence for Euripides, nor of Amyntor's curse upon Phoenix, just as there is nothing in Homer of Amyntor blinding Phoenix in punishment; the latter is attested indirectly just once among Euripides' fragments (F 816.2; but see F 815 and note) and in one contemporary source (Aristophanes, Acharnians 421 = test. iiia), but later expressly (test. iva[1] below).

Euripides may have introduced the blinding to the story, then. In his version, moreover, Phoenix refused his mother's pleading, only to be falsely accused of rape by the concubine (test. iic, iiid, iva[1] below). Whether or not this element too was Euripides' invention, it became so dominant in later retellings and references that the text of Homer was altered to accommodate it (see test. iic). Euripides' purpose is plain, to maximize the pathos of Phoenix's tragedy and, so the fragments suggest, to create room for much introspection and agony in the disillusioned Amyntor (F 803a, 804–5, 807), together with tense argument between father and son over the concubine's allegations (F 809–11). The concubine (brief fragment F 818) is probably meant in F 808 as the 'fiercest evil of all', rather than Amyntor's wife, of whose anger nothing is attested in the fragments, only in Homer. At the end Phoenix is condemned and blinded (F 816.2) before going, voluntarily or not, into exile (F 817, cf. 816.1–6). If Chiron indeed came in person, it is tempting to assign F 812 and 813a to him as an attempt at mediation between Phoenix and Amyntor after the blinding. F 814 cannot be placed.

406

The only vase painting perhaps to be associated with the play, an Apulian crater of c. 350 B.C. (LIMC no. 2, Trendall–Webster III.3.42, Todisco Ap 167, Taplin no. 80) shows Peleus arriving to take the blinded Phoenix to Chiron.

Brief fragments: F 817a 'is inferior to' (from a verse in a damaged papyrus anthology, possibly confused with Medea 76); F 818 'a woman not to be wed' (i.e. a concubine). Other ascriptions: F 1064; F 1067 (see on F 812: also ascribed to Hippolytus Veiled).

Date: earlier than Aristophanes' Acharnians of 425 B.C., where vv. 418–22 refer to the rags of (Euripides') Phoenix (cf. F 816.1–6); the metrical criteria permit no more precise dating (Cropp–Fick 88). Phoenix is yet another play from Euripides' earlier period when 'bad women' and their troubles were common (see Webster 77, Jouan 1989–90).

The story motif is broadly that of 'Potiphar's Wife' (see Papamichael and cf. Stheneboea, Introduction). It was popular with tragedians, from Sophocles in the 5th century to Astydamas II in the 4th; Menander, Samia 498–500 alludes to it. An oblique indication that Euripides' play itself was frequently performed in the 4th century is found in Demosthenes 19.246 (test. v): responding to his opponent Aeschines' quotation of F 812 (see there), he names actors who had and had not appeared in it. Ennius seems to have adapted Euripides' play in his Latin Phoenix (frs. 125–133 Jocelyn). The comedian Eubulus produced a Phoenix, perhaps dependent upon Euripides.

407

ΦΟΙΝΙΞ

test. iia

Φοῖνιξ, [ο]ῦ ἀρ[χ]ή[·
ὦ πλοῦτε, ὅ[σῳ μὲν ῥ]ᾶ[ιστον εἶ β]άρος
φ[έ]ρε[ιν· ἡ δ᾽ ὑπό]θεσις·
Ἀ]μυ[ντ.]ρο[
βα]σι[λ

P. Oxy. 2455, ed. E. Turner (1962), fr. 14 col. xvii.
2 = F 803a.1 below

test. iic

᾽τῆ πιθόμην καὶ ἔρεξα᾽· Ἀριστόδημος ὁ Νυσαιεύς, ῥήτωρ
τε ἅμα καὶ γραμματικός, φεύγων τὸ ἔγκλημα, ἐπενόησε
γραφὴν τὴν ᾽τῆ οὐ πιθόμην οὐδ᾽ ἔρξα᾽. καὶ οὐ μόνον γε
ηὐδοκίμησεν, ἀλλὰ καὶ ἐτιμήθη ὡς εὐσεβῆ τηρήσας τὸν
ἥρωα. πρὸ δὲ αὐτοῦ Σωσιφάνης τὴν τοιαύτην εὗρε γρα-
φήν. καὶ Εὐριπίδης δὲ ἀναμάρτητον εἰσάγει τὸν ἥρωα
ἐν τῷ Φοίνικι. ταῦτα ἱστορεῖ Ἁρποκρατίων ὁ Δίου δι-
δάσκαλος.

Schol. on Homer, *Iliad* 9.453; more briefly Eustathius on the
same verse

408

PHOENIX

test. iia

Phoenix, which begins 'O wealth, (how much the easiest) weight (you are to bear!)'; the plot is as follows: Amyntor . . . king . . .

test. iic

'I obeyed her and did so' *(i.e. Phoenix obeyed his mother's request to lie with his father's concubine).* Aristodemus of Nysa, a rhetorician and literary scholar,[1] in a defence against the accusation, invented the reading 'I did not obey her, nor did I do it'. Not only did he succeed *(i.e. in being 'acquitted' by his audience),* but he was also honoured for safeguarding the hero *(i.e. Phoenix)* as dutiful. Before him Sosiphanes[2] had invented a reading like this, and Euripides brings this hero on stage as guiltless in the *Phoenix*. This is told by Harpocration the teacher of Dios . . . [3]

[1] 4th c. A.D.? Presumably he was reconstructing Phoenix's self-defence in a rhetorical performance. [2] A 4th c. B.C. tragedian from Syracuse (*TrGF* 1 no. 92), if the name here is correct. [3] A Homeric scholar, apparently, otherwise unknown; the Greek is unlikely to mean 'Harpocration of Dion [in Macedonia], a teacher'.

EURIPIDES

test. iiid

. . . Φοῖνιξ ὁ Ἀμύντορος . . . ὑπὸ τοῦ πατρὸς ἐτυφλώθη καταψευσαμένης φθορὰν Φθίας τῆς τοῦ πατρὸς παλλακῆς. Πηλεὺς δὲ αὐτὸν πρὸς Χείρωνα κομίσας, ὑπ᾿ ἐκείνου θεραπευθέντα τὰς ὄψεις βασιλέα κατέστησε Δολόπων.

Apollodorus 3.13.8; (with minor differences of detail) Schol. on Plato, *Laws* 931b

test. iva[1]

Ἀναγυράσιος δαίμων· ἐπεὶ τὸν παροικοῦντα πρεσβύτην καὶ ἐκτέμνοντα τὸ ἄλσος ἐτιμωρήσατο Ἀνάγυρος ἥρως. Ἀναγυράσιοι δὲ δῆμος τῆς Ἀττικῆς. τούτου δέ τις ἐξέκοψε τὸ ἄλσος. ὁ δὲ τῷ υἱῷ αὐτοῦ ἐπέμηνε τὴν παλλακήν, ἥτις μὴ δυναμένη συμπεῖσαι τὸν παῖδα διέβαλεν ὡς ἀσελγῆ τῷ πατρί. ὁ δὲ ἐπήρωσεν αὐτὸν καὶ ἐγκατῳκοδόμησεν. ἐπὶ τούτοις καὶ ὁ πατὴρ ἑαυτὸν ἀνήρτησεν, ἡ δὲ παλλακὴ εἰς φρέαρ ἑαυτὴν ἔρριψεν. ἱστορεῖ δὲ Ἱερώνυμος . . . ἀπεικάζων τούτοις τὸν Εὐριπίδου Φοίνικα.

Hieronymus of Rhodes, *On Tragedians* fr. 32 Wehrli, in Photius α 1432 Theodoridis and other lexica

803a (= 813 N)

⟨ΑΜΥΝΤΩΡ?⟩

ὦ πλοῦθ᾿, ὅσῳ μὲν ῥᾷστον εἶ βάρος φέρειν·
πόνοι δὲ κἂν σοὶ καὶ φθοραὶ πολλαὶ βίου
ἔνεισ᾿· ὁ γὰρ πᾶς ἀσθενὴς αἰὼν βροτοῖς.

Stobaeus 4.31.74; v. 1: P. Oxy. 2455 fr. 14.2–3 (see test. iia above); Stobaeus 4.31.10

PHOENIX

test. iiid

... Phoenix son of Amyntor ... was blinded by his father when Phthia his father's concubine falsely accused him of rape. Peleus took him to Chiron,[1] who treated his eyes and made him king of the Dolopians.

[1] The centaur with superhuman medical and other powers, often an intermediary between gods and men; cf. Introduction to *Peleus*.

test. iva[1]

'The Anagyrasian deity': because the hero Anagyrus revenged himself upon the old man who lived nearby and had cut down his grove. The Anagyrasians were a deme of Attica. One of its men cut down this hero's grove, and the hero maddened the man's concubine with lust for his son; when she was unable to get the son's consent she traduced him to his father for lewd advances. The father blinded the son, and confined him to a building. In the outcome, the father hanged himself and the concubine threw herself into a well. Hieronymus recounts this ... with a comparison to Euripides' *Phoenix*.[1]

[1] A similar reference to Euripides is made in Aelian fr. 246 Hercher = test. ivb.

803a (= 813 N)
(Beginning of the play)

⟨AMYNTOR?⟩[1]

O wealth, how much the easiest weight you are to bear! Yet many of life's toils and disasters are in you too, for men's whole life is frail.

[1] Possibly Amyntor, anxious about Phoenix' actions, if not already aware of them: cf. F 803b, 804–5.

411

EURIPIDES

803b (= 806 N)

⟨ΑΜΥΝΤΩΡ?⟩

ἀλλ᾽ οὔποτ᾽ αὐτὸς ἀμπλακὼν ἄλλον βροτὸν
παραινέσαιμ᾽ ἂν παισὶ προσθεῖναι κράτη,
πρὶν ἂν κατ᾽ ὄσσων κιγχάνῃ σφ᾽ ἤδη σκότος,
εἰ χρῇ διελθεῖν πρὸς τέκνων τιμώμενος.

Stobaeus 4.1.16

3 κιγχάνῃ Monk: τυγχάνῃ Stob.   σφ᾽ ἤδη Collard (σφε
Diggle, ἤδη Wecklein): με καὶ Stob.: μέλας Grotius   4 εἰ
χρῇ . . . τιμώμενος Vitelli: εἰ χρὴ . . . νικώμενον Stob.

804

⟨ΑΜΥΝΤΩΡ?⟩

μοχθηρόν ἐστιν ἀνδρὶ πρεσβύτῃ τέκνα
(one or more lines lost)
δίδωσιν, ὅστις οὐκέθ᾽ ὡραῖος γαμεῖ·
δέσποινα γὰρ γέροντι νυμφίῳ γυνή.

Stobaeus 4.22.109; v. 3 = Aristophanes, *Women at the Thes-
mophoria* 413; lacuna Kannicht; there have been many conjec-
tures in the text without lacuna, e.g. μοχθηρὸν ὅστις . . . νέαν |
δίδωσι θυγατέρ᾽· οὐκέθ᾽ ὡραῖον γαμεῖν (Barrett). Heath consid-
ered vv. 2–3 a separate fragment, and in v. 2 suggested δείλαιος
for δίδωσιν.

805

⟨ΑΜΥΝΤΩΡ?⟩

ὦ γῆρας, οἷον τοῖς ἔχουσιν εἶ κακόν.

Stobaeus 4.50.74

803b (= 806 N)

⟨AMYNTOR?⟩[1]

But having made the mistake myself, I would never advise
another man to attach power to his sons before darkness is
already reaching down over his eyes, if he desires to go on
being honoured by his children.[2]

[1] Cf. F 803a and note. [2] Cf. *Phaethon* 160–2. Text inse-
cure, but the general sense is certain; v. 3 as printed is very similar
to *Hipp.* 1444 (Grotius gives 'black darkness reaches down'). In v.
4 Stobaeus' 'if (he) must go on being dominated . . .' is impossible.

804

⟨AMYNTOR?⟩

Children are burdensome for an elderly man . . . *(one or
more lines lost)*[1] . . . gives . . . who marries when no longer
in his prime; for a wife rules over an aged bridegroom.

[1] For the suggested loss of text Kannicht compares *Danae* F
317 (cited only a little later by Stobaeus in this same chapter 4.22
entitled 'One must have regard to the ages of those joining in
marriage'). For v. 2 without a break Heath conjectured 'Whoever
marries when no longer in his prime is pitiful'. Barrett's major al-
terations give 'It is burdensome when someone gives a young
daughter to an elderly man; it is no longer time for him to marry.'
Cf. F 807.

805

⟨AMYNTOR?⟩

Old age, what an evil you are for those who have you!

(806 N = 803b above)

807

πικρὸν νέᾳ γυναικὶ πρεσβύτης ἀνήρ.

Stobaeus 4.22.116; Clement of Alexandria, *Miscellanies* 6.2.14.6, with attribution to Aristophanes (= F 616 *PCG*), and with αἰσχρὸν for πικρὸν

808

γυνή τε πάντων ἀγριώτατον κακόν.

Stobaeus 4.22.191

809

. . . πεῖραν οὐ δεδωκότες,
μᾶλλον δοκοῦντες ἢ πεφυκότες σοφοί . . .

Stobaeus 2.15.11

810

μέγιστον ἄρ' ἦν ἡ φύσις· τὸ γὰρ κακὸν
οὐδεὶς τρέφων εὖ χρηστὸν ἂν θείη ποτέ.

Stobaeus 4.30.7

811

τἀφανῆ
τεκμηρίοισιν εἰκότως ἁλίσκεται.

Clement of Alexandria, *Miscellanies* 6.2.18.3

(806 N = 803b above)

807

An elderly husband is a bitter thing for a young wife.

808

. . . and a woman is the fiercest evil of all.[1]

1 Probably the concubine rather than Amyntor's wife (see Introduction). A similar expression at *Oedipus* F 544.

809

. . . having given no proof, seeming wise rather than being so by nature . . .

810

So nature is the most important thing: no one would ever make evil into good through a good upbringing.[1]

1 For this axiom cf. *Antigone* F 167, *Dictys* F 333, F 1068; and for the 'nature versus nurture' debate in relation to morality, prominent in Euripides' day, e.g. *Hippolytus* 921–2, *Hecuba* 592–602, *Suppliant Women* 911–7.

811

What is unclear may reasonably be grasped by judging evidence.[1]

1 Cf. *Oenomaus* F 574 with note.

812

ἤδη δὲ πολλῶν ἠρέθην λόγων κριτὴς
καὶ πόλλ᾽ ἁμιλληθέντα μαρτύρων ὕπο
ἐναντί᾽ ἔγνων συμφορᾶς μιᾶς πέρι.
κἀγὼ μὲν οὕτω χὤστις ἔστ᾽ ἀνὴρ σοφὸς
5 λογίζομαι τἀληθές, εἰς ἀνδρὸς φύσιν
σκοπῶν δίαιτάν θ᾽ ἥντιν᾽ ἐμπορεύεται
(one or more lines lost)
ὅστις δ᾽ ὁμιλῶν ἥδεται κακοῖς ἀνήρ,
οὐ πώποτ᾽ ἠρώτησα, γιγνώσκων ὅτι
τοιοῦτός ἐστιν οἷσπερ ἥδεται ξυνών.

Aeschines 1.152 (with paraphrase in 153); vv. 1–6: Stobaeus
2.15.25 (see on F **813a); vv. 7–9: Demosthenes 19.245–6 (a re-
joinder to Aeschines); Diodorus 12.14.1; Stobaeus 2.33.1; many
later rhetoricians or reflections (some with aberrant attributions
or texts)

3 ἐναντί᾽ Valckenaer, West: τἀναντί᾽ Aeschin., Stob.
6 ἐμπορεύεται Aeschin.: ἱμερεύεται (i.e. ἡμ-) Stob.   lacuna
Meineke

(813 N = 803a above)

**813a (= fr. adesp. 515 N)

καὶ τῷδε δηλώσαιμ᾽ ἄν, εἰ βούλοιο σύ,
τἀληθές, ὡς ἔγωγε καὐτὸς ἄχθομαι,
ὅστις λέγειν μὲν εὐπρεπῶς ἐπίσταται,
τὰ δ᾽ ἔργα χείρω τῶν λόγων παρέσχετο.

Stobaeus 2.15.25a ms. L, joined without lemma to F 812.1–6;
vv. 3–4: Stobaeus 3.13.14 ms. L, joined without lemma to *Phoeni-
cian Women* 527–8; assigned to *Phoenix* by Hense

PHOENIX

812[1]

In the past I was chosen as judge in many arguments,
and realised that many opposite contentions were made
by witnesses about a single incident. I myself, and every
wise man, reason the truth as follows, by examining a man's
nature and the life he trades in . . . *(one or more lines lost)*   5
. . . ;[2] but I've never yet questioned one who enjoys associ-
ating with bad men, realising that he is like the very men
whose company he enjoys.[3]

---

[1] Aeschines cites these verses from the defence made in Eu-
ripides' play when Phoenix's conduct towards his father was tra-
duced. He does not state that they were spoken by Phoenix (and
the young Phoenix could not have gained long experience of judg-
ing arguments), but many editors make him the speaker. F 1067
has been attached to F 812 by some; if that is correct, its beginning
'I know your son . . .' makes the attribution to Phoenix impossible.
Probably the speaker is a third party (as also of F 813a), and that
points to Chiron: see Introduction.   [2] Stobaeus has 'the life
he daily follows'. Meineke supposed text lost because Aeschines'
paraphrase is fuller at this point.   [3] Cf. *Bellerophon* F 296,
Erechtheus F 362.21–3 with note.

(813 N = 803a above)

**813a (= fr. adesp. 515 N)

And I would show him the truth, were you willing; for I
myself too find the man hard to bear who knows how to
speak plausibly, but whose actions prove worse than his
words.[1]

---

[1] For the speaker see note 1 on F 812.

EURIPIDES

814

ΧΟΡΟΣ

φθόνον οὐ σέβω, φθονεῖσθαι
δὲ θέλοιμ' ἂν ἐπ' ἐσθλοῖς.

Stobaeus 3.38.14, attributed to the Chorus

815

⟨ΑΜΥΝΤΩΡ?⟩

δμωσὶ⟨ν⟩ δ' ἐμοῖσιν εἶπον ὡς †ταυτηρίαις
πυρίδες καὶ διηπετῆ κτεῖναι†

Erotian δ 27

1 καυτήρια (or -ίοις) editors   2 διειπετῆ editors (cf.
Hyps. F 752h.31)

816

⟨ΦΟΙΝΙΞ⟩

καίτοι ποτ' εἴ τιν' εἰσίδοιμ' ἀνὰ πτόλιν
τυφλὸν προηγητῆρος ἐξηρτημένον
ἀδημονοῦντα συμφοραῖς, ἐλοιδόρουν
ὡς δειλὸς εἴη θάνατον ἐκποδὼν ἔχων.
5 καὶ νῦν λόγοισι τοῖς ἐμοῖς ἐναντίως
πέπτωχ' ὁ τλήμων. ὦ φιλόζωοι βροτοί,
οἳ τὴν ἐπιστείχουσαν ἡμέραν ἰδεῖν
ποθεῖτ' ἔχοντες μυρίων ἄχθος κακῶν.
οὕτως ἔρως βροτοῖσιν ἔγκειται βίου·
10 τὸ ζῆν γὰρ ἴσμεν, τοῦ θανεῖν δ' ἀπειρίᾳ
πᾶς τις φοβεῖται φῶς λιπεῖν τόδ' ἡλίου.

PHOENIX

814

CHORUS

I don't esteem envy, but I should wish to be envied for honourable deeds.

815

⟨AMYNTOR?⟩

I told my servants to . . . (*text incurably corrupt*) . . . [1]

[1] Editors have conjectured to create such sense as 'to lay out hot irons' in v. 1 and '(make them) gleaming bright' in v. 2, supposing that Amyntor has ordered the blinding of Phoenix.

816

⟨PHOENIX⟩

And yet if ever I saw a blind man tied to a guide and in anguish at his misfortune,[1] I used to abuse him for a coward in resisting death. And now I have fallen foul of my own words, poor wretch! O mortal men and your love 5 for life, who long to see the following day when you are burdened by untold troubles! This is how desire for life presses upon mortal men: we know what living is, but through inexperience of death every one of us fears to 10 leave the sunlight here.[2]

[1] See Introduction on the blinding of Phoenix in this play.
[2] Cf. *Polyidus* F 638 with note; conversely, *Meleager* F 533.

Stobaeus 4.53.10 ms. S; vv. 9–11 (ἔρως—ἡλίου) Stob. ms. A

3 ἀδημονοῦντα Wyttenbach, Musgrave: ἃ δαιμόνων ταῖς Stob.   8 ποθεῖτ' Musgrave: πόθον Stob.

817

⟨ΦΟΙΝΙΞ⟩

σὺ δ᾽, ὦ πατρῷα χθὼν ἐμῶν γεννητόρων,
χαῖρ᾽· ἀνδρὶ γάρ τοι, κἂν ὑπερβάλλῃ κακοῖς,
οὐκ ἔστι τοῦ θρέψαντος ἥδιον πέδον.

Stobaeus 3.39.10; v. 3: Chrysippus, *On Negatives* fr. 180.17
von Arnim

817

⟨PHOENIX⟩

And you, fatherland of my ancestors, farewell! Truly, even
if a man has trouble to excess, there is no soil more pleasing
to him than that which reared him.

PHRIXUS A *and* B

Van Looy (1964), 132–84 (French résumé, 315–20) and in ed. Budé VIII.3.339–71; Diggle, *TrGFS* 161–5 (*Phrixus A* test. iia, F 818c, *Phrixus B* test. iia, F 819, *Phrixus A/B* F **822b).

W. Schadewaldt, *Hermes* 63 (1928), 1–14 (= *Hellas und Hesperien* I².505–15), before publication of the hypotheses; Webster 131–6; Aélion (1986), 135–41, cf. (1983), I.277–81; C. Riedweg, *CQ* 40 (1990), 124–36; Gantz 176–80, 183–4; *LIMC* VII.i.398–404 'Phrixos und Helle'; Taplin 215–7.

Euripides' authorship of two Phrixus plays, not one alone, was thinly attested and long doubted until papyrus hypotheses to both were recovered (test. iia of each below; a still unpublished fragment of a Phrixus *hypothesis may belong to either: W. Luppe, APF 50 [2004], 218). These and other evidence compel us to conclude that the two plays had similar plots.[1] The myth of Athamas son of Aeolus (a*

---

[1] The only Euripidean parallel lies in the two Hippolytus plays, one of which was however a significant revision of the other, and produced (it seems) not long after it. We have no such information about the Phrixus plays, and no sure guide to their relative dates. Euripides' other paired plays named for Alcmeon, Autolycus, Iphigenia and Melanippe have quite distinct plots.

son of Hellen: see Melanippe Wise) *was complex, unstable, and full of deadly intentions, successes, and escapes (it is well analysed by Gantz 176–80, cf. Van Looy 339–46); Euripides used it also in his* Ino. *Its other chief figures were Athamas' first wife Nephele ('Cloud'), their two children Phrixus and Helle, and after Nephele's death or ascension into the sky, his second wife Ino, who is as prominent in the Phrixus plays as in her own (but there in a very different story).*

We have two continuous accounts of the Phrixus incident dramatized by Euripides, Apollodorus 1.9.1 (= Phrixus A *test. iib below*) and Hyginus, Fab. 2 and 3 (= Phrixus B *test. iib below*): Ino attempted to destroy her stepchildren Phrixus and Helle (her 'stepmother's evil design' is mentioned in Pindar, Pythians 4.162; cf. F 824 here); she induced the women who had charge of the next year's seed-corn to render it sterile by roasting; when it was sown and no crop grew, and Athamas consulted Delphi, Ino suborned the envoy into reporting falsely that crops would be restored if Athamas' son Phrixus were sacrificed to Zeus. Thus far Apollodorus and Hyginus agree (cf. Ovid, Fasti 3.853–8), but then they diverge. In Apollodorus, Athamas is forced by the people to sacrifice Phrixus, but he is rescued by his mother Nephele who descends from the sky and gives him and Helle a golden-fleeced ram on which to escape (similarly Ovid 859–68). In Hyginus 2.2–4, Phrixus offers himself voluntarily for sacrifice (cf. Pherecydes, FGrH 3 F 98 = Schol. on Pindar, Pythians 4.162, a variation attributed to Sophocles in one of his two Athamas plays: see TrGF 4.99–100); he is about to be killed when the envoy to Delphi reveals Ino's evil design; she is given to Phrixus to put to death, but is saved by her appeal to Dionysus (she had 'nursed' the god as an infant, cf. Ino, Intro-

*duction); then in Hyginus 3.1 Dionysus puts Phrixus and
Helle in wild country to be killed by his ranging maenads,
but Nephele descends and gives them the golden-fleeced
ram to carry them to Colchis (this concurs closely with
Apollodorus). As to Helle, she falls from the ram into the
sea named after her as the Hellespont (Apollodorus), but
Phrixus reaches Colchis where he sacrifices the ram and
places its fleece in the temple of Ares (Hyginus 3.1; cf.
Apollodorus at end, and Ovid 869–76).*

*Two other allusions to the story provide additional or
discrepant detail: according to the Scholia on Aristoph-
anes, Clouds 257, Sophocles in a second Athamas play had
Athamas volunteering his own sacrificial death, appar-
ently in place of, or atonement for, that of Phrixus, but he
was rescued by Heracles; and in Herodotus 7. 197.1 Atha-
mas, not Ino alone, contrives sacrificial death for Phrixus,
while in 197.3, after Phrixus' escape, perhaps comparably
with Sophocles, Athamas himself is to be made a public
sacrifice in an act of purification. Nothing of this survives
in our evidence for Euripides, however.*

*These variations in myth and sources complicate even
notional reconstruction of the two plays, for the very few
fragments which are attributed definitely to one or other
(respectively F 818a, and F 819, 820, 820a, 820b) frustrat-
ingly do not help to differentiate their plots. Editors since
Nauck have left almost all the other fragments (F 822–38)
unassigned, as they may come from either play. This much
may be said, however: in both plays, Phrixus is rescued by
Nephele: in A (if this is the play reflected in Apollodorus),
from the sacrifice; in B (since Hyginus concurs with its hy-
pothesis), from Dionysus after Ino has invoked him. In
both, almost certainly, Phrixus' escape led to threatened
death for Ino (F **822b.8–16 and 824 may reflect her dan-*

ger). Uncertain or unknowable are (1) in which play, if either, Phrixus volunteered his own death (Phrixus A test. iia.20–3 may point to it, and F 833 could relate to such a moment; conversely F 832 is a protest against unjust death); (2) when an old man under interrogation reveals Ino's plan, against her denials (F **822b), was this also the servant who in that play (it seems from Hyginus 2.3) took pity upon Phrixus at the moment of sacrifice; and did his revelation coincide with, or precede, a descent by Nephele? Van Looy 352–4 suggests A for the pity and B for the voluntary sacrifice; but it is not unparalleled for Euripides to crowd into a single play three such favourite elements as a humanly motivated plan foiled by humanly motivated remorse, a voluntary as opposed to an involuntary sacrifice, and a divine rescue (cf. Iphigenia in Aulis).

Two definite differences between the plays hardly help reconstruction: (1) Phrixus A was set in Thessaly (test. iia.5; cf. F 822a, usually left unassigned, which uses a Thessalian name for a serf), while Phrixus B was set in Boeotia (Orchomenus: test. iia.4). (2) It appears from Phrixus B test. iia.14–16, cf. Hyginus 2.3–4, that Ino when detected is handed over to Phrixus for punishment, and that this is when Dionysus saves her. Was that then the end of Phrixus B, her rescue reported by the god himself, while Phrixus A ended with Nephele's rescue of Phrixus? Nephele certainly, and possibly even Dionysus, might close either play with prophecies for Phrixus' arrival in Colchis with the ram, and for Helle.

Of the other, mostly sententious, fragments F 825, 826, 828 and 829 may bear upon Athamas' responsibilities amid the threat of starvation, but again in either play; for F 835 see 'Other ascriptions' below.

Brief fragments: F 836 'beard of fire' (cf. Aeschylus, Agamemnon 306); F 837 'offspring' (of animals) either 'driven together' (i.e. herded) or 'driven up and down' (i.e. in ploughing); F **837a 'ram' (with the golden fleece); F 838 mention of Aretias, an island in the Black Sea inhabited by the lethal Stymphalian birds, possibly a prophesied detail of Phrixus' flight to Colchis on the ram.

Other ascriptions to Phrixus A: F 912b (appended to F 835 in its sources: see note there) and adesp. F 490 '(s)he paid the penalty for the trouble (s)he began' (appended to F 835 at Stobaeus 1.3.15a): these are assigned to Phrixus A by Riedweg 134–6, who argues that because F 820b belongs to Phrixus B, it must be a rewriting of F 835. Other ascription to Phrixus B: F 1007c.

Date: the metrical criteria suggest only an insecure inference that Phrixus B may come from the middle to late 420s, and that Phrixus A was therefore probably earlier than that: see Cropp–Fick 88–9.

Apart from Sophocles' lost plays (above), an Athamas by Aeschylus (F 1–4a) and a Phrixus by Achaeus (F 38) are known. Another Phrixus was produced at the Dionysia of 340 by an incompletely identified poet (perhaps Timocles: see TrGF 1, 86 T 3). The story, especially of the escape on the golden ram, was popular in art; two late-4th c. Italian craters have composite scenes which may show acquaintance with Euripides: LIMC no. 1 (= Todisco Ap 159, Taplin no. 81) has Phrixus about to be sacrificed but touching a ram, with Ino and Helle present, and, in tragic costume, Athamas and a Tutor, with Nephele aloft; LIMC no. 26 (= Todisco P 3) has Phrixus and Helle flying on the ram, with both Nephele and Dionysus depicted. For modern times see OGCMA 240–1.

ΦΡΙΞΟΣ Α

test. iia (Hypothesis)

Φρί[ξο]ς πρῶτος, οὗ ἀρχή·
εἰ μὲν τόδ᾽ ἦμαρ [π]ρῶτον ἦν κακουμ[έ]-
νῳ· ἡ δ᾽ ὑπόθεσις·
Ἀθάμας υἱὸς μὲ[ν] ἦν Αἰόλου, βασιλεὺς
5 δὲ Θετταλίας· ἔ[χω]ν δὲ παῖδα[ς] ἐκ
Νε]φέλης Ἕλλη[ν τε κ]αὶ Φρίξον, [σ]υν[ῴ-
κησ]εν Ἰνοῖ τῆ[ι] Κάδμου, παῖδα[ς
.]ο[· κα]τὰ δὲ τῶν προ-
γόνω[ν ἐπιβουλὴν] ἐμηχανᾶτο καθά-
10 περ φο[βουμένη, μὴ τ]ὸν τῆς μητρυιᾶς

1–12, 19–23: P. Oxy. 2455 fr. 14, ed. E. Turner (1962), re-ed.
Van Looy (1964), 180–4, Austin, *NFE* 101; cf. H. Lloyd-Jones,
Gnomon 35 (1963), 441–2, W. Luppe, *ZPE* 51 (1983), 25–8. 1–18:
P. Oxy. 3652, ed. H. M. Cockle and P. J. Parsons (1984); both
papyri re-ed. W. Luppe, *APF* 32 (1986), 5–13, van Rossum-
Steenbeek 204, 221–2, Diggle, *TrGFS* 161 (1–18 only). We repro-
duce the text as edited by Kannicht in *TrGF*.

2 = F 818c.1 below   5 Θεσσαλίας 3652: -ῶν 2455
6–7, after Φρίξον: [.] . . [| . . .]εν Εἰνῶι (or -οῖ) τη[. . . . . .]υ

428

PHRIXUS A

test. iia (Hypothesis)

The first *Phrixus*, which begins, 'If this were (my) first day of
trouble'; its plot is as follows: Athamas was the son of Aeolus,
and king of Thessaly; (with) Helle and Phrixus, his children   5
from Nephele, he (lived with) Ino the daughter of Cadmus;[1]
... child(ren) ... Against his previous children Ino contrived
(a plot), inasmuch as she feared ... the cruel ... of a step-   10

---

[1] Lloyd-Jones in P. Oxy. 2455 suggested 'he (lived with, *or*
brought in [as a second wife]) Ino the child of Cadmus'. Luppe in
P. Oxy. 3652, assigning 'child(ren)' to the next clause, restored
'and furthermore (he married as his second wife) Ino (the daugh-
ter) of Cadmus', and supplied the same verb in 2455.

πα[P. Oxy. 2455, whence [σ]υν[ώκησ]εν Ἰνοῖ τῆ[ι Κάδμο]υ
πα[ιδί *or* [ἐ]πή[γαγ]εν Ἰνὼ τὴ[ν Κάδμο]υ πα[ῖδα Lloyd-Jones:
ἔτι δε[   ] Ι Κάδμου παιδ_[P. Oxy. 3652, whence ἔτι δὲ
[ἐπέγημεν Ἰνὼ τὴν] Κάδμου· παῖδα[ς . . . Luppe, with
[ἐ]πέ[γημ]εν Ἰνὼ τὴ[ν Κάδμο]υ· πα[ῖδας . . . in 2455 (which
does not have ἔτι δὲ): cf. e.g. Schol. on Lycophron, *Alexandra*
1284 Νεφέλην . . . ἐπέγημε   9 ἐπιβουλὴν] Parsons in 3652
10 φο[βουμένη Luppe in 2455

429

πικρὸν .[   ]η· συγκαλέ-
σασα γὰρ τῶν [Θετταλῶν γ]υνα[ῖκας ὅρ-
κοις κατησφαλ[ίσατο φρύγειν σπέρμα πύρι-
νον ἐπὶ τὴν χε[ιμερινὴν σποράν· τῆς δὲ
15 ἀκαρπίας ⟦αγε.[
λυσιν, εἰ Φρίξος [σφαγείη Διΐ· τὸν γὰρ
εἰς Δελφοὺς ἀπ[ἄγγε-
λον ἔπεισε⟨ν⟩ ὡς .[

*13 lines missing, then a few letters from the end of 19 and be-
ginning of 20, then:*

20   κ]ινδυν[
διδον[.]ων[ἀ]ναγκαιό[-
τερον ἡγησά[με]νος ἢ πατρὶ κίνδυνον [
ἐπιστήσαν[τ .] διὰ γυναῖκα————————[

11 πικρὸν θ[άνατου πάθ]η Parsons in 3652   12 P. Oxy.
2455 ends at]υνα[12–17 ex. gr. Cockle in 3652 (cf. test. iib
below and *Phrixus B* test. iib)   15 αγε. deleted in 3652
19–23 restored from 3 fragments of 2455 by Luppe, *ZPE* 51
(1983), 25–8   23 ἐπιστήσαν[τι] or -σαν[τα] διὰ: all letters
are uncertain

test. iib

τῶν δὲ Αἰόλου παίδων Ἀθάμας, Βοιωτίας δυναστεύων, ἐκ
Νεφέλης τεκνοῖ παῖδα μὲν Φρίξον, θυγατέρα δὲ Ἕλλην.
αὖθις δὲ Ἰνὼ γαμεῖ, ἐξ ἧς αὐτῷ Λέαρχος καὶ Μελικέρτης
ἐγένοντο. ἐπιβουλεύουσα δὲ Ἰνὼ τοῖς Νεφέλης τέκνοις
ἔπεισε τὰς γυναῖκας τὸν πυρὸν φρύγειν· λαμβάνουσαι δὲ
κρύφα τῶν ἀνδρῶν τοῦτο ἔπρασσον. γῆ δὲ πεφρυγμένους
πυροὺς δεχομένη καρποὺς ἐτησίους οὐκ ἀνεδίδου· διὸ

mother;[2] calling the women (of the Thessalians) together, she
secured an oath (that they would roast the seed corn) for the
(winter sowing) . . . and deliverance (from?) barren crops if   15
Phrixus (were sacrificed to Zeus);[3] for she persuaded the (en-
voy . . .) to Delphi that . . . *(13 lines missing, then a few letters
from the end of 19 and beginning of 20, then:)* . . . danger . . .   20
giving . . . deeming (him) a closer relative (to himself?)[4] than
to his father who had imposed danger (on him?) because of a
woman. *(end of hypothesis)*

[2] Perhaps 'feared (she might suffer) the cruel (death) of a step-
mother' (Parsons).   [3] Cf. the same phrase in test. iib, with
note there.   [4] Perhaps Phrixus deeming Melicertes a closer
relative (see test. iib and *Phrixus B* test. iib (3), and *Ino* Introduc-
tion and test. iii (5)): so Luppe (1983). Less probably, 'deeming it
(i.e. the sacrifice) more necessary'.

test. iib

Of Aeolus' children Athamas, while ruling Boeotia, fathered
on Nephele a son Phrixus and a daughter Helle. Later he
married Ino, and from her were born his sons Learchus and
Melicertes. In a plot against Nephele's children Ino per-
suaded the women to roast the (seed) corn; they took it with-
out the men's knowledge, and did so. When the soil received
roasted grains it would not produce annual crops. Therefore

Apollodorus 1.9.1

πέμπων ὁ Ἀθάμας εἰς Δελφοὺς ἀπαλλαγὴν ἐπυνθάνετο
τῆς ἀφορίας. Ἰνὼ δὲ τοὺς πεμφθέντας ἀνέπεισε λέγειν ὡς
εἴη κεχρησμένον παύσεσθαι τὴν ἀκαρπίαν, ἐὰν σφαγῇ
Διὶ ὁ Φρίξος. τοῦτο ἀκούσας Ἀθάμας, συναναγκαζό-
μενος ὑπὸ τῶν τὴν γῆν κατοικούντων, τῷ βωμῷ παρ-
έστησε Φρίξον. Νεφέλη δὲ μετὰ τῆς θυγατρὸς αὐτὸν
ἀνήρπασε, καὶ παρ' Ἑρμοῦ λαβοῦσα χρυσόμαλλον
κριὸν ἔδωκεν, ἐφ' οὗ φερόμενοι δι' οὐρανοῦ γῆν ὑπερ-
έβησαν καὶ θάλασσαν. ὡς δὲ ἐγένοντο κατὰ τὴν μεταξὺ
κειμένην θάλασσαν Σιγείου καὶ Χερρονήσου, ὤλισθεν
εἰς τὸν βυθὸν ἡ Ἕλλη, κἀκεῖ θανούσης αὐτῆς ἀπ' ἐκείνης
Ἑλλήσποντος ἐκλήθη τὸ πέλαγος. Φρίξος δὲ ἦλθεν εἰς
Κόλχους . . .

818c (= 821 N)

⟨ΑΘΑΜΑΣ⟩

εἰ μὲν τόδ' ἦμαρ πρῶτον ἦν κακουμένῳ
καὶ μὴ μακρὰν δὴ διὰ πόνων ἐναυστόλουν,
εἰκὸς σφαδάζειν ἦν ἂν ὡς νεόζυγα
πῶλον χαλινὸν ἀρτίως δεδεγμένον·
5   νῦν δ' ἀμβλύς εἰμι καὶ κατηρτυκὼς κακῶν.

Galen, *On the Doctrines of Hippocrates and Plato* 4.7.11
citing Posidonius fr. 165 Edelstein–Kidd; translated by Cicero,
Tusculan Disputations 3.67; v. 1 = test. iia.2–3; vv. 1–2 cited by
Tzetzes on Aristophanes, *Frogs* 1225 as the opening of 'the sec-
ond *Phrixus*' (see on F 819); vv. 1 and 3 cited in many lexica for the
word σφαδάζειν. Assigned to Athamas by Van Looy.

5 κακῶν Galen: -οῖς Valckenaer

Athamas sent to Delphi and enquired about release from the lack of produce. Ino however persuaded those who had been sent to say that the oracle had responded that the lack of crops would end if Phrixus were sacrificed to Zeus.[1] On hearing this Athamas, compelled by the land's inhabitants, had Phrixus stand ready at the altar. Nephele however snatched him away together with her daughter; she got from Hermes a ram with a golden fleece and gave it them, on which they were borne through the heaven across land and sea; but when they reached the sea lying midway between Sigeum and the Chersonese, Helle slipped off into the deep; and because she died there the water was called the Hellespont after her; but Phrixus reached the land of the Colchians . . .

[1] This myth provided an aetiology for the particular sacrifices made to Zeus at Halus in Thessaly (Herodotus 7.197.1–3) and on Mt. Laphystius in Boeotia ([Plato], *Minos* 315c; Schol. on Apollonius Rhodius 2.652–4).

818c (= 821 N)

⟨ATHAMAS⟩

If this were the first day of my troubles, and I were not on a long voyage through suffering, it would be natural to choke like a newly-yoked colt that has just taken the bit;[1] but now I am dulled and broken in to trouble.

[1] For the metaphor cf. *Aeolus* F 41.

ΦΡΙΞΟΣ Β

test. iia (Hypothesis)

Φρίξος δ[ε]ύ[τ]ερος, οὗ ἀρχή·
Σειδώνιον ποτ' ἄστυ Κάδμος ἐκλιπών·
  ἡ δ' ὑπόθεσις·
Ἀθάμας ἐν Ὀρχομε[νῷ δυνασ]τεύων
5 Ἰ]νοῖ τῇ Κάδμ[ο]υ συν[ᾤκει, δύο] παῖδας
ἐκ Ν]εφέλης προγ[ε]γεν[νηκὼς Ἕλλην τε
καὶ Φ]ρίξον· οἷς μ....[

remains of lines 8–13, including 11 Ἀθ[αμα- *and* 13 Φρί[ξ-,
then 14 lines missing, then:

        ] τῷ ἐπιβο[υλ]ευομέν[ῳ·
15 ἡ δὲ τὸν Διόνυσον] ἐπικαλε[σα]μένη τ[ὸν
θάνατον διώλισθεν· ἐμμανεῖς γὰρ π[οι-

P. Oxy. 2455, ed. E. Turner (1962), fr. 17 cols. xix–xx; re-ed.
Austin, *NFE* 102, van Rossum-Steenbeek 224, Diggle, *TrGFS*
164; cf. H. Lloyd-Jones, *Gnomon* 35 (1963), 442, W. Luppe, *APF*
30 (1984), 31–7 and 39 (1993), 13.

2 = F 819.1 below (ποτ' F 819.1: τότ' P. Oxy.)   4–7 cf.
Phrixus A test. iia.4–7   4 δυνασ]τεύων Diggle: βασι]λευών

PHRIXUS B

test. iia (Hypothesis)

The second *Phrixus*, which begins, 'Leaving the city of Sidon
once upon a time, Cadmus . . .'; its plot is as follows: Athamas
exercising power in Orchomenus[1] lived with Cadmus' daugh-
ter Ino, having previously fathered two children with   5
Nephele, (Helle and) Phrixus; to whom . . . *(remains of six
lines, including the names* Athamas *and* Phrixus, *then 14 lines
missing)* . . . (Phrixus) the object of (Athamas') design; but
(Ino) invoked the aid (of Dionysus) and evaded this death:[2]   15

---

[1] In Boeotia; the hypothesis to *Phrixus A* has him ruling
in Thessaly: see Introduction.   [2] 'evaded manifest death',
Turner. Ino had been a 'nurse' of the newly-born Dionysus; in *Ino*
she had joined his rites at Delphi (see test. iib (4) below and *Ino*
test. iii with note).

Turner   5 συν[ῴκει, δύο] Luppe (1993)   6 προ-
γ[ε]γεν[νηκὼς ῞Ελλην τε Parsons (see Lloyd-Jones 442)
15 end Luppe (1984): ἐπικαλέ[σασ]α ἐναρ[γῆ Turner

EURIPIDES

ήσας [ὁ] Δ[ι]όνυσος Φρίξον τε καὶ Ἕλλην τὴ[ν
ἀδε[λ]φ[ὴ]ν προηγάγετο εἰς τὴν ἔρημ[ο]ν
ὡ[ς] παρανάλωμα τῶν μαινάδων ποι-
20 ήσων· Νεφέλη [δ]ὲ καταπτᾶσα καὶ διαρ-
πάσασα τοὺ[ς] ἑαυ[τῆ]ς κριὸν ἔδωκε[ν] αὐ-
τοῖς ὁδηγε[ῖν] εἰ[ς Κόλ]χο[υ]ς————————

18 P. Oxy. has the gloss χω[ρὰν] beneath ἔρημ[̣]ν· ἔρημ[ο]ν
Luppe (1984): ἐρήμ[η]ν Diggle   19 beg. Luppe (1984):
ὥ[σ]περ ἀνάλωμα Turner   22 ὁδηγε[ῖν] Luppe (1984):
ὁδηγῆ[σαι] κ[αλ]ῶς Turner

test. iib

2. INO. Ino Cadmi et Harmoniae filia, cum Phrixum et Hel-
len ex Nebula natos interficere uoluisset, init consilium cum
totius generis matronis et coniurauit ut fruges in sementem
quas darent torrerent, ne nascerentur; ita ut, cum sterilitas et
penuria frugum esset, ciuitas tota partim fame, partim morbo
interiret. (2) De ea re Delphos mittit Athamas satellitem, cui
Ino praecepit ut falsum responsum ita referret: si Phrixum
immolasset Ioui, pestilentiae fore finem; quod cum Athamas
se facturum abnuisset, Phrixus ultro ac libens pollicetur se
unum ciuitatem aerumna liberaturum. (3) Itaque cum ad
aram cum infulis esset adductus et pater Iouem comprecari
uellet, satelles misericordia adulescentis Inus Athamanti
consilium patefecit; rex facinore cognito, uxorem suam Ino et
filium eius Melicerten Phrixo dedidit necandos. (4) Quos cum
ad supplicium duceret, Liber pater ei caliginem iniecit et Ino
suam nutricem eripuit.

436

for Dionysus maddened Phrixus and his sister Helle and led
them far into the wilderness to cause their incidental death[3] at
the hands of his maenads.[4] Nephele flew down however and   20
seized her children, and gave them the ram to conduct them
to the Colchians. *(end of hypothesis)*

[3] 'as if to cause their death', Turner.   [4] I.e. as victims of
maenads ranging in search of 'living flesh'.

test. iib

2. INO. Ino the daughter of Cadmus and Harmonia wished
to kill Phrixus and Helle the children of Nephele; so she en-
tered on a design together with the matrons of her entire
clan, and conspired that they would roast the corn they were
to give for seed, to prevent its germination. The result was that
when there was barrenness, and a dearth of corn, the entire
population began to die, partly of famine, partly of disease.
(2) Athamas sent a dependant to Delphi about the situation;
Ino instructed him to bring back a false response, as follows: if
(Athamas) sacrificed Phrixus to Zeus,[1] there would be an end
to the pestilence. When Athamas refused to do this, Phrixus
spontaneously and gladly promised that he alone would free
the population from misery. (3) So when Phrixus had been
wreathed and brought to the altar, and his father meant to in-
voke Zeus' aid, the dependant out of pity for the youth re-
vealed Ino's design to Athamas. With the crime discovered,
Athamas handed his wife Ino and her son Melicertes over
to Phrixus to put to death. (4) When Phrixus was taking
Melicertes to execution, Father Dionysus threw a mist over
them and snatched away Ino, who had been his nurse.[2]

[1] See note on the similar phrase in *Phrixus A* test. iib above.
[2] See note on Ino's rescue in test. iia above.

EURIPIDES

3. PHRIXUS. Phrixus et Helle insania a Libero obiecta cum
in silua errarent, Nebula mater eo dicitur uenisse et arietem
inauratum adduxisse . . . eumque natos suos ascendere iussit
et Colchos . . . transire ibique arietem Marti immolare.

Hyginus, *Fab.* 2.1–4 and 3.1

819

⟨ΙΝΩ?⟩

Σιδώνιόν ποτ' ἄστυ Κάδμος ἐκλιπών,
Ἀγήνορος παῖς, ἦλθε Θηβαίαν χθόνα
Φοῖνιξ πεφυκώς, ἐκ δ' ἀμείβεται γένος
Ἑλληνικόν, Διρκαῖον οἰκήσας πέδον.
5 ἢ δ' ἦλθ' ἀνάγκῃ πεδία Φοινίκης λιπών,
λέγοιμ' ἄν. ἦσαν τρεῖς Ἀγήνορος κόροι·
Κίλιξ, ἀφ' οὗ καὶ Κιλικία κικλήσκεται,
Φοῖνίξ ⟨θ'⟩, ὅθενπερ τοὔνομ' ἡ χώρα φέρει,
καὶ Κάδμος . . .

vv. 1–2 (Σιδώνιόν–παῖς): Aristophanes, *Frogs* 1225–6 with
Schol. identifying this as the opening of 'the second *Phrixus*';
vv. 1–6: Tzetzes on *Frogs* 1225, attributing it rather to 'the first
Phrixus' (see on F 818c); v. 1 (= test. iia.2 above): Plutarch,
Moralia 837e, Lucian 12.33; v. 3: Plutarch, *Moralia* 607b; vv. 6–9
(ἦσαν—Κάδμος): Schol. on *Phoenician Women* 6. Prologue as-
signed to Ino by Welcker.

1 ποτ' sources: τότ' P. Oxy. 2455 (test. iia.2 above)
3 ἀμείβεται Tzetzes: ὁρίζεται Plut.   6 τρεῖς Tzetzes: γὰρ
Schol.   8 ⟨θ'⟩ Valckenaer   9 καὶ Κάδμος Schneide-
win: καὶ Θάσος Schol.: Θάσος τε Bothe

438

3. PHRIXUS. When Phrixus and Helle were wandering in a forest after Dionysus visited madness upon them, their mother Nephele is said to have come and brought them a gilded ram; she ordered her children to mount it and to cross over to the Colchians . . . and there to sacrifice the ram to Ares.

819

⟨INO?⟩[1]

Leaving the city of Sidon once upon a time, Cadmus the son of Agenor came to the land of Thebes—born Phoenician, but his line changed to Greek after he began to live on Dirce's plain. Under what necessity he came, after leaving Phoenicia's land, I'll gladly tell. Agenor had three sons: 5 Cilix, from whom Cilicia is in fact named, (and) Phoenix, the origin of that land's name (i.e. Phoenicia), and Cadmus . . .[2]

[1] The most likely speaker (see next note); a god has also been suggested.   [2] Agenor sent all three sons to search for his daughter Europa (F 820 (a)); although they did not find her, none returned home, and they gave their names to their new lands. The restoration of Cadmus' name in v. 9 after its occurrence in v. 1 seems inescapable, especially if Ino is the speaker: she will go on to tell of her birth from him, and this play's setting is Orchomenus in Boeotia, near Thebes which Cadmus founded. Thasos' name perhaps came from a variant tradition concerning Agenor's descendants, e.g. Herodotus 6.47.1, Schol. on *Phoenician Women* 6, 217.

EURIPIDES

820

(a) (Ταῦρος) ... οὗτος λέγεται ἐν τοῖς ἄστροις τεθῆναι διὰ τὸ Εὐρώπην ἀγαγεῖν ἀπὸ Φοινίκης εἰς Κρήτην ἀσφαλῶς διὰ τοῦ πελάγους, ὡς Εὐριπίδης φησὶν ἐν τῷ Φρίξῳ.

(b) (Εὐρώπη) ... ἐξ ἧς ἔσχεν υἱὸν τὸν Μίνω, καθὼς καὶ Εὐριπίδης ὁ σοφώτατος ποιητικῶς συνεγράψατο, ὅς φησιν ὅτι Ζεὺς μεταβληθεὶς εἰς ταῦρον τὴν Εὐρώπην ἥρπασεν.

(a) [Eratosthenes], *Catasterisms* 14, cf. Schol. on the Latin Aratus 167–8, p. 211.8 Maass, Schol. on Germanicus, *Aratea*, p. 135.18 Breysig, Hyginus, *Astronomy* 2.21 (b) John Malalas, *Chronicles* 2.7 Thurn = 2.8 Jeffreys–Scott, adduced by Bentley to *Phrixus* rather than *Cretans* (see note on the translation of F 820 (a))

820a (= 827 N)

χρῄζων ἀνοῖξαι μὲν σιροὺς οὐκ ἠξίουν.

Etymologicum Genuinum AB 'σιρός' (= *Etym. Magnum* p. 714.16 Gaisford)

ἠξίουν *Et. Gen.* B: ἠξίου *Et. Gen.* A, *Et. Magn.*

820

(a) (Taurus) . . . he is said to have been placed among the stars because he brought Europa from Phoenicia to Crete safely over the ocean, as Euripides says in *Phrixus*.[1]

(b) (Europa) . . . from whom (Zeus) got his son Minos, as the very learned Euripides has recorded poetically; he says that Zeus was transformed into a bull and carried off Europa.

[1] Euripides tells of Europa's passage to Crete also at *Hypsipyle* F 752g.18–23, cf. *Cretans* F 472.1–2 (in both places without mention of the bull-Zeus who abducted her).

820a (= 827 N)

Though I desired to open the corn stores, I did not think it right.[1]

[1] Probably Athamas, who instead sought advice from Delphi. The alternative reading with 'you' for 'I' gives the words to someone accusing him, perhaps Ino, as part of her plot against Phrixus.

820b

ὦ θνητὰ παραφρονήματ' ἀνθρώπων, μάτην
οἵ φασιν εἶναι τὴν τύχην ἀλ[λ' οὐ] θεούς·
ὡς οὐδὲν ἴστε, κεἰ λέγειν δοκεῖτέ τι·
εἰ μὲν γὰρ ἡ [τύ]χη 'στίν, οὐδὲν δεῖ θεῶν,
5 ε[ἰ] δ' οἱ θεοὶ [σθένουσιν], οὐδὲν ἡ τ[ύχη].

Florentine Gnomology, PSI 1476 no. 8 Bartoletti (= Austin, *NFE* fr. 154), attributed to 'the second (*Phrixus*)'; vv. 1–2, 4–5: John the Lydian, *On Months* 4.7; vv. 4–5 paraphrased in *Florilegium Monacense* 108 Meineke

(821 N = 818c above)

820b

Oh, the delusions of mortal men, who vainly say that chance exists, but (not) gods! You men know nothing, even though you think your words are sound: for if chance exists, there is no need of gods; but if the gods (have strength), chance is nothing.

(821 N = 818c above)

ΦΡΙΞΟΣ A or B

822

col. ii   ὦ πρόσπολο[ι *a few more traces*
fr. 1   στυγνα[*traces*

          μελεα[*traces*

δότε δ' εἰς θαλάμ[ου]ς εἰς δέμνια [

5   οἰ‹κ›τροτατα *a few letters*

       ἐπὶ γὰρ ἄχεσιν ἄχεα τάδε[

       κύματι δ' ὡς ἔπι κῦμα κυλ[ίνδεται

       εἰς ἐμὰ δώματα καὶ κ . . [

       θεῶν τις οἰκ.[*traces*

             〈ΧΟΡΟΣ?〉

10   καὶ μὴν [. .]ιον βαρο . . . [

        nothing certainly intelligible

        κἀγω.[*a few letters*

        δμῶες [*a few letters*

        nothing certainly intelligible

PHRIXUS A *or* B

822

Possibly the start of an episode: Athamas is already present (19), and may have sung vv. 1–9; Ino (cf. 15, 16, 22, 32) enters at v. 19 after her female attendants (20; also 1, 13?) have chanted vv. 10–18;[1] she and Athamas then converse:

⟨ATHAMAS?⟩

. . . O handmaidens . . . hateful . . . miserable . . . give . . . into (her?) chamber to the couch . . . most pitiable . . . For here   5
are woes upon woes . . . they roll on like wave upon wave into my house and . . . one of the gods . . .

[1] These handmaidens may in fact be the main chorus, rather than a secondary one.

P. Oxy. 2685 ed. J. Rea (1968), col. ii frs. 1–2, apparently continuous (a few letters survive from col. i and from seven tiny separated fragments: see on 34–7); vv. 35–8: Stobaeus 4.22.15 (and 4.22.25 cited in Antipater fr. 63 von Arnim)

10 μὴν [conj. Rea, reading μηδ[almost certainly in P. Oxy.

15   βασίλεια δεσ . . ηδ[
         ἄλοχος [σ]τε[ί]χει· τί π.[
         τί δὲ σημαίνει και[νὸν
         μήθ᾽ ὧδ . . . ειτω[

                    〈ΙΝΩ〉

         Ἀθάμας, ὅρα τάδ᾽, εἰ τισ[
20   φέρουσιν αἵδε πρόσπολοι δ[
         λιποῦσαν οἴκους τἄμ᾽ ἐμε.[
         τάδ᾽ οὖν πατήρ μοι Κάδμο[ς
         φερνὰς δέδωκεν νῦν τε[
            ] . . [. . . .]ε μόσχον ξα[
25   traces of one more line
         few if any lines lost

col. ii fr. 2   a few letters from four lines (26–29), then:
30   ψυχην[traces
         ταυτ.[traces

                 〈ΑΘΑΜΑΣ〉

         γύναι, τ[. .]πεις δ[
         πόσιν . [ ] . . ρον[
         φεύγειν π[ρ]οδοῦσαν οτε[
35   γυνὴ γὰρ ἐ[ν] κακ[οῖ]σι καὶ νό[σοις πόσει
         ἥδιστόν ἐ[σ]τι δώματ᾽ ἢ[ν οἰκῇ καλῶς
         ὀργήν τε πραΰνου[σα καὶ δυσθυμίας
         ψυχὴν μεθιστᾶ[σ᾽· ἡδὺ κἀπάται φίλων.
         τούτων δ᾽ ἄκοντα[

446

⟨CHORUS?⟩

Look! . . . And I . . . servants . . . the queen . . . (your) wife   15
approaches. What . . . ? And what fresh trouble does she in-
dicate . . . neither . . .

⟨INO⟩

Athamas, see these . . . if . . . the handmaidens here are   20
carrying . . . when I left the house . . . my . . . ² So my
father Cadmus . . . gave me these as dowry, and now . . . a
heifer . . . *(traces of five lines)* . . . (his) life . . . . . . these . . .   30

⟨ATHAMAS⟩

Lady . . . husband . . . to flee when you have betrayed . . .
For a wife is most pleasing to her husband amid trou-
bles and upsets if she manages his house well, both sooth-   35
ing his anger and changing his spirits from gloom.³
Friends' deceptions too are pleasing.⁴ Of these . . . unwill-

---

² Vv. 19–20 are too damaged to reveal what 'these' (cf. 22, 40?)
are; perhaps Ino is bringing out fine things from her dowry (23),
and a heifer (24), to accompany the proposed sacrifice of Phrixus
(note 'life', 30).   ³ Cf. F 823, and Jocasta in *Oedipus* F
*545a.8–9.   ⁴ Text and sense insecure; Schmidt offered
'Friends' consolations . . .'

---

16 [σ]τε[ί]χει Handley   17 και[νὸν West   34–7 P.
Oxy. fr. 4 adds a few letters to those in fr. 2   35 κακοῖσι καὶ
νόσοις Stob. 15: νόσοισι καὶ κακοῖς Stob. 25   38 ἡδὺ
κἀπάται Stob. 25: ἡδὺν· καὶ ἀπαντᾶ Stob. 15 mss. SM (ἄπαντα
ms. A): ἡδὺ κἀπῳδαὶ F. W. Schmidt

447

40   τὸ κτῆμα· καὶ γὰρ α[
    〚τέρψιν παρασχοι[〛
    ἐγὼ δ᾽ ὁμοίως ωσα[
    ὅταν μὲν ...[
    remains of three more lines; minimal further remains in
    frs. 3–9

    41 verse deleted in P. Oxy.

822a (= 830 N)

λάτρις, πενέστης ἁμὸς ἀρχαίων δόμων

Athenaeus 6.246c; Eustathius on Homer, Iliad 16.865

**822b

ΙΝΩ

σὺ δ᾽ οὖν] ἔλεγχ᾽, εἰ τ[ο]ῦτ᾽ ἐν ἡδονῇ τί σοι.

ΑΘΑΜΑΣ

σὲ δ᾽ ἐνν]έπειν χρὴ π[ά]ντα τἀληθῆ, γέρον.

ΠΡΕΣΒΥΣ

φάσκω] παρούσης ταῦτα κἀπούσης, ἄναξ,
ἐκ τῆσ]δε χειρὸς σπέρμα δέξασθαι τόδε
5   σπείρε]ιν τ᾽ ἀρούρας· ὤφελον δὲ μὴ λαβεῖν.

PSI 1474 col. i, ed. G. Vitelli, *Révue Egyptologique* 1 (1919), 47–9 and (with Vitelli's aid) A. Vogliano, *RFIC* 4 (1926), 206–17 and 5 (1927), 79, with attribution to *Phrixus*; cf. W. Schadewaldt, *Hermes* 63 (1928), 1–14 (= *Hellas und Hesperien* I².505–15), identifying dialogue and speakers; Page, *GLP* 170–3 (no. 32); Van Looy (1964), 156–64; Diggle, *TrGFS* 163 (attributed to *Phrixus A*)

ing . . . the possession; for truly . . . ⟦ . . . would provide   40
delight . . . ⟧[5] And likewise I . . . whenever . . .

[5] The line containing these words is deleted in the papyrus.

822a (= 830 N)

. . . a servant, a serf[1] of my ancient house . . .

[1] *penestēs*, a Thessalian labourer, whether bondsman or
captive (cf. *Children of Heracles* 639): so perhaps Athamas is
speaking (*Phrixus B* is set in Boeotia, but Thessaly was his native
country). Kannicht identifies this serf as the old man who in F
**822b.3–5 confesses to have received the roasted seed-corn from
Ino; he therefore moved Nauck's fr. 830 forward.

**822b

INO

Test the matter (then), if this gives you any pleasure![1]

ATHAMAS

And (you) must speak the whole truth, old man.

OLD MAN

(I declare),[2] my lord—whether she is present or not—that
I received this seed (from her) hand and sowed the
ploughfields. How I wish I had not taken it!   5

[1] As Athamas tries to learn the true source of the sterile seed-
corn, Ino defiantly lies until the Old Man half-confirms that
her object was to kill Phrixus and Helle (13–15).   [2] A pres-
ent tense as in v. 15, rather than Wilamowitz's 'I will speak'.

---

1 σὺ δ᾽ οὖν] Vogliano   3 φάσκω] Collard: λέξω]
Wilamowitz   4 ἐκ τῆσ]δε Vogliano

ΙΝΩ

ἀπώμο]σ'—ὅρκου τ' ἐκτὸς οὐ ψευδῆ λέγω —
μὴ τοῦτ'] ἐμῆς τόνδ' ὠλένης λαβεῖν πάρα.

ΑΘΑΜΑΣ

......]ι σπεύδου[σα] δύστηνος φόνον
......] πολίταις ἢ [τέ]κνοισι τοῖς ἐμοῖς·
10   c. 11 letters]ν σπ[έρ]μα τίς δίδωσί σοι;

ΠΡΕΣΒΥΣ

6–7 letters] τὸν αὐτὸν μῦθον· ἐκ τίνος δ' ἐγὼ
... δι]ώλλ[υν ...]ιδε δοῦλος ὢν σέθεν;
.....] τάχ', ἢν τοῦδ' ἀνδρὸς ἄρσενος τύχῃς,
τὼ παῖδ]' ἀποκτείνουσ'· ἐγὼ δ' ἔτ' ἐν σκότῳ
15   κρύπτω] τὰ πλείω, πόλλ' ἔχων εἰπεῖν ἔπη.

ΙΝΩ

τάδ' εἰσακ]ούεις ἄλοχος οἷ' ὑβρίζεται;

ΠΡΕΣΒΥΣ

c. 9 letters] βλέπω γε τοῦδ' ἐς ὄμματα
c. 7 letters]εικη προσμένων ψευδῆ λέγω

6 ἀπώμο]σ' Schadewaldt   7 μὴ τοῦτ'] Blumenthal: μὴ
τῆς γ'] Schadewaldt   λαβεῖν πάρα Dodds: χερὸς λαβεῖν
PSI: θέρος λαβεῖν Radt   9 δεινὸν] or τῆς γῆς] Collard
(e.g.)   11 κυκλεῖς] Kannicht (e.g.)   12 δι]ώλλ[υν
Wilamowitz   13 γνώσῃ] Schadewaldt: πείσῃ] Collard
τάχ' ἂν ... τύχοις Schadewaldt   14 τὼ παῖδ'] Schadewaldt
16 τάδ' εἰσακ]ούεις Kannicht (σὺ δ' etc. Schadewaldt)
18 κοὐ πήματ'] εἰκῆ Page (εἰκῆ Schadewaldt): ἀ]εικῆ Vogliano

INO

(I do swear)—and regardless of an oath I speak no false-
hood—that this man did (not) take (it) from my hand.[3]

ATHAMAS

(*to Ino*) . . . eager, you wretch, to bring . . . death[4] upon the
people or upon my children . . . (*to Old Man*) Who gave you
the seed?   10

OLD MAN

(*to Athamas*) . . . the same story.[5] Why . . . was I wanting to
destroy . . . when I am your slave? (*to Ino*) . . . soon,[6] if you
find your husband here a real man, for your killing (his two
children).[7] (I keep) the greater part still (hidden) in dark-
ness, however, although I have much I might say.   15

INO

Do you hear how your wife is being abused?

OLD MAN

. . . I look him in the eye . . . awaiting . . . I speak falsehood.[8]

---

[3] We print the emendations of Blumenthal and Dodds; but note
Radt's 'take the crop from my hand'.   [4] Perhaps 'a (terrible)
death', or 'the people (of the land)', Collard.   [5] '(You keep
repeating) the same story', Kannicht.   [6] '(You'll know)
soon', Schadewaldt; '(You'll suffer) soon', Collard   [7] Text
and sense insecure, but the Old Man's apparent threat, that Ino
will find she has 'a real man' to deal with, is echoed in F 829
(speaker there unknown).   [8] Text beyond repair so far; Page
introduces the necessary negative, 'And I speak (no) falsehood
though rashly expecting to suffer' (but 'rashly' is awkward;
Vogliano's earlier suggestion would give 'though expecting to suf-
fer vilely').

EURIPIDES

823

⟨ΧΟΡΟΣ?⟩

δίκαι᾽ ἔλεξε· χρὴ γὰρ εὐναίῳ πόσει
γυναῖκα κοινῇ τὰς τύχας φέρειν ἀεί.

Stobaeus 4.23.31; Van Looy suggested the Chorus as speaker.

824

⟨ΙΝΩ⟩

ὡς οὐδὲν ὑγιές φασι μητρυιὰς φρονεῖν
νόθοισι παισίν, ὧν φυλάξομαι ψόγον.

Stobaeus 4.22.197

2 ὧν Stob.: ὃν Nauck

825

κρείσσων δὲ βαιὸς ὄλβος ἀβλαβὴς βροτοῖς
ἢ δῶμα πλούτῳ δυσσεβῶς ὠγκωμένον.

Stobaeus 4.31.94

826

δι᾽ ἐλπίδος ζῇ καὶ δι᾽ ἐλπίδων τρέφου.

Etymologicum Genuinum AB ʼζῆθιʼ (= *Etym. Magnum* p. 410.44 Gaisford)

452

823

⟨CHORUS?⟩

He spoke justly: a wife should always join the husband of her bed in bearing their troubles.[1]

[1] A continuation of the exposure of Ino—or, if it means 'She (Ino) spoke justly', part of her attempted deception of Athamas? For the sentiment cf. F 822.35–8 with note.

824

⟨INO⟩

Men say that stepmothers have no good intentions towards another's children[1]; I shall be on my guard against such men's blame.

[1] Lit. 'bastard children', i.e. stepmothers regard their husbands' previous offspring as illegitimate and are hostile to them (cf. *Aegeus* F 4). For Ino's enmity in this episode cf. Pindar, *Pythians* 4.162, Ovid, *Fasti* 3.853; in a different episode, see *Ino*, Introduction. In v. 2 Nauck suggested 'blame which I shall be on my guard against'.

825

A little harmless prosperity is better for men than a house bloated by riches into irreverence.[1]

[1] A cliché: *Hippolytus Veiled* F 438, *Melanippe* F 504 etc.

826

Live in hope and sustain yourself with hopes![1]

[1] Possibly Ino taunting Athamas if he does not sacrifice Phrixus.

EURIPIDES

(827 N = 820a above)

828

αἱ γὰρ πόλεις εἴσ᾽ ἄνδρες, οὐκ ἐρημία.

Stobaeus 4.1.4

829

ἀνδρὸς δ᾽, ὃς εἶναί φησ᾽ ἀνήρ, οὐκ ἄξιον
δειλὸν κεκλῆσθαι καὶ νοσεῖν αἰσχρὰν νόσον.

Stobaeus 3.8.7

1 so Nauck: ἀνὴρ δ᾽ ὃς εἶναι φής, ἀνδρὸς Stob. mss. SA
(ἀνδρὸς δ᾽ ms. M)   2 δειλὸν Macarius, Gesner: δειλῶ(ν)
Stob.

(830 N = 822a above)

831

πολλοῖσι δούλοις τοὔνομ᾽ αἰσχρόν, ἡ δὲ φρὴν
τῶν οὐχὶ δούλων ἐστ᾽ ἐλευθερωτέρα.

Stobaeus 4.19.39

832

εἰ δ᾽ εὐσεβὴς ὢν τοῖσι δυσσεβεστάτοις
εἰς ταὔτ᾽ ἔπρασσον, πῶς τάδ᾽ ἂν καλῶς ἔχοι;
ἢ Ζεὺς ὁ λῷστος μηδὲν ἔνδικον φρονεῖ;

[Justin], *On Monarchy* 5.8.

3 rejected by Wilamowitz as a late interpolation, on linguistic
grounds

454

PHRIXUS A *or* B

(827 N = 820a above)

828

. . . for cities are their men, not a wilderness.[1]

[1] A famous axiom, e.g. Sophocles, *Oedipus* 56–7, Thucydides 7.77.7. The speaker (Ino again, as in F 826?) means Athamas' city, if its inhabitants die of starvation.

829

It is unworthy of a man who says he is a real man to be called cowardly and to suffer a shaming affliction.[1]

[1] I.e. a treacherous wife whom he tolerates: the Old Man wanted Athamas to prove himself a 'real man' by punishing Ino (F **822b.13–14), but Van Looy thinks Ino may be the speaker here, 'having changed her tone'.

(830 N = 822a above)

831

For many slaves their name is a thing of shame, but their mind is freer than those who are not slaves.[1]

[1] Cf. *Melanippe Captive* F 495.41–3 with note.

832

If I who am reverent to the gods were acting the same as very irreverent men, how would this be well—or has the most excellent Zeus no sense of justice?[1]

[1] Possibly Athamas recoiling from sacrificing Phrixus (Van Looy). V. 3 is suspect: see opposite.

833

ΦΡΙΞΟΣ

τίς δ᾽ οἶδεν εἰ ζῆν τοῦθ᾽ ὃ κέκληται θανεῖν,
τὸ ζῆν δὲ θνήσκειν ἐστί; †πλὴν ὅμως† βροτῶν
νοσοῦσιν οἱ βλέποντες, οἱ δ᾽ ὀλωλότες
οὐδὲν νοσοῦσιν οὐδὲ κέκτηνται κακά.

Stobaeus 4.52.38; for attribution to the play see also on
Polyidus F 638.

2 δῆλον ὡς Hense

834

καὶ γὰρ πέφυκε τοῦτ᾽ ἐν ἀνθρώπου φύσει·
ἦν καὶ δίκη θνήσκῃ τις, οὐχ ἧσσον ποθεῖ
πᾶς τις δακρύειν τοὺς προσήκοντας φίλους.

Stobaeus 4.54.11

835

ὅστις δὲ θνητῶν οἴεται τοὐφ᾽ ἡμέραν
κακόν τι πράσσων τοὺς θεοὺς λεληθέναι,
δοκεῖ πονηρὰ καὶ δοκῶν ἁλίσκεται,
ὅταν σχολὴν ἄγουσα τυγχάνῃ Δίκη.

Sextus Empiricus, *Against the Experts* 1.274 and 287; Stobaeus 1.3.15a, appending another verse (15b) now separated as adesp. F 490 (see Introduction, 'Other ascriptions'); [Justin], *On Monarchy* 3; Clement of Alexandria, *Miscellanies* 5.14.121.2 (whence Eusebius, *Preparation for the Gospel* 13.13.47); the last three append F 912b. Clement and Eusebius cite the fragment as if from Diphilus (see F 136 *PCG*).

3 καὶ δοκῶν Sextus: κἀδικῶν Stob.

833

PHRIXUS

Who knows if what is called death is life, and living, dying?
†Except however† those among men who see the light of
day become ill, while the dead have no illness and own no
troubles.[1]

[1] Perhaps Phrixus offering himself for sacrifice; cf. *Phrixus B*
test. iib (Hyginus) 2.2. We translate literally as 'become ill' and
'have no illness', but others metaphorically, as 'suffer afflictions'
and 'have no afflictions'. Vv. 1–2 closely resemble *Polyidus* F 638,
and attribution between the two plays is confused in the sources:
see there. For the unidiomatic 'Except however' Hense suggested
'It is clear that . . . '

834

In fact this is in a man's born nature: every man longs no
less to weep for dear friends, even for one who is justly put
to death.[1]

[1] Perhaps spoken by a servant instinctively pitying Ino (Van
Looy).

835

Whoever of mortal men thinks that in doing wrong from
day to day he has escaped the gods' notice, believes wicked
things, and is caught out in his belief[1] whenever Justice
happens to be at leisure.[2]

[1] Sextus' reading, more stylish (and more difficult) than
Stobaeus' 'in his wrongdoing'.   [2] Cf. *Philoctetes* F 800 with
note. Here Ino's plot has presumably been discovered and is about
to be punished.

CHRYSIPPUS

H. Van Looy in ed. Budé VIII.3.373–89.

Wilamowitz, *Kleine Schriften* I.176–85; C. Robert, *Oidipus* (Berlin, 1915), 396–410; E. L. de Kock, *AC* 5 (1962), 15–37; Webster 111–3, 298; Trendall–Webster III.3.16–18; H. Lloyd-Jones, *The Justice of Zeus* (Berkeley, 1983²), 113–23, and *CQ* 52 (2002), 1–14; Aélion (1986), 29–34; *LIMC* III.i.286–9 'Chrysippos I', and VI.i.185–7 'Laios'; W. Poole in A. Powell (ed.), *Euripides, Women and Sexuality* (London, 1990), 136–50; Gantz 488–92, 544–5; D. Mastronarde, *Euripides. Phoenissae* (Cambridge, 1994), 11–14, 31–8; M. L. West, in J. Griffin (ed.), *Sophocles Revisited* (Oxford, 1999), 39–44; T. K. Hubbard in J. Davidson et al., *Greek Drama III: Essays in honour of Kevin Lee* (London, 2006: *BICS* Suppl. 87), 223–44.

The subject was Laius' abduction and rape of Pelops' adolescent (in some accounts illegitimate) son Chrysippus while in exile from Thebes and a guest of Pelops at Pisa in Elis. This is indicated explicitly by Cicero and Aelian (test. iva–c below), and references to 'Laius' or 'Laius in the tragedy' amongst the sources of F 839a (Plutarch), 840 (Clement) and 841 (Albinus) no doubt allude to this play. The drama, then, involved Laius' struggle and failure to control his desire for Chrysippus, the abduction and rape, and

459

*Chrysippus' death. Later summaries of the myth add some likely details. Laius fell in love with Chrysippus as he first arrived at Pisa, and carried him off after failing to seduce him; Pelops lamented his son's abduction and cursed Laius, praying he should remain childless or be killed by his own son (*Hypoth. Phoenician Women *no. 8(a) Mastronarde); Laius abducted Chrysippus while teaching him to drive a chariot (*Apollodorus 3.5.5: cf. Athenaeus 13.602 *and vase-paintings mentioned below); Chrysippus committed suicide (*Schol. Phoenician Women *1760).*

According to Aelian (test. iva below, and Historical Miscellany *13.5) Euripides portrayed Laius as the first Greek to practise pederasty; other authors cite Laius as the standard example of it. There is no clear evidence for the story in any form before Euripides. Some think it must have been mentioned in the lost epic* Oedipodeia *and in Aeschylus' Laius (the first play of his Theban tetralogy), and that the epic story appears in* Schol. Phoenician Women *1760 (the so-called Peisander scholion) which attributes the affliction of Thebes by the Sphinx to the wrath of Hera incurred by the rape of Chrysippus (for all this see especially Lloyd-Jones). But it seems at least as likely that, as Robert argued, Euripides invented the story, modelling it on the abductions of Ganymede by Zeus, Pelops by Poseidon (Pindar,* Olympians *1.37–42), and Chrysippus himself by Zeus (Praxilla F 5 PMG). An alternative story from Euripides' time is that Chrysippus was murdered for political reasons by his half-brothers Atreus and Thyestes, encouraged by their mother Hippodamia (Hellanicus F 157, cf. Thucydides 1.9.2; Plato,* Cratylus *395b3;* Schol. Eur. Orestes *5). In two mythographic sources ('Dositheus'* FGrH *290 F 6 = [Plutarch],* Moralia *313d–e; Hyginus,*

Fab. 85) *the murder story is combined with the abduction story in what is probably a Hellenistic concoction, perhaps a tragedy: Chrysippus is retrieved from Laius by his father or half-brothers and then killed by the latter with encouragement from Hippodamia, who ends up killing herself in remorse.*

The testimonia suggest the following tentative and incomplete outline. Laius' arrival at Pisa and first encounter with Chrysippus may have been related in a prologue speech (speaker uncertain). F 839a may come from an anapaestic introductory scene (like Medea 96–203). F 840 and 841 suggest a scene where Laius struggled with his desire before resolving on the abduction. F 842 looks like Chrysippus defending his virtue, possibly in response to Laius (but F 840 was not necessarily addressed to Chrysippus). The chariot-abduction, rape and suicide will have followed, presumably reported to Pelops by an eyewitness. F 843 looks like this witness or the chorus-leader consoling Pelops on the loss of his son. The chorus's 'philosophical' F 839 has been associated either with the debate on Laius' desire or, more probably, with a consolation of Pelops (see the note on this fragment below). The play may have ended with the return of Chrysippus' body and Pelops' curse. Nothing can be said about other characters, but the chorus is likely to have been citizens of Pisa friendly to Pelops. As in Archelaus, there is no trace of a female character (Hippodamia appears only in the murder story).

Brief fragments: F 838a (two letters from the play's first line cited in a hypothesis); F 843a 'Be assured I am silent'; F 844 'Crying 'Eia!' (i.e. 'Get on!'—Laius to his chariot-horses?). Other ascriptions: adesp. F 379 and 380, quoted by Plutarch immediately after F 840 and 841: 'My soul *yields now and no longer resists, like an anchor's fluke dragged through sand by the surge'; '. . . as a ship is tied to the land by ropes, and the wind blows—but my cables do not hold'.*

The play seems to have portrayed Laius' action as wrong, Chrysippus as an innocent victim, and the outcome (suicide and curse) as disastrous. It is not so clear whether it implied a condemnation of pederasty as such, or only of Laius' use of force and violation of hospitality to achieve his object; F 840 and 841 might point in either direction. Poole (149) compares Laius with the Phaedra of the extant Hippolytus, whereas Hubbard finds it significant that 'mankind's first pederast was also the first child rapist', and infers that Euripides' play can be associated with a middle-class reaction against the Athenian elite's continuing fashion for pederasty. If the play ended with Chrysippus' suicide and Pelops' curse, and without any kind of rehabilitation for Laius, Hubbard's view may well be near the mark, although some sympathy for Laius as a tragic figure may still have been suggested.

The fragments are too few for metrical dating, and the linking of Chrysippus with Oenomaus (involving Pelops) and Phoenician Women (involving Laius' descendants) in a fragmentary hypothesis to the latter need not suggest that these three plays formed a trilogy (see Mastronarde 11–14, 36–8). Nor is the anecdotal linking of the play with Agathon (test. ivc) of any documentary value. An apparently simple plot and the topic of sexuality may suggest a relatively early work like Cretans, Stheneboea, Phoenix, Aeolus, and both versions of Hippolytus. An allusion to Laius' sexuality by Aristophanes (F 453) and a comic Chrysippus by Strattis may reflect Euripides' play. The *chariot abduction appears several times in 4th c. South Italian and Etruscan art (see* LIMC, *Todisco Ap 164, 176, 210, 203, 231, Taplin no. 82). We have only titles from a tragic* Chrysippus *ascribed to Diogenes the Cynic (4th c.) and another by the Alexandrian poet Lycophron (early 3rd c.). Whether the five brief fragments of Accius'* Chrysippus *should be used in reconstructing Euripides' play (as for example by Webster and Poole) is quite uncertain. For Pacuvius see the note on F 839 below.*

ΧΡΥΣΙΠΠΟΣ

test. iva

Λάιος δὲ ἐπὶ Χρυσίππῳ, ὦ καλὲ Εὐριπίδη, τοῦτο οὐκ
ἔδρασε, καίτοι τοῦ τῶν ἀρρένων ἔρωτος, ὡς λέγεις αὐτὸς
καὶ ἡ φήμη διδάσκει, Ἑλλήνων πρώτιστος ἄρξας.

Aelian, *Nature of Animals* 6.15 (for context see the note opposite)

test. ivb

Quis aut de Ganymedi raptu dubitat quid poetae uelint, aut
non intellegit quid apud Euripidem et loquatur et cupiat
Laius?

Cicero, *Tusculan Disputations* 4.71, discussing the Greeks'
acceptance of pederasty

test. ivc

ἤρα δέ φασι τοῦ αὐτοῦ Ἀγάθωνος τούτου καὶ Εὐριπίδης ὁ
ποιητής, καὶ τὸν Χρύσιππον τὸ δρᾶμα αὐτῷ χαριζόμενος
λέγεται διαφροντίσαι.

Aelian, *Historical Miscellany* 2.21

CHRYSIPPUS

. . . Laius did not do this (i.e. kill himself) over Chrysippus, O admirable Euripides, even though he was the very first of the Hellenes to practise love for men, as you yourself say and tradition tells us.[1]

[1] Aelian compares Laius' behaviour in Euripides' play with that of a dolphin which fell in love with a handsome young man but accidentally caused his death as they swam together; in his grief the dolphin threw himself onto the shore and expired beside the body of his loved one.

test. ivb

Who doubts what the poets mean when they refer to the abduction of Ganymede, or does not understand what Laius in Euripides says and desires?

test. ivc

They say the poet Euripides too was in love with this same Agathon, and devised the play *Chrysippus* in order to please him.

EURIPIDES

839

ΧΟΡΟΣ

Γαῖα μεγίστη καὶ Διὸς Αἰθήρ,
ὁ μὲν ἀνθρώπων καὶ θεῶν γενέτωρ,
ἡ δ' ὑγροβόλους σταγόνας νοτίας
παραδεξαμένη τίκτει θνητούς,
5   τίκτει βοτάνην φῦλά τε θηρῶν,
ὅθεν οὐκ ἀδίκως
μήτηρ πάντων νενόμισται.
χωρεῖ δ' ὀπίσω
τὰ μὲν ἐκ γαίας φύντ' εἰς γαῖαν,
10   τὰ δ' ἀπ' αἰθερίου βλαστόντα γονῆς
εἰς οὐράνιον πάλιν ἦλθε πόλον·
θνήσκει δ' οὐδὲν τῶν γιγνομένων,
διακρινόμενον δ' ἄλλο πρὸς ἄλλου
μορφὴν ἑτέραν ἀπέδειξεν.

vv. 1–7: Sextus Empiricus, *Against the Experts* 6.17; vv. 8–14: Philo, *On the Eternity of the World* 30 (VI.82.14 Cohn); v. 1 and parts of vv. 8–14 are quoted by Philo in three other places, and with minor variants by several other authors; only Clement of Alexandria (*Miscellanies* 6.2.24.4) identifies both author and play; all of vv. 1–14 are paraphrased in Latin by Vitruvius, *On Architecture* 8 Pref. 1, and imitated by Lucretius 2.991–1009; cf. also Pacuvius, *Chryses* (*Chrysippus*?) frs. 21–23 d'Anna

5 βοτάναν (-ην Nauck) Ed. Müller: δὲ βορὰν Sextus
13 ἄλλου Corsinus: ἄλλο Philo and others: ἄλλῳ Bernays

839

CHORUS

Earth, greatest one, and Aether, realm of Zeus—he the
begetter of human kind and gods, while she, receiving
his damp moisture-spreading drops, bears mortals, bears
vegetation and the families of beasts, and so is rightly con-   5
sidered mother of all. Those things that were born from
earth return to earth, and those that grew from ethereal
seed go back to the heavenly region. None of those things   10
that come into being perishes, but one is separated from
another and exhibits a different form.[1]

[1] This fragment was widely cited in antiquity for its 'philo-
sophical' ideas (see apparatus opposite). Its dramatic context is
uncertain. The description of the propagation of life through the
heterosexual intercourse of Sky and Earth (vv. 1–7) might be a re-
sponse to Laius' claim that his homosexual desire is compelled by
'nature' (F 840). The doctrine that 'nothing perishes' (vv. 8–14)
might have been offered to Pelops as a consolation for Chrysip-
pus' death. The ideas in vv. 1–7 are implied in Hesiod's story of the
separation of Sky from Earth (*Theogony* 154–206), and explicit in
e.g. *Works and Days* 563 (Earth as mother of all), Aeschylus F 70
(Zeus identified with Sky/Aether) and F 44 (intercourse of Sky
with Earth); in Euripides cf. *Antiope* F 182a, 195, *Melanippe Wise*
F 484 and 487, F 898.7–13, F 985. Those in vv. 8–14 reflect 5th c.
thought, especially Empedocles and Anaxagoras; see also on F
941. What returns to the aether is the life-breath or soul, e.g. *Sup-
pliant Women* 532–4, 1140, *Helen* 1014–6, *Erechtheus* F 370.71–
2, F 971: see further Egli 94–103; R. Gagné, *HSCP* 103 (2007),
12–13; W. Burkert, *Babylon, Memphis, Persepolis* (Cambridge
MA, 2004), 112ff. (development of the idea in Greece and neigh-
bouring cultures).

EURIPIDES

**839a (p. 632 N)

λήθη δὲ φίλων, λήθη δὲ πάτρας

Plutarch, *Moralia* 750a and (first three words) 77c, with reference to Laius

λήθη . . . λήθη Plut. 750a: λήθη Plut. 77c (in both quotations the case is determined by the context)   φίλων Plut. 77c: λόγων Plut. 750a

840

ΛΑΙΟΣ

λέληθεν οὐδὲν τῶνδέ μ' ὧν σὺ νουθετεῖς,
γνώμην δ' ἔχοντά μ' ἡ φύσις βιάζεται.

Clement of Alexandria, *Miscellanies* 2.15.63.2; v. 2: Stobaeus 2.7.10a (= Chrysippus, *On Passions* fr. 389 von Arnim); Plutarch, *Moralia* 446a

841

ΛΑΙΟΣ

αἰαῖ, τόδ' ἤδη θεῖον ἀνθρώποις κακόν,
ὅταν τις εἰδῇ τἀγαθόν, χρῆται δὲ μή.

Albinus, *Introduction to Plato* 24; Plutarch, *Moralia* 33e and 446a; Stobaeus 3.3.33; and elsewhere as a proverb

1 θεῖον: δεινὸν F. W. Schmidt, also found in a citation of the proverb in Gregorius Palamas' *Prosopographia* (*PG* vol. 150, 1357b)

CHRYSIPPUS

**839a (p. 632 N)

. . . forgetfulness of friends, forgetfulness of homeland . . .

840

LAIUS

None of this advice you are giving me has escaped me, yet though I am mindful of it, nature compels me.

841

LAIUS

Alas, this truly is a godsent(?)[1] evil for men, when someone knows the good but does not practise it.

[1] Perhaps better 'a terrible evil' (F. W. Schmidt). Cf. Phaedra's reflections on this topic, *Hippolytus* 375ff.

842

†γνώμη σοφός μοι† καὶ χέρ᾽ ἀνδρείαν ἔχων
δύσμορφος εἴην μᾶλλον ἢ καλὸς κακός.

Stobaeus 4.21.20

1 γνώμη (or –ην) σοφός τ᾽ ὢν Blaydes   γνώμην σοφὴν
μὲν Collard   ἔχων Stobaean excerpts in cod. Escorial. X-1-13:
ἔχειν Stob.

843

ὦ δέσποτ᾽, οὐδεὶς οἶδεν ἄνθρωπος γεγὼς
οὔτ᾽ εὐτυχοῦς ἀριθμὸν οὔτε δυστυχοῦς.

Stobaeus 4.41.13

CHRYSIPPUS

842

I would rather be ugly but wise in judgment(?)[1] and with a valiant arm, than handsome and cowardly.

[1] The translation reflects Blaydes' conjecture; the Greek phrase does not make sense. Collard suggests 'with wise judgement and a valiant arm'.

843

Master, no one born human knows the measure of his good fortune, nor of his misfortune.

FRAGMENTS OF

UNIDENTIFIED PLAYS

(F 845–1106)

*Most of these fragments are attributed simply to Euripides
by their sources, or (if marked **) by modern conjecture. F
846, 850–6, 858, 860 are attributed to named plays either
questionably or wrongly. Many possible attributions are
mentioned in the notes to our translations (see also 'Other
ascriptions' in our Introductions to the named plays).*

*Brief fragments, mostly from ancient lexica identifying
unusual words, or words used unusually, or interesting
turns of phrase: (845 N = Alope F 112a, 845a N–Sn = 881a
below), 855 'burgeonings' (see Hypsipyle F 766), 860 'red
sea' (said to refer to the Red Sea, but more likely 'sea red
with blood'), 869 'a free gift' (with no gratitude or return
expected), 870 'the serpent's bloodshot eye', 872 'an un-
boastful statement', 873 'an unboastful declaration', 881a*

(= 845a N–Sn, damaged papyrus) 'the strength of (Apollo or Poseidon?)', 925a 'tearings of cheeks (in grief)', 926a (= fr. adesp. 152 N) 'I knew how to explain this clearly', 928c (damaged papyrus) 'of men, if . . .', 931 'lotus-wood night-ingales' (i.e. auloi, woodwind instruments often made from lotus wood), 932 'an Aeginetan market' (nickname for a flea-market, Aegina being a cosmopolitan trading centre), 955 'Demeter's servant' (Hecate), 955a 'a faint voice', 955b 'a big sea-urchin', 955g 'a flower of a singer' (Orpheus), 955k 'from beginning to end', 989 'lot, the child of fortune', 989a 'the gods' heralds' (birds observed in augury), 999 'unageing virtue', 1000 'Zeus protector of kin', 1002 'with logs of pine', 1003 'release the close-timbered doors' (adapted in Aristophanes, Acharnians 479), 1005 'I am my own man', 1011 'What need has come upon the house?' (adapted in Aristophanes, Clouds 30), 1088 'you have said an old-fashioned (i.e. simple-minded) thing', 1094a 'difficult to live (through)', 1094b (= 1122 N) a corrupt word apparently meaning 'eye' ('gleamings' or 'rays' has been conjectured), 1095 'wheedling' (rare feminine form), 1095a 'wife' (anomalous genitive form), 1095b (= 1123 N) 'useless' (but elsewhere in Euripides 'unabating' or 'undaunted'), (1096 N = Andromeda F 155a), 1096a (= 955e N–Sn) 'I am alive again', 1096b 'to be going to uproot', 1097 'take yourself off!', 1097b (= 955i N–Sn) 'delicate' (said to imply 'different' or 'new'), 1098 'limb-strengthening' (wine), 1098b 'indistinct' (a voice), 1098c 'murderess', 1098d (= 1098a N–Sn) 'growing' (a person's body), 1099 'chafing' (a horse against the bit), 1100 'excellence of education', 1100a 'a (wooden) box', 1101 'sacrificial' (a robe), 1102 'Xanthian' (from Xanthos on the island of Lesbos), 1103 'guest-killer' or 'host-killer', 1103a 'grape-bloom' (for

which Euripides used 'dew' as a metaphor), 1104 'acted as sponsor' (unusual tense-form), 1105 'to chine (an animal during a sacrifice)', 1106 'down' (as in 'thistledown', but meaning 'chaff').

(845 N = *Alope* F 112a)

846

Αἴγυπτος, ὡς ὁ πλεῖστος ἔσπαρται λόγος,
ξὺν παισὶ πεντήκοντα ναυτίλῳ πλάτῃ
Ἄργος κατασχὼν . . .

Aristophanes, *Frogs* 1206–8 with Schol.; possibly from *Archelaus* (see note opposite)

(847, 848 N = *Bacchae* fr. i and fr. dub. i Diggle)

(849 N = *Trojan Women* 117)

850

ἡ γὰρ τυραννὶς πάντοθεν τοξεύεται
δεινοῖς ἔρωσιν, ἧς φυλακτέον πέρι.

Stobaeus 4.8.4, with mistaken attribution to Euripides' *Electra*

851 (= *Children of Heracles* fr. fals. iv Diggle)

τάρασσε . . . ὁμοῦ τὰ πράγματα | ἅπαντα

Schol. on Aristophanes, *Knights* 214–5 (τάρασσε καὶ χόρδευ᾽
ὁμοῦ τὰ πράγματα | ἅπαντα) attributes some such phrase to
Children of Heracles.

---

1 The ancient attributions of F 851, 852.1–2, 852a and 853
to *Children of Heracles* are probably mistaken: see W. Allan, *Euripides: The Children of Heracles* (Warminster, 2001), 128–9,
225–7.

(845 N = *Alope* F 112a)

846

Aegyptus, as the most widespread account has it, reaching Argos by seafaring oar with his fifty sons . . .[1]

[1] For Aegyptus see also F 881. This fragment is the first of the Euripidean prologue openings subverted by Aristophanes in *Frogs* 1198ff. with the conclusion 'lost his little oil jar' (cf. *Meleager* F 516 with note). The scholia on *Frogs* say that it was attributed by 'some' to *Archelaus*, but that a different opening (F 228) appeared in the Alexandrian text of that play. The Alexandrian editor Aristarchus suggested that F 846 might have been the original opening, suppressed by Euripides because of Aristophanes' mockery (cf. on *Meleager* F 515). Alternatively, F 228 might have been composed for a later reperformance of the play; this possibility is favoured by Scullion (2006: see bibl. for *Archelaus*), who doubts the assumption of many scholars (including Harder, Gibert, Kannicht) that the attribution of F 846 to *Archelaus* was mistaken.

(847, 848 N = *Bacchae* fr. i and fr. dub. i Diggle)

(849 N = *Trojan Women* 117)

850

Tyranny is targeted from all sides by terrible desires; one must protect it carefully.[1]

[1] I.e. (probably), tyrants must constantly guard against the threats of envious competitors. The fragment is cited by Stobaeus as a 'criticism of tyranny'. In *Heracles* 65–6 the same point is given a more positive spin: tyrants are fortunate to be so envied.

851 (= *Children of Heracles* fr. fals. iv Diggle)[1]

Throw . . . all their affairs into confusion . . .

852 (= *Children of Heracles* fr. fals. i Diggle)
ὅστις δὲ τοὺς τεκόντας ἐν βίῳ σέβει,
ὅδ' ἐστὶ καὶ ζῶν καὶ θανὼν θεοῖς φίλος·

* * *

ὅστις δὲ τὸν φύσαντα μὴ τιμᾶν θέλῃ,
μή μοι γένοιτο μήτε συνθύτης θεοῖς
5 μήτ' ἐν θαλάσσῃ κοινόπλουν στέλλοι σκάφος.

vv. 1–2: Orion, Euripidean Appendix 7 Haffner, without play-attribution; Stobaeus 4.25.2, with attribution to Euripides' *Children of Heracles*; vv. 3–5: Orion, Euripidean Appendix 8 Haffner, marked off from no. 7 only by a double colon

852a (= 949 N = *Children of Heracles* fr. fals. v Diggle)
. . . καὶ τοῖς τεκοῦσιν ἀξίαν τιμὴν νέμειν . . .

Orion, Euripidean Appendix 11 Haffner, combined with *Children of Heracles* 297–8 but without play-attribution; similarly Stobaeus 4.25.3, with attribution to *Children of Heracles*

853 (= *Children of Heracles* fr. fals. ii Diggle)
τρεῖς εἰσιν ἀρεταὶ τὰς χρεών σ' ἀσκεῖν, τέκνον,
θεούς τε τιμᾶν τούς τε φύσαντας γονῆς
νόμους τε κοινοὺς Ἑλλάδος· καὶ ταῦτα δρῶν
κάλλιστον ἕξεις στέφανον εὐκλείας ἀεί.

Stobaeus 3.1.80, with attribution to Euripides' *Children of Heracles* (to *Antiope* in ed. Trincavelli)

852 (= *Children of Heracles* fr. fals. i Diggle)[1]
Whoever respects his parents . . . during his life is dear to
the gods both in life and after death.

* * *

Whoever refuses to honour his father, may that man never
share in my sacrifices to the gods, nor launch a ship with
me on a shared sea-voyage.

[1] See above on F 851, and apparatus opposite.

852a (= 949 N = *Children of Heracles* fr. fals. v Diggle)[1]
. . . and to allot due honour to one's parents . . .

[1] See above on F 851, and apparatus opposite.

853 (= *Children of Heracles* fr. fals. ii Diggle)[1]
There are three virtues you should practise, child: to hon-
our the gods, the parents who begot you, and the common
laws of Greece. If you do these things, you will always have
good repute, the fairest of crowns.

[1] See above on F 851, and apparatus opposite

EURIPIDES

854 (= *Heracles* fr. dub. i and *Children of Heracles*
fr. fals. iii Diggle)

τὸ μὲν σφαγῆναι δεινόν, εὔκλειαν δ' ἔχει·
τὸ μὴ θανεῖν δὲ δειλόν, ἡδονὴ δ' ἔνι.

Stobaeus 3.7.8, with attribution to Euripides' *Heracles*; Plutarch, *Moralia* 447e without attribution

(855 = *Hypsipyle* F 766)

856 (= *Iphigenia at Aulis* fr. dub. iii Diggle)

ἀλκυόνες, αἳ παρ' ἀενάοις θαλάσσας
κύμασιν στωμύλλετε,
τέγγουσαι νοτίοις πτερῶν
ῥανίσι χρόα δροσιζόμεναι . . .

Aristophanes, *Frogs* 1309–12 with Schol. attributing all or
part to *Iphigenia at Aulis*

854 (= *Heracles* fr. dub. i and *Children of Heracles*
fr. fals. iii Diggle)

To be sacrificed is dreadful, but brings renown. To avoid
death is cowardly, but there's pleasure in it.[1]

[1] Stobaeus' attribution to *Heracles* is probably just a mis-
take. Luppe suggested a connection with the alternative text of
Heracles represented by F **953c, but in that play Heracles'
family is not offered a glorious death. A play in which a young per-
son accepts sacrifice on behalf of the community is more likely,
e.g. *Erechtheus* or *Phrixus B* (or *Children of Heracles* if our text of
it is indeed defective).

(855 = *Hypsipyle* F 766)

856 (= *Iphigenia at Aulis* fr. dub. iii Diggle)[1]

You halcyons, who chatter by the sea's e'er-flowing waves,
moistening, bedewing your wings with flecks of spray . . .

[1] Halcyons are kingfishers, in myth the product of the trans-
formation of Alcyone and her husband Ceyx. This fragment is
the beginning of a parody of Euripides' choral lyric style in
Aristophanes' *Frogs* 1309–22 (which also includes *Meleager* F
528a, *Electra* 435–6, and *Hypsipyle* F 765a; cf. also F 765). It is
not clear how much of the wording is Euripides' own, and the pre-
cise source (if it was a single Euripidean passage) is uncertain. A
lost passage of *Iphigenia at Aulis* (as suggested by the scholia) is
unlikely since this play was produced two months after *Frogs*.
Some have suggested the broadly similar *Iphigenia in Tauris*
1089–93, or *Hypsipyle* (since Aristophanes associates the singer
of his parody with the heroine of that play).

EURIPIDES

857 (= *Iphigenia at Aulis* fr. dub. i Diggle)

⟨ΑΡΤΕΜΙΣ⟩

ἔλαφον δ' Ἀχαιῶν χερσὶν ἐνθήσω φίλαις
κεροῦσσαν, ἣν σφάζοντες αὐχήσουσι σὴν
σφάζειν θυγατέρα.

Aelian, *Nature of Animals* 7.39, with attribution to Euripides'
Iphigenia

858

ὦ θερμόβουλον σπλάγχνον . . .

Aristophanes, *Acharnians* 119, mistakenly attributed by the
Schol. there to *Medea*

(861 N = *Thyestes* F *397b)

862

('ἐνιαυτός' . . . εἴρηται) ὁθούνεκα
ἐν ⟨αὐτὸς⟩ αὑτῷ πάντα συλλαβὼν ἔχει.

Achilles, *Introduction to Aratus'* Phaenomena 19

863

ἥκει δ' ἐπ' ὤμοις ἢ συὸς φέρων βάρος
ἢ τὴν ἄμορφον λύγκα, δύστοκον δάκος.

Aelian, *Nature of Animals* 14.6

857 (= *Iphigenia at Aulis* fr. dub. i Diggle)

⟨ARTEMIS⟩

And I shall place in the Achaeans' own hands an antlered deer, which they will slay, proclaiming that they are slaying your daughter.[1]

[1] Probably from an ending of *Iphigenia at Aulis* earlier than the one found in the extant text, but nevertheless inauthentic: see D. Kovacs in the Loeb *Euripides* VI.161.

858

O (my) hot-tempered heart . . .[1]

[1] Wrongly attributed to *Medea* by an ancient commentator; possibly from another play about Medea, *Peliades* or *Aegeus*.

(861 N = *Thyestes* F *397b)

862

(The year is called *eniautos*) because it comprehends everything 'within itself' (*en autos hautōi*).[1]

[1] A false etymology (cf. *Pirithous* F 3 with note in the Appendix): *en-* has been identified with the root **eno-* 'year', the remainder less confidently with (*i*)*au-* 'rest': hence 'year-rest', 'turn of the year'?

863

He has come bearing a hefty boar on his shoulders, or the unsightly lynx, a beast that gives birth with difficulty.[1]

[1] Or perhaps 'born with difficulty'; hardly 'born for mischief' (LSJ). The fragment, almost certainly from a satyr play, may perhaps refer to Heracles returning with Cerberus in *Eurystheus* (cf. S. Goins, *RhM* 132 [1989], 401–3; questioned by Pechstein 347–8).

EURIPIDES

(864 N = *Auge* F *272a)

865

Φήμη τὸν ἐσθλὸν κἂν μυχοῖς δείκνυσι γῆς.

Aeschines, *Against Timarchus* 128; Suda φ 269

866

ἀλλ' ἥδε μ' ἐξέσωσεν, ἥδε μοι τροφός,
μήτηρ, ἀδελφή, δμωΐς, ἄγκυρα στέγης.

Alexander, *On Figures* 1.10

**866a

ἀλλ' †ἐξέπεσε† πορθμὶς ἐλατίνῳ πλάτῃ.

Anaxilas F 22.17 *PCG*, ascribed to Euripides by U. Reinhardt, *RhM* 114 (1971), 329–33, noting the strongly Euripidean character of the last three words. Kannicht in *TrGF* limits the fragment to these words.

ἐξέπεσε Athenaeus 13.558c quoting Anaxilas: ἐξέπλευσε Porson: ἐξέπεσεν ‹ἡ› πορθμὶς Kaibel (metrically implausible for tragedy)

867

ἀλλ' ἄγχιμος γὰρ ἥδε Φοιβεία γυνή . . .

Anecdota Graeca I.340.24 Bekker = Photius α 292 Theodoridis

868

. . . θεοὶ χθόνιοι
ζοφερὰν ἀδίαυλον ἔχοντες ἕδραν
φθειρομένων, Ἀχεροντίαν λίμνην . . .

484

(864 N = *Auge* F *272a)

865

Fame marks out the virtuous man, even in the bowels of the earth.[1]

[1] Fame is identified as a goddess, and her influence noted, in Hesiod, *Works and Days* 760–4.

866

But this woman has rescued me; she is my nurse, my mother, sister, servant, and my family's anchor.[1]

[1] Cited to illustrate the rhetorical figure called *epimonē* ('dwelling on', 'elaboration'). Cf. Homer, *Iliad* 6.429–30; Eur. *Hecuba* 280–1, *Alcmeon in Psophis* F 72.

**866a

The boat †escaped?† by means of its pine-wood oars.[1]

[1] Ascription to Euripides is conjectural, and should perhaps be limited to 'by means of its pine-wood oars' (see opposite). For the verb Porson suggested 'sailed out (of danger)'.

867

But here close by is the woman possessed by Phoebus . . .[1]

[1] Possibly Cassandra in *Alexander*.

868

. . . gods of the earth below, possessing the murky abode of the dead from which none return, the marsh of Acheron . . .

Anecdota Graeca I.343.31 Bekker

EURIPIDES

871

αἱματοσταγεῖ

κηλῖδι τέγγῃ

Photius α 622 Theodoridis (cf. α 618) ≈ *Anecdota Graeca* I.362.9 Bekker

874

οὔ σοι παραινῶ μηχανωμένη κακὰ
ἐχθροῖσι σαυτῇ προσβαλεῖν ἀλάστορα.

Photius α 901 Theodoridis = *Anecdota Graeca* I.382.31 Bekker

875

ὦ Κύπρις, ὡς ἡδεῖα καὶ μοχθηρὸς ‹εἶ›.

Anon., *On Barbarism and Solecism* p. 291.5 Nauck (= *Anecdota Graeca* III.239 Boissonade)

876

. . . τρομὸν δράμημα γηραιοῦ ποδός

Anon., *Analyses of Homeric Words* δ 76 Dyck

877

ἀλλ᾿ αἰθὴρ τίκτει σε, κόρα,
Ζεὺς ὃς ἀνθρώποις ὀνομάζεται.

Anon., *Analyses of Homeric Words* ζ 7 Dyck, and other lexica

871

You are wet with the stain of dripping blood.

874

I advise you *(feminine)* not to set an avenger against your-self while plotting harm to your enemies.

875

O Cypris, how pleasurable—and how mischievous—you are!

876

. . . the unsteady running of (my?) aged foot

877

But Aether bore you, maiden, which men name Zeus.[1]

[1] The identity of this maiden daughter of Zeus is uncertain: perhaps Athena (traditionally born from his head), or Dikē (Justice), who wanders clothed in mist to observe men's misdeeds (Hesiod, *Works and Days* 222–4, 256–62)? For the association of Zeus with Aether see on *Chrysippus* F 839. The sources of F 877 explain that Zeus is so named because the aether 'seethes' (*zei*) with fire, but it is not clear that Euripides offered this etymology. See further on F 941.

878

τίς ἔσθ' ὁ μέλλων σκόλοπος ἢ λευσμοῦ τυχεῖν;

Choeroboscus, *Orthography* in *Anecdota Graeca Oxon.*
II.258.3 Cramer

879

ὁ λῷστος οὗτος καὶ φιλοξενέστατος

Anon. Lexicon, *Anecdota Graeca Oxon.* II.452.17 Cramer

(880: see *Scyrians*, after F 684)

881

(a) Βῆλος . . . βασιλεύει μὲν Αἰγύπτου . . . καὶ αὐτῷ
γίνονται παῖδες δίδυμοι, Αἴγυπτος καὶ Δαναός, ὡς δέ
φησιν Εὐριπίδης, καὶ Κηφεὺς καὶ Φινεὺς προσέτι.

(b) ὁ Εὐριπίδης ε΄ φησὶ παῖδας εἶναι Βήλου, Αἴγυπτον,
Δαναόν, Φοίνικα, Φινέα, Ἀγήνορα.

(a) Apollodorus 2.11   (b) Schol. on Aeschylus, *Suppliant
Women* 318

(882 N = Homer, *Iliad* 16.391)

882a

ἥδιστον φάος ἡμέρας

Aristophanes, *Knights* 973 with Schol.

878
Who is the one about to be impaled or stoned?

879
. . . this excellent and most hospitable man. . .[1]

[1] Perhaps an ironic reference to the murderous Busiris or Sciron in the satyr play *Busiris* or *Sciron*, as Wilamowitz inferred from the vocabulary: cf. Pechstein 347–8.

(880: see *Scyrians*, after F 684)

881
(*a*) Belus . . . ruled Egypt . . . , and had twin sons Aegyptus and Danaus, and according to Euripides, Cepheus and Phineus also.

(*b*) Euripides says there were five sons of Belus: Aegyptus, Danaus, Phoenix, Phineus, Agenor.[1]

[1] Aegyptus ('the Egyptian') and Danaus ('the Danaan') were generally identified as sons of Belus and descendants of Io and Zeus. Cepheus is best known as father of Andromeda (see our Introduction to *Andromeda*), Phineus as Cepheus' brother in that story, Phoenix (the 'Phoenician') and Agenor as alternative fathers of Cadmus and Europa (cf. *Cretans* F 472.1, *Hypsipyle* F 752g.18–22). The traditions about them were very variable: see Gantz 208–12. The genealogy implied in F 881 differs substantially from that given in *Archelaus* F 228a and may reflect, more or less accurately, Euripides' *Andromeda*.

(882 N = Homer, *Iliad* 16.391)

882a
. . . the light of day most pleasing . . .

**882b

οὐδὲν γὰρ ὧδε θρέμμ᾽ ἀναιδὲς ὡς γυνή.

Inferred from Aristophanes, *Lysistrata* 369 (exact wording uncertain)

883

ἀλλ᾽ αἰσχρὸν εἰπεῖν καὶ σιωπῆσαι βαρύ.

Aristophanes, *Lysistrata* 713 with Schol.

(884 N = *Telephus* F 696.13)

885

ἄληθες, ὦ παῖ τῆς θαλασσίας θεοῦ;

Schol. on Aristophanes, *Frogs* 840

888

βέβληκ᾽ Ἀχιλλεὺς δύο κύβω καὶ τέσσαρα.

Aristophanes, *Frogs* 1400 with Schol., and derivatives (see note opposite)

**888a

αἱρήσομαι γὰρ ὅνπερ ἡ ψυχὴ θέλει.

Aristophanes, *Frogs* 1468; identified as Euripidean by van Leeuwen

**882b

No creature is so shameless as a woman.

883

But it's disgraceful to tell, and burdensome to keep quiet.

(884 N = *Telephus* F 696.13)

885

Is that really so, son of the sea goddess?[1]

[1] Achilles, son of Thetis, a character in *Telephus* and *Scyrians*, possibly also in *Palamedes*. The colloquial 'ἄληθες;' is usually indignant or contemptuous.

888

Achilles has thrown two ones and a four.[1]

[1] A poor dice-throw, perhaps metaphorical. In *Frogs* the verse is spoken by Dionysus as if it came from Euripides. Hellenistic scholars could not locate it in any extant play, and made various unlikely guesses at a Euripidean source (*Telephus, Philoctetes, Iphigenia at Aulis*). If genuine, it may have come from a play lost before their time. On the attribution of the fragment and its status as a 'proverb' see W. Buehler, *Zenobii Athoi proverbia* (Göttingen, 1987–), V.130–7 (on 2.51).

**888a

I'll choose the one my soul desires to choose.[1]

[1] Spoken by Dionysus preparing to choose between Aeschylus and Euripides. Van Leeuwen's attribution to Euripides, based on the verse's tragic diction, remains doubtful.

EURIPIDES

888b

... αἱ σοφαὶ ξυνουσίαι ...

Aristophanes, *Women at the Thesmophoria* 21 with Schol. (see further opposite)

**889

πεσεῖν ἐς εὐνὴν καὶ γαμήλιον λέχος

Aristophanes, *Women at the Thesmophoria* 1122; identified as Euripidean by Barnes and others, rejected by Wilamowitz and doubted by Rau

**889a (= fr. adesp. 68 N)

τί δ᾽ ἔστιν, ὦ παῖ; παῖδα γάρ, κἂν ᾖ γέρων,
καλεῖν δίκαιον ὅστις ἂν ...

Aristophanes, *Wasps* 1297–8 (cf. *Women at the Thesmophoria* 582); identified as Euripidean by Fritzsche

889b

ἔχει τελευτήν, ἧσπερ οὕνεκ᾽ ἐγένετο.

Aristotle, *Physics* 194a32 with commentary of John Philoponus, *CAG* XVI.236.7, 237.29, 309.15

---

1 Death as the natural outcome for mortals: cf. *Hypsipyle* F 757.924–7. Aristotle quoting the verse complains that it misrepresents death as the *objective* of life.

888b

. . . associations with the wise . . .[1]

[1] 'What a fine thing these associations with the wise are!', exclaims Euripides' kinsman in *Women at the Thesmophoria*. The scholiast suggests that Aristophanes alluded to the sentence 'Rulers are wise through association with wise men', and supposed that Euripides wrote it (as did Antisthenes and Plato: cf. *Republic* 568a–b, *Theages* 125b), although it actually belonged to Sophocles' *Ajax the Locrian* (F 14). The scholiast allows that it might have occurred a second time in an unpreserved play of Euripides; that is possible, but it seems more likely that Aristophanes alluded to a sentence of Euripides that merely resembled that of Sophocles. For discussion (favouring ascription of Aristophanes' sentence to both authors) see M. Joyal, *Symbolae Osloenses* 67 (1992), 69–79.

**889

To fall into her bed and nuptial couch.[1]

[1] Spoken by 'Euripides' impersonating Perseus rescuing Andromeda, so possibly one of the many quotations from *Andromeda* in that scene although the Scholia do not identify it.

**889a (= fr. adesp. 68 N)

What is it, child—for even an old man can justly be called 'child' if he . . .[1]

[1] In *Wasps* the Chorus-leader addressing the slave Xanthias completes this with 'if he takes a beating'. The same pattern of address provides a different joke in *Women at the Thesmophoria* 582–3. The pattern is probably Euripidean, its application to an 'old man' probably Aristophanic.

889b

He has reached his end, for the sake of which he was born.[1]

890

λόγων δίκαιον μισθὸν ἂν λόγους φέροις,
ἔργον δ᾽ ἐκεῖνος ἔργον ⟨ὃς⟩ παρέσχετο.

Aristotle, *Eudemian Ethics* 1244a11

(891 N = *Suppliant Women* 440)

892

ἐπεὶ τί δεῖ βροτοῖσι πλὴν δυοῖν μόνον,
Δήμητρος ἀκτῆς πώματός θ᾽ ὑδρηχόου,
ἅπερ πάρεστι καὶ πέφυχ᾽ ἡμᾶς τρέφειν;
ὧν οὐκ ἀπαρκεῖ πλησμονή· τρυφῇ δέ τοι
5   ἄλλων ἐδεστῶν μηχανὰς θηρεύομεν.

Athenaeus 4.158e; Aulus Gellius, *Attic Nights* 6.16.6 citing Chrysippus fr. mor. 706 von Arnim; vv. 1–3: Sextus Empiricus, *Against the Experts* 1.271; Musonius Rufus p. 45.5 Hense (in Stobaeus 3.40.9); Eustathius on Homer, *Iliad* 11.631. Several other sources cite the passage in part.

893

ἀρκεῖ μετρία βιοτά μοι σώφρονος τραπέζας,
τὸ δ᾽ ἄκαιρον ἅπαν ὑπερβάλλον τε μὴ
προσείμαν.

Athenaeus 4.158e; v. 1: Philo, *Every Good Man is Free* 145

894

τἀλλότρια δειπνεῖν τὸν καλῶς εὐδαίμονα

Theopompus fr. 35 *PCG* (in Athenaeus 4.165b)

890

For words the return you can fairly expect is words; action is earned by one who provided action.

(891 N = *Suppliant Women* 440)

892

Why, what do mortals need but just two things, Demeter's grain and running water to drink—things which are at hand and were made to give us nourishment? But their abundance does not satisfy us; we are choosy and hunt for ways of contriving different foods.

893

A moderate sustenance from a modest table suffices me; all that is out of place or excessive, may I reject!

894

. . . that the truly fortunate man eats the dinners of others.[1]

[1] Quoted by a parasite in comedy as from Euripides; 'eats the dinners' may be the parasite's words rather than Euripides'.

EURIPIDES

895

ἐν πλησμονῇ τοι Κύπρις, ἐν πεινῶντι δ᾽ οὔ.

Athenaeus 6.270b; Schol. on Theocritus 10.9. Many sources cite the verse or its first four words anonymously as a proverb.

896

Βακχίου φιλανθέμου
Αἴθοπα πεπαίνοντ᾽ ὀρχάτους ὀπωρινούς,
ἐξ οὗ βροτοὶ καλοῦσιν οἶνον αἴθοπα.

Athenaeus 11.465b

897

παίδευμα δ᾽ Ἔρως σοφίας ἐρατῆς
πλεῖστον ὑπάρχει,
καὶ προσομιλεῖν οὗτος ὁ δαίμων
θνητοῖς πάντων ἥδιστος ἔφυ·
5   καὶ γὰρ ἄλυπον τέρψιν τιν᾽ ἔχων
εἰς ἐλπίδ᾽ ἄγει. τοῖς δ᾽ ἀτελέστοις
τῶν τοῦδε πόνων μήτε συνείην
χωρίς τ᾽ ἀγρίων ναίοιμι τρόπων.
τὸ δ᾽ ἐρᾶν προλέγω τοῖσι νέοισιν
10   μήποτε φεύγειν,
χρῆσθαι δ᾽ ὀρθῶς, ὅταν ἔλθῃ.

Athenaeus 13.561a

895

Cypris (i.e. sexual desire) comes with fullness, not when you're hungry.

896

. . . Aethops ('Tawny'), ripening flower-loving Bacchus' late-summer vine rows, whose name men give to tawny wine.[1]

---

[1] Cited by Athenaeus to show that Euripides called one of the Sun-god's horses Aethops. Some scholars therefore assign it to *Phaethon* (cf. *Pha.* 175 with note).

897

Love is the fullest education in lovely wisdom. He is the pleasantest of all the gods for mortals to consort with, for he possesses a pleasure that brings no pain, and so leads 5 them to hope. May I not be among those uninitiated in his toils, and may I also keep clear of his savage ways! To the young I say, never flee the experience of love, but use it 10 properly when it comes.[1]

---

[1] For the content of this fragment cf. *Theseus* F 388 with note.

898

τὴν Ἀφροδίτην οὐχ ὁρᾷς ὅση θεός;
ἣν οὐδ᾽ ἂν εἴποις οὐδὲ μετρήσειας ἂν
ὅση πέφυκε κἀφ᾽ ὅσον διέρχεται.
αὕτη τρέφει σὲ κἀμὲ καὶ πάντας βροτούς.
5 τεκμήριον δέ, μὴ λόγῳ μόνον μάθῃς
{ἔργῳ δὲ δείξω τὸ σθένος τὸ τῆς θεοῦ}·
ἐρᾷ μὲν ὄμβρου γαῖ᾽, ὅταν ξηρὸν πέδον
ἄκαρπον αὐχμῷ νοτίδος ἐνδεῶς ἔχῃ·
ἐρᾷ δ᾽ ὁ σεμνὸς οὐρανὸς πληρούμενος
10 ὄμβρου πεσεῖν εἰς γαῖαν Ἀφροδίτης ὕπο·
ὅταν δὲ συμμιχθῆτον ἐς ταὐτὸν δύο,
φύουσιν ἡμῖν πάντα καὶ τρέφουσ᾽ ἅμα,
δι᾽ ὧν βρότειον ζῇ τε καὶ θάλλει γένος.

Athenaeus 13.599f; Stobaeus 1.9.1; vv. 1, 3 and parts of 7–10
cited or paraphrased individually in various places

**898a (= fr. adesp. 98 N)
ἐγὼ δὲ φεύξομαί ‹γ᾽› ἐλεύθερος γεγώς;

Athenaeus 14.658f; attributed to Euripides' *Telephus* by
Wilamowitz

898

Do you not see how great a goddess Aphrodite is? You could neither tell nor measure how great she is, and how far her power extends. She nurtures you and me and all mankind. Here is an indication, so you may learn it not just through words {but I may show you the goddess's 5 power in action}: through Aphrodite's influence the earth yearns for rain when her parched surface, infertile through drought, stands in need of moisture, and in turn the majestic sky, filled with rain, yearns to fall upon the earth; and 10 when these two come together and commingle, they generate and nurture all the things for us through which the human race lives and thrives.[1]

[1] Attributed to *Hippolytus Veiled* by Matthiae and others (cf. the extant *Hipp.* 447–50). Euripides here imitates Aphrodite's speech in Aeschylus, *Daughters of Danaus* F 44. See further on *Chrysippus* F 839.1–7.

**898a (= fr. adesp. 98 N)
And shall I flee, I who am freeborn?[1]

[1] Apparently a question, at least in Athenaeus' context. Wilamowitz's ascription of the verse to Euripides, and specifically to *Telephus*, because of its similarity with Aristophanes, *Acharnians* 203 ('And I for my part shall flee the Acharnians') is far from certain.

EURIPIDES

899

εἴ μοι τὸ Νεστόρειον εὔγλωσσον μέλος
Ἀντήνορός τε τοῦ Φρυγὸς δοίη θεός,
οὐκ ἂν δυναίμην μὴ στέγοντα πιμπλάναι,
σοφοὺς ἐπαντλῶν ἀνδρὶ μὴ σοφῷ λόγους.

vv. 1–3 (εἴ—δυναίμην): Athenaeus 15.665a; vv. 3–4: Plutarch, *Moralia* 502c; Stobaeus 3.4.29

1 μέλος Athen.: μέλι Barnes: μένος West

900

ὤφειλε δ᾽ εἴπερ ἔστ᾽ ἐν οὐρανῷ ⟨　⟩
Ζεὺς μὴ τὸν αὐτὸν δυστυχῆ καθιστάναι.

Athenagoras, *Plea for Christianity* 5.1

⟨κρατῶν⟩ Meineke: others locate the omission earlier in the verse

901

πολλάκι μοι πραπίδων διῆλθε φροντίς,
εἴτε τύχα ⟨τις⟩ εἴτε δαίμων τὰ βρότεια κραίνει,
παρά τ᾽ ἐλπίδα καὶ παρὰ δίκαν
τοὺς μὲν †ἀπ᾽ οἴκων δ᾽ ἐναπίπτοντας
5　ἀτὰρ θεοῦ†, τοὺς δ᾽ εὐτυχοῦντας ἄγει.

Athenagoras, *Plea for Christianity* 25.1; imitated in Latin by Claudian, *Against Rufinus* 1.1–3 and 12–14

500

899

Were god to give me the eloquent song of Nestor or of Phrygian Antenor, I could not fill a leaky vessel, pouring wise words into a man who is not wise.[1]

[1] In short, 'It's futile to offer wisdom to fools'. Nestor and Antenor were advisers of Greeks and Trojans respectively in the war at Troy (cf. Homer, *Iliad* 1.247ff., 3.146ff., 7.347ff.; Plato, *Symposium* 221c8). The Greek word for 'song' does not usually denote oratory, so Barnes' 'eloquent honey' (i.e. honeyed eloquence) may be preferable: cf. *Iliad* 1.249, '(Nestor) from whose tongue flowed speech sweeter than honey'. West suggests 'eloquent power' (i.e. powerful eloquence).

900

If Zeus really exists . . . in the sky, he ought not to have made the same person unfortunate.[1]

[1] Perhaps 'exists (holding sway)' (Meineke), but there are many other possibilities. In v. 2 '(always) unfortunate' seems to be implied. Similar sentiments and wording: *Phoenician Women* 86–7, *Helen* 1448. For Zeus allocating nothing but misery to some people, cf. Homer, *Iliad* 24. 527–33.

901

Often the question has gone through my mind, whether it is some kind of chance or some god that ordains human events, and against expectation, against justice, brings some † . . . from their homes,†[1] and others prospering.

[1] Unexpected and undeserved misfortune is contrasted with unexpected and undeserved prosperity, but the corrupt and meaningless text has not been convincingly restored.

902

τὸν ἐσθλὸν ἄνδρα, κἂν ἑκὰς ναίῃ χθονός,
κἂν μήποτ᾽ ὄσσοις εἰσίδω, κρίνω φίλον.

Basil, *Letters* 63.1; Schol. on Iamblichus, *On the Pythagorean Life* 237; Procopius of Gaza, *Letters* 156; first three words cited in Julian, *Letters* 34; the whole paraphrased in Cicero, *On the Nature of the Gods* 1.121 (= Chrysippus fr. mor. 635 von Arnim) and Themistius, *Orations* 22.275b

903

ἄφρων ἂν εἴην εἰ τρέφοιν τὰ τῶν πέλας.

Choeroboscus, *Scholia on Theodosius' Introductory Rules of Inflection*, p. 260.31 Hilgard (*Gramm. Gr.* IV.2), and later lexica.

904

ἀλλ᾽ ἄκρας εὐηθίας
ἅπτοιτ᾽ ἂν ὅστις τὴν φύσιν νικᾶν θέλει.

Choricius 32.135

905

μισῶ σοφιστήν, ὅστις οὐχ αὑτῷ σοφός.

Cicero, *Letters to Friends* 13.15.2; Plutarch, *Life of Alexander* 53.2 and *Moralia* 1128b; Lucian, *Apology* 5; [Menander], *Monostichs* 457; there are other allusions, and a Latin version in Ennius, *Medea* (fr. 105 Jocelyn).

906

ψῦχος δὲ λεπτῷ χρωτὶ πολεμιώτατον.

Cicero, *Letters to Friends* 16.8.2

902

The virtuous man, even if he lives far from my country,
even if I never set eyes on him, I count as my friend.

903

I would be foolish if I took care of my neighbours' busi-
ness.[1]

[1] Cited for the 1st person optative form τρέφοιν, paralleled in
classical Greek only in Cratinus F 60 *PCG* (ἁμάρτοιν).

904

Anyone wanting to overcome nature would be extremely
naive.

905

I detest a clever man who is not clever for his own benefit.[1]

[1] Assigned by some to *Aegeus* because of the similarity with
Ennius fr. 105 (see opposite with our Introduction to *Aegeus*).

906

Cold is most hostile to a delicate skin.

907

κρέασι βοείοις χλωρὰ σῦκ᾽ ἐπήσθιεν
ἄμουσ᾽ ὑλακτῶν, ὥστε βαρβάρῳ μαθεῖν.

Clement of Alexandria, *Protrepticus* 7.76.5, with reference to
Heracles feasting; v. 1 rephrased in Athenaeus 7.276f and Plu-
tarch, *Moralia* 668a

908

τὸ μὴ γενέσθαι κρεῖσσον ἢ φῦναι βροτοῖς.
ἔπειτα παῖδας σὺν πικραῖς ἀλγηδόσι
τίκτω; τεκοῦσα δ᾽ ἢν μὲν ἄφρονας τέκω,
στένω ματαίως εἰσορῶσά ⟨νιν⟩ κακούς,
5 χρηστοὺς δ᾽, ἀπολλῦσ᾽· ἢν δὲ καὶ σεσωμένους,
τήκω τάλαιναν καρδίαν ὀρρωδίᾳ.
τί τοῦτο δὴ τὸ χρηστόν; οὐκ ἀρκεῖ μίαν
ψυχὴν ἀλύειν κἀπὶ τῇδ᾽ ἔχειν πόνους;

Clement of Alexandria, *Miscellanies* 3.3.22.2; v. 1: Stobaeus
4.52.37

908a (= fr. adesp. 111 N)

ἔμοιγε νῦν τε καὶ πάλαι δοκεῖ,
παῖδας φυτεύειν οὔποτ᾽ ἀνθρώπους ἐχρῆν
πόνους ὁρῶντας εἰς ὅσους φυτεύομεν.

Clement of Alexandria, *Miscellanies* 3.3.22.3

907

(Heracles) was eating green figs along with portions of ox-flesh, howling unmusically enough for a barbarian to notice it.[1]

[1] Perhaps from the satyr play *Syleus:* cf. test. iiia there.

908

Not to be born is better than life for mortals. Shall I then bear children with the bitter pains of childbirth? If I do so and give birth to foolish children, I lament vainly as I watch them turn out bad; or if they are good, I lament when I see them die—or if they survive, my poor heart is worn down   5
with fears for them. What then is so valuable in this? Is it not enough to have the distress of a single soul, and to bear the pains that it incurs?[1]

[1] 'Better not to be born': *Cresphontes* F 449, Sophocles, *Oedipus at Colonus* 1224–37. 'Better not to have children': *Oenomaus* F 571, and F 908a below.

908a (= fr. adesp. 111 N)

Now and long since it seems to me, mortals should never beget children, seeing what great troubles we beget them for.[1]

[1] See above on F 908.

908b (= fr. adesp. 112 N)

ὦ δυστυχεῖν φὺς καὶ κακῶς πεπραγέναι,
ἄνθρωπος ἐγένου καὶ τὸ δυστυχὲς βίου
ἐκεῖθεν ἔλαβες, ὅθεν ἅπασιν ἤρξατο
τρέφειν ὅδ᾽ αἰθὴρ ἐνδιδοὺς θνητοῖς πνοάς·
5   μή νυν τὰ θνητὰ θνητὸς ὢν ἀγνωμόνει.

Clement of Alexandria, *Miscellanies* 3.3.22.4

908c (= fr. adesp. 116 N)

ἴτω τὸ δεινὸν <   > ὑπερφρονῶ
ὁθούνεκ᾽ ἀρετὴ τῶν ἐν ἀνθρώποις μόνη
οὐκ ἐκ θυραίων τἀπίχειρα λαμβάνει,
αὐτὴ δ᾽ ἑαυτὴν ἆθλα τῶν πόνων ἔχει.

Clement of Alexandria, *Miscellanies* 4.7.55.1, without attribution; vv. 2–4: ms. Vienna phil. Gr. 253 fol. 250 (unedited gnomology, cf. H. Mette, *Hermes* 102 [1974], 505–6), with attribution to Euripides

1 ἴτω τὸ δεινὸν τοῦτο, κινδύνων ὑπερφρονῶ (unmetrical) Clement

(909 N = *Oedipus* F *545a)

(910: see *Antiope*, at end)

911

χρύσεαι δή μοι πτέρυγες περὶ νώτῳ
καὶ τὰ Σειρήνων πτερόεντα πέδιλ᾽ ἁρμόζεται,
βάσομαί δ᾽ ἀν᾽ αἰθέρα πουλὺν ἀερθεὶς
Ζηνὶ προσμείξων.

908b (= fr. adesp. 112 N)

You, who were born to suffer misfortune and be in misery—you were made human and got your life's ill fortune from the moment when this aether began to nurture all mortals by giving them breath.[1] So don't reject mortal experience when you are a mortal!

[1] For the association of the life-breath or soul with the aether see on *Chrysippus* F 839.

908c (= fr. adesp. 116 N)

Let danger come . . . I think nothing of (it?),[1] for virtue alone amongst human attributes does not win its rewards from others but has itself as its own prize for its labours.

[1] In Clement's unmetrical paraphrase, 'Let this danger come; I think nothing of perils.'

(909 N = *Oedipus* F *545a)

(910: see *Antiope*, at end)

911

Golden wings are on my back, and the Sirens' winged sandals are being fitted to my feet. I shall be lifted upward into the broad heaven, into the company of Zeus.[1]

[1] The wings of song. Satyrus absurdly claims that Euripides here declared his intention of leaving Athens for the court of Archelaus in Macedonia. Wilamowitz and others have assigned the fragment to Amphion in *Antiope*.

Satyrus, *Life of Euripides*, P. Oxy. 1176 fr. 39 col. xvii.30–xviii.8; Clement of Alexandria, *Miscellanies* 4.26.172.1. The phrase χρύσεαι πτέρυγες is used allusively elsewhere.

EURIPIDES

912

σοὶ τῷ πάντων μεδέοντι χλόην
πελανόν τε φέρω, Ζεὺς εἴτ᾽ Ἅιδης
ὀνομαζόμενος στέργεις· σὺ δέ μοι
θυσίαν ἄπυρον παγκαρπείας
5 δέξαι πλήρη προχυταίαν.
σὺ γὰρ ἔν τε θεοῖς τοῖς Οὐρανίδαις
σκῆπτρον τὸ Διὸς μεταχειρίζεις
χθονίων θ᾽ Ἅιδῃ μετέχεις ἀρχῆς.
πέμψον δ᾽ ἐς φῶς ψυχὰς ἐνέρων
10 τοῖς βουλομένοις ἄθλους προμαθεῖν
πόθεν ἔβλαστον, τίς ῥίζα κακῶν,
τίνι δεῖ μακάρων ἐκθυσαμένους
εὑρεῖν μόχθων ἀνάπαυλαν.

Clement of Alexandria, *Miscellanies* 5.11.70.3; vv. 1–3: Satyrus, *Life of Euripides*, P. Oxy. 1176 fr. 37 col. iii.9–14

12 τίνι δεῖ (Grotius) . . . ἐκθυσαμένους Valckenaer, Musgrave: τίνα δὴ . . . ἐκθυσαμένοις Clement

912a (= 1130 N = adesp. F 623)

ποῖος δ᾽ ἂν οἶκος τεκτόνων πλασθεὶς ὕπο
δέμας τὸ θεῖον περιβάλοι τοίχων πτυχαῖς;

Clement of Alexandria, *Miscellanies* 5.11.75.1. The fragment has been widely regarded as a Hellenistic Jewish forgery (see *TrGF* 2.169 on adesp. F 617–24, with bibl.). Euripidean authorship was asserted by Wilamowitz and is considered possible by Kannicht, *TrGF* 5.1029 on F 1129–31.

912

To you, ruler of all—whether you favour the name Zeus or Hades—I bring fresh greenery and liquid meal; accept, I beg you, this unburned offering of all kinds of produce, poured forth in abundance. For you wield the sceptre of   5 Zeus amongst the gods of heaven, and also share with Hades the rule of those within the earth. Send into the light the souls of the dead for those who wish to learn the trials awaiting them—whence they have grown, what is the   10 root of their woes, which of the gods they should appease with sacrifice and so find respite from their tribulations.[1]

[1] A necromantic prayer seeking revelations from the spirits of the dead (cf. Aeschylus, *Persians* 638–42). Zeus Chthonios, ruler of the Underworld, 'can be be conceived as an extension of Zeus, or as a chthonic counterpart of Zeus' (M. L. West on Hesiod, *Works and Days* 465).

912a (= 1130 N = adesp. F 623)

What house shaped by builders could enclose the divine form within its enfolding walls?[1]

[1] Widely regarded as a Hellenistic Jewish forgery designed to show monotheistic tendencies in Euripides (see apparatus opposite). The language is not un-Euripidean, and the thought perhaps not less Euripidean than that of *Heracles* 1345–6 ('the god who is truly a god has no needs . . . '), with which Clement cites this fragment.

912b (= 1131 N = adesp. F 624)

ὁρᾶθ', ὅσοι νομίζετ' οὐκ εἶναι θεούς,
δὶς ἐξαμαρτάνοντες οὐκ εὐγνωμόνως.
εἰσὶν γὰρ εἰσίν. εἰ δέ τις πράσσει καλῶς
κακὸς πεφυκώς, τὸν χρόνον κερδαινέτω·
5 χρόνῳ γὰρ οὗτος ὕστερον δώσει δίκην.

[Justin], *On Monarchy* 3; vv. 1, 3–5: Clement of Alexandria,
Miscellanies 5.14.121.3 (whence Eusebius, *Preparation for the
Gospel* 13.13.47); appended to *Phrixus* F 835 in all the sources.
Authenticity doubted as for F 912a, reasserted by C. Riedweg,
CQ 40 (1990), 124–36 with the textual alterations below.

1 θεούς Riedweg: θεόν sources   3 εἰσὶν γὰρ εἰσίν
Riedweg: ἔστιν γὰρ ἔστιν sources

913

τίς [. .] . .οθεος [κ]αὶ [. .]ραδαίμω[ν]
ὃς τάδε λεύσσων οὐ προδι[δ]άσκει
ψυχὴν [αὑ]τοῦ θεὸν ἡ[γε]ῖσθαι,
μετεωρολόγων δ' ἑκὰς ἔρριψεν
5 σκολιὰς ἀπάτας, ὧν τολμηρὰ
γλῶσσ' εἰκοβολεῖ περὶ τῶν ἀφανῶν
οὐδὲν γνώμης μετέχουσα;

vv. 1–6 (damaged): Satyrus, *Life of Euripides*, P. Oxy. 1176 fr.
38 col. i.16–30; vv. 2, 4–7: Clement of Alexandria, *Miscellanies*
5.14.137.2

1 [ἀτι]μόθεος [κ]αὶ [βα]ρυδαίμω[ν] Murray and Hunt
(Clement paraphrasing has δυσδαίμων ἄθλιός τε)   2 προ-
δι[δ]άσκει Satyrus: θεὸν οὐχὶ νοεῖ Clement (condensing vv. 2–3)
5 τολ[μηρὰ Satyrus: ἀτειρὰ (i.e. ἀτηρὰ) Clement

912b (= 1131 N = adesp. F 624)

See, all you who think the gods do not exist, how you are doubly[1] in error with your poor judgment! They exist indeed, they exist. And if anyone evil is prospering, let him enjoy the time of his prosperity; for in due course he will pay the penalty.[2]

[1] Both denying the existence of the gods and thinking crimes can go unpunished.   [2] Authenticity doubted as for F 912a (see apparatus opposite). Riedweg shows that, but for the sources' monotheistic 'God' and 'He exists', the language and thought are thoroughly Euripidean, e.g. *Phrixus* F 835 (with which the sources of this fragment combine it), *Oenomaus* F 577, and F 991, F 1007c below. The all-seeing eyes of Zeus and the gods were a poetic commonplace after Hesiod, *Works and Days* 267–9. Contrary ideas in *Bellerophon* F 286.1–12, *Melanippe* F 506.

913

Who (is the) god-(forsaken?) and (heavy?)-fortuned man who on seeing these things does not train his soul to recognize god, having cast far away the false deceptions of those who study the heavens, whose rash tongues guess randomly about the unknown and have no measure of judgement?[1]

[1] An 'orthodox' chorus welcomes the punishment of irreligious behaviour, as e.g. *Heracles* 757–9. 'Those who study the heavens' are 'atheistic' natural scientists such as Anaxagoras, Diogenes of Apollonia, and 'Socrates' as travestied in Aristophanes' *Clouds:* cf. Egli 15–18. In v. 5 Clement has 'pernicious' rather than 'rash'.

914

κακὸν γυναῖκα πρὸς νέον ζεῦξαι νέαν·
ὁ μὲν γὰρ ἄλλης λέκτρον ἱμείρει λαβεῖν,
ἡ δ᾽ ἐνδεὴς τοῦδ᾽ οὖσα βουλεύει κακά.

Clement of Alexandria, *Miscellanies* 6.2.8.4

1 νέαν is suspected: see note opposite.

915

νικᾷ δὲ χρεία μ᾽ ἡ κακῶς τ᾽ ὀλουμένη
γαστήρ, ἀφ᾽ ἧς δὴ πάντα γίγνεται κακά.

Clement of Alexandria, *Miscellanies* 6.2.12.4; vv. 1–2
⟨γαστήρ⟩ are adapted by Diphilus fr. 60.2–3 *PCG* as reported by
Athenaeus 10.422b

916

ὦ πολύμοχθος βιοτὴ θνητοῖς,
ὡς ἐπὶ παντὶ σφαλερὰ κεῖσαι,
καὶ τὰ μὲν αὔξεις, τὰ δ᾽ ἀποφθινύθεις·
κοὐκ ἔστιν ὅρος κείμενος οὐδεὶς
5   εἰς ὅντινα χρὴ τέλεσαι θνητοῖς,
πλὴν ὅταν ἔλθῃ κρυερὰ Διόθεν
θανάτου πεμφθεῖσα τελευτή.

Clement of Alexandria, *Miscellanies* 6.2.13.8

917

            ὃς οἶδ᾽ ἰατρεύειν καλῶς,
πρὸς τὰς διαίτας τῶν ἐνοικούντων πόλιν
τὴν γῆν ⟨τ᾽⟩ ἰδόντα τὰς νόσους σκοπεῖν χρεών.

Clement of Alexandria, *Miscellanies* 6.2.22.2

914

It's bad to marry a young woman to a young man. For he desires to bed another, and she, deprived of his bed, devises mischief.[1]

[1] Most editors have thought these lines should refer to the marriage of a young man with an *old* woman, since the very corrupt text of Epicharmus F 167 *PCG*, which Clement says they imitated, has been interpreted to this effect, and v. 1 as it stands is almost identical with *Aeolus* F 24.1. Neither objection is compelling: cf. G. Giangrande, *AC* 73 (2004), 215–6.

915

I am subdued by need and by my damnable belly, the source of all miseries.[1]

[1] A reminiscence of Homer, *Odyssey* 17.286–7; cf. *Od.* 7.216–8, 18.53–4. Perhaps spoken by Telephus impersonating a beggar in *Telephus* (Welcker, Hartung), but other ragged heroes or satyr play figures are possible.

916

O mortal life, full of afflictions, how treacherous you are at every point, building up some things and diminishing others! There is no boundary laid down for mortals where they can reach an end, except when death's cold termina-   5
tion comes, dispatched by Zeus.

917

The man who knows how to heal well must look to the lifestyles of a city's inhabitants and to their land when he examines their illnesses.[1]

[1] Hippocratic doctrine: cf. *On Airs, Waters and Places* 1. Attention to the specific nature of a disease is recommended in *Bellerophon* F 286b.1–3.

513

EURIPIDES

918

πρὸς ταῦθ᾽ ὅτι χρῇ καὶ παλαμάσθω
καὶ πᾶν ἐπ᾽ ἐμοὶ τεκταινέσθω·
τὸ γὰρ εὖ μετ᾽ ἐμοῦ
καὶ τὸ δίκαιον ξύμμαχον ἔσται,
5   κοὐ μή ποθ᾽ ἁλῶ κακὰ πράσσων.

Adapted in Aristophanes, *Acharnians* 659–64; original in
Suda π 40 (v. 5 also in α 1404); vv. 1, 3–5: Clement of Alexandria,
Miscellanies 6.14.113.1; vv. 1–3: Cicero, *Letters to Atticus* 8.8.2 (v.
3 also in 6.1.8); vv. 3–4 (τὸ γὰρ—δίκαιον): Marcus Aurelius 7.42

919

κορυφὴ δὲ θεῶν ὁ περὶ χθόν᾽ ἔχων
φαεννὸς αἰθήρ

Cornutus, *Compendium of Greek Theology* 20

(920 N = *Auge* F 265a)

(920a N–Sn = *Licymnius* F 479)

921

ἀωρὶ πόντου κύματ᾽ εὐρέος περῶν

* * *

σμικραῖσιν αὐτοὺς ἐπιτρέπουσιν ἐλπίσιν

* * *

τριδάκτυλον σῴζει σφε πεύκινον ξύλον

Reconstructed from [Dio Chrysostom], *Orations* 64.9–10
(now ascribed to Favorinus)

514

918

In reply let him plot whatever he wants and contrive anything against me. Good will be on my side, and justice will be my ally; and never shall I be caught acting badly.[1]

[1] Possibly from *Telephus* along with many other passages parodied by Aristophanes in *Acharnians*. Bergk thought of someone opposing Odysseus, Wilamowitz of the dispute between Agamemnon and Menelaus (F 722–3, also anapaestic).

919

. . . and the gods' summit, gleaming aether which surrounds the earth . . .

(920 N = *Auge* F 265a)

(920a N–Sn = *Licymnius* F 479)

921

. . . crossing *(sing.)* unseasonably the broad sea's waves . . .

* * *

. . . they entrust themselves to slender hopes . . .

* * *

. . . a pinewood plank three fingers thick preserves them . . .[1]

[1] Quoted by Favorinus as parts of a single speech. On the temptations and dangers of seafaring see e.g. Hesiod, *Works and Days* 641–5, 663–88, Solon F 13.43–6.

EURIPIDES

(922 N = *Lamia* F 472m)

923

οὐκ ἐγγυῶμαι, ζημίαν φιλεγγύων
σκοπῶν· τὰ Πυθοῖ δ' οὐκ ἐᾷ με γράμματα.

Diodorus Siculus 9.10.4

1–2 ζημίαν φιλεγγύων σκοπῶν Herwerden (-αν -ον -ῶν
Seyffert): ζημία φιλέγγυον σκοπεῖν Diod.

924

μή μοι λεπτῶν θίγγανε μύθων
⟨μή μοι⟩, ψυχή· τί περισσὰ φρονεῖς,
εἰ μὴ μέλλεις
σεμνύνεσθαι παρ' ὁμοίοις;

Dionysius of Halicarnassus, *On Arrangement of Words* 4.25

925

λέγει δὲ καὶ Εὐριπίδης περὶ τῆς γενέσεως αὐτοῦ τὸν
τρόπον τοῦτον· Ἥφαιστον ἐρασθέντα Ἀθηνᾶς βούλεσθαι
αὐτῇ μιγῆναι, τῆς δὲ ἀποστρεφομένης καὶ τὴν παρθενίαν
μᾶλλον αἱρουμένης ἔν τινι τόπῳ τῆς Ἀττικῆς κρύπτε-
σθαι, ὃν λέγουσι καὶ ἀπ' ἐκείνου προσαγορευθῆναι
Ἡφαιστεῖον· ὃς δόξας αὐτὴν κρατήσειν καὶ ἐπιθέμενος
πληγεὶς ὑπ' αὐτῆς τῷ δόρατι ἀφῆκε τὴν ἐπιθυμίαν, φερο-
μένης εἰς τὴν γῆν τῆς σπορᾶς· ἐξ ἧς γεγενῆσθαι λέγουσι
παῖδα, ὃς ἐκ τούτου Ἐριχθόνιος ἐκλήθη.

[Eratosthenes], *Catasterisms* 13; similarly in Latin Hyginus,
Astronomy 2.13

(922 N = *Lamia* F 472m)

923

I make no pledges, considering the penalties for those who indulge in them;[1] and the words inscribed at Delphi forbid me.[2]

[1] Reading and sense uncertain. The transmitted text is hardly possible: 'It's a penalty to observe one who indulge in pledges.'
[2] 'Pledge brings ruin' is said to have been one of the precepts inscribed on the Temple of Apollo at Delphi; cf. Plato, *Charmides* 165a with Schol. citing the younger Cratinus F 12 *PCG*.

924

Don't touch subtle arguments, (don't touch them,) my soul! Why think too cleverly, unless you want to put on airs amongst your fellows?[1]

[1] Disdain for 'subtle' (i.e. sophistic) thinking and argument, e.g. *Medea* 529, *Hippolytus* 921–4; cf. Aristophanes, *Clouds* 319–22.

925

Euripides too speaks of his (i.e. Erichthonius') birth in this way: Hephaestus lusted for Athena and wanted to have intercourse with her, but she turned away, preferring to keep her virginity, and hid in a place in Attica which they say is named 'Hephaesteum' after him. He attacked her, expecting to subdue her, but was struck by her with her spear and released his lust, his seed being spent on the ground. From it, they say, a child was born who because of this was called Erichthonius.[1]

[1] For the 'earthborn', semi-serpentine Erichthonius (distinguished in Athenian myth from the hero Erechtheus although they were probably once identical) cf. *Ion* 21, 267–8, 999–1000; Gantz 77–8, 233–7, 239. His name suggests 'rich-earth' (*eri-,*

(925b N–Sn = *Alcestis* 608)

926

γλώσσῃ διαψαίρουσα μυκτήρων τόπους

Etymologicum Genuinum AB 'διαψαίρουσα' (= *Etym. Magnum* p. 782.8 Gaisford) and other lexica

926b (= 1116 N)

(*a*) Euripides autem montem esse altissimum adfirmat, qui Atlans uocetur.

(*b*) Εὐριπίδης δὲ τὸν Ἄτλαντα ὄρος εἶναί φησιν ὑπερνεφές.

(*a*) Eusebius, *Chronicle* (tr. Jerome), p. 37b.17 Helm

(*b*) George Syncellus, *Chronography* p. 283 Dindorf (p. 175 Mosshammer)

927

ἔνδον γυναικῶν καὶ πρὸς οἰκέτας λόγος.

Aristophanes of Byzantium fr. 316 Slater

928

οὐ γὰρ ἀσφαλὲς
περαιτέρω τὸ κάλλος ἢ μέσον λαβεῖν.

Galen, *Protrepticus* 8

chthon-), but some ancient sources connect it with *eris* ('strife': his struggle with Athena) or *erion* ('wool', with which in one version of the story she wiped his semen from her thigh). The likeliest context for Euripides' telling of the story would be *Erechtheus*, but other plays are possible, especially those on Athenian subjects.

(925b N–Sn = *Alcestis* 608)

926

. . . cleaning the area of its nostrils with its tongue . . .[1]

[1] Description of a beast, probably in a messenger speech. Naber suggested the Chimaera in *Bellerophon*. *Theseus* (Minotaur), *Aegeus* (Marathonian Bull), *Andromeda* (sea monster) or *Eurystheus* (Cerberus) could also be considered (but the masc. διαψαίροντα in a description of the Minotaur in *Theseus* F **386b.7 is probably just a coincidence).

926b (= 1116 N)

(*a*) Euripides asserts that there is a very high mountain, which is called Atlas.

(*b*) Euripides says that Atlas is a mountain that rises above the clouds.

927

Women's conversations (should be) indoors and with their household.[1]

[1] Cf. *Meleager* F 521 with note.

928

It is unsafe to have beauty beyond the average.[1]

[1] Similarly Ennius, *Melanippa* fr. 118 Jocelyn; hence Hartung assigned this fragment to *Melanippe Wise*.

928a

ὁ πρῶτος ἡμῖν τῶν ἐν οὐρανῷ θεῶν
βωμοὺς ἱδρύσας εὐαγῆ τ᾽ ἀγάλματα
γλ[υ]πτοῖσι τέχνης ζωοποιήσα[ς] τύποις
ἑνὸς κατημέλησεν ὡς οἶμαι τότε,
5 ὃς τοῦ μεγίστου καὶ θεῶν ὑπερτάτου
Πλούτου στεφήρη βωμὸν οὐχ ἱδρύσατο.
remains of one more line

Florentine Gnomology, PSI 1476 no. 3 Bartoletti = Austin,
NFE fr. 153

928b

ὦ Ζεῦ, τί τοῦτ᾽ ἐφόδιον ἀνθρώποις δίδως,
τοῖς μὲν πονηροῖς πᾶσι τὴν εὐγλωσσίαν,
τοῖς δ᾽ οὖσι χρηστοῖς ἀδυναμ‹ε›ῖν ἐν τῷ λέγειν;

Florentine Gnomology, PSI 1476 no. 20 Bartoletti = Austin,
NFE no. 156

929

ἑῷος ἡνίχ᾽ ἱππότης ἐξέλαμψεν ἀστήρ

Hephaestion, Metrical Handbook 15.17, illustrating the verse-
type called 'Euripidean'

929a (= fr. adesp. 187 N)

δισσὰ πνεύματα πνεῖς, Ἔρως.

Hermias on Plato, Phaedrus 230e (p. 34.3 Couvreur); para-
phrased in Lucian 49.37

928a

The man who first established for us altars of the heavenly
gods, and fashioned sacred lifelike images of them in art-
fully carved sculptures, neglected one thing when he did
so in my opinion: he established no garlanded altar for
Wealth, the greatest and highest of gods . . . *(remains of one*   5
more line) . . .

928b

Zeus, why do you give men this endowment for life's jour-
ney—a ready tongue to every wicked man, but inability in
speaking to those who are good?[1]

1 Cf. *Alexander* F 56 with note.

929

. . . when the dawn star on her chariot shone forth . . .[1]

1 Cf. *Phaethon* 63–4 with note.

929a (= fr. adesp. 187 N)

You breathe two kinds of breath, Eros.[1]

1 Inspiring two kinds of love, uncontrolled and temperate: cf.
Theseus F 388 with note.

929b (= *Aeolus* fr. 14 N)

Ἕλλην γάρ, ὡς λέγουσι, γίγνεται Διός,
τοῦ δ᾽ Αἴολος παῖς, Αἰόλου δὲ Σίσυφος
Ἀθάμας τε Κρηθεύς θ᾽ ὅς τ᾽ ἐπ᾽ Ἀλφειοῦ ῥοαῖς
θεοῦ μανεὶς ἔρριψε Σαλμωνεὺς φλόγα.

Heraclides of Crete, *Cities of Greece* 3.3

930

οἴμοι, δράκων μου γίγνεται τὸ ἥμισυ·
τέκνον, περιπλάκηθι τῷ λοιπῷ πατρί.

Hermogenes, *On Invention* 4.12

(933 N = *Eurystheus* F 379a)

934

νοῦν ἔχοντος ⟨   ⟩
φίλον πρίασθαι χρημάτων πολλῶν σαφῆ.

Libanius, *Letters* 571.3

1 ⟨ἦν ἄρα⟩ Porson

929b (= *Aeolus* fr. 14 N)

Hellen, they say, was a son of Zeus, Aeolus of Hellen, and
Aeolus' sons were Sisyphus, Athamas, Cretheus, and Sal-
moneus who in his madness hurled the god's flame by
Alpheus' stream.[1]

[1] Musgrave attributed this prologue fragment to *Aeolus*, but
it is now clear that that play's Aeolus had no connection with the
son of Hellen (see *Aeolus* Introduction and test. ii). Suggested
alternatives include *Sisyphus* (Valckenaer), *Melanippe Captive*
(Mette), *Peliades* (Kannicht). For the sons of Aeolus see Gantz
171–83 with 808–10 (genealogies). Salmoneus, father of Tyro, im-
personated Zeus with his thunderbolt and was duly struck down
by him. The river Alpheus bounded Zeus's great sanctuary at
Olympia.

930

Alas, half of me is becoming a serpent. Child, embrace the
remainder of your father![1]

[1] Hermogenes' attribution of this to Euripides, and his as-
sumption that it comes from a tragedy, may well be mistaken; satyr
play or comedy seem more likely. Valckenaer assigned it to the
highly dubious *Cadmus* (see there), comparing Cadmus' words to
his wife in Ovid, *Metamporhoses* 4.583–5.

(933 N = *Eurystheus* F 379a)

934

. . .[1] of a sensible man to give a lot of money for a true
friend.

[1] '(So it's characteristic) of a sensible man', Porson (the Greek
imperfect tense expressing recognition of a general truth).

EURIPIDES

(935 N = *Alexander* F 62f)

936

οὔκ· ἀλλ' ἔτ' ἔμπνουν Ἀίδης μ' ἐδέξατο.

Lucian 38.1

937

μὴ κτεῖνε· τὸν ἱκέτην γὰρ οὐ θέμις κτανεῖν.

Lucian 28.3, together with F 938 and verses from *Orestes* and *Bacchae*. See note opposite

938

νῦν οὖν ἔκατι ῥημάτων κτενεῖτέ με;

Lucian 28.3 (see on F 937)

939

ὦ παγκάκιστοι, χθόνια γῆς παιδεύματα

Lucian 21.1, together with F 940 and 940a in a pastiche of tragic verses which he seems to ascribe to Euripides (*Orestes* 1–3 adapted and *Heracles* 538 precede): see further opposite.

940

τί δ' ἔστι; πρὸς χορὸν γὰρ οἰκείων ἐρεῖς.

Lucian 21.1 (see on F 939)

940a (= fr. adesp. 293 N)

οὐκ οἶσθ', ἐπεί τοι κἂν ἐκώκυες μέγα.

Lucian 21.2 (see on F 939)

UNIDENTIFIED PLAYS

(935 N = *Alexander* F 62f)

936

No; I was still alive when Hades received me.[1]

[1] Probably Heracles in *Pirithous* (Welcker, Wilamowitz) or *Eurystheus* (Wagner: cf. F 371).

937

Don't kill me: it's unlawful to kill a suppliant![1]

[1] F 937 and 938, quoted adjacently by Lucian, have been attributed to Alexander in the altar scene of *Alexander* (cf. F 62i) by Snell and Hartung respectively. The attributions are plausible but far from certain.

938

So now you're going to kill me on account of my words?[1]

[1] See on F 937 above.

939

You total villains, earthbound offspring of earth![1]

[1] Presumably the Titans (cf. [Aeschylus], *Prometheus Bound* 205), although Lucian's Zeus is complaining about philosophers who doubt the existence of the gods and thus (cf. 21.3) resemble the rebellious Giants and Titans. It is hard to identify a suitable Euripidean context, if indeed this verse is rightly ascribed to Euripides.

940

What is it? You'll be telling it to a band of friends.

940a (= fr. adesp. 293 N)

You don't know; if you did, you'd certainly be wailing loudly.

EURIPIDES

941

ὁρᾷς τὸν ὑψοῦ τόνδ' ἄπειρον αἰθέρα
καὶ γῆν πέριξ ἔχονθ' ὑγραῖς ἐν ἀγκάλαις;
τοῦτον νόμιζε Ζῆνα, τόνδ' ἡγοῦ θεόν.

Lucian 21.41; Stobaeus 1.1.2; Heraclitus, *Homeric Allegories* 23.7; Achilles, *Commentary on Aratus'* Phaenomena, p. 82 Maass; Athenagoras, *Plea for Christianity* 5.1; Clement of Alexandria, *Miscellanies* 5.14.114.1; Probus on Virgil, *Eclogues* 6.31. Partial citations elsewhere. Cicero translates the whole fragment, *On the Nature of the Gods* 2.65.

**941a

ὅμως τἀληθὲς οὐ προδώσομεν
εἴξαντες ὄκνῳ.

Lucian 49.31

(942 N = *Hypsipyle* F 765c)

942a

Ἀθάναν αὐτὴν παρὰ το 'ἀθάνατον' Εὐριπίδης καλεῖ.

John Lydus, *On Months* 4.22

(943 N = 1111a below)

944

καὶ Γαῖα μῆτερ· Ἑστίαν δέ σ' οἱ σοφοὶ
βροτῶν καλοῦσιν ἡμένην ἐν αἰθέρι.

Macrobius, *Saturnalia* 1.23.8, and in part (Ἑστίαν—βροτῶν νομίζουσιν) Anatolius, *On the First Ten Numbers* p. 30 Heiberg

941

You see this boundless aether high above, holding the earth about in its moist embrace? Consider this to be Zeus, think of this as god![1]

[1] Attributed to *Thyestes* by Valckenaer and others since both Cicero and Probus compare it with Ennius, *Thyestes* fr. 153 Jocelyn (*aspice hoc sublime candens, quem uocant omnes Iouem*, 'Look upon this shining heaven, which all call Jove'); but the similarity is not compelling. For the philosophical idea of the moist aether enveloping and supporting the Earth cf. *Trojan Women* 884, F 919, F 944; Egli 84–6.

**941a

Yet we shall not give in to fear and betray the truth.

(942 N = *Hypsipyle* F 765c)

942a

Euripides calls her 'Athana' by association with *athanaton* ('immortal').[1]

[1] For names explained by etymologies cf. *Alexander* F 42d with note.

(943 N = 1111a below)

944

. . . and mother Earth, whom the wise amongst men call Hestia, as 'seated' in the aether.[1]

[1] Another etymology (see on F 942a), relating the name Hestia to the verb *hēsthai*, 'to be seated'. Several such etymologies of her name can be found; cf. also Plato, *Cratylus* 401b–d. The fragment is quoted to exemplify the idea of Hestia as the immobile centre or 'hearth' of the cosmos (hence her identification with Gaia/Earth). Anatolius suggests the idea was widespread in early

(944a N–Sn = Chaeremon, *TrGF* 1, 71 F 42)

945

ἀεί τι καινὸν ἡμέρα παιδεύεται.

Orion 8.1 Haffner

946

εὖ ἴσθ᾿, ὅταν τις εὐσεβῶν θύῃ θεοῖς,
κἂν μικρὰ θύῃ, τυγχάνει σωτηρίας.

Orion, Euripidean Appendix 2 Haffner

(947 N = *Aeolus* F 13a)

948

θεοὺς ἀρέσκου· πᾶν γὰρ ἐκ θεῶν τέλος.

Orion, Euripidean Appendix 6 Haffner

(949 N = 852a above)

950

ὡς ἡδὺ πατέρα παισὶν ἤπιον κυρεῖν
καὶ παῖδας εἶναι πατρὶ μὴ στυγουμένους.

Orion, Euripidean Appendix 13 Haffner

Greek philosophy, and that Euripides derived it from Anaxagoras (= 59 B 20b DK; cf. Archelaus 60 B 1a DK). For the identification with Gaia cf. Sophocles F 615. Pythagoreans placed a fire (rather than Earth) at the centre of the cosmos, and called this its 'hearth' (Philolaus 44 A 17 and B 7 DK). See also F 941 above with note.

(944a N–Sn = Chaeremon, *TrGF* 1, 71 F 42)

945

A day always teaches something new.

946

Be assured, whenever someone sacrifices piously to the gods, even if the sacrifice is small, he gets protection.

(947 N = *Aeolus* F 13a)

948

Placate the gods, for every fulfilment comes from them.

(949 N = 852a above)

950

How pleasing it is for children to have a kind father, and for a father not to find his children hateful.

EURIPIDES

951

ἢν οἱ τεκόντες τοῦτο γιγνώσκωσ' ὅτι
νέοι ποτ' ἦσαν, ἠπίως τὴν τῶν τέκνων
οἴσουσι Κύπριν, ὄντες οὐ σκαιοὶ φύσιν.

Orion, Euripidean Appendix 14 Haffner

952

ὅστις πατὴρ πρὸς παῖδας ἐκβαίνει πικρός,
τὸ γῆρας οὗτος τερματίζεται βαρύ.

Orion, Euripidean Appendix 15 Haffner

(953 N = Com. adesp. F 1000 *PCG*)

**953a

*A single badly damaged leaf with a scholarly commentary
on a play, almost certainly Euripidean: lines 1–13 appear
to evaluate its composition; then lines 14–18 are the begin-
nings of five verses which may not be continuous and are
perhaps a sample of its gnomic content.*

πρόσαντες οὐδέν ἐ[στι
15 ἄπαντα δ' αυτη κα[
τὸ μὲν πονηρὸν η[
κακοὺς κολάζειν [
γ]έλωτα κινεῖν .[
traces of one more line

P. Amherst 2.17; see *TrGF* 5.940–1 and especially W. Luppe,
Anagennesis 2 (1982), 245–61 for a fuller description (including
255–7 on attributions).

951

If parents recognize that they were young once, they will bear their children's love affairs mildly, for they are not naturally stupid.[1]

[1] For the sentiment cf. *Dictys* F 339.

952

A father who turns out sour towards his children makes a burdensome old age his end.

(953 N = Com. Adesp. F 1000 *PCG*)

**953a

Beginnings of five verses quoted in a scholarly commentary, perhaps not continuous:
Nothing (is) adverse[1] . . . and everything . . . (for her; *or* and she . . . everything) . . . villainy . . . to punish base men[2] . . .   15
to provoke laughter(?)[3] . . .

[1] Probably an opening line; cf. *Orestes* 1 'There is almost nothing so terrible . . . ', *Stheneboea* F 661.1.   [2] These words happen to begin *Sciron* F 678.2, so that for a time this line was attributed to that play.   [3] 'laughter' is not securely read.

953b

Part of a prologue speech from the same collection as Alcmene F *87b,* Archelaus F 228a *and* Hypsipyle F 752a: *remains of seven lines*

ὡς μὴ μὲν ἡμῖν τοῦδε ....[
πα[ῖ]δες τὸ λῶστον· εἰ δὲ .[
10 κα.....ει σαφῶς π......[...].ν τόδε,
ἀλλ᾽ οὐκ ἐάσει μ᾽, ὡς ἔοικ.[.]..[...]νος
παισὶν συνελθεῖν καὶ λογ..[...]ων.....ν:
'κακῶς ὄλοιο, πρίν ποτ᾽ εἰς ἐμοὺ[ς δό]μους
ἐλθεῖν πατρῳο[.]σ.....[....]...λιπών,
15 ὡς ἐν δόμοις τ᾽ ὀχληρὰ ...[....].. δίδως
στένων, δακρύων καὶ κατο[ικτίρ]ων τύχας.'
remains of three more lines

P. Hamburg 119 col. ii, ed. E. Siegmann (1954); vv. 8–19 re-ed. Austin, *NFE* 84

8 reading of μὴ and articulation of ὡς μὴ μὲν are uncertain 12 λόγων [φίλ]ων τυχεῖν Siegmann 14 πατρῴο[υ]ς Siegmann: πατρῴο[ν] Mette 15 καὶ [ἔξωθ]εν Siegmann: καὶ [ἐν πόλ]ει Mette

**953c

From near the start of possibly a complete play text (see opposite):

953b

Part of a prologue speech, possibly Thyestes speaking about Atreus in Thyestes, *if that play concerned the famous banquet (see Introduction there):*

. . . *(remains of seven lines)* . . . so that this man's(?) sons may not . . . what is best for us/me.[1] But if . . . this . . . , but   10
. . . (he) will not allow me, it seems, to meet with (his?) sons and . . . :[2] 'May you perish miserably, before you ever come into my ancestral(?)[3] home . . . leaving . . . , for you are causing trouble in the house and (abroad, *or* in the city?),   15
moaning, weeping and lamenting your misfortunes' . . . *(remains of three more lines)* . . .

[1] Or possibly '. . . so that my sons may not . . . what is best from this man'.   [2] Siegmann's tentative reading gives 'and to enjoy friendly words (from them)'; but it seems more likely that the phrase introduced a hostile direct address in vv. 13–16 (the double colon at the end of v. 12 probably indicates this).   [3] This makes the Greek adjective plural (Siegmann). Mette's singular links it with a missing following word, 'leaving your ancestral . . .'

**953c

These 3rd c. B.C. papyrus fragments have been identified by various scholars as coinciding with, or similar in content to, the parodos and first episode of Euripides' Heracles. *They seem to represent an alternative version of this play (see Luppe cited on p. 536). Fr. 1 has the ending of a prologue scene and a chorus entry in a form quite different from the extant text; frs. 4, 3, 7 and 2 col. i correspond closely to the extant* Heracles *136–70 (end of parodos, Lycus' entry and speech, first line of Amphitryon's reply); frs. 6, 5 and 2 col. ii seem to continue Amphitryon's reply in an alternative form, but fr. 2 col. ii ends with the extant first*

EURIPIDES

Col. 1

fr. 1

        ]ερεις γνώρισμα κα.[
        ]ει σαφῆ δερκόμεθα.[
        ]...βεις σπουδῇ γε λα[

                ⟨ΧΟΡΟΣ⟩
        ]. πολλοῖς ἄλγεσιν ἤδη τ..[

5   ]υ πέμψαντας ταῖσδ᾽ ἐπι..[
        ]. καὶ ἰσήλικ᾽ ἐμοὶ χρόνον [
        ]ντες π[ο]λιοὶ πολιῷ φω[
        ].. γηραιοῦ βήματος ὀρ[μη
        remains of 22 more lines

1 φ]έρεις Turner   2 ἀλλ᾽] εἰ (e.g.) Kannicht
3 πεδο]στιβεῖς (e.g.) Kannicht

Col. 2
frs. 3, 4, 7: parts of *Heracles* 136–43, 146–60 and 160–5
with minor variants

Col. 3
fr. 2 col. i: ends of *Heracles* 167–70 with minor variants
fr. 6: parts of nine lines, very damaged; vv. 5–6 and 8 corre-
spond to *Heracles* 183–4 and 186 but the rest differ from
the adjacent lines.

fr. 5   *traces of one line*
        ἐλ]άσσονός τι τ[
            ] Κάδμου γα[ῖα
        τοῖς] Ἡρακλείοις παρα[

*line of Lycus' response. Each column had about 30 lines
(cf. fr. 1), so Amphitryon's speech here had only about 32
lines rather than the 66 of the extant text. Luppe maintains
that this alternative version was composed by Euripides
himself and may even have preceded the extant version. It
is at least as likely that it is an adaptation made for a later
production.*

Col. 1: . . . (you bear?) a mark of recognition . . . (but if?) we
see clearly . . . (on foot?) in haste . . .

<CHORUS>
. . . with many griefs already . . . having sent *(acc.)* (upon?)   5
these . . . . . . and having . . . *(nom.)* a time equal to my age
. . . gray-haired (with?) gray . . . the pace of my aged foot . . .
(remains of 22 more lines) . . .

Cols. 2–4: ~ Heracles *136–70 (see above), then parts of
Amphitryon's speech in alternative form including:*

fr. 5: . . . something of lesser . . . (O all you land?) of Cadmus
. . . (come, stand by the offspring?) of Heracles . . . him . . .
terrible (things?) . . .

EURIPIDES

5   ] τ᾽ ἐκεῖνον δειν[
    traces of one more line

        3 ὦ πᾶσα] Kannicht (cf. *Heracles* 217)   4 παρα[γενοῦ
    βλαστήμασι (e.g.) Kannicht (cf. *Heracles* 219)

    Col. 4
fr. 2   traces of one line
col. ii θαυμαστ[
    δράσειεν οὗτος [
    κενὴν δ᾽ ἅμιλλαν [
5   ..] την τίθεσθαι μ[

            ⟨ΛΥΚΟΣ⟩
    σὺ μὲν λ]έγ᾽ ἡμᾶς οἷ[ς πεπύργωσαι λόγοις

        6 = *Heracles* 238

    P. Hibeh 179, ed. E. Turner (1955), re-ed. R. Kannicht, *ZPE*
    21 (1976), 117–33; see also W. Luppe, *ZPE* 95 (1993), 59–64
    (with summary of preceding discussions); R. Janko, *ZPE* 136
    (2001), 1–6

            **953d
    Dialogue lines perhaps from a scene of Cresphontes *(see
    opposite):*

fr. 2 col. ii: . . . amazing (things) . . . (would?) this man do . . . ,
and . . . to set up a vain contest . . .

<LYCUS>
Abuse me, for your part, with these words with which you
have buttressed yourself . . . (= *Heracles* 238)

**953d

The style of this Hellenistic papyrus text suggests Euripi-
des (or possibly Sophocles) as author. Its first editor F. Mal-
tomini suggests the play may be Cresphontes *where, in*
Hyginus' summary of the story (test. iia), after Cresphon-
tes returned in disguise from Aetolia claiming the reward
offered by Polyphontes for his own murder, 'an old man
who had been a messenger between mother and son came
to Merope weeping and saying he was not with the family
friend and had disappeared'. In col. 1 the references to a
'reward', a 'token', and 'Aetolia' are consistent with this
possibility, as are the appearance of a grieving mother (11–
14) and her son's old tutor (16), with whom she presumably
conducts the dialogue in col. 2. But identification and re-
construction remain problematic, especially since col. 1
may be incomplete and changes of speaker are unclear in
both col. 1 and col. 2 (where paragraphi indicating
changes may have been lost at vv. 22, 23, 26). Maltomini
suggests we have Polyphontes responding cautiously to
Cresphontes' demand for the reward (1–10), then after
their exit Merope reacting despairingly to the news of her
son's death (11–14), then the tutor delivering his puzzling
news to Merope (15–33); but he admits that this makes for
a rather compressed dramatic development. An alternative
might be that Cresphontes delivered his false news first to
Merope (though Hyginus' summary does not reflect this)

EURIPIDES

col. 1

] πιστόν, εἴ τίς ἐστι σοι

traces of one line

]‸ς μισθὸν ο‸‸ρ‸[

σύ]μβολον κ‸‸‸‸‸‸

remains of three lines

]‸νον εἰς Αἰτωλίαν

]ε πρὸς δόμους ἰών

10

]‸δ᾽ ἐπ᾽ ἐξόδοις ἐμαῖς

τῆ]ιδ᾽ ἐν ἡμέρᾳ

]ς ἀφιγμένη

θ]άνατος, ὦ τάλαιν[᾽ ἐγώ

κ]ακὸν τόδ᾽ οὐ κακόν

15

]‸ς μεμνήμεθα

]‸‸ ἐμοῦ παιδὸς τροφόν

trace of one more line

possibly some lines lost before col. 2

col. 2   *Sixteen line-beginnings, some with one or two words pre-
served (and speaker changes marked in 29–32), including:*

18 ὦ πρέσβ[υ   20 ζῶντα   21 οὐκ οἶδα

25 λάθρᾳ   27 ἀπὼν 28 ἧκεν   29 — πάντας

30 — κοὐκ ειδ‸[31 — θαυμάστα   32 — αἰαῖ

P. Munich 340, ed. F. Maltomini (1986)

and that vv. 1–10 represent the end of such a scene. An early encounter between Merope and her long-lost and as yet unrecognized son would be in keeping with a plot of this kind (cf. Electra, Iphigenia in Tauris, Ion, Antiope, Hypsipyle).

col. 1: . . . loyal, if there is anyone (loyal) to you . . . *(one line)* . . . reward . . . token(?) . . . *(three lines)* . . . into Aetolia . . . going *(masc.)* to the house . . . on my departure . . . on this   10
day . . . having arrived *(fem.)* . . . death, wretched that I am . . . this evil (that is?) not evil . . . we/I remember . . . . . . my   15
son's tutor(?) . . . *(trace of one more line, and possibly some lines lost before col. 2)*

col. 2: Old man, . . . living *(masc.)* . . . I do not know . . .   21
secretly . . . being absent *(masc.)* . . . has come . . . — All . . .   29
— And . . . (did?) not (see?) . . . — Amazing things . . .   32
— Alas . . .

**953e

Perhaps from an anthology of dramatic scenes or speeches:

]ν ἐλευ[θ]εροι[

]μα τοῦ νεανίου

]αντα σὺν κείνῳ πόνους

]ν δοῦλον ἐν δόμοις ἔχειν

5   ]ν· οἱ δὲ σοῦ κακίονες

] καὶ κρατοῦσι δωμάτων

]σι· σὺ δὲ τί προσδοκῶν ποτε

]νει· μὴ μεθῇ σ' ἐλεύθερον

π]ολλάκις δὲ νουθετεῖ

10   ] οἴκοισι πολ[ε]μιώτατος

ἐγώ σ' ἔθηκα] δοῦλον ὄντ' ἐλεύθερον

].…αν ἢ γένοιτ' ἔτι

ε]ὑμαρῶς ἐλεύθερον

]…[ ]..[ ].ργοις· κέαρ

15   εὖ λέ]γων οὐ παύομαι

].[ ]της πατὴρ μὲν οὖν

]μ' ἔδωκας εἰς δόμους

] γιγνώσκεις ἀνήρ

].α[λ]λάξειέ τις

20   ἐλε]ύθερον

P. Oxy. 3215 fr. 1, ed. E. Lobel (1977), with damaged or missing brief marginal 'scholia' (see on 15); v. 11 (= fr. adesp. 74 N): Aristotle, *Sophistic Refutations* 166a35 and derivatives, identified here by Mette. Vocabulary, style and subject are characteristically Euripidean, and fr. 2 of the papyrus has *Hecuba* 223–8.

15 εὖ λέ]γων restored by Kannicht from a marginal gloss εὐλογῶν   παύ‹σ›ομαι Kannicht

**953e

Perhaps from an anthology of dramatic scenes or speeches:
. . . free . . . of the young man . . . hardships with him . . . to
have a slave in the house . . . Those worse than you . . . and   5
control houses . . . Whatever are you expecting, yourself . . .
not to let you go free . . . he frequently advises . . . most hos-
tile to the house . . . . . . I set you free when a slave . . . or   10
might still be . . . free easily . . . (your?) heart . . . I do not
stop praising . . . as a father however (?) . . . you gave me to   15
the house . . . you know as a man (?) . . . someone might (*or*
would) exchange . . . free . . .[1]

[1] It is impossible to establish clearly the relationship of the
persons mentioned (there may be dialogue between them from v.
11 onward). The issues of good and bad slaves and masters are
common in Euripides, e.g. *Alexander* F 48–51, *Antiope* F 216–8;
with the thought in vv. 5–6 cf. *Melanippe* F 495.40–3 with our
note. In v. 15 Kannicht proposes 'I will not stop . . .', for the future
tense in such expressions is common in Euripides while the pres-
ent would be unique. Assigned by some to either of the *Alcmeons*
(cf. F 86.6).

EURIPIDES

(**953f: see *Hippolytus Veiled*, after F 446)

**953m

*From an anthology of tragic lyrics, P. Strasbourg WG 306
cols. iii.26–36 and iv (both badly damaged) together with
some very small fragments which we mostly omit. Each
line had originally about 70 letters; the lyrics were written
continuously like prose, but with occasional signs for ends
of metrical units, sentences and/or voice-parts (see vv. 29,
42 in col. iv; for a full presentation of this very problematic
text see M. Fassino, ZPE 127 [1999], 1–46, esp. 26–44, a
large-scale re-edition of the papyrus, or TrGF 5.952–5). P.
Strasb. WG 305 col. ii and 306 col. iii.1–25 have Medea
841–65 and 1251–92, WG 307 has Phoenissae 1499–1581
and 1710–36: this helps confirm the impression from the
lyric style that our fragment is Euripidean; Ino has been
strongly suggested by Fassino 40–4.*

col. iii (end): *ends of vv. 1–10, including* 1].ρα πολλὰ
τίκτει *and* 10 σω]τῆρι φίλων

col. iv (*complete: at the ends vv. 11–19 lack about 40 let-
ters, 20–26 an undetermined number of letters, 27–46
about 25–30 letters*):

ἦλθες ἰὼ τάλαιν᾽ ἔβας ἵνα τῶν προτ[
..[...]σα λιμένας· τάδε σοι μεγάλων δι[
.[c. 7 letters].τος δόμοισι πελάζει ....[
τάλαιν᾽ ἄφρον γύναι· ἀπὸ μὲν ὀμμ[άτων
15 ἐκ δὲ λευκῶν χερῶν δυσέκνιπτον αἶμ[α

542

(**953f: see *Hippolytus Veiled*, after F 446)

**953m

*From an anthology of tragic lyrics. In the long lyric se-
quence in col. iv three voices seem to be singing: a chorus
(11) perhaps as far as 28; then a woman and mother (ad-
dressed in 11, 14 etc.) perhaps from 28 to 46; lastly, her
husband (40) who may be 'the king'. The woman appears to
have threatened to kill her children (23–4?), and then to
have done so (36–7); her husband arrives too late (46). Sev-
eral words are lost at the end of every line in col. iv, so it is
impossible to identify the structure of the exchange or the
metres; but the commonest rhythm, dochmiac, as usual
conveys extreme alarm and passion. Possibly from* Ino *(see
opposite).*

col. iii (end): . . . generates many . . . *(8 lines)* . . . saviour(?)
of friends . . . (10)

col. iv: You went, O you poor woman, you went away where
. . . of those before(?) [   ] a haven. This (is) for you . . . of
great [   ] is approaching the house [   ] Poor (*or* cruel),
foolish woman! . . . from (your?) eyes [   ] and blood(?)
hard to wash away from white arms (15) [   ] What superi-

---

10 σω]τῆρι Diggle   12 stop after λιμένας editors

τίς ἂν ὑπερβολὰ λόγων ἐκπίθοι τα[.].[
ἰαλέμων γὰρ οὔπω γέμει στέγος κα[
κυκλώσεταί σφε πολυπόνων [.]...[
μένους, ὀλομένα δ᾽ αυτ...[
20 συμμαχων γάμους δυσ[......]οι.[c. 9 letters].κοπαδ[
   c. 7 letters]α.[.]..[   ].....(.)[.....].π[.]ονους..[
    c. 24 letters   ]αιωντ[.].[..]λασμω[
φρενὶ μ[ά]ργῳ [   ]οντατ[.]...ενομονα[
τὸν αὑτᾶς γόνον [   ].ιον[[.]]κτ.[ ].ε..(.)εφη[
25 τ᾽ ἄλλος δαίμων [   ]ων λα[.....]..[
πάλαι τὸ Κάδμ[.].[   ].οιστικ.[..]..ποιστικ.[
των δάκρυ᾽ α...[.....].[.]...ετο ἄρ᾽ οὔτε πόλις οὔτε
   δωμ[α
χθονὸς θεοῖσι μῖσος [....(.)]..η..πόλει ἐξενεγκεῖν
   ἄφθονα ..[
αἴτιος[ ]—[   ]μοι μοι φυγᾷ φυγᾷ φυγᾷ βοασο[
30   ]νον χθονός τ᾽ Ἀχαιῶν· ἰὼ Ζεῦ τε.[
...]ἰὼ δάϊο[ι   ] τέκνου κακιστα ἐξάγιστον τύμ[βον
αἱματοσταγ[δώμασι]ν ἐν πατρῴοισιν δεδειγμένον
   .(.)[
φανερὸν ὄμμα δυσπ[ρόσ]οπτον φίλοις ἐμοί τε
   ταλαίνα .[
δεον ἔσχατον πενθῶ[ν].[.] ὦ [π]υροθήκτων ἐγχέων
πλ[αγαί c. 24 letters κά-
35 ματοι δυσώνυμοι πα[c. 8 letters]μοισι μόχθοις
ασεπαι.[

ority in words would convince [   ] For the house is not yet
full of laments [   ] of very harsh . . . will encircle it [   ] (of
passion?) . . . and . . . accursed (*probably* 'you, the accursed
woman')[1] [   ] (disastrous)[2] union (of allies?) [   ] (20)
[(21, 22)   ] with frenzied mind [   ] her (*or* your) own
child [   ] and another deity (*or* destiny) [   ] (25) Anciently
the . . . of Cadmus [   ] tears . . . neither city nor house [   ] a
detestation to the land's gods . . . to bring unenviable (*or*
plentiful) . . . to the city [   ] responsible . . . (*new speaker?*)
. . . (Oh?) me, me . . . cry out . . . in flight, in flight, in flight[3]
[   ] . . . (of?) the land of the Achaeans. O Zeus [   ] (30) O
(my) enemies! . . . my child's accursed tomb most evilly [   ]
dripping with blood . . . displayed (in) my ancestral (home)
[   ] a face clear and painful to see for my dear ones and for
my poor self [   ] . . .[4] the worst of sorrows . . . O (the
strike?) of fire-sharpened spears [   ] exertions ill-omened
. . . by efforts [   ] (35) . . . to have done, you did:[5] poor . . . of

---

[1] 'accursed': 'destroyed' is possible, with no certain refer-
ence.   [2] Kannicht's supplement.   [3] The triple repeti-
tion of 'in flight' is without sure parallel; it may be a copyist's error.
[4] The beginning of v. 34 is not yet understood; 'it being neces-
sary' was hazarded by Diggle.   [5] e.g. '(what you should not)
have done, you did', Fassino.

---

17 γέμει Diggle: γεμοι P. Strasb.   19 μένους translated,
but -μένους possible   ὀλομένα translated, but ὀλόμενα possi-
ble   20 δυσ[γάμους Kannicht   24 αὐτᾶς translated,
but αὐτᾶς possible   31 τύμ[βον Lewis   32 δώμασι]ν
ἐν Schadewaldt, Fassino   34 δέον (e.g.) Diggle   πενθῶ[ν and
ὦ (Kannicht) [π]υροθήκτων Fassino   πλ[αγαί editors
34–5 κά]ματοι Diggle   35 e.g. ἅ σ' οὐ χρῆν Fassino

ῥέξαι ἔρεξας· τάλαινα [.....]. τεκέων κτενεῖς σφιν [
τέκνων σὰν γονάν· ὢ λεύ[σιμα] λεύσιμα τοῦδε
    παιδὸς [
μέλη· τί φράσω; τί φῶ; τί β[οάσω κ]ακόν; ὢ τάλας
    τοδε [
ἀχήσω· βέβακέ μοι χερνίβ[ων χάρις] ἄθεος οἴχεται
    πόλις α[
40 ζει πτήξει τὰς ἐμὰς π.[....(.)]να βασιλεὺς
        εὐμέλαθρο[ς
    θρον ἐμὸν ἄποτμον ..[....(.)].ν ἀβίοτον ἀνέρα νυν.[
    οὐχ ὅσιον εἴσεται σφαλεντε.[..(.)]. — τόδ' αὖ τόδ'
        αὖ κα[κὸν
    ἀοίδιμον πετομένα ...[..(.)] ὀλοφύρομαι τ.[..].κ.[
    τὰ μὲν ἐνθάδ' ἐρῶ, τὰ δὲ .[...(.) ἄ]λγε' ἀλγέων
        διάδ[οχ]α [
45 χρυσέων τ' ἄστρων πη[.....(.)] λάβοιμι πυρσὸν
        ...[
    ποτὶ τὸν αἰθέ[ρα ...]π [.....]η φιλίας ἀλόχου
        θάνοιμι [

a further scrap (fr. aa in TrGF) *has 5 lines including*
    4 ὀψόμεθα, 5 -φθόγγος

37 λε[ύσιμα] Fassino   38 μέλη or -μέλῆ   β[οάσω
κ]ακόν Diggle   39 χερνίβ[ων χάρις] Kannicht
41].ν ἀβίοτον editors (or].να βίοτον)   42 σφαλεντε. not
convincingly interpreted   44 ἐρῶ Diggle (ερω insecure):
perhaps ὀρῶ Collard

(?) your children . . . will you kill . . . for(?) them [   ] the children you bore? Oh, (to be punished) by stoning, by stoning[6] . . . this boy's [   ] (limbs?). What am I to think? What am I to say? What evil (am I to cry out)? O the poor child, . . . this [   ] I shall cry aloud . . . favour for my rites is lost! The city is gone, abandoned by the gods[7] [   ] will crouch (at?) my . . . the king in his fine palace [   ] (40) my ill-fated, unlivable . . . husband [   ] He will not know of impious . . . (brought low?). *(new speaker?)* Here is more evil, more [   ] for song in my flight . . . I wail [   ] I shall speak[8] of what is here, and . . . the pain that succeeds pain [   ] I wish I might seize . . . blazing . . . of golden stars [   ] (45) to the sky[9] . . . May I die . . . (of *or* for?) my dear wife . . .

(fr. aa) . . . we shall see (4) . . . -voiced (5)

6 Public execution for shedding kindred blood and so endangering the public good: cf. e.g. *Orestes* 14.   7 Metre suggests this phrasing rather than 'favour for my rites is lost, abandoned by the gods'.   8 Or perhaps 'I see . . .'   9 A conventional tragic wish to escape catastrophe through miraculous ascent of the heaven, e.g. *Phaethon* 270–2.

EURIPIDES

954

Et Euripides: Qui incontinentes sunt, et redundat in eis ma-
lum inimicitiae et iniustitiae, mali sunt; in quibus autem op-
posita praeualent, uirtute praediti. In aliis uero ita quasi ae-
qualis sit commixtio, ita ut nulli sint qui omnia mala habeant
sine ullo bono.

Philo, *Questions and Answers on* Genesis, IV.202 ed. J. B.
Aucher (1826) in Latin translation from Armenian (Philo's Greek
text does not survive): see R. Marcus, *Philo. Supplement* I (Loeb
Classical Library, 1953), 497–8; R. Kannicht, *TrGF* 5.956; F.
Jouan in ed. Budé VIII.4.556.

**954a

⟨ΧΟΡΟΣ⟩
πρὸς σὲ πελάζω
τὸν ὀπισθοβάτην πόδα γηροκομῶν.

Philodemus, *On Poems*, P. Herc. 1081a fr. 16 (R. Janko, *Philo-
demus on Poems* I [2000] 442–3, fr. 212)

955c
Ἄφιδνε, γαίας υἱὲ τῆς ἀμήτορος

Photius α 1196 Theodoridis

955d
ὡς ἀμφιπρύμνω δύο μ᾽ ἐλέγχετον λόγω.

Photius α 1361 Theodoridis

954

And Euripides (says): Those who are without self-control, and in whom the evil of enmity and injustice overflows, are evil, while those in whom the opposites prevail are imbued with virtue. In others, however, there is a mixture such that it nears equality, with the result that there are none who are completely evil without any good in them.

**954a

⟨CHORUS⟩

I approach you, favouring a dragging foot in my old age.[1]

[1] From an anapaestic entry 'march' by an elderly chorus, cf. *Cresphontes* F 448a.73–6 and F 953c.4–8.

955c

You, Aphidnus, son of the motherless earth . . .[1]

[1] The ancestor of the Attic deme Aphidna. Theseus entrusted Helen to his care when he abducted her from Sparta; the fragment may relate to this episode, or to a later one in which Aphidnus protected Helen's twin brothers Castor and Pollux. Earth is the mother of all life (cf. *Chrysippus* F 839.3–7 with note) and as the oldest of divine powers thus herself motherless.

955d

Two arguments refute me fore and aft![1]

[1] I.e. on two counts simultaneously; the metaphor is from a boat steerable from both ends, easily reversible.

EURIPIDES

(955e N–Sn = 1096a)

(955f N–Sn = *Andromache* 1249)

**955h
ἄννδρα δ' ᾠκηκὼς ἄναξ
κριωπὸς Ἄμμων δάπεδα θεσπίζει τάδε.

Photius α 2153 Theodoridis

(955i N–Sn = 1097b)

956
πραγμάτων ἄλλων ποτὲ συμπεσόντων,
εὔξῃ τοιοῦτον ἄνδρα σοι παρεστάναι.

Plato, *Letters* 1.309d

957
μικρὸν φρονεῖν χρὴ τὸν κακῶς πεπραγότα.

Plutarch, *Moralia* 28c; Patmos Florilegium 3 Livrea

958
τίς δ' ἔστι δοῦλος τοῦ θανεῖν ἄφροντις ὤν;

Plutarch, *Moralia* 34b, 106d and other sources, esp. Cicero, *Letters to Atticus* 9.2a.2

959
⟨ΧΟΡΟΣ⟩
ἐγὼ δ' οὐδὲν πρεσβύτερον
νομίζω τᾶς σωφροσύνας,
ἐπεὶ τοῖς ἀγαθοῖς ἀεὶ ξύνεστι.

(955e N–Sn = 1096a)

(955f N–Sn = *Andromache* 1249)

**955h

The lord with a ram's face, Ammon, who inhabits waterless plains, makes this prophecy.[1]

[1] The ram-faced Egyptian god Ammon (Herodotus 2.42.3–6) doubled as 'Zeus' in his famous desert oracle (*Alcestis* 115–16, *Electra* 734–5). The fragment may come from either prologue or exodos of a play set in mythic 'Africa'; *Andromeda, Busiris, Phaethon* have been suggested.

(955i N–Sn = 1097b)

956

Should other circumstances ever befall you,

you will pray for such a man to stand by you.

957

The man who has come off badly must be humble-minded.[1]

[1] Cf. *Alcmeon* F 81 with note.

958

Who is a slave if he does not worry about death?

959

〈CHORUS〉

I myself think nothing more important then moderation, since it is always associated with good men.

Plutarch, *Moralia* 36c; Stobaeus 3.3.29. Cf. F 960 and note.

EURIPIDES

960

⟨ΧΟΡΟΣ⟩

traces at line-end

δρά[σαν]τ'· ἔνι γὰ[ρ] π[ό]νος· ἀλλ'
ὅτ[ῳ] πάρεστιν τὸ πονεῖν
τῶν τ' ἀγαθῶν κεκλῆσθαι
5 φίλος ὢν ἐμ[ὸ]ς λεγέσθω[·]
τί μάταν βροτοὶ δ[ὲ] πολλ[ὰ
πέπασθε πλούτῳ τε δοκεῖτ'
ἀρετὰν κατεργάσεσθαι;
τί] δ', εἴ τιν' Αἴτν[α]ς ⟨τε⟩ πάγον
10 Π[αρ]ίαν τε πέτραν
χρυσήλατον ἐν θαλάμοις ἔχοιτε
πασάμενοι πατρώ[ι]οις·
οὔ τοι τ[ό] τε μὴ πεφυ[κὸς

* * *

ἐν ἐσθλοῖς δὲ καθήσεσθ' ἄνολβοι.

vv. 1–13: Satyrus, *Life of Euripides*, P. Oxy. 1176 fr. 38 col.ii;
vv. 6–8 and 14: Plutarch, *Moralia* 36c, directly after F 959

6–8 τιμὰν τὰν τέτασθε πλούτῳ δ' ἀρετὰν κατεργασάσθω
(-άσασθαι eds.) δοκεῖτ' Plut., continuing directly into 14
9–10 τιν' ... Π[αρ]ίαν ed. pr.; τὸν ... Π[ιερ]ίαν Wilamowitz
13 P. Oxy. col.ii breaks off here; the number of missing lines is
unknown.

961

φεῦ, τοῖσι γενναίοισιν ὡς ἅπαν καλόν.

Plutarch, *Moralia* 84f and *Life of Pompey* 73.7

552

960

⟨CHORUS⟩

. . . doing (it); for there is work involved. But the man who
can work hard and be named amongst good men, let him
be called friend of mine! Why though, you mortal men,   5
have you acquired many things in vain, and why do you
think that with wealth you will achieve virtue? And what if
you were to acquire and keep in your ancestral halls some
hard mass from Etna and Parian marble worked round   10
with gold?[1] I tell you, what is not natural (will) not . . . (*text
missing*) . . . but without prosperity you will sit among good
men.

[1] The question appears to be rhetorical: 'even were you to
possess such valuable natural substances, what claim to virtue
would you or could you make?' In vv. 9–10 Wilamowitz's conjec-
ture creates allusion to such substances from two 'divine' moun-
tains, Etna (Hephaestus) and Olympus (Pieria, home of all the
gods). The differences in Plutarch's text suggest adaptation. The
lyric metre is mainly choriambic.

961

Ah, yes! Everything is good in the eyes of honourable
men.[1]

[1] Or perhaps 'Everything that honourable men do is fine'. The
quotation may be deliberately incomplete. In *Moralia* Plutarch
applies it to identifying virtue generally, in the *Life* to finding it in
servants and service.

962

. . . ἀλλ᾽ ἐπ᾽ ἄλλῃ φάρμακον κεῖται νόσῳ·
λυπουμένῳ μὲν μῦθος εὐμενὴς φίλων,
ἄγαν δὲ μωραίνοντι νουθετήματα.

Plutarch, Moralia 102b; vv. 2–3: Moralia 69d and Sotio in
Stobaeus 4.48.30

1 ⟨ἀλλ᾽⟩ ἄλλ᾽ etc. Gataker

963

μηδ᾽ εὐτύχημα μηδὲν ὧδ᾽ ἔστω μέγα,
ὅ σ᾽ ἐξεπαρεῖ μεῖζον ἢ χρεὼν φρονεῖν,
μηδ᾽ ἤν τι συμβῇ δυσχερές, δουλοῦ πάλιν·
ἀλλ᾽ αὐτὸς αἰεὶ μίμνε τὴν σαυτοῦ φύσιν
5 σῴζων βεβαίως ὥστε χρυσὸς ἐν πυρί.

[Plutarch], Moralia 102e, briefly reflected in Libanius, Letters
557.5

964

ΘΗΣΕΥΣ

ἐγὼ δὲ ⟨   ⟩ παρὰ σοφοῦ τινος μαθὼν
εἰς φροντίδας νοῦν συμφοράς τ᾽ ἐβαλλόμην,
φυγάς τ᾽ ἐμαυτῷ προστιθεὶς πάτρας ἐμῆς
θανάτους τ᾽ ἀώρους καὶ κακῶν ἄλλας ὁδούς,
5 ἵν᾽ εἴ τι πάσχοιμ᾽ ὧν ἐδόξαζον φρενί,
μή μοι νεῶρες προσπεσὸν μᾶλλον δάκοι.

962

. . . there are different remedies set for different conditions: for a man in sorrow, a kindly word from friends;[1] for excessive folly, warnings.

[1] Cf. *Phrixus* F 822.4 with note, F 1079.2.

963

Let no success be so great that it will excite you to pride greater than is proper; nor, in turn, if any reverse occurs, become its victim. Rather, stay always the same, maintaining your own nature steadfastly like gold in fire.

964

THESEUS

I learned . . . from a wise man: I kept my mind turned to anxieties and misfortunes, presenting to myself exile from my fatherland, and untimely death, and other paths of misery, so that, should I suffer any of the things I imagined in   5
my thoughts, nothing might befall me unexpectedly and hurt me the more.[1]

[1] All the sources attribute the lines to 'Theseus in Euripides'. *Aegeus, Hippolytus Veiled, Theseus* itself, or *Pirithous* have been suggested. The ideas are commonplace, e.g. *Phrixus* F 818c (cited after F 964 by Galen and Cicero) and Terence, *Phormio* 241–6. Galen and Cicero repeat Posidonius' attribution of them first to Anaxagoras (see 59 A 33 DK).

[Plutarch], *Moralia* 112d; Galen, *On the Doctrines of Hippocrates and Plato* 4.7.9 citing Posidonius fr. 165 Edelstein–Kidd; translated (probably from the same source) by Cicero, *Tusculans* 3.29, with v. 2 repeated at 3.58

4 κακῶν [Plut.], cf. *mali* Cicero: κακὰς Galen

EURIPIDES

965

ὅστις δ᾽ ἀνάγκῃ συγκεχώρηκεν βροτῶν,
σοφὸς παρ᾽ ἡμῖν καὶ τὰ θεῖ᾽ ἐπίσταται.

[Plutarch], *Moralia* 116f; Epictetus, *Encheiridion* 53. The last
letters of both lines are found in vv. 5–6 of P. Petrie 2.49 (which
has 43 line-ends or beginnings, unattributed).

966

βίος γὰρ ὄνομ᾽ ἔχει πόνος γεγώς.

[Plutarch], *Moralia* 120a

967

⟨ΧΟΡΟΣ⟩

πρὸς τὴν Ἀφροδίτην
εἴης μοι, μέτριος δέ πως
εἴης μηδ᾽ ἀπολείποις.

Plutarch, *Moralia* 132a

(968 N = *Alexander* F 62h)

969

οὐ βούλομαι πλουτοῦντι δωρεῖσθαι πένης,
μή μ᾽ ἄφρονα κρίνῃς ἢ διδοὺς αἰτεῖν δοκῶ.

Plutarch, *Moralia* 384d; v. 1 a little differently, and v. 2 almost
identical: *Comparison of Menander and Philistion* 2.49–50 Jaekel

965

Any mortal man who has gone along with the inevitable is wise in our eyes, and understands the gods' will.[1]

[1] Similarly *Melanippe* F 505.

966

Life is called 'life' though in reality it is toil.[1]

[1] Life 'a disaster', *Alcestis* 802; 'a struggle', *Suppliant Women* 550.

967

⟨CHORUS⟩
(praying to Aphrodite)
Be with me, but in moderation, and do not abandon me![1]

[1] A commonplace concerning love, e.g. *Helen* 1105–6. On the need for moderate love cf. *Theseus* F 388 with note.

(968 N = *Alexander* F 62h)

969

As a poor man I do not wish to make presents to a rich one, in case you judge me foolish or I seem to be making a request through my gift.[1]

[1] Plutarch records that these verses were thought to be said 'by Euripides to Archelaus' (the king of Macedon), but few scholars therefore ascribe them to *Archelaus*.

EURIPIDES

(970 N = *Melanippe Wise* F 481.11)

971

ὁ δ' ἄρτι θάλλων σάρκα διοπετὴς ὅπως
ἀστὴρ ἀπέσβη, πνεῦμ' ἀφεὶς ἐς αἰθέρα.

Plutarch, *Moralia* 416d and (ὁ δ'—ἀπέσβη) 1090b
2 ἀπέσβη Plut. 416d: ἀπέστη Plut. 1090b

972

πολλαῖσι μορφαῖς οἱ θεοὶ σοφισμάτων
σφάλλουσιν ἡμᾶς κρείσσονες πεφυκότες.

Plutarch, *Moralia* 20f and (in part) 431a; Stobaeus 3.3.36

973

μάντις δ' ἄριστος ὅστις εἰκάζει καλῶς.

Plutarch, *Moralia* 432c, paraphrased at 399a; Arrian, *Anabasis*
7.16.6; Appian, *Civil War* 2.152; Cicero, *Letters to Atticus* 7.13.4,
translated in *On Divination* 2.12; other citations

974

τῶν ἄγαν γὰρ ἅπτεται
θεός, τὰ μικρὰ δ' εἰς τύχην ἀφεὶς ἐᾷ.

Plutarch, *Moralia* 811d, slightly adapted at 464a
2 ἀφεὶς Plut. 464a: ἀνεὶς Plut. 811c: παρεὶς Kannicht

975

χαλεποὶ πόλεμοι γὰρ ἀδελφῶν.

Plutarch, *Moralia* 480d; Aristotle, *Politics* 7.1328a15

558

(970 N = *Melanippe Wise* F 481.11)

971

The one whose bodily strength was flourishing just now is quenched[1] like a swift comet; he has given up his breath to the heaven.

[1] Paraphrased with 'has passed away' by Plutarch 1090b. Similar alternative readings at *Medea* 1218, where 'breath to the heaven' also occurs: cf. *Chrysippus* F 839.8–11, *Suppliant Women* 531–6. The fragment is assigned to *Phaethon* by some (cf. *Pha.* 214–5).

972

The gods trip us up with clever devices of many forms: for they are superior in nature.[1]

[1] The gods 'trip us up': *Archelaus* F 254.1, *Auge* F 273.

973

The best prophet is one who figures things well.

974

For the god seizes on excess, but lets small things pass and leaves them to chance.[1]

[1] For this commonplace cf. adesp. F 353 (Zeus), Cicero, *Nature of the Gods* 2.167. The variant readings have almost identical meaning.

975

Wars between brothers are cruel.[1]

[1] Probably from a choral passage (anapaestic metre), possibly from *Telephus* (cf. *Tel.* F 722–3 and perhaps 713).

EURIPIDES

976

ἀκόλασθ᾽ ὁμιλεῖν γίγνεται δούλων τέκνα.

Plutarch, *Moralia* 526c; Diogenes Laertius 4.35

977

ἡ γὰρ σιωπὴ τοῖς σοφοῖσ⟨ιν⟩ ἀπόκρισις.

Plutarch, *Moralia* 532f; [Menander], *Monostichs* 307 Jaekel

978

εἰ δ᾽ ἦσαν ἀνθρώποισιν ὠνητοὶ λόγοι,
οὐδεὶς ἂν αὑτὸν εὖ λέγειν ἐβούλετο·
νῦν δ᾽—ἐκ βαθείας γὰρ πάρεστιν αἰθέρος
λαβεῖν ἀμισθί—πᾶς τις ἥδεται λέγων
5 τά τ᾽ ὄντα καὶ μή· ζημίαν γὰρ οὐκ ἔχει.

Plutarch, *Moralia* 539b; vv. 1 and 3–4 partly paraphrased in
Philodemus, P. Herc. 1471 col. xviiib.2 Olivieri, and vv. 3–4 in P.
Herc. 425 fr. iv.81–3 (= Philodemus, *Rhetorica* II.101 Sudhaus)
and 1573 fr. 3.27–31 (= II.68 Sudhaus: vestigial)

4 ἀμισθί Plut.: ἀμοχθεί Phil. 425 (missing from 1573)

979

οὔτοι προσελθοῦσ᾽ ἡ Δίκη σε, μὴ τρέσῃς,
παίσει πρὸς ἧπαρ οὐδὲ τῶν ἄλλων βροτῶν
τὸν ἄδικον, ἀλλὰ σῖγα καὶ βραδεῖ ποδὶ
στείχουσα μάρψει τοὺς κακούς, ὅταν τύχῃ.

Plutarch, *Moralia* 549a and (vv. 3–4) 549d; Stobaeus 1.3.21
(text adulterated)

976

The sons of slaves make undisciplined company.

977

Silence is an answer in the eyes of the wise.[1]

[1] I.e., wise people understand a silent response as well as they understand a spoken one.

978

If men had to buy words, no one would be wishing to praise himself; but now, since one may take them from heaven's depth without a fee, everyone delights in saying both what is fact and what is not: for there is no penalty.[1]

[1] Plutarch claims implausibly that Euripides was here blending inappropriate praise of himself with his proper tragic concerns.

979

I tell you, Justice will not attack you—never fear!—and strike you to your core, nor the unjust among the rest of mankind; but she will come silently and at a slow pace to seize the wicked, whenever she does.[1]

[1] Cf. *Philoctetes* F 800 with note.

980

τὰ τῶν τεκόντων σφάλματ' εἰς τοὺς ἐκγόνους
οἱ θεοὶ τρέπουσιν.

Plutarch, *Moralia* 556e and 562e

981

εἰ δὴ πάρεργον χρή τι κομπάσαι, γύναι,
οὐρανὸν ὑπὲρ γῆς ἔχομεν εὖ κεκραμένον,
ἵν' οὔτ' ἄγαν πῦρ οὔτε χεῖμα συμπίτνει·
ἃ δ' Ἑλλὰς Ἀσία τ' ἐκτρέφει κάλλιστα γῆ
5 δέλεαρ ἔχοντ' ἐς ‹τήνδε› συνθηρεύομεν.

Plutarch, *Moralia* 604e, combined with *Erechtheus* F 360.7–10

1 δὴ Grotius: δὲ Plut.: δ' ἐν παρέργῳ Kvičala   γύναι Stephanus: γυναῖκες Plut.: φίλαι Musgrave   4–5 γῆ . . . ἔχοντ' ἐς ‹τήνδε› Collard: τῆς . . . ἔχοντες Plut.: γῆς (Reiske) . . . ἔχοντες ‹τῆσδε› Ellis (κάλλιστ' ἀεὶ | τῆς γῆς Musgrave)

982

πολλοὺς δὲ βροντῆς πνεῦμ' ἄναιμον ὤλεσεν.

Plutarch, *Moralia* 666c; Theon of Smyrna, *Explanation of Mathematics* p. 47.24 Hiller

983

οἶνος περάσας πλευμόνων διαρροάς

Plutarch, *Moralia* 699a; Macrobius, *Saturnalia* 7.15.22

---

1 Plutarch supports Plato's idea of wine and other liquids being completely ingested through the lungs (*Timaeus* 70c, 91a) by cit-

980

The gods turn the errors of fathers onto their descendants.[1]

[1] Cf. *Alcmeon* F 82.

981

If indeed one should boast of something secondary, lady,[1] we have a good, temperate climate over our land, where neither heat nor cold occurs to excess;[2] and the finest things grown by Greek and Asian soil that lure us, we seek to gather (to our own land here) . . .[3]

[1] Text emended by Grotius and Stephanus. Kvičala suggested 'boast something incidentally', Musgrave 'dear women' ('women', Plutarch).   [2] Athens' temperate climate: *Medea* 829–30, 837–9; Sophocles, *Oedipus at Colonus* 674–91.   [3] For Athens gathering the world's finest products cf. [Xenophon], *Constitution of Athens* 2.7, Thucydides 2.38.2, Isocrates 4.42, Hermippus F 63 *PCG*. We have tried to heal Plutarch's corrupt text plausibly. Kannicht follows Reiske and Ellis with 'the finest things . . . , we gather through the attraction of this land' ('having always the attraction of our land', Musgrave).

982

The blast of thunder kills many without bloodshed.[1]

[1] Suggested for *Phaethon* by Matthiae; cf. F 786 there.

983

. . . wine that has passed through the channels of the lungs.[1]

ing this fragment along with Eupolis F 158 *PCG* and Eratosthenes fr. 25 Powell; and Macrobius copies him. Plutarch 1047d cites also Alcaeus fr. 347a L-P. Ancient medicine was not unanimous on this point, and we must allow for imprecise understanding of all the body's conduits.

984

τὴν σωτηρίαν οἴκοι καὶ παρ' αὐτῶν ἔχοντες
ἄλλην θέλουσιν εἰσαγώγιμον λαβεῖν.

Plutarch, *Moralia* 713d

985

ὁ πετόμενος ἱερὸν ἀνὰ Διὸς
αἰθέρα γοργοφόνος

Plutarch, *Moralia* 747d

986

πλούτῳ χλιδῶσα θνητὰ δή, γύναι, φρόνει.

Plutarch, *Moralia* 755b

δή (Xylander) . . . φρόνει Nauck: δ' ὦ . . . φρονεῖς Plut.:
χλιδῶσαν . . . δεῖ . . . φρονεῖν Blaydes, West

987

εἴθ' ἦν ἄφωνον σπέρμα δυστήνων βροτῶν.

Plutarch, *Moralia* 801f

(988: see *Cretans*, after F 472g)

990

Εὐριπίδης διορίζεται θέρους τέσσαρας μῆνας καὶ χει-
μῶνος ἴσους
    φίλης τ' ὀπώρας διπτύχους ἦρός τ' ἴσους

Plutarch, *Moralia* 1028f

984

Those who have security at home and from their own resources

want to get more brought in from outside.

985

(Perseus) the gorgon-slayer who flies up into Zeus's sacred heaven.[1]

[1] Lyric verses, cited by Plutarch to illustrate free poetic rhythm imitating the sense. For Zeus's heaven cf. *Chrysippus* F 839.1 with note.

986

As you luxuriate in wealth, lady, keep your thoughts mortal.[1]

[1] Cited in a story of an amorous and rich widow abducting a handsome youth. Plutarch's 'you keep . . .' (a statement) must be wrong; 'you must keep' (Blaydes, West) is very possible.

987

If only the offspring of wretched mankind lacked a voice.[1]

[1] Cf. *Hippolytus Veiled* F 439.1–2, which follows this fragment in Plutarch.

(988: see *Cretans*, after F 472g)

990

Euripides distinguishes four months equally of summer and winter,

and two equally of friendly autumn and spring.[1]

[1] Similar length for the seasons at Hippocrates, *Airs, Waters and Places* 10.

991

ἀλλ᾽ ⟨ἔστιν⟩ ἔστι, κεἴ τις ἐγγελᾷ λόγῳ,
Ζεὺς καὶ θεοὶ βρότεια λεύσσοντες πάθη.

Plutarch, *Moralia* 1040b

992

ἀμφίπολος Ἄρεος ἀνιέρου

Plutarch; *Life of Antony* 90.3

993

φίλων λαβεῖν ⟨γὰρ⟩ πεῖραν οὐ σμικρὸν κακόν.

Plutarch, *Life of Fabius Maximus* 17.4

994

εἰ δὲ θανεῖν θέμις, ὧδε θανεῖν καλόν,
εἰς ἀρετὴν καταλυσαμένους βίον.

Plutarch, *Life of Marcellus* 33.4 and *Moralia* 24d

(994a N–Sn = Chaeremon, *TrGF* 71 F 42)

995

πολλοῖσ⟨ι⟩ πολλήν, δὶς τόσοις δὲ πλείονα

Plutarch, *Life of Solon* 22.2

991

But there really are, there really are, even if one laughs at the saying, Zeus and the gods noticing mankind's sufferings.[1]

[1] Cf. F 912b with note.

992

. . . a priest of unholy Ares . . .[1]

[1] Plutarch applies this image to the brutal Macedonian general Demetrius Poliorcetes ('the Besieger'). Ares the war-god violates all sanctities: Aeschylus, *Seven against Thebes* 343–4.

993

For to put friends to the test is no small evil.

994

If it is right to die, it is good to die like this, ending one's life bravely.[1]

[1] Cited as a maxim for those dying in battle, even amid victory.

(994a N–Sn = Chaeremon, *TrGF* 71 F 42)

995

. . . much (land) for many, and more for twice as many . . .[1]

[1] Applied by Plutarch to Sparta under the rule of Lycurgus; if Euripides himself was describing Sparta, the fragment may go with *Temenidae/Temenus* F 727e (first quotation).

EURIPIDES

(996 N = *Cretans* F 472a)

(997 N = *Cretans* F 472b.29)

998

(Πελοποννήσιοι) †αἰεὶ πρασίμοχθοί τινες† καὶ οὔποτε
ἥσυχοι δορί

Polybius 5.106.4

ἀεὶ | περισσόμοχθοι κοὔποθ᾽ ἥσυχοι δορί conjectured for
Euripides by Heimsoeth

(1001 N = *Theseus* F 386aa)

(1004: see *Cretans*, after F 472g)

1006

οὐχ ἑσπέρας, φάσ᾽, ἀλλὰ καὶ μεσημβρίας
τούτους ἀφεστήκασιν ἡμέραν τρίτην.

Priscian, *Institutions of Grammar* 18.166 and 194; (μεσημ-
βρίας—ἀφεστήκασιν) *Etymologicum Symeonis* α 1122 Las-
serre–Livadaras

1007

λευκοὺς λίθους χέοντες αὐχοῦσιν μέγα.

Photius λ 307 Theodorides = Suda λ 529 and 536; cf.
Zenobius, *Proverbs* 1.275 Bühler

χέοντες Naber: ἔχοντες Phot., Suda

(996 N = *Cretans* F 472a)

(997 N = *Cretans* F 472b.29)

998

(The Peloponnesians) . . . †people always selling their effort†[1]
and never at rest under arms.

[1] The term is doubtful in form and inaccurate of the Spartans,
and the wording is unmetrical; Heimsoeth restored metre and
sense with 'always excessive in effort'.

(1001 N = *Theseus* F 386aa)

(1004: see *Cretans*, after F 472g)

1006

Not only in the evening, they say, but also at midday they
have held these men off into the third day.[1]

[1] Cited for the unusual grammar of the verb 'hold off'. Euripi-
des' context is obscure (a battle?).

1007

They smelt bright ores with great pride.[1]

[1] Text and translation insecure, but 'smelt' (Naber) seems
much more pointed than the sources' 'possess'. Photius and the
Suda gloss 'ores' (lit. 'rocks') with 'gold and silver'.

EURIPIDES

1007a + b

Βοσπό]ρου πέρα

Νείλου] τε ναυστολοῦσι χρημάτων χάριν

ἀστρο[σκο]ποῦντες [̣ ̣]λίαν τρικυ[μί]αν

θύραθεν [̣ ̣] θέλοιμ᾿ ἂν (a few more letters)

5 χρυσοῦν [τὸν] Ἴστρον [τόν] τε Βόσπο[ρον λα]βών.

Satyrus, *Life of Euripides*, P. Oxy. 1176 fr. 38 col. iii.8–20

1–2 suppl. Wilamowitz: ρου̅περαν[P   3 [οὐ]λίαν
Schorn   4 [οὐ] Hunt   5 first [τὸν] von Arnim, second
Schorn: [παρ᾿] . . . [εἴ]τε . . . [τρί]βων Arrighetti

1007c

⟨—⟩

λ]άθρᾳ δὲ τούτων δρωμένων, τίνας φοβῇ;

⟨—⟩

τοὺς μείζονα βλ[έ]ποντας ἀ[ν]θρώπων θεούς.

Satyrus, *Life of Euripides*, P. Oxy. 1176 fr. 39 col. ii.8–14

1007d

κτήσασθ᾿ ἐν ὑ[σ]τέροισιν εὔ[κ]λειαν χρόνοι[ς]

ἅ]πασαν, ἀντλή[σαν]τες ἡμέρας [πόν]ον

ψ[υ]χαῖς (further traces)

Satyrus, *Life of Euripides*, P. Oxy. 1176 fr. 39 col. iv.33–8

2 ἅ]πασαν . . . ἡμέραν Hunt

1007a + b

. . . beyond (the Bosporus) and (the Nile) for the sake of wealth they sail the . . . huge wave, keeping watch on the stars.[1]

I would (not?) wish . . . away from home . . . taking (the) golden Danube and (the) Bosporus.[2]

[1] Wilamowitz' supplements in vv. 1–2 are probable. In v. 3 'huge wave' is literally 'third (and greatest) wave of three'; Schorn's supplement 'deadly' is possible. Satyrus could have been quoting one fragment or two, but editors have tried to restore a transition between vv. 3 and 4, unconvincingly (the papyrus has no punctuation); text may have been lost, or omitted, between them.   [2] Text and translation uncertain, especially the word-order in 'the golden Danube': hence Arrighetti's 'spending time (near the) golden Danube or Bosporus'. The adjective connotes a trade route of valuable goods (cf. 2).

1007c

⟨—⟩

If these things are done secretly, whom do you fear?

⟨—⟩

The gods, whose view is greater than men's.[1]

[1] Satyrus suggests a Socratic pedigree for the idea in v. 2, but see F 912b above with note. The fragment is attributed to *Phrixus B* by Van Looy, to Critias (cf. Appendix below, F 19) by H. Yunis, *ZPE* 75 (1988), 39–46.

1007d

Get yourselves every glory in later times, after you have endured the day's toil to its end in your hearts . . .[1]

[1] Cf. *Archelaus* F 233, 236–7, 240, *Licymnius* F 474, etc. Satyrus says Euripides is urging 'Spartan' endurance on young men. Hunt's conjecture gives 'Get yourselves glory . . . after you have endured toil all day . . .'

1007e + f

remains of one line
κα]ὶ [τῶ]ι τεκόν[τι] π[α]τρὶ δυσμενέστατοι·
δόμων γὰρ ἄρχε[ι]ν εἰς ἔρωτ' ἀφιγμένοι
τοῖς φιλτάτοις κυρ[ο]ῦσι πολεμιώτατοι·
5 σμικρ[οὶ] γέροντι πα[ῖ]δες ἡδίους πατρί.

Satyrus, *Life of Euripides*, P. Oxy. 1176 fr. 39 col. vi.1–15

5 separated from 1–4 by the first editors of P. Oxy.

(1007g N–Sn was a mistaken reconstruction from
P. Oxy. 1176 fr. 2 col. i.1–12)

**1007h
κ]αὶ νόσων [. . (.)] . αν ἐν θαλά[μ]οις
ἕξεις ζό[αν] δίκαν ἀνε[. .]ν·
remains of one more line

1 νόσων [Kannicht: νόσῳ [earlier editors
1–2 ἐρή]μαν . . . ἀνέ[χω]ν Austin

Satyrus, *Life of Euripides*, P. Oxy. 1176 fr. 40

1008
τί σιγᾷς; μῶν φόνον τιν' ἠργάσω;

Schol. on Aeschylus, *Eumenides* 276–8

1009
γλαυκῶπίς τε στρέφεται μήνη.

Schol. on Apollonius Rhodius 1.1280–1

1007e + f

. . . *(remains of one line)* . . . and very hostile to the father who got them; for when they have come to desire to rule a house, they prove to be the worst enemies of those dearest to them: small sons are more pleasant for an elderly father.[1]

[1] The fragment has been ascribed to *Danae* because of its affinity to F 316–7.

(1007g N–Sn: see opposite)

**1007h

. . . and in your halls you shall have a life (without) afflictions, (upholding) justice . . . *(remains of one more line)* . . .[1]

[1] Austin's bold supplements are translated; but attribution to Euripides is insecure, and Austin thinks of comedy.

1008

Why are you silent? You've not committed some bloodshed?[1]

[1] Silence ascribed to a killer's fear of spreading his pollution by speaking: *Ixion* F 427, *Heracles* 1218–9; cf. *Orestes* 75–6.

1009

. . . and the moon orbits, bright-faced.[1]

[1] Anapaestic metre; possibly a chorus is setting a scene.

1009a

.... ἄ]κοντι σὺν κλαδα[ρῷ
πή]δησε κοῦφα ποδ[....(.)

P. Oxy. 2260 col. ii.10–13 (unidentified commentary on gods
and their names)

1 κλαδα[ρῷ Kannicht   2 κοῦφα ποδ[οῖν Kannicht:
κοῦφ᾽ ἀπὸ Δ[ιὸς Lobel

1010

ἤπειρον εἰς ἄπειρον ἐκβάλλων πόδα

Schol. on Apollonius Rhodius 4.71 and many lexicographic
sources, e.g. Photius η 212 Theodoridis

1012

ἀεί ποτ᾽ <ἐστὶ> σπέρμα κηρύκων λάλον.

Schol. on *Orestes* 896

1013

τὸ μὲν τέθνηκε σῶμα, †τοῦτο δ᾽ ἀναβλέπει†.

Schol. on *Troades* 632

1 ἀναβλέπει Schol.: αὖ βλέπει Cobet

1014

πόλεως μὲν ἀρχῷ, φωτὶ δ᾽ οὐκ ἔτη πρέπον

Schol. on Homer, *Iliad* 6.239, citing the grammarian
Herodian

1009a

... (Athena) with brandished spear leapt lightly (with her feet?) ...[1]

[1] Athena's birth 'fully armed' from Zeus's head: hence Lobel's suggested reading in 2 'lightly from (Zeus's ...)'. The fragment is lyric.

1010

... departing to the limitless mainland[1]

[1] Cited to illustrate the supposed derivation of the noun ἤπειρος 'mainland' from the adjective ἄπειρος 'limitless' (as opposed to a circumscribed island).

1012

Heralds (have) always (been) a talkative breed.[1]

[1] A commonplace, e.g. *Suppliant Women* 462, cf. 426, 458.

1013

The body is dead, †but this (... ?) is reviving.†[1]

[1] The Greek is unmetrical but easily corrected with Cobet's 'this one ‹however› is alive'; then either 'this' refers to some body-part ('eye' has been suggested, e.g. of Andromeda's dragon apparently killed by Perseus but reviving), or the whole meaning is quite different: 'That body is dead, but this (body) is however reviving'.

1014

... appropriate to the ruler of a city, but not to a common citizen ...

EURIPIDES

1015

ἀεὶ δὲ μήτηρ φιλότεκνος μᾶλλον πατρός·
ἡ μὲν γὰρ αὑτῆς οἶδεν ὄνθ', ὁ δ' οἴεται.

Schol. on Homer, *Odyssey* 1.215 Ludwich and 4.387 Dindorf; Stobaeus 4a.24.24, and other sources

1015a (= 1128 N)

ὁ δὲ Εὐριπίδης πρὸς τῇ Ἐρυθρᾷ θαλάσσῃ τὴν Νησαίαν φησὶν εἶναι.

Schol. on Phlegon of Tralles, *Wonders*, *FGrH* 257 F 36, ch. 3.10 (see *FGrH* IIB. 1176, app. on 24)

1017

τὸν εὐτυχοῦντα καὶ φρονεῖν νομίζομεν.

Schol. on Pindar, *Nemeans* 1.3; Stobaeus 1.6.12 (without ascription) = [Menander], *Monostichs* 726 Jaekel

1018

ὁ νοῦς γὰρ ἡμῶν ἐστιν ἐν ἑκάστῳ θεός.

[Menander], *Monostichs* 588 Jaekel and Tzetzes, *Commentary on the Iliad* p. 53.6 Hermann have the complete verse; only three of many other sources attribute their incomplete text to Euripides, esp. Schol. on Pindar, *Nemeans* 6.7 and Nemesius of Emesa, *On the Nature of Man* 42 (pp. 348–9 Matthiae). See note on the translation.

1019

†δούλοισι γάρ τε ζῶμεν οἱ ἐλεύθεροι.†

Schol. on Pindar, *Pythians* 4.72

1015

A mother always loves her children more than a father does, for she knows they are hers, while he (only) thinks so.

1015a (= 1128 N)

Euripides says that Nesaea is by the Red Sea.[1]

[1] 'Red Sea' could mean the Persian Gulf or Indian Ocean as well as what we call the Red Sea. The scholiast himself places Nesaea, famed for its horses, inland in eastern Persia ('between Susiana and Bactria'), while Herodotus 7.40.3 had placed 'the Nesaean plain' in Media.

1017

We consider the successful man to have good sense too.

1018

Our mind in each of us is a god.[1]

[1] Paraphrased as 'our mind exercises supreme provision for us (as if it had this function of a god), but no god does' by Nemesius (c. A.D. 400), who just possibly knew Euripides' context. Other sources interpret the verse in various ways, presumably out of context. The mind is equated with specific gods at e.g. *Trojan Women* 886 (Zeus), 988 (Aphrodite). On the broad sense of *nous* ('mind') in such passages see C. Wildberg, *ICS* 24–25 (1999–2000), 254–5, and for related philosophical ideas Egli 88–90.

1019

†For we who are free live by (*or* through?) slaves.†[1]

[1] Cited to illustrate Pindar's description of servants as freeing their masters from toil. The general sense is thus clear, but grammar and metre are faulty.

EURIPIDES

1020

ὁ δ᾽ ἐσφάδᾳζεν οὐκ ἔχων ἀπαλλαγάς.

Schol. on Sophocles, *Ajax* 833

1021

Εὐριπίδης τρεῖς γενονέναι φησὶν τὰς ἐν Δωδώνῃ πελει-
άδας.

Schol. on Sophocles, *Trachiniae* 172

1022

. . . secundum Euripidem, in cuius tragoedia dicit Furia se
non esse unius potestatis, sed se Fortunam, se Nemesin, se
Fatum, se esse Necessitatem.

Servius on Virgil, *Aeneid* 7.337; cf. [Dio Chrysostom], *Orations* 64.8 (now ascribed to Favorinus)

(1023 N = *Antiope* F 182a)

1024

ἔπει[τ]α χρῆσθαι [
ὅσοι δοκοῦσιν ου [
εἰδὼς ὁθ[ο]ύνεκα[
φθείρουσιν ἤθ[η χρήσθ᾽ ὁμιλίαι κακαί.

P. Hibeh 7 fr. 1.91–4; v. 4: Paul, *I Corinthians* 15.33, whence
Clement of Alexandria, *Miscellanies* 1.14.59.3; attributed to Eu-
ripides by Socrates, *History of the Church* 3.16.26; other citations
and reflections

1020

He was in convulsions, without release from them.[1]

[1] Cited to illustrate the term 'convulsion' in the suicidal Ajax's hope for a quick and easy death; but Euripides may have been describing epilepsy.

1021

Euripides says that the doves at Dodona were three in number.[1]

[1] The priestesses of Zeus' famous oracle at Dodona (*Melanippe Captive* F 494.15) were called 'Doves' because they sat at or on the oak trees there and interpreted as 'prophecy' the movements and sounds of the leaves.

1022

. . . according to Euripides, in whose tragedy the Fury says that she is possessed of not just one power, but that she is herself Fortune, herself Retribution, herself Fate, herself Necessity.[1]

[1] Attributed to *Alcmeon in Psophis* by Wilamowitz, supposing that one of the Furies persecuting Alcmeon might have appeared there.

(1023 N = *Antiope* F 182a)

1024

. . . and then to use . . . all those who seem . . . knowing that . . . bad company ruins good morals.[1]

[1] Cf. *Erechtheus* F 362.21–3 with note.

(1025 N = *Peleus* F 617a)

1026

τὰ πλεῖστα θνητοῖς τῶν κακῶν αὐθαίρετα.

Stobaeus 2.8.11 (attribution to Euripides inferred); [Menander], *Monostichs* 758 Jaekel

1027

παῖς ὢν φυλάσσου πραγμάτων αἰσχρῶν ἄπο·
ὡς ἢν τραφῇ τις μὴ κακῶς, αἰσχύνεται
ἀνὴρ γενόμενος αἰσχρὰ δρᾶν· νέος δ' ὅταν
πόλλ' ἐξαμάρτῃ, τὴν ἁμαρτίαν ἔχει
5 εἰς γῆρας αὐτοῖς τοῖς τρόποισιν ἔμφυτον.

Stobaeus 2.31.2

1028

ὅστις νέος ὢν Μουσῶν ἀμελεῖ,
τόν τε παρελθόντ' ἀπόλωλε χρόνον
καὶ τὸν μέλλοντα τέθνηκεν.

Stobaeus 2.31.24

1029

οὐκ ἔστιν ἀρετῆς κτῆμα τιμιώτερον·
οὐ γὰρ πέφυκε δοῦλον οὔτε χρημάτων
οὔτ' ἀσφαλείας οὔτε θωπείας ὄχλου.

* * *

ἀρετὴ δ' ὅσῳ περ μᾶλλον ἂν χρῆσθαι θέλῃς,
5 τοσῷδε μείζων αὔξεται τελουμένη.

(1025 N = *Peleus* F 617a)

1026

Most of men's troubles are incurred by their own choice.

1027

When you are a child, keep yourself from shameful acts: for if someone is not badly brought up, he is ashamed to do shameful things when he becomes a man; but when a young man does wrong frequently, he has wrongdoing implanted in his very nature until old age.[1]

[1] Exactly comparable are *Suppliant Women* 911–7.

1028

Any man who in his youth neglects the Muses has perished for the time that is past and is dead for the future.[1]

[1] Sometimes ascribed to *Antiope*; cf. F 910 there (at end), which also has anapaestic metre.

1029

There is no possession more valuable than virtue: it is no slave either to money or cautious safety or a mob's flattery ... The more you are willing to practise it, the more it will grow greater and be perfected.

Orion, Euripidean Appendix 22a Haffner; Stobaeus 3.1.6

3 ἀσφαλείας Stob.: εὐγενείας Orion   4 lacuna here, Meineke; vv. 4–5 moved to *Oedipus*, near F 542, by Gomperz (see there)

1030

ἀρετὴ μέγιστον τῶν ἐν ἀνθρώποις καλόν.

Stobaeus 3.1.13

1031

τὸ μὴ εἰδέναι ⟨σε⟩ μηδὲν ὧν ἁμαρτάνεις,
ἔκκαυμα τόλμης ἱκανόν ἐστι καὶ θράσους.

Stobaeus 3.4.2

1032

τὸ δ᾽ ὠκὺ τοῦτο καὶ τὸ λαιψηρὸν φρενῶν
εἰς συμφορὰν καθῆκε πολλὰ δὴ βροτούς.

Stobaeus 3.4.21, ed. Trincavelli and one minor ms. only
2 text reconstructed by editors

1033

εὖ γὰρ τόδ᾽ ἴσθι, κεἴ σ᾽ ἐλάνθανεν πάρος,
τὸ σκαιὸν εἶναι πρῶτ᾽ ἀμουσίαν ἔχει.

Stobaeus 3.4.20, ed. Trincavelli only

1034

φεῦ φεῦ, τὸ νικᾶν τἄνδιχ᾽ ὡς καλὸν γέρας,
τὰ μὴ δίκαια δ᾽ ὡς ἀπανταχοῦ κακόν·
καὶ γλῶσσα φλαύρα καὶ φθόνος τοῦ μὴ φθονεῖν
ὅσῳ κάκιον μὴ καλῶς ὠγκωμένοις.

1030

Virtue is the greatest good of those that men have.

1031

That (you) know nothing of your mistakes is sufficient to kindle your audacity and bravado.

1032

This swift and hasty thinking quite often commits men to disaster.

1033

For know this well, even if it escaped you before: stupidity is first of all boorish.[1]

[1] I.e. indifferent to the Muses (F 1028).

1034

Well! How fine a reward it is that justice prevails, and how everywhere evil that injustice does so! And how much worse is a mean and envious tongue than having no envy for those who are dishonourable in their ostentation![1]

[1] The just man (v. 1) witholds envy for those described in vv. 3–4, while the unjust one (v. 2) reveals himself in feeling envy for them. For 'impious ostentation' (v. 4) see *Phrixus* F 825. Adesp. F 279g. 4 (see app. crit.) is incoherent and may represent an unhappy adaptation of Euripides.

Stobaeus 3.9.14; vv. 3 and perhaps 4 resemble and were possibly the model for vv. 8–9 of adesp. F 279g, a recently destroyed inscription of c. 200 B.C. in Armenia re-edited by Kannicht in *TrGF* 5.1122

3 φλαύρα Stob.: φαύλη adesp. F 279g   4 so Stob.: . . .] δικαίως μὴ καλῶς ὡρισμένος adesp. F 279g

1035

δύστηνος ὅστις τὰ καλὰ <καὶ> ψευδῆ λέγων
οὐ τοῖσδε χρῆται τοῖς καλοῖς ἀληθέσιν.

Stobaeus 3.12.1

1036

πότερα θέλεις σοι μαλθακὰ ψευδῆ λέγω
ἢ σκλήρ᾽ ἀληθῆ; φράζε· σὴ γὰρ ἡ κρίσις.

Stobaeus 3.13.1

1037

ἀτὰρ σιωπᾶν τά γε δίκαι᾽ οὐ χρή ποτε.

Stobaeus 3.13.6

1038

ὀργαὶ γὰρ ἀνθρώποισι συμφορᾶς ὕπο
δειναί, πλάνος τε καρδίᾳ προσίσταται.

Stobaeus 3.20.26

1039

ὁ θυμὸς ἀλγῶν ἀσφάλειαν οὐκ ἔχει.

Stobaeus 3.20.38

1035

It is a wretch who speaks fair lies and does not employ these good truths.[1]

[1] The text has been doubted; for the general sentiment cf. *Antiope* F 206.1–4, and the next fragment.

1036

Do you wish me to tell you gentle lies or hard truths? Say: the decision is yours.

1037

But one should never keep silent when what one has to say is just!

1038

Men's anger from disaster is terrible, and their hearts begin to lose their way.[1]

[1] Stobaeus gives this fragment as 'from the same' as his previous citation, which is *Archelaus* F 258, so that some editors assign F 1038 also to that play.

1039

A heart aggrieved is unstable.[1]

[1] Lack of context prevents secure translation, but the fragment is immediately preceded in Stobaeus by *Medea* 1079–80, famously ambiguous verses about the heart's passion overcoming deliberation.

EURIPIDES

(1040 N = 1113a below)

1041

κρινεῖ τίς αὐτὸν πώποτ᾽ ἀνθρώπων μέγαν,
ὃν ἐξαλείφει πρόφασις ἡ τυχοῦσ᾽ ὅλον;

Stobaeus 3.22.6

1 κρινεῖ Valckenaer: κρίνει Stob.

1042

ἅπαντές ἐσμεν εἰς τὸ νουθετεῖν σοφοί,
αὐτοὶ δ᾽ ὅταν σφαλῶμεν οὐ γιγνώσκομεν.

Stobaeus 3.23.5; unattributed in other sources

1043

οὐδεὶς ἔπαινον ἡδοναῖς ἐκτήσατο.

Stobaeus 3.29.31 (where confusion in the lemmata caused past editors to assign the fragment to Carcinus, TrGF 70 F 11); derived anthologies

1043a

οὐκ αἰσχρὸν οὐδὲν τῶν ἀναγκαίων βροτοῖς.

Stobaeus 3.29.56; attached by Clement of Alexandria, Miscellanies 4.7.53.3 and [Plutarch] Moralia 110f to unattributed lines now known to be Hypsipyle F 757.920–7; cited singly by [Plutarch], Moralia 117d

1 οὐκ αἰσχρὸν οὐδὲν Stob.: οὐ δεινὸν οὐδὲν Clem.: δεινὸν γὰρ οὐδὲν [Plut.]

(1040 N = 1113a below)

1041

Who among men will ever judge himself great, when a chance cause can wipe him away completely?[1]

[1] Authenticity is doubted because of the prosaic vocabulary of 'chance cause' and 'completely' (contrast the same idea as styled in *Peleus* F 618).

1042

We are all wise in giving advice, but we don't realise it when we ourselves go wrong.[1]

[1] Cf. *Alcmene* F 102.

1043

No one has acquired fame though indulging in pleasures.

1043a

Nothing that happens through necessity is shameful for mankind.

1044

οὔτ᾽ ἐκ χερὸς μεθέντα καρτερὸν λίθον
οἷόν τ᾽ ἐπισχεῖν οὔτ᾽ ἀπὸ γλώσσης λόγον.

Stobaeus 3.36.14a (where corruption caused its attribution to
Menander); reflected, perhaps partly paraphrased, in Plutarch,
Moralia 507a

2 οἷόν τ᾽ ἐπισχεῖν one minor ms. of Stob.: ῥᾷον κατασχεῖν
other mss.: Plut. paraphrases with ῥᾴδιον . . . κατασχεῖν and
κρατῆσαι δυνατόν

1045

μὴ κάμνε πατρίδα σὴν λαβεῖν πειρώμενος.

Stobaeus 3.39.2, continuous with 39.1 (= *Temenidae* F 729);
separated by editors

1046

πολλοῦ γὰρ χρυσοῦ καὶ πλούτου
κρείσσων πάτρα σώφρονι ναίειν·
τὸ δὲ σύντροφον ἁδύ τι θνητοῖς
†ἐν βίῳ χωρεῖ†.

Stobaeus 3.39.4

4 deleted by Grotius

1047

ἅπας μὲν αἰθὴρ αἰετῷ περάσιμος,
ἅπασα δὲ χθὼν ἀνδρὶ γενναίῳ πατρίς.

Cited by Musonius Rufus, as noted at Stobaeus 3.40.9

1 αἰθὴρ West: ἀὴρ Stob.

1044

Just as it is not possible[1] to stop a heavy stone once released
from the hand, so it is not possible to recall a word released
from the tongue.

1 Stobaeus' alternative 'easier' gives awkward sense; Plutarch's
paraphrase has 'easy' or 'possible'.

1045

Do not weary in your efforts to recover your fatherland!

1046

Living in his fatherland is superior for a sensible man to
much gold and wealth, and what is familiar is (*or* †contin-
ues in life as†) something pleasing to men.[1]

1 For the idea of v. 3(–4) cf. *Phoenix* F 817. Anapaestic metre,
probably therefore a chorus. The obelized words translate
with great difficulty, and are unmetrical, so deletion (Grotius) or
deeper corruption is suggested.

1047

Just as the whole heaven is open to an eagle's crossing, so
the whole earth is his fatherland to a man of nobility.[1]

1 The idea in v. 2 was a commonplace (e.g. *Phaethon* F 777),
found in the pre-Socratic philosopher Democritus 68 B 247 DK
(Stobaeus 3.40.7).

1048

οὐκ ἔστιν οὐδὲν τῶν ἐν ἀνθρώποις ἴσον.
χρῆν γὰρ τύχας μὲν τὰς μάτην πλανωμένας
μηδὲν δύνασθαι, τἀμφανῆ δ᾽ ὑψήλ᾽ ἄγειν.

* * *

ὅστις κατ᾽ ἰσχὺν πρῶτος ὠνομάζετο
ἢ τόξα πάλλων ἢ μάχῃ δορὸς σθένων,
τοῦτον τυραννεῖν τῶν κακιόνων ἐχρῆν.

Stobaeus 4.1.13; v. 1 = *Hecuba* 805 (cited at Stobaeus 4.41.34)

4–6 detached as a separate fragment by Matthiae; placed before *Eurystheus* F 378 by Gomperz; all of F 1048 moved there by Pechstein

1048a (= 1107 N)
                    ἄρχεσθαι χρεὼν
κακοὺς ὑπ᾽ ἐσθλῶν καὶ κλύειν τῶν κρεισσόνων.

Stobaeus 4.2.1, unattributed in the mss. but confidently assigned by editors (Stob. 4.2.2 is Euripidean: see note on the translation)

(1049 N = *Oedipus* F 554a)

1050

ἀλλ᾽ οὐ πρέπει τύραννον, ὡς ἐγὼ φρονῶ,
οὐδ᾽ ἄνδρα χρηστὸν νεῖκος αἴρεσθαι κακοῖς·
τιμὴ γὰρ αὕτη τοῖσιν ἀσθενεστέροις.

Stobaeus 4.7.4

1048

There is nothing at all that is equitable in human affairs;
fortunes that shift randomly about should have no power,
but should lead clear distinction to the heights . . . The man
whose name was first for might, either brandishing bow
and arrow or showing strength in spear-fighting—he it is
who should be ruling over his inferiors.[1]

[1] Logical continuity is lacking between vv. 1–3 and 4–6, proba-
bly due to loss of text, or of a fresh heading in Stobaeus.

1048a (= 1107 N)

Base men should be ruled by noble ones, and obey those
who are stronger.[1]

[1] The fragment appears to repeat the 'class values' of F
1048.4–6, cf. 1050.2–3. The next fragment in Stobaeus (4.2.2) is
Dictys F 337, similar in sentiment; so too is *Dictys* F 334.4–5, so
that Hense suggested assigning F 1048a to that play; but the
theme occurs also at e.g. *Aegeus* F 8.

(1049 N = *Oedipus* F 554a)

1050

It is unfitting however, in my opinion, for a ruler or a man
of quality to start feuding with base men; for this does hon-
our to those of lesser consequence.[1]

[1] Cf. *Dictys* F 334, and above on F 1048a.

1051

σὺν τοῖσι δεινοῖς αὔξεται κλέος βροτοῖς.

Stobaeus 4.10.7 and derivatives

1052

νεανίας γὰρ ὅστις ὢν Ἄρη στυγῇ,
κόμη μόνον καὶ σάρκες, ἔργα δ᾽ οὐδαμοῦ.
ὁρᾷς τὸν εὐτράπεζον ὡς ἡδὺς βίος·
{†ὅ τ᾽ ὄλβος ἔξωθέν τίς ἐστι πραγμάτων†}
5 ἀλλ᾽ οὐκ ἔνεστι στέφανος οὐδ᾽ εὐανδρία,
εἰ μή τι καὶ τολμῶσι κινδύνου μέτα·
οἱ γὰρ πόνοι τίκτουσι τὴν εὐανδρίαν,
ἡ δ᾽ εὐλάβεια σκότον ἔχει καθ᾽ Ἑλλάδα,
τὸ διαβιῶναι μόνον ἀεὶ θηρωμένη.

Stobaeus 4.10.26; v. 3: Athenaeus 14.641c; vv. 6–8: P. Herc. 1384 col. 6.1–6, unattributed (A. Antoni, *Cronache Ercolanesi* 34 [2004], 30–4); v. 7 ≈ *Archelaus* F 237.3

4 deleted by Herwerden, Wilamowitz

1053

μισῶ δ᾽ ὅταν τις καὶ χθονὸς στρατηλάτης
μὴ πᾶσι πάντων προσφέρῃ μειλίγματα.

Stobaeus 4.13.14, continuous with *Bellerophon* F 287; separated by Barnes

1051

Men's fame increases with their dangers.

1052

The young man who detests War is merely long hair and flesh, his actions of no account. You see how pleasant is the life which enjoys a good table; {†and that prosperity is remote from affairs†} but there's no wreath of glory or true manhood in it, unless people actually venture upon   5
something with a risk: it is hard effort which creates true manhood, while caution remains in obscurity amongst the Greeks, always seeking only to live a long life.[1]

[1] These are the sentiments of *Archelaus* F 237 (where v. 3 is identical with v. 7 here; such innocent duplications are not rare in Euripides). The criticisms in vv. 1–3 and 5 strongly resemble those of overfed, 'useless' athletes at *Autolycus* F 282. For vv. 5–9 cf. *Suppliant Women* 314–6, 323–5.

1053

I hate it too when a country's general does not use winning ways towards everybody in everything.[1]

[1] Cf. *Temenus* F 744, fairness to all. Conversely, Agamemnon's ingratiating behaviour while seeking election as general is criticized in *Iphigenia at Aulis* 337–42.

EURIPIDES

(1054 N = *Andromeda* F 138a)

1055

οἰκοφθόρον γὰρ ἄνδρα κωλύει γυνὴ
ἐσθλὴ παραζευχθεῖσα καὶ σῴζει δόμους.

Stobaeus 4.22.9

1056

οὐ πάντες οὔτε δυστυχοῦσιν ἐς γάμους
οὔτ᾽ εὐτυχοῦσι· συμφορὰ δ᾽ ὃς ἂν τύχῃ
κακῆς γυναικός, εὐτυχεῖ δ᾽ ἐσθλῆς τυχών.

Stobaeus 4.22.70

1 ἐς γάμους Nauck: ἐν γάμοις Stob.

1057

μακάριος ὅστις εὐτυχεῖ γάμον λαβὼν
ἐσθλῆς γυναικός, εὐτυχεῖ δ᾽ ὁ μὴ λαβών.

Stobaeus 4.22.72

(1058 N = *Antigone* F 162a)

1059

δεινὴ μὲν ἀλκὴ κυμάτων θαλασσίων,
δεινὴ δὲ ποταμοῦ, καὶ πυρὸς θερμοῦ πνοαί,
δεινὸν δὲ πενία, δεινὰ δ᾽ ἄλλα μυρία,
ἀλλ᾽ οὐδὲν οὕτω δεινὸν ὡς γυνὴ κακόν·

Stobaeus 4.22.136; vv. 1–4: *Life of Aesop* 32 Perry (with minor textual differences); vv. 1–2 apparently reflected in P. Oxy. 684.13–16

UNIDENTIFIED PLAYS

(1054 N = *Andromeda* F 138a)

1055

A good wife joined with him restrains a husband who is ruining his house and property, and saves the home.

1056

Not all men are unfortunate in marriage, nor all fortunate; but it is disastrous for any who gets a bad wife, while any who gets a good one is fortunate.[1]

[1] Euripides' supposed misogyny (F 1056–60 here) was caught in comedy and hence in the biographical tradition: see *TrGF* 5.99–101, T 108a–111b.

1057

Blessed the man who has had the luck to get a good wife, and lucky the one who has not got one at all.

(1058 N = *Antigone* F 162a)

1059

Terrible is the might of the sea's waves, terrible a river's, and hot fire's blasts; terrible is poverty, and terrible are countless other things—but nothing is so terrible an evil as

---

1 ἀλκὴ Stob.: ὀργὴ or ὀργαὶ *Life*: ἀκμαὶ (seemingly) γὰρ εἰσ[. . . .]αυμάτων (i.e. κ]αυμάτων or]κυμάτων) P. Oxy.
2 δεινὴ Grotius: δειναὶ . . . ποταμοῦ Stob.: δειναὶ or πολλαὶ . . . ποταμῶν *Life*: δειναὶ in both v. 1 and v. 2, Musgrave

5 οὔτ᾽ ἂν γένοιτο γράμμα τοιοῦτον γραφῇ
οὔτ᾽ ἂν λόγος δείξειεν. εἰ δέ του θεῶν
τόδ᾽ ἐστὶ πλάσμα, δημιουργὸς ὢν κακῶν
μέγιστος ἴστω καὶ βροτοῖσι δυσμενής.

5–6 οὔτ᾽ . . . οὔτ᾽ West: οὐδ᾽ . . . οὐδ᾽ Stob.   γραφῇ Stob.:
γραφεῖ Nauck

1060

ἐχθροῖσιν εἴη πολεμίαν δάμαρτ᾽ ἔχειν.

Stobaeus 4.22.141 ms. S; mss. MA combine it with no. 140 (=
Oedipus F 544)

1061

μοχθοῦμεν ἄλλως θῆλυ φρουροῦντες γένος·
ἥτις γὰρ αὐτὴ μὴ πέφυκεν ἔνδικος,
τί δεῖ φυλάσσειν κἀξαμαρτάνειν πλέον;

Stobaeus 4.23.10

2 ἔνδικος Gesner: εν δος or ἔνδος or ἔνδον Stob.

1062

γυναικὶ δ᾽ ὄλβος, ἢν πόσιν στέργοντ᾽ ἔχῃ.

Stobaeus 4.23.15

a woman;[1] there could be no such picture drawn,[2] nor 5
could speech describe it. If this is the fabrication of some
god, he should know that he is the greatest craftsman of
evil, and malevolent to mankind.[3]

[1] Vv. 1–3 form a 'priamel'; cf. *Danae* F 316 with note. In v. 2
the sources have the impossible 'blasts of a river (*or* of rivers)',
economically salvaged by Grotius; Musgrave, on the basis of the
Life, suggested 'the rages of the sea's waves, and those of a river
. . .' 'Hot fire's blasts' are presumaby from volcanoes: cf. [Aeschy-
lus], *Prometheus Bound* 365–71 (Mt. Etna).   [2] The Greek
expression is strained; Nauck conjectured 'picture for (i.e. 'by') an
artist'; there are many other conjectures.   [3] Note 'mankind',
as in Hesiod, *Theogony* 570, not 'males' as in *Works and Days* 56,
82. Woman is 'fabricated' by Hephaestus, *Theogony* 571, *Works
and Days* 70; by Prometheus, Menander F 508.5–6.

1060

I wish a hostile wife on my enemies!

1061

We waste our effort keeping guard on the female sex: when
a woman is herself not naturally law-abiding, what use is
there in guarding her, and compounding our error?[1]

[1] Cf. F 1063.2–11, *Danae* F 320.

1062

It is happiness for a woman if she has a loving husband.

1063

δεῖ πυνθάνεσθαι γὰρ σὲ νῷν χἠμᾶς σέθεν.
τὸ μὲν μέγιστον, οὔποτ᾽ ἄνδρα χρὴ σοφὸν
λίαν φυλάσσειν ἄλοχον ἐν μυχοῖς δόμων·
ἐρᾷ γὰρ ὄψις τῆς θύραθεν ἡδονῆς·

5   ἐν δ᾽ ἀφθόνοισι τοῖσδ᾽ ἀναστρωφωμένη
βλέπουσά τ᾽ εἰς πᾶν καὶ παροῦσα πανταχοῦ
τὴν ὄψιν ἐμπλήσασ᾽ ἀπήλλακται κακῶν·
{τό τ᾽ ἄρσεν αἰεὶ τοῦ κεκρυμμένου λίχνον.}
ὅστις δὲ μοχλοῖς καὶ διὰ σφραγισμάτων

10 σῴζει δάμαρτα, δρᾶν τι δὴ δοκῶν σοφὸν
μάταιός ἐστι καὶ φρονῶν οὐδὲν φρονεῖ·
ἥτις γὰρ ἡμῶν καρδίαν θύραζ᾽ ἔχει,
θᾶσσον μὲν οἰστοῦ καὶ πτεροῦ χωρίζεται,
λάθοι δ᾽ ἂν Ἄργου τὰς πυκνοφθάλμους κόρας·

15 καὶ πρὸς κακοῖσι τοῦτο δὴ μέγας γέλως,
ἀνήρ τ᾽ ἀχρεῖος χἠ γυνὴ διοίχεται.

Stobaeus 4.23.26a, combined with Menander F 816 *PCG*; vv.
2–7: Choricius, *Orations* 8.52 with implicit attribution to Euripides

1 so Nauck: ἐκπυνθάνεσθαι τ᾽ ἀρσένων δ᾽ ἡμᾶς σέθεν Stob.
2 ἄνδρα χρὴ Chor.: ἄνδρ᾽ ἢ (or ἦ) or ἀνδρὶ Stob.   4 followed in Chor. by ἐρᾷ δ᾽ ἀκούειν ὧν φυλάττεται κλύειν
8 deleted by Wecklein   10 δρᾶν τι Tyrwhitt: δ᾽ ἀνδρὶ Stob.

1063

You must learn from us two, therefore, and we from you.[1]
The biggest thing is, a wise husband should never keep his
wife too much under guard in his inner house; for her eyes
long for the pleasure that is out of doors.[2] If she wanders
freely and ungrudged among those things, however, and   5
looks at everything and is present everywhere, her eyes are
sated and she is kept from trouble. {A male too is always
prurient about what is hidden.}[3] The husband who keeps
his wife safe by means of bars and seals, imagining that he
is doing something wise, is a fool and his thinking makes no   10
sense; for any of us who has her heart abroad is off faster
than an arrow or a bird on the wing, and would evade the
clustered eyes of Argus[4]—and there's much to laugh at
here, as well as trouble: the husband is helpless, and his   15
wife is gone.

[1] One of two women appears to be arguing with a repressive husband; cf. F 1061. With the whole fragment compare *Andromache* 929–53.   [2] There is an awkward transition in the Greek from v. 4 'the pleasure' to v. 5 (literally) 'among these things ungrudged', which the intervening verse in Choricius may have been intended to ease ('and she longs to listen to things she is guarded from hearing'). The 'pleasure' in v. 4 is that of attractive men.   [3] V. 8 was probably added to contrast male desires with female.   [4] The many-eyed and unsleeping guard set by Hera over the girl Io, the object of Zeus' desire: *Prometheus Bound* 678–9 etc.

1064

ἀλλ' ἴσθ', ἐμοὶ μὲν οὗτος οὐκ ἔσται νόμος,
τὸ μὴ οὐ σὲ μῆτερ προσφιλῆ νέμειν ἀεὶ
καὶ τοῦ δικαίου καὶ τόκων τῶν σῶν χάριν.
στέργω δὲ τὸν φύσαντα τῶν πάντων βροτῶν
5 μάλισθ'· ὁρίζω τοῦτο, καὶ σὺ μὴ φθόνει·
κείνου γὰρ ἐξέβλαστον· οὐδ' ἂν εἷς ἀνὴρ
γυναικὸς αὐδήσειεν, ἀλλὰ τοῦ πατρός.

Stobaeus 4.25.27

6 οὐδ' ἂν εἷς ἀνὴρ Stob.: ἄνδρα δ' οὐδ' ἂν εἷς West

1065

καὶ τῶν παλαιῶν πόλλ' ἔπη καλῶς ἔχει·
λόγοι γὰρ ἐσθλοὶ φάρμακον φόβου βροτοῖς.

Stobaeus 2.4.4

1066

εἰ τοῖς ἐν οἴκῳ χρήμασιν λελείμμεθα,
ἡ δ' εὐγένεια καὶ τὸ γενναῖον μένει.

Stobaeus 4.29.40

600

1064

Know this, however: it will be my rule always to hold you dear, mother; it is what right requires, and a return for your giving me birth. Yet I cherish the father who begot me beyond all mankind: this is what I have determined, and you are not to grudge it; for it was from him that I sprang, and   5 no man would call himself a woman's son, but his father's.[1]

[1] For the invariable and much prized Greek rule of naming sons for their male ancestors see *Electra* 933–5, Sophocles F 564; for the father, not the mother, as the true parent see Aeschylus, *Eumenides* 658–61. In v. 6 West aimed at better idiom with 'no one would name a man for a woman'. The fragment has been suggested for *Phoenix* where Euripides, differently from Homer, portrayed Phoenix as not guilty of seducing his father's concubine at his mother's request (see *Phoenix*, Introduction and test. iic).

1065

And many sayings of the ancients are well; noble words are a remedy for men's fears.

1066

If we have fallen short in our house's wealth, at least our high birth and name for nobility remain.[1]

[1] 'We' probably means 'I'. Cf. *Archelaus* F 232, *Temenidae* F 739, *Electra* 37–8. A possible reflection of these verses in Accius, *Telephus* fr. 7 Dangel has prompted assignment to Euripides' play (the ragged Telephus pleading his case, F 697–8?).

1067

τὸν σὸν δὲ παῖδα σωφρονοῦντ᾽ ἐπίσταμαι
χρηστοῖς θ᾽ ὁμιλοῦντ᾽ εὐσεβεῖν τ᾽ ἠσκηκότα·
πῶς οὖν ἂν ἐκ τοιοῦδε σώματος κακὸς
γένοιτ᾽ ἄν; οὐδεὶς τοῦτό μ᾽ ἂν πίθοι ποτέ.

Stobaeus 4.29.47

1068

οὐ γάρ τις οὕτω παῖδας εὖ παιδεύσεται,
ὥστ᾽ ἐκ πονηρῶν μὴ οὐ κακοὺς πεφυκέναι.

Stobaeus 4.30.3

1069

<—>

χρυσοῦ σε πλήθει, τούσδε δ᾽ οὐ χαίρειν χρεών;

<—>

σκαιὸν τὸ πλουτεῖν κἄλλο μηδὲν εἰδέναι.

Plutarch, *Moralia* 20d; v. 2: Stobaeus 4.31.59

1070

ὅστις δὲ λύπας φησὶ πημαίνειν βροτούς,
δεῖν δ᾽ ἀγχονῶν τε καὶ πετρῶν ῥίπτειν ἄπο,
οὐκ ἐν σοφοῖσίν ἐστιν, εὐχέσθω δ᾽ ὅμως
ἄπειρος εἶναι τῆς νόσου ταύτης ἀεί.

Stobaeus 4.35.4

---

[1] I.e. the griefs of v. 1: see on F 1071.

1067

I know your son as virtuous, as associating with good men, and as practising piety. How then could he become bad from the kind of person he is? No one will ever persuade me of that![1]

[1] Loss of context makes the translation of vv. 3–4 insecure; some render 'How could a bad son be born from such a person?', as if the question is put to a grandfather about his virtuous son's son. The question as we translate it has been thought to refer to Hippolytus in *Hippolytus Veiled*, or to Phoenix in *Phoenix* (F 810, F 812.4–9; cf. F 1064 with note).

1068

No one is going to bring up sons so well that bad ones are not born from base fathers.[1]

[1] Cf. *Phoenix* F 810 with note.

1069

⟨—⟩

Ought you to delight in plentiful gold, but these men not?

⟨—⟩

Being rich and knowing nothing else is foolish.[1]

[1] I.e. 'these men have not the knowledge or sense to manage riches, but I have'; Plutarch's context is the need to agree with the better of two conflicting positions.

1070

The man who says that griefs harm men, and that they should hang themselves in nooses or throw themselves from cliffs, is not among the wise; all the same, let him pray never to experience this malady.[1]

1071

λῦπαι γὰρ ἀνθρώποισι τίκτουσιν νόσους.

Stobaeus 4.35.10

1072

μέλλων τ᾽ ἰατρὸς τῇ νόσῳ διδοὺς χρόνον
ἰάσατ᾽ ἤδη μᾶλλον ἢ τεμὼν χρόα.

Stobaeus 4.38.2

1073

οὐ χρή ποτ᾽ ὀρθαῖς ἐν τύχαις βεβηκότα
ἕξειν τὸν αὐτὸν δαίμον᾽ εἰς ἀεὶ δοκεῖν·
ὁ γὰρ θεός πως, εἰ θεόν σφε χρὴ καλεῖν,
κάμνει ξυνὼν τὰ πολλὰ τοῖς αὐτοῖς ἀεί.
5 θνητῶν δὲ θνητὸς ὄλβος· οἱ δ᾽ ὑπέρφρονες
καὶ τῷ παρόντι τοὐπιὸν πιστούμενοι
ἔλεγχον ἔλαβον τῆς τύχης ἐν τῷ παθεῖν.

Stobaeus 4.41.8

7 τῆς τύχης Gomperz: τὴν τύχην Stob.

1074

βέβαια δ᾽ οὐδεὶς εὐτυχεῖ θνητὸς γεγώς.

Stobaeus 4.41.41

1075

θνητὸς γὰρ ὢν καὶ θνητὰ πείσεσθαι δόκει·
θεοῦ βίον ζῆν ἀξιοῖς ἄνθρωπος ὤν;

Stobaeus 4.44.31; v. 1: Arsenius 30.7 (*CPG* II.458.12)

604

1071

Griefs generate maladies[1] for men.

[1] Either mental distress (e.g. F 962, 1070.4, 1079.1 and 3) or physical affliction (e.g. Phaedra, *Hippolytus* 159).

1072

And a doctor who delays and gives the disease time has already cured it more than through surgery.

1073

The man on the path of steady success should not think that he will enjoy the same luck for ever, for the god—if one should use the name 'god'—seems generally to grow weary of supporting always the same men. Mortal men's prosperity is mortal; those who are arrogant and assure   5
themselves of the future from the present get a test of their fortune through suffering.

1074

No mortal is born to sure success.

1075

Since you are mortal you must expect also to suffer as mortals do; do you claim a god's life when you are human?

1076

πάντων ἄριστον μὴ βιάζεσθαι θεούς,
στέργειν δὲ μοῖραν· τῶν ἀμηχάνων δ' ἔρως
πολλοὺς ἔθηκε τοῦ παρόντος ἀμπλακεῖν.

Stobaeus 4.44.53

1077

πέπονθας οἷα χἄτεροι πολλοὶ βροτῶν·
τὰς γὰρ παρούσας οὐχὶ σῴζοντες τύχας
ὤλοντ' ἐρῶντες μειζόνων ἀβουλίᾳ.

Stobaeus 4.44.18

1078

ἀνδρῶν τάδ' ἐστὶν ἐνδίκων τε καὶ σοφῶν,
κἂν τοῖσι δεινοῖς μὴ τεθυμῶσθαι θεοῖς.

Stobaeus 4.44.36; [Plutarch], *Moralia* 116f, attributed to Aeschylus

1 ἐνδίκων Stob.: ἐναρέτων [Plut.]   2 κἂν τοῖσι δεινοῖς
Stob.: ἐν τοῖς κακοῖσι [Plut.]

1079

οὐκ ἔστι λύπης ἄλλο φάρμακον βροτοῖς
ὡς ἀνδρὸς ἐσθλοῦ καὶ φίλου παραίνεσις·
ὅστις δὲ ταύτῃ τῇ νόσῳ ξυνὼν ἀνὴρ
μέθῃ ταράσσει καὶ γαληνίζει φρένα,
5   παραυτίχ' ἡσθεὶς ὕστερον στένει διπλᾶ.

Stobaeus 4.48.23

1076

Best of all not to force the gods, but to be content with one's lot. Desire for the impossible makes many lose what they have now.

1077

You have suffered just as many other men have too: they did not conserve the good fortune they already had and were ruined in a foolish desire to have greater.

1078

This is the conduct of righteous and wise men: even amid their dangers, not to be angry with the gods.[1]

[1] [Plutarch]'s variations are typical of the habits of ancient citation, either too reliant upon memory or too willing to adjust an illustration to a context: in v. 1 'virtuous' (this word found only later than Euripides) instead of 'righteous', and in v. 2 'troubles' instead of 'dangers'.

1079

Men have no other remedy for their grief than the comfort of a good man and friend;[1] the man who is familiar with this malady, and stirs and (then) tries to calm his mind with drink, gets immediate pleasure but later laments twice as much.[2]

[1] Friendly words as a remedy for grief: cf. F 962.
[2] Drink as relief from mental hurt: Sophocles F 758. In v. 4 'stirs' is suspect ('soothes', Wakefield).

---

4 μέθη Valckenaer: μεθῆς or μεθ' ἧς Stob.   ταράσσει Stob.: μαλάσσει Wakefield

(1080 N = 1113b below)

1081

τύμβῳ γὰρ οὐδεὶς πιστὸς ἀνθρώπων φίλος.

Stobaeus 4.58.1

1082

Ζεὺς γὰρ κακὸν μὲν Τρωσί, πῆμα δ᾽ Ἑλλάδι
θέλων γενέσθαι ταῦτ᾽ ἐβούλευσεν πατήρ.

Strabo 4.1.7

(1083 = *Temenidae/Temenus* F 727e)

1084

ἥκω περίκλυστον προλιποῦσ᾽ Ἀκροκόρινθον,
ἱερὸν ὄχθον, πόλιν Ἀφροδίτας.

Strabo 8.6.21; reflected in Plutarch, *Moralia* 767f

1085

. . . Εὐριπίδης τὸν Μαρσύαν φησὶ
τὰς διωνομασμένας
ναίειν Κελαινὰς ἐσχάτοις Ἴδης τόποις.

Strabo 13.1.70

---

[1] Marsyas was the satyr whom Apollo flayed after his presumptuous challenge to the god's musical prowess (so attribution to a satyr-play is suggested, but tragic narrative is quite possible). Strabo is contesting Euripides' location of Celaenae by Mt. Ida near Troy; it lay near the source of the Meander in Phrygia (Herodotus 7.26.3).

(1080 N = 1113b below)

1081

No man's friend stays faithful to his tomb.[1]

---

[1] Cf. *Temenidae* F 736.3.

1082

For father Zeus planned these things, wanting evil for the Trojans and disaster for Greece.[1]

---

[1] A divine explanation of the Trojan War, like *Electra* 1282–3, *Helen* 1639–42. According to the *Cypria* (fr. 1 West), Zeus wanted to reduce the Earth's excessive population. The fragment has often but improbably been assigned to the prologue or exodos of *Alexander* (C. Bussi, *Sileno* 30 [2004], 45–56 favours the prologue).

(1083 = *Temenidae/Temenus* F 727e)

1084

To come here I have left Acrocorinth bounded by two seas, the sacred hill, city of Aphrodite . . .[1]

---

[1] Entry of a chorus of Corinthian women, possibly temple servants (comparable motive for a chorus in *Cretans* F 472); the Greek metre (ionic in v. 1) is solemn. Plutarch's context is a famous Corinthian prostitute ('city of Aphrodite', cf. *Sciron* F 676; Pechstein assigns the fragment to this play). This confirms the sense 'bounded by two seas' (the Saronic and Corinthian gulfs, overlooked by the acropolis of Corinth) against Strabo's interpretation 'flowing all round with water' (from springs and wells).

1085

Euripides says that Marsyas inhabited

the widely famous Celaenae, in the farthest parts of Ida.[1]

EURIPIDES

1086

ἄλλων ἰατρὸς αὐτὸς ἕλκεσιν βρύων

Suda ε 3691; (unattributed) Plutarch, *Moralia* 71e, 88c, 481a, 1110e; Galen, *On Maintaining Health* 5.1.9; many other citations

1087 *TrGF* (1087 N = adesp. F 562a)
εὐφημία γὰρ παρὰ σπονδαῖσι κάλλιστον.

Suda ε 3795 (cf. ε 3735) = Aelian fr. 267 Hercher (= fr. 265 Domingo-Forasté)

1089

σῶσαι γὰρ ὁπόταν <ἄνδρα> τῷ θεῷ δοκῇ,
πολλοὺς πόρους δίδωσιν εἰς σωτηρίαν.

Theophilus, *To Autolycus* 2.8.4 (p. 50 Marcovich)

1 ὁπόταν <ἄνδρα> Nauck: <θνητὸν> δοκῇ Ferrari: δοκῇ <τινα> Grotius   2 πολλοὺς πόρους Nauck: πολλὰς προφάσεις Theoph.

1090

ἀνέχου πάσχων· δρῶν γὰρ ἔχαιρες.

Theophilus, *To Autolycus* 2.37.4 (p. 93 Marcovich), followed by F 1091 and 1092

1091

νόμος τὸν ἐχθρὸν δρᾶν, ὅπου λάβῃς, κακῶς.

Theophilus (see F 1090)

νόμος Grotius: νόμου Theoph.

1086

He treats others while a mass of wounds himself.

1087 *TrGF* (1087 N = adesp. F 562a)

Holy silence is best at the pouring of libations.[1]

[1] Metre uncertain, perhaps lyric.

1089

When the god decides to save (a man), he provides many
ways to safety.[1]

[1] Euripidean authorship has been doubted on grounds of
style.

1090

Endure now that you are suffering (harm), for you were
happy in doing (it).[1]

[1] Probably from a chorus; the metre is anapaestic.

1091

It is the custom to harm one's enemy, wherever you catch
him.[1]

[1] A commonplace: see F 1092 and e.g. *Heracles* 585–6, *Ion*
1046–7. Grotius' 'It is the custom' is needed to fit Theophilus' con-
text of retaliation sanctioned by custom and approved by poets (he
does not mention formal retaliation in law); the transmitted read-
ing gives '. . . to harm the law's enemy . . .'. Without this correction
Euripidean authorship is open to doubt on grounds of style.

1092

ἐχθροὺς κακῶς δρᾶν ἀνδρὸς ἡγοῦμαι μέρος.

Theophilus (see F 1090)

1093

. . . διωκομένη ὑπὸ Πηλέως ἡ Θέτις μετήλλαττεν ἑαυτὴν ὡς ὁ Πρωτεὺς εἰς διαφόρους ἰδέας· . . . κατέσχεν αὐτὴν ἐν σηπίας μορφῇ καὶ ἐμίγη αὐτῇ, ὅθεν καὶ Σηπιὰς χώριον Μαγνησίας Θετταλικῆς.

Tzetzes on Lycophron, Alexandra 175, cf. 178

1093a

503   Ἕλενος . . .

505   μόνος προσῆλθεν Ἕλλησι καὶ λέγει τὰς μαντείας . . .

506   . . . ὁ δ᾽ Εὐριπίδης λέγει,

507   ἀνθ᾽ οὗπερ ὁ Δηΐφοβος ἔλαβε τὴν Ἑλένην,
       ὁ τούτου σύναιμος, φθονῶν τοῖς Ἕλλησιν ἐπῆλθε.

Tzetzes, Chiliades 6.503–8

1094

Euripides ait ideo nomen additum esse Andromachae, quod ἀνδρὶ μάχεται.

Varro, On the Latin Language 7.82 citing Ennius, Andromache fr. 35 Jocelyn (see note opposite)

1092

I think it a man's part to harm his enemies.

1093

(Euripides said that) when Thetis was pursued by Peleus, she changed herself like Proteus into different forms . . . he seized her when in the form of an octopus and lay with her, as a result of which the place in Thessalian Magnesia (is called) Sepias.[1]

[1] *Sepia* was one Greek name for an octopus. Tzetzes' attribution of this testimony has been strongly questioned

1093a

Helenus . . . went alone to the Greeks and told them the prophecies . . . and Euripides says, in retaliation for Deiphobus taking Helen, his brother out of jealousy approached the Greeks.[1]

[1] Helen had been married to Deiphobus rather than Helenus after the death of Paris. In some accounts it was this that caused Helenus to reveal to the Greeks how Troy could be taken, but in others, including Euripides' *Philoctetes* (test. iii(c), F 789b (2)), he was captured by them and compelled to reveal it. Tzetzes' attribution of the alternative story to Euripides is questionable.

1094

Euripides says that Andromache was given her name because she 'fights a man'.[1]

[1] *Andro-mache* is Greek 'man-fight'. No known myth has her fighting a man, but her physical resistance to her second 'husband' Neoptolemus, the enforced successor to her first husband Hector (whom Neoptolemus' father Achilles had killed), may be implied. For such etymologies cf. *Alexander* F 42d (cited with this fragment by Varro) with note.

DOUBTFUL OR SPURIOUS
FRAGMENTS
(F 1107–1132)

These fragments are attributed to Euripides by one or more sources (including the first named for each below), but the attributions are either unlikely or false. See the notes to the translations.

Brief fragments: F 1114 'a common mind' or 'the mind of a market orator', F 1117 'the course of evil lives' (?), F 1124 'one another' (meaning 'themselves', as in Suppliant Women *676?), F 1125 'go and be damned!', F 1126 'secret agents', F 1127 'to strip (a traveller of his clothes)'.*

DOUBTFUL OR SPURIOUS FRAGMENTS

(1107 N = 1048a above)

(1108, 1109 N: see *Rhesus* above)

(1109a N Suppl. = *Andromache* 158)

1110

Ζεὺς ἐν θεοῖσι μάντις ἀψευδέστατος ...
καὶ τέλος αὐτὸς ἔχει.

Aristides, *Orations* 2.166 with Schol.

(1110a N–Sn = *Iphigenia at Aulis* 80)

1111

κρίμνη σεαυτὴν ἐκ μέσης ἀντηρίδος.

Etymologicum Genuinum AB α 932 Lasserre–Livadaras;
other sources have the phrase whole or (mostly) curtailed

1111a (= 943 N)

πυριγενὴς δὲ δράκων ὁδὸν ἡγεῖται τετραμόρφῳ
ζευγνὺς ἁρμονίᾳ πλούτου πολύκαρπον ὄχημα.

Macrobius, *Saturnalia* 1.17.58

1 τετραμόρφῳ Wilamowitz: ταῖς τετραμόρφοις | ὥραις
Macrob.

(1107 N = 1048a above)

(1108, 1109 N: see *Rhesus* above)

(1109a N Suppl. = *Andromache* 158)

1110

Zeus is the most unerring prophet among the gods . . . and himself possesses the fulfilment.[1]

[1] The Scholia indicate a short break in the sense. The attribution is doubted on metrical grounds (the combination of iambic trimeter and dactylic half-verse is rare but possible in Euripidean lyric). West assigns the fragment to Archilochus (F 298 *IEG*), but attribution to Euripides is reasserted by A. Casadio, *Museum Criticum* 25–8 (1990–3), 31–5.

(1110a N–Sn = *Iphigenia at Aulis* 80)

1111

Hang yourself from the middle of a beam.[1]

[1] Addressed to a woman; for such suicides cf. *Hipp.* 769, 779, 802 etc. So forthright a command suggests comedy rather than tragedy.

1111a (= 943 N)

And the fire-born serpent leads the way, yoking its produce-laden wagon of abundance to a fourfold harmony.[1]

[1] Cited by Macrobius to illustrate the naming of the Sun's sinuous path through the ecliptic as 'the serpent', identified with the Python slain at Delphi by the sun-god Apollo. 'The fourfold harmony are the four seasons, which the Sun, the fire-dragon, has yoked to his wagon, and which bring the blessing of the earth's produce' (Wilamowitz, correcting the transmitted interpolation 'with the fourfold seasons in harmony'). Thought and dactylic verse-form suggest a mystical source much later than Euripides' time.

1112

ἔδει γὰρ ἡμᾶς τοῖς θεοῖς θύειν, ὅταν
γυναῖκα κατορύττῃ τις, οὐχ ὅταν γαμῇ.

Melissa Augustana 56.18 Wachsmuth; Excerpta Vindobonensia 39 Meineke, unattributed

1113

ἡ φύσις ἑκάστῳ τοῦ γένους ἐστὶν πατρίς.

Stobaeus 4.29.35, attributed to Euripides only in ed. Trincavelli; [Menander], Monostichs 295 Jaekel

1113a (= 1040 N)

ὅταν ἴδῃς πρὸς ὕψος ἠρμένον τινὰ
λαμπρῷ τε πλούτῳ καὶ γένει γαυρούμενον
ὀφρύν τε μείζω τῆς τύχης ἐπηρκότα,
τούτου ταχεῖαν νέμεσιν εὐθὺς προσδόκα.

Stobaeus 3.22.5; varied and expanded in many other citations

1113b (= 1080 N)

ὦ γῆρας, οἵαν ἐλπίδ᾽ ἡδονῆς ἔχεις,
καὶ πᾶς τις εἰς σὲ βούλετ᾽ ἀνθρώπων μολεῖν·
λαβὼν δὲ πεῖραν, μεταμέλειαν λαμβάνει,
ὡς οὐδὲν ἔστι χεῖρον ἐν θνητῷ γένει.

Stobaeus 4.50.40

1112

We should be sacrificing to the gods when one of us digs a grave for his wife, not when he marries.[1]

[1] Deemed comic by some editors, but kept for Euripides by Kassel–Austin in *PCG* VIII.514.

1113

The nature he has from his birth is each man's fatherland.[1]

[1] Attribution is missing in the mss. of Stobaeus (supplied in ed. Trincavelli), as for the preceding citation there (= adesp. com. F 902 *PCG*).

1113a (= 1040 N)

Whenever you see someone lifted to the heights and exulting in the splendour of wealth or birth, with brows raised in pride too great for his fortunes, immediately expect swift retribution for him.[1]

[1] Vocabulary, style and metre show Euripides not to be the author.

1113b (= 1080 N)

Old age! What hope you hold of pleasure—and every man wishes to reach you! But when he experiences you, he has regret, for there is nothing worse in human existence.[1]

[1] Metrical features show Euripides not to be the author, and style points to comedy (source of most citations in Stobaeus 4.50.32–50, on old age).

DOUBTFUL OR SPURIOUS FRAGMENTS

1115

λιγυρῶς δὲ οὐ λέγει ἡδέως κατὰ τὸν Εὐριπίδην 'ἡδονὴ πανταχοῦ ἐστι καὶ πάντα δι' ἡδονῆς γίνεται', ἀλλὰ λιγὺ τὸ ὀξύ.

Schol. on Dionysius Thrax, *Art of Grammar, Gramm. Gr.* I.3.475.33 Hilgard

(1116 N = 926b above)

1118

Quae hic mala putantur, haec sunt in caelo bona.

Lactantius, *Divine Institutions* 5.15.11 (= Lactantius fr. 2 in *Fr. Poet. Lat.* Büchner-Blänsdorf)

1119

ὀχληρὸς δὲ ξένος ὄψιος μολών.

Macarius 6.83 (*CPG* II.199.4)

1121a

Εὐριπίδης ἔφη τὸν ἥλιον διὰ τὴν γῆν γενέσθαι καὶ τὸν οὐρανὸν ὁμοίως.

Olympiodorus, comm. on Aristotle, *Meteorologica* 353a24 (*CAG* XXX.2.129.24)

1115

The word λιγυρῶς does not mean 'pleasantly', as in Euripides' 'pleasure is everywhere and everything comes into being through pleasure', but λιγύ is that which is piercing.[1]

[1] Mysterious: the quotation from Euripides does not include the word he is said to use in a wrong meaning, nor is it metrical.

(1116 N = 926b above)

1118

Things which are here thought bad are good in heaven.[1]

[1] Paraphrased as Euripides' by Lactantius. Euripidean authorship is defended by W. Theiler and (with F 1128a) M. L. West. Similar paradoxes at *Hippolytus* 411–2 and *Ion* 449–51.

1119

A guest who comes late is troublesome.[1]

[1] The words yield no metre, and probably reformulate *Alcestis* 540.

1121a

Euripides said that the sun came into being on account of the earth, and the sky likewise.[1]

[1] Aristotle remarked that the ancients had formulated the primacy of the earth 'in rather tragic and solemn style', and his commentator Olympiodorus endorsed 'tragic' with this statement attributed (without evidence) to Euripides; compare *Chrysippus* F 839 with note.

DOUBTFUL OR SPURIOUS FRAGMENTS

(1122, 1123 N = 1094b, 1095b above)

(1128 N = 1015a above)

1128a
τὰ καλὰ καὶ τὰ μὴ καλὰ
καλῶς ἔχουσιν.

Tzetzes on Aristophanes, *Wealth* 600

1128b
ἐκτυπεῖτο δὲ
ἐμβὰς γερόντων εὐρύθμοις προβήμασιν.

Aristophanes, *Wealth* 758–9, where Tzetzes asserts parody of Euripides

**1128c
δεῦρ' ἐλθέ· σὺν σοὶ τἄλλα βούλομαι φράσαι.

Schol. on Aristophanes, *Birds* 1647; assigned to Euripides by West

ἐλθέ· σὺν σοὶ Schol.: ἐλθ'· ἐς οὖς σοι Wilamowitz, comparing *Ion* 1520–1

1128d
διὰ λύπην καὶ μανία ⟨γὰρ⟩ γίγνεται
πολλοῖσι καὶ νοσήματ' οὐκ ἰάσιμα.

Anonymous Byzantine text (A. Sideras, *Hellenika* 38 [1987], 190); but the lines with γὰρ included = Philemon F 106.2–3 *PCG* (from Stobaeus 4.35.1)

(1122, 1123 N = 1094b, 1095b above)

(1128 N = 1015a above)

1128a

Good and not good are well.[1]

[1] Tzetzes illustrates hyperbole in Euripides; for the phrasing cf. *Orestes* 492. Possibly authentic: see on F 1118 above.

1128b

. . . and the old men's slippers were noisy with their rhythmic steps forward.[1]

[1] Comic mockery of the entry of elderly chorusmen, e.g. *Cresphontes* F 448a.73–6; 'were noisy' and 'rhythmic steps forward' are modelled on Euripidean expressions.

**1128c

Come here! I want to talk the rest over with you.[1]

[1] 'to say the rest into your ear', Wilamowitz.

1128d

Through grief madness and incurable afflictions also come to many people.[1]

[1] Metre bars ascription to Euripides, with or without the supplement; but for grief as affliction see on F 1079.3.

DOUBTFUL OR SPURIOUS FRAGMENTS

(1129 N = adesp. F 622)

(1130, 1131 N = F 912a, 912b above)

(1132: see *Danae*, Appendix)

DOUBTFUL OR SPURIOUS FRAGMENTS

(1129 N = adesp. F 622)

(1130, 1131 N = 912a, 912b above)

(1132: see *Danae*, Appendix)

APPENDIX:
CRITIAS OR EURIPIDES?

PIRITHOUS, RHADAMANTHYS, TENNES, and a SISYPHUS(?)

TrGF 1 43 Critias T 1–4, F 1–21, with Addenda in *TrGF* 1² (1986), 341–5 (chiefly F 4a) and *TrGF* 5.1107–8 (chiefly F 20a); cf. B. Gauly in *Musa Tragica* 108–25 (with Kannicht's participation). Earlier, Critias 88 B 10–29 DK; A. M. Battegazzore in Battegazzore and M. Untersteiner, *Sofisti. Testimonianze e Frammenti IV* (1962), 274–317; see also under *Pirithous* and *Sisyphus* below.[1]

Wilamowitz, *Analecta* 159, 161–6, *Kleine Schriften* IV.534 (orig. 1907), 446–7 (orig. 1927), 481–2 (orig. 1929), and a letter of 1907 responding to Kuiper (see bibl. for *Pirithous* below), published by J. M. Bremer and W. M. Calder III, *Mnemosyne* 47 (1997), 179–81, 211–6; A. Lesky, *Die tragische Dichtung der Hellenen* (Göttingen, 1972³), 525–6; D. V. Panchenko, *Vestnik Drevnei Istorii* 151 (1980), 144–62; B. Gauly in *Musa Tragica*, 108–9; Pechstein 289–319 with bibliography, and in Krumeich

---

[1] Nauck in 1889 assigned the then known fragments of *Pirithous, Rhadamanthys* and *Tennes* to Euripides, and the *Sisyphus* fragment to Critias along with those ascribed to him without play titles. Jouan and Van Looy excluded the four plays altogether from their Budé edition of Euripides (see ed. Budé VIII.1.xv).

(1999), 552–5; C. Collard, *Tragedy, Euripides and Euripideans* (Exeter, 2007), 55–68 (orig. 1995) with bibliography.

These four fragmentary plays are attributed in modern editions to the intellectual Critias, a slightly younger associate of Socrates who was politically active in the last years of Euripides' life; he became notorious as one of the 'Thirty Tyrants' who briefly controlled Athens under Spartan rule in 404–3, and was killed resisting overthrow in 403. Some scholars however follow the majority of ancient sources in attributing the plays to Euripides.

    I. THE EVIDENCE. *Sisyphus* and *Tennes* appear among Euripides' plays in the papyrus collection of hypotheses P. Oxy. 2455, and in the list of play titles P. Oxy. 2456 (see *TrGF* 5.60, T 8; the part of this list which might have contained *Pirithous* and *Rhadamanthys* is missing). A *Sisyphus* by Euripides is known as part of his production of 415 (see under *Sisyphus* above), and is listed in the damaged Piraeus catalogue inscription (see *TrGF* 5.58–9, T 7a); *Pirithous* may perhaps have stood there also where only an initial P remains (no entries for R or T survive)

    The following fragments are attributed in the sources to Euripides: *Pirithous* F 1 (hypothesis and text), 3, 4, 6, 10, 12–14 (F 2 is attributed uncertainly to Euripides or Critias, F 11 simply to a *Pirithous*; F 4a, 5 and 7–9 are from a single papyrus without attribution, but F 4a and 5 are clearly from a play featuring Pirithous); *Rhadamanthys* F 15 (hypothesis) and F 16–18; *Tennes* F 20 (hypothesis) and F 21 (in F 20a, a myth summary, Euripides may have been named as a poet who told Tennes' story). The sole source of the *Sisyphus* fragment as a whole (F 19) attributes it to Critias (without a play title), but some lines from it are elsewhere attributed to Euripides, and their speaker named as Sisyphus.

Against Euripidean authorship of *Pirithous*, *Rhadamanthys* and *Tennes* is the statement in the ancient *Life of Euripides* (see *TrGF* 5.47, T 1.IA(9)) that these three plays are not authentically his—but no alternative author is named.

The following are attributed to Critias: *Pirithous* F 2 (to Critias or Euripides, see above), *Sisyphus* F 19 as a whole (see above), and four fragments cited without attribution to any play (Critias F 22–25).[2] It is inferred from Plato, *Critias* 108b and *Charmides* 162d (Critias T 1a and 1b in *TrGF*) that Critias composed for the tragic theatre.

Further major considerations may be briefly listed: (*a*) Only one other play named *Pirithous* is known, by Euripides' contemporary Achaeus (a single two-word fragment survives, *TrGF* 20 F 36). No other *Rhadamanthys* or *Tennes* is known. (*b*) The survival of papyrus fragments of narrative hypotheses and/or texts of *Pirithous*, *Rhadamanthys* and *Tennes* favours Euripides rather than any other poet, given his huge preponderance among papyrus fragments of tragedy. (*c*) The compatibility with Euripidean practice of some features of vocabulary, style and metre

---

[2] F 22? (= 2 N): 'Time has a remedy for all anger.' F 23 (= 3 N): 'The man who in associating with his friends does everything to gratify them, makes their immediate pleasure into enmity for time to come' (see further under *Pirithous*, Other Ascriptions). F 24 (= 4 N): 'It is dreadful when a man without sense thinks he is sensible.' F 25 (= 5 N): 'It is better to have wealth and its stupidity share one's home than poverty with its wisdom.'

in the fragments is disputed. *(d)* The compatibility with Euripidean thought and expression of some philosophical and 'metaphysical' concepts in *Pirithous* F 3 and 4 is disputed. *(e)* Since Euripides did write a satyric *Sisyphus*, the most debated questions are whether F 19 should be attributed to him, and to this known play, rather than to a *Sisyphus* by Critias for which there is no evidence at all, and whether the atheistic character of F 19 is consistent with Euripides' reputed atheism (rather than Critias's), as perceived in antiquity and mentioned in the sources which attribute parts of this fragment to Euripides, and consistent with satyric style and ethos overall.

II. SUMMARY DISCUSSION. The attribution of all four plays to Critias stems from repeated insistence by Wilamowitz between the years 1875 and 1929. He put the statement in the ancient *Life* of Euripides that '*Tennes*, *Rhadamanthys* and *Pirithous* are inauthentic' alongside the ancient attribution of a satyric *Sisyphus* and its two surviving fragments to Euripides, and of the *Sisyphus* fragment (without play title) to Critias. In a theory of magisterial economy, he declared that Critias had composed a tetralogy consisting of all four plays, in which *Sisyphus* was satyric; because Critias almost disappeared from the record after his infamous career and death, the entire tetralogy became associated with Euripides;[3] Alexandrian scholars (echoed in the *Life*) had tried to correct this false

---

[3] Although unconvinced by Wilamowitz's argument, Gauly 109 well observes that such a transfer of all four plays into the Euripidean corpus might explain why so many of the fragments are attributed to him, and why narrative hypotheses to *Pirithous*, *Rhadamanthys* and *Tennes* have surfaced under his name.

attribution, and we should respect them, given the general care and accuracy of their information. Wilamowitz claimed that *Pirithous, Rhadamanthys* and the *Sisyphus* fragment are inconsistent with Euripides' style and thought. He also contended that the very fewness of the dramatic fragments ascribed to Critias strengthened his case: 'the less well attested author is likely to be the true one'. Lastly, he supposed that the two very brief fragments of Euripides' *Sisyphus* (F 673–4) were wrongly attributed, possibly through a miscopying of the title of the similarly satyric *Syleus*, or that the play itself is entirely lost.

The chief aspects of the dispute are as follows: *(a)* *Pirithous, Rhadamanthys* and *Tennes* are linked only in the *Life*'s statement that they are not authentically Euripidean; their association with one another, and with the *Sisyphus* fragment at all, let alone all together in a tetralogy by Critias, was and remains purely hypothetical, despite the uncertain attribution of *Pirithous* F 2 to both poets. So long as we do not know why some Alexandrian scholar(s) disqualified the three plays for Euripides, their status is best regarded as uncertain. *(b)* Can the huge preponderance of attributions of the three named plays to Euripides (both hypotheses and book fragments) be set aside, especially when there is so little evidence that Critias wrote tragedy at all, and when the only play named as his is *Pirithous*, in the disputed attribution of F 2? *(c)* Judgments on matters of language, metre and thought which disqualify Euripides as author of the three plays (chiefly Wilamowitz, Panchenko) will always be contested (see Kuiper and Page on *Pirithous*, and Pechstein), but their attribution to Critias does not follow in any case; and Critias' authorship of the *Sisyphus* fragment has been contested on the same grounds (Davies, Pechstein). One particular argument against Euripides' authorship of this fragment is the occurrence within its 42 verses of two certain instances of verse enjambement through a final prepositive word (13, 27) and one doubtful one (18): there are barely more than half-a-dozen instances of this phenomenon in dialogue in the whole of Euripides' surviving work.[4] *(d)* Scholarship remains evenly divided, whether the 'atheistic' *Sisyphus* fragment is compatible with Euripides' thought: Battegazzore, Winiarczyk and Obbink deny it; Dihle, Scodel and Pechstein accept it; Davies reached no conclusion.[5] *(e)* If all four plays are 'returned' to Euripides, how is it explicable that some parts of them were attributed to Critias? Would the four unassigned book fragments (F 22–25) be plausibly the only survival of his dramatic activity?

In sum, Lesky's reserve about Wilamowitz's theory looks more and more sensible. Collard has shown how overwhelming was the testimony for Euripidean authorship, and that it should be respected (while retreating a little in 2007 for the *Sisyphus* fragment on the ground of

---

[4] This consideration was first advanced by Dover, some years before his separate discussion of *Pirithous*, but it is not conclusive: ὅπως = 'so that' with enjambement (v. 13) has seven clear parallels in Euripides (including *Telephus* F 738; also = 'like' in F 971). ἵνα with enjambement (v. 27) has no parallel in Euripides, but five in Sophocles and four in *Prometheus Bound*. τε καὶ ending v. 27 is unparalleled in Euripides (four times in Sophocles), but is in a probably interpolated and also corrupt passage.   [5] Features of the plot and dramaturgy of *Pirithous* which seem to bear on the dispute are mentioned below in the Introduction to that play.

metre). It seems best to conclude that on the evidence at present available the question of authorship must remain unresolved; so too the question whether the *Sisyphus* fragment was satyric, and whether it may after all belong, if not to Euripides' known *Sisyphus*, then perhaps to another of his satyr plays such as *Autolycus A* (Pechstein, 1999; cf. P. Cipolla [bibl. for *Sisyphus* below], 247–68).

PIRITHOUS

TrGF 1 43 Critias F 1–14, with F 4a in Vol. 1² (1986), 349–51; B. Gauly in *Musa Tragica* 109–20; Battegazzore (1962: see general bibl. above), 280–305 and in Battegazzore and others, *Corpus dei papiri filosofici greci e latini* 1* (1989), 442–66; Diggle, *TrGFS* 173–5 (F 1, 4a, 5, 7); G. Alvoni, *Hermes* 134 (2006), 290–300 (F 1, Hypothesis).

K. Kuiper, *Mnemosyne* 35 (1907), 354–85 (for Wilamowitz's response to Kuiper see general bibl. above); Page, *GLP* 120–3 (no. 15); H.-J. Mette, *ZPE* 50 (1983), 13–19; D. F. Sutton, *Two Lost Plays of Euripides* (Frankfurt, 1987), 5–106; Gantz 277, 291–5; K. J. Dover, *Aristophanes. Frogs* (Oxford, 1993), 54–5; *LIMC* VII.i.232–42 'Peirithoos' nos. 69–91, cf. V.i.182 'Herakles' nos. 3515–9 and VII.i.922–51 'Theseus' nos. 291–9.

On the authorship of *Pirithous* see the Introduction to this Appendix. For ascription to Euripides see also Kuiper, Page, Mette, Sutton, and for ascription to Critias, Dover. A further study is promised by Alvoni 290 n. 3 ('pseudo-Euripidean').

The close friendship between Theseus and Pirithous, already implicit in their brief pairing at Homer, Odyssey *11.631, is regularly attested in art and literature from the 6th century onwards (Gantz 277, 291–2, LIMC VII.i.232–3). The story of their joint descent into Hades to recover*

Persephone (abducted by Hades) as Pirithous' future wife, and of their imprisonment and release, became increasingly varied from the mid-5th century into late antiquity (Gantz 293–5). This background to the play is summarized along with its plot in the narrative hypothesis preserved by the Byzantine Ioannes Logothetes. It ends by stating that both Theseus and Pirithous were rescued by Heracles, and it is probably the source of the scholia on the Byzantine Tzetzes, Chiliades 4.911 (p. 573 Leone), which attribute the double rescue to Euripides and imply that a different version was commoner, in which Pirithous was intended as food for Cerberus and could not be rescued (so too Tzetzes on Aristophanes, Frogs 142a; the double rescue reappears in e.g. Diodorus 4.26.12 and Hyginus, Fab. 79.3; Heracles' rescue of Theseus alone during the same labour also occurs in Euripides' Heracles 610–9, 1221–2, and the single rescue persists in e.g. Horace, Odes 4.7.27–8: on this whole topic see Alvoni 294–5). The play's dominant theme of friendship under severe trial (here between all three main persons: F 1, Hypothesis, end; F 6, 7) is frequent in Euripides; it helps to suggest his authorship (Mette, Sutton), but cannot prove it.

Some of the fragments can be given a dramatic context. F 2–4 are from the entry chant of the Chorus, comprised apparently of dead initiates of the Eleusinian Mysteries (see note on F 2); they come to pour offerings to the underworld powers, but celebrate also physical and metaphysical aspects of the world above. F 1, Heracles' arrival in Hades and greeting by its 'gatekeeper' Aeacus, was for a time taken as the play's opening (so Snell in the first edition of TrGF 1); such a dialogue is not securely attested at the very beginning of a Euripidean prologue, and was therefore taken also to disqualify him from authorship, but it

is much more likely that the play began by presenting
Theseus and the already fettered Pirithous, and that Hera-
cles arrived perhaps immediately after the Chorus' entry
chant.[1] F 4a and 5, Heracles' meeting and exchange with
Pirithous, would follow; here it may be suggestive for the
tone of the play that Pirithous appears to attribute the
cause of his own punishment in Hades to his being the son
of Ixion who was similarly arrogant towards the gods (F
5.12–20)—but the text breaks off here, and it is possible
that Pirithous admitted comparable arrogance in himself
in entering Hades. In probably a further episode Theseus
would appeal to Heracles for rescue for both himself and
Pirithous (F 7). The book fragment F 6 seems also to belong
to this scene. The gnomic F 10 and 12 may well come from
this part of the play too, but the gnomic F 11 cannot be lo-
cated. That is all we have; the many representations in art
of the three heroes in the underworld give no sure help in
reconstructing the play (see LIMC).

Brief fragments: Critias F 13 (= Eur. fr. 599 N) 'pretext'
and F 14 (= Eur. fr. 600 N) 'distress' (a verb). Other ascrip-
tions: Eur. F 865, 868, 912 (also ascribed to Cretans or
Oedipus), 936 (also to Eurystheus), 955c, 964 (of these all
but F 912 mention or allude to Hades); Critias F 23;[2] and,
most significantly, adesp. F 658 comprising two related pa-
pyrus fragments, P. Köln 2 with remains of twelve lines
possibly describing the rescue of Theseus and Pirithous as

---

[1] Wilamowitz himself had come to such an opinion: see TrGF
5.1107 and Gauly 110–1, who adds that a prologue which immedi-
ately presented Heracles is unlikely in a play named for Pirithous.
But W. Luppe, Philologus 140 (1996), 217 holds to the older view.
[2] Suggested for Pirithous, in the vicinity of F 7, by Diels–Kranz;
for the content see note 2 in the Introduction to this Appendix.

a struggle facing Heracles greater than that with Cerber-us,[3] and PSI inv. 3021 with damaged ends of twelve lines in which Persephone may be foretelling to Theseus or Piri-thous the return to the living world of Theseus and also Pirithous;[4] Cockle (see under F 4a below) inclines to accept both fragments for the play (and for Euripides), but Snell–Kannicht in TrGF 2.241 decline attribution even to Critias on the ground of 'late' vocabulary.

It cannot be known whether the play was a tragedy or a satyr play. In favour of the first may be the similarity with Prometheus Bound, *in which Prometheus is fettered apparently like Pirithous. A temptation to think the second may lie in the parodic scenes in Aristophanes,* Frogs *285–95 and especially 464–78, 605–73, where Dionysus-Heracles encounters Hades' gatekeeper (named as Aeacus in the mss., as in F 1 here: on this point see Dover [bibl. above]). It has been suggested that if* Pirithous *is Euripidean, it may have been 'prosatyric' like* Alcestis.

Art in the modern period has concentrated on the more famous episode of Theseus and Pirithous at the Wedding of the Centaurs (OGCMA II.902–3).

---

[3] Vv. 1–5 seem to be stichomythia: 1 ' . . . the curse of the Sown Men . . . '; 2 ' . . . you thought . . . the unyielding dog'; 3 ' . . . struggle . . . , not a wrestle with a beast'; 4 ' . . . to go . . . a most glorious struggle'; 5 ' . . . I shall destroy . . . ', then 6 ' . . . a bold heart . . . ', 9 ' . . . ruler (?) . . . ', 10 ' . . . expecting . . . '   [4] 'a place . . . you *(sing.)* together with Heracles . . . daughters [i.e. the Erinyes?] . . . hero [i.e. Heracles?] . . . is not fated . . . darkness. He will go even beneath the earth . . . as helper *(or* conductor) . . . (from?) the bounds which permit no return. A gorgon-face(?) with . . . eyes (will manifest itself?) to you *(sing.)*, fearsome with menace, of an undead thing . . . it will overcome my husband [i.e. Pirithous] . . . darkness . . . *(one line)* . . . (in?) the hidden depth . . . '

639

ΠΕΙΡΙΘΟΥΣ

1, Hypothesis (~ Euripides pp. 546–7 Nauck)

Πειρίθους ἐπὶ τὴν Περσεφόνης μνηστείαν μετὰ Θησέως
εἰς Ἅιδου καταβὰς τιμωρίας ἔτυχε τῆς πρεπούσης· αὐτὸς
μὲν γὰρ ἐπὶ πέτρας ἀκινήτῳ καθέδρᾳ πεδηθεὶς δρακόν-
των ἐφρουρεῖτο χάσμασιν, Θησεὺς δὲ τὸν φίλον ἐγκατα-
λιπεῖν αἰσχρὸν ἡγούμενος βίον εἶχε τὴν ἐν Ἅιδου ζωήν.
ἐπὶ δὲ τὸν Κέρβερον Ἡρακλῆς ἀποσταλεὶς ὑπὸ Εὐρυσθέ-
ως τοῦ μὲν θηρίου βίᾳ περιεγένετο, τοὺς δὲ περὶ Θησέα
χάριτι τῶν χθονίων θεῶν τῆς παρούσης ἀνάγκης ἐξέλυ-
σεν, μιᾷ πράξει καὶ τὸν ἀνθιστάμενον χειρωσάμενος καὶ
παρὰ θεῶν χάριν λαβὼν καὶ δυστυχοῦντας ἐλεήσας φί-
λους.

(For the rest of F 1 see after F 4 below)

Ioannes Logothetes, Commentary on [Hermogenes], *Means of
Rhetorical Effectiveness* 28 (ed. H. Rabe, *RhM* 63 [1908], 144–5);
Gregory of Corinth, Commentary on the same treatise, *Rhet. Gr.*
VII.1312–13 Walz; cf. Diggle, *TrGFS* 172; W. Luppe, *Philologus*
140 (1996), 216–9 (textual history and status of this hypothesis);
G. Alvoni, *Hermes* 134 (2006), 290–300 (edition from a new

PIRITHOUS

1, Hypothesis

To woo Persephone, Pirithous went down with Theseus into
Hades and met with fitting punishment: he himself was fet-
tered to an immovable seat upon rock and guarded by gaping
serpents,[1] but Theseus held it shameful to abandon his friend
there and went on with the existence in Hades as his life.[2]
When Heracles was sent by Eurystheus to fetch Cerberus he
overcame the beast by force,[3] and through the favour of the
underworld gods released Theseus and his companion from
their predicament: in one act he worsted his opponent, re-
ceived favour from the gods, and took pity on friends in mis-
fortune.

(For the rest of F 1 see after F 4 below)

[1] The vocabulary in 'fettered . . . serpents' is almost certainly
borrowed from the play; but 'immovable seat' may allude to the
posture forced upon those facing execution at Athens, for in some
accounts Pirithous is set to be eaten by Cerberus (like Andromeda
by a sea-monster).   [2] The expression has been questioned
(but cf. F 7.5–10, and F 12 for the idea) and altered: 'willingly
chose the life in Hades' Nauck, 'willingly went on with the life in
Hades' Wilamowitz.   [3] Cf. Euripides' satyric *Eurystheus*.

recension of the mss.). Attributed by these sources to Euripides' *Pirithous*.

βίον εἶχε all mss. (so Alvoni: βίον εἶχε earlier read wrongly in the most important one): ἑκὼν εἵλετο Nauck: ἑκὼν εἶχε Wilamowitz

2 (= Eur. fr. 592 N)

ΧΟΡΟΣ

. . . ἵνα πλημοχόας τάσδ᾽ εἰς χθόνιον
χάσμ᾽ εὐφήμως προχέωμεν.

Athenaeus 11.496a, attributed to 'the author of the *Pirithous*, whether he is Critias the tyrant or Euripides'

3 (= Eur. fr. 594 N)

ΧΟΡΟΣ

ἀκάμας τε χρόνος περί τ᾽ ἀενάῳ
ῥεύματι πλήρης φοιτᾷ τίκτων
αὐτὸς ἑαυτόν, δίδυμοί τ᾽ ἄρκτοι
ταῖς ὠκυπλάνοις πτερύγων ῥιπαῖς
5   τὸν Ἀτλάντειον τηροῦσι πόλον.

Clement of Alexandria, *Miscellanies* 5.6.36.1, attributed to 'tragedy'; v. 5: Schol. on Aristophanes, *Birds* 179, attributed to Euripides' *Pirithous* and slightly adapted

2 (= Eur. fr. 592 N)

CHORUS

. . . so that we may pour these ewers in reverent silence into earth's chasm.[1]

[1] From the entry song of the Chorus, continued in F 3–4. Athenaeus names the ewers as those used on the final day of the Eleusinian Mysteries, and it is inferred that the Chorus therefore comprised dead initiates; *Cretans* F 472 has a similar entry by a ritual Chorus. Diodorus 4.25.1 and Apollodorus 2.5.12 tell that Heracles thought it wise to be initiated in the Mysteries before descending into Hades. Cf. *Heracles* 613.

3 (= Eur. fr. 594 N)

CHORUS

Time is unwearying; full in its ever-flowing stream it goes its round begetting itself;[1] and the twin bears[2] with the swift traverse of their beating wings keep watch on Atlas' vault of sky.

[1] In the Greek *heauton* 'itself' imitates *eniauton* 'year', thus Time regularly begets its own regular and measured length. For the etymology cf. especially Eur. F 862 and Hermippus F 73 *PCG*, with Egli 51–3 who traces the thought to Heraclitus. See also on the next fragment.   [2] Ursa Major and Minor, in the northern sky.

643

APPENDIX

4 (= Eur. fr. 593 N)

ΧΟΡΟΣ

σὲ τὸν αὐτοφυῆ, τὸν ἐν αἰθερίῳ
ῥύμβῳ πάντων φύσιν ἐμπλέξανθ',
ὃν πέρι μὲν φῶς, πέρι δ' ὀρφναία
νὺξ αἰολόχρως ἄκριτός τ' ἄστρων
5 ὄχλος ἐνδελεχῶς ἀμφιχορεύει . . .

Clement of Alexandria, *Miscellanies* 5.14.114.2, attributed to
Euripides' *Pirithous*; vv. 1–4 (τὸν ἐν αἰθερίῳ etc.): Satyrus, *Life
of Euripides* P. Oxy. 1176 fr. 37 col. II, implicitly attributed to Eu-
ripides; vv. 1–2: Schol. on *Orestes* 982, attributed to Euripides'
Pirithous, and (disordered) Schol. on Apollonius Rhodius 4.143,
cf. on 1.1134, both naming Euripides' *Pirithous*

1, cont'd (= Eur. fr. 591 N)

ΑΙΑΚΟΣ

ἔα, τί χρῆμα; δέρκομαι σπουδῇ τινα
δεῦρ' ἐγκονοῦντα καὶ μάλ' εὐτόλμῳ φρενί.
εἰπεῖν δίκαιον, ὦ ξέν', ὅστις ὢν τόπους
ἐς τούσδε χρίμπτῃ καὶ καθ' ἥντιν' αἰτίαν.

Ioannes (F 1, Hypothesis above) continues immediately with
this fragment; Gregory has only vv. 6–10 before the Hypothesis;
v. 9 is attributed by them to both Euripides' *Pirithous* and
his *Melanippe Wise* (= F 481.1), and by Hermogenes (citing only
v. 9) to Euripides. Re-edited by G. Alvoni, *Philologus* 152 (2008),
40–7.

PIRITHOUS

4 (= Eur. fr. 593 N)

CHORUS

You, who generate your own self, who entwine the nature
of all things in heaven's whirl, round which the light of day,
round which night's spangled darkness and the countless
host of stars dance perpetually . . .[1]

[1] According to Clement these verses addressed Mind, as cre-
ator of the universe (this theory of Mind was associated with the
pre-Socratic Anaxagoras, whose influence on Euripides was as-
serted in Satyrus' *Life*: see apparatus opposite); but Time has also
been suggested as the addressee, as in F 3, or Zeus himself. F 3
and 4 are a semi-scientific, semi-mystical evocation of the elemen-
tal world (and a ground for argument about the authorship of
the play, as noted in the Introduction to this Appendix). Egli 49–
53 notes the equation of Time with Olympus (i.e. Zeus) in the fa-
mous Derveni papyrus (P. Derv. col. XXX.3) and its representation
as a creative force in Orphism (1 B 12 and 13 DK).

1, cont'd (= Eur. fr. 591 N)[1]

An entry scene later in the play:

AEACUS

What? What's this? I see someone toiling in haste towards
me here, and with a very brave heart. Stranger, it is right
you should say who you are, and for what reason you ap-
proach this place.

[1] Quoted with the Hypothesis above by its sources, but almost
certainly following F 2–4 (see Introduction).

ΗΡΑΚΛΗΣ

5 οὐδεὶς ὄκνος πάντ' ἐκκαλύψασθαι λόγον·
ἐμοὶ πατρὶς μὲν Ἄργος, ὄνομα δ' Ἡρακλῆς,
θεῶν δὲ πάντων πατρὸς ἐξέφυν Διός·
ἐμῇ γὰρ ἦλθε μητρὶ κεδνὰ πρὸς λέχη
Ζεύς, ὡς λέλεκται τῆς ἀληθείας ὕπο.
10 ἥκω δὲ δεῦρο πρὸς βίαν, Εὐρυσθέως
ἀρχαῖς ὑπείκων, ὅς μ' ἔπεμψ' Ἅιδου κύνα
ἄγειν κελεύων ζῶντα πρὸς Μυκηνίδας
πύλας, ἰδεῖν μὲν οὐ θέλων, ἆθλον δέ μοι
ἀνήνυτον τόνδ' ᾤετ' ἐξηυρηκέναι.
15 τοιόνδ' ἰχνεύων πρᾶγος Εὐρώπης κύκλῳ
Ἀσίας τε πάσης ἐς μυχοὺς ἐλήλυθα.

8 κεδνὰ πρὸς λέχη Dobree: κεδνὴ (i.e. -ῇ) πρὸς λέχος Ioann.
and (some mss.) Greg.   14 τόνδ' ᾤετ' ἐξηυρηκέναι Stahl,
Wilamowitz: τὸν ἔδωκ' ἐξηνυκέναι Ioann.

4a

⟨ΠΕΙΡΙΘΟΥΣ?⟩

δρακοντ[
τηνου[
ὀργὴν .[
ἐπίσταμ[αι

ΧΟΡΟΣ

5 ὀψὲ ξυνεὶς [....]ο..[
θεοὺς σέβεσθ[αι

PIRITHOUS

HERACLES

I do not shrink from revealing my whole story. My country   5
is Argos, and my name Heracles, and I am the son of Zeus,
father of all gods: for Zeus, as is truly told, came to a splen-
did union with my mother. I have come here under com-
pulsion, yielding to the commands of Eurystheus, who   10
sent me with orders to bring the Hound of Hades alive to
Mycenae's gates—not because he wished to see it, but he
thought he had invented in this a task beyond my accom-
plishment. In pursuit of this business I have circled the in-   15
most parts of all Europe and Asia.[2]

---

[2] Presumably searching for an entrance to Hades.

4a

‹ PIRITHOUS?›

. . . serpent(s)[1] . . . anger . . . (I) know . . .

CHORUS

Your understanding is late . . . to respect the gods . . .   5

P. Oxy. 3531, ed. H. M. Cockle and others (1983), a separated
part of P. Oxy. 2078 (F 5 and 7 below); re-ed. R. Kannicht, *TrGF*
1² (1986), 349–51, cf. B. Gauly in *Musa Tragica* 114; Diggle,
TrGFS 174–5. Names (or changes) of speakers were entered by a
second hand.

6 σέβεσθ[αι an attractive supplement, but the papyrus is
insecurely read

ΗΡΑΚΛΗΣ

Ἰξίονος πα[ῖ, πο]λλὰ δ[
εἶδον λόγῳ τ᾽ ἤκουσα [
οὐδ᾽ ἐγγὺς οὐδέν᾽ ἠ[σθόμην
10 τῇ σῇ πελάζοντ᾽ ἀλ[λ-
δυσπραξίᾳ τοὺς π[
σκῆψιν τίν᾽ ἢ τίν᾽ [
ἄτης ἀπρούπτως᾽ .[

ΠΕΙΡΙΘΟΥΣ

ἥδ᾽ οὐκέτ᾽ ἐστ᾽ ἄσημος [οὐδ(ὲ)
15 ὀνειρατώδης ἀλλ᾽ ο[
Ἕλλην· ἰδεῖν δὲ τὸν λέ[γοντα
οἷός τ᾽ ἂν εἴην. πέπτατ[αι
ἀχλὺς πάροιθε τῶν ἐμῶ[ν
ἄθλους ἐρωτᾷς τοὺς ἐμο[ὺς
20 γλώσσης γὰρ ἠχὼ τῆσδε πρ..[

ΗΡΑΚΛΗΣ

οὐδέν τι πάντως θαῦμ[α
ἀπεστερῆσθαί <σ᾽> ἐστὶν α..[
καὶ φθέγμα καὶ σχῆμα .[
πολλαὶ διῆλθον τῆς ἐ[μῆς
25 καὶ σῆς· ἀναμνήσω δε.[

9 ἠ[σθόμην τύχῃ ποτὲ Parsons   10 ἀλ[λ᾽ ὑπερβάλλεις
μακρῷ West   12 τίν᾽ ἢ τὶν᾽ [Cockle   15 ὅ[σον γ᾽
ἐπεικάσαι Diggle: ὁ [φωνήσας τάδε Maehler   16 λέ[γοντα
Handley   23 end ἡμέραι Parsons   24 ἐ[μῆς ὁμιλίας
Cockle: ἐ[μῆς ἀπαλλαγῆς Collard

648

PIRITHOUS

HERACLES

Son of Ixion, many . . . have I seen and heard told . . . (but?
I have learned) of no one (ever) closely approaching your
(misfortune); but in harshness of outcome (you far sur-   10
pass) those . . . what excuse or what . . . (for?) ruin unfore-
seeably . . .

PIRITHOUS

This (voice) is no longer unintelligible (nor) . . . dream-like,
but . . . (is?) Greek.[2] I would be able to see the (speaker) . . .   15
(but?) a mist has spread before my (eyes?) . . . You ask
about my ordeal . . . : for an echo of those words . . .[3]   20

HERACLES

It is absolutely no wonder . . . that (you) are deprived . . .
(my?) voice and appearance . . . Many (days?) . . . of (my
and) your . . .[4] have lapsed. I will remind (you) . . .   25

---

[1] Guarding Pirithous (see Hypothesis).   [2] Presumably
Heracles' voice (cf. v. 23); but Cockle suggests Pirithous may
imagine the voice of an approaching Fury (cf. v. 26) or 'gorgon-
face' (cf. adesp. F 658 in the Introduction, 'Other ascriptions',
note 4), like the 'monster' heard and feared in the apparent parody
of *Pirithous* at Aristophanes, *Frogs* 285–95 (see Introduction, at
end).   [3] Pirithous has heard Heracles' question in v. 19 only
with difficulty.   [4] Cockle suggests '(my and) your (acquain-
tance)', for this line is (so far) the only indication from myth that
Heracles and Pirithous had met before; Kannicht suggested that
'separation' might suit better, whence Collard's conjecture.

APPENDIX

σίγησον· ἀρ[(α)
φων[
της[

26 σίγησον· ἀρ[(α) Mette: σειγησιναρ[P. Oxy.

5

⟨ΠΕΙΡΙΘΟΤΣ⟩

beginnings of six lines including 1 ἐσφηλα[4 ἐλθὼν .[
5 Ἑλλην[6 βωμω..[, then:
θεὸς δὲ μανια[
ἔπεμψεν ἄτη[ν
νεφέλην γυναικ[
10 ἔσπειρεν εἰς τοὺς Θε[σσάλους
θυγατρὶ μίσγοιτ' ε[
τοίων δὲ κόμπω[ν
ποινὰς θεοῖς ἔτεισεν [
μανίας τροχῷ περι[
15 οἰστρη[λ]άτοισιν ᾧχ[ετ(ο)
ἄπυστο[ς] ἀνθρώποι[σιν οὐδέ νιν τάφος
ἔκρυψεν, ἀλλὰ Βορε[άσιν πνοαῖς
διεσπα[ρ]άχθη σῶμ[α

P. Oxy. 2078, ed. A. S. Hunt (1927), fr. 1 (frs. 2 and 3 are F 7 below; frs. 4 and 5, in which hardly a word can be read, are F 8 and 9, omitted here); re-ed. A. Körte, *APF* 10 (1932), 50–3; Page, *GLP* 120–5 (no. 15); Gauly in *Musa Tragica* 116–17; Diggle, *TrGFS* 175–6.

PIRITHOUS

Quiet! ... voice ... ?[5]

5 Mette's supplement suggests a possible continuation: 'Quiet! (Do you hear) a voice ... ?', as if of some approaching terror.

5

⟨PIRITHOUS⟩

beginnings of six lines including 1 (they?) brought low *or* ruined   3 coming   5 (a?) Greek   6 altars, *then*: The god however ... (with?) madness ... sent ruin ... a cloud as wife ... sowed (a report) among the (Thessalians)   10 (that?) he had lain with the daughter ... For such boasts ... he paid the gods penalty ... (for his?) madness on a wheel ... (he was gone?) ... (in?) frenzied ... vanished from   15 men's knowledge (and no tomb) hid him, but his body was torn apart (by?) northern (blasts). ... my father (was de-

---

15 ὤχ[ετο (χ *insecure*): ὤχ[μασεν Housman   16 *end* Körte   17 *end* Housman   18 σῶμ[α *read by* Cockle: σ[υ]ν μ[Hunt

πατὴ[ρ ἁ]μαρτὼν εἰς θε[οὺς ἀπώλετο
20 ἐγὼ [δ' ἐκ]είνου π[ή]ματα [

19 end Körte: 18–19 τήνδε δὴ τίσιν | . . . εἰς θε[οὺς ἐκτήσατο
Diggle

6 (= Eur. fr. 595 N)
αἰδοῦς ἀχαλκεύτοισιν ἔζευκται πέδαις.

Plutarch, *Moralia* 96c (mentioning Theseus and Pirithous in a
treatise on friendship) and 482a and 533a, all without attribution;
and at 763f with attribution to Euripides

7

ends of three dialogue trimeters, including 3 πόνου, *then:*
c. 9 *letters*] σοι το .[. . . . .] ἡδὺ ν[ῦ]ν δοκεῖ

⟨ΘΗΣΕΤΣ?⟩
5 οὐκ   ]τος, Ἡράκλεις, [σὲ] μέμψομαι
c. 9 *letters*]η, πιστὸν γὰρ ἄνδρα καὶ φίλον

P. Oxy. 2078 (see under F 5) frs. 2 (vv. 1–32) and 3 (vv. 33–39)

5 οὐκ supplied by Körte

stroyed) for his offence to the gods. I . . . his sufferings . . .[1]   20

[1] Pirithous recounts the cruel price his father Ixion (a Thessalian) paid the gods for his (mad?) boasting that he had seduced Cronus' daughter Hera, the wife of Zeus; but it appears from 'cloud as wife' that Zeus deceived him with a phantom (as in Pindar, *Pythians* 2.21–42; for Ixion's arrogance and Zeus's deception cf. Eur. *Ixion* test. ii–iii and F 426–7). While myth generally tells of Ixion's endless torture on the wheel, some accounts (and some art) have him associated with winds or, as apparently in vv. 17–18, torn apart by them. Editors' supplements in this fragment depend largely on their differing accommodation of such variant detail. In v. 15 Housman's 'he rode (i.e. rode the wheel)' makes a grim metaphor from mastering a horse. In vv. 18–19 Diggle suggests '(This was indeed the punishment) my father (got) for his offence . . .'

6 (= Eur. fr. 595 N)

He (i.e. Theseus) is joined (to me?) in the unforged fetters of a sense of honour.[1]

[1] Possibly Pirithous explaining Theseus' selflessness to Heracles (cf. F 7.6–7). Cf. the two friends' 'invisible bond' in Apollonius Rhodius 1.102.

7

ends of three dialogue lines, including 3 labour, *then:*
. . . now seems pleasant to you.

⟨THESEUS?⟩
. . . , Heracles, I will (not) blame (you) . . . . . . for (it is   5

αἰσχρὸν πρ]οδοῦναι δυσμ[εν]ῶς εἰλημμένον.

⟨ΗΡΑΚΛΗΣ⟩

σαυτῷ τε,] Θησεῦ, τῇ τ᾽ Ἀθηναίων πό[λει
πρέπουτ᾽ ἔλεξας· τοῖσι δυσ[τυ]χοῦσι γὰρ
10 ἀεί ποτ᾽ εἶ σὺ σύμμαχος· σκῆψιν [δ᾽ ἐμ]οὶ
ἀεικές ἐστ᾽ ἔχοντα πρὸς πάτραν μολεῖν.
Εὐρυσθέα γὰρ πῶς δοκεῖς ἂν ἄσμενον,
εἴ μοι πύθοιτο ταῦτα συμπράξαντά σε,
λέγειν ἂν ὡς ἄκραντος ἤθληται πόνος;

⟨ΘΗΣΕΥΣ⟩

15 ἀλλ᾽ οὗ σὺ χρῄζεις π[c. 9 letters] ἐμὴν ἔχεις
εὔνοιαν, οὐκ ἔμπλ[ηκτον, ἀλλ᾽ ἐλ]ευθέρως
ἐχθροῖσί τ᾽ ἐχθρὰν [καὶ φίλοισι]ν εὐμενῆ.
πρόσθεν σ᾽ ἐμοὶ τ[c. 12 letters]ει λόγος,
λέγοις δ᾽ ἂν [....].[c. 12 letters]ους λόγους.

⟨ΗΡΑΚΛΗΣ⟩

20 ὦ φ[ίλτατ(ε)

vv. 21–39: *further trimeters from a continuing dialogue
(perhaps joined by Pirithous), with a few words read at or
towards their ends:*

ὑ]πηρετῶ
]. θν[η]τῶ[ν] φρένας
] γνώμης ἄτερ
25   τοῦ]τό σοι φίλον

7 beg. Hunt   14 λέγειν Housman: λέξειν P. Oxy.
20 so Kannicht

shameful) to betray a true and faithful friend when he has
been seized malevolently.

⟨HERACLES⟩

Theseus, your words become (both yourself) and the city
of the Athenians; for you have ever been an ally of those
in misfortune. It is unseemly however that I should   10
return to my fatherland with an excuse;[1] for how gladly
Eurystheus would say—do you not think?—if he learned
that you had shared this labour with me, that I had strug-
gled with the task but left it unfulfilled!

⟨THESEUS⟩

But what you desire . . . you have my goodwill, not from im-   15
pulse (but) freely, in enmity to enemies and good intention
(towards friends). The word (is?) that in the past you . . . to
me, and now, if you please, say . . . (the same?) words.

⟨HERACLES?⟩

O (my good friend?) . . .   20

Heracles and Theseus seem to have continued their dia-
logue, and Pirithous may have joined in; only a few further
words can be read securely (speakers indeterminable):
22 I serve   23 the minds of mortal men   24 without

---

[1] Theseus appears to have offered Heracles help in overcom-
ing Cerberus, but Heracles fears that Eurystheus would discount
a labour which he had not completed alone, and impose another
(as he did with the Hydra and Augeas' stables: Apollodorus 2.5.2,
2.5.5). Theseus may have offered help in the hope of its being re-
turned with the release of Pirithous and himself (see Hypothe-
sis). In v. 7 Hunt's '(it is shameful)' matches the Hypothesis well
('Theseus held it shameful . . . ').

]δικώτατ᾽ αἰτιᾷ θεούς
]η πᾶς [ἀ]νέρριπται κύβος
]‥οντα μὴ μάταιον ᾖ
]ην ἔχω ‥εξα[‥] δὲ χρή
30   ]μαθεῖν ὅτου[

mutilated ends of ten further lines, including
34]αλλαγην, 37]ι θεῷ, 38] νερτέρων

   26 ἐκ]δικώτατ᾽ or ἐν]δικώτατ᾽ Körte

10 (= Eur. fr. 598 N)
οὐκ ἀγυμνάστῳ φρενὶ
ἔρριψεν, ὅστις τόνδ᾽ ἐκαίνισεν λόγον,
ὡς τοῖσιν εὖ φρονοῦσι συμμαχεῖ τύχη.

Stobaeus 2.8.4, attributed to Euripides' *Pirithous*; v. 3:
[Menander], *Monostichs* 637 Jaekel, cf. Menander F 500.1 *PCG*

1 beg. ὁ πρῶτος εἰπών Stob., deleted by Wilamowitz

11 (= Eur. fr. 597 N)
τρόπος δὲ χρηστὸς ἀσφαλέστερος νόμου·
τὸν μὲν γὰρ οὐδεὶς ἂν διαστρέψαι ποτὲ
ῥήτωρ δύναιτο, τὸν δ᾽ ἄνω τε καὶ κάτω
λόγοις ταράσσων πολλάκις λυμαίνεται.

Stobaeus 3.37.15, attributed to *Pirithous*

12 (= Eur. fr. 596 N)
οὔκουν τὸ μὴ ζῆν κρεῖσσόν ἐστ᾽ ἢ ζῆν κακῶς;

Stobaeus 4.53.23, attributed to Euripides' *Pirithous*

resolve   25 (this) is dear to you   26 he accuses the
gods most (un?)justly   27 the die is wholly cast
28 that it may not be in vain   29 I have . . . and/but . . .
ought . . .   30 to learn whose(?) . . .   34 change *or* re-
lease   37 to/for the god   38 of the dead

10 (= Eur. fr. 598 N)

There was no unpractised mind in the man who coined and
threw out this saying, that fortune is an ally to those of good
sense.

11 (= Eur. fr. 597 N)

A good character is surer than a law: no orator would ever
be able to distort it, whereas often one of them defiles the
law with words which cause confusion high and low.

12 (= Eur. fr. 596 N)

So isn't not living superior to living in dishonour?[1]

---

[1] Perhaps part of Theseus' argument for refusing to abandon
Pirithous (see note on F 7).

RHADAMANTHYS

TrGF 1 43 Critias F 15–18; B. Gauly in *Musa Tragica* 120–1 (F 17 only).

Gantz 259–60; J. Davidson, *AC* 68 (1999), 247–52; *LIMC* VII.i.626–8 'Rhadamanthys'.

On the authorship of *Rhadamanthys* see the Introduction to this Appendix.

Rhadamanthys (a pre-Hellenic name) is best known as one of the sons born by Europa to Zeus after he had carried her to Crete, and as a wise lawgiver who after his death resided happily in the Elysian Fields (Homer, Odyssey 4. 563–5) or the Islands of the Blessed (Pindar, Olympians 2.75), or became one of the judges in the Underworld (first in Plato, Gorgias 523e). There was also a tradition, possibly as early as the 5th century, that he married Heracles' mother Alcmene after her first husband Amphitryon's death, either in the Isles of the Blessed or in Boeotia where he had come to live in exile (on all this see LIMC and Gantz, and on the marriage with Alcmene, Davidson). The story implied in the hypothesis fragment describing the play's ending (F 15 below) shows no connection with any of these traditions. It involves the deaths of Zeus's twin sons Castor and Pollux, of whom one or both are usually said to have been killed by the sons of Aphareus in a dispute over the daughters of Leucippus; as a result, they attained a shared immortality (see Gantz 323–8). How Rhadamanthys and his daughters could be associated with the deaths of Castor, and why the daughters should have been deified, is entirely unclear.

ΡΑΔΑΜΑΝΘΥΣ

15 (Hypothesis)

[Πο-
λυδεύκους, ἀνηρέθη μονομαχήσας.
Ῥ]αδαμάνθυος δ᾽ ἐπὶ μὲν τῇ νίκῃ [χ]αί-
ρ]οντος, ἐπὶ δὲ ταῖς θυγατράσιν ἀ[λ-
γ]οῦντος Ἄρτεμις ἐπιφανεῖσα πρ[οσ-
5 έταξε τὴν μὲν Ἑλένην ἀ[μφοτέροις
τοῖς ἀδελφοῖς τοῖς τεθν[ηκόσι τὰς
τιμὰς καταστήσασθαι, [τὰς θυγα-
τέρας δ᾽ αὐτοῦ θεὰς ἔφησε γ[ενέσθαι.

_____

PSI XII.1286 col. ii.1–8, ed. V. Bartoletti (1951: previously C.
Gallavotti, *RFIC* 11 (1933), 177–88); re-ed. Austin, *NFE* 92, van
Rossum-Steenbeek 202. The same papyrus has parts of the hy-
potheses to the extant *Rhesus* and to *Scyrians*.

16 (= Eur. fr. 658 N)

οἳ γῆν ἔχουσ᾽ Εὐβοΐδα πρόσχωρον πόλιν

RHADAMANTHYS

15 (Hypothesis)

. . . (after?) Polydeuces (died)[1] . . . he (Castor) was killed fighting alone. Rhadamanthys rejoiced at the victory but grieved for his daughters; but Artemis appeared and instructed Helen to establish the rites honouring (both) her dead brothers, and [5] declared that his daughters (had become) goddesses.[2] (*end of hypothesis*)

[1] Sense supplied by Snell. [2] For a similar outcome compare *Erechtheus* F 370.55ff.

16 (= Eur. fr. 658 N)

. . . who possess the neighbouring state, the land of Euboea . . .[1]

[1] The traditional possessors of Euboea were the Abantes (Homer, *Iliad* 2.536); 'neighbouring' presumably means next to Boeotia, which was sometimes associated with Rhadamanthys (see Introduction above).

Strabo 8.3.31, with attribution to Euripides' *Rhadamanthys*

APPENDIX

17 (= Eur. fr. 659 N)

〈ΡΑΔΑΜΑΝΘΥΣ?〉

ἔρωτες ἡμῖν εἰσὶ παντοῖοι βίου·
ὁ μὲν γὰρ εὐγένειαν ἱμείρει λαβεῖν,
τῷ δ᾽ οὐχὶ τούτου φροντίς, ἀλλὰ χρημάτων
πολλῶν κεκλῆσθαι βούλεται πατὴρ δόμοις·
5 ἄλλῳ δ᾽ ἀρέσκει μηδὲν ὑγιὲς ἐκ φρενῶν
λέγοντι πείθειν τοὺς πέλας τόλμῃ κακῇ·
οἱ δ᾽ αἰσχρὰ κέρδη πρόσθε τοῦ καλοῦ βροτῶν
ζητοῦσιν· οὕτω βίοτος ἀνθρώπων πλάνη.
ἐγὼ δὲ τούτων οὐδενὸς χρῄζω τυχεῖν,
10 δόξαν 〈δὲ〉 βουλοίμην ἂν εὐκλείας ἔχειν.

Stobaeus 2.8.12, with attribution to Euripides; vv. 1–8: Stobaeus 4.20b.61, with attribution to Euripides' *Rhadamanthys*; v. 4: Schol. on *Orestes* 1197, with attribution to Euripides

18 (= Eur. fr. 660 N)

οὐδεὶς γὰρ ἡμᾶς 〈ὅστις〉 ἐξαιρήσεται.

Anecdota Graeca I.94.1 Bekker, with attribution to Euripides' *Rhadamanthys*

〈ὅστις〉 Van Dam

RHADAMANTHYS

17 (= Eur. fr. 659 N)

⟨RHADAMANTHYS?⟩

The desires we have for our lives are of all kinds. One man
yearns to get nobility, while another cares nothing for this
but wishes to be called the father of great riches[1] in his
house. Another is pleased to say nothing honest based on
careful thought, and to influence those around him with 5
evil bravado; and others again among men seek shameful
profits rather than virtue. Such are the ways in which
human life can err; but I want to get none of these things
myself, and would rather have the renown of a good repu-
tation.[2]

[1] I.e. the creator of ancestral wealth for his heirs (Snell).
[2] For the fragment's 'priamel' form cf. *Danae* F 316 with note.
These may have been the play's opening lines, as F 285 may have
opened *Bellerophon*.

18 (= Eur. fr. 660 N)

(There is) none (who) shall dispossess us.[1]

[1] Perhaps one of the Disocuri, or of Aphareus' sons, laying
claim to the disputed girls?

TENNES

TrGF 1 43 Critias F 20–21, with F 20a in *TrGF* 5.1108–9.

Jouan (1966), 303–8; Gantz 591–2; *LIMC* VII.i.893 'Tennes'; M. Huys, *ZPE* 152 (2005), 203–8; M. Polito in A. Mele et al., *Eoli ed Eolide: tra madrepatria e colonie* (Naples, 2005), 187–99.

On the authorship of *Tennes* see the Introduction to this Appendix.

Ten(n)es, eponym of the island of Tenedos off the coast of the Troad, was probably a pre-Greek god in origin. Greek myth made him a migrant from the mainland and founder of the polis of Tenedos. His story is told fairly consistently in numerous mythographic sources.[1] *It may have been told at least in part in the epic* Cypria, *although it is not mentioned in Proclus' summary of that poem. Tennes and Hemithea (in some accounts Leucothea) were the children of Cycnus, a ruler in the area of Troy; their mother died, and Cycnus' second wife tried to seduce Tennes; when he rejected her advances, she accused him of assaulting her*

---

[1] Chiefly Conon *FGrH* 26 F 1.xxviii, Apollodorus, Epit. 3.24; for a thorough list and a recently published ostracon text from Egypt see Huys 203 and Polito 191, 193, 197–8; on the ostracon also W. Luppe, *APF* 51 (2005), 65–6.

*and with support from an aulos-player persuaded Cycnus
to set both Tennes and his sister adrift in a chest which
floated to the nearby island of Leucophrys (F 20a.5).*[2]
*Cycnus learned that he had been deceived and attempted a
reconciliation, but Tennes prevented him from landing on
the island. Tennes' merits caused him to be made the is-
land's ruler, and it was renamed Tenedos in his honour.
He was eventually killed by Achilles when the Achaeans
landed there on their way to Troy.*

*The hypothesis (F 20) shows that the play told the story
of the false accusation and Cycnus' discovery of the truth,
differing from most accounts insofar as the island is re-
named by Cycnus at Apollo's command rather than by
Tennes himself or his people. Apollo no doubt intervened
with this command at the play's conclusion, and probably
excused Cycnus in view of his wife's treachery; Tennes' re-
jection of a reconciliation may have been overlooked.*

Aeschylus may have composed a Tennes *concerning the
Achaean landing on Tenedos and the death of Tennes: see
Radt in TrGF 3, pp. 343 (with refs.) and 479–80 (F 451o =
P. Oxy. 2256. frs. 51–3), and Polito (2005), 197 n. 68.*

*The story of Tennes is not certainly depicted in art: see
LIMC 'Tennes'.*

---

[2] Compare the stories of Danae and Perseus (*Danae, Dictys*)
and one version of the story of Auge and Telephus (*Auge,* Intro-
duction). Other elements of this story are familiar in Euripides,
especially that of 'Potiphar's Wife' in *Hippolytus Veiled, Sthene-
boea* etc.

ΤΕΝΝΗΣ

20 (Hypothesis)

one very fragmentary line

....]κλείσας [

[μ]άρτυρα των[

σάμενος· τα[

5 μετεμέλη[   ]...ι τ[ὸ]ν Τ[έ]ν-

νην ἤκουσεν ἐπὶ τὴ[ν] ἀντιπέρα νῆσον

σεσῶσθαι· προειπό[ν]τος δ' Ἀπόλλωνος

τὴν μὲν νῆσον Τένεδον προσηγόρευσεν,

τ]ὴν δὲ ψευσα[μέν]ην γυναῖκα ἀπέκτεινεν.

_____

P. Oxy. 2455 fr. 14, ed. E. Turner (1962); re-ed. Austin, *NFE* 97, W. Luppe, *APF* 35 (1989), 7–10 with 39 (1993), 15–16

2 κλείσας [εἰς λάρνακα Turner   3–4 [μ]άρτυρα τῶν [διαβολῶν αὐλητὴν ποιη]σάμενος Turner
5 μετεμέλη[σε (sc. Κύκνῳ) Turner: μετεμελή[θη Luppe

TENNES

20 (Hypothesis)

. . . shutting . . . witness of the . . . [1] (he) relented . . . he heard that Tennes had safely reached the island opposite. At Apollo's command he named the island Tenedos and killed the wife who had deceived him. *(end of hypothesis)*

[1] Turner suggested 'shutting (them in a chest)' and '(mak)ing (an aulos-player) a witness of the (slanders)'.

APPENDIX

20a (Myth summary)

τῇ ἀδελφῇ .( )[
τα θάλατταν [ἡ δὲ
λάρναξ κατάγ[εται θείᾳ
γνώμῃ τῇ τό[τε μὲν ἐπικα-
5 λουμένῃ νήσ[ῳ Λευκόφρυϊ,
Τενέδῳ δὲ ὕστ[ερον ἀπ' αὐτοῦ
προσαγορευθε[ίσῃ. οὕτως
Μύρτιλος καὶ Ε[ὐριπίδης?

P. Hamburg 199, ed. B. Kramer and D. Hagedorn (1984), col.
ii, from a mythographic commentary on Homer, *Iliad* 1.38–9; re-
ed. R. Kannicht, *TrGF* 5.1108; cf. W. Luppe, *ZPE* 56 (1984), 31–2

7 οὕτως Luppe: ἱστοροῦσιν (too long) ed. pr.   8 ε[or θ[
P. Hamb.: Ε[ὐριπίδης or Θ[εόπομπος Kannicht

21 (= Eur. fr. 695 N)

φεῦ·
οὐδὲν δίκαιόν ἐστιν ἐν τῷ νῦν γένει.

Stobaeus 3.2.15, with attribution to Euripides' *Tennes*

20a (Myth summary)

. . . (with?) his sister . . . the sea . . . The chest was (brought) ashore by (divine) intention on the island then named (Leu-   5
cophrys) but later Tenedos (for Tennes): thus Myrsilus[1] and E(uripides?).[2]

[1] A historian from Lesbos (*FGrH* no. 477).   [2] Kannicht suggests either E(uripides) or Th(eopompus) (i.e. the historian Theopompus of Chios), and thinks it more likely that the mythographer would add a poet rather than another historian.

21 (= Eur. fr. 695 N)
Alas, the present generation is wholly without justice.

SISYPHUS(?)

TrGF 1 43 Critias F 19; B. Gauly in *Musa Tragica* 120–3;
Battegazzore (1962: see general bibl. above), 304–15; M.
Davies *BICS* 36 (1989), 16–32; Diggle, *TrGFS* 177–9, cf.
Prometheus 22 (1996), 103–4; Pechstein 185–92, 289–318,
319–44, and in Krumeich 552–61; P. Cipolla, *Poeti minori
del dramma satiresco* (Amsterdam, 2003), 225–69.

A. Dihle, *Hermes* 105 (1977), 28–42; D. F. Sutton, *CQ*
31 (1981), 33–8; R. Scodel, *The Trojan Trilogy of Euripides*
(Göttingen, 1982), 124–8; M. Winiarczyk, *Wiener Studien*
100 (1987), 35–45; D. Obbink, *Philodemus on Piety. Part I*
(Oxford, 1996), 353–5; Voelke 358–62.

On the authorship of this fragment see the
Introduction to this Appendix. See also Battegazzore,
Sutton, Winiarczyk, Obbink for ascription to Critias, and
Dihle, Scodel, Pechstein for ascription to Euripides.

*Neither the presumed title of this play nor its single frag-
ment—if it is indeed by Critias and not from Euripides'
Sisyphus—permits any inference about its plot, nor is it
certain that the play was satyric; on all these issues see the
Introduction to this Appendix. Textual uncertainties in the
fragment itself permit quite differing translations at some
places (vv. 11–13, 16, 18–19, 25–6, 28, 33, 37–9), and these*

in turn permit and affect (or reflect) differing views of its authorship. We have translated it as objectively as we can.
    Other ascription: Euripides F 1007c (see there).

ΣΙΣΥΦΟΣ(?)

19 (= Critias fr. 1 N)

ΣΙΣΥΦΟΣ

ἦν χρόνος ὅτ' ἦν ἄτακτος ἀνθρώπων βίος
καὶ θηριώδης ἰσχύος θ' ὑπηρέτης,
ὅτ' οὐδὲν ἆθλον οὔτε τοῖς ἐσθλοῖσιν ἦν
οὔτ' αὖ κόλασμα τοῖς κακοῖς ἐγίγνετο.

5 κἄπειτά μοι δοκοῦσιν ἄνθρωποι νόμους
θέσθαι κολαστάς, ἵνα δίκη τύραννος ᾖ
<   > τήν θ' ὕβριν δούλην ἔχῃ·
ἐζημιοῦτο δ' εἴ τις ἐξαμαρτάνοι.

ἔπειτ' ἐπειδὴ τἀμφανῆ μὲν οἱ νόμοι
10 ἀπεῖργον αὐτοὺς ἔργα μὴ πράσσειν βίᾳ,

Sextus Empiricus, *Against the Experts* 9.54, attributed to Critias (no play is named); vv. 1–2, 17–18 (and 9–16 in paraphrase): Aetius, *Opinions* 1.7.2, attributed to Sisyphus in Euripides; vv. 33–4: Chrysippus fr. phys. 1009 von Arnim, attributed to Euripides; v. 34: Philo, *On Dreams* 1, unattributed; v. 35: see below

7 ‹γένους βροτείου› Grotius   10 ἀπεῖργον Normann:
ἀπῆγον Sext.

SISYPHUS(?)

19 (= Critias fr. 1 N)

SISYPHUS

There was a time when human life was disordered and bestial, and subservient to might;[1] when there was neither reward for good men, nor on the other hand punishment for bad. And then, I think, men established laws which were   5
punitive, so that justice might be sovereign . . . *(a phrase missing)*[2] . . . and keep aggression in servitude; and if any man did wrong, he was punished.[3]

Then, when the laws were preventing men from doing violence openly, but they did it in secret, that was the mo-   10

---

[1] For 5th c. ideas of man's progress from chaos to order, gradually moving away from thinking it the gift of gods towards rationalizing it as man's own achievement, see e.g. W. K. C. Guthrie, *History of Greek Philosophy* III (Cambridge, 1969), 60–3 or A. J. Podlecki, *Aeschylus: Prometheus Bound* (Oxford, 2005), 16–27.   [2] Perhaps 'be sovereign (over the human race)' (Grotius).   [3] For law, founded upon custom and eventually codified, see e.g. Guthrie 117–31 or M. Gagarin, *Early Greek Law* (Berkeley, 1986), 51–2.

APPENDIX

λάθρᾳ δ᾽ ἔπρασσον, τηνικαῦτά μοι δοκεῖ
<   > πυκνός τις καὶ σοφὸς γνώμην ἀνὴρ
θεῶν δέος θνητοῖσιν ἐξευρεῖν, ὅπως
εἴη τι δεῖμα τοῖς κακοῖσι, κἂν λάθρᾳ
15 πράσσωσιν ἢ λέγωσιν ἢ φρονῶσί <τι>.
ἐντεῦθεν οὖν τὸ θεῖον εἰσηγήσατο,
ὡς ἔστι δαίμων ἀφθίτῳ θάλλων βίῳ
{νόῳ τ᾽ ἀκούων καὶ βλέπων, φρονῶν τε καὶ
προσέχων τε ταῦτα καὶ φύσιν θείαν φορῶν}
20 ὃς πᾶν τὸ λεχθὲν ἐν βροτοῖς ἀκούς<σ>εται,
<τὸ> δρώμενον δὲ πᾶν ἰδεῖν δυνήσεται·
'ἐὰν δὲ σὺν σιγῇ τι βουλεύῃς κακόν,
τοῦτ᾽ οὐχὶ λήσει τοὺς θεούς· τὸ γὰρ φρονοῦν
ἔνεστι<ν αὐτοῖς>.' τούσδε τοὺς λόγους λέγων
25 διδαγμάτων ἥδιστον εἰσηγήσατο
ψευδεῖ καλύψας τὴν ἀλήθειαν λόγῳ.
ναίειν δ᾽ ἔφασκε τοὺς θεοὺς ἐνταῦθ᾽ ἵνα
μάλιστ᾽ ἂν ἐκπλήξειεν ἀνθρώπους ἄγων,

12 <πρῶτον> Enger: <ἄγαν> Steffen   13 θεῶν Wecklein,
δέος Petit: γνῶναι δὲ ὃς (or δέοσῃ) Sext. mss.   15 <τι>
Scaliger   18–20 so Normann, emending Sext. (18–20) and
Aet. (18)   18–19 deleted by Blaydes and Diggle, the latter
obelizing καὶ προσέχων τε ταῦτα   19 τε ταῦτα Sext.: τὰ
πάντα Grotius: τε πάντῃ West   21 <τὸ> Scaliger
24 ἔνεστι<ν αὐτοῖς> Heath   25 ἥδιστον is suspect:
κύδιστον Haupt, Diggle: κράτιστον Mutschmann   27 ναί-
ειν Pierson: αἰεὶ Sext.   28 ἐκπλήξειεν Grotius: ἐξέπληξεν
Sext.   ἄγων Sext.: λέγων Grotius

ment, I think, when . . . (*a word missing*) . . . some shrewdly
intelligent and clever man invented[4] for mankind fear of
gods, so that there might be something to frighten bad
men even if they do or say or think (something) in secret.
From that time therefore he introduced belief in gods— 15
that there exists a divine power flourishing with indestruc-
tible life {and hearing and seeing with a mind, and both
thinking and ?attending to? these things, and bearing a
godlike nature}[5] which will hear everything that has been
said among men, and will be able to see everything that is 20
being done. 'Further, if you silently plan some evil, this will
not escape the gods' notice: for there is intelligent aware-
ness in (them).' In saying these words he introduced the
most pleasant[6] of teachings, hiding the truth with words of 25
falsity; he asserted that the gods lived in a place that would
especially terrify men when he made them aware of it,[7] the

---

[4] The notion of a 'first inventor' for many aspects of man's material
and intellectual development dates from the 5th c., e.g. Gorgias B
11a.30 DK; cf. our Introduction to *Palamedes*. In v. 12 Enger sug-
gested 'when (first) . . .'; Steffen's 'some (too) shrewdly intelligent
. . .' adds a hint of cynicism to the 'atheistic' account which follows.
[5] Text as printed in *TrGF*, with Normann's emendation of numer-
ous errors in Sextus and Aetius; but this is still unsatisfactory and
obelized in part by Diggle. Vv. 18–19 are redundant in language,
and partly duplicate v. 20, so Blaydes and Diggle deleted them.
[6] If correct, this is ironic, as is 'most glorious' (Haupt, Diggle);
'strongest' Mutschmann.   [7] Lit. 'when he led (i.e. directed)
them to it'; many editors reject this as flat or even corrupt. Grotius'
alteration giving 'when he told them of it (cf. 24 'saying these
words') is best, but not compelling.

ὅθεν περ ἔγνω τοὺς φόβους ὄντας βροτοῖς
30 καὶ τὰς ὀνήσεις τῷ ταλαιπώρῳ βίῳ,
ἐκ τῆς ὕπερθε περιφορᾶς, ἵν' ἀστραπὰς
κατεῖδεν οὔσας, δεινὰ δὲ κτυπήματα
βροντῆς τό τ' ἀστερωπὸν οὐρανοῦ σέλας,
Χρόνου καλὸν ποίκιλμα, τέκτονος σοφοῦ,
35 ὅθεν τε λαμπρὸς ἀστέρος στείχει μύδρος
ὅ θ' ὑγρὸς εἰς γῆν ὄμβρος ἐκπορεύεται.
τοίους πέριξ ἔστησεν ἀνθρώποις φόβους,
δι' οὓς καλῶς τε τῷ λόγῳ κατῴκισεν
τὸν δαίμον' οὗτος ἐν πρέποντι χωρίῳ,
40 τὴν ἀνομίαν τε τοῖς νόμοις κατέσβεσεν
(some details omitted by Sextus)
οὕτω δὲ πρῶτον οἴομαι πεῖσαί τινα
θνητοὺς νομίζειν δαιμόνων εἶναι γένος.

30 ὀνήσεις Musgrave: πονήσεις Sext.   32 κατεῖδεν
Sext.: κατεῖδον Snell   33 σέλας Chrys.: δέμας Sext.
35 ἄστερος Sext.: ἡλίου Nauck, comparing Schol. on Eur.
Orestes 982 Εὐριπίδης μύδρον λέγει τὸν ἥλιον   37–40 de-
leted by Pechstein (40 Luppe)   38–9 τῷ λόγῳ . . . οὐκ Sext.
(οὗτος Diels): τῶν λόγων . . . οὕνεκ' Diggle

very source from which he knew they have their fears and
their benefits[8] for their miserable life—from the rotating   30
vault above them, where he observed[9] lightnings and terri-
ble crashes of thunder, and the starry gleam[10] of heaven,
the beautiful and spangled work of Time, a skilled ar-
chitect, and from where the sun-star's brilliant, glowing
mass[11] comes, and the wetting rain begins its way to earth.   35
Such were the fears he established all round for mankind,
and thanks to these fears this man did a fine job in his story
of settling divine power in a fitting place, and quenched
lawlessness with the laws.[12] . . . (some details omitted by   40
Sextus) . . . In this way, I think, someone first persuaded
mortal men to believe in the existence of a race of divine
powers.

[8] Musgrave's 'benefits' (i.e. the sun and rain of vv. 33–6) makes
a contrast with 'fears'. Sextus' 'ordeals' emphasizes men's miseries
from the sky (31–3).   [9] 'he observed' conveys the man's
exploitation of what caused fear; 'they observed' (Snell) is matter-
of-fact.   [10] Chryssippus' 'gleam' is more pointed than Sextus'
'frame, structure', though the latter half-epic metaphor is not un-
apt for Time as a 'skilled architect' (see on *Pirithous* F 594.1–2).
[11] A metaphor from the smithy, attributed in the *Orestes* scholia to
the Pre-Socratic speculator Anaxagoras' influence on Euripides
(see on *Pirithous* F 593). A reference to the sun, rather than bril-
liant stars or comets (Diggle), suits the contrast with 'wetting rain'.
[12] Vv. 37–40 are deleted by Pechstein and Luppe as a confused
and interpolated summary of vv. 1–36. Diggle tried to ease the
expression, and Sextus' corrupt text, with 'he did well, for the sake
of his fiction, to settle . . .'

INDEX OF NAMES
AND PLACES

Some indirect references are included. Play-titles or their obvious abbreviations refer to the introductions and/or testimonia for a play; references such as '(t. ii)' draw attention to a specific testimonium. Numbers refer to fragments, double numbers (e.g. 370.3) to verses within the longer fragments; 'App.' to the Appendix. Fragments printed out of numerical sequence or listed as 'brief' in a play-introduction are identified by the name of the play to which they belong, e.g. 1132 (*Dan.*); 514 (*Mel.W.* brief).

Abantes: App. 16
Abas: 228a.5
Acastus: *Peleus; Prot.;* 647; 652?
Achaeans: *Pal.; Tel.;* 696.15; 789d(7); 857; 953m.30. See also Greeks
Achelous, R.: *Alcm.Ps.;* 753
Acheron, R.: 868
Achilles: *Scyr.; Tel.;* 683a; 880 (*Scyr.*); 716; 717–8?; 727.95–101?; 727c; 885; 888
Acrisius: *Dan.;* 228a.8; 316; 1132 (*Dan.*)
Acrocorinth: 1084
Acropolis of Athens: 370.3; 481.10
Actor: *Phil.* (t. ivb)

Adonis: 514 (*Mel.W.* brief)
Adrastus: 558; 752f.34; 753c.20; 757.917
Aeacus: (father of Peleus) *Peleus* (gatekeeper of Underworld) App. *Pir.;* App. 1
Aegeae, in Macedonia: *Arch.*
Aegean Sea: 752f.27; 759a.1624
Aegeus: *Aeg.;* 386b.10
Aegina, island: 752g.7; 932
Aegisthus: *Thy.?*
Aegyptus: 846; 881
Aeolia: 481.3–6
Aeolian Isles: *Aeol.; Mel.C.*
Aeolus: (ruler of Aeolian Isles) *Aeol.;* 13a–41 (son of Hellen) *Mel.W., Phrix.;* 481.2, 14; 485; 500?; 510?; 929b

681

NAMES AND PLACES

Danaus: 228; 881
Danube: 1007a+b
Dawn (Eos): 771; 773.64
Deidameia: *Scyr.;* 682
Deio (Demeter): 370.34, 109
Deiphobus: *Alex.;* 62a–d; 1093a
Deipyle: *Oeneus;* 558; 753c.21
Delphi, Delphic oracle:
  Alcm.Ps.; Erech.; Phrix.; 1132.7
  (*Dan.*); 472b?; 752; 923
Demeter: 370.102; 781.268;
  892; 955. *See also* Deio
Dictys: *Dict.;* 332; 342
Diomedes: *Oeneus; Scyr.; Phil.;*
  558; 559; 565
Dione: 177; 228a.22
Dionysus: *Antig.; Antiope; Ino;*
  Thes.; Hyps.; Phrix.; 175
  (*Antiope*); 177–9; 203; 586;
  752; 752a; 752g.35;
  758a.1085; 888a. *See also*
  Bacchus; Bromius; Zagreus
Dirce: *Antiope;* 175 (*Antiope*);
  221; 223.6, 60–4, 80–5, 111–
  5; 819
Discord (Stasis): 453.20
Dodona: 228a.20; 367; 494.15;
  1021
Dolopians: *Phoen.*
Doves (priestesses at Dodona):
  1021

Earth (Gaia; Ge): 24b; 61b; 86;
  154; 182a; 195; 223.94; 316;
  370.45; 415; 953f.12
  (*Hipp.V.*); [448]; 1004 (*Cret.*);
  484; 533; 586; 839; 898; 919;
  939; 841; 944; 955c; 1121a

Echinades, isles: *Alcmene;* 87b
Echo: *Andr.;* 114; 118
Edonian women: 759a.1571
Egypt: *Busir.;* 228; 881
Eileithyia: 696
Electryon: *Alcmene; Licym.;* 89;
  228a.15
Eleusis: *Alope; Erech.*
Eleutherae: *Antiope;* 179; 175
  (*Antiope*)
Elis: *Chrys.;* 727e.13–14
Enipeus, R.: 14
Eos. *See* Dawn
Epeus: *Epeus*
Epigoni: *Alcm.Ps.;* 559
Epopeus: *Antiope*
Erechtheids: *Erech.;* 358; 360;
  370.65–89
Erechtheum: 370.90–91
Erechtheus: *Erech.;* 349–370;
  481.10
Erichthonius: 925
Erinyes. *See* Furies
Eriphyle: *Alcm.Ps.;* 71;
  752k.16–17
Eris. *See* Strife
Eros (Love): 136; 269; 430; 663;
  758a.1106; 897; 929a
Ethiopia, Ethiopians: *Andr.;*
  Pha.; 147; 228; 228a.11; 349;
  771
Etna, Mt.: 960
Euboea: App. 16
Eumolpus: *Erech.;* 360.48;
  370.15?, 100
Euneos: *Hyps.;* 752c; 757.845;
  759a
Europa: 472.1; 820

Silenus: *Autol.; Eurys.; Scir.;*
  282a; 373; 674a; 676?
Sirens: 116; 911
Siris: *Mel.C.* (t. iib); 495.15
Sirius: 779.175
Sisyphus: *Autol.; Sis.;* App. *Sis.;*
  661.17; 929b; App. 19
Sky. *See Index of Topics,*
  Heaven
Sparta: *Tem.* (t. ii–iii); 681a;
  723; 995?
Sphinx: *Oed.;* 178; 540; 540a
Stasis. *See* Discord
Stheneboea: *Bell.; Sthen.;* 304a;
  661; 664; 665; 666?; 671
Sthenelus: *Oeneus;* 89; 228a.13
Strife (Eris): 453.21
Sun: 112a (*Alope* brief); 228;
  472e.49; 540; 727e; 765b?;
  783 (*Pha.* brief); 929; 1111a;
  1121a; App. 19.35. *See also*
  Helios
Syleus: *Ther.?; Syl.*
Symplegades. *See* Clashing
  Rocks

Tantalus: 223.102
Taphians or Teleboans:
  Alcmene; Licym.; 87b
Taurus: 820
Tegea: *Auge;* 727c.31
Telamon: 530
Teleboans. *See* Taphians
Telephontes: *Cresph.* (t. ii)
Telephus: *Auge; Tel.;* 271b?;
  696–727c
Temenus: *Arch.; Tem.;* 228a.17–
  25
Tenedos, island: App. *Tenn.*

Tennes: App. *Tenn.*
Teuthrania: 476
Teuthras: *Auge;* 696.10
Thebes, Thebans: *Alcmene;*
  Antig.; Licym.; Oed.; Chrys.;
  69; 87b; 178; 223.78–116;
  752f.32; 752h.37–40; 819. *See*
  also Seven against Thebes
Themisto: *Ino;* 411; 415
Theseus: *Aeg.; Alope; Eurys.;*
  Hipp.V.; Thes.; Scir.; App.
  Pir.; 10; 11a; 260?; 379a?;
  386b.11; 386c; 439–40; 953f
  (*Hipp.V.*); 531; 531a; 676?;
  964; App. 6; 7; 12?
Thessaly, Thessalians: *Ino;*
  Ixion; Hipp.V. (t. iib); *Mel.W;*
  Peliad.; Peleus; Prot.; Phrix.A;
  422; 481.3–6; 822a; 1093;
  App. 5
Thestius: 515 (sons of) *Meleag.;*
  530
Thetis: *Peleus; Scyr.;* 885; 1093
Thoas: (father of Hypsipyle)
  759a.1595–7, 1625, 1632 (son
  of Hyps.) *Hyps.;* 752c; 752e;
  757.845
Thrace, Thracians: *Arch.;*
  Erech.; 360.48; 366?; 369;
  370.13; 752g.2,10; 759a.1619
Thyestes: *Thy.; Cret.W.; Pleis.?;*
  396; 462?; 953b?
Time: 222; 303; App. 3; 4?;
  19.34
Tiresias: *Alcmene; Alcm.C.*
Tiryns: *Sthen.;* 696
Tisamenus: *Tem.*
Tisiphone, d. of Alcmeon:
  Alcm.C.; 73a

INDEX OF NARRATIVE AND
DRAMATIC FEATURES

For explanation of references see headnote to Index of Names and Places. Asterisk indicates a related entry in Index of Topics.

Aetiologies: *Alope; Andr.;*
Antiope; Arch.; Erech.; Ino (t.
iib); *Licym.; Hyps.; Pha.;*
Phrix. A (t. iii)

Animals: (constructed) *Cret.;*
Epeus (feed babies) *Alope;*
Auge; Mel.W. (formerly hu-
man) *Mel.W.* (miraculous)
Bell.; Cret.; Oenom.; Sthen.;
Phrix. (monstrous) *Aeg.?;*
Andr.; Thes.; Hipp.V.; Cret.;
Meleag.; Sthen. (used in kill-
ing) *Antiope.* See also Mon-
sters; Staging

*Babies, newborn: *Antig.* (t. iia)
(concealed) *Aeol.; Auge;*
Dan.(?); *Mel.W.; Scyr.* (ex-
posed) *Aeol.; Alex.; Alope;*
Antiope; Auge; Mel.W.?; Oed.
(set adrift) *Auge?; Dan.*

*Barbarians: *Andr.; Busir.;*
Erech.; Tel.; Pha.; Phil.

*Beauty: (female) *Alcm.C.;*
Alope (t. iib); *Andr.; Antiope*
(t. iii (a)); *Auge* (t. iia); *Dan.*
(F 1132); *Lam.; Mel. W.* (t. i);
Meleag. (male) *Alex.; Hipp.V.;*
Chrys.

Bestiality: *Cret.*

Betrayal: *Alcm.Ps.; Andr.?;*
Arch.; Oenom.; Phrix. B (al-
leged) *Pal.*

Blinding: *Mel.W.?; Oed.; Phoen.*

*Brothers: *Aeol.; Alex.; Alcm.C.;*
Dict.; Thy.; Cret.W.?; Pal.;
Pleis.?; Tem.; App. *Rhad.*
(twins) *Antiope; Ino; Mel.W.;*
Mel.C.; Hyps. (b.-in-law)
Alcmene; Oed.

Burial, forbidden: *Antig.*

Cannibalism: *Thy.?; Cret.W.?;*
Meleag. (F 537)

Catasterism: *Andr.* (t. iiia (a),
iiib); *Mel.W.* (t. vb)?; F 820

691

INDEX

692

Cret.W.?; Mel.C.; Syl.; Hyps.;
Sis.

Escapes: Andr.?; Thes., Cret.?;
Sthen.; Phrix.

*Exile: Arch.; Dict.; Thy.;
Hipp.V.; Cresph.; Licym.;
Mel.C.; Phoen.; Chrys.; Hyps.
(after murder) Aeg.; Alcm.Ps.;
Alcmene; Bell.; Mel.W. (t. i);
Oed.?; Peleus; Sthen.; Syl.

Famine: Phrix.

*Fathers: Aeg.; Aeol.; Alex.;
Alcm.Ps.; Alcm.C.; Alope;
Andr.; Auge; Dan.; Erech.;
Thes.; Thy.?; Ino; Hipp.V.;
Cret.W.; Licym.?; Mel.W.;
Oenom.; Peliad.; Polyid.;
Prot.; Scyr.; Tem.?; Pha.;
Phoen.; Phrix.; Chrys. See
also Parricide

*Feasting: Andr.?; Thy.?;
Cret.W.; Syl.

Filicide: Meleag.; Pleis.?; F
953m? (indirect) Aeol.;
Hipp.V. (near-) Aeg.; Alex.

Fishermen: Dict.; Sthen.

Flying: Bell.; Andr.; Dict.;
Cret.?; Sthen.; Phrix.

Foundations (cities, families,
dynasties) Aeol.; Alcm.C.;
Alope; Andr.; Antiope; Arch.;
Auge; Dict.; Cresph.; Mel.C.;
Oenom.; Tem. See also Aetiol-
ogies; Cults founded

*Friendship: Tel.; App. Pir.

Games: Alex.; Hyps.

*Gods: (punish offences etc.)

Andr.; Bell.; Ixion; Cret.;
Meleag.; Pha.; App. Pir. (res-
cue dependants) Auge?;
Erech.; Thes.; Hyps.; Phrix.
(speak prologue) Alex.?;
Alcm.C.; Alcmene?; Erech.;
Ino?; Cret.?; Meleag. (F
517)?; Prot.? (in 'second pro-
logue') Prot. (at play-end)
Aeol.?; Alcmene?; Alcm.Ps.?;
Alcm.Cor.?; Alope; Andr.;
Antig.?; Antiope; Arch.;
Auge?; Bell.; Dan.?; Dict.?;
Erech.; Thes.; Ino?; Ixion;
Hipp.V.; Cresph.?; Cret.?;
Mel.W.; Mel.C.?; Meleag.;
Pal.?; Scyr.?; Hyps.; Pha.;
Phil.?; Phrix; App. Rhad.;
Tenn. See also Deification;
Rape; Seduction

Grandson(s): Alope (t. iib);
Arch.; Oeneus; Peleus?;
Hyps.

*Heralds: Busir. (t. iiib); Erech.;
Tel.?; Pha.

Heroes: (born) Alcmene; Alope;
Auge; Dan.; Mel.W.; Scyr.
(claim birthright) Aeg.; Alex.;
Antiope; Cresph.; Oeneus;
Tem. (adopted by kings)
Auge; Mel.C.; Oed. (heroic
exploits) Aeg.?; Alope?;
Andr.; Arch.; Bell.; Busir.;
Dict.; Eurysth.; Thes.;
Meleag.; Oed.; Oenom.;
Sthen.; Scir.; Syl.; App. Pir.
(deaths) Alcm.Ps.; Bell.;
Hipp.V.; Meleag.; Pal.; Pha.

Monsters, monstrous animals: *Andr.; Bell.; Eurysth.; Thes.; Hipp.V.; Cret.; Meleag.; Scir.; Sthen.;* App. *Pir. See also* Ogres

*Mothers: *Alex.; Alope; Andr.; Antiope; Dict.; Erech.; Ino; Cresph.; Mel.W.; Mel.C.; Meleag.; Oed.; Tel.; Hyps.; Pha.?; Phoen.?; Phrix. See also* Illicit pregnancy/childbirth; Matricide

Murder: *Alcm.Ps.; Antiope; Busir.; Ixion; Thy.?; Cresph.; Oeneus; Oenom.; Sthen.; Scir.* (attempted) *Antiope; Arch.; Mel.C.* (of children) *Thy.?; Ino; Lam.* (judicial) *Pal.* (of kin) *Alope?; Cret.?; Licym.?; Mel.W.?; Meleag.;* (of kin, near-) *Aeg.; Alex.; Alcmene; Antig.; Auge; Dan.; Cresph. See also* Matricide; Parricide; Plots (death; revenge); Sacrifice (human)

Nurses: *Aeol.; Alope; Auge; Dan.?; Ino; Hipp.V.; Cret.; Mel.W.; Meleag.; Prot.?; Sthen.; Scyr.; Hyps.*

*Oaths: *Erech.* (F 370.70); *Thes.* (t. iiia)?; *Hipp.V.; Phrix. A* (t. iia)

*Old age: *Aeg.; Oeneus; Peliad.; Peleus?; Pha.; Phoen. See also* Chorus (older men)

Ogres: *Busir.; Eurysth.; Ther.; Lam.; Scir.; Syl.*

*Oracles: *Alcm.Ps.* (2); *Alcmene* (F 87b); *Arch.* (t. iiia; F 228a); *Auge* (t. iib); *Dan.; Erech.* (t. ii); *Cret.W.; Cret.* (t. *iiia); *Oed.; Polyid.* (t. iva); *Scyr.* (t. iia); *Syl.* (t. iiic); *Tel.* (2); *Tem.* (t. i); *Phrix.*

Parricide: *Oed., Peliad.*

Peasants, herdsmen: *Alope; Antiope; Autol.; Thes.* (F 382); *Mel.W.; Oeneus* (F 561–2); *Phil.*

Plots: (to kill hero) *Aeg.; Alex.; Andr.?; Arch.; Dict.; Eurysth.; Hipp.V.; Mel.C.; Pal.; Peleus; Phrix.; Pleis.?; Sthen.* (to gain revenge) *Antiope* (2); *Arch.; Bell.*(?); *Thy.; Ino; Cresph.; Pal.; Sthen.*

Poisoning: *Aeg.*

Political or contemporary resonance: *Alcm.C.?; Antiope; Arch.; Bell.?; Erech.; Cresph.; Oenom.; Pal.; Scyr.?; Tem.; Hyps.; Phil.*

*Pollution: *Alcm.Ps.; Auge; Ixion; Oed.; Prot.* (F 648); *Phrix.?*

*Priestesses: *Auge; Erech.; Peliad.?*

Prophecies: *Alex.; Mel.W.* (F 481); *Meleag.; Phil. See also* Divination; Gods (at play-end); Oracles

*Prostitution: *Scir.*

*Purification: *Alcm.Ps.; Ixion; Peleus; Sthen.*

INDEX

Ragged figures: *Bell.; Thy.* (t. ii); *Ino?; Cret.W.; Oeneus* (t. iia); *Tel.; Phil.*

*Rape: (by god) *Alcm.C.; Alcmene; Alope; Antiope; Dan.; Mel.W.* (by man) *Auge; Autol.?; Syl.* (of goddess) *Ixion* (homosexual) *Chrys.* (falsely alleged) *Hipp.V.; Peleus; Sthen.; Phoen.;* App. Tenn.

Recognition: (with reunion) *Aeg.; Alex.; Alcm.C.; Alope; Antiope; Auge; Cresph.; Mel.C.; Oed.; Hyps.* (with reversal) *Oed.* (tokens) *Aeg.; Alope; Auge; Hyps.*

Rejuvenation: *Peliad.; Peleus?*

Restoration to life: *Polyid.* See also Underworld, returns from

Reversals: *Aeg.; Alex.; Antiope; Arch.; Ino; Cresph.* (2); *Mel.C.; Phrix.*

Rhetorical display: *Autol.* (F 282); *Bell.* (F 285–6); *Erech.* (F 360–2); *Mel.W.* (t. iia); *Mel.C.* (F 494). See also Debate scenes; Dissembling rhetoric; Sophistic argument

Ritual activity: *Antiope* (F 175); *Auge; Cresph.* (t. iia); *Cretans* (F 472); *Erech.* (F 350–1); *Ino; Pha.; Prot.; Phrix.;* App. Pir. (F 2). See also Sacrifice

*Sacrifice: *Cresph.; Syl.* (t. iiia); *Hyps.; Pha.* (human) *Andr.; Busir.; Erech.; Phrix.*

Sanctuary (at altar etc.): *Alex.; Alcmene; Antiope; Dict.; Cret.?; Oed.* (F 554a)?; *Tel.*

Satyrs: *Antiope* (F 210); *Autol.; Busir.; Epeus?; Ther.; Lam.; Sis.; Scir.; Scyr.; Syl.*

'Second prologue': *Prot.*

*Seduction: (of girl by god) *Lam.* (of girl by man) *Cret.W.; Scyr.* (of wife by man) *Thy.* (of youth by woman, attempted) *Hipp.V.; Peleus; Sthen.; Phoen.;* App. Tenn. See also Rape

*Seercraft: *Polyid.; Hyps.*

*Sexual topics. See Bestiality; Homosexuality; Illicit pregnancy/childbirth; Incest; Love Stories; Marriage; Prostitution; Rape; Seduction; Women.

Sisters: *Aeol.; Alcm.C.; Antig.; Erech.; Pha.* (F 782); *Phrix.;* App. Tenn.

*Slave characters: *Alex.; Alcmene* (F 94); *Arch.* (t. iiia); *Dan.* (F 1132); *Cresph.* (F 448a); *Hipp.V.* (t. iib); *Mel.C.* (F 495); *Oed.* (F 541); *Prot.; Phrix.B* (t. iib, cf. F 822b?). See also Chorus (slave women); Enslavement; Nurses; Tutors

*Snakes: *Polyid.* (t. iva); *Hyps.*

*Sons: (adult) *Aeg.; Aeol.; Alex.; Alcm.Ps.; Alcm.C.; Antig.; Antiope; Dict.; Hipp.V.; Cresph.; Licym.?; Mel.C.; Meleag.; Oed.; Pleis.?; Tem.;*

696

*Hyps.; Pha.; Phoen.; Phrix.;
Chrys.* (children) *Ino;
Polyid.;* F 953m? (infants)
*Aeol.; Alope; Auge; Dan.;
Mel.W.; Scyr.; Tel.; Hyps.*
(adopted) *Erech.; Mel.C.; Oed.*
See also Filicide; Recognition

Sophistic argument: *Ixion;
Cresph.* (F 451); *Cretans*
(F 472e); *Chrys.;* App. *Sis.*
(F 19)

Staging, special features: (animals) *Bell.; Eurysth.* (cave-entrance) *Antiope; Phil.* (earthquake) *Erech.* (eccyclema)
Bell.?; Ixion? (fire) *Alcmene?;
Pha.?* (immobile figures)
Andr.; App. *Pir.* (masks)
Mel.W. (t. va); *Oed.; Phil.;
Phoen.?;* (mēchanē) *Andr.;
Bell.; Ixion?; Cret.* (see also
Gods, at play-end) (off-stage
voice) *Andr.* (rainstorm)
Alcmene (wheel) *Ixion.* See
also Death on stage

*Stepmothers: *Aeg.; Alcm.C.;
Hipp.V.; Ino; Mel.C.; Phrix.;*
App. *Tenn.*

Stoning: *Pal.*

*Suicide: *Aeol.* (2); *Erech.; Ino*
(2); *Hipp.V.; Mel.C.; Meleag.;
Oeneus* (t. iiib)?; *Prot.; Chrys.*

*Supplication: *Erech.; Hipp.V.?;
Cret.?; Sthen.; Tel.; Hyps.*

Theft: *Autol.* (t. iv); *Phil.*

Time, dramatic: *Alcm.Ps.; Oed.;
Pal.; Sthen.*

Transportation (of heroines and
children to distant lands):
Auge; Dan.; Mel.W.?; Mel.C.

Transvestism: *Scyr.*

Treachery. See Betrayal

*Trials (judicial): *Alcmene;
Hipp.V.; Cret.; Pal.; Hyps.;
Phoen.*

Trickery: *Alcmene; Autol.; Dan.*
(F 1132.29ff.); *Sis.*

Tutors: *Cresph.; Pha.*

Twins. See Brothers

Uncles: *Andr.?; Antig; Mel.C.;
Meleag.; Oeneus*

*Underworld, returns from:
Eurysth.; Prot.; App. *Pir.*

Usurpers: *Cresph.; Oeneus;
Peliad.*

Veiling: *Hipp.V.; Hyps.* (F
757.874, 883)

*Vengeance: *Alcm.Ps.; Alcmene*
(F 87b); *Meleag.; Oeneus.* See
also Plots (vengeance)

*War as dramatic context: *Arch.;
Epeus; Erech.; Licym.?; Pal.;
Scyr.; Tel.; Tem.; Hyps.; Phil.*

*Women: (conflict between) *Ino;
Mel.C.; Meleag.* (sexual transgressions) *Hipp.V.; Cret.W.;
Cret.; Pel.; Sthen.* See also
Beauty; Concubines; Daughters; Marriage; Mothers;
Nurses; Priestesses; Sexual
topics; Sisters; Stepmothers;
Veiling

Wounded figures: *Bell.; Tel.;
Phil.*

INDEX OF TOPICS

For explanation of references see headnote to Index of Names and
Places. Asterisk indicates a related entry in Index of Narrative and
Dramatic Features.

Abstinence: 446; 1132.18
 (*Dan.*)
Abuse, verbal: 334; 661.28;
 712–3; 816.3; 822b.16;
 953c.42
Acquisitiveness (*pleonexia*): 425
Advice: 317; 362; 440; 603;
 754b.14; 757.920–49; 803b;
 840; 874; 1042. *See also* De-
 liberation
Aether. *See* Heaven
Alphabet. *See* Writing
Ambitious activity
 (*polypragmosynê*): 193; 576;
 (787–9)
Anger: *Thes.* (t. iiia); 31; 62a.9–
 12; 257; 259; 287; 1132.63
 (*Dan.*); 472e.43; 654; 711;
 718; 746; 757.823, 836–7;
 760; 799; 822.36; 858; 1038–
 9; 1078
Association: 296; 341; 462. *See
 also* Company
Astronomy, Astrology: 397b;
 483; 913

Athletes, Athletics: 105; 201;
 282; 785. *See also* Games
Aulos: 370.8; 556; 931 (brief)
Autochthony: 360.7–13; 925

*Babies: 272a; 316; 323; 514
 (*Mel.W.*, brief)? (exposure of)
 46.2; 485. *See also* Childbirth
Bad character(s): 59; 60; 61c;
 75; 166; 222; 293; 303; 326;
 333; 402; 414; 419; 564; 606;
 617; 643; 692; 721; 760a;
 953a; 954; 1027; 1067–8 (as-
 sociation with) 296; 341;
 362.19–20; 609; 812.7–9;
 1024 (in politics) 201;
 362.28–31; 512; 626; 643–4;
 678; 738 (women) 493;
 494.22–9; 497; 657
*Barbarians: 124; 366; 370.13;
 696.14; 719; 796; 907
Bastards: 141; 168; 377;
 495.20?; 824
'Bears' (at Brauron): 767 (*Hyps.*
 brief)

INDEX

INDEX

Sculpture: 125; 752c; 928a

Sea: 316.2; 636; 670; 759a.1601–3; 856; 860 (brief); 1059.1

Seafaring: 417; 494.9; 669; 759a.1604–7; 773.79–86; 789a; 846; 852; 921; 1007a–b

Seasons: 752a.4; 862; 990; 1111a

*Seduction: 11a?; 661.7–14

Seercraft: *Polyid.* (t. iva); 635–6; 757.857, 864, 889–90. *See also* Prophecy

Self-control: 62a.17; 362.33; 365; 388; 413; 446; 453.9; 503; 505; 757.875–7, 882–3; 948; 929a (lack of) 201; 272b; 362.22–3; 841; 954; 976

Self-love: 452

Self-praise: 978

Sentries: 589

*Sexual desire, love: 23; 26; 136; 138; 138a; 161–2; 269; 322; 324; 1132.19 (*Dan.*); 331; 339–40; 362.24–7; 388; 400; 428; 430; 472e.6–26; 524; 547; 661.21–5; 663; 665; 875; 895; 897–8; 929a; 951; 967

Shame: 19; 436; 457; 524; 746; 1027; 1043a; App. 6

Ships: 89; 304; 355; 708a; 752g.4–14; 758c.7; 774.124–6; 866a; 955d

Silence: 29; 126; 219; 334; 413; 773.101–18; 796; 883; 977; 1008; 1087; App. 2

Simplicity: 473

Sky. *See* Heaven

Slander: 56; App. 20?

*Slaves, slavery: 48–51; 57; 61a; 62a–d; 86; 129a; 142; 175.10 (*Antiope*); 216–8; 245; 251; 261; 375; 410; 495.19, 37–8; 561; 688; 719; 752f.17; 752h.22–3; 754b.16; 754c.5; 759a.1606; 773.54–8, 90–4; 822a; 822b.12; 953e; 976; 1019 ('freedom' of) 831; 958 (nobility in) 62b.31; 495.40–3; 511 (relations with masters) 50–1; 85; 93; 313; 529; 689

*Snakes: 752f.23–5; 754a; 757.902–5; 870 (brief); 930; 1111a; App. 1 hyp.; 4a.1

Song: 182a; 187; 187a; 192; 202; 223.90–7; 369; 453.19; 472g; 752f.9–14, 19–28; 907; 911 (victory-) 62d.53; 370.5–10 (wedding-) 752h.4–9; 773.88–100; 781.227–44

*Sons: 15; 62d.30; 75; 83–4; 167; 298; 317.6; 318; 333; 338; 339; 345; 360.22–33; 362.1–4; 518; 527; 773.46–53; 775a; 781.286–8; 803b; 953b; 1007e–f; 1067

Speech, freedom of: 362.18–20; 410; 412; 703; 706; 737; 797; 1036–7

Spoils of war: 266; 370.19?

Stasis: 173; 267; 282.24–8; 453.21–3

*Stepmothers: 4; 824

Strength, physical: 24b; 199; 201; 290; 450; 525; 732; 971

Stupidity. *See* Ignorance

TOPICS

*Suicide: 362.26; 656; 1070; 1111
Sun: (course of) 228.5; 397b;
    765b?; 779; 1111a (heat/light
    of) 316.1; 540.7; 772; 816.11;
    App. 19.35
*Supplication: 351; 435?; 513?;
    661.7, 15; 757.856–60; 937
Swans: 773.77–8
Sympathy: 33; 119–20
Symposium: 468. *See also*
    Cottabus; Feasting
Syrinx: 773.71

Talk: 61b.1; 170; 219; 297.5;
    362.18–20; 394; 470?; 473;
    610; 927; 1012
Temperance. *See* Self-control
Temples: 170; 264a; 472.4–8;
    752c; 752h.20–1, 27–8; 794;
    912a; 923
Thunder: 472.11?; 982;
    App. 19.32
Time: 38a; 42; 45; 60; 61b; 192;
    222; 223.107; 291; 303–4;
    441; 759a.1582; 800; 1072;
    App. 3; 4?; 19.34
Toil. *See* Hardships
Torches: 62h; 90; 411; 472.12;
    752
Toys: 272; 752d.2
Transformation. *See* Metamor-
    phosis
Travel: 752h.15–19
*Trials (judicial): 88a
Trophies: 370.12
Truth: 206; 289; 313; 396; 439;
    441; 812; 813a; 822b.2; 941a;
    1035–6
Tyrants, tyranny. *See* Rulers

Ugliness: *Autol.* t. iv; 282a;
    545a; 842
Ululation: 351
*Underworld: 370.62; 371;
    448a.56; 450; 456?; 638; 868;
    912; 936; App. 1. *See also*
    Death etc.
Unmanliness: 183–8; 239; 288;
    362.34; 453.5; 683a; 829;
    1052. *See also* Manliness
Upbringing. *See* Education

*Vengeance: 448a.44, 69–70;
    559; 874
Vice. *See* Bad character(s)
Vines: 370.85; 530.3; 758b.4;
    765; 896
Virtue: 7; 9; 11; 60; 61c; 62i; 75;
    138; 163; 296; 377; 446; 463;
    473; 494.28–9; 497.6; 505;
    527; 542; 543.5; 545a.2; 572;
    734; 853; 865; 902; 908c; 918;
    954; 960.6–14; 961; 1029–30;
    1047; 1067

*War, warfare: 16; 185; 200;
    282.18–23; 289; 352–3;
    370.23; 728; 731; 759a.1623;
    975; 992; 1052.1
Water: 223.83–5; 114; 228.2;
    316.3; 367; 370.86; 656?;
    727e.5; 752f.17; 752h.29–32;
    757.891–2; 892
Wealth: 7; 20–1; 54; 55; 61b.10;
    92; 96; 137; 142; 191; 198;
    232; 235; 247–9; 252; 285.3–
    10; 322; 326–7; 354; 362.7,
    11–15; 378; 395; 417; 419–20;
    438; 453.15; 462; 502; 504;

709